STUDIES

IN THE ANTHROPOLOGY OF

NORTH AMERICAN INDIANS

The Comanche Indians are one of the most widely known yet least understood groups on the plains. Although much has been published on Comanche
history and culture, this is the first in-depth historical study of the changes
and continuities in Comanche political organizations from their earliest interactions with Europeans to their settlement on a reservation in present-day
Oklahoma.

Based on the critical analysis of documentary material from historical
and anthropological archives in Spain, Mexico, and the United States, the
study focuses on the different ways the Comanche tribes—the Yamparikas,
Jupes, Kotsotekas, Quahadas, Penatekas, Tenewas, and Nokonis—organized
and reorganized around the changing resources of hunting, warfare, trade, and
diplomacy. It also examines the ways the Comanches were portrayed by
contemporary governmental authorities, the popular media and folklore, and
by anthropologists and historians, and on how those perceptions and
misperceptions influenced the political relations between the Comanches and
Euroamericans.

Beyond the detailed histories of each of the Comanche tribes, it also
raises larger questions about political processes. What are the origins and
fates of political organizations? Why do peoples come together? Why do they
disperse? In classical political philosophy, tribes, nations, and ethnic groups
have clear, unchanging boundaries; their origins are mythical and unknow-
able, and their collapse is pathological. In contrast, using the record of the
Comanches, this study argues that political formation and re-formation is not
only normal but frequently ignores existing political and ethnic boundaries.

THOMAS W. KAVANAGH is Curator of Collections at the William Hammond
Mathers Museum, Indiana University. He has published articles in such
journals as *Visual Anthropology* and *Plains Anthropologist.*

THE COMANCHES
A History
1706–1875

Thomas W. Kavanagh

Published by the University of Nebraska Press
Lincoln and London

In cooperation with the American Indian Studies Research
Institute, Indiana University, Bloomington

Library of Congress Cataloging-in-Publication Data
Kavanagh, Thomas W., 1949–
[Comanche political history]
The Comanches: a history, 1706–1875 / Thomas W. Kavanagh.
p.   cm.—(Studies in the anthropology of North American Indians)
Originally published: Comanche political history. 1996.
Includes bibliographical references.
ISBN 0-8032-7792-X (pbk.: alk. paper)
1. Comanche Indians—History.   2. Comanche Indians—Politics and government.
3. Comanche Indians—Government relations.   I. Title.   II. Series.
E99.C85K39   1999
978′.0049745—dc21
99-28160   CIP

Contents

Maps and Illustrations

Maps

Plates

Figures

Tables

Preface

I first met Comanches at the Smithsonian Institution's 1970 Festival of American Folklife, which featured the Indians of Oklahoma. One Comanche participant, Francis Joseph Attocknie—better known to Comanches as Joe A— was demonstrating flute making; I later came to know him as a respected historian and I grew to value both his knowledge and his friendship. After graduating from the University of New Mexico, I joined the staff of the Smithsonian's Indian Awareness Program; we produced the "Native Americans" portion of the Festival of American Folklife and we served as cultural consultants to the Bureau of Indian Affairs, the Department of Commerce's Economic Development Administration, and the U. S. Congress's American Indian Policy Review Commission. When I joined the program, the director was Cherokee, married to a Comanche, and I was drawn into the small Comanche community of Washington, D. C., for socializing and hand games; when Oklahoma Comanches came to Washington on tribal business, there was after-dinner conversation and storytelling. Whenever possible, I visited a widening circle of Comanche friends in Oklahoma, attending the Comanche Homecoming powwow, and camping at the Anadarko Fair.

In 1972 several Comanche elders asked me if I could find any documentary mention of the Tedapukunu—the *tuepukunuu* 'little ponies'—the old-time men's society recently revived to honor returned Vietnam war veterans. Although I could find but few documentary references to the group, the request piqued my interest and I began what has become a continuing search for documentary sources relating to the Comanches. That summer I joined the Little Ponies as an associate—non-Indian—member. In 1976, as a part of the Bicentennial Festival of American Folklife, the Smithsonian Institution contracted with the Comanche Tribe of Oklahoma to produce a major presentation; for this, Joe A and others revived the *tuwinuu* 'black knives', the Yamparika men's society.

In 1976, I went to George Washington University for a Master's degree in anthropology; for my thesis I spent the summer of 1979 in Oklahoma studying the Little Ponies and their role in the modern powwow for (1980). My arrival coincided with the beginnings of a major political dispute, but I managed to carry out my research, powwowing on weekends and talking to people during the week, all the while aware of the growing political tensions, but not explicitly focusing on them. In the months after I left—moving to Arizona to coordinate the Hopi commemoration of the Tricentennial of the Pueblo Revolt of 1680—the Comanche dispute came to a head. Elected officials were recalled amid charges of financial irregularities and more general criminal fraud; there were numerous creative, though anonymous, photocopied political posters; rumors spread overnight. The political process culminated with the occupation of the tribal offices by one faction, shutting down tribal operations for a time.

In fall 1981, I returned to the University of New Mexico to continue graduate school, intending to extend my earlier study of the powwow into a dissertation. But on my first trip back to Oklahoma in 1982, several Comanche friends—including Joe A, who provided lodgings in the camper-trailer behind his house—suggested that it would be of more value to them for me to investigate the continuing political dispute, so I switched to that focus. Later trips to Oklahoma and to the Federal Archives and Records Center in Fort Worth, 1983–84, added information about the modern controversy, the course of events, and the trajectory of processual developments.

I found that the dispute had deep historical roots. Both groups in the 1980 controversy—one called itself the Grassroots, the other was generally unnamed—were often called the Yes people and the No people. Those names referred to positions taken during the mid-1960s when the Yes Comanches favored political separation from the Kiowa-Comanche-Apache (KCA) confederation legitimized by the 1867 Medicine Lodge Treaty, while the No Comanches favored continued association. Further research uncovered the Comanche side of disputes in the 1950s about representation on the KCA committee. (For a Kiowa version of these events, see Levy 1959.) Those disputes were, in turn, related to controversies in the 1930s about acceptance of the Oklahoma Indian Welfare Act—the version of the Indian Reorganization Act designed specifically for the legal conditions of Oklahoma—and the writing of separate tribal and joint KCA constitutions. Ultimately, the documentary trail of Comanche political disputes reached back into the nineteenth century, with quarrels over allotment, Peyotism versus Christianity, and the opposition of Quanah Parker and other more "traditional" pre-reservation leaders (Hagan 1976).

At about the same time, and somewhat by accident, I discovered the gold mine of archival records from the other end of recorded Comanche history. Since the earliest Euroamerican contacts with Comanches were with the Spaniards of New Mexico, and I was in New Mexico, I decided to examine those original sources. At first I did not expect to find much material on the Comanches from the early periods—the general feeling among Plains scholars seemed to be that contacts between Spaniards and Comanches were fleeting and hostile—but I soon discovered that the Spanish Archives of New Mexico held a wealth of detailed information on Comanche–Euroamerican interaction. Thereafter, for days and weeks on end I haunted the now-former Coronado Room of Zimmerman Library where I found photocopies of the Spanish, Mexican, and Territorial Archives of New Mexico, the Michael Steck Papers, and the Béxar Archives of Texas, as well as selected documents from the Mexican Archivo General de la Nación–Provincias Internas, and the Spanish Archivo General de Indias (Seville). On trips to Washington, I located records of Anglo-American interaction with Comanches in the National Archives and the National Anthropological Archives of the Smithsonian. All of those materials would have been of great interest to Joe A; he often spoke of going to Mexico to pursue Comanche connections there. Unfortunately he passed away in 1984.

Besides extending the historical record into the eighteenth century, those materials allowed two other dimensions to the analysis. Many recent analyses of American Indian politics have utilized the concept of "factionalism" to explain political disputes, most recently Schusky (1994); both Jones (1968; 1972) and Hagan (1976) used factionalism to explain aspects of Comanche politics. Indeed, the late nineteenth and early twentieth century history I was uncovering seemed close to the model of "pervasive factionalism" suggested by Siegel and Beals (1960). However, the earlier history was not of a singular Comanche "tribe"; rather there were multiple independent political units, each following its own interpretation of its own best interests. That seemed to confirm a suggestion I had made in my thesis, that the "bands" of traditional Comanche analysis were better viewed as political "tribes"; independently, Melburn Thurman (1980) came to much the same conclusion at about the same time.

In addition, the historical records, particularly those of Spanish and Mexican New Mexico and Texas, contained significant details on the political and especially the economic interactions between Comanches and Euroamericans, and I was able to analyze the political resources available to Comanche political actors in a degree of detail usually unavailable to researchers in American Indian history.

After completing my PhD dissertation (1986)—a work best viewed as an incomplete draft of the present book—I continued to seek Comanche documents at the Smithsonian, the American Museum of Natural History in New York, and in private hands. The analysis of those materials has forced a postponement of the examination of the modern political disputes: one must know the past before analyzing the present. But publication of this book does not end my connection with Comanches. Indeed it is only a preliminary to the study of the reservation period and more contemporary politics. In the meantime, I continue to collaborate with Comanche people on topics ranging from the implementation of the Native American Graves Protection and Repatriation Act, the continuing political and constitutional reorganization of the Comanche Nation, the origins and development of the symbolism of the Native American Church, and the contemporary powwow. Therefore, the present book is part of an ongoing cooperative study of the Comanche sociocultural system and process.

As in any such effort, a great many people have rendered invaluable assistance. Unfortunately, many of my first Comanche friends are *kehewanuu*, no longer with us, and normally it would be improper to mention their names. Nevertheless, it is important to acknowledge their support, and I ask forgiveness for naming them. I am especially grateful for the continuing assistance of the families of Francis Joseph Attocknie and of Haddon Nauni. I must also acknowledge Raymond Nauni, Sr., George "Woogie" Watchetaker and his wife Eva, Edward Yellowfish, the Reverend Robert Coffee, and Ernest "Nig" Mihecoby. Of those who are still with us, I would like to acknowledge the friendship of the Reverend Dr. Reaves Nahwooks and his wife Clydia, who first introduced me to Comanches; of Sonny, Marlene, and Billy Fodder, who taught me to dance on their front porch; of Leonard Riddles, Doc Tate Nevaquayah, Elton Yellowfish, George Kishketon, and Wallace Coffee, all of whom have encouraged me to undertake the study, spent many hours talking about the old—and not-so-old—days, answering my questions, and allowing me to dance with them. Sam DeVenney has shared both his photograph collection and his knowledge of those old faces. Other Comanches in Cache, Walters, and Apache, too numerous to mention here, as well as those in Washington, D. C., Lincoln, Nebraska, and Stillwater, Oklahoma answered my endless questions, allowed access to personal records, and supported my research with good will.

Special thanks are owed to Waldo R. Wedel, E. Adamson Hoebel, and Gustav G. Carlson, who allowed unprecedented access to their notes and photographs.

I am grateful to Mauricio J. Mixco of the University of Utah for assistance in translating Pedro Vial's 1785 journal.

Further thanks go to the staffs of the National Archives and Records Centers in Washington, D.C. and Fort Worth; the National Anthropological Archives, which provided plates 3, 5, 6, and 8, the Anthropology Department Library and the interlibrary loan office of the Natural History branch library of the Smithsonian Institution; the now-consolidated Coronado and Anderson rooms, Zimmerman Library, University of New Mexico; the Bancroft Library of the University of California, Berkeley; the Western History Collection of the University of Oklahoma; and the Department of Anthropology of the American Museum of Natural History. Towanna Spivey of the Fort Sill Museum has gone out of his way to provide access to the William S. Soule photographs in his collections, and made available the previously unpublished view of Terheryaquahip's village (plate 7). Similarly, the American Philosophical Society in Philadelphia provided access to E. Adamson Hoebel's 1933 field notes, including the photograph of his sketch of Pinero's *pianu?upai* (figure 2.1). The British Museum provided the previously unpublished photograph of Prick in the Forehead and Paruasemena (plate 4), and the British Library provided the photographic copy of Bernardo Miera y Pacheco's 1778 map of New Mexico (map 2).

My old friend, companion across a parking lot, and now editor, Ray DeMallie, who once taught me the difference between physical and cultural anthropology, and who has now taught me the intricacies of formatting a manuscript for publication, has been extremely patient with my efforts to finish this book. Linguist Jean O. Charney graciously corrected my efforts at writing Comanche names and provided a brief overview of the Comanche language sound system. Ultimately, however, I must accept responsibility for any deficiencies in the lingustic renderings as my own.

Notes on the Comanche Sound System

Jean O. Charney

The Comanche language has many of the same sounds as Spanish and English, and a few sounds that are different. This overall similarity has made it possible for many of the Comanche names and terms recorded in the archives to be recognized and transposed into an orthography that is fairly close to the actual sounds of Comanche. When both a good written representation and a more or less accurate translation of a name or term exist, we have often been able to analyze that name or term. However, because the individuals who wrote down those words were varyingly skilled in their ability to represent alphabetically the sounds they heard, and often did not leave a translation, some of the names in the historical records still lack analysis or phonetic transcription.

The Comanche consonants *p*, *t*, *k*, *m*, *n*, *w*, *y*, *s*, and *h* are much like their Spanish and English counterparts. Like Spanish, the consonant *b* ranges from its English counterpart to a sound more like v; and *r* is a briefer sound than both the Spanish and the English r. The letters *kw* and *ts* stand for sounds that English has—*kw* is like qu in words like 'quit'. Although Spanish does not have *kw*, Spaniards often attempted to record the sound as qu; however, qu is normally sounded in Spanish as *k*. This can lead to difficulties in recognizing a word or name. Thus the name recorded in 1786 as Piaquegipe is not **piakehipe* but is *piakwahipʉ*. The sound *ts* occurs within English words, as in 'cats'. Neither Spanish nor English have *ts* at the beginning of words, but many readers will be familiar with the sound from words like 'tsar'. The Spaniards sometimes represented *ts* as ch. Comanche has the glottal stop *ʔ* in which the air leaving the lungs is stopped momentarily, deep in the throat. English speakers use a glottal stop in words like 'uh-oh'. The Spaniards represented the sound *h* both with a g as in "-gipe" *-hipʉ* noted above, or with a j as in "jupe" *hupe*.

The vowels of Comanche and English and Spanish are in most cases similar, although the linguists' rendering of those vowels do not correspond one-to-one with the way the vowels are written in English or Spanish. The vowels *i*, *e*, *u*, *o* and *a* are the same as English vowels in this way: *i* stands for the vowel in 'beet'; *e* stands for the vowel in 'pay'; *u* stands for the vowel in 'fool'; *o* stands for the first vowel in 'sofa'; and *a* stands for the vowel in 'mall'.

A capital letter represents a voiceless vowel—a vowel that is expressed with a puff of air (if one watches the speaker's lips one can see the shape of the vowel). Voiceless vowels become regular vowels when they are stressed. We have not marked stress, because the main stress in a Comanche word almost always falls on the first syllable of the word.

Comanche also has a vowel that does not exist as a "real" vowel in English or in Spanish, although the sound is often heard in unstressed English vowels. The vowel is *ʉ*, and it sounds like the uh sound in words like 'number'. The vowel *ʉ* has been transcribed in a number of ways. For instance, the words Yamparika and Kotsoteka both contain *tʉhka* 'eater'; both transcriptions are attempts to represent a vowel that is not represented by a letter in either English or Spanish.

Those words, Yamparika and Kotsoteka, are also examples of two sound changes in the Comanche language, one linguistic, the other historical. For many grammatical suffixes, the initial consonants *p* and *t* can be changed to *b* and *d* respectively when they follow certain stems. Of the words that appear in this book, this feature is most obvious in the word Yamparika. It is composed of two separate words, *yampa*, the pan-Shoshone word for the edible root *Perideridia gaidneri*, and *tʉhka* 'to eat'. Put together to form 'root eater' *yamparʉhka*, the *t* of -*tʉhka* is sounded like an *r*.

The second sound change in the word Yamparika is historical. In the almost two centuries represented in this history there have been changes in the way Comanche sounded. This is most obvious in the absence in modern Comanche of a feature that was present in eighteenth-century Comanche, and is still present in Shoshone. Called pre-nasalization, consonants would be nasalized—pronounced with a preceding *m*, *n*, or *ng*—within stems and following certain stems and affixes. For instance, the ethnonym 'root eater' was recorded by eighteenth-century Spaniards as Yamparika *yamparʉhka*; as noted above, a modern Comanche would say *yaparʉhka*; that is, *yampa* has become *yapa*. Similarly, the ethnonym 'buffalo eater' was recorded in the eighteenth century as Cuchanteca *kutsontʉhka*, while a modern Comanche would say *kutsotʉhka*; *kutson*- became *kutso*-.

In Comanche words, stress normally falls on the first syllable, e.g., *yámparʉhka*.

1

Introduction

This book asks the general question, What are the origins and fates of political organizations? Why do people come together? Why do they disperse? It addresses that question through an examination of the historical Comanche political organizations, the ways the *numunuu* 'people', as individuals and as groups, organized and reorganized themselves to achieve their goals, and the conditions in the wider natural and social environments that influenced the short- and long-term political successes of those organizations. It examines the political economy, the interactions among the cultural structures of society, the politics of social organization, and the economics of diplomacy, trade, and warfare. Its approach is ethnohistorical, combining the methods of historiography with the concepts of anthropology in the analysis of documentary materials.

The Problem of the Comanches

Understanding the Comanches has long been problematical for Euroamericans. For the 170 years from the earliest reported contact with Comanches in 1706 to their settlement on the reservation in 1875, the basic problems were particulars: Who were the Comanches? What were the names of their groups, and how many were there? Who were their leaders, and who were not? Sometimes those questions were addressed formally and explicitly, sometimes informally and implicitly. For instance, in 1786 the Comandante Inspector of the Provincias Internas of the Viceroyalty of New Spain, Joseph Antonio Rengel, asked Texas governor Antonio Cabello:

> When you go among the Comanches, try to find in their combinations all
> the news possible on the mutual customary interest of their rancherías;
> the force of each one; the territory which they ordinarily occupy; the
> names of the captains which govern them; which ones are distinguished
> in authority and following; the principles on which the superiority of
> their command is established, if by election or by inheritance; the
> personal character of their chiefs, with respect to the influence which
> they have and could have on the negotiations of their nation. [Rengel
> 1786]

During the next century, others addressed similar questions both through day-
to-day reports of interactions with Comanches and through more formal
surveys such as Rengel asked of Cabello.

Those reports produced a mass of specific data. From the earliest documentary mention in 1706, a variety of labels have been used to represent the
contexts of Comanche social and political life. The Spaniards and the Mexicans of New Mexico and Texas used the term *ranchería* 'scattered village'
to refer to the local residential groups, and such terms as *parcialidad*
'division' or 'faction', *rama* 'branch', and less often *tribu* 'tribe' or *nación*
'nation', to refer to political organizations comprised of several rancherías.
They seldom referred to the Comanches as a cultural-political whole—that is,
to a single sociopolitical unit of Shoshone speakers on the southern Plains.
Indeed, when the Spaniards and Mexicans of Texas used the term Comanche,
they usually meant those who were nearby; those who were farther off—although acknowledging that they shared the same language and many
customs—were designated by labels such as Yamparika. Anglo-Americans
generally used the simple term band to refer to the full range of Comanche
sociopolitical units, with tribe often, but not always, referring to the cultural-
linguistic whole. But Anglo-Americans were unclear about whether that
whole was politically united. For instance, in 1818, David Burnet reported
that "the tribe known among us by the term Comanchees, is divided into three
great parties . . . the three parties collectively acknowledge one head or grand
chief" (Wallace 1954:121–24); on the other hand, twenty years later, in 1838,
George W. Bonnell, commissioner of Indian affairs for the Republic of
Texas, first paralleled Burnet's words, "Each party or tribe is under the
command of one or more chiefs, who are in turn subject to the control of one
principal chief" (Bonnell 1838). But he went on,

> The Comanche nation is, perhaps, the most perfect democracy on the
> face of the earth; everything is managed by primary assemblies, and the
> people have a right to displace a chief and elect a successor at pleasure.
> . . . With such a state of things it cannot be expected that there would be
> much harmony in their councils; and their war councils not infrequently

terminate with a battle between the different tribes. This sometimes produces permanent enmities and the chief of the disaffected tribe . . . separates from the nation and sets up for himself. [Bonnell 1838]

Bonnell did not attempt to reconcile the questions raised by those two characterizations, between parties "under command" and "subject to control" of chiefs, and their right to "displace a chief . . . at pleasure."

At the same time, Euroamericans differentiated among Comanches along a number of dimensions. Sometimes geographic designations were used. To the New Mexican Spaniards, the Comanches of Texas were Orientales 'easterners'; less frequently, to Texas Spaniards, Mexicans, and later Anglo-Texans, the Comanches of New Mexico were Occidentales 'westerners'. Some Anglo-Americans and Anglo-Texans used the opposite set of cardinal direction terms, speaking of northern, middle, and southern Comanches, often with the implication that those terms referred to political organizations. Beginning in the mid-1750s, ethnonyms—group names, both in Comanche and in translation—were used to refer to Comanche groups, and lists of names were gathered by bureaucrats, soldiers, and travelers (table 1.1). Interestingly, there is little evidence that, once compiled, the lists were ever used to inform later observers or policy considerations.[1]

Similarly, Comanche leaders have been designated by a variety of terms. The most common terms used by the Spaniards and Mexicans were *capitan* 'captain' and *capitancillo* 'little captain'; *jefe* (or *gefe*) 'chief' was rare. At any one time, a small set of specific individuals were consistently labeled *general* or *principal* by the Spaniards and Mexicans (table 1.2). Anglo-Americans used the simple term 'chief'; Anglo-Texans sometimes distinguished 'war chief' from 'peace chief' or from the unmarked term. As with the Spanish terms *general* and *principal,* a small but relatively consistent set of individuals were labeled principal chief by Anglo-Americans (table 1.2).

In contrast to the particular questions of the pre-reservation era, for later anthropologists and historians, the problem of the Comanches has been in the generalizations. To the first generation of American anthropologists, the Comanches were one of the "True Plains" peoples, sharing with the Sioux, Cheyennes, Kiowas, and others a "typical" domestic economy based on the full-time horse-mounted exploitation of the buffalo and the use of the tipi, the travois, and other features (Wissler 1914). But further investigation revealed a problematical aspect: the Comanches apparently lacked the political structures—authoritative leaders, men's societies that assumed periodic police functions, and annual ceremonies such as the Sun Dance—that were also held to be typical of, if not ecologically adaptive to, Plains life (Oliver 1962). According to the standard ethnography of the Comanches:

Table 1.1.
Comanche Ethnonyms Recorded before 1875

Marín 1758	Miera 1778	Mendinueta 1778[a]	Anza 1786[b]	Burnet 1818[c]
Pibian	Cuchan Marica	Yamparica	Cuchanec or Cuchanteca	Yamparacks
Yamparica	Yamparika	Come Civalos	Yamparica	Comanche
Jumanes	Jupes	Gente de Palo	Jupes	Tenewa
Panana	Piviones			

Padilla 1820[d]	Ruíz 1828	Berlandier 1830[e]	A. P. Chouteau 1838	Ruíz 1840[f]
Yucantica	Yamparika	Comanche	Padokah	Oriental
Yambarica	Comanche	Yamparica	Cochetaker	Yamparicu
		Yucantica	Yamparika	Juez
			"or Comanche"	Tanemaez

P. M. Butler 1846	P. M. Butler and M. B. Lewis 1846	Fitzpatrick 1847b	Neighbors 1852	Pike 1861a, b
Nonah	Cochetaker	Yampatickers	Koochetaker	Peneteghca
Yamparicka	Yampeucos	Cootsentokara	Nonaum	Noconi
Tenawish	Hoish	Penoe-entokara	Tenawash	Cochotihca
Penateca	Tenaywosh		Parkeenaum	Yaparihca
Hooish	Cuschutexca		Itchitabuddah	Mooche
	Noonah		Haunenaune	Kewihchemah
	Noconee		Hois or Peneteka	Tichaikane
			Nokoni	Paabo
			Taniewah	

García Rejón 1865	Butler, Singer, and Leyendecker 1867	Tatum 1870 d	Kimball 1872
Yaparehca	Kotsoteka	Penateka	Noconee
Cuhtsteca	Penadojka	Yamparika	Yamparica
Pacarabo	Danemmi	Ditsahana	Titcathkina
Noconi	Jui	Dinama	Tamenerind
Napuat or Quetahtore	Yapareska	Nokoni	Tiniema
Titsakanai	Muvinabore	Yapaine	Quahahdahs
Sianabore	Qushodojka	Mutsha	Cochetethcas
Penande	Quageyoke		

[a] Thomas 1940 [c] Wallace 1954 [e] Berlandier 1969
[b] Thomas 1932 [d] Hatcher 1919 [f] Ruíz 1921

Table 1.2.

Comanche Principal Chiefs Recorded before 1875

Kotsotekas in New Mexico

Ecueracapa	Encanguane	Canaguaipe	Quegüe	Cordero	Mowway
1786-1793	1793-	1797-	1805- ?	1821-1826-?	1849?-1875

Kotsotekas in Texas (Comanches Orientales)

Camisa de Fierro	Cabeza Rapada	Zoquine	Sofais	Chihuahua	Cordero
-1786	-1786	1787-	1787-	1801-1806	1806-1821

Hois and Penatekas in Texas

Muguara	Mopechucope	Sanaco	Ketumsee	Tosawa
-1840	-1849	1849-1855	1855-1861	1865-1875
		Potsanaquahip		
		1849-1862- ?		

Jupes and Yamparikas

Toro Blanco	Paruanarimuco	Somiquaso	Paruaquita	Toro Echicero
-1785	1786-1797?	1805- ?	?-1810-1826- ?	1829-?

Shaved Head	Bistevana	Paruasemena
1855-1857	1861	1853-1872

Tenewas

Paruakevitsi	Tabequena	Pahayuko	Puhiwitiquasso
1820-1832	1834-1839	1844-1855	1865-1875
	Isacony		
	1835-1837		

Nokonis

Quinahewi	Terheryaquahip
1861-1866	1861?-1875

SOURCE: Kavanagh 1986

> "Tribe" when applied to the Comanches is a word of sociological but not
> political significance. . . . The tribe consisted of a people who had a
> common way of life, but that way of life did not include political
> institutions or social mechanisms by which they could act as a tribal unit.
> There was in the old days no ceremonial occasion or economic enterprise
> that pulled all the far-flung bands together for a spell, be it ever so brief.
> There was no chieftain or group of chieftains to act for the tribe as a
> whole. There was no tribal council. [Wallace and Hoebel 1952:22]

Similarly, Harold Driver noted, "most of the Plains peoples achieved tribal
integration, but a few such as the Shoshoni speaking Comanche, never got
beyond the band stage" (1969:299). As stated by Symmes C. Oliver: "The
Comanche *were* different from the other True Plains tribes, and this fact
demands explanation" (Oliver 1962:71; emphasis in original).

As if in response to Oliver's call, scholars began to offer solutions to the
Comanche "anomaly," emphasizing in various degrees historical, cultural, or
ecological factors. The historical—really diffusionist—explanations pointed
to a recent arrival of the Comanches on the Plains to argue that they had not
had time to borrow the typical Plains traits that had been developed by earlier
peoples (Hoebel 1940, 1954:129; Oliver 1962:74; Eggan 1980; Lowie 1982:
191). There were two cultural explanations; one pointed to the linguistic connections between the Comanches and the other Shoshone speakers of the
Great Basin to argue that they had "not completely shed their Shoshonean
heritage"; the second argued that the "Comanche placed such a high value on
individual freedom that government was held to a minimum" (Tefft 1960:
110). The ecological explanations were somewhat more complex, but generally argued that since ecological conditions influenced social organization,
and since the Comanches did not share the typical Plains traits as did the
other True Plains tribes, they must not have shared precisely the same ecological niche as the other groups (Oliver 1962:73). Several factors have been
suggested to describe that different ecological niche. Some scholars have
suggested that since there was an abundance of bison and less harsh
conditions on the southern Plains, there was no need for the political controls
required on other parts of the Plains (Ralph Linton, quoted in Wallace and
Hoebel 1952:235; Colson 1954).

Recently, a number of scholars have argued the opposite. Extrapolating
from ecological data from the late nineteenth and early twentieth centuries,
and from comparisons with other hunting groups, such as subarctic caribou
hunters, they have argued that the southern Plains, and particularly Comanchería—the territory of the Comanches—had a significantly lower ecological
carrying capacity than other parts of the Plains and therefore could support
only the relatively small and dispersed populations and minimal organizations

as were reported in the standard ethnography (W. R. Brown 1987; Bamforth 1988). Using much the same data, D. L. Flores (1991:480) has argued that the southern Plains could have supported significant numbers of bison, which in turn could have—other factors being equal—supported even larger human populations than were historically reported. He did not, however, make any extrapolations from that data to its implications for Comanche organization.

Oliver suggested two other ecological factors that might have influenced Comanche social organization: first, because they were "widely scattered," not all Comanches lived on the Plains proper; second, some Comanche bands were "more involved with horses" than were others (1962:72). Both factors suggested that only some Comanches were True Plains people.

Although offered as generalizations, and although some degree of validity may be granted to all of those explanations of the Comanche problem, each provides only a particularistic solution, and each presents particularistic problems. The historical explanations argued that the Comanches had not been resident on the Plains long enough to borrow or develop the typical Plains traits developed by others. But of all Wissler's "True Plains" peoples, the Comanches have the longest documented existence as horse-mounted Plains peoples; they had horses when the Cheyennes still lived in earth lodges. The first cultural argument invoked an unspecified "Shoshonean heritage" to explain the Comanches' lack of political organization, but the details of that alleged heritage are more stereotypical than analytical; the second cultural argument invoked an alleged Comanche "individualism," but other than the assertion that Comanches were individualists—presumably in contrast to the collectivism of other peoples—no positive examples of Comanche individualism, or indeed of other Plains groups' contrasting collectivism, have been offered. The ecological explanations argued that the southern Plains did not offer the same conditions as did the central and northern Plains, but there has been no agreement on either the general conditions allegedly common to the Plains as a whole nor to the specific variations of Comanchería. For instance, neither Linton nor Colson offered data for their conclusion that there was an abundance of bison on the southern Plains. Conversely, for both Brown and Bamforth, the use of environmental data from the southern Plains of the 1890s and later to model the environmental relations of the 1840s, the relatively unquestioning use of reported Comanche population estimates, and the focus on the bison as the sole political-economic resource, raise significant problems with their analyses. Although Oliver's argument that because of differing economies, only some Comanches were True Plains people is important, he made no attempt to specify either which Comanche groups were Plains peoples and which were not, or what he meant by "more involved with horses."[2]

Oliver's lack of specificity—common to many of the recent scholars of Comanchería as well—is particularly unfortunate in light of the continuing interest in the names and numbers of Comanche sociopolitical groups by anthropologists (table 1.3).[3] However, in contrast to the earlier band lists which, once compiled, remained unstudied, later researchers soon noticed variations among their lists, and between those lists and the historical records—some lists included new names, others omitted names—and they began to offer explanations for the differences.

Interestingly, some of the earliest notices of Comanche ethnonymic variation originated from Comanches themselves. In September 1865, while gathering comparative vocabularies for the Smithsonian Institution, army surgeon D. J. MacGowan interviewed the Comanche delegates—unfortunately unnamed—attending a council with former Confederate Indians at Fort Smith, Arkansas. MacGowan noted—apparently based on comments by the Comanches—that there seemed to be many synonyms in Comanche, which he attributed to the "custom of tabooing the name of deceased men," so that names might change over time. As an example he noted:

> One of the bands that entered into a treaty with the Rebels under Albert Pike is set down in the printed copy as Nokoné [sic], which means moving or roaming. Since that time one of their number, Pootnokoné (solitary roamer) [koni 'to turn' or 'return'] deceased and the band has assumed as its proper designation Tsihkiahnoyekahde [tʉtsʉ noyʉkanʉʉ 'bad campers'], not staying in one place, wanderers, retaining indeed the meaning of the tabooed term.[4] [MacGowan 1865]

Interestingly, although this story was often repeated in later years, the ethnonym Nokoni continued to be recorded in direct references to a Comanche group while the ethnonym tʉtsʉ noyʉkanʉʉ apparently was not.

The next year Charles Bogy and W. R. Irwin reported speaking to some Comanche chiefs at Fort Zarah on the Arkansas River who told them, "This tribe at present embraces seven bands, there were formerly nine but two have merged with others" (Bogy and Irwin 1866b). Unfortunately, they reported neither the names of the chiefs nor the names of the bands that had merged.

In 1880 the Nokoni Comanche leader Coby (kobe 'wild horse'), passing through Washington while on an inspection tour of Carlisle Indian School and the East (W. C. Clark 1988), was interviewed by Walter J. Hoffman of the Smithsonian Institution's newly formed Bureau of Ethnology. In the process of giving a list of Comanche "gentes," Coby mentioned that several names had changed:

Table 1.3. Comanche Ethnonyms and Equivalences Recorded and Suggested after 1875

Hoffman 1880	E. L. Clark 1881	ten Kate 1885a	Mooney 1896		Lowie 1912	Curtis 1907–30	
Iampairika	Penetethka	Yampateka	Detsanayuka	Motsai	Yappai =Yapareka	Detsanayuka	=Yamparika
Penetekai	Caschotethka	Penetaka	=Nokoni	Pagotsu	=ontsontiwiwa	=Nokoni	Penateka
Kostshotekai	Nocony	Tenewa	Ditsakana	Peneteka	Noyeka	Yapa	=Penande
Tistshinoieka	Yapparethka	Nokoni	=Widyu	=Penande	=Nokoni	=Yamparika	Tanume
Kuahadi	Quahada	Kwadatitchasko	=Yapa	=Tayuwit	=Tanomo	=Ketseteka	Qasiner
Tiniema	=Quahehuke	Kohstchoteka	=Yamparika	=Tekapwit	Kwaare	=Qahadi	Katate
Titsakanai	Yaparexka	Pohonim	Kawatsina	=Kubaratpat	Kotsuteka	Metsai	Muvinabore
			Kotsai	Pohoi	Penateka	Pagotsu	
			Kotsoteka	Tanima	=Tekapwait		
			Kwahari	Tenawa			
			=Kwahadi	=Tenawit			
				Waiih			

R. N. Richardson (1933)	Hoebel (1940)		Wallace and Hoebel (1952)		Thurman (1980)	
Penateka	no'yeka	tasipenanɜ	Penatɜka	Pagotsu	Penateka	
Yamparika	=dɜ'tsanɔ'yeka	ɔteta'o	=Teyuwit	=Panaixtɜ	= Hois	
Kotsoteka	=nɔ'koni	páhuaix	=Tekapwai	Pahuraix	= Yupe	
Nokoni	kwɜhɑɹenɔ	=par-ke-na-um	=Kuβaratpat	=Parkeenaum	= Tenewa	
Tenewa	=kwahihekene	kutsueka	=Penanɜ	Wia'nɜ	Yamparika	
Tanima	yápaina	mutanɜ	=ho'is		Cuchantica	
Kwahari	=yep	wi'a'nɜ	Noyeka		= Nokoni	
=Kwahadi	=Yamparika	wɔ'ai	=Nokoni		= Quahada	
=Quahehuke	=Distakana	panaixtɜ	=Dɜtsanɔyeka			
	=Widyu	tɜsakɜnan	Kutsueka			
	penanɜ:		Kwaharena			
	=penatɜke		=Kwahihɜkene			
	=hois					

The Tis-tshi-no-i-e-ko—Bad movers or Poor Travelers—were formerly called No-kó-ni—movers, but the reason of this [change] was not known. It is possible that the change of name may have been due to the cause as in the following example:

> The Ui-ú-i-ni-em [*widyunʉʉ*] Awl people, was the former name of the Tí-tsa-ka-nai [*tʉtsahkʉnanʉʉ*], but an individual of that gens, having the same name, died, whereupon the present name was adopted, for the reason that the name of a deceased person is never mentioned.[5]

The former name of the Ku-a-ha-di was Na-ó-ni-em or Ridge people, but no reason of the change is known to the informant.

After removing to the southern country, a large party of Comanches remained near the headwaters of the streams to catch wild horses. This band was called Pá-ka-tsa—headwater people—and was composed of individuals from the several other gens, but when they again joined their respective bands the name ceased. [Hoffman 1880][6]

In his book on sign language, William P. Clark (1885) published portions of a letter written to him in 1881 by Edward L. Clark, interpreter at the Kiowa Agency, who had been along on Coby's trip to the East. Among other brief comments about various bands, E. L. Clark cited comments made by Straight Feather, *siʔa tsinika*, usually spelled Ceachinika, a seventy-year-old Penateka (*pihna tʉhkaʔ* 'honey eater') local band chief:

> At what period of time the Pen-a-teth-kas band of the Comanches separated themselves from the main body is not definitely known, but as there is a well-authenticated tradition that the Pen-a-teth-kas had wandered off a great distance and were entirely lost to the other bands, and that long afterwards they were discovered by the Yap-pa-reth-kas ['root eater'] and Qua-had-da ['antelope'] warriors. . . . The original name of Qua-had-da was 'Qua-he-huk-e', meaning 'back shade', because they inhabited the plains or a country without timber or trees, where no shade could be had, and during hot weather they shaded their face by turning their backs to the sun. [E. L. Clark 1881; W. P. Clark 1885:119]

The linkage of Que-he-huke and Qua-had-da is another example of synonymous names, although neither E. L. Clark nor Ceachinika gave a reason for the change. Of more lasting influence on the Comanche literature was Ceachinika's suggestion of differential migrations in Comanche history—that the Penatekas had been long separated from other Comanches.[7]

James Mooney stated that the Comanches "have, or still remember, thirteen recognized divisions or bands, and may have had others in former times.

Of these all but five are practically extinct" (Mooney 1896:1044). He listed some twenty names, in alphabetical order, with several names given as correlated synonyms. Those he suggested might be due to either the taboo on using the names of the dead such as mentioned by MacGowan and Hoffman, or the extinction and annihilation of groups in battle.

In a week of fieldwork in 1912, Robert Lowie recorded nine ethnonyms, not counting variant spellings, as well as a number of nicknames, which paralleled but did not exactly duplicate Mooney's list (Lowie 1912). In his publication based on those notes, however, and although in many respects exactly reproducing them, he reported only four ethnonyms and did not even hint that names might change (Lowie 1915).

In 1926 Edward Curtis reported, "At the climax of their existence the Comanche were apparently divided into ten or more bands, but through tribal disintegration this band organization is almost lost." Although his list included synonyms and nicknames, he offered no reason other than "tribal disintegration" for the alternate names (Curtis 1907–30, 19:187).

Texas historian Rupert N. Richardson (1933) generally bypassed the question of ethnonymic variation, arguing for a permanence to Comanche political organization: "The tribe was divided into a number of bands, or permanent tribal parts. . . . Chiefs might come and go, but the bands remained, and selected new chiefs to carry on the leadership" (R. N. Richardson 1933:16). After repeating Mooney's list in a footnote, he noted, "It is impossible to identify all the bands, or to describe with any detail and precision more than about half of them" (1933:18), and he then gave brief descriptions of several groups. Ultimately, he noted several sources of variation: the "Kwahari or Kwahadi . . . cannot be identified until towards the close of the pre-reservation period" because of their "wild and independent way of living"; at another point he suggested that the names Jupe and Tenewa referred to the same group (1933:21).

In 1933, the Santa Fe Laboratory of Anthropology sponsored a summer field session among the Comanches; they recorded a number of ethnonyms, many previously unrecorded. In 1940, one member of that party, E. Adamson Hoebel, summarized the discussions of band lists recorded since 1875; paralleling R. N. Richardson's argument, he argued that it was futile to attempt to specify "precisely how many Comanche bands there were" because "what constituted a Comanche local group is not a problem to be settled by monistic definition. Only the larger bands received permanent recognition and a name" (Hoebel 1940:12). That disclaimer aside, he then presented a list based on the names given by his Comanche consultants in 1933, regardless of size and with partial correlations to the lists of Neighbors, Mooney, and Lowie.

In 1952 Hoebel teamed up with Texas historian Ernest Wallace to produce a popular ethnography. They noted that Anglo-Americans—they generally ignored Spanish materials—frequently used geographical terms to refer
to Comanches, but that "as they . . . came to know the Comanches better, the
practice was replaced by the use of definite band names" (Wallace and
Hoebel 1952:24). Their discussion of those names drew heavily on Hoebel's
earlier work and on R. N. Richardson's history; they repeated Hoebel's statement that "only the larger bands received permanent recognition and a name,"
and their description of the "five outstanding divisions" (1952:25–31) is an
almost verbatim repetition of Richardson's discussion (1933:18–21).

In 1959 George E. Hyde, after a lifetime of library research, attempted a
historical synthesis of the Plains peoples "from the prehistoric period to the
coming of the white man." Unfortunately, his efforts resulted in more confusion than clarity. Most of his explanations of Comanche ethnonyms were
based on name equivalences of doubtful validity and on the migration hypothesis drawn from Ceachinika's account, which he transposed and made into
a "Yamparika" tradition. One of his more inventive implications was what
might be called a "worm hole"[8] on the Arkansas River into which peoples
sometimes drifted to emerge decades later with a new identity. Thus, without
any further evidence, he equated the eighteenth-century "Yupes"[9] with the
nineteenth-century Kwahadas, arguing that "when the large Kwahari Comanche tribe moved south of the Arkansas it was lost. There is not one clear reference to this tribe until after 1860, when it suddenly emerged again as a
most powerful Comanche group" (1959:212).

Karl Schlesier (1972) utilized the Comanche migration hypothesis to explain the demise of the archaeological complex known as the Dismal River
culture. From published historical sources, beginning with Ceachinika's
account of an early separation of the Penatekas from other groups, he ad-
duced waves of migration corresponding to "the final withdrawal of Comanche groups still in the Green and Yampa Rivers into the High Plains of
eastern Wyoming" (1972:119). Through a series of name equivalences,
Schlesier came to the proposition that, after 1762:

> Comanche distribution, on a generally northwest to southeast axis from
> northern Colorado to the Middle Red River, would have been the
> following (proceeding south to north): Penateka, Kwahadi, Kotsoteka,
> Yupe [sic], and Yamparika. All recorded Comanche bands of the 19th
> century would have originated from these five principal divisions of the
> 1750s to 1780s. [1972:127]

However, some of those names—such as Penateka and Kwahada—were not
recorded until the middle of the nineteenth century, and one name—Jupe—

had disappeared in the interim. Schlesier offered no process other than migration to explain the appearance of names; unlike Hyde, he had no worm hole on the Arkansas River.

In 1980 Melburn Thurman revived the nickname hypothesis in a new form. He acknowledged that "confusion has surrounded the Comanche 'divisions' because of substantial variations in their reported numbers" (Thurman 1980, 5:6), but he rejected Wallace and Hoebel's suggestion that "as they . . . came to know the Comanches better" Euroamericans used "definite band names" (1952:24). He argued that "the late increase in names does not indicate an increased knowledge of the Comanches, but rather a confusion of synonymous terms" (Thurman 1980, 5:7). Moreover, in contrast to Mooney's, Curtis's, or Hyde's open-ended lists of equivalences, Thurman specifically argued that "at least from the late eighteenth century, Comanches seem to have been organized into three divisions" (1980, 5:7); thus he reduced all of the ethnonymic variation to three sets of synonyms.

Most recently, Morris Foster (1991) has taken issue with the basic premise of the band lists, the assumption that the ethnonyms referred to discrete sociopolitical organizations recognized by Comanches. Instead, he argued that although Comanche language ethnonyms were "frequent designations" by Euroamericans in the eighteenth and nineteenth centuries, they did not label any Comanche political reality. Rather, like the lumping of the native population of the Americas under the sign *Indian,* Euroamerican use of Comanche language ethnonyms was politically motivated, occurring only "when it suited [Euroamerican] purposes in trade or diplomacy." For Foster the ethnonyms were merely a "handy gloss on the internal organization of the larger community" (1991:57) and, if anything, referred only to temporary identities, perhaps actualized in social gatherings, but with no enduring political reality; "Comanche social structure is best understood as the strategic movement and organization of personnel among different social groups, regulated by means of periodic multigroup gatherings" (Foster 1991:70).

Some degree of validity may be granted to most of those diverse explanations for ethnonymic variation. Certainly, people might get together for specific purposes and be given names, some of which were remembered long after the people had dispersed; certainly, some names—and their referent groups?—may have had a continuity throughout the century and three-quarters of pre-reservation recorded history; certainly, people refrained from mentioning the names of deceased relatives out of grief and mourning; certainly, some groups were wiped out in sudden attacks by enemies; certainly, groups may have been called by different names and nicknames, and there may even have been differences in terms of reference, address, and self-designation; certainly, there was often confusion about the level of organization on which

a particular named political unit operated; and certainly, contemporary politics, as well as inherited culture, played an important role in the way Comanches perceived themselves and in how Euroamericans perceived Comanches.
Nonetheless, as a set, like Ceachinika's story of Penateka origins, and like the
explanations of why Comanches differed from the other "True Plains" tribes,
without reference to more general sociopolitical processes, those explanations
are little more than particularistic rationalizations of specific events whose
applicability to wider situations is problematic.

A similar—but shorter—narrative describes historical and anthropological interest in Comanche leadership. None of the nineteenth-century anthropologists commented upon the issue; for them the existence of Comanche
"chiefs" was apparently a given. Similarly, in the early twentieth century
Texas historian Rupert N. Richardson gave almost no attention to it; his comments on political leadership were limited to the above quoted, "Chiefs might
come and go, but the bands remained, and selected new chiefs to carry on the
leadership" (1933:16), and "a treaty would be made . . . with a number of
Comanche braves led by a certain great chief who described himself as 'head-
chief of all the Comanches' . . . [and the government] might continue to labor
under the impression that they had made a treaty with the 'entire Comanche
nation'" (1933:23-24).

However, in more recent years the concept of Comanche chiefs has
fallen into disrepute. For E. A. Hoebel, interest in the political leadership process was summarized in a Comanche's comment from 1933, "I hardly know
how to tell about them; they never had much to do except hold the band together. . . . He just got that way" (1940:18). And once "that way," for
Hoebel, "the influence of the peace chief was limited to internal and civil
matters only. No peace chief could stop a war party from taking the trail.
Peace making was the prerogative of war leaders" (1940:19). Most recently,
Morris Foster has argued that although "some Comanche leaders were able to
acquire a degree of authority that approximated control over a division," for
the most part,

> the leaders who from time to time represented divisions or suprabands
> [sic] to Euro-American authorities were intermediaries with limited
> authority. They dealt with Euro-Americans on specific matters relating to
> Comanche-Euro-American interactions and were not "paramount" or
> "principal" leaders in the way that we usually employ those terms.
> [1991:68]

But again, while each of those discussions may have some validity, each
fails a crucial test. Here the objection is the opposite to that raised to the
explanations of the Comanche "anomaly" and to the ethnonymic variation

noted above: while those were particularities without generalizations, these are generalizations without particulars. Both Richardson and Foster claimed that the "chiefs" who signed treaties had no influence or authority beyond a specific diplomatic context, but they gave no supporting examples; without such references, their generalizations remain as untested hypotheses. At the same time, given that the historical documents often include specific details about the Comanche individuals involved in interactions, and that sets of documents show the continuities of specific individuals across time (table 1.2), the conclusions of Richardson and Foster raise the questions, in Foster's terms, How are those individuals and their actions to be evaluated? Were they indeed little more than intermediaries with no political roles beyond the immediate interaction or were they political leaders whose influence extended across time and space?

It would seem that if the former hypothesis were correct, then there should be a great many more such individuals named in the historical record than the relatively few we find, with the extreme case being that there should have been be a new "spokesman" for each incident in the 170 years of pre-reservation interaction. That there was not suggests some sort of selection process at work. Since there is no evidence that Euroamericans were doing the selecting, it must have been done by Comanches. At the same time, there is evidence from both ends of pre-reservation Comanche history, from the 1780s and from the 1870s, that many Comanche "spokesmen" were also political leaders both of local and of larger sociopolitical groups.

Finally, in both Richardson's and Foster's approach there are unanswered questions. Richardson noted that "a treaty would be made . . . [*with*] *a certain great chief*" (1933:23, my emphasis); similarly, Foster argued that "*some Comanche leaders* were able to acquire *a degree of authority* that approximated control over a division" (1991:70, my emphasis). The questions are, first, the particulars: Which "great chief"? Which "Comanche leaders"? What "authority"? Are Richardson's and Foster's conclusions based on the generalization of historical materials or on theoretical preconceptions? Then come the generalizations: How did a man become a "great chief"? Under what conditions could a man acquire a "degree of authority"? Then, using Foster's terms, How are those conditions related to the "strategic movement and organization of personnel" between groups? How regular—historically recurring—were those conditions? Often enough to be called normal? Rare enough to be abnormal? Once again, are those conclusions based on ethnohistorical analysis or on preconceptions?

Tribes as Processual Political Organizations

Anthropological conceptualizations of political organization developed within the Western intellectual tradition that viewed society as sacred, auto-chthonous, and primordial. For political philosophers from Plato through St. Augustine, Machiavelli, Montaigne, Hobbes, Locke, Adam Smith, J. S. Mill, and beyond, the theoretical problem was not the origin of groups, but the establishment and maintenance of the best form of government within them. For the American revolutionaries, both the original Founding Fathers and the less successful southern Confederates, the implications of the founding of "new nations" upon a general theory of political organization were masked by a rhetoric in which "the people"—or "the state"—was seen as an entity preexisting the political reformation.

Europeans viewed non-Western peoples in similar terms. They lived in "tribes," which, like the "nations" of "civilized peoples," had existed from the beginning, with clear and unchanging boundaries. Membership was by birth —the word race was often used in reference to both the uncivilized tribes and to the civilized nations—and their cultures were believed to be homogeneous and unchanging. Moreover, in contrast to the rational politics of nations, the relations of tribes one to another were seen as traditional, ancient, and irra-tional. For instance, in 1835, justifying a treaty-making expedition to the southern Plains, Secretary of War Lewis Cass said of the southern Plains peoples, "It is believed that hereditary feuds have existed there for a long suc-cession of years and that many of the tribes have received as an inheritance that state of hostility in which they are placed" (Cass 1835). The key words in that statement were not "feud," or "inheritance," or "succession of years," or even "state of hostility in which they are placed," all of which implied a passive aspect to Indian existence; rather the key word is "believed", for it was the Anglo-American's belief that the Indians were in a "state of hostility" one to another that impelled their own actions to end those "hostilities." Cass was not the first, nor would he be the last, to substitute belief in place of con-temporary political and economic analysis.

It was in that philosophical milieu that anthropology developed. All the major schools of anthropological thought implicitly, if not explicitly, viewed bounded and primordial society as the locus of social and cultural activity and thus passed over questions and implications of the temporal origins of parti-cular societies. The nineteenth-century evolutionists focused on the evolution of particular institutions, such as technology, marriage, or law, while ignoring the temporal context of the social units that manifested those institutions. Similarly, for the diffusionists, from the extremes of the Kulturkriese to the more moderate Boasians, cultural elements washed over preexisting societies, changing them internally yet leaving the boundaries intact. In both Spencer's organic analogy and the Durkheimian problem of the maintenance of social order, the collapse of society was a pathological condition to be avoided. Well into the twentieth century, for both mainstream American cultural and British social anthropology, bounded tribes, however fictive in ethnographic or historical reality, were the focus of anthropological activity.

That is not to say that all anthropological researchers viewed all societies in such a fixed way, although the exceptions were rare and sporadic. In 1884 Frederick Engels noted that "the formation through segmentation of new tribes and dialects was still proceeding in America until quite recently" (Engels 1884:82). Some thirty years later, Clark Wissler noted that "the facts indicate Blackfoot bands to be social groups, or units, frequently formed and even now taking shape by division, segregation, and union, in the main a physical grouping of individuals in adjustment to sociological and economic conditions" (Wissler 1911:3). Unfortunately, neither Engels nor Wissler elaborated on the details of the "segmentation" process, let alone "division" or "union."

In the ensuing years, several anthropologists noted processual aspects to political organization. In 1937 Fred Eggan described historic Plains societies as going through a "series of social units—the elementary family, the extended family, the household, the band, the society [sodality], and the tribe," alternating in an annual cycle (Eggan 1937:82). A decade later Demitri Shimkin (1947) detailed the similar annual cycle of the Wind River Shoshones, and a decade after that, Fred Gearing (1958, 1962) offered this generalization: "The social structure of a human community is not a single set of roles and organized groups, but is rather a series of several sets of roles and groups which appear and disappear according to the tasks at hand" (Gearing 1958: 1148). But however powerful Eggan's, Shimkin's, or Gearing's models were, they had in common the implicit assumption that from one cycle to the next, the forming and reforming units included the same individuals—or at least they did not explicitly note the contrary possibility that individuals might, for whatever reason, decide to associate with other groups. Be that as it may, none of those studies immediately influenced wider social or political theory; neither Eggan, Shimkin, nor Gearing were cited in Joan Vincent's (1990) history of political anthropology.

Somewhat more influential in establishing the direction of anthropological studies of political systems were the neo-evolutionary typologies proposed by Marshall Sahlins (1961, 1968) and Elman Service (1962). Inspired by Julian Steward's (1955) concept of "levels of integration," they proposed four energy levels of general cultural evolution: band, tribe, chiefdom, and state. Although often misperceived as a static typology, for Sahlins and Ser-

vice—Sahlins especially[10]—units on the tribal and chiefdom levels were explicitly dynamic and processual. In that schema tribes were defined as groups
of residential units linked by cross-cutting sodalities, kinship ties, voluntary
associations, or political affiliations; chiefdoms were defined by the institutions of economic redistribution, of goods flowing to a center from which
they were redistributed outward. The dynamic aspect of those organizations
resulted from the temporal nature of those institutions and mechanisms—
sodalities and redistribution—which might not always be in operation. Rather,
they could be called into action whenever the need arose to organize and inte-
grate a wider population. In Sahlins's initial example the primary context for
tribal integration was competition, particularly intergroup conflict. At the
cessation of hostilities, "a tribe will automatically return to the state of dis-
unity—local autonomy—and remain there when competition is in abeyance"
(1961:326). The clear implication was that tribal boundaries were themselves
variable, depending upon the perception of intergroup conflict, and therefore
subject to political process and debate. Similarly, chiefdoms, ranging from
"big men" to "chiefs," were dynamic and processual. Theoretically, a big
man's network formed around him as a center, and collapsed at his death or
retirement. On the other hand, chiefdoms were based on the exploitation and
redistribution of more enduring resources, and could have longer durations,
although they too might collapse; Sahlins suggested that one cause of collapse
might be rebellion against a perceived indiscreet siphoning off of redistributional resources by a bureaucratic elite (Sahlins 1963). Unfortunately, although
the Steward-Sahlins-Service model of levels of integration is widely cited, the
dynamic processual elements of that model are often overlooked, particularly
by writers of introductory textbooks.

   At the same time, it is unfortunate that Sahlins and Service chose to label
their second level as they did, for it soon became embroiled in the confusion
engendered by conflicting uses of the term tribe in anthropology and in
everyday life. Commonly, tribe is used to refer to the units of "primitive"
peoples, with the belief that tribes encompassed shared language, territory,
and culture. Unfortunately, there has been no anthropological consensus about
that belief. While some anthropologists have used tribe to designate culture-
sharing units, they have noted that some tribes—such as the Comanches
(Hoebel 1940)—need not be politically organized as a single unit; other writers—such as Sahlins and Service, at least initially—limited its use to a very
specific kind of political organization.

   On the other hand, the leading critic of any use of "tribe" in anthropology was Morton H. Fried, who in a series of papers—one republished
three times in as many years—and books inveighed against almost all uses of
the word (Fried 1966, 1967, 1968, 1975a, 1975b, 1983); after race, he wrote,

tribe was "the single most egregious case of meaninglessness" in anthropology, often leading to a "a thicket of difficulties for analysis" (1968:4). Although Fried's argument was not impartial—he had proposed his own typology for political evolution[11]—it has been influential, and many scholars, including lawyers (Weatherhead 1980; see also Sturtevant 1983 and Clifford 1988), are now conscious of its implications—although again, those implications have generally been ignored by the writers of introductory anthropology and political science textbooks.

Given the problems with the word *tribe,* why use it at all? Sturtevant (1983)—probably overly focusing on Fried rather than on Sahlins and Service as the source of the problematical anthropological usage—suggested that American anthropologists allow *tribe* to remain a term in the lexicon of politico-legal relations between Indians and the federal government, while choosing an appropriate alternative term from some suitably exotic language for technical use. Unfortunately, other than his suggestion of the Chinese *buluo,* there is no likely candidate. There is a need for a term to label the span of political types between uncentralized bands and centralized chiefdoms (Lewellen 1983:25); that is, between the multiple organizations that follow variations of a common cultural structure, but that have little political or economic coordination either within or between them beyond basic reciprocity, and the centralized decision-making organizations whose internal political economies are based on redistribution. Tribe seems to be as good a term as any to cover that multidimensional span, provided it is used consistently. Indeed, as Robert Lowie noted, "The term 'tribe' may be used in a political sense [i.e., referring to autonomous political units] . . . *provided* we remember that linguistic and political groups need not coincide. . . . It is necessary to be clear whether the term 'tribe' is to be understood politically or linguistically" (1952:7; emphasis in original).

Moreover, the processual aspect of tribe—or whatever label we choose to apply to that kind of structure and its on-the-ground organization—must not be overlooked. Contemporary political organizations are phases in ongoing political processes of organization and reorganization at least as much as they are enduring units of cultural structure. To understand contemporary tribes, one must understand not only their histories, but the contemporary social, political, economic, and cultural fields within which they act.

A Processual View of Political Organization

The modern anthropological study of politics focuses on the "processes involved in determining and implementing public goals and [on] the differential
achievement and use of power by the members of the group concerned with
those goals" (Swartz, Turner, and Tuden 1966:7). That definition implies a
number of characteristic qualities that define an action as political: it is public
rather than private, it concerns goals, it is groupwide, and it involves a
focusing of power. Although each of those attributes of politics is of some
present concern, my primary focus is on the various publics involved in
political actions, on the varying social, temporal, and spatial dimensions of
the groups involved in setting and achieving goals, and on the processes by
which those publics are achieved, maintained, or denied.

Although politics is defined as groupwide, the definition of the relevant
group can be itself a goal of political action. Thus, a politically relevant
public need not be a whole society or even a major segment of it; indeed,
often society itself can be defined only by reference to the people concerned
with its continuing political goals, however general those goals may be.
During day-to-day social interaction, most actions and goals are focused by
immediate small-group concerns. At the other extreme, some political actions
might concern an entire regional population made up of several linguistic or
cultural units, whose goals are vague and generalized.

Fred Gearing's model of the "structures for Cherokee politics" (Gearing
1958, 1962) is extremely useful for a processual understanding of political
organization and reorganization. In Gearing's example, a co-resident population—an idealized eighteenth-century Cherokee village—was not a single
polity. Rather, it organized and reorganized itself depending upon its recurrent goals, its tasks at hand. For most economic activities, the household provided the structural pose, and the population was divided into many household organizations. For some purposes, the population organized itself as
corporate clans or clan segments. For other purposes, the population might
unite with other villages to form larger decision-making groups. Concur-
rently, some groups might decide not to follow the reorganization and might
split off, join with others, or even legitimate a new group. With each change
of pose, albeit structured according to the common culture, new groups, new
publics, were realized, with coincident changes in the kinds of goals and
activities subject to public discussion, coordination, and organization. But a
change of pose did not mean that the concerns of other poses were forgotten.

However, political organizations are not always as provided for in the
structural maps. As Raymond Firth noted, the process of operationalizing
structural cultural models into the on-the-ground organization of people-in-

groups is mediated by "the magnitude of the situation (as in men and materials), the alternatives open for choice and decision, and the time dimension" (Firth 1954:12). The inability to organize a sufficient work force for the task at hand, whether caused by a simple quantitative lack of personnel or by the leader's own lack of charismatic or administrative abilities, can have profound effects on the continued existence of the organization. The presence of alternatives, either in the form of alternate structural models or of alternate resources on which to base modified, alternative, or competitive organizations, can affect organizational strength. Finally, there is the time dimension, both in cyclical and in absolute terms; organizing a berry-picking party in January will lead to the same failure as organizing a mammoth-hunting party in 1995.

To generalize, when situations requiring organization are enduring, the organizations formed to meet those situations will endure; when changing environmental situations are predictable, as in a predictable seasonal round, organizational change will be predictable, with parallel changes in the allocation of sociopolitical power and authority. At the extreme, the exhaustion of a resource must result in the collapse of organizations based on its exploitation. Within that framework, sociopolitical history is the trajectory described by the establishment, the development, and possibly the collapse of organizations structured according to particular social-cultural models exploiting specific and definable resources.

In this light, each of the pre–1875 band lists can be interpreted as a temporal, though often partial, cross-section of ongoing sociopolitical processes; and the combined lists (table 1.1) can be interpreted as an outline of Comanche political history, recording the emergence, continuity, and sometimes decline and disappearance of sociopolitical groups. Furthermore, seen in processual terms, the preliminary answer to the question of how many Comanche groups there were is that one must specify a time period. During the eighteenth and nineteenth centuries there were multiple Comanche political organizations with distinct processual political histories. The specific question is, What were those histories? The general question is, What were the conditions in the wider natural and social environments that influenced their short- and long-term political successes—the particular histories—of those organizations?

The Structure of the Book

The following chapters describe Comanche political structure and its resulting on-the-ground organizations as they existed between 1706 and 1875. Chapter 2 details some of the structures of Comanche politics—the values, norms, and rules of public behavior, the kinds of political actors and political groups recognized by Comanches. It concludes with a general discussion of Comanche domestic and political economies. In the course of documented Comanche history, four political-economic resource domains can be identified, derived from (1) the exploitation of the buffalo and the horse, (2) warfare, (3) the control of trade, and (4) the solicitation and distribution of Euroamerican political gifts. But because those resources were differentially available— temporally, geographically, and politically—different political organizations emerged from their exploitation.

Informed discussion of ethnohistorical processes requires a knowledge of the historical actions that impelled those processes. Unfortunately, the published historical coverage of the Comanches has been uneven, and many incidents supposedly well-known, upon examination turn out to be at best confused or at worst contrived. There are numerous references to the Comanches in the literature on the Spanish borderlands (e.g., Bolton 1914; Thomas 1929a, 1929b, 1929c, 1932, 1935, 1940), but the focus was not on the Comanches themselves, and no general synthesis of Comanche history was attempted. Elizabeth A. H. John (1975) discussed eighteenth-century Euroamerican-Comanche relations in New Mexico and Texas in the context of general Euroamerican-Indian relations in the Southwest, but she ended her discussion about 1795. While Rupert N. Richardson (1933) briefly overviewed Comanche-Spaniard relations, his main focus was on post-Mexican Texas relations; his treatment of relations in New Mexico and elsewhere was minimal. Conversely, Charles Kenner (1969) treated Comanche relations in New Mexico, but not elsewhere. Although Wilbur Nye's histories of the southern Plains wars (Nye 1968, 1969) were based on extensive interviews with the aged Indian survivors, they were limited to the American military perspective.

In light of the uneven coverage, I have devoted much space to a detailed narrative synthesis of the history of Comanche political organizations from the time of earliest historical mention in 1706 to the Comanches' restriction to the reservation in 1875. I have divided the whole into five broad periods of political adaptation, stabilization, and change, discussed in chapters 3 through 7. The breaks between periods correspond to major changes in the Comanches' political-economic environment: first contact and interaction with Euroamerican leading to the treaties with the Spaniards in 1785–86, the Mexican

Revolution of 1821, the treaty with the Texas Republic in 1844, the American Civil War, and the restriction to the reservation in 1875. Although those periods and period breaks might seem to be based on Euroamerican rather than Comanche actions, they were significant events that marked changes in the resource bases of Comanche politics and thus relate to the presence or absence of resources; that the resources happen to have been other humans adds a degree of complexity and interest to the interactions but does not alter the basic political-economic relationship. Moreover, during several of those periods Comanches were often much better at manipulating Euroamericans than Euroamericans were at manipulating Comanches.

Within each period, utilizing different political-economic resources, the various Comanche organizations followed distinct but interacting historical and processual trajectories. Therefore, each chapter is divided into sections, each tracking a particular political group or groups. Each chapter concludes with an overall analysis of Comanche political organization during the period, emphasizing the quantitative dimensions of Comanche political resources and the changes in divisional organization that resulted from changes in the resource bases. The final chapter summarizes the political histories of the several divisions and suggests wider implications of this study.

Sources

The anthropological data for this study come from several sources. I have known Comanches since 1970; more-or-less formal fieldwork was conducted over some eighteen months between 1979 and 1986, with informal visits before and since. In addition I have sought out the unpublished notes of previous anthropologists who worked with Comanches: W. J. Hoffman (1880), Robert H. Lowie (1912), E. Adamson Hoebel, Waldo R. Wedel, and Gustav G. Carlson. The latter three were members of the 1933 Santa Fe Laboratory of Anthropology Field School under the direction of Ralph Linton. Hoebel's notes from that summer are held by the American Philosophical Society in Philadelphia; Wedel's and Carlson's are held by the National Anthropological Archives of the Smithsonian Institution. Linton left no notes, but some of his correspondence relating to the field party is held by the Museum of New Mexico's Laboratory of Anthropology. Since Linton, Hoebel, Wedel, and Carlson were present at many of the same interviews, their notes are a check upon one other. I have correlated their notes and am preparing a complete text for publication.

Historical archival sources on the Comanches include the records of the Spanish and Mexican periods of New Mexico, available on microfilm as the

Spanish Archives of New Mexico (cited here as SANM) and the Mexican Archives of New Mexico (MANM). Another photographed version of the Mexican period documents, called the New Mexico Archives (NMA), is in bound book format at the University of New Mexico. The Béxar Archives of Spanish and Mexican Texas (BA) are held by the University of Texas at Austin and are available on microfilm. Photocopied—photographed as well as microfilmed—documents from the Mexican Archivo General de la Nación (AGN) and its subunits Historias, Californias, and especially the Provincias Internas (AGN-PI) are housed at several North American repositories. In bound book format, copies of AGN documents relating to New Mexico are held by the University of New Mexico. Microfilmed copies of documents from the AGN were also examined at the University of Oklahoma Western History Collection and at the H. H. Bancroft Library at the University of California at Berkeley. Documents from the Spanish Archivo General de Indias in Seville (AGI) were examined on microfilm at the University of Oklahoma Western History Collection.

Archival sources in English include the records of the Bureau of Indian Affairs and those of the various military departments and districts of the West and Southwest held by the National Archives and its branches; microfilmed and original documents were examined at the National Archives in Washington and at the Fort Worth Federal Records Center. Originals, photocopies, and microfilms of the Kiowa Agency records were examined at the Oklahoma Historical Society (OHS-KA) in Oklahoma City. Other repositories include the National Anthropological Archives (NAA) of the Smithsonian Institution and the Albert Pike Collection in the Library of the Supreme Council, 33°, Ancient and Accepted Scottish Rite, Washington, D.C.

The principal documents I have utilized in this study are the direct, and where possible primary, reports of diplomatic meetings, military campaigns, daily diaries of comings and goings, and inventories of supplies purchased and of political gifts distributed. In those contexts, the degree to which cultural bias might impinge upon the facts of whether or not a certain person was present at a certain time, what he said—given the adequacy of interpreters—what was said to him, when he left, what gifts he was given, or what he traded for, is less than in the potentially more culturally loaded descriptions of intent, motivation, or meaning given from a distance in time, space, and degree of contact such as are contained in summary accounts and secondary reports.

At the same time, the historical literature on the Comanches is replete with accounts whose historical accuracy is at best unreliable and at worst fabricated. Although Thomas Streeter (1983) and Melburn Thurman (1982) have discussed several spurious Comanche captivity narratives, the reliability of other sources has seldom been examined. I have subjected all the historical materials I cite, both published and unpublished, to a basic historiographic critique: can it be shown that the author had first-hand knowledge of the events he reported? That process has produced some surprises. For example, many scholars accept the accounts of George Catlin, Josiah Gregg, and Randolph B. Marcy as valid descriptions of the Comanches. But careful examination raises doubts about their reliability as expert witnesses. For instance, there are serious discrepancies between Catlin's description of the meeting between the Comanche chiefs and the U.S. Dragoons in 1834 (Catlin 1841) and the reports of the official reporters (Wheelock 1835; Hildreth 1836; Perrine and Foreman 1925), especially concerning the identity of the "principal chief." Given that the Dragoons were attempting to open diplomatic relations with the Comanches, it would have been important for them to know and to report the names of those with whom they had dealt. Catlin, on the other hand, was concerned with creating a romantic image of the Indian. Moreover, Catlin had been detained in the sick camp and was not even present during the meetings. Thus, at best his published account must be considered garbled hearsay.

Josiah Gregg's general description of Comanche political relations (J. Gregg 1844) is often cited as authoritative (see, e.g., Hoebel 1940:20). Although Gregg was in the Santa Fe trade for over a decade, about 1830–40, only two incidents of direct contact with Comanches can be attributed to him, an apparently not uncommon statistic for the Santa Fe trade during that period. Thus, unless shown otherwise by further research, his general information on the Comanches must also be considered hearsay.

Finally, although Randolph Marcy considered himself an expert on the Comanches—in 1852, when preparations were under way for an expedition to explore the headwaters of the Red River, Marcy recommended himself for its command because of his "acquaintance with the several bands of Comanches who frequented that country and the knowledge he possessed of their language" [Foreman 1937:xii]—in his voluminous writings (Marcy 1849, 1866; Foreman 1937, 1939) he described only two incidents of direct contact and gave contradictory details in different books. Thus, without additional collaboration from other witnesses, it is difficult to judge the extent of Marcy's first-hand knowledge of Comanches and the amount of faith to put in any particular statement.

I have generally avoided the reminiscences by early settlers and the various compendia of "Indian depredations" (DeShields 1886, 1912; Wilbarger 1889; J. H. Brown 1899; J. H. Jenkins 1958). Most of the former were composed years if not decades after the events in question, often with no resources other than faulty memory as a guide; in the few cases I cite, they are given in the form "according to . . ." Likewise, most of the depredation narratives are based on reminiscences rather than on documentation. Moreover, the authors freely copied among themselves without citation (J. H. Jenkins 1958:xix). But even more than the reminiscences, the depredation stories often contain chronological and other errors; although those are generally too numerous and trivial to comment upon here, a few will require asides from the narrative flow.

There were, however, individuals who had much more intimate and longlasting relations with Comanches, and their reports have correspondingly greater authority. For instance, José Francisco Ruíz lived with Comanches from at least 1812, if not earlier, and between 1821 and 1835 he was often in more or less constant contact with them. Thus, his descriptions have an authority unsurpassed by any other historical writer.

Ultimately, there are also documentary sources produced by Comanches themselves. While at the Smithsonian Institution, 1987–92, I was able to recover a manuscript family history, based on oral traditions and other research, written by Joe Attocknie (Attocknie 1965). Through the generosity of the Attocknie family, I have quoted from that manuscript here; I am preparing an edited text for publication.

I have paid special attention to two kinds of citations. This is a study of political organizations; therefore I have paid special attention to political ethnonyms. Although I agree with Morris Foster that the ethnonyms *may be* "problematic glosses on the internal organization of the Comanche community" (1991:37–38), the pre-1875 band lists may also be more or less accurate reflections of the Comanche totality as understood by contemporary observers. Therefore, the best strategy to evaluate those possibilities is not to ignore the ethnonyms and their changes through time, to a priori label them as mere artifacts of Euroamerican political misconceptions without need of further discussion, but rather it is to seek an understanding of the ways those names were applied by both Comanches and Euroamericans.

At the same time, since I view politics as culturally mediated individual actions, I have tried to identify and follow individuals; this is also an attempt to respond to Robert Berkhofer's observation, "Even for those peoples like the Cherokees or the Iroquois . . . we still do not possess specific lists of personnel and issues over time" (1971:374). In this, I also follow the advice given to me by Joe Attocknie: "History without names is just stories." I have retained names in the Comanche language for the simple reason that the Comanches are one of the few Plains Indian groups whose personal names were not translated into English when they were transformed into family names; therefore, familiarity with the original Comanche names is necessary for anyone interested in the Comanches. Whenever possible, at the first appearance of a name I have given a normalized phonemic spelling and an English gloss. For the most part I have retained the spelling of names as they first appear; I have, however, after initial quoted appearances, removed the syllabic hyphens common in English transcriptions of Indian names as a typographic barbarism that refuses to recognize the names as real words (Deloria 1970:27).[12]

2

Comanche Political Culture

Comanches have organized and oriented their actions as individuals, and as individuals in groups, toward a variety of compelling goals: to participate in collective religious rituals; to gather together in social interactions; to exploit resources—buffalo, horses, Euroamericans; to resist competition by others—Kiowas, Cheyennes, Euroamericans. Sometimes they have organized because they have been persuaded by politicians or other zealots that they have common goals and interests. All were organized according to shared models of the world and how to get things done in it.

Comanche society was, in Fried's sense, a "rank society." That is, there were "fewer positions of valued status than persons capable of filling them. A rank society has means of limiting the access of its members to status positions they would otherwise hold on the basis of sex, age, or personal attributes" (1967:52). For Comanches, the "means of limiting access . . . to status positions" was through the ideals of 'honor' or 'respect'.[1]

In turn, honor created an authority—the "belief that [its holder] is more capable, more able than [others], and that therefore they are well-advised to place the decision-making rights in his hand" (R. N. Adams 1966:6). Traditionally, the normative route to honor was primarily, for both males and females (D. E. Jones 1972), through *puha* 'medicine power'; secondly, for males,[2] through honor obtained in war; and thirdly, again for both males and females, through the maintenance of social relations by the distribution of wealth, of "prestige accrued through generosity" (Wallace and Hoebel 1952:131). War honors and *puha* were closely linked; as one of the 1933 consultants noted, "no man won great honors without having medicine" (Comanche Field Party: Naiya, July 6).[3]

Puha could be obtained through the vision quest, *puhahabitu* 'lying down for power', at a place known for power. The 1933 consultants were nearly

28

unanimous in their agreement that one did not just go on a vision quest, waiting, as it were, for the first passing spirit. Rather, one must know what power one was searching for; as Post Oak Jim said, "If a person keeps going to a lonely place with no definite idea of what he wants, his mind may be led into evil thoughts" (Comanche Field Party: July 14). Thus, a searcher often went to the grave of a known *puhakatu* 'possessor of power' in search of his power.

Medicine power obtained in a vision could be shared with others, forming small-scale medicine societies. The 1933 Comanche Field Party consultants indicated some variation in their size and extent; Post Oak Jim said that power could be shared with no more than twelve others and that a man could belong to several such groups (Comanche Field Party: July 14), but George Koweno reported that such groups were composed of only six members and that a man could belong to only one group (Comanche Field Party: July 21). But the 1933 consultants also noted that not all men had *puha*; according to Naiya, "Some men had no medicine. They were afraid to go where there was great danger" (Comanche Field Party: July 6).

To be a *tekwuniwapI* 'warrior' or 'hero' (from *tekwa* 'to speak') required a war record. Kwasia (Comanche Field Party: July 5) noted that "the most honorable man was he who had killed the most enemies in fighting." That paralleled a comment made almost two centuries earlier by New Mexico governor Francisco Marín del Valle, "Their leader is the one who had killed the most enemies" (Marín 1758).

Tahsuda gave the following story, which can be exemplary of a young man's rise to leadership:

[A young man] asked his father for permission to go on a war-party. His father said, "OK, take this pony and lead it from the mule. When you're in enemy territory, ride the pony fast aways and then stop. Do this four times and he will never tire."

They camped and sent a lookout up a hill. The lookout saw two tipis on the other side. He went down and reported that three people were returning to those tipis and had seen him. The party went around the hill and saw three families fleeing, three women ahead of three men. They chased them and shot. One man on a fast horse carried on the rear guard action. The boy drove at him on the next sally and speared him. The other two dismounted and started shooting with guns. He speared them both. He looked back and saw his party coming all strung out. The first man up counted coup. They took scalps and mounted them on long poles and returned to camp and gave the victory dance.

The next morning, women dressed like warriors and came to the hero's tipi and danced. Some lifted up the sides of the tipi and saw him sitting there. His relatives and parents had brought gifts and had piled them outside. The leader of the women dancers went in and took the first gift; then she distributed the gifts saying, "We're seeking for something that you threw away, or are going to throw away." His father gave two horses.

The boy went off on another war party as leader. He worked his horse as before. The party met another band looking for war like they were. These were Utes. The parties faced each other. The boy rode out and made a circle before the other band. Their chief chased him back. Then he had one of his followers repeat the tactic. When their chief followed up, the boy rode up and speared him. He rode into the enemy and killed two more. His band followed him in and they broke up the enemy. They returned to the dead and took scalps and looted the bodies. They took anything they wanted, and then returned to the main camp. There was a big victory dance almost till morning and a Shakedown Dance in the morning at the boy's tipi. His father gave three horses this time.

After the Horse Dance,[4] they went on a raid again. They clashed with Osages. There were three chiefs with the Osages. The boy charged and killed the three. There was a general melee and the Osages fled. They took the scalp-lock off the Osages. There were more dances and the father gave four horses. [Comanche Field Party: no date; Hoebel 1940:26–28]

Although Tahsuda did not generalize his story, saying only that a chief "just got that way" (Hoebel 1940:18), a century earlier, in 1832, Jean Louis Berlandier gave a generalized description of a warrior's ascent, based on information from José Francisco Ruíz:

When a warrior wins great honor by mastering his enemy with the knife in face-to-face combat, he covers himself with glory, there is talk of his achievement in council, and as his deeds increase in daring, he gains a degree of respect from his fellows and visibly takes on authority. Little by little, the public confidence in him grows. Then finally, in one of these public assemblies where the pipe passes from hand to hand as the men deliberate, he is addressed as "captain," and he acquires the rights to that position. An old man from the council, or the village crier, tells the whole village of his glorious deeds, and as a sign of respect to the mighty warrior, the other men of the village, as well as the women, refrain from smoking before him. Slowly, and almost imperceptibly, he gains power and prestige and is finally named chief. [Ruíz 1828:39]

War honors were visually represented in several ways. They could be painted in war records and summarized either in stripes on leggings or in headdresses. In the conclusion of Tahsuda's story of the young hero, started above, three years later, when the boy was nineteen years old, they gave him a war-bonnet. They had a buffalo-hide tipi set up and painted with white clay. The floor was all smoothed out. There were buffalo-hide robes and blankets spread out. The warriors entered. The leader was in the west. They went to the north of the door and fell back. They entered according to seniority on this status. The boy entered and took his place at left of the leader. The chief got up and made a talk: "This man has done brave deeds. What's more, I honor him ahead of myself. Hereafter he is chief in my stead. This is merely a bunch of feathers given by your friends." Then they gave him a bonnet on his head. There were two rows of feathers as a special honor. The boy went to the first position instead of the usual place to the south of the door. [Comanche Field Party: no date; Hoebel 1940:26–28]

Another headdress was the otter-fur cap, whose wearers, according to Post Oak Jim, must go on every raid made by the cap wearers; sometimes fur caps had buffalo horns, an even higher honor (Comanche Field Party: July 24). Particularly brave warriors, as well as members of the Big Horse Society, carried spears decorated with a ruff of crow feathers, recorded by Wedel as *woinutsik nahaihkorohkO* ['spear with a necklace of crow feathers'] (Comanche Field Party: Kwasia n.d.). Another form was the crooked lance, recorded by Lowie (1912) as "patsukuwe kwitowi," that is, *patso?ikowe kwitubi* 'otter wrapped' (fig. 2.1). A third symbol of a warrior's bravery was the *pianu?upai* 'big whip', a notched wooden club with a leather lash, carried only by the bravest men. Apparently the last pre-reservation-era *pianu?upai*s were held by Chivato and his brother Pinero (Hoebel recorded his name as Pinedaboi); both were Lipan Apaches by birth who lived with Comanches in the 1870s, then with Mescaleros, and returned to the Comanches about 1890. Pinero gave his *pianu?upai* to Ralph Linton in 1933, saying that Linton's war record outmatched his own (Wallace and Hoebel 1952:272) (fig. 2.2 and plate 1). Its current location is unknown.[5]

The conjunction of medicine power and war honors created the authority to influence the direction of social and political actions; "Comanches tended to attribute moral rightness to the braver man" (Hoebel 1940:55). According to Ralph Linton, "Power seems to be about equally divided between great warriors and great Medicine Men. An individual who is both is unassailable" (Linton 1933). That social power was not "skill authority" (R. N. Adams 1966:6) based on personal knowledge or abilities in the matter at hand, but functioned in contexts beyond those from which the authority was derived.[6] For instance, the *pianu?upai* was carried, not in war, but in society dances to whip the dancers. Similarly, a war record could be used to overbalance an otherwise uncertain negotiation. In one classic case reported by Kwasia,

Fig. 2.1. Wakini's sketch of a *patso?ikowe kwitubi* in Robert Lowie's field notes. Courtesy American Museum of Natural History.

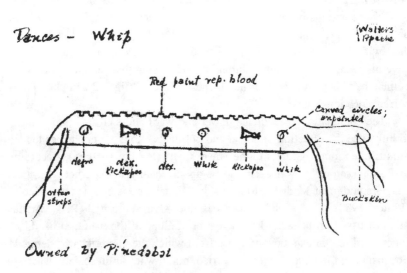

Fig. 2.2. E. A. Hoebel's sketch of Pinero's *pianu?upai*. Courtesy American Philosophical Society Library.

Plate 1. Chivato and his *pianuʔupai*. Photographer unknown, before 1930. Courtesy Sam DeVenney.

Plate 2. Pinero (second from right) and his *pianɨ?ɨpai*. Photograph by Waldo R. Wedel, August 1933. Courtesy National Anthropological Archives, Smithsonian Institution.

just before the allotment of Indian lands, one man beat another to a certain choice half section of land. The one who had the claim threatened to kill the other if he caused any disturbance. The latter countered with another threat of violence. The case was settled by Quanah Parker [then a judge on the Court of Indian Offenses] who called in two old warriors to determine the war records of the respective parties to the dispute. One warrior was late in coming, so Parker sent Kwasia, who was then chief of Indian police to see him for his record. One of the disputants (the first party) accompanied the policeman. There he said to the warrior, "which is better, me or this other fellow," thinking that thus asked the warrior would give him the credit.

"Alright," said the warrior, "you asked me, I'll speak out plain. This other fellow is the better man. I was in a battle where I saw him get off his horse and help a dismounted comrade from the midst of the enemy. He is a brave man and did a great deed. You better look out or he'll whip you or kill you." The man with the best record for bravery won the decision and the loser gave up his claims to the land. In this case if he could have shown braver deeds he could have kept the land. [Comanche Field Party: July 5; Hoebel 1940:55]

Another secondary context for the use of a war record was by the "champion at law" (Hoebel 1940:59), when an aggrieved party enlisted the services of a brave man, not as advocate but as enforcer.

Authority was not a fixed and permanent mark, but was subject to constant measurement and testing, and formal competitions were a recognized aspect of Comanche social life. According to Kwasia:

If a man were throwing a feast, a braver man could come and stand by and tell the people of his bravery. Then he asked the promoter of the feast if he had anything better to boast of. If he did, the late comer retired. Otherwise, if the second had the bravest feats to his credit, he took over and promoted the feast, getting the honor at the actual giver's expense. [Comanche Field Party: July 5]

Competitions could also involve medicine power. According to Post Oak Jim, "In the old days, a group could get together and compare powers" (Comanche Field Party: July 13). He later elaborated:

At certain times the tribe [sic] gathered so men could show their powers. Once a man with nɨnɨpʉhiʔ [the "little people"] power came along. He said he would do his power at night. So they gathered at a lodge late one night. The man took his bow and arrows, and the nɨnɨpʉhiʔ touched each one. Then he sent a man outside to shoot four arrows in any direction he wished. The man shot the arrows, then the nɨnɨpʉhiʔ man went out to get them. A streak of lightning pointed at each one, and each shaft was illuminated. One was fired in each direction. The man got all but the east one, which was stuck in a tree; he said they would get it the next morning.

The next man stuck an eighteen-inch stick in the ground, and put a blanket over it. He then pulled the blanket off and a big plum tree loaded with plums sprang forth. This man had power for doctoring pregnant women; he couldn't approach a menstruating woman.

The third man sent a man to bring in a large grape leaf and lay it on the ground beneath the knee of the preceding magician. Then he told the latter to lift it up. He did so and found a baby under the leaf. Crest fallen, he crawled out of the tipi on his hands and knees and left.

The meeting was here interrupted by a medicine man who wanted a peyote meeting, because he didn't believe in it. So he put up a tipi and held a meeting. He went into the tipi when the moon came up. The man who wanted the meeting sat beside the chief on the west wall. He said he saw a man with big knife and bloody scalp come into view as the moon rose; the higher the moon, the nearer the apparition. The man was terribly frightened. He tried to tell the chief, who was singing, that he wanted to get out and go home. At the end of the meeting, the chief put sage leaves on the fire and smoked the lodge up. The man was finally brought around; he said he still didn't think anything of peyote, but he didn't care to go through the experience again. [Comanche Field Party: July 25]

Political Statuses and Roles

Several Comanche terms designated political statuses, leaders, and officers, although a degree of indeterminacy existed among them. In the most general sense, the root *nomUne* (*noo* 'camp', 'move', *muhne* 'to lead') referred to the camp leader; *nomUnekatʉ* or *nomUnewapI* is a 'leader' or 'officer'. A more common term was *paraibo*, generic for 'chief', 'primary', or 'principal'; 'one with authority'. According to Nemaruibitsi (Comanche Field Party: August 8), the 'first' or 'chief' wife was *paraibo kwʉhʉ*. Gatschet (1893) and Detrich (1894) recorded "maimiana paraivo" and "mimeah paraivo" as 'war chief' (both *mahi* 'war', *mia* 'go', *na* nominalizing suffix). Joe Attocknie classed paraivo as *ʉrʉ paraibo* 'good' or 'peaceful' chief, and *woho paraibo* 'mean' or 'dangerous' chief (pers. comm.). In 1873 Cyrus Beede, the chief clerk of the Office of Indian Affairs Central Superintendency, was called "tosa paraivo" 'white chief' (Haworth 1873b); in 1884 Albert Gatschet (1884) recorded *taivo paraibo* as 'white man chief'. Gatschet also recorded *paraibo nanemane* as 'chief of one tribe' (he gave *nanamane* [*naʔnʉmʉnʉʉ*, that is, *na* reflexive pronoun, *numu* 'Comanche', *nuu* plural] as 'family, relations, member of the tribe'). A decade later he gave *tubitsi paraibo* 'real chief' as 'head chief' (Gatschet 1893).[7]

The extent of a *paraibo*'s authority has long been problematical for Euroamericans; in 1758, Governor Marín of New Mexico sketched the problem in outline: "some obeyed him, others did not" (Marín 1758). However, interpreting the basis of those differences has proven difficult. For some observers, the situation was simple: Comanches were perverse savages, having no laws: in 1821, Juan Antonio Padilla, a Spaniard stationed at Béxar, said they were "governed by the person most noted for bravery, intrepidity, and ferocity," but "they obey him when they wish, without noting him. And if they follow him to war, it is because of the love they have for murder and theft" (Hatcher 1919:55). For others, the situation was cultural: Comanche chiefs lacked the explicit "socially recognized privilege" of applying "absolute coercive force" (Hoebel 1940:47). In 1818, David Burnet suggested that there was a pragmatic dimension:

> Compulsion is seldom exercised on a refractory culprit; and when imperious circumstances require it be done, it is effected by a convention of chiefs whose personal influences become auxiliary to an otherwise impotent authority. [Wallace 1954:124-25]

Except for Padilla's invocation of savagery, I suggest that all three of those dimensions are involved. As noted above, one basis of Comanche social standing was war honors—Marín's "bravery [and] intrepidity." That in turn provided a basis for authority, the culturally defined ability to influence the behavior of others. But there were limits to that authority; in parallel to the modern anthropological definition of politics as "the processes involved in determining and implementing *public* goals and [on] the differential achievement and use of power by the members of *the group concerned with those goals*" (Swartz, Turner, and Tuden 1966:7; my emphasis), Comanche culture at least normatively recognized a difference between the private and domestic, and the public and political, although where a particular incident fell on that continuum would have been a matter of political debate. Finally, there were pragmatic dimensions to the exercise of authority, with political actors weighing their various options singly and in concert.[8]

Nonetheless, there are several historical cases documenting the use of both threatened and actual coercive force by political leaders. In 1753 it was reported that a chief told his own brother to leave his village or be punished, saying, "he did not wish his people to experience another defeat such as [one caused by the brother]" (Thomas 1940:116). In 1785 Toro Blanco, principal fomentor of continued hostilities against New Mexico, was assassinated and his followers scattered by the followers of Ecueracapa, proponent of peace (Thomas 1932:299). In 1853 Julius Froebel observed, "In the evening before dark, Okhakhtzomo exhibited his authority by ordering our Indian visitors to leave the camp and return home. To some, who did not obey immediately he applied his horsewhip" (Froebel 1859:266). And in 1858 a Comanche left the Texas reservation on a raid into Mexico; "When he returned . . . with 12 horses, a council of chiefs was called to consider the matter and the culprits were informed that if they repeated the act they would all be instantly shot. Since that time no parties have left the reserve" (Leeper, Sr., 1858f:175).

It remains an open question whether those chiefly actions were based on the *paraibo'* s own authority and *puha*, or whether through consensus achieved in council, compromise, persuasion, passive agreement not to disagree or the more active counterpart, withdrawal, those *paraibos* came to act on the authority of the public—although that latter case seems to parallel Burnet's 1818 above noted comments about "compulsion . . . effected by a convention of chiefs" (Wallace 1954:124–25). Each alternative is possible, but the available data are often not detailed enough to make a determination from among the possibilities.

At the same time, it has been argued (e.g., Foster 1991:68) that inasmuch as the cited incidents involved relations with Euroamericans in one form or another, they were thereby atypical and did not represent normal interaction between Comanches. While it is certainly true that those incidents involved Euroamericans, the degree of influence Euramericans may have had on the situations also remains open. To assert that there was no influence is to insist that Comanches lived in a vacuum; conversely, to insist *a priori* that contact with Euroamericans always and everywhere evoked extraordinary, extralegitimate, or even extra-cultural responses is to imply that the Euroamerican records of that interaction are always and everywhere invalid representations of normal modes of interaction; such a conclusion undermines the foundations of the ethnohistorical project, the dialogue between ethnography and documentary history. Since we cannot now ask the participants about their motivations and influences, unless cultural, pragmatic, or political influence can be infered from other evidence, our concern must be the effect those actions had on the course of Comanche political history. For the present, suffice it to say that there are documented incidents in which chiefs used authority both normatively and pragmatically.

The status of *paraibo* can be contrasted with that of *tekwawapI* or *tekwakatI*, from *tekwa* 'talk' or 'speech'; the first form is 'talker', the second 'he has speech', that is, the camp crier.[9] The term sometimes used by Spaniards and a few Anglo-Texans to refer to speakers was *tlatolero*, derived from the Comanches' Uto-Aztecan linguistic relative, Nahuatl *tlatoa* 'to speak'.

Among the Aztecs it had political connotations, and *tlatoani* 'great talker' was a royal title.

There are several historical references that emphasize the distinction between political leaders and announcers. In reporting his 1785 talks with Comanches, the French-Spanish voyager Pedro Vial clearly distinguished between the men with whom he treated and those who announced the results of those meetings: "They [the chiefs] ordered their *tlatoleros* to send word to all those of their respective divisions," and "The *tlatoleros* [spent the day] in talking . . . in order for them to know what has happened" (Vial and Chavez 1785). In 1836 Anglo-Texan John Cameron stated, "The results of the council are proclaimed to all the tribe by order of the principal chief through the medium of a person called 'Talotero' [*sic*] appointed then for the purpose" (Lamar 1921, 1:475). In 1851 Ketumsee, then a local band chief and later the principal Penateka chief, apologized for not having "some one to speak and reply for him" (Winfrey and Day 1959–66, 3:145).

Although the statuses of *paraibo* and *tekwawapI* are distinct, decision maker and consensus former as opposed to announcer and articulator of decisions, they were not necessarily distinct persons: "The announcer would be the chief of the band, who called out and announced the move" (Comanche Field Party: Naiya, July 24); "A chief . . . decided when to move camp, and would go out and announce, 'Listen, listen, we are going to move camp. The grass is getting short, and we must move to the next creek. The place has already been chosen'" (Comanche Field Party: Howard White Wolf, July 31). During a 1786 treaty council with Governor Juan Bautista de Anza of New Mexico, Tosapoy (either *tosa po?e* 'white road' or *tosa poi* 'white eye') was the designated speaker for the Comanches, giving a carefully prepared speech (Thomas 1932:304); Tosapoy was also listed as leader of a residential group, and was thus presumably a *paraibo*. In 1828, while bison hunting with a group of Texas Comanches, Jean Louis Berlandier recorded that "after a quiet night . . . at 6 o'clock . . . the Captain-Speaker (called Tlatolero) was already beginning to tell the entire tribe in a loud voice what they ought to do and at what time the march [would] have to be resumed. At sunrise he repeated his speech and advised them, above all, to be considerate with us" (1844:178). Berlandier's "Captain-Speaker" is an evocative combination of the two roles, but unfortunately, Berlandier did not further discuss the incident, and it is not clear whether the speaker was the band chief. In 1933, however, Post Oak Jim did not give the role even that much structure: a man "might get in the habit, and would get out every morning and announce" (Comanche Field Party: July 19).

Sociopolitical Implications of the
Search for Social Standing

With the beginnings of social standing came the possibility of a good marriage, and thus a widening involvement in kinship-based political support networks; according to Rhoda Asanap, "Women liked to marry a warrior for his
name, and because he had many horses" (Comanche Field Party: July 7).
Elopement did take place, and sometimes the couple "fixed things up" themselves (Comanche Field Party: Herman Asanap, June 30–July 1), but usually
marriage choices were carefully considered by the families. According to
Herman Asanap, "A man sometimes requested the father of a promising
youth, an honorable boy, to give him as a son-in-law" (Comanche Field
Party: June 30–July 1). Conversely, "A man with two or three sisters would
try to marry one of them to an industrious man, so that his brother-in-law
could provide him with game" (Comanche Field Party: Post Oak Jim, July
19). Although denying the existence of bride price, the 1933 consultants
acknowledged bride service. As stated by Herman Asanap, "A son-in-law had
certain duties toward his father-in-law. . . . A man gave a portion of the kill
to his father-in-law, usually the best of the game" (Comanche Field Party:
June 30–July 1). Naiya echoed that, saying, "A man always divided up his
game with his father-in-law and other kin. . . . A man would always cut a certain choice piece of meat from the kill for his father-in-law. He always asked
his wife to take her father's portion to him, he never took it over himself"
(Comanche Field Party: July 7). Those kinship support networks in turn
became the basis of wider political organizations.

Other support networks developed as politically active individuals forged
independent links, often framed in terms of *haits* 'formal friend' or *tubitsinahaitsInuu* 'true friends' (male only). According to Post Oak Jim, "True
friends were closer than actual brothers, especially in time of battle, because
if a man lost something belonging to himself he was less bothered than if he
lost something belonging to someone else. So long as there was any life left
in a fallen warrior, his brother couldn't desert him in battle" (Comanche Field
Party: July 19). Other friendship relations were not as formalized, but they
involved similar reciprocal support; "the poor were your friends, if you fed
them" (Comanche Field Party: Naiya, July 8).

On a more pragmatic level, social standing required the maintenance of
followers and supporters; honorable persons were expected to be liberal in the
distribution of wealth, with the expected reciprocal return of political support.
The distribution of wealth required the production of wealth, and was thus the
basis of Comanche political economy.

Structural Poses and Levels of
Sociopolitical Integration

Comanche sociopolitical structure was composed of several structural poses
in four levels of integration. The levels were the nuclear family, the extended
family, the residential local band, and the political division (Kavanagh 1980,
1986; Thurman 1980). Units on those levels were linked by sodalities—political support groups, small-scale medicine societies, and large-scale military
societies—and the scale of the units and sodalities increased with the level of
integration. The Spaniards and Mexicans generally recognized those levels;
Anglo-Americans generally did not.

Although there are several accounts of travelers encountering single Comanche families or camps of only a few tipis, the nuclear family was usually
not an independent entity but cooperated with others to form a bilaterally extended household; Joe Attocknie used the word *numunahkahni* 'the people
who live together in a household' to refer to such groups (Kavanagh 1986);
the *numunahkahni* is coordinate with Hoebel's "extended family group" and
his otherwise undefined "group of relatives" (1940:14). There are no limits to
the size of groups that could be called *numunahkahni*, although the nonrecog-
nition of relatives beyond two generations above and three below, or beyond
two intervening marriage relationships, could limit the interactions of members at the extremes (Gladwin 1948:76).

The 1933 consultants described patrilocal residence as the normative pattern, offering an economic rationalization:

> When a married young man had living parents, he always took his wife
> to his own people. They lived near the wife's parents only when the man
> had no living parents. If the man's parents had accumulated much stock,
> he stayed and took care of the stock when they died; he remained in the
> same band. If a father dies, his sons must take care of his stock, there-
> fore, he can't be with his wife's folks. [Comanche Field Party: Naiya,
> July 7]

But they also noted exceptions. For instance, according to Naiya, "If his
parents had little or no wealth he might, at their death, transfer to his wife's
band" (Comanche Field Party: July 7). During the period before Frank
Chekovi's father's death, Frank's married brother lived not with his own relatives but with his wife's people (Comanche Field Party: Frank Chekovi,
August 2). Howard White Wolf added a touch of romantic love, noting that
sometimes if the father objected to a choice of wife, a man "would leave his
people and go to live with his wife's people rather than give up the girl" (Comanche Field Party: August 4).

A representative *numunahkahni* was described in 1836 by a ransomed captive, Sarah Ann Horn:

> There were three branches of the family in which I lived residing in separate tents. One branch consisted of an old woman and her 2 daughters, one of whom, was also a widow. The next was a son of the old woman who claimed me as his property and the third was a son-in-law of the old woman. In the family to which I belonged there were 5 sons and no daughters. [Rister 1955:157]

That *numunahkahni* exhibited two types of postmarital residence: the old woman's son remained at home, as did two daughters, one of whom brought her husband. Similar *numunahkahni* groups could be identified in the 1990s.

Local residential bands, called *rancherías* by the Spaniards, comprised one or more *numunahkahni,* one of which formed its core, and which cooperated in the exploitation of resources. That is probably the situation to which Hoebel referred when he commented that "the identity of the 'extended family group' was submerged in the more embracing organization of the band, but not wholly lost" (Hoebel 1940:14). But individuals and nuclear families—as well as whole *numunahkahni*—could, for a variety of reasons, move between local bands. There were also otherwise unrelated nuclear families and individuals attached to a group. Joe Attocknie noted that when his great-grandfather, Uphuhe *(upuitu* 'sleeper') stole Wuhyahkeh, a curly haired women of the *aanuu*, the Crows, they went to live with Comanches in Texas. After several years, they then attached themselves to Paruasemana's *(parua* 'bear', *sumaru* 'ten', *nu* nominalizer) band (Attocknie 1965).

Although it may be assumed that local bands were named, and although it is probable that many of the unique names that appear in the historical record are local band names, it is seldom possible to attach ethnonyms to specific historical local populations, or conversely, to give local band affiliations to specific individuals.[10]

Because the local band comprised one or more *numunahkahni,* most local band members were related to one another; some modern Comanches feel that membership in the same local band implied kinship, with the English term cousin used to designate a close but unspecified relationship. Since marriage between relatives was prohibited, Hoebel's suggestion (1940:12) that marriage was "to a great extent within the [local] band" is incorrect. The most common exceptions to this pattern were the marriages of peripheral men to core women, which established a more permanent status for the man within the local band. Such was the case when the son of Uphuhe and Wuhyahkeh, Attocknie *(ata* 'other', *kahni* 'house', sometimes given as "Lone Tipi") married Paruasemana's granddaughter (Attocknie 1965).

The central man in the core *numunahkahni* was the local band headman, the *paraibo*, sometimes called by the Spaniards capitancillo, rarely capitan chiquito, but both 'little captain'. Joe Attocknie recognized the *paraibo*'s central position in political organization: "The size of a personage's following is an almost accurate indication of his leadership qualities" (Attocknie 1965). Through a combination of *puha,* hunting skill and military bravery, political skill and charisma, and control of trade and other economic activities, he attracted judicious marriages for members of his own family and *numunah-kahni* and maintained peripheral families and individuals in personal support relations; conversely, if he was unable to maintain his supporters, they would look elsewhere. It was in those kinds of actions that there was, to use Morris Foster's phrase, a "strategic movement and [re-]organization of personnel among different social groups" (1991:70; see also Kavanagh 1989). Futhermore, in that light, Tahsuda's remark that the *paraibo* had little to do but "hold the band together" (Hoebel 1940:18) takes on new meaning: holding the band together was a major task and took considerable skill.[11]

As elements in a political arena involving groupwide interests, village movements, cooperative hunts, the general context of trade, and matters of immediate war, peace, and intergroup relations were political issues to be discussed publicly. Other matters, such as berry picking, hide tanning, and the specifics of trade, domestic affairs, marriage arrangements (including the collapse of those arrangements in divorce), *nanawokU* (damages for adultery), and even murder, were private matters (Hoebel 1940:49). In the event the private and domestic became public and political, as when a *nanawokU* feud began with a refusal to pay damages, or in retaliation for damages taken, "the chief usually stepped in and tried his best to quiet things down" (Comanche Field Party: Post Oak Jim, July 24).

The adult men of a village formed its council, although not all men participated all the time (Comanche Field Party: Post Oak Jim, July 19). Informal meetings, called "smoke lodges," occurred almost every night.[12] As described by Post Oak Jim:

> The men smoked every night in this group. Here representatives of different bands met to talk, sometimes the chief was also there. Sometimes young men attended. The announcer was present to see what was going on. The next morning, he announced the plans that they would be moving out in two or three days. Then the chief would get out on the last morning and help announce. [Comanche Field Party: July 19]

Smoke lodges were places of gossip. According to Jean Louis Berlandier, "It is at these meetings that they exchange their deepest secrets and it is here that an adulteress is usually discovered. The guilty man is almost never killed; the aggrieved husband usually thrashes him and takes some of his horses and mules" (1844:178). According to Robert Neighbors, here were discussed "war and women" (Neighbors 1848).

More formal meetings discussed matters of public concern. They were begun with ceremonial smoking:

> In order to transact any important business or receive any important communication from another tribe, the principal chief always convokes the lesser ones of his tribe to meet in general council when each occupies the seat corresponding to his grade, and after many ceremonies peculiar to themselves on such occasions, the tobacco pipe is introduced into the assembly, and after passing around, and each taking a "whiff." The object for calling the convention is made known by the principal chief; previously placing a sentinel at the door of the tent to impede the approach of any to disturb their serious meditation. . . . The same ceremonies are observed previously in issuing an order for the removal of the camps. [John Cameron, 1836, in Lamar 1921, 1:475]

José Francisco Ruíz also described council rituals:

> When a council is to be held it is held in the Chief's tent, and called and managed in the following manner. A fire is built in the center of the Chief's tent, and in the back part of the tent opposite the door is a small enclosure made up of green branches of trees. The Chief takes the principal seat and sends the crier to give notice to all the warriors to come to the council of the pipe. He goes out and cries through the town "Come to the pipe, the pipe is ready." A sentinel is placed at the door and they come to the door one at a time and say "here I am, what seat shall I occupy?" The answer is given by the Chief, on the right or left, as the case may be and he enters and seats himself accordingly; each one as he enters divesting himself of the ornaments and clothing he wears and depositing them in the enclosure in the back part of the tent. All the men having entered and seated themselves in this manner (no woman is allowed to attend) a profound silence reigns in the meeting, while the preparation is making [sic] for commencing the ceremony.
>
> The Chief then fills his pipe from a pouch in which he carries tobacco mixed with leaves of another quality, everyone holding his nose to prevent inhaling the smoke before the ceremony commences. The Chief then lights the pipe and draws a mouthful of smoke, then turns his face towards heaven and blows out the smoke which ascends to the top of the tent. This is intended as an offering to the sun. He again fills his mouth and turning his face towards the earth blows the smoke downward and then blows smoke first to the right then to the left. After this he draws from the pipe four times and swallows the smoke, then passes the

pipe to the next person. . . In this way the pipe is passed all around and smoked by every one in the same manner as by the chief, each one after smoking rubbing himself all over. This is continued until three pipes of tobacco are consumed, the Chief carefully preserving the ashes.

Consultation then commences. It is determined how long they shall occupy their position, when they shall move their encampment and where they shall re-encamp, etc. If any person arrives during the council from another town or from an expedition, the crier announces it to the Chief, who orders that he be summoned to appear. He then presents himself without speaking to any person in the town until after he has passed through the same ceremonies of smoking. He then tells whence he comes, his adventures, the news he brings, etc., which the crier communicates by shouting through the town. [Ruíz 1921:222]

Because local bands were as much kinship units as they were networks of political linkages between the *paraibo* and his supporters, and inasmuch as a son or other kinsman was already a part of the existing network, there could be a lineal succession to the status of local band *paraibo* following kinship lines.[13] Unfortunately, one of the problems in Comanche ethnohistory is that the kinship relations of chiefs one to another are virtually unknown, and thus that dimension of politics is unclear. The exception are the kinsmen of Paruasemena, the Yamparika principal chief of the 1860s and 1870s (plate 3; fig. 2.3). At least one of Paruasemena's sons, Kotsoekavit *(kotso ekavitU* 'red buffalo')* was a reknowned warrior. Two other sons or step-sons, Esananaka *(isa nanaka* 'wolf's noise' or 'wolf's howl')* and Hitetsi *(hai tʉtsi* 'little crow')*, a grandson, Cheevers (probably *tsivis,* probably from the Spanish *chiva* 'goat' although Joe Attocknie insisted that the name really was *tsii puh-se* 'little pitied one') and Cheevers's brother-in-law Attocknie, were local band leaders in the late 1870s and into the reservation period. The brothers Tabenanaka *(tabe* 'sun' *nanaka* 'noise' 'sun's noise')*, Esiturepu *(esi* 'grey' *tʉehpʉ?rʉ* 'child')*, and Pohocsucut *(puha kwasu?u katU* 'possessor of a medicine shirt')*, their brother-in-law Esarosavit *(isa tosavitU* 'white wolf')*, and another, Paruaquitsquip *(parua kutsUkwepu* 'chewing elk')*, were possibly related although the links cannot now be established. Several of the latter were also local band leaders as well as major political players.

Interestingly, several of those sets of brothers and brothers-in-law were leaders of local bands; that is, except for the internal succession of Esananaka by Attocknie, those kinsmen were not members of the same local bands. That suggests that since networks were at least minimally differentiated into centers and supporters, then brothers—particularly politically ambitious brothers—could find themselves caught between the pragmatics of their own network politics and the normative demands of mutual support. One solution

Plate 3. The Yamparika core leadership, ca. 1885. Standing, Cheevers, Ahdosy, Attocknie. Seated, Tabenanaka, Tabeyetchy, Pohocsucut. Ahdosy was a Nokoni. Photographer unknown. Courtesy National Anthropological Archives, Smithsonian Institution.

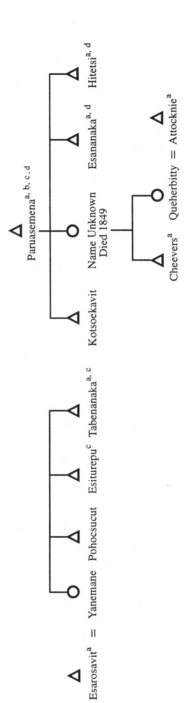

Fig. 2.3. Kinship relations among the Yamparika core leadership, ca. 1854–85.

[a] Local band leader
[b] Signer of the Treaty of Fort Atkinson
[c] Signer of the Treaty of the Little Arkansas
[d] Signer of the Treaty of Medicine Lodge

would be withdrawal by one brother, leading to the establishment of a new, relatively independent local band, albeit with the possibility of wider political connections to other bands through kinship links. In this sense the concept of the "solidarity of brothers" (Straus 1994) takes on a political dimension.

There was a range of men's and women's sodalities—nonresidential associations that have some corporate functions or purposes (Service 1962: 13)—that is, political, medicine, and soldier societies. Already discussed were the political support networks centered around a *paraibo*. Medicine societies were small groups of individuals—men or women—who shared the same *puha* (Hoebel 1940:40; Wallace and Hoebel 1952:165; Thurman 1987:553). At the other extreme were soldier societies. There is essential agreement on the names of three of the latter groups: *pibiapukunuu* (*pibia* 'big' plural, *puku* 'horse', *nuu* plural) 'big horse people'; *tuepukunuu* (*tue* 'little') 'little horse people' or 'little ponies'; and *tuwinuu* (*tu* 'black', *wi* 'knife', *nuu* plural) 'black knife people', also called 'crows' or 'ravens' from their black feather emblems (W. P. Clark 1885:355; ten Kate 1885a:128; Scott 1898; Lowie 1912, 1915). Several other sodality names have also been reported, including Lobo 'wolves' (Berlandier 1969), Afraid of Nothing (W. P. Clark 1885:355), "wontsi" or Swift Fox—probably *waaʔneʔ* 'fox'—(W. P. Clark 1885:355; Lowie 1912), Gourd (W. P. Clark 1885:355), Buffalo Bull (W. P. Clark 1885: 355; Lowie 1912), and Crow Tassel (Hoebel 1940:31), but whether those latter names were synonyms, referred to otherwise unreported groups, or designate dances (i.e., choreography as opposed to social groups) is unclear. It does seem clear, however, that Hoebel's discussion of the Crow Tassel group, based on data from Jeannette Mirsky, probably represents a short-lived medicine group rather than a major soldier society.[14]

Ethnohistorical information on the soldier societies is scanty and often contradictory. Ruíz and Berlandier reported that the Lobos had the "no-flight" rule (Ewers 1969, 1972); as such they were paralleled in the Afraid of Nothing group cited by W. P. Clark (1885). Lowie's consultants in 1912 implied that the primary ritual context of those sodalities was a ceremony to recruit volunteers for revenge war expeditions. They also suggested that there was an association of the societies with particular "bands," apparently meaning divisions (Lowie 1912). However, other observers reported that, with the possible exception of the association of the *tuwinuu* with the Yamparikas, a society might "include men from every band" (Scott 1898:11).

Lowie's notes of a conversation with Wakini include the following comments:

"Big Horses" used dew claw rattles. Very few Big Horses. Appointed in travelling by leader of people while marching. These Big Horses acted as guides of march. Another badge consisted of neck skin of buffalo worn as a sash, near knee. They have [nothing] to do with buffalo hunt. . . .

Big Horses had little different song from other songs. Never danced by themselves.

Big Horses took ekwipca (red body paint) [*ekwipIsaʔ* 'red rock'] and painted bodies down to waist and had rattle, shook them.

Took hawk and sparrow hawk feathers tied to back of head so they would flutter as they moved. BH remained in office every time people were on march as long as they pleased. No function outside of marching. [Wakini] saw them in action himself.

BH were never young men. [Wakini] never saw more than 20. Main function was to make peace with another tribe. [Lowie 1912]

As noted by Wakini, the sodalities sometimes performed police functions. Joe Attocknie gave two examples of police actions, both involving the *tuepukunuu*:

Warriors who disregarded the hunting policy of the [1874 Adobe Walls] expedition had the results of their hunt taken away from them.[15]
    Nohkahnsuh was a very daring older warrior although he had one very badly crippled leg. He left the main body and killed a buffalo and butchered it. He loaded the meat on a horse and went back to join the war party. The "Little Horse" warriors saw him coming with his load of meat. A group headed for him to take away his meat. As they drew up and started cutting the straps and ropes holding up his meat, Nohkahnsuh held up his hand and told them:

Wait, you young warriors, wait! Way up north, on the Cimarron River, I met an enemy Osage tribesman. Before witnesses I scalped this enemy Osage while he was still alive, unharmed and watching me. I left him alive after I took off his scalp so he could live to tell about it. Now then, if any of you young warriors can tell of your own battle act that can better mine, you can take my meat.

The Little Horse warriors after a silent wait, quietly withdrew and Nohkahnsuh kept his meat. [Attocknie 1965]

According to Agent Haworth:

Soon after reaching the camp of collection, those of them who did not want to engage in war and found what the real object of the collection was, determined to return to the agency, but found when they undertook it that such a move had been anticipated. . . . The warriors of the Comanche and Cheyenne had determined to prevent any returning, even if the killing of them was necessary to do it. . . . Some of the Penatekas were first, later then some of Horseback's band, following some of the Yamparikas. [Haworth 1874o]

Joe Attocknie's account was fuller, and specified that the "warriors" were not an undifferentiated mass, but were the *tuepukunuu*:

The Little Horse society were seeing that no warriors reneged on their obligation [to go on the expedition]. Those warriors prodded the stragglers, dealing harshly with any shirkers.

[Mahseet (*masiito* 'fingernail') a Penateka, started to go home.] Attocknie saw the Little Horses strike down Mahseet's tipi; they also confiscated his entire horse herd. Mahseet recognized Attocknie and called to him, "I am too old for any more war, I have too many children, but still I am being subjected to this authority." Attocknie, being not only a member of another band [the Yamparika] but also another society, the *Tuwinuu*, was in no position to help Mahseet.

Word of Mahseet's treatment at the hands of the Little Horse warriors reached the ears of Asehabit, [a] chief of the Penatekas. This chief immediately followed the expedition, overtaking it, and demanded Mahseet's horses. The Little Horses rejected his demand, and when he grew belligerent one of their members, a young warrior named Pahvotaivo (*pabotaiboo?* 'white/clear man') subjected the Penateka chief to a severe horse whipping with his riding quirt.

Yellowfish [Attocknie's future son-in-law], a member of the Little Horse [Little Pony] society, was in a position to see the raising and falling of Pahvotaivo's arm as he lashed [Esihabit]. Tears of rage rushed to [Esihabit's] eyes at this humiliation but he was helplessly outnumbered and surrounded by the warlike Little Horses. Quanah, the war party leader, and who was a member of the Little Horses, hurried up and intervened. He said that the horses should be given to Asehabit and so he was allowed to drive them away. [Attocknie 1965]

E. A. Hoebel's comments about the Cheyenne Elk Soldiers, who once took power unto themselves to act in a law-making and law-enforcing capacity, are apposite in the evaluation of the case of the Little Ponies vs Mahseet:

Can anyone deny that the Elk Soldiers were in effect sitting as a court for the entire tribe? The test is, first, one of responsibility. That they knew. It is, second, one of authority, that they acheived. It is, third, one of method. Unhampered by a system of formal precendent . . . they recognized that the rule according to which they were settling this case was new and so they annouced it. [Hoebel 1954:24]

In the case of the Little Ponies and Mahseet, the Little Ponies were clearly acting in the name of the entire party. Because they had the responsibility of patrolling the line of march, they had the socially recognized privilege of applying sanctions: they had authority. Moreover, they had precedent: they had the prior announced ultimate sanction, that of killing transgressors. Only the two leaders, Isatai and Quanah, had superior authority. Thus, when Quanah intervened on behalf of Mahseet, the Little Ponies tempered their justice.

War parties were both intra- and interband efforts. There are numerous documentary references to small groups, such as "17 Comanches—strapping youths without a chief" (Loomis and Nasatir 1967:363). More substantial war parties were organized by warriors of repute. As described by Ruíz in 1828, the leader of the proposed expedition

> traveled from village to village recruiting warriors. Upon entering a village, singing and drumming, he proceeded to the chief's lodge, and the warriors and elders of the village assembled. After smoking, they were asked to explain their proposed expedition. If the chief agreed to participate, he again smoked, and the camp crier announced the decision to the village. . . . The [one] who assembles the [war party] is the chief in charge of the whole war operation, and all the other chiefs take orders from him in matters concerning overall strategy. The chief gives the signal to retreat should the circumstances require such a move. The chief has to be the last man to abandon the field of battle. If the fight is won, the chief takes credit for the victory and is lavishly praised, but if the action results in defeat, he is blamed for it and his life is threatened. . . . The participating village chiefs recruit their own men for the expedition. . . . Each chief leads his own men, taking care not to counter the overall strategy previously agreed upon. Each chief has to watch out for his men, rescue them even at the risk of his own life, and see that individual fighters do not become surrounded by the enemy. [Ewers 1972:11–12]

That idealized description of chiefs in charge of warrior contingents echoes the description of a joint Comanche-Spaniard war expedition against Apaches in 1786 as given by Comanches in the form of a card or "tally sheet." The card shows five groups, an advance party of 31 warriors, and four other parties of 114, 88, 64, and 50 men respectively, each headed by previously identified local band chiefs and denoted by crooked lances, held point down; the chiefs were indicated by name; their political positions are known from other references. In front of the whole was the principal chief, armed with a sword (Thomas 1929b).[16]

The division was the maximal level of aboriginal Comanche political organization. The Spaniards used the terms *tribu* 'tribe', *parcialidad* 'division' or 'faction', *rama* 'branch', and less often *nación* 'nation' to refer to this level.[17] When Anglo-Americans recognized them at all, they generally called them bands, thus confusing them with the local residential units; there are also a few references in English that use the term tribe for this level of organization. Divisions were political organizations composed of local residential bands linked by kinship and sodality ties and recognizing a commonality of interest in group affairs, war, peace, and trade. Although they were not residential units, there are a number of documentary references to large, and therefore probably divisional, gatherings. One such example neatly represents a politically coordinated but dispersed pattern: in 1786 eight Kotsoteka (*kuhtsutʉhka* 'buffalo eater') rancherías were in an area of forty leagues square between the Canadian and the Pecos rivers. The largest contained 157 lodges, another had 155, and the smallest was "of thirty tipis"; there was a total of 700 lodges. In those, "the number of men of arms . . . [was] three and four in each, and of women and children seven and eight" (Thomas 1932:321). With that estimate of 12 individuals per lodge, the largest ranchería contained 1,884 people, the second largest 1,860, and the smallest 350, with a total population of 8,400. Even with the lower estimate of 5 individuals per lodge common in later years, 3,000 people were in those dispersed camps. The previous winter a gathering of some "600 camps" (that is, lodges) met at the Casa de Palo, literally the 'house of wood', the area known as the Big Timbers, on the Arkansas below modern La Junta, Colorado (Thomas 1932:73). In 1788 Pedro Vial visited a camp of 372 lodges (Loomis and Nasatir 1967:321); using Vial's estimate of 8 individuals per lodge, that camp contained almost 3,000 people.[18]

Those nucleated camps often had explicit political purposes. The 1785-86 winter gathering met to discuss peace with the Spaniards. War-planning meetings were reported in the Wichita Mountains in 1791 (Nava 1791), 1809 (M. Salcedo 1810; Manrrique 1810a), and 1825 (Twitchell 1914, 1:346). In the winter of 1793 Kotsoteka Comanches met "along the [Canadian River] for the purpose of naming a general" (Simmons 1967:31). In 1797 more than "1,000 men at arms" met with New Mexico governor Chacón at Pecos Pueblo for the same purpose (Chacón 1797a). Similarly, in 1849 the Texas Penatekas met in council to elect a principal chief (L. H. Williams 1849).

That there were ceremonials associated with those divisional gatherings is likely, but details are scanty. Conversely, that Comanches held large ceremonials is undoubted, but again, most details are unknown, including details of timing, of ritual, and (most important for present purposes) of political activities coincident with the ceremony. One Comanche ceremony was called *piakne nʉhkana* 'big house dance', or "nekado" *nʉʉkado* 'our sun dance' (ten

Kate 1885a:127) from the Kiowa name [*kado*] for their tribal ceremony. As described by Post Oak Jim in 1933, and as reported by Linton (1935), that Comanche sun dance included several ritual actions, animal-calling ceremonies, masked ritual clowns, mock battles and buffalo hunts, and curing and foretelling, as well as the public announcements, demonstrations, and transfers of medicine power (Comanche Field Party: Post Oak Jim, July 17, 19).[19]

One historically important ceremony with political implications took place in May 1874, during which an attack on invading Anglo-American buffalo hunters was planned. The nature of the ritual is unclear; such details of that ceremony as are known are given in chapter 7. All contemporary references called it a medicine dance; Linton (1935) was apparently the first to call it a "sun dance or medicine dance," as did Nye (1969 [1937]:190) and Hoebel (1941). Hoebel further stated that it was the "first and only" such Comanche ceremony. That is clearly a mistake. Linton (1935) had noted that there were several such ceremonies "held at irregular intervals," the last in 1878. Ten Kate (1885b:394) reported that preparations for a dance in 1883 were aborted by the inability to obtain a buffalo bull for the center pole. Joe Attocknie (1969) listed the leaders of six remembered Yamparika sun dances, including at least one led by a woman. Moreover, although the 1933 notes contain several mentions of both sun dance rituals—including Post Oak Jim's account, which formed the basis of Linton's 1935 report—and of the 1874 ceremony, there are no linkages between them. It is almost as if the 1933 consultants felt that the 1874 ceremony was not a *piakne nuhkana*.

Although individuals usually recognized a cultural affinity with other Comanches, cultural and linguistic differences between divisions must have existed, arising as much from normal sociocultural processes as from the ethnogenetic political processes involved with differentiating "us" from "them." Unfortunately, pre-reservation sociopolitical affiliations became obsolete soon after the establishment of the reservation, before extensive anthropological fieldwork was conducted. Thus it was not possible to observe the differences in action, and such differences as may have existed cannot be now sorted out from the general Comanche data. Linguist Elliot Canonge attempted to note "clan," that is divisional, differences in vocabulary, pronunciation, and semantics, but he was neither systematic nor consistent, and although his linguistic executors, Robinson and Armagost (1990), have generally accepted his attributions, they are not without question.

As political support networks, divisions focused on their principal chief, selected from among the component local band chiefs. The Spaniards referred to him as *general*, sometimes *jefe principal* 'principal chief', or rarely *primer caudillo* 'first chief'. In contrast to Tahsuda's comment, "We did not elect them" (Hoebel 1940:18; Wallace and Hoebel 1952:211)—probably referring to *paraibo*s in general, although the specific comment does not appear in the field notes—there are several documentary references to divisional elections, but details of the process are unknown.[20] One account states that a divisional chief was chosen "by a plurality of votes," but without further comment (Chacón 1797a). Although Spaniards were present at that and several other elections, there is no evidence that the elections were influenced by their presence. Indeed, of the thirty divisional principal chiefs recorded between 1786 and 1875 (table 1.2), in only one case is there clear evidence of Euroamerican involvement in their selection: in 1806 the Texas Kotsoteka Comanches were told, "It is proper that [they] elect and propose . . . a Chief of all their division" (N. Salcedo 1806a). Beyond that, however, there was no recorded Spanish involvement in the election. One other case of less direct Euroamerican involvement occurred in 1786, when a multidivisional party seeking peace with New Mexico was told to select a single individual to represent them all (Thomas 1932:299). However, as that was a multi-divisional organization, it was historically unique, and ultimately the attempt by the Spaniards to create a principal chief for all Comanches was unsuccessful.

On the other hand, the Spaniards' perception of their own role in Comanche politics was clearly stated in 1804, "The election of the General of the Comanches does not depend on the Governor of the province, who only ratifies the one who has been elected by all of the Captains" (Chacón 1804). Moreover, there are several cases in which individuals who claimed to be the divisional principal chief were passed over in favor of others, with apparently more legitimate claims in Comanche terms, but there is no evidence that a candidate favored by Spaniards was ever installed in place of one favored by Comanches.

Thus, there is no indication that factors other than traditional Comanche values were involved in the selection of principal chiefs. For instance, the chief and spokesman selected in 1786 was already the "most celebrated and most distinguished chieftain" of the Kotsotekas (Thomas 1932:322). In later years, although the ability to get along with Euroamericans was of value in ensuring the continuation of trade and other support, prior proof of such ability does not appear to have been of primary importance in the selection of principal chiefs; only three principal chiefs can be clearly identified in the documentary records prior to their emergence as principal chiefs. The conclusion is obvious: if they were creations of Euroamerican intervention, they should be visible in the documents before their selection as principal chief. That they are not suggests that they were not.

Although there is no evidence that Euroamericans explicitly intervened in Comanche political processes, once those processes had been completed, in accordance with their own customary practice, the Spaniards presented principal chiefs with symbols of authority, including silver-headed canes, flags, medals, and other prestigious goods. There was nothing comparable to that practice during the Anglo-American periods; indeed, whereas the Spaniards gave only one medal per group, to the so-called medal chief, the symbolic currency of medals as emblematic of political leadership was debased by the Anglo-American practice of almost unlimited distribution of medals by both Indian agents and traders to any and all friendly comers.

Divisional interests could continue beyond the actual divisional gatherings; thus divisional principal chiefs might act in the name of the division beyond the context of divisional interaction. Furthermore, since principal chiefs were also local band chiefs, they often lived in relatively small villages. For instance, in 1808 the Kotsoteka principal chief was found in a camp of only thirty lodges (Loomis and Nasatir 1967:490). Some thirty years later, according to Noah Smithwick, Texas colonist of the mid-1830s, the camp of the "principal chief" of the southern Comanches "was not nearly so large as I had expected, there being only about fifty lodges and not over one hundred warriors" (Smithwick 1899:124). It was also true, however, that individual and local interests could diverge from divisional interests, resulting in more or less successful political fission.

Relations between divisions varied greatly, ranging from mutual support and intermarriage to professed if not explicit antagonism. The specific reasons for those variations are generally unclear, although the two inter-related prime movers in Comanche political history—the competitive search for social standing and the competitive search for political resources—inevitably must have been involved. However, the ultimate interdivisional calumny—that the Penateka were "distinct enough to help the United States troops against other Comanches" (Wallace and Hoebel 1952:26)—finds little support in the documentary record.[21]

The Comanche sociopolitical system closely matched that generalized for the whole Plains by Fred Eggan: "a series of social units—the elementary family, the extended family, the household, the band, the society, and the tribe" (1937:82), which alternated in an annual resource exploitation cycle. Interestingly, the archival documents do not indicate that the Comanche pattern followed seasonal changes. The large divisional gatherings occurred at all times of the year, including midwinter. Similarly, other activities, trading, raiding, and so forth, occurred throughout the year. It remains uncertain whether that reflects ecological conditions unique to the southern Plains or the vagaries of the documentary record.

Viewed from the Comanche perspective, the *paraibo* was the central man in the political-economic organization, both the local band and the division, and he took all the credit or the blame for the contingencies of history. Comparatively, the *paraibo* was in the middle of the multidimensional continuum between the political types of big man and chief (Sahlins 1963). Since there could be a succession of *paraibo*s within organizations based on enduring resources, the *paraibo* was something more than an individual big man whose network collapsed with his death or retirement, but still something less than a kingly chief whose legitimacy was based on an inherited ideological connection to the supernatural.

Structurally, a *paraibo*'s authority was coincident with the traditional Comanche distinctions between public and private affairs. Pragmatically, given the relative freedom of movement between residential groups, a chief was circumscribed in his ability to compel individuals to follow a particular course of action. Although geographical distance could negatively define the extent of a chief's power, it was no hindrance to agreement upon common interest. That is, ultimately—albeit tautologically—chiefs had power over those whom they could influence in particular directions, but they lacked that power over those they could not. Whether any particular individual came under that power was as problematic for Comanche politicians of the eighteenth and nineteenth centuries as it is for the ethnohistorian in the twentieth.

In contrast to the Arapaho case as presented by Loretta Fowler (1982), and as seconded for the Comanches by Morris Foster (1991), there is no evidence that the Comanches who interacted with Euroamericans were structurally limited to intermediary roles, *tekwawapI* 'speaker', merely articulating consensus, and with but limited authority to act on their own. Rather, the interactions between Comanches and Euroamericans presented three possibilities: the Comanche individual came as (1) a *paraibo*, who was already a *puhakatu*, a possessor of power—spiritual and political—in his own right; (2) a *tekwawapI*, a speaker for others; or (3) a seeker of power, hoping to gain from the interaction. Each was possible, and indeed examples of each type were recorded in the historical record; thus each encounter must be analyzed individually to determine which interpretation is appropriate.

Above all, the *paraibo* was of necessity a politician, pursuing his own goals as fervently as those of his group. New organizations, both local bands and divisions, could form through the establishment and exploitation of new resources. Through a series of successful chiefs, an organization—either a local band or a whole division—could exist beyond the lives of its individual members, and could approximate a corporate unit. Conversely, a politically unlucky leader could precipitate a schism.

Comanche Domestic and Political Economies

The most successful *paraibos* must have derived their support from several resources; to base all of their power on a single resource was to court disaster. In Comanche terms, a *paraibo*'s most important resources were his *puha* and his war record; following those were his kinsmen and his peripheral supporters. In pragmatic terms, of equal importance to the recognition of real and fictive kinship ties in the maintenance of social networks was the distribution of gifts such as those given in the Shakedown Dance. Such distributions required sufficient access to and control of material resources. In the course of recent Comanche history, four such resources can be identified, derived from (1) the exploitation of the buffalo and the horse;[22] (2) military campaigns, based either on coups and war honors or on the redistribution of war booty; (3) the control of trade, which could involve either controlling trade itself or controlling traders and the redistribution of pretrade gifts; (4) the possession and redistribution of Euroamerican political gifts. Those domains were not clearly circumscribed, and indeed they often transformed into one another as, for example, when trade items included not only buffalo products but war booty, captives, and horses. Comanche political organizations were thus derived from the interrelations of several different resources. Details of the latter two will be given in the following chapters; it is necessary to discuss here the antecedents of the first two.

Since earliest times resource domains on the Plains have been derived from the buffalo. Unfortunately, there are no first-hand descriptions of Comanche hunting until well into the nineteenth century, long after the addition of the horse. But several general inferences can be made from other sources. Although individual or small-group stalking is no doubt of extreme antiquity, the most productive prehorse hunting technique was the trap, fall, or pound (Ewers 1955:302-4). The archaeological evidence for the productivity of pre-horse buffalo hunting techniques reaches back to at least the Olsen-Chubbock event, about 8,500 B.C. That day almost 200 animals were killed; the 150 fully butchered animals yielded some 60,000 pounds of "usable" meat, plus another 10,000 pounds of tallow, marrow, and "variety" meat. Depending upon several variables, including the amount of meat eaten per day per person, the percentage of meat preserved, and the presence of dogs, the product could have fed 50 people—with no dogs—for more than three months, or 100 people and 100 dogs for twenty-two days (J. B. Wheat 1972:121). Even then, only 75 percent of the kill was butchered, 150 animals out of 200 killed; fuller utilization of the kill might have added another several thousand pounds of meat, with concomitant increase in either the supportable population or the duration of the organization, but not both.

Such hunts required organization and coordination. They required investment in an infrastructure, at least a knowledge of the potentials of the terrain
for traps or falls, a greater investment of labor for corrals, pounds, and drive
lines. They required an ideology and social structure that could mobilize and
organize the combined labor of a number of people. Ethnohistorically reported communal pounds and drives among horse-poor Plains groups were
under the direction of the "pound-maker," often, but not necessarily, a sha-
man, who distributed the meat and hides to all present for further processing
and final consumption. Such an economy was redistributional, with a flow
into and out of a center. In turn, the control of that redistribution would have
been the source of political power.

Depending on specific conditions, a trap needed at least twenty-four
grown males (Frison 1971:89). Lowie (1909) reported that the horse-poor
Assiniboines made drive lines two miles long that were manned every ten
feet; that is probably an overgeneralization, for at such figures some 2,112
people would have been required for the lines. But even at twice the distance
between drivers, several hundred people would have been needed. However,
depending upon the successes of the hunts, such large numbers of people
could have been supported by the technology, and there is ethnohistorical
evidence for large assemblages. Arthur notes that "the Assiniboine were
noted for their large winter camps," often in the range of 200–300 lodges
(1975:111). At 8 persons per lodge, about 1,600–2,400 people could have
been in those camps.

Proto-Comanche Shoshones had been resident on the Plains for a long
time (Wright 1977); the linguistic unity of Eastern Shoshonean, as against its
divergences from the other Shoshonean languages, suggests that their movement to the Plains began about A.D. 1500 (Shimkin 1940). That date corresponds to an apparent period of increased precipitation, which led to a parallel
increase in the buffalo population and thereby to an increase in the size,
number, and duration of the human groups who could exploit the herds
(Reher 1977).

There is no reason to doubt that the proto-Comanche Shoshones knew
the techniques for managing a communal hunt: rabbit and antelope drives are
of considerable antiquity in the Basin. But in the Basin such activities were of
necessity rare: it would take several years for a rabbit population to become
re-established after a rabbit drive. Movement to the richer Plains would have
affected the duration and political power derived from communal hunts; on
the Plains hunts could be more regular, and, as Charles Reher notes, "more
formalized, institutionalized social structures would be expected to arise
among groups aggregated every year, as opposed to groups averaging only
one or two cooperative ventures in 10 or 20 years" (1977:22).

It was into such a situation that horses were introduced. The initial effect of the horse would have been to expand the range of search parties and to ease the job of maneuvering the animals to the traps. The horse thus would have added a new source of economic and political power: by controlling access to his horses, a horse owner—there are no reports of communal ownership of horses—could control access to the products of the hunt. As the horse population grew, the necessity for cooperation in buffalo hunting decreased: individual horse-mounted buffalo hunters could produce as much as pedestrian communal hunts with significantly less infrastructural and structural costs. Thus, in political terms, the horse democratized access to the buffalo, transforming its economic role from being the basis of the political economy to being primarily an object in the domestic economy.[23]

However, other processes intervened. The largest post-horse hunts were the so-called running hunts, in which mounted hunters charged a herd in a coordinated attack under the direction of a chief hunter and with the enforcement of hunt rules by a police force. The political importance of those hunts lies not in their productive activity—a single horse-mounted hunter had a more efficient input-output ratio—but in their restrictions upon production. As in the coincident economic revolution in Euroamerica, access to the means of production was only one aspect of political power; restricting the access of others was equally important in maintaining power. That is what the men's societies did in their function as police. As Ewers noted of the Blackfeet:

> Police regulation of the summer hunt . . . preserved the fiction of equal opportunity for all. Actually, it enabled the owner of the fastest running horse to get first chance at the herd and deprived the poor man, who owned no buffalo horse, of the right to hunt. It is obvious that under such conditions the poor would have been much worse off than they would have been under pre-horse conditions, when every family participated actively in the hunt and shared of its spoils, unless special provisions were made for their benefit. The Blackfoot adopted two measures necessary for the welfare of the poor: (1) the loaning of buffalo horses . . . and (2) the presentation of outright gifts of meat. [1955:305]

In adding to the prestige of the already wealthy, those "special provisions" served to maintain the existing distribution of social power as well as drawing supporters into the circle of power. Thus, although buffalo retained an importance in the household domestic economy and in the cosmology after the introduction of the horse, they constituted a direct political resource domain only insofar as access was controllable.

That Comanche sodalities functioned as police is attested to by Joe Attocknie's story of Nohkahnsuh and the Little Ponies noted above. In further support is Naiya's story of a man

> who took advantage of the rest. People were waiting for the light. This
> man went out and shot but didn't skin a few animals, planning to do that
> later. The rest of the people came up, and immediately knew who was
> guilty, so they took knives and cut up the animal's inside and rendered
> them unfit for food.
>
> They always tried to watch when near the bison to prevent early
> killing; they especially watched doubtful characters if they were known.
> The chief appointed watchers, but there was no regular police. [Coman-
> che Field Party: July 7]

Unfortunately, Naiya did not specify whether the Comanche "watchers" were
anything more than simply the mass of the people, nor it is clear what he
meant by "regular police," that is, whether he meant to imply that there were
no police at all, or that he was comparing them to the agency police of which
his friend and fellow consultant, Kwasia, had been a member.

The advent of the horse meant that controlling access to the buffalo was
transformed from a direct to an indirect political resource domain; that is,
only insofar as the domestic economy affected the wider public political
climate did the buffalo retain a political significance. By the first third of the
nineteenth century the precipitation cycle had reversed, initiating a general
decline in the buffalo carrying capacity and leading to increased pressures on
the herds from the human population. That pressure was exacerbated by the
forced migration of eastern Indians. Later, commercial hide hunters not only
decimated the remaining herds, but bypassed the Indians as producers of
hides, whose trade that had been an important source of individual income
and whose control was a valuable political resource domain for their chiefs.

Given an increased population in the period 1500–1800, there would also
be increased intergroup pressures; thus, one would expect wars of territorial
exclusion, and with increasingly structured military actions (Reher 1977:35).
The appearance of stockaded villages on the Middle Missouri during that
period, antedating the horse, suggests such pressures. Increased tensions
would also place a value on military capability; significantly, both Shimkin
(1941) and Sutton (1986) argue that Shoshone military organization was the
decisive factor in their expansion through the Basin and out onto the Plains.
Pre-horse Shoshone battles on the Plains were fought between opposing lines
of what may be called heavy infantry, armored and with shields, who shot
arrows at each other from the protection of a shield wall until "one chief
decided to substitute shock for fire" and ordered a charge. The battle then
ended with a hand-to-hand melee (D. Thompson 1916; Secoy 1953:34).

Among the Comanches, warfare was not simply an arena in which to demonstrate bravery; it could be a direct material resource as a source of war booty. Although the Comanches in 1933 agreed that the leader of a war party set the order of the distribution of the loot, there was some confusion about the normative order of distribution. Wedel recorded Herman Asanap (Comanche Field Party: June 30-July 1) as stating that "booty from a raid was divided up in a rote order. The leader selected his portion first, then others in order set by leader. The leader observed the industry of the men on the party, which one got wood most willingly, carried water, aided in camp." Hoebel's notes quote Asanap as saying, "After the raiders are safely away from enemy, the leader picked the two or three most industrious for first choice, then his assistants got to pick. The chief got last choice, though if there is not enough to go around a second time, he may get the balance." Howard White Wolf agreed with that latter statement, "They divide[d] the loot as soon as they were safe from immediate pursuit. The bravest fighting man had the first choice, others followed, the *nomUne* ['leader'] usually last" (Comanche Field Party: August 1). Whatever the order was, there was a redistribution from a definite center.

The horse would not have immediately disrupted the aboriginal military patterns. Along with the horse came the heavy-cavalry tactics of the Spaniards, including mass shock attacks by leather-armored horsemen (Secoy 1953:18). Like the heavy-infantry tactics of prehorse battles, the cavalry tactics depended on discipline and coordination for their effectiveness and required definite leadership. But the use of such heavy-cavalry tactics by Indians would have been constrained until the number of horses available surpassed a certain undefinable risk level; if horses were primarily used in hunting, there was a risk to their economic value in using them in warfare. Later, however, the general mode of acquisition of the horse by raiding emphasized the light-cavalry tactics stereotypical of later Plains warfare. Such coordinated efforts were maintained for the large-scale wars. Moreover, soon after the introduction of the horse came that of the gun, both providing a long-range defense against the shock tactics of heavy cavalry and emphasizing the value of light tactics.

Shimkin (1947) described the interaction of these forces: "More horses would have meant closer pursuit of the buffalo, better defense in war . . . but also less fodder per head, consequently more frequent moving, and temptation to horse raiders. Fewer horses would have meant longer stays, but poorer defense, less close pursuit of the buffalo" (1947:268). Thus, by devaluing the prestige system built on the relative number of horses owned, by devaluing the need for social nucleation in hunting, and by straining the immediate resources, the increased absolute numbers of horses served as an atomizing force. Counterposed were forces stressing societal maintenance. In particular, the increased population density brought about both by internal population growth and by migration to the Plains by peripheral peoples brought increased pressures toward military organization and tribal nationalism.

That general Plains-wide developmental trajectory formed a backdrop for the specific trajectory of Comanche political organizational change. The initial impetus for the Comanche move south was probably the desire to obtain horses (R. N. Richardson 1933:19). That move also brought contact with Euroamerican goods, often mediated through other Native American middlemen, whose control became an important basis of political power. Warfare and raiding remained a viable and necessary source of political power, but the ability of a leader to get along with Euroamericans could dramatically increase his and his people's access to their goods. But because the Comanche divisions had differential relations with the different Euroamericans, there were different resulting organizations.

3

First Euroamerican Contacts,

1706–86

New Mexico, 1706–60

The earliest documentary references to the Comanches apparently date from 1706. In July of that year Sergeant-Major Juan de Ulibarrí, on his way to retrieve apostate pueblo Indians living in the Plains Apache rancherías in eastern Colorado, was told by the caciques of Taos Pueblo that Utes and Comanches were about to raid the pueblo. After sending word of the threat to Governor Francisco Cuervó y Valdés, Ulibarrí waited for a week. When no attackers appeared, he continued on to the Apaches. There he was told of repeated and damaging Comanche attacks (Thomas 1935:16, 61, 76). Meanwhile, Governor Cuervó reported to his superiors that he was surrounded on all sides by hostile Indians; those on the north included Utes and Comanches (Hackett 1923–37, 3:382). Since no one—neither the Taoseños nor the Apaches, Ulibarrí nor Cuervó—expressed surprise at the appearance of Comanches on their borders, it is probable they were known to the New Mexicans before that time, but details are so far unknown.[1]

In the decade after 1706 Comanches must have had contacts with the Spaniards of New Mexico, but details are unknown. In the summer of 1716 Utes and Comanches visited several New Mexican settlements; although there were no reports of hostilities, the Spaniards feared that they were spying out weaknesses in the defenses. In reaction, a force of presidial soldiers and militia, led by Captain Cristóbal de la Serna, attacked a Comanche and Ute

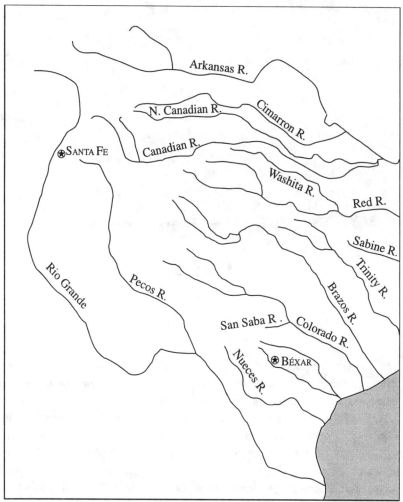

Map 1. The southern plains.

village in the San Antonio mountains, about one hundred miles northwest of Santa Fe. Many Indians were captured and sent as slaves to Nueva Viscaya. When rumors spread that the governor had personally profited from the sale, he was required to repurchase the captives. However, many had died of smallpox; others had been baptized and thus could not be sent back to "paganism" (F. Martínez 1716).

For the next three years, although they kept the Plains Apaches under constant attack, Comanches apparently did not venture near the Rio Grande. In the summer of 1719, a horse herder in Arroyo Hondo was attacked; later a boy and four horses belonging to Captain Serna were run off from his ranch along the Rio Embudo north of Santa Fe; whether Serna's property was attacked because of his involvement in the 1716 battle or simply because he owned horses is not known, but at a council of war the Spaniards decided that both Utes and Comanches were probably involved in the raid on the Rio Embudo, and both should be punished. In September an expedition found traces of two camps near modern Pueblo, Colorado, one of 60 fires, the other of 100, but there were no encounters (Valverde y Cosio 1719).

At that council, Captain Serna offered a brief summary of the history of Comanche-Spaniard relations. Although his comments are best seen as an attempt to place the events in a general context rather than as references to specific events, they have become the source of much later confusion. Serna noted that Comanches had been known in New Mexico "since the time when the Marques de la Peñuela governed this kingdom" and that they had come to New Mexico "to beg peace. . . . this was given them" (Valverde y Cosio 1719). Later scholars, indirectly citing Serna's report, and thereby apparently—but not explicitly—noting that the Marques de la Peñuela had been appointed governor in 1705, have argued that the Comanches "were unquestionably identified in New Mexico in 1705" (Wallace and Hoebel 1952:8) or that "Comanches made their first recorded visit to Taos in 1705" (Kenner 1969:28). Although Peñuela was indeed appointed governor in 1705, he did not take office in Santa Fe until 1707 (Barnes, Naylor, and Polzer 1981:105). Moreover, there are no recorded contacts with Comanches during his tenure. Thus the 1706 reports, during the administration of governor Cuervó y Valdez, remain the earliest mentions of Comanches in the documentary record. Based on the comment "They came to beg peace. . . . this was given them," it is sometimes stated that a formal treaty with the Comanches was concluded at that time (e.g., Thomas 1935:27). However, there is no evidence for actual contact in 1706, nor of a formal treaty at that time.

Meanwhile, Comanches were becoming involved in the international relations between the various European powers in America. However, for a number of reasons, the magnitude of their immediate involvement has been obscured by a basic confusion of ethnonyms. French exploration of the North American west had began in the 1680s, and French maps from that time and later include references to a powerful group called "Padouca." A number of expeditions were sent from Louisiana in the late 1710s and early 1720s to reach them. At least one, led by Étienne Véniard de Bourgmont, did reach some Padoucas in the fall of 1724 to whom Bourgmont presented a French flag and other goods (Margry 1886, 6:398-449).

The identity of the Padoucas has long been a problem for historians. Some scholars (e.g., Folmer 1942; John 1975:) have argued that they were Comanches; however, as Grinnell (1920), Secoy (1951), and Hyde (1959:83) have pointed out, since the ethnonym "Padouca" only occurs in documents from the east, French and later Anglo-American, it is more likely that before about 1750, the ethnonym referred to Plains Apaches. After that date, and after the Comanches had driven the Apaches from the Plains, it was applied with decreasing frequency to Comanches.

In 1726 and again in 1727 there were rumors of Frenchmen assisting Comanches against Apaches (Thomas 1940:14-15), as well as helping Apaches against Comanches (Thomas 1935:257), but there is no firm evidence of the nature of those relationships, if they existed at all.

For most of the 1720s there were only indirect notices of Comanches in the Spanish records. In early 1723 they made their heaviest attacks to date on the Apache rancherías; Governor Juan Domingo de Bustamente went in pursuit but did not catch them (J. D. Bustamente 1724). Later that year, after a Ute and Comanche attack on Jicarilla Apaches, Bustamente again pursued, recovering sixty-four captives (Thomas 1935:208). The ferocity of the attacks on the Apaches was such that by the end of the decade many had sought the relative safety of Pecos Pueblo, but Comanches followed and were soon attacking the pueblo itself. By the end of the eighteenth century the struggle between Comanches and Apaches had assumed legendary proportions: in 1784, in recounting the history of the southern Plains, Texas governor Domingo Cabello recorded that some sixty years earlier (i.e., ca. 1724) the Apaches had been routed from the southern Plains in a nine-day battle at El Gran Cierra de el Fierro 'The Great Mountain of Iron', somewhere northwest of Texas (Cabello 1784d). There is, however, no other record, documentary or legendary, of that fight.

At the same time, there are indications of a different kind of interaction. In 1725, brigadier Pedro de Rivera Villalón was sent on an inspection tour of northern New Spain. He arrived in Santa Fe on June 4, 1726, and remained there until late August, making a detailed study of the presidial organization and conducting an inquiry into the Villasur massacre (Thomas 1935:219-45). It is possible that he saw both Apaches and Comanches—in the spring of 1727, Governor Bustamente noted that "during the past year of '26, Brigadier Don Pedro de Rivera being engaged in the inspection . . . it happened that a group of Apaches . . . brought prisoners who were Comanches" (Thomas 1935:257). Unfortunately, Rivera made no specific entries in his diary during that period (Rivera 1946:73-74). Later, at El Paso, he wrote a "brief description" of New Mexico, including the first ethnographic comments on the Comanches. He noted:

Each year at a certain time, there comes to this province a nation of Indians very barbarous, and warlike. Their name is Comanche. They never number less than 1,500. Their origin is unknown, because they are always wandering in battle formation, for they make war on all the Nations. They halt at whichever stopping place and set up their campaign tents, which are of buffalo hide and carried by large dogs, which they raise for this purpose. The clothing of the men does not pass the navel, and that of the women passes the knee. And after they finish the commerce which brought them there, which consists of tanned skins, buffalo hides, and those young Indians which they capture (because they kill the older ones), they retire, continuing their wandering until another time. [Rivera 1946:78–79]

Although it is not clear how Rivera obtained this information, it is as interesting as much for what it left out as for what it included. For example, he noted that Comanches bred large dogs to carry their "campaign tents" (tipis) and described the Comanches' clothing. He also mentioned that they visited Santa Fe "at a certain time," implying a regular trade, and specified that they traded tanned hides, buffalo robes, and captives. However, it was then only three years since the Comanches' major attacks on the Apaches, only two years since the alleged fight at the Gran Cierra de el Fierro, and barely one year since the reports of Comanche-French interaction, yet Rivera made no comment on any of those events.[2]

There are other, more indirect, indications of Comanche-Spaniard interactions in the 1730s, but again the available details are more tantalizing for what they do not say than for what they do. The primary example is in a criminal case brought against Diego de Torres, lieutenant to the alcalde mayor of the Chama district, by Juan García de la Mora, for allegedly trading with Comanches "before the time set for the regular trade" (Twitchell 1914, 2:205; Cruzat y Gongora 1735);[3] in turn, Torres charged García with the same crime. While the testimony is replete with charges and countercharges of falsehood and fraud, this much seems clear: on April 1, 1735, a group of five or six "ranchos"—probably tents—of Comanches had appeared at Torres's house with hides and other articles for trade. They waited until mid-afternoon for either Torres or the alcalde mayor to "open the fair or ransoming as was customary"; when neither appeared, they returned to Ojo Caliente. Meanwhile, the alcalde mayor sent Torres a note saying that since it was Holy Week, in order not to profane the sacred times, he should not open the trade until after Easter. According to one of Torres's witnesses, he received the note and showed it to García, who said he would go anyway. García did and therefore traded illegally at least one, and perhaps two small swords for some buffalo hides. Then Torres sent a "Cumanche infiel," a pagan Comanche, who may have been his servant, with some—possibly ten —cuchillos (knives) made in San Juan Pueblo, to Ojo Caliente to purchase hides. When the servant arrived at Ojo Caliente, he saw many other buffalo robes purchased from the Comanches, and he assumed that the trade had been properly opened. Thus he traded his knives for ten buffalo hides; that is, one knife for one hide. The testimony of that "Cumanche infiel," unfortunately unnamed, was interpreted by a Christian Indian who was fluent in "the Castillian language and in the Comanche idiom." Both Torres and García were convicted; Torres forfeited his buffalo hides, which were given to the new church in Santa Cruz de la Cañada; García was fined ten pesos, applied to the cost of the sacramental lights in the church.

The tantalizing hints in the testimony suggest that by 1735 Comanches were regular visitors to the upper Rio Grande and that there were already established customs for dealing with them, such as official regulations for the conduct of the "feria o rescate" 'fair or ransoming'; unfortunately, the content of those regulations is unknown. Thus, although the timing of the Comanches' visit during Holy Week was probably merely coincidental, it is unclear whether Torres's and Garcia's actual offenses were trading before the official opening of the fair or trading during Holy Week. While it is not known whether the Christian Indian interpreter was himself Comanche—he was at least familiar with both the Comanche and Spanish languages—it does seem that at least one Comanche, still pagan, was a valued servant, and was even trusted to travel to a Comanche ranchería on his master's business; moreover, he could give testimony in a court of law. Additionally, the rate of exchange was one knife for a buffalo robe.

The testimony contained one other hint of changed relations in and around New Mexico. For the first three decades of the eighteenth century, Comanches and Utes had been described as allies. Now, in several asides to the general trend of testimony, the Utes were described as "enemies" of the Comanches. No further details are known.

French involvement with the Plains Indians continued through the 1730s; one Frenchman—his name was unrecorded—allegedly even lived with Comanches. According to secondhand accounts, he reported fifty or sixty villages "scattered about, caring for the many horses which they get from New Mexico" (Hackett 1931–46, 3:348). Nothing more is known of his life with the Comanches; moreover, his information was not always reliable: he reported that New Mexico was only a few days distance from Illinois. However, if his general story was true, he was apparently the earliest Euroamerican to voluntarily sojourn with the Comanches.

In 1739 the brothers Pierre and Paul Mallet, with eight companions, made an overland journey from the Illinois country to New Mexico. They met a few Indians, including a rather unfriendly group of Lalitanes, presumably Comanches, northeast of New Mexico (Margry 1886, 6:455–62; Hackett

1931–46, 3:346–52). After an informal nine-month confinement in Santa Fe, the Mallets were allowed to leave. Traveling down the Canadian and Arkansas rivers to Louisiana, they visited another group of Lalitanes, with whom they traded for horses (Margry 1886, 6:461).

Mooney (1896:1043, 1898:167) suggested that the ethnonym Lalitanes and its homophones Iatan, Ietan, Aliatan, and Halitane—and the typographical error Tetau—derive from a nasalization of the ethnonym Ute. On that earlier page, however, he noted that the Wichita ethnonym for the Comanches was *na'taa'* 'snake'. I suggest that the two terms Lalitanes and *na'taa'* are the same. However, its reference to any specific Comanche political organization is uncertain, and it is probably unwise to attempt a more specific identification of them. Hyde (1959:99, 201) argued that the ethnonym referred to a combined Ute and Apache (but not Comanche?) group of "trading Indians" who traveled between the northern and southern Plains. Although the suggestion is intriguing, there is little other evidence for the existence of such a group.

The Mallets' relatively good reception in New Mexico gave encouragement to the French Louisiana authorities, who sent them back toward New Mexico with letters of introduction proposing the establishment of a formal trade relation. Unfortunately, when the Mallets' canoe overturned in the Red River, all their papers were lost, forcing them to return to Louisiana; they spent the next ten years extolling the virtues of New Mexico to all who would listen (Hackett 1931–46, 3:335). Back in New Mexico, Governor Gaspar Domingo de Mendoza's lenient treatment of the Mallets was severely censured, and later French visitors were not so kindly treated. In 1742 the leader of a party of nine was shot in the Santa Fe plaza; in 1744 another visitor, arrested at Pecos, was sent south to Mexico (Lummis 1898:127).

Comanche–New Mexico hostilities surfaced again in the 1740s, but the immediate causes are unknown. A 1742 New Mexican military campaign against them was unsuccessful (Mendoza 1742); a later expedition went down the Arkansas River as far as the Wichita villages, but without making contact (Bolton 1914, 1:48, 1915:398). In 1746, because many Taoseños continued to trade with Comanches, possibly even informing them of the movements of troops, Governor Joachín Codallos y Rabal closed the trade with the Comanches and declared a mandatory death penalty for any Taoseño going more than a league from the pueblo without a license (Codallos y Rabal 1746).

In June of that year Pecos Pueblo repulsed a major Comanche attack, and a force of militia and pueblo auxiliaries, led by the lieutenant governor, Bernardo de Bustamente, pursued them some leagues from the pueblo. Turning to meet the attack, the Comanches fought a pitched battle, losing more than sixty warriors to the Spaniards' nine. Two weeks later Galisteo

Pueblo was attacked. In October 1747 a large party of Comanches and Utes attacked Abiquiu in the Chama Valley, driving away its inhabitants (Twitchell 1914, 2:233); Governor Codallos claimed to have pursued the attackers, killing or capturing several hundred (Bancroft 1889a:251). In January 1748 Comanches again attacked Pecos, and although Codallos had been forewarned and again met them in pitched battle, only the timely arrival of reinforcements from Santa Fe saved the governor from defeat. In that fight many Comanches wore leather or rawhide armor, carried large shields, and fought with lances, bows and arrows, and clubs (Lummis 1898:77).

Meanwhile, at the opposite end of Comanchería, other Comanches established peace with the Wichitas living on the Arkansas River. Through them, the Comanches were contacted by French traders from Louisiana, who supplied Euroamerican goods in return for meat, hides, and tallow. It is not clear how the Comanche-Wichita-French relations were formalized, and it is tempting to suggest that events at opposite ends of Comanchería were linked—that in the absence of the Spanish trade, the Comanches turned to the French—but there is no evidence for such a linkage. Furthermore, such an argument would imply that the Comanches had a unified politico-economic decision-making organization that made policy and rationally allocated resources. It is more likely that the Comanches in the east, whether or not they knew of events in the west, saw the French trade as an economic opportunity for themselves.

Soon Frenchmen were again trying to reach New Mexico. In February 1748 the parish priest at Taos reported that Panfito—the first Comanche mentioned by name in the historical records, although the meaning of the name is unknown—and six others had come to the pueblo seeking tobacco and saying that their women were busy tanning hides and that they would soon arrive to trade. Almost as an aside, Panfito reported that thirty-three Frenchmen had recently visited his village and given them "plenty of muskets" in exchange for mules. Although most of the traders had returned to the east, two had stayed with the Comanches and wanted to visit Taos when the village came in to trade (Lummis 1898:127).

The New Mexicans greeted the report of the French traders in Comanche villages with alarm, but of more immediate importance was the question of trade at Taos: the expected arrival of Panfito's ranchería showed that the trade ban was having only minimal effect. At a midyear council to determine whether the trade ban should be ended, many officials argued that as a whole the Comanches were unreliable; nonetheless their trade in hides, meat, and horses had become necessary to the well-being of the province (Bancroft 1889a:249). The official outcome of that meeting is unclear, both in terms of the long-range policy and of Panfito's impending visit, but the pragmatic result was that trade was again allowed at Taos.

In April 1749, upon receiving word that Comanches were again coming in to Taos, Governor Codallos sent his lieutenant, Bustamente, to Taos "in order to be represented." While there, Bustamente was much surprised when three Frenchmen came forward and asked to be taken to Santa Fe to see the governor. They had, individually, deserted from Canada and made their way to Arkansas Post where they had heard stories of New Mexico from resident Euroamericans, probably including the Mallet brothers. Joining forces, they had gone first to the Wichitas and then to the Comanches, 150 leagues beyond. They had spent some six months with the Comanches, moving little by little while hunting buffalo and other animals. The Indians had been reluctant to let them go on, wishing them to help with a war against the Aa Nation, but finally the Comanches had agreed to bring them to New Mexico.[4]

In their initial statements to the Spanish authorities, the Frenchmen spoke of only three Comanche rancherías, one of eighty-four tents and 800 people, the other two of forty and twenty-three tents, respectively (Hackett 1931–46, 3:299–308). When officials in Mexico questioned the validity of the threat to New Mexico by such a small number of Comanches, the Frenchmen were reinterrogated. They then described other rancherías of buffalo skin tents, each housing "three, four, or five men of arms," totaling about 2,000 men. They used "arrows, lances, hatchets, and a few muskets which the Jumanes give them along with their ammunition," but they counted only five muskets, and the Indians lacked powder and ball. Finally, in what is perhaps the earliest explicit mention of the social effects of the introduction of the horse to the Plains, they noted that the rancherías were "dispersed, with their large droves of horses, for which reason they could not live together, having to seek sufficient pasturage and water for their horses" (Hackett 1931–46, 3: 317).

On December 12, 1749, Comanches attacked Galisteo Pueblo, killing eight men (Kessell 1979:380). Several days later ten Comanche "ranchos"— tents—came to Taos to trade. Governor Tomas Vélez Cachupín, thinking they might be the Galisteo attackers, ordered Carlos Fernández, lieutenant alcalde mayor of Taos, to hold a council of war to determine whether they should be punished. The wheels of Spanish authority ground exceedingly slowly, and it was not until the first of the year that the council got under way. After interviewing several witnesses, the council determined that the Comanches who attacked Galisteo—led by Grulla Larga 'large crane' and had included Pasionosabisti (possibly literally *pasi ono* 'sand creek' but also possibly referring to the Red River, *tuibitsi* 'young man' or 'warrior'), Ojatara (*oha* 'yellow', *tarʉ* 'spots' or 'holes'), Quanacani (*kwana katʉ* 'he has a smell'), Esembuie (possibly *isa pui* 'wolf's eye', but *puʔe* is 'road', giving 'wolf's road', the Milky Way), and Luis the Apostate—were not the Comanches who had visited Taos. Moreover, since the Galisteo attackers had come with Utes, a two-front war was not advisable. Ultimately, since all the Comanches, both the attackers and the Taos visitors, were now well beyond the Arkansas River and out of reach of the meager forces at Taos, no action was taken (Fernández 1750).

In late February 1750 three more Euroamericans, two Frenchmen and a native Spaniard, arrived at Taos. Seven years before, the Spaniard Felipe de Sandoval had been en route to Mexico by ship when he had been captured by the English and had spent two years at hard labor in Jamaica. From there he had escaped aboard a French ship to Louisiana where he had spent five years at Arkansas Post as a hunter. There he heard about New Mexico from the Mallets. Accompanied by "four Frenchmen, a sergeant, and a German" (Hackett 1923-37, 3:321), Sandoval had traveled two months up the Arkansas River to the Wichita villages. From there, with twenty Wichitas, they had gone on an unsuccessful search for the Comanches. The others had turned back after three weeks; Sandoval had been on the verge of returning also when he came across a young Comanche man going to the Wichita villages to trade horses. After receiving a musket and a hand-axe for his three horses, the young man offered to guide Sandoval to New Mexico. Four days beyond the Wichita village, they reached the main Comanche ranchería "at the foot of a mountain whence issues a river called Case," probably the Arkansas (Thomas 1940:20). The village contained 400 tents, with large numbers of horses, mares, mules, and asses. Of the inhabitants, he said:

> [They are] a very barbarous people, heathen, very disorganized, and obeying no head; but they are well supplied with arms such as arrows, hatchets, lances, swords, and a few muskets. . . . Comanches came to this ranchería from several others which I did not see, and went from it to the others. . . . there were many rancherías in different places, which according to the seasons, are moved from time to time in search of pasturage, wood, water and buffalos. [Hackett 1931-46, 3:323]

A number of other Indians and Euroamericans visited the Comanches while Sandoval was in residence. Once twenty Wichitas and two Frenchmen spent five days trading muskets, hatchets, glass beads, and ammunition for buffalo hides, horses, and slaves. While they were there, a German and another Frenchman visited, also guided by Wichitas. Those latest Euroamericans wanted to visit New Mexico but were dissuaded because they were Protestants, and the Spaniards "had the Inquisition." In early February 1750, when a Comanche from another ranchería came by intending to go to New Mexico, Sandoval and the remaining Frenchmen joined him. After seven days travel in "easy stages," they came upon another ranchería on the plains east of Taos, and taking three days to cross the Sangre de Cristo Mountains, they arrived at Taos (Hackett 1931–46, 3:324).

By 1750 Wichitas had mediated a truce between Comanches and Pawnees, and in 1751 Wichitas, Pawnees, and Laytannes (Comanches?)—reported as armed with spears and mounted on "caparisoned," probably meaning "armored," horses—joined in an attack on the Grand Osages. In response the Osages sought both Illinois Indian and French assistance, but the French military commandant at Fort Chartres argued that the attackers were only avenging themselves for years of Osage attacks; moreover, the Comanches were now also allies of the French, and it would not do to attack allies (Thwaites 1908:88).

Meanwhile, the Spaniards of New Mexico were reevaluating their relations with the Comanches. In 1750 Governor Vélez Cachupín reviewed the situation thus:

> Although the Comanche nation carries on a . . . trade with us, coming to the pueblo of Taos, where they hold their fairs and trade in furs and in Indian slaves whom they take from various nations in their wars, and in horses, mares, mules, knives, belduques, and other trifles, as always, whenever the occasion offers for stealing horses or attacking the pueblos of Pecos or Galisteo, they do not fail to take advantage of it. During the five-year term of my predecessor, Don Joaquín Codallos, as many as 150 of the Pecos perished at their hands. . . . On the occasions when the Comanches have entered Taos . . . I have reproached them for their malice and lack of good faith toward us. They excuse themselves by blaming others of their nation, saying that among them are warlike captains who commit outrages and those who are well disposed are unable to prevent them. [Hackett 1931–46, 3:328]

Here, while noting that the Comanches did trade with New Mexico, Vélez Cachupín took the opportunity to argue that they were also the source of much difficulty. There is a problem in interpreting that evaluation, however: as John Kessell (1979:379) pointed out, the Pecos book of births and deaths for the period 1743–49 records only fifteen deaths attributed to Comanches, plus another twelve from the 1746 attack. Thus Vélez's summary was probably more an attempt to inflate the problems of the province than a faithful reporting of conditions under his predecessor.

But despite the disadvantages, it was better to have the Comanches as friends than as enemies; it was even more important to have them as a buffer between New Mexico and the French. Therefore, with the dual inducements of trade and swift military retaliation, Vélez Cachupín set out to establish a lasting peace. In July 1750 a ranchería of some 130 men in forty tents came to Taos to trade hides and captives. Vélez Cachupín, "persuaded by opinion that I should not close completely the door to their trade," allowed the trade fair to take place. He did, however, threaten that he would declare war upon them if they attacked Pecos or Galisteo (Thomas 1940:111).

Although those chiefs made "the necessary promises," the following November, spies and sentries notwithstanding, another group of Comanches, armed with bows, spears, and 16 muskets, attacked Pecos. Vélez Cachupín and a force of presidial soldiers, militia, and pueblo Indians followed them out to the plains. After the attacking force split up, the governor followed the main body of 145, cornering them at a pond in a box canyon where the Comanches formed a defensive wall with their horses and body-size shields. During the night 44 surrendered, including 6 women. At three in the morning, by moonlight, the remaining warriors attempted to force their way out but were unsuccessful. At daylight Vélez Cachupín found he had 49 prisoners and over 150 horses and mules; the rest of the Indians were dead. Except for 4 prisoners kept as hostages, he released the others, with tobacco and ten arrows for hunting on their return home, and admonished them to make a permanent peace or the Taos trade would be cut off again and they would be pursued until "completely destroyed" (Thomas 1940:68-74).

In December several Comanches visited Taos with their chief, El Nimiricante Luis; Demitri Shimkin (1980) has translated his name as *neme reka* [*numu tuhka*] 'man eater'. It is possible that he was the Luis the Apostate who had allegedly attacked Galisteo in 1749. Vélez Cachupín sent them tobacco and repeated his policy of peace or war. According to later reports, on their return to Comanchería they and other chiefs spent the winter in council. Much time was given to discussions of the history of their relations with the Spaniards. They finally decided that their triumphs of the past were nothing compared to the damages inflicted by the "boy captain." Nimiricante himself tried to obtain the release of several women taken from Abiquiu four years earlier and still held captive by El Oso 'The Bear', possibly his own brother. Although Nimiricante offered to trade an Apache woman for one of the women, El Oso refused, and Nimiricante ordered him to leave or be punished, saying "he did not wish his people to experience another defeat such as the present one." For his part, El Oso, described as the "little king of them all," said he would bring his ranchería to Taos only if presents in unlimited quantities were given (Thomas 1940:114-17).

In February 1751 the New Mexicans received another shock from the east. That month, in another winter passage of the Plains, Pierre Mallet and three companions came to Pecos to complete their aborted mission of 1740, carrying letters from the governor of Louisiana and from several merchants in New Orleans. Traveling up the Red River from Natchitoches, they met no

Indians until they were six days out from Pecos, when they met some one hundred Comanches armed with bows and arrows, swords and lances, wearing leather jackets and mounted on caparisoned horses. At first those Comanches seemed friendly, but soon they began to denigrate the Euroamericans and would not let them pass. On a pretext, they got the party to fire their muskets, then stole the saddlebags containing their letters of introduction. Mallet had to trade a musket for the return of just the endorsement on his governor's letter. As a final tribulation, on their arrival in Santa Fe they were arrested, sent south to El Paso—where their remaining goods, including their clothes, were sold to a local soldier, painter, and cartographer, Capt. Bernardo Miera y Pacheco (Kessell 1979:389)—and they were sent south to Mexico City and ultimately to Spain (Hackett 1931–46, 3:334–63).

In the spring a small Comanche ranchería arrived at Taos. While there, two of the four hostages held from the previous November's battle, one of whom was said to be the son of Quanacante—possibly Quanacani, the alleged attacker of Galisteo in 1749—recounted the good treatment they had received at the hands of the Spaniards. In an attempt to strengthen the Comanches' "inclination for peace," Vélez Cachupín released his remaining hostages. In July another group of thirty men in ten tents came to Taos with word of the chiefs' decision to seek peace. The chiefs would wait until "the poplar leaves fell," when they would have booty and captives to sell. A week later, messengers came in from El Oso to apologize for the attacks on Galisteo, which had been done "against his will," and to ask for more tobacco. Unfortunately, while they were in Taos, five other Comanches stole horses from the Rio Arriba—the upper Rio Grande. Pursued by the settlers, two were killed and a third wounded, and one of the settlers was killed. El Oso's messengers mourned the loss and acknowledged that some individuals would not follow the advice of their chiefs.

In August 1752 two more Frenchmen arrived at Pecos from the Illinois country with nine horses and seven loads of goods, intending to open trade. Unfortunately, because of the lack of a competent interpreter, the details of their journey are unclear. They had started with eight other companions, but the others had turned back at the Pawnee villages. Continuing on, they met a few Indians, including some Comanches whom they "regaled plentifully" and some Carlana and Jicarilla Apaches on the Gallinas River, who guided them to Pecos. Like the Mallets before them, they were arrested, their goods confiscated, and they were sent south (Hackett 1931–46, 3:364–70).

When Vélez Cachupín left office in 1754, he prepared detailed instructions and suggestions for his successor, Francisco Marín del Valle: the governor should personally attend the Taos fair, as much for appearance's sake as for the necessity to settle disputes immediately. He should have a strong guard and appear in his best uniform. When the Comanches arrive at the fair, the chiefs should be called together for a smoke and a council. A guard should be placed on their ranchería and horse herd to prevent thefts. Above all, if the Comanches were to declare war, only the skillful use of the army would restore the situation; although a few easy victories might be achieved, the province could not afford an extended war and might, in the meantime, drive the Comanches to a dependence upon the French (Thomas 1940:129–43).

Marín left few records of interactions with Comanches, but interactions cannot be ruled out. Bernardo Miera y Pacheco, enticed by Marín from El Paso to be alcalde mayor of Pecos and Galisteo, said he went on three campaigns against Comanches between 1756 and 1760 (Auerbach 1943:121), but he gave no further details. In a 1758 report on conditions in New Mexico, Marín gave evidence of a knowledge of Comanches, although whether it was based on first-hand interations is unknown. In that report, he gave the so-far earliest discussion of the internal political differentiation of the Comanches, and the earliest documentary use of Comanche language ethnonyms. He noted that "the nations exterior to this province are the Comanches, comprising the Pibian, Yamparicas, Jumanes, and Panana, and other names, but all are under the name of Comanche." Marín's first ethnonym seems close to *pibia* 'large' (plural), but is an otherwise unknown ethnonym. The second is the Comanche name Yamparika *yampa tuhka* 'root eaters'. The latter two are generic terms, usually applied to various Caddoan groups, Wichitas and Pawnees, but whose specific identities in this context are unclear. Marín also commented, "This nation is very inconstant in their words." Their leader was "the one who had killed the most enemies," and although some obeyed him, others did not. That is, although identifying the basis of Comanche leadership as originating in war honors, it should not have been surprising that some individuals did not "obey" the chiefs; considering his confused listing of groups, they were, quite simply, not their leaders. Finally, he noted that they traded buffalo skins and other items through the Wichitas to the French for guns, powder, ammunition, and "offensive weapons" (Marín 1758).

The only direct evidence of interaction during Marín's tenure was a battle near Ranchos de Taos, south of the pueblo. Although the details are unclear, the precipitating incident seems to have been in the summer of 1760. After the Taoseños had entertained visiting Comanches, they announced that the two dozen fresh scalps used in the dance were from Comanches. The source of those scalps is unknown—there were no reports of recent actions between Comanches and Pueblo—but in retaliation for the insult, in August a Comanche war party, reported to number several thousand, attacked the pueblo. Repulsed by the fortress-like defenses, they continued to the Spanish

settlements in the Taos valley. Many settlers had taken refuge in the Villalpando house, near Ranchos de Taos, south of the Indian pueblo. After a day-
long siege by the Indians, about fifty women and children were taken
captive.[5] Governor Marín made a desultory attempt to follow but traveled
only as far as Taos itself. Later, with a reported 1,000 Utes, pueblos, and
militia men, he spent twenty-five days in the field, but without incident (I.
Armijo 1929:291 -92). Similarly, Marín's interim successor, Manuel Portillo
de Urrisola, spent a month in the field, but without encountering any Comanches.

In December 1761 eleven Comanches, led by Onacama—possibly *ona*
'salt', *kamatu* 'taste'—arrived at Taos, saying that their ranchería of some
sixty tents would arrive three days later for trade. Portillo gathered a small
force and went to meet them. While some of his solders guarded the camp, a
group of men—Portillo called them chiefs—met with Portillo in the pueblo.
Saying that although most of the captives from the Villalpando house were
held in other rancherías, they did have seven with them, whom they would
trade for a horse each. Portillo declined the offer, saying he would rather give
them "powder and ball," and seized the men. One, who was sent back to
bring the captives, spread the alarm and began organizing a defense. Leaving
the rest under guard, Portillo rushed to the camp and attempted to take
charge. However, as soon as he left, the men attacked the guards, took several
guns, and fled across the rooftops in a hail of musket fire; one was killed outright and several wounded. They finally barricaded themselves in the stable,
where they kept up a steady fire all night. Meanwhile, the camp itself was
surrounded.

The next morning a messenger came out carrying a cross and a white
flag, asking for the release of the prisoners and an opening of trade. Portillo
countered that before he would agree, they must give their own horses as hostages. When the Comanches refused and broke off the talks, the governor
opened fire with a small cannon. Although the Indians outnumbered the
Spaniards, and they returned the fire, they were finally forced to flee. While
the Spaniards chased the fugitives, Utes pillaged the camp, capturing, it was
claimed, more than a thousand horses and over three hundred women. Meanwhile, when the prisoners in the stable still refused to surrender, Portillo had
it set afire; the fire smoldered all day, and that night the four remaining Comanches broke out. Three were immediately killed, and the fourth, although
badly wounded, managed to escape (I. Armijo 1929:294; E. Adams 1953:
218).

Portillo hoped that his "glorious victory" would make the Comanches
think twice about again attacking New Mexico. However, it had the opposite
effect: the Comanches called a council of war to plan retaliation. During the

council, six of the women captured at Taos the previous December arrived with important news. Tomas Vélez Cachupín was back in Santa Fe, reappointed for a second term, and was seeking to overturn the previous seven years of bad feelings. The Comanches dispatched a delegation of nine leading men, armed with muskets, two pounds of powder each, bows and arrows, lances, and tomahawks, with an escort of sixty warriors, to determine whether the report was true.

In the council that followed, the Comanches complained about the treatment they had received from Vélez's successors. While acknowledging the validity of their complaints, the governor pointed out that both sides had acted in an "insane" manner. But the discord between Comanches and Spaniards arose not out of a general policy, but from the acts of particular pernicious individuals "who exist in all republics" (Thomas 1940:151). He promised to punish any Spaniard who abused the trade and suggested that the first step should be a mutual exchange of captives taken since 1760. In turn, the Comanche delegation promised to discuss the governor's propositions and to return again in July.

The delegation made positive identification of Vélez Cachupín, but two chiefs wanted further confirmation. Thus, in early June another delegation of nineteen people, eleven men, including four chiefs, the eldest of whom was reported to be the "high priest or medicine man," five women, and three children, arrived in Taos and was sent on to Santa Fe. They were received by Vélez Cachupín and, seeing for themselves that he had returned, asked to see some of the Comanche prisoners. Thirty-one captives were brought together, and each of the delegation was allowed to select one to be returned. They were all given tobacco and were sent home with a pueblo Indian escort (Thomas 1940:153). Unfortunately, there is no record of a return Comanche visit, whether they released their captives as promised, or whether Vélez Cachupín's second term matched the good relations of his first. What is certain is that the peace did not last much beyond his second departure in 1767.

The details of the new collapse of Comanche-Spaniard relations are once again unclear. In late 1767 the new governor, Pedro Fermín de Mendinueta, had hopes of "achieving peace with the Comanche nation," but he was wary of their "reliability." He established a new garrison of fifty soldiers at the Cerro de San Antonio, about one hundred miles northwest of Santa Fe (Thomas 1940:159). His vigilance was soon rewarded. In May 1768 six Comanches came to Taos under a white flag, bringing with them a young captive Spaniard, saying that their ranchería would soon be coming in for trade; on June 2, 400 Comanches camped near Taos. Meanwhile, another 100 Comanches attacked Ojo Caliente. But at the crossing of the Rio Grande, they were unexpectedly confronted by the new garrison. The Comanches turned and fled, some drowning in the river, others spreading the alarm to the Comanche ranchería still at Taos, the occupants of which also fled, killing five settlers and one Taoseño who had gone to the ranchería for private trade. Governor Mendinueta followed with the militia but was unable to overtake the Comanches.

It was not clear whether the two groups were part of a coordinated attack; Mendinueta argued that they were. He also reported that the captive, left behind in Taos, said that the Comanches were armed with guns obtained from the Wichitas and that they had recently received seventeen horseloads of firearms. If true, he argued, since Louisiana was now Spanish, those guns could only have come from English traders.

On September 26 a group of twenty-four Comanches appeared at Ojo Caliente, taunting the garrison, which gave chase and killed all but one. From him, Mendinueta learned that a chief had "raised himself up among that nation with the appearance and accouterments of . . . a little king" (Thomas 1940:167). He had a guard of armed men, pages to help in mounting and dismounting, a sun shade of buffalo hide, as well as two "confidants" to carry out his orders, one of whom was among those killed at Ojo Caliente. A month later, after raiding in the vicinity of Picurís, some five hundred Comanches again attacked Ojo Caliente. Their leader wore a headdress with a single green horn on his forehead. Personally leading a charge upon the fortified plaza, he was met by a musket volley and killed. From the efforts made to recover his body, Mendinueta later inferred that he was the "little king" and that the attack had been in retaliation for the death of his lieutenant at Cerro de San Antonio the previous month (Thomas 1940:167).

Comanches in Texas, 1743–74

Although the Comanches had been known to the Spaniards of New Mexico since the first decades of the eighteenth century, contact with Spaniards in Texas did not occur until much later, coming through both the Wichita alliance and attacks on the Lipan Apaches. The earliest known direct report dates from 1743, when three Comanches passed Béxar[6] on their way to find Apaches (Morfi 1935, 2:294). However, the extent of penetration below the Red River is unclear.

By the mid-1750s the Osage advance to the Arkansas River had forced the Wichitas from the Arkansas to the Red River, which in turn drew their Comanche allies closer to the Lipan Apaches. The Texas Spaniards reacted to that move with near hysteria, and it is difficult to separate fact from rumor. The allied Comanches and Wichitas were blamed for raids on Apaches near

the San Sabá mission-presidio and for the March 16, 1758, attack on the
presidio itself. The repulse of Colonel Diego Ortiz Parilla's retaliatory attack
on the Taovaya village on the Red River below Cache Creek was attributed in
part to the presence of both Comanches and French (H. E. Allen 1939)—
although the presence of both is problematic. When new missions for the
Lipans were established on the Nueces in late 1761, they too were attacked.
In October 1762 a party of several hundred Norteños—the Nations of the
North, an indefinite name used by the Spaniards of both New Mexico and
Texas to refer to the Indians north of their settlements—possibly including
Comanches, visited San Antonio and promised not to molest any of the mis-
sionized Apaches (Morfi 1935, 2:402; Faulk 1969:19; Tunnel and Newcomb
1969:169). Nonetheless, raids against the Apaches continued throughout the
rest of the decade. Although the Comanches were often suspected of involvement, there is no hard evidence for it.

   In 1763 France was forced to cede Louisiana to Spain, but there was no
immediate change in the flow of goods through the Wichitas to the Comanches, as much because of the reluctance of French Louisianans to change
allegiance as because of their reluctance to give up the lucrative trade. By
1770 Spain had managed to establish some authority in Louisiana, mostly by
adopting French policies and by persuading former French officials to serve
the new authorities. One of those, Athanase de Mézières, lieutenant governor
of Natchitoches, was detailed to attempt to establish peace with the various
Nations of the North. In the summer of 1770 de Mézières arranged for a conference with Comanches and Wichitas at the Cadodachos village on the Red
River. However, upon his arrival the Wichita chiefs told him that the Comanche chiefs had decided not to attend and had in fact turned upon their former
allies (Bolton 1914, 1:210); the cause of that about-face is not clear.

   De Mézières had hopes of restoring relations. In October 1771 Taovaya
chiefs said they would try to prevent Comanches from committing hostilities
"as they had formerly done." But they also noted that the Comanches had
agreed to peace in New Mexico and would be unlikely to take up arms
against the eastern provinces (Bolton 1914, 1:257).

   In February 1772 four Comanches, three women and a girl, came into
Béxar under a white flag. Hoping to win the favor of their chief, Evea—he
was also called Pubea; the name is possibly related to either *evi* 'blue', or to
to the modern exclamation *ubia* 'oh, my!'—the first Comanche mentioned by
name in the Texas records, Governor Juan María de Ripperdá sent two of the
women home with presents, detaining the other two as hostages. In April one
of the messengers returned with six other relatives. After being reunited with
the hostages, they left loaded with presents. They also managed to make off
with 400 pack animals from the Béxar horse herd. Half of the animals, as

well as several of the women, were recovered. Apaches later attacked the retreating raiders, killing all but the former messenger. She and the other recaptured Comanches were sent as prisoners to Coahuila (Bolton 1914, 1:274).

That same spring de Mézières began a tour of the Indian tribes up the
Red River from his headquarters in Natchitoches. At the Wichita village, relocated to the Brazos because of Osage pressures, he met with a delegation of
some five hundred Comanches, including Evea himself, whom he called the
"principal chief" (Bolton 1914, 1:273). After their meeting the chief accompanied de Mézières and a number of Wichita and Taovaya chiefs to meet
Governor Ripperdá, the Comanches going in part to try to retrieve the women
now held in Coahuila.

While in Béxar, de Mézières wrote a report on his trip. Although he did
not detail his conversations with the Comanches, he did make several important observations about them. They were divided into several "tribes or
bands," which he named as "Naitanes, Yarambicas, etc." The former is the
Wichita ethnonym Snake; the latter is clearly Yamparika. Each group was
headed by "chiefs or captains," among whom Evea was "generally recognized" as foremost. However, because of their dependence on the "cattle"—
buffalo—they lived in small groups, and their chiefs could neither prevent nor
redress any damages caused by errant individuals (Bolton 1914, 1:297).

Here de Mézières's general notation of the absence of chiefly political
power contrasts with his earlier specific characterization of Evea as "principal
chief." His immediate explanation for the lack of power is based on a geographic argument, that because the rancherías were dispersed, chiefs could
not control everyone. Although that may have been the case, it was not an
absolute; political power is cultural, based on a rational-cultural assessment of
alternatives, of which geographical distance is only one variable.

The particular notice of chiefly powerlessness may also be de Mézières's
attempt to rationalize recent events. Upon arriving in San Antonio, he found
that there had been many raids in the vicinity; only the night before, more
than one hundred animals had been taken from Mission La Concepción. De
Mézières assured the governor that none of Evea's party was implicated, but
when the raiders were overtaken after a three-day pursuit, they were found to
be Comanches. Ripperdá wanted to execute them, an action with which the
Wichita and Taovaya chiefs concurred. Evea persuaded the governor to spare
them, although the chief himself gave them a "severe and extended punishment" (Bolton 1914, 1:315). Ripperdá harangued the Comanches, showing
them the false flag of truce carried by the women in February and recounting
the recent raids. Evea, publicly embarrassed, agreed to Ripperdá's threat of
execution for future transgressors, and although admitting that he could not
speak for his "dispersed and large nation," he promised to try to persuade the

other chiefs to become friends with the Spaniards (Bolton 1914, 1:333). The Wichita chiefs themselves promised to keep an eye on the Comanches (Bolton 1914, 1:321).

In the spring of 1773 Comanches attacked the Apache rancherías around Béxar, forcing their abandonment and driving the Apaches deep into Coahuila and Nueva Vizcaya. That fall Béxar was hit in the largest raids yet in Texas, followed by raids on Laredo, where more than 350 horses were taken. In an effort to stem the raids, in October 1773 a trader from Opelousas, Louisiana, J. Gaignard—his first name is unknown—was sent up the Red River to attempt to establish peace with the Comanches. After wintering with the Caddos, he reached the Taovaya village in early 1774. Finding three Naitanes there, he gave them a gift of tobacco for their chief. Five weeks later, after other Comanches had passed through from a raid against the Apaches, an unnamed chief arrived, saying that the "great chief," unfortunately also unnamed, had received the tobacco and had smoked it with a "good heart." A week later eleven more Comanches, identified as Manbarica—that is, Yamparika—arrived, saying that they were glad to see Gaignard, as it had been eight years since they had seen Frenchmen, and they hoped that would mean a reopening of trade.

Gaignard had been ordered to travel to the Comanche village itself, but the Taovaya chiefs would not let him pass their village (Bolton 1914, 2:88). In early June, forty more Comanches arrived at the Taovaya village, telling Gaignard that as soon as the great chief had returned from fighting the Apaches, he would receive them. A week later another Comanche appeared, saying that the great chief had prepared thirty "cabins"—the meaning is unclear—for the embassy, but as before, the Taovayas would not let the Spaniards proceed. Gaignard was especially disappointed; he had been told that the Comanche village was thirteen days' travel away, a distance equal to that between the Taovaya village and Santa Fe, and he had hoped to persuade the Comanche chief to take him on to New Mexico. That distance accords with the five weeks it took for the tobacco to be taken to the great chief and word of its receipt to return, and it places the principal village on the upper Red River in the vicinity of Palo Duro Canyon or the middle reaches of the north Canadian River.

In early July the great chief, presumably Evea, arrived with "the whole nation." Considering the presumed distance to their village, they must have left their village even before the earlier messengers had arrived at the Taovaya village. Gaignard immediately called a council with the chiefs of the Taovayas and the Comanches. Saying that there were no longer any differences between the Frenchmen and the Spaniards, he argued that the chief should "firmly grasp the hand of the Spaniard" and that the chief should forbid any of his young men from warring on the Spaniards. He gave the chief a number of symbolic gifts, a flag "as a sign of peace," a "Limbourg blanket . . . to cover the blood . . . and to make them white and clean," knives "to stop up the crooked trail [so that] all nations should travel the same roads, straight and free," and tobacco "to be smoked by the young men, so that the war may be at an end." The chief responded by saying that he was glad to have the flag; it would facilitate travel among the Spaniards. By his talk, he would ensure peace: if any Comanches attacked the Spaniards, they would not be considered part of his people. Although admitting that there were some Comanches who stole Wichita and Spanish horses, he condemned their actions (Bolton 1914, 2:93-94).

Several days later five Comanches arrived from Béxar, saying that other Comanches had been surprised while stealing horses, and five were killed. When the village began to mourn, the chief ordered them to stop, saying that since the raiders had refused to listen to him, the Spaniards had done right; the weeping stopped.

In his report Gaignard made several brief observations about the Comanches. He said they had no fixed villages, but followed wild animals for their living; their commerce was in captives and buffalo hides, which they traded for "trifles," including tobacco, knives, axes, and beads. According to Gaignard, they were composed of four groups "which are never together," and that meeting was the only time he had seen them all (Bolton 1914, 2:94-95); unfortunately, other than using the ethnonyms Naitane and Manbarica, he did not name the groups.

New Mexico, 1769–79

Interactions between Comanches and New Mexicans continued, but the documentary evidence is scattered. In 1769 Comanches raided Picurís, sacking the church and taking the vestments and the written records, most of which were recovered later in tattered condition (E. Adams and Chavez 1956:92). In February 1771 Governor Mendinueta arranged a truce with some Comanches (Bancroft 1889a:259), possibly the "peace" referred to that year by Taovayas in Texas (Bolton 1914, 1:257), but again, while some kept the peace, others raided. By the summer of 1773 Comanches were raiding throughout New Mexico. In July some five hundred hit Pecos; there were five separate raids on Picurís and four on Galisteo. Others went to Taos to trade (Thomas 1940: 44).

The summer of 1774 again brought mixed interactions: four attacks and one trading expedition. The first was on June 22, when a group of Comanches killed two Picuriseños and ran off the horse herd of Nambé. They were pursued and forced to scatter. In July a reported 1,000 Comanches came down the Chama River as far as Santa Clara Pueblo. During the attack on Santa Cruz de la Cañada, the alcalde mayor, together with some of the settlers, barricaded themselves in a fenced field. They managed to kill the Comanche leader; in repeated but unsuccesful efforts to recover his body, the Comanches lost twenty-three dead.

The third attack came on August 15, when 100 Comanches attacked Pecos. A force of pueblos and militia pursued. Five days later, and some seventy leagues distant, they attacked a village of "so many tipis . . . they could not make out where they ended." The initial attack carried well into the village, causing panic. However, when the Comanches realized how small the attacking force was, they counterattacked. The Spaniards formed a defensive square and held out all day. Late in the afternoon the Spaniards again attacked, driving the Comanches from their positions, retiring again in "good order." That night the Comanches were tricked into fleeing when a former captive shouted to them that the Spaniards were only the vanguard of a much larger force. Another escaped captive reported that 40 Comanches had been killed, including 7 chiefs. At the same time, while that battle was raging, another 200 Comanches attacked Albuquerque, where they killed 5 men and 400 sheep and ran off the horses. Since the local militia had gone on a campaign against the Navajos, there was no pursuit. A week later about 60 Comanches came into Taos to trade, ransoming 6 captives and exchanging 140 animals, as well as meat and salt (Thomas 1940:169-72).

Following those battles, Governor Mendinueta began planning a campaign against the Comanches. To prevent word from leaking out through contacts in Taos, any Comanche visitors were to be arrested and taken to Santa Fe. Almost immediately, eight men and eleven women arrived and were taken into custody. At Las Truchas, in the mountains above Taos, they were confined for the night in the watchtower. When guards came in to light a fire for warmth, the Comanches overpowered them and took over the tower. After a night-long siege the tower was set afire, but none surrendered.

In the campaign that followed, Carlos Fernández, veteran of more than sixty years in New Mexico and former alcalde mayor of both Santa Cruz de la Cañada—it is not clear if he was the alcalde who barracaded himself in the field—and of Taos, led some 600 soldiers, militia, and pueblo Indians. On September 23, about fifty leagues from Santa Fe, when the advance scouts were surprised, Fernández turned north, hoping to avoid an ambush while gaining time to lay one himself. On the twenty-sixth he found signs of a ranchería traveling south and on the twenty-seventh, signs of a ranchería moving north; he assumed they were made by the same group. Then on the twenty-eighth, still going north, Fernández attacked a ranchería of some eighty lodges. The inhabitants erected a breastwork near a miry pond; after a two-hour fight, 115 women and children surrendered; 18 men had escaped (Thomas 1940:174). There is no evidence from Mendinueta's summary report that the ranchería Fernández attacked had been directly involved in any recent raiding. Indeed, it is possible that the expedition had not been tracking a single group, instead following one, then another, before attacking a third.

Other than stating that it was "50 leagues" from Santa Fe, the report does not locate the battle. Some scholars have placed it on the plains east of Santa Fe (Thomas 1932:62; Campa 1942:14). Others are more specific and have placed it at Las Orejas del Conejo—the 'rabbit ears'—between the arroyo Don Carlos and the Colorado River, or on the Staked Plains near the source of the Colorado River (A. Espinosa 1907:12). However, Juan de Dios Peña's military service record reported the battle, in which Peña was wounded, as at Guanjantolla, clearly the Comanche language toponym *waha toya* 'two mountains', the Spanish Peaks, about 140 miles—50 leagues—northeast of Santa Fe at Raton Pass (Peña 1805).[7]

There were other contacts in 1775. On May 1 a Comanche party struck Pecos; two weeks later a party composed of "a chief and seven rancherías"— here probably meaning tipis—came to Taos seeking trade, but because they had not gone to Santa Fe first to make peace with the governor, their trading petition was refused. The next day, as Taoseños were going to their fields, they stumbled on about one hundred Comanches lying in ambush. Deprived of the surprise factor, the attackers were put to flight, losing three. Mendinueta argued that the two groups were part of a "depraved" plan to attack the pueblo. Two weeks later Nambé was hit: four were killed, two girls were taken captive, and the horses were run off. On June 23, when Comanches advanced as far as Alameda on the Rio Grande, residents of nearby Sandia Pueblo gave chase. After a long ride the Comanches turned on the exhausted pursuers, killing thirty-three. Another pursuit was organized the next day. Following the trail, they unexpectedly came upon the Comanche village in a canyon and immediately attacked to prevent the erection of breastworks. They were repulsed and settled down to a night-long siege, broken off the next day. That same day an attack on Pecos was repulsed, as was one on Galisteo on August 10. Later that year Governor Mendinueta admitted that although there were more than 600 guns in the province, as well as 150 pairs of pistols, there were not enough horses to mount an active pursuit of raiders, nor even enough to ensure the repopulation of the horse herd (Thomas 1940: 180–84).

In the summer of 1776, the Franciscan brothers Atanasio Domínguez and Silvestre Vélez de Escalante, and cartographer Bernardo de Miera y Pacheco, were sent from Santa Fe to find an overland route to Monterey, California. Traveling northwestward from Santa Fe, they eventually reached the Green River in what is now Utah before turning back. While in the north, they heard constant rumor of Comanches, particularly Yamparikas, but had no contact (Auerbach 1943; Bolton 1950; Chavez 1976).

In the summer of 1777 Comanches again struck New Mexico. The small community of Tomé, south of Isleta, was particularly hard hit, losing twenty-one men killed in May and thirty killed in August (E. Adams and Chavez 1956:154). In another attack, on November 14, 1778, a Comanche force was repulsed with losses of twenty killed and many wounded; forty animals were recovered from the attackers. Later New Mexico folk history attributed that devastating raid to the refusal of the alcalde to fulfill a promise to give his daughter to the Comanche chief. Elsewhere, after Comanches attacked Abiquiu, killing eleven and wounding three settlers and taking twenty-six animals, thirty or more Comanches were killed in the pursuit, and many animals were recovered (Rubio 1778).

In late 1777 and early 1778, in an effort to reach a policy decision on the various threats to northern New Spain—Apaches and Navajos on the west, and the Comanches and other Nations of the North on the east—Teodoro de Croix, comandante general of the newly organized Provincias Internas of northern Mexico, called a series of councils of war with officials of the frontier provinces, which were held at Monclova, Béxar, and Chihuahua (Bolton 1914, 2:147-70; Thomas 1940:193-211). At each council the participants were asked for information about the enemy tribes, the history of their relations with the Spaniards, their internal political divisions, the number of warriors they had, and other details. Although there was extensive discussion of the Apaches, there was relatively little about the Comanches and their allies. The participants in the Monclova meeting, in December 1777, declined to give information about the Comanches, citing the "lack of personal knowledge" (Bolton 1914, 2:155). At Béxar, in January 1778, the participants estimated that besides some 2,300 warriors in the Nations of the North, there were another 5,000 Comanches, "whose name is applied generally to various groups of Indians" (Cabello 1784d, Bolton 1914, 2:166). The third meeting, in Chihuahua City the following June, generally concurred in the latter opinion. Former New Mexico governor Mendinueta commented that the Comanches who attacked New Mexico numbered only 1,500 and were divided into three "congregations," known in New Mexico as the Yamparika, Gente de Palo 'people of the timber', and Come Civolos 'buffalo eaters' (Thomas 1940:201).

Although the lack of information about the Comanches among the participants in the first two meetings is understandable given the distances that still separated Comanches from most Spaniards, Mendinueta's silence at the Chihuahua meeting is regrettable, particularly since his three "congregations" matched Comanche groups identified on a set of maps drawn by Bernardo de Miera y Pacheco of his explorations with the Domínguez–Vélez de Escalante expedition of the previous year. Miera had already produced maps for the New Mexico authorities in 1758 and 1760 (Kessell 1979:167, 507–12) and would make at least one more (Thomas 1932; E. Adams and Chavez 1956:4). But whereas the earlier maps simply marked the territory to the northeast of New Mexico as Tierra de Cumanchis, the Domínguez–Vélez de Escalante maps gave greater detail, with several comments about the people and places encountered, including Comanches.

Three versions of the Domínguez–Vélez de Escalante maps were made, with several copies of one version (C. I. Wheat 1957–63, 1:94–116). On all the maps, clusters of tipis are used as icons for nomadic Indians. However, there are significant differences between the various versions and copies. Although cartographically different, version A in the British Library, probably produced in 1777 to accompany the official report of the Domínguez–Vélez de Escalante expedition, and version B in the Ministro de Guerra in Madrid (both reproduced in Auerbach 1943) have similar legends. On the far north, along the "Rio de los Yamparigos" of version B (version A was unlabeled) was a tipi cluster with the legend, "Land of the Yampatica Comanches who are the ultimate [word unclear] of the North." Then extending down the front range of the Rockies are three clusters. The "Cumanchis Pivianes," possibly Marín's Pibian, are noted but there are no named geographical features nearby. The "Cumanchis Jupis" (*hupe* 'timber') are near a river labeled "this could be the Missouri," but it seems to be the Platte. Along the Nepeste[8] River—the Arkansas—was a cluster labeled "Tierra de Cumanchis Nacion vago" [version B has "vaga"]; the Spanish is ungrammatical—it could be 'Land of the Roaming [or Vague] Comanche Nation', or possibly 'Land the Comanche Nation Roams." On the plains east of the mountains is a long legend:

> Unknown land of the Comanchis. This nation is very warlike and cruel. It has made itself master of the buffalo plains from the land of the Yamparikas to the province of Texas. It is very skillful in the handling of horses. It has dispossessed the Apache Nation of all its lands, becoming master of those as far as the frontier of the provinces of our King. These two said nations are those which for many years have been in a continual state of war against this kingdom, the one from the north and east, and the other from the south and west, and have brought about such panic that they have left no towns, cities or ranches of the Spaniards unattacked.

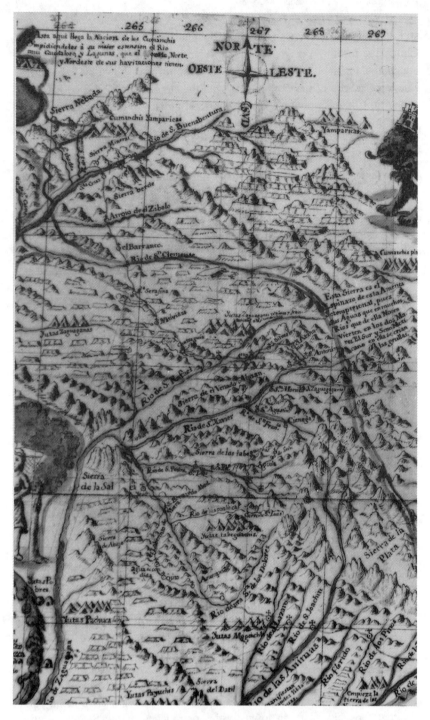

Map 2. Detail of Bernardo Miera y Pacheco's 1778 map of the Domínguez-Velez de Escalante expedition. Courtesy British Library.

Esta Nacion Cumanche, hace pocos años se apareció primero á las
Yutas, dicen salió por la banda de el Norte Rompiendo por entre
barias Naciones, y dhos Yutas los trujeron á hacer Cambios con los
Españoles, traian multitud de Perros, Cargados con sus Pieles
y tiendas; se hicieron de Caballos y Armas de fierro, y se
han abilitado tanto, á el manejo de el Caballo, y á ellas que
abentajaban á todas las Naciones en su agudeza y Ani
mo, se han echo Sᵣ y dueños de todos Campos de
los Zibolos, quitandoselos á la Nacion Apache, la
que era la mas dilitada que se ha conocido en
America, han destruido muchas Naciones della, y
las que han quedado, los han arrinconado á las fron
teras de las Provincias de Nᵗᵒ Rey. Causa porque se
experimentā tantos daños, pues los sala, en primer
mantenimiento los obliga la necesidad á mantener
se con Caballos y Mulas.

Plano Geographico, de
la tierra descubierta, nueva
mente, á los Rumbos Norte
Noroeste, y Oeste, del Nue vo
Mexico. demarcada por mi Don
Bernardo de Miera y Pacheco que
entró ahacer su descubrimiento, en com
pañia de los RRᵉˢ PPᵉˢ fr. Francisco Ata
nacio Doming͠ y Fr. Silbestre Veles, segun
consta en el Diario y Derrotero que se hizo
y se remitió á S.M. por mano de su Virrei con
Plano á la letra: El que dedica Al Sᵣ D. Teo
doro de la Crois, del Insigne Orden Teutonica
Comandante General en Gefe de Linea y
Provincias de esta America Setemp
trional, por S.M. hecho en S. Phᵉ
el Real de Chiguagua. Año
de 1778.

Cumanchis Yupis

Sierra del Almagre

Sierra de las
Grullas

Rio de Napeste.

Sierra
mojada

Rio de Animas

Cumanchis Cuchas Maria

Yabajoo

El Baltalque

Rio del Norte

Las tres
Mesas

Rio de la Xara

Sierra blanca

Cerro

Version C, dated 1778, exists in four copies; one (reproduced here as map 2) is in the British Museum, another is in the Archivo General de la Nación in Mexico City (reproduced with "corrections" in Bolton 1950); there are also two tracings in the Library of Congress in Washington. As a set, the four have the same legends, different from versions A and B, as well other minor differences from versions A and B.

For instance, all copies of version C omit the Rio de los Yamparigos altogether, and in place of "Land of the Yamparicas" was the longer statement:

> The Nation of the Comanches reaches to here. The wide river[9] and lakes impede their major extension on the west, north and northeast of their habitations.

The comment is particularly interesting since it implies that the Comanche expansion was towards the Basin, rather than away from it.

The four copies of version C give slightly different placements for the Comanche tipi clusters. The Yamparicas are still on the far north; although the British Library copy shows two clusters of tipis labeled "Cumanchis Yamparicas," the Mexico City copy as reproduced in Bolton (1950) shows only one. The "Cumanchis Pivianes" are again indefinately located along the front range. However, the "Cumanchis Jupis" have been moved to the Napeste River, while the fourth cluster, labeled "Roaming Comanches" on versions A and B, are placed below the Purgatoire and relabeled "Comanches Cuchun Marica" (*kuhtsutuhka* 'buffalo eaters'[10]); on both Library of Congress tracings that cluster was labeled "Apaches Cuchan Marica." Finally, the long legend on version C is rewritten:

> This Cumanche nation some years ago appeared first to the Yutas. They say they left the northern border, breaking through several nations and the said Yutas took them to trade with the Spaniards, bringing a multitude of dogs loaded with their hides and tents. They acquired horses and weapons of iron, and they have had so much practice in the management of horses and arms, that they excel all other tribes in agility and spirit, making themselves lords and masters of all the buffalo country, wresting it from the Apache Nation, who were the most extensive known in America, destroying many Nations of them and those which remain have been pushed to the frontiers of the Provinces of Our King. Because they have experienced many losses, lacking their primary means of support, necessity compels them to maintain themselves with horses and mules.

Thus, in both versions of the long legend, in very broad strokes, Miera outlined his understanding of the history of Comanche–Spaniard relations. The most interesting comments are the echoes of Brigadier Rivera's 1726 comment about the use of dogs for transport, and the final sentence about eating horses.[11] However, that final sentence is ambiguous: were the subjects of the sentence the Comanches or the Apaches? If Comanches were meant, it seems unlikely they would have been characterized as "lords" of the buffalo country. In contrast, if the Apaches were meant, inasmuch as they had been driven from their lands, and thus would have been forced to eat horses, the sentence does make some sense. It may also be be noted that Apaches were reported eating horses as early as 1630 (Opler 1983:384).

The more significant question is how much trust should be placed in Miera's political cartography. Was the change from "Land of the Comanches" on the earlier maps to specific divisional locations merely the result of the different scale of the maps, or did it reflect increased knowledge? Comparing versions A and B with all copies of version C, what caused the relocation of the Jupis from the Platte to the Arkansas, and the relabeling of the "Comanches . . . Vago/a" to "Cumanches Cuchun Marica"? Inasmuch as the group closest to New Mexico would presumably have had the most interactions with that province, they should have been the best known to the New Mexicans; why their ethnonym was not the first recorded is unclear. It is possible that, given the coincidence that version C was drawn in Chihuahua while de Croix's third council was meeting in that city, Miera was influenced by Mendinueta—after all, "Cuchun Marica" *kuhtsutuhka*, is 'buffalo eater', Mendinueta's term 'come civolos'—or vice versa. At the same time, and whichever way the influence may have traveled, given the evidence of Mendinueta's testimony and Miera's maps, it seems probable that the New Mexicans had a wider knowledge of Comanche political organization—at least of the ethnonyms—than the surviving documents reveal; unfortunately the extent of that knowledge is unknown.

Among the questions asked at the councils at Monclova, Béxar, and Chihuahua was "What benefits might come from making war on these nations [Comanches, Wichitas, etc.], allying ourselves with the Lipanes, or vice-versa" (Bolton 1914, 2:151). After much discussion, little of it apparently informed by first-hand knowledge of the Indians, it was decided that an alliance with the Comanches against the Apaches would end both wars. The councils also recommended that de Mézières be detailed from Louisiana to review all of the correspondence and minutes from the three councils and to draw up a plan for the proposed alliance (Bolton 1914, 2:169).

Thus, in his initial report describing the various Indian nations, focusing mainly in the Indians of Texas, de Mézières noted that although the Comanches were "the most populous, modest, and valiant of the tribes on the borders," their "great propensity to steal" masked those virtues. He argued that their behavior was not due to any natural perversity but was the result of their nomadic lifestyle. Losing horses on seasonal migrations and lacking both agriculture and Euroamerican trade, they had no resort but to thefts from Texas and Mexico, which, in turn, could be prevented only by establishing trade or by the more expensive alternative of military action (Bolton 1914, 2:174).

There was renewed military activity in New Mexico in the spring of 1779. In June Tomé was again the target of Comanche raids, with thirty killed. On July 10 a large group of Comanches attacked a Ute village, now enemies, near San Luis Lake in southern Colorado. They were repulsed with a loss of twelve, including a chief (Thomas 1932:127). In early August Juan Bautista de Anza, the new governor of New Mexico, organized a retaliatory campaign against the raiders. Mustering some 500 army, militia, and pueblo Indian auxiliaries, later joined by 200 Utes and Apaches, he traveled up the west side of the Rio Grande northward to the headwaters of the Arkansas River. There they surprised a village of about 120 tents—with Anza's esti-mate of 6 or 8 men per lodge, possibly 700 men—killing 18 Comanches, wounding many more, and capturing 64 women and children, 500 horses, and more wealth than 100 horses could carry off.

From the captives, Anza learned that their chief, or "captain-general," Cuerno Verde 'green horn', along with four other "principal captains" and a host of others, had gone to attack New Mexico sixteen days before. Anza caught up with him late on September 2, near the foot of what is now called Greenhorn Peak. A brief skirmish was fought that night. The next day, while Anza was directing the movement of his forces, the Comanche leader, identi-fiable by his "insignia and devices" of a green-horned headdress, came out between the lines to taunt the Spaniards. Anza planned a risky strategy: he split his force, hoping to draw the Comanche leader and his retinue of about forty men into a pincer. The trap failed, but Cuerno Verde, his son, and four other chiefs were killed, including one called Aguila Bolteada 'jumping eagle', called Cuerno Verde's "sumo pujacante" (*sumʉ?* 'one, someone', *puhakatʉ* 'possessor of power'). Satisfied with the extent of that victory, Anza returned to Santa Fe. Both Cuerno Verde's headdress and that of Aguila Bolteada were sent as trophies to Comandante General Croix (Thomas 1932: 142, 1941:109).

There were thus possibly three Comanche leaders called Cuerno Verde mentioned in the eighteenth century records of New Mexico: the "little king" with a headdress of a green horn killed at Ojo Caliente in 1768, the chief said by the drama *Los Comanches* to have been killed by Fernández at the Spanish Peaks in 1774, and Anza's opponent. It is tempting to suggest that they were relatives; Anza himself noted that his Cuerno Verde hated the Spaniards "because his father who also held the same command and power met death at our hands" (Thomas 1932:136). However, since the specifics of the father's death are unknown, linkage with either of the previous holders of the name is uncertain. Some thirty years after the battle, Pedro Bautista Pino wrote that Anza's opponent was "Tabivo Naritgante (brave and handsome)" (Carroll and Haggard 1942:131); Shimkin (1980:234) translated that name as *taivo* 'man' (possibly with implications of 'alien man') *naricut* [*narɨkatɨ*] 'danger possessor'.[12] The divisional affiliations of all three are unknown. Some scholars (e.g., John 1975:520) have suggested that Anza's opponent was Yamparika, but since both the 1774 and the 1779 battles were in the area indicated on Miera's map as occupied by the Jupes, both chiefs may have been of that division.

It was a bad time for the Comanches near New Mexico. While Anza was in the field, Comanches—probably those led by Cuerno Verde—attacked Taos, but the pueblo had been forewarned, and the attackers were repulsed with a loss of ten killed and many wounded. In addition, Anza's Ute auxiliaries, who had left after the fight of September 2, surprised a small camp of seven Comanche men and nine women and children; all but one child were killed (Thomas 1932:138). Thus, the Comanches lost at least thirty-eight killed, sixty women and children, and some five hundred horses captured. Juan de Dios Peña brought back from that campaign thirty-four prisoners, "small and large, of both sexes" (Peña 1805).

Nonetheless, Anza let it be known that he was willing to negotiate for a permanent peace. However, other events intervened. In the smallpox epidemic of 1780–81, several thousand pueblo Indians were reported to have died (Simmons 1979:193), but its effect upon Comanches is unclear. There were tentative negotiations in 1783 (Croix 1783), but no definite actions were taken.

The Comanche Peace in Texas, 1778–86

Initial Texas Spaniard efforts toward arranging a peace with the Comanches fared little better than those in New Mexico. During the spring and summer of 1778, de Mézières traveled among the Indian tribes on the northern borders of Texas to persuade them to join in an expedition against the Apaches. Among his party was a young Comanche, said to be a leading man, wounded and captured near Béxar, who went along as guide and interpreter. At the Taovaya village on the Red River they met a party of eight Comanches who reported that others had recently raided between Béxar and the Presidio del Rio Grande, taking at least one scalp and many horses. Since the Béxar ranches were becoming more vigilant, they had turned southward toward Laredo. Given the evidence of continued hostility, de Mézières decided not to continue on to the Comanche camps. Rather, he sent his young interpreter with the message that the recent thefts were the last straw and that in the future the Comanches would be blamed for any and all raids on Spanish settlements (Bolton 1914, 2:200).

De Mézières then returned to Natchitoches by way of the new town of Bucareli on the Trinity River. After staying a few days, he resumed his journey; but on the very day that he left Bucareli, a party of Comanches arrived. As reported by the local authorities, thirty Comanche warriors appeared on the outskirts of the town and stole some horses. Alarmed, the inhabitants mustered, and chased the Indians as far as the Brazos, killing three (Bolton 1915b:432). However, de Mézières heard a different story from the Comanches. The party had been on a peaceful mission, with Evea's own son in charge. It was after they had set their own horses out to graze that the panicked citizens of Bucareli attacked them (Bolton 1914, 2: 233). Whatever the actual motivations were, Comanches retaliated against Bucareli throughout the fall and winter of 1778–79, ultimately forcing the abandonment of the settlement (Bolton 1915b:435).

Both de Mézières and Evea had hopes of restoring relations. By the spring of 1779 they had made several contacts with each other through the interpreter from the summer before and through a Comanche woman, sent to Bucareli by way of the Tawakonis. Evea himself sent word through the Anadarko chief that, although he was angered by the Bucareli attack, most of the raiding was, in fact, carried out by a small band who had broken away from his authority. De Mézières accepted that explanation, noting that the size of the attacking parties was small, between five and ten men, and that there were few attacks on Béxar; if the entire Comanche nation were hostile, there would have been more serious attacks (Bolton 1914, 2:289). De Mézières planned another journey up the Red River for the following summer but was seriously injured by a fall from his horse; he died that autumn.

In late 1779 Comanches made several raids on the Lipan Apaches northwest of Béxar, doing no damage but raising the Spaniards' fears. On January 1, 1780, citizens and militia from Béxar attacked a party of Comanches on the Guadalupe River. Nine Comanches were killed, and the Spaniards brought back trophies, including bows and arrows, guns, an English hatchet, lances, and several feathered headdresses (Cabello 1780a). Comanche retaliation was not immediate but came in force. In June they attacked a cattle drive intended to resupply Nacogdoches (Cabello 1780b). A large party was reported above the Guadalupe, attacking and breaking up ranches with impunity. In August a group of Tejas Indians told Governor Domingo Cabello that the attacks originated in two large villages of "Namborica"—probably Yamparika—on the upper Colorado, and were in retaliation for their losses the previous January (Cabello 1780c).

Comanche raids continued through 1781, and the Texans were unable to mount a response. In December Governor Cabello received word of a Comanche village on the Medina River north of Béxar. He organized a small force and sent them to attack the village, later estimated to contain eighty men, women, and children. The Comanches saw the attackers and were thereby forewarned. In the battle that followed, some men formed a defense, while the rest escaped to a nearby hill. The Comanches lost eighteen men killed, including their chief, who wore a horned headdress and a scalp-ornamented shirt; his horse also wore a horned headdress. In the remains of the village the Spaniards found clothing and jewelry identifiable as belonging to victims from the vicinity of Béxar, apparent evidence that those Comanches had participated in the recent raids (Cabello 1781).

The Texans feared retaliation, and Cabello maintained a constant reconnaissance to discover any attempts at revenge. Although there were signs— smoke signals and tracks—that Comanches were nearby, there was no direct contact for almost eighteen months, possibly due to the smallpox of 1780-81, but there is no direct evidence.

In the spring of 1783, a large Comanche encampment was sighted at Arroyo Blanco on the Guadalupe River. Cabello raised a small party to meet them, but the Comanches, again forewarned, did not wait for an attack. They fled, stopping once, and then fled again, leaving behind the frames of forty tipis. According to the scout's estimate of ten persons per tipi, some four hundred people were thus homeless (Cabello 1783). For the rest of the summer, although Indian signs were evident around Béxar, there was no clear contact with Comanches. In the summer of 1784 a detachment of Spaniards chasing a Wichita raiding party came across forty Comanches on the Guadalupe; ten were killed and as many captured, as were all the horses. Claimed as a victory, it again raised the prospect of retaliation, although none occurred (Cabello 1784d).

One event in the summer of 1784 was to have minor but continuing influence on the course of Comanche-Euroamerican interactions. In July, during a period of crisis with various Wichita groups, a young man, Francisco Xavier de Chavez, appeared at Béxar. He was a New Mexican captured by Comanches and later sold to Taovayas. He had been along with one of their raiding parties that had been harassing Béxar that summer and had managed to escape (John 1975:649). After a brief interview Cabello quickly realized his importance as a means of communicating with the Indians around Béxar (Cabello 1784a). It must be acknowledged, however, that the extent of his knowledge both of the languages he was called upon to translate and of the customs of the people he was asked about is difficult to estimate and therefore remains problematic.

During that same time, larger issues again confronted Comanche-Texan relations. When the Anglo-American Revolution ended in 1782 it brought about a change in political relations throughout North America. Although the Spaniards had aided the rebels in the revolution, favorable provisions acknowledging their assistance, such as limiting the territory of the new republic to the existing states and protecting the northern borders of New Spain, Louisiana, and the Floridas against encroachment, were not included in the treaty ending the war.

By 1783 the Spaniards had begun major efforts to establish alliances with the Indian groups along their borders to counter the expansionist Anglo-Americans. Comandante General Croix and his successors, Felipe de Neve and Joseph Antonio Rengel, wished to break the Comanche-Wichita alliance (Thomas 1932:72), but it is not clear whether any serious efforts were made in that direction. More successful were several small-scale efforts undertaken by Governor Cabello of Texas. Since 1780 he had sent several individuals north in efforts to contact the Comanches and other Nations of the North. None were particularly successful until late summer 1784, when he licensed Juan Baptista Bousquet, a trader from Louisiana, to seek the source of a silver ore he had seen in the Wichita villages years before; he was also instructed to tell the chiefs of the Wichitas, the Taovayas, and the Tawakonis that the Spaniards still desired peace (Cabello 1784b).

Soon after his departure, rumor circulated that Comanches, Taovayas, and Wichitas were mustering to attack any Spaniards or Lipans they happened to meet (Cabello 1784c). Although nothing came of that report, it caused much anxiety in Texas. Thus there was great relief when Bousquet returned in February 1785 with four Wichita and Taovaya chiefs who wanted to restore positive relations. They especially wanted Cabello to recognize a new Taovaya "medal chief" (the former chief had died), but they also complained about Comanche raids: en route their own horses had been taken by Comanches, and they had to proceed on foot. Cabello was impressed by their professions of friendship and sent them home with what modest presents he could spare (Cabello 1785a).

Three other Euroamericans accompanied Bousquet from the north: Pedro Vial, Alfonso Rey, and Antonio Mariano Valdés. Valdés was from Béxar; Vial and Rey were natives of France, speaking only moderate Spanish. Of the three, Vial was to prove most valuable. He was a blacksmith who made lances and repaired guns for the Indians; it was even rumored that he had taught gunsmithing to an Indian. Despite Vial's lack of close familiarity with either the Comanches or the Spanish language, he was to become a major intermediary between the Texas Spaniards and the Indians. Because of their potential knowledge and expertise about the Norteños, Cabello pardoned Valdés, Vial, and Rey for any illegal acts they might have committed, and he settled them in Béxar.

In the spring of 1785 Vial and Chavez offered to visit the Comanches in hopes of ending the hostilities. On June 16 Cabello gave them a set of instructions—unfortunately, so far undiscovered—and on June 17 they were issued four hundred pesos worth of gifts and subsistence (Cabello 1785b). On their return they prepared a detailed account of their extraordinary journey (Vial and Chavez 1785). Although it was attributed to both Vial and Chavez, its content shows it to be the product of Vial himself. The document is apparently Vial's long sought "diary" of his expedition to the Comanches, but it is not a day-by-day account of events and distances traveled; rather it is an after-the-fact report, dated November 15, 1785, in numbered paragraphs, each a single sentence long and with little further punctuation.

According to the diary, in July 1785, having been commissioned by Cabello, Vial and Chavez traveled to Nacogdoches to pick up Guersec, the newly recognized Taovaya medal chief, Eschas, the Wichita chief, and a party of their people to act as guides and intermediaries. Setting out from Nacogdoches, they passed the Tierra Blanca—the 'white land'—where the road split to the Tawakoni, Yscani, and Flechazos villages; ten days later they reached the Taovaya village where Vial had formerly lived and where Guersec had his home.

Unsure how to proceed, Vial send a small party ahead, which soon returned with a Comanche "captain"—unfortunately unnamed, perhaps no more than a *tekwɨniwapI* 'war leader'—who had been leading a horse-stealing party against the Osages. But he was glad to turn aside to escort the party to his village. Thus, on August 31 they came into sight of a great ranchería, situated on a broad plain along the Red River. Guersec and Eschas put on their uniforms and medals, and on seeing them, about two hundred Comanches in "two bands or files" came out on horseback, firing their "few muskets." Vial had a Spanish flag unfurled and returned the salute in kind; when the two groups met, "they embraced us, and took us hand in hand."

Although Vial called it the primary ranchería of the Comanches, the two principal chiefs were not present, so the tlatoleros 'speakers' were sent throughout the "11 or 12 rancherías which comprise the Comanche Oriental," calling the chiefs and principal men to a parlamento principal 'general council'.

The two Spaniards were taken to a large tent, in front of which they placed their flag; Guersec and Eschas were taken to another. Their horses and mules, which had been carrying gifts, were unloaded and set out to graze, and they were given buffalo meat, venison, fruits, and "papas"—literally potatoes but probably one of the several edible roots that grow on the plains—in abundance. The captain who had led them to the village told them he was going on to his own village, but would return for the meeting to come, and he advised them not to leave their tent until then. Guersec and Eschas, however, were well known among the Comanches and were allowed to move freely within the village. They took advantage of this freedom to spread word of the purpose of their visit.

The Comanches were worried, however. They asked whether any of the visitors were sick; only recently, they said, two-thirds of their people had been killed by smallpox—possibly referring to the 1780-81 epidemic.[13] Vial responded that the sickness had been brought by Frenchmen from La Zarca;[14] moreover, since the Spaniards had been there, the sun had not been darkened but was always clear and bright.

By about a week later, the two principal chiefs had arrived; one Vial called "the Captain of the Camisa de Hierro[15] ['iron shirt'] (because he dressed in a Cota de Maya ['coat of mail'] which he had taken from an Apache captain)"; the other was called "the Captain of the Cabeza Rapada ['shaved head'] for having the middle in that mode."[16] There were another ten or so "little captains." Vial gave them all presents of his tobacco, knives, vermilion, and beads, but he was careful to give proportionately to rank lest he run out of goods.

On September 10, with Guersec and Eschas in their uniforms, and displaying the Spanish flag, Vial and Chavez were taken to a large circle composed of an "infinity of men, women, and children"; Camisa de Hierro and Cabeza Rapada and the other chiefs sat on the ground in the center. Sitting beside them, Vial lit a "great pipe," and after smoking, passed it to Guersec and Eschas and then to the Comanches. After that "indispensable ceremony," Vial stood and in the Taovaya language, "which they all understood very perfectly," began a long speech giving his version of the history of their expedition.

He began by noting, "This is not the first occasion that my companion and I have been among you." He recounted that Chavez had been captured by Comanches, then sold to Taovayas. After those people had been killed, he had gone to Béxar to be among his own people. Vial himself had traveled among their rancherías as a trader with merchandise from the Rio de la Zarca (the Arkansas). Thus, he said, he and Chavez, were known as good and truthful people.

While living with the Indians, they heard that the Capitan Grande de San Antonio—Governor Cabello—was very valiant and protected all those who came under his care, they went to see him, and indeed, they were treated as well as his own people if not better. They had heard that Cabello was planning to make his annual presents to the chiefs and people of the friendly nations. But they had also heard that he was going to equip his troops with many horses, good arms, powder and ball, to make "incessant war" on the Comanches. When Vial and Chavez had thought about the good treatment they had received from the Comanches and Taovayas, "tears came to us that you were not included in the regalo." They remembered "that many times you do not have a knife to cut meat, a pot to cook in, nor a grain of powder with which to kill deer or buffalo for your food." Thus they determined to demand that the "Capitan Grande to have you included in the gifts that he was going to give to the friendly nations."

At that suggestion, Vial said, Cabello became very angry. The Comanches had, he said, killed many people who, without arms, had gone to hunt on the Plains; "anyone who would do that was a people without a good heart, without valor." After much talk, Vial and Chavez had persuaded Cabello that the "Comanches were good people, very generous, and very friendly to their friends." "Is this certain?" he had asked; it was "muchisima verdad" 'extremely true', they answered.

Therefore, Cabello had asked Vial and Chavez to take these words to the Comanches:

If they want to be my friends, and friends of the Spaniards, I will promise not to kill them, and to stop sending my soldiers, those who make war on them. And if they want to come to San Antonio to talk to me, I will give them my hand in advance, like friends, as also they would be to the other nations who are my friends, except the Lipans and Apaches, with whom I do not want anyone to be friends, but to make continual war against them.

Two days later, as Vial and Chavez had prepared their loads of tobacco, knives, beads, and vermilion, Cabello had repeated to them his desire to make peace. Moreover, he wanted them to be not just friends with the Spaniards, but also to make war on the Apaches and Lipans, who stole many horses and mules and killed the cows on which the people lived, and also to carry the war to the Osages, who disrupt the lives of many people. If that were done, he, Cabello, "would forget the many deaths which they had caused among my people, as they must forget those which my people did to them." To ratify the truth of those actions, and to hear that they were indeed Cabello's words, they should send two or three chiefs to return with Vial and Chavez, and Cabello would give the chiefs his hand and would give them presents. Finally, if they would be his friends, he would send traders to their rancherías who would provide their necessities in trade for the skins and the other things that they would sell. In addition, every year the chiefs and principals of the Comanche Nation should come to San Antonio for a "regalito," a small gift-giving. Thus, they would maintain a brotherlike peace, without one hurting the other. With those words Vial ended his speech. They were seconded by Guersec, the Taovaya: "All that the Spaniards have said of the Capitan Grande is true."

Throughout the rest of that day, the tlatoleros were heard speaking of the events; they continued into the night, when all of the streets of the rancheria were lit up, and there was such a noise that Vial and Chavez could not sleep. At daybreak Guersec and Eschas returned from an all-night meeting; they said they had persuaded all of the chiefs and principal people to make peace with the Capitan Grande and the Spaniards.

The next day, September 11, the emissaries were again brought to the council circle, where Cabeza Rapada replied to their speeches. He said:

> We have heard with great favor the good words which have been sent to us by our Father, the Capitan Grande, which we embrace in our hearts. And we see that there has been no wind, nor has the Sun been shadowed, nor has the smoke of the pipe twisted while they were spoken. It is a signal that what you, and the Capitan Grande say is true. . . . [we will] forget the deaths of our fathers, sons, and brothers caused by the Spaniards . . . and from now on the war with our brothers the Spaniards is finished, we will not kill, nor make any raids, nor rob. And there will be three little captains from our nation named to go with you to hear what the Capitan Grande says about the mode of establishing the peace.

There were two large war parties out, one attempting to take the horse herd of San Antonio and La Bahia, the other going against the Lipans. "But as soon as they return we will no more leave against the Spaniards." They were glad that "the Capitan Grande, does not like the Apaches and Lipans, against whom we have warred whenever we find them"; they had only one request: "that he not oppose that we make war on the Lipans, our ancient enemies." Finally, they would "go to give news to our companions and brothers the Yambericas, so that also they can have friendship with the Spaniards of Santa Fe as well as San Antonio."

With that, "there was a great cry and shout of all the circle, and of those who were outside it." Taking it as a signal that they had agreed to the peace, Vial and Chavez retrieved the flag from the center of the circle and were returned to their tent, accompanied there by Cabeza Rapada and Camisa de Hierro.

The next two days were spent preparing to return. One of Cabello's instructions to Vial had been to discover the whereabouts of two Spaniards, Miguel George Menchaca, son of a prominent family, and another named

José Solis, both taken captive in December 1781. The matter was not only one of recovering relatives, but had military importance. In 1783 a man who had identified himself as Menchaca, and had been so identified by a member of the Menchaca household, was seen near Béxar in company with a party of Comanches looking for horses. Such troops as could be mounted had been sent in pursuit but they had had no luck finding him (John 1975:644–46). However, the Comanches reported to Vial that they had killed Miguel "the day after the action with the Spaniards on December 6 of that same year"—presumably Cabello's fight on the Medina River in 1781—"out of anger at seeing so many Comanches killed and wounded." Solis, on the other hand, had been held captive by a principal chief and had since been passed to the Yamparicas where he had many friends.

According to Cabello's instructions, Vial was also to attempt the ransom of an individual of the "A Nation" said to be held captive, but the Comanches responded that there was no such person among them; he could only be among the Yamparicas, "because only they war on that nation, whom they know as Maxa and Utos, who are of the same division in the manner of the Lipans and Apaches."

Their mules and horses were returned, well treated and loaded, and at dawn on September 14 they set out to return to San Antonio. The party included the three captains, their women, Guersec and Eschas and their people, and some other Comanches who were going to visit the Taovayas. For more than a league from the village, they were accompanied by all the chiefs, great and small, and more than three hundred men, who then "gave the hand as a signal of departure." The Comanche village must have moved from the banks of the Red River during the two weeks Vial was resident, although he made no mention of it, for three days later, on September 17, they again reached the river. There, Guersec and Eschas left with their people and the other Comanches, charging Vial to "give many memorials to their Father." They also asked the three captains to return via their villages, so that they could tell what had happened.

That left the three captains and their women. Because "they did not want to meet any Lipans," they went through woods and lands so rough that they lost two mules and four horses. Two weeks later, on September 29, they arrived at Béxar, and at four in the afternoon the Comanches "went into the first house they had ever entered" and were presented to Governor Cabello.

Vial's report concludes with a "Description of the Comanche Nation." Because it is one of the earliest first-hand accounts of the Comanches, I quote it almost in its entirety:

The Comanche Nation has no fixed villages because they have many horses, because of which it is necessary to find places to pasture them, and which have buffalo and deer, for that is their food, and clothing, and with which they make the tents in which they live from the buffalo hides which they make white, and very strong, useful, and durable.

Their rancherías are organized by the captains, who, each [one] endeavoring to have his own [ranchería], they do not have a fixed number of subjects, but only those who can adjust to the spirit of each captain. The two most famous in that nation, the one named Camisa de Hierro, and the other Cabeza Rapada, to whom they listen with much respect and attention from their respect among them as the most valiant of all. There are another ten little captains who govern and order their respective rancherías. They are nevertheless, subject to the two greatest.

The smallpox made great havoc among them, having reduced much of the nation, and nevertheless they would have about 2000 warriors, and many women and children.

The nation known as Comanche lives from the borders of New Mexico to this province of Texas as far as El Paso, and for this is known as the Easterners.

On the northwest are the western Comanches, known as Yambericas. They differ from the Easterners only in the cut of the hair. They possess the same language, and see each other as brothers, and companions, and aid each other in their wars when necessary. They are said to be twice as many as the Orientales, and distant about 150 leagues.

The Eastern Comanches have as friends the Taovayas and Wichitas, and are also found among the Tawakonis, Yscanis, and Flechazos [Echaros?], but not so much as among the others. They have much trade in salt, which they lack, and for which they frequently come to trade. They have as enemies the Apaches and Lipans and the Osages, who steal many horses from them.

Their arms are arrows, lances, and some guns and ammunition provided by the Taovayas and Wichitas, who also provide them to the Yambericas, who also get them from the nations known as Kansas, Guahes, and Guitavoiratas who are situated in the north, and who in turn are provided by the traders who come from New Orleans and Illinois, and who are installed along the Missouri River.

The Yambericas have as friends the aforesaid Nations, and the Spaniards of New Mexico, which, they say, is five days distant. Their enemies are the Maxá (which are here called A) and Utos, with whom they are always at war.

The eastern Comanches are good looking, and of well built bodies, and well dressed. They are valiant, and of a rational mind, from which arises much generosity, and good hearts with his friends and even with his captives, of whom, during the season we were among them, they had no more than 10 men, according to the old ones, nor any who left their masters, the source of their captivity, but who had been totally made into Comanches.

These eastern Comanches are those who had made the war of many years against this province, extending their hostility to Coahuila, due to the protection that distance provides them, it being as far from there as their usual campgrounds. It is 16 or 18 days to the extinct presidio at Saba through very reasonable country. Because of its ruggedness, it provides shelter when they withdraw after a raid.

From what we have learned while among this nation, theirs should be a lasting peace as long as they are treated fondly and warmly when they come to visit this Presidio and care is taken to make an annual gift to the captains and principals of the nation, without neglecting the youths; and to maintain a trader for them and have the Taboyaces and Wichitas urge them to keep good relations.

We believe that they will do whatever is wished, especially if their compatriots, the Yambericas, also enter into the peace, providing both with gifts which is what we can say about these Indians. For in the end, their temperament is ambitious and acquisitive and they are very fond of being given the equivalent of what they might obtain through pillage, theft, and the raids which they carry out when at war. [Vial and Chavez 1785]

Vial's report would be an extraordinary document if only for the account of his motivations and actions in seeking the peace; but its appeal to honor, valor, and "good hearts" is unique in the documentary history of Euroamerican-Comanche relations. It also includes significant ethnographic detail on Comanche political processes. However, evaluation of those details requires evaluation of Vial's knowledge of the Comanches, a requirement that the document also fulfills. Moreover, since Vial was later called upon to perform important missions to the Comanches, and his comments thereon are the basis of many modern conclusions about Comanche political relations, the extent of his knowledge of the Comanches is important.

Vial admitted that his contacts with Comanches had been minimal: he said that although he had "traveled among" them as a trader, he had lived primarily among the Taovayas, attested to by his use of that language as the medium of interaction. Finally, there is the fact that after their arrival at the Comanche village, he and Chavez were confined to a tipi, while Guersec and Eschas, being "well known," were allowed the run of the village. Thus, although Vial may have been acquainted with Comanches, he was not particularly familiar with them. He had a general knowledge of the southern and eastern Plains, but some of his specific knowledge is debatable.

The general proceedings of the council are interesting. Vial presented his case to a general council apparently composed of the whole ranchería, seated in a circle. Then the chiefs—and Guersec and Eschas—spent the night in a special council. The next day Camisa de Hierro announced their decision to the assembly, which approved it with shouts of affirmation. Thus, it seems that although the presentation was to the general council, the debate on the merits of the proposition was not open to all, but took place during the all-night session, in executive session, as it were. Unfortunately, Vial was not invited to that session. Finally, Vial's companions on his return journey apparently represent the only documented case in which persons other than principal chiefs were sent as emissaries to arrange a truce, although they may have been local band chiefs.

Vial was the earliest observer to mention Comanche pipe ceremonies, although the symbolism of windless days, unclouded sun, and untwisted smoke are unattested elsewhere. Similarly, Vial was the earliest observer to use the term *tlatolero* to refer to camp criers, and he was clear about their distinction from the captains as political leaders. Vial explicitly distinguished the Comanches of Texas, to whom he exclusively attributed the ethnonym, from the Yamparikas of New Mexico; that was to become a common Texas distinction in later years, although his claim of a difference in hair styles is unattested elsewhere. His report of the Comanche's claim that two-thirds of the division had died of smallpox, probably referring to the epidemic of 1780–81, is interesting but unverifiable; his own claim that even after the epidemic they had 2,000 warriors is probably an exaggeration.

Of the other ethnonyms mentioned, Guaxes and Guitavoiratas are unknown, although the former is possibly *aguayes*, that is Pawnee. The identity of the "A [or Aa] nation" has long been problematic in Plains ethnohistory; some scholars have suggested that the Aa's were Caddos (Loomis and Nasatir 1967:424) or even Arapahos (Thomas 1940:109). Joe Attocknie (1965) suggested, based on the similarity of the name to *aa* 'horn' that they were Crow, *aanuu* 'horn people'. Vial was the only eighteenth-century source to explicitly identify them with the "Maxa" or Mahas, that is, Omahas. That identification is strengthened by Vial's other linkage of the Mahas with the "Utos," probably Otoes, both on the Missouri River and both "of the same division in the manner of the Lipans and Apaches." Since both Otoe and Omaha are Siouan languages—Omaha is Dhegiha, Otoe is Chiwere—the analogy is apt.

Vial's analysis of the political organization of rancherías is interesting, and its implications are surprisingly modern and processual. As sets of individuals, rancherías were "followers of the captains"; that is, membership was political, not ascribed. Moreover, since a goal of each captain was to have his own ranchería (that implies that captain was applied not only to existing local band chiefs, but to all important men, *tekwuniwapI*, for whom the goal of heading a local band had yet to be achieved), there was a constant movement of people—chiefs had no "fixed number of subjects"—between rancherías. Ultimately, rancherías were composed of "those who [could] adjust to the spirit of each captain"; there was a constant political process of mutual adjustment between chief and band member. He does seem clear in numbering the eastern Comanches in "ten or twelve rancherías," a number that corresponds to the "ten or so little captains."

Vial's report is the first mention of the two principal chiefs, Camisa de Hierro and Cabeza Rapada; the former would become the focus of much later confusion. It is not at all clear whether Vial had known either of them previously. Although the phrase "Cota de Maya" is capitalized in the manuscript, it is not clear whether it was intended as a name. Vial is also the only source for the origin of the name in the "Coat of Mail which he had taken from an Apache captain."

In October 1785 a treaty was formalized with the Texas Comanche delegates who had accompanied Vial. It stipulated that Spaniards and Comanches would act as brothers and friends, and enemies of the same enemies, particularly the Lipan Apaches. Further, "since the Spanish would . . . provide them with goods in exchange for hides," no foreign traders would be allowed. Finally, there would be an annual distribution of presents to both "chiefs and principal tribal members as a proof and manifestation of our good will." As a symbol of their authority, the Comanche chiefs were given canes of office, similar to the silver-headed canes used by Spaniards throughout the hemisphere as symbols of local authority (Faulk 1964:65). They were also given captain's uniforms, guns, and other items, including white flags with the Burgundian cross (Cabello 1785c).

Soon after the delegation left Béxar, other Comanches began arriving. The first were two young men who told of the great celebration at the news that peace had been established, particularly in the rancherías of the principal chiefs Camisa de Hierro and Cabeza Rapada. The two youths said that after they had decided to come and visit, their own "Capitan Grande" —unnamed, but one of the three delegates who had come with Vial—sent them to tell Cabello of the reception, and he sent along one of the guns recently given to the delegation as his credential. The youths stayed a week, having many conversations with Cabello, but the governor did not report details (Cabello 1785d).

Within a week another party of sixteen youths and three women arrived; they were led by another of the three chiefs from the previous October, who was wearing his uniform and carrying his cane. They had been out hunting horses and Apaches and decided to try to sell their booty at Béxar. In the ensuing trade they exchanged skins, meat, and two Apache children captured in Sonora for horses, belduque knives, and the loaves of hard sugar called piloncillos, all at "well regulated prices" (Cabello 1786a). During the following weeks, still other parties arrived to visit Cabello, including the brother of Cabeza Rapada—who may have been a cousin or indeed a *tubitsinahaitsInuu*, all of whom could have been called brother in Comanche. There were so many visitors that Cabello built a small wattle-and-daub jacalon structure to house them all (Cabello 1786b).

In all of those negotiations and meetings, neither Vial nor Governor Cabello directly named the three Comanches. Later, and based on information from the New Mexico Comanches, Governor Anza of New Mexico reported that Cabello had met first with Oxinicante, Taninchini, and Paruatuosacante, that later Tazaniquinta had visited Cabello, and that finally Ysayabenohe had visited (Thomas 1932:320). The first and third are clearly *ohinikatu* 'left hand' and *paruatuakatu* 'he has a young bear'; the meanings of the second and the last two names are unclear. Also unclear is the relation of those names to the order of visits to Béxar; although the first list of three names seems to correspond to the "three captains who came in October," correlation of the other two names with Cabello's visitors is not possible.

In January 1786 Comandante Inspector of the Provincias Internas Joseph Antonio Rengel instructed Cabello:

> When you go among the Comanches, try to find in their combinations all the news possible on the mutual customary interest of their rancherías; the force of each one; the territory which they ordinarily occupy; the names of the captains which govern them; which ones are distinguished in authority and following; the principles on which the superiority of their command is established, if by election or by inheritance; the personal character of their chiefs, with respect to the influence which they have and could have on the negotiations of their nation. [Rengel 1786]

In April Cabello (1786c) responded to each of Rengel's points, numbering his replies more or less in order. Although brief and synoptic, his extended discussion of Comanche political organization merits some discussion here. Inasmuch as there is no evidence that Cabello visited Comanches in their own country, his sources are probably the interviews with the Comanche visitors to Béxar and the report of his emissaries, Pedro Vial and Francisco Xavier de Chavez. Cabello wrote as follows:

1) On their Customs.

Following that which is known of this nation, the most colorful and warlike of those who inhabit the North, with a generous spirit; when they have friendship, they are expressive and friends with their friends, although delicate in the mode which they must be treated.

Many of them worship a shield ["una piel de animas" 'a skin of spirits'(?)] which they bring with them to war and which they believe has the power to protect them from being killed or wounded.

If any disgrace occurs, they attribute it to having made some offense to this idol, such as not offering food or the smoke of tobacco each time they smoke, or allowing women in their ceremonies when they take the pipe in hand. Some are dedicated to adoring a buffalo horn, others to the bear, others to the beaver, and others to the various birds whose skins and feathers they take with them.

Marriages are celebrated with four women if they can maintain them. Fathers sometimes give their daughters to one who is distinguished in valor and in actions against his enemies or is outstanding in generosity, and [such men] often marry the rest of the sisters that they can support with the buffalo and deer. . . . They are extremely jealous and for any motive kill their women; and in any case they treat them as if they were slaves.

Behind the confusion there are several elements of validity in that description, for example, the power of invulnerability possessed by shields, the medicine ceremonies, including the use of the pipe, and the wearing of *puhakatʉ* 'medicine possessing' skins and feathers. With a modernization of language, the description of marriage practices could serve as a minimal synopsis of the economics of Comanche social organization.

2) What reciprocal interest has one for the other Rancherías.

The trade and interest that some rancherías have with others is that the Eastern Comanche take horses which they acquire in their wars and rapines to the rancherías of the Western Comanches who are known by the name of Yamberika, who barter for guns, powder, balls, lances, cloth, jars, knives. etc, which the Western Indians acquire from the Kansa, Quita, Quirate, and Aguayas. Intervening also is the trade in buffalo hides with and without hair, which benefits them and they prepare very well.

This statement reflects the view of trade as seen from Texas, hence the suggestion that the Yamparikas were closer to the sources of Euroamerican goods than were Texas Comanches. Although that suggestion is suspect—the New Mexico Comanches were actually closer—the understanding of the sources of Comanche horses in raiding and their destination in trade is valid. The referent of the ethnonym Kansa is clear; the Aguayas were Pawnees. The ethnonyms Quita—possibly *kwita* 'excrement'—and Quirate are unknown.

> 3) What force has each one.

> In respect to the force of each ranchería, it is not possible to investigate the number of tents which compose each, nor the number of rancherías because they are accustomed to subdivide according to the mode of the territory in which they exist. Because of the necessities of the buffalo hunt on which they maintain themselves, their whole force lives separately, lacking firearms, which are in short supply. But none are situated in incommodious areas or in which they are covered by their enemies. They send out small separate parties to observe if they might be attacked, and systematically move from one part to another without maintaining a fixed place or sowing seed, but living off of nothing but buffalo meat and deer, and of the search for the root of a type of sweet potato which abounds in much of the territory through which they travel.

Cabello's excuse for his lack of population estimates is, after Vial, perhaps the earliest recognition that Comanche groups periodically divided and coalesced. In contrast to the rationale given by the Frenchmen who visited New Mexico in 1749—that rancherías were dispersed "having to seek sufficient pasturage and water for their horses" (Hackett 1931–46, 3:317)—Cabello focused on the buffalo as producing the same result. Yet despite being so scattered, he argued there was no area within their territory that the Comanches could not defend. Moreover, he said, they were constantly on the lookout for enemies—although the recurrent surprise attacks on Comanche villages might belie the effectiveness of their vigilance. Finally, Cabello is the first to note the continuing economic reliance on root vegetables in Comanche domestic economy.

> 4) What territory do they ordinarily occupy.

> The rancherías of the eastern Indians commonly stay above the river that some name the Colorado, and others that of the palisade which passes by Natchitoches to disgorge into the Mississippi, whence they pass to the head of the Brazos de Dios, about 100 leagues from one to the other. In their wanderings, they often visit a stopping place called the Gran Salina ('great salt') where they make salt to trade with the Tawayazes and Wichitas who for lack of it have much regard for it.

Cabello obviously meant the Red River, sometimes called the Colorado. Although Comanches were often later reported as visiting the Salt Plains of the Salt Fork of the Arkansas River, as well as the Salinas area east of the

Manzano Mountains in New Mexico, Cabello was the first—and apparently only—notice of Comanche salt making.

5) What are the names of the Captains who Govern them.

The names of the captains of whom notice has been made are of the first place Cota de Maya or Camisa de Yerro [sic]; the second Cabeza Rapada; and those of the second class are El Lobito; El Sonnillo; Quinacaraco; El Quaguangas; La Boca Partida; El Español; El Surdo, and El Manco. It was not possible to learn the names of the other three or four of the second class.

Translation of those names presents some difficulties. Those in the first class include 'Coat of Mail or Iron Shirt', seconded by 'Shaved Head'. Of the second class, the first seems to be 'The Small Wolf'; the third is clearly *kwina korohkO* 'eagle sash/neckpiece'. Guaquangas is possibly *wakwakwasI* 'trotter'. La Boca Partida seems to be 'The Broken Mouth'. Rounding out the second class were The Spaniard, The Deaf One, and The One Armed. The first two were named by Vial, but it is not clear where Cabello obtained the other names.

6) What distinguishes them in authority and following.

The captains of greatest following and authority are known by the Eastern Comanche in the first place el Camisa de Fierro [sic], or Cota de Maya, and in the second, Cabeza Rapada, and another ten or twelve which form the second class, as above noted.

Here, in repeating the same information from question 5, Cabello avoided answering question 6 altogether.

7) On what principles do they establish the superiority of command, by election or inheritance.

Command and superiority is established in the two aforesaid captains by election and vote of the whole eastern nation by having signaled the distinctions in war against their enemies by which they acquire all the regard of their nation, and the following which they have, in such a way that in their gatherings that they always promise to give their vote.

In this answer, Cabello became the first to report an explicit election to the position of divisional principal chief. He also echoed Governor Marín of New Mexico in stating that Comanche man's social standing was dependent upon his war record. At the same time, although it is probable that there were diverse political relations between leader and follower, as well as bargainings for aid and assistance, Cabello's comments seem to have somewhat of a monarchist's view of the crassness of electioneering.

> 8) What is the personal quality of these chiefs and of the influence that they have and could have in the politics of their nation.

> As the aforesaid two great captains have not come to this Presidio of San Antonio de Béxar, the governor has not been able to determine their character, but in his experience with the six lesser captains who had come to the ratification, it was a generous spirit which manifested great care towards the Spaniards which the Captains of the other friendly nations of the north, observing the [efforts] with enough respect those Indians who had brought for their following, nevertheless he knows these subjects do not have all the subordination which is required.

Underneath that verbiage, Cabello admitted, first, that even considering the "lesser captains" who came to visit Béxar, he did not know enough about the Comanches "to determine their character," and, second, that the chiefs did not have the kinds of authority—or rather, conversely, that the other Indians did not have the subordination that in Spanish eyes should have been accorded them.

Throughout 1786 Comanches came to visit Béxar, bringing news from Comanchería; Camisa de Hierro continued to promise to visit but never appeared. In mid-July a small group of Comanches brought news that Cabeza Rapada had been killed by Mescaleros and Lipan Apaches along the southern Pecos River (Cabello 1786d).

The Comanche Peace in New Mexico, 1785–86

Meanwhile, in New Mexico Governor Anza was having increased inter-action with Comanches.[17] On July 12, 1785, eight Comanche captains, with 170 men at arms and more than 200 members of their families visited Taos Pueblo seeking a trade fair. Under the watchful eye of the Taos alcalde, they traded four slaves, many skins, rawhides, meat, and more than 60 horses (Rengel 1785). Two weeks later representatives of several other rancherías visited, and by October at least two trade fairs had been held in Taos. The visitors told Anza that although they were in favor of peace, the main source of belligerence was the Jupes and Yamparikas, particularly a chief called Toro Blanco 'White Bull'. In reply, Anza told them that he would not meet with them unless they chose a single individual to represent all Comanches.

Thus, in November 1785 at the Casa de Palo on the Arkansas River, near modern Pueblo, Colorado, some "600 camps," probably meaning lodges or at most *nʉmʉnahkahni* groups, mostly Kotsotekas, but with some Jupes and Yamparikas, met to discuss Anza's proposals and to select a representative to speak for them (Thomas 1932:295). That role fell to

> the captain most distinguished as much by his skill and valor in war as by his adroitness and intelligence in political matters, who because of his notable war-like spirit had acquired the name Contatanacapara, which signifies one without equal in military achievements. [Thomas 1932:295]

A major confusion exists in the analysis and evaluation of that leader's identity. Initially, Anza reported his Comanche name as Contatanacapara, which "signifies one without equal in military achievements" (Thomas 1932: 295). Later he translated the name into Spanish as Grulla en Cruz, which Thomas (1932:325) translated as 'crane on the cross'; Armagost (1989) gave the Comanche as *koontyta?nikypa?a* 'crane on a stake'. He was more commonly referred to as Ecueracapa 'leather cape'. According to Anza—or at least according to Pedro Garrido y Duran's summary account of "the documents [up to July 15, 1786] which it cites" (Thomas 1932:294–321)—he was also called Cota de Malla (or Maya) 'coat of mail', a name similar in meaning to Ecueracapa, but not exactly the same. The latter name was also applied to the Texan also known as Camisa de Hierro; the similarity was to cause much confusion.

The Kotsotekas also plotted to do away with Toro Blanco. Details are minimal, but by late 1785 he had been assassinated and his followers scattered (Thomas 1932:299).

In early December a New Mexican Indian was captured by Comanches while hunting buffalo. When it was discovered that he could understand Comanche, he was pressed into service as a messenger. After witnessing their councils, he was sent back to Santa Fe, accompanied by Paraginanchi—Anza gave the name as Ears of Sorrel Deer; it was probably either *arʉkʉ* 'deer' or *parʉhʉya* 'elk' [*pa* 'water' *tʉhʉya* 'horse'], *nakI* 'ear'—with word of Ecueracapa's "full power." The council also suggested that Ecueracapa should come to visit Anza in Santa Fe. After hearing their report, Anza sent him back, accompanied by a party of New Mexicans, with gifts of a horse and a headdress of "fine scarlet cloth" for Ecueracapa (Thomas 1932:297).

In January 1786 fugitive members of Toro Blanco's ranchería attacked Pecos Pueblo, killing one resident. They escaped but were captured by Ecueracapa's people, and Ecueracapa himself killed their leader. Later that month a Comanche delegation led by Paraginanchi and Cuetaninaveni, the latter translated as The Maltreated One, with several other Comanche men and women, visited Santa Fe to apologize for the attack and to prepare for the upcoming meetings.

On February 25 Ecueracapa arrived in Santa Fe to a ceremonious welcome. Meeting with Anza at the Palace of the Governors, he restated essentially the same peace proposals as had been made in Texas: peace should rule
the relations between Comanches and Spaniards, there should be free access
to Santa Fe and its trade, and there would be a joint war on the Apaches.
Finally, Ecueracapa requested that he be given a token "to prove to the scattered rancherías that they were admitted to peace." Agreeing to the proposals,
Anza suggested that Ecueracapa be "elevated above all other chiefs" and
recognized as "principal chief" of all the Comanches, to which Ecueracapa
readily agreed. They decided to formalize the agreement later at Pecos Pueblo
(Thomas 1932:301). Three days later the Comanches met Anza at a formal
session at Pecos Pueblo. Present were thirty-one of the principal men of the
Kotsotekas, including Ecueracapa and eleven chiefs, seated "according to
order" (table 3.1).

Tosapoy was designated speaker, *tekwawapI*, for the Comanches. In a
prepared speech he thanked the governor for accepting the peace proposals
and asked that the past hostilities be forgotten. He was particularly concerned
about commerce and deeply regretted the violence that had marked trade
fairs, promising to abide by the agreements. He ended by handing over, on
his knees, a captive, Alejandro Martin, captured eleven years before at Tomé
(Thomas 1932:304).

Governor Anza then answered Ecueracapa's proposals. In the king's
name he agreed to the peace, provided the Comanches themselves also kept
the peace. Trade fairs were to be reformed, and Ecueracapa himself was
granted free and unhampered access through Pecos to Santa Fe. In token of
the Spaniards' recognition of Ecueracapa's status as Comanche "General,"
Anza presented him with a sabre and a Spanish flag. Additionally, the
governor loaned his personal cane to serve as Ecueracapa's "staff of office"
until it could be replaced by another. The staff was to be "exhibited in all the
rancherías to prove that they were admitted to peace." That duty was
entrusted to Tosacondata, the second "in authority." The meeting ended with
"the Comanches making in the soil a hole which they refilled with various
attendant ceremonies . . . [and] buried the war on their part." They then
adjourned for a trade fair at which "more than six hundred hides, many loads
of meat and tallow, fifteen riding beasts, and three guns" changed hands.
Anza reported the whole proceedings to his superior and waited for authority
to move ahead with the peace (Thomas 1932:301–6).

For the rest of that spring and into the summer, Comanches visited Santa
Fe as never before, and their interactions that summer laid the groundwork
for continuing political relations. Although Ecueracapa claimed to represent
all Comanches in New Mexico, Anza was anxious to know whether he held

Table 3.1

The Seating Order at the 1785 Pecos Conference

NAME	ANZA'S TRANSLATION	MODERN RETRANSCRIPTION
Ecuercapa		
Tosacondata	White Crane	*tosa* 'white', *koto* 'crane'
Tosapoy	White Road	*tosa* 'white', *puʔe* 'road', or *pui* 'eye'
Hichapat	The Crafty One	*isapʉ* 'liar', *tʉ* nominalizing suffix
Paraginanchi	Ears of Sorrell Deer	*arʉku* 'deer', or *parʉhʉya*'elk', *nakl* 'ear
Cuetaninaveni		
Quihuaneantime	He Gnaws his Master	*kʉyuʔne* 'to chew', *tumi* 'owner of an animal'
Sonocat	Many Peppers	*soo* 'many', *a* 'horn', *katʉ* 'possessor'
Canaguipe	Poor Woman	*kana* 'poor', *waʔihpʉ* 'woman'
Pisimampat	Decayed Shoe	*pisi* 'odor', *napʊ* 'shoe', *tʉ* nominalizing suffix
Toyamancare	Seated on the Mountain	*toya* 'mountain', *ma* 'on', *karʉ* 'sit'
Ticinalla	Ugly Game	*tʉtsʉ* 'bad, ugly', *narʉ* 'game'

SOURCE: Thomas 1932:303

the authority he claimed. Since snows prevented the Jupes, Yamparikas, and eastern Kotsotekas from attending the Pecos meeting, the treaty technically included only the western Kotsotekas. In mid-April two Jupes visiting Taos—Chamanada, also called Chama, later translated as The Boy (although that meaning is unclear) and Querenilla, which Anza noted as "signifying one who works miracles" (but that meaning, too, is unclear)—told Anza that three hundred tipis of Jupes and Yamparikas were searching for Ecueracapa to verify the peace. After "regaling" the visitors for several days, Anza sent them on, accompanied by Francisco Xavier Ortiz, with instructions to investigate the progress of the peace (Thomas 1932:308).

On May 9 Tosacondata returned from his embassy, bringing three others, Huanacoruco (*wane korohkO* 'fox sash'), Tosaparua (*tosa parua* 'white bear') and Pasahuoques (*pasa huhku* 'dry dust'); the latter two were identified by Anza as Yamparikas, and Huanacoruco was later identified as a Kotsoteka, but that is questionable. Tosacondata reported that "he went through all the rancherías of his group, the Kotsoteka in many of the Jupe and some of the Yamparica . . . in all he had announced peace, exhibited the cane in testimony of it and of his trust. They had seen it and accepted it with the greatest appreciation" (Thomas 1932:311).

Tosacondata also brought Ortiz's report. The emissary had visited eight Kotsoteka rancherías between the Colorado and Pecos Rivers, with a total of 700 lodges. The largest, under Ecueracapa, had 157, the second largest, under

Canaguaipe, had 155, and the smallest had 30. Ortiz estimated there were 12 persons per lodge, the same as estimated in 1750. At that rate, there were 1,884 people in the largest ranchería, 1,860 in the second, and 360 in the smallest. In all, Ortiz found that indeed Ecueracapa was extended "great respect . . . in consequence of some superiority" (Thomas 1932:323)

On May 16 Tosapoy returned, bringing three Jupe chiefs, Ysaquebera, Tuchuparua, and Encatine. The first name was given as Long Wolf, possibly *isa* 'wolf', *pa?a* 'long'; however, in modern Comanche, *pa?a* occurs as a prefix, not as a suffix; moreover, since *ke* is the negative, *isa ke pa?a* would seem to be 'not long wolf'. The second name was given as Bird Bear, probably *tuuhutsu* 'crow', *parua* 'bear'. The third name was given as Beetle, probably *ekatunuu?* 'red bug' (Thomas 1921:327). Anza told them that the season for war on the Apaches was rapidly diminishing, but that there were plenty of enemies either in the Sierra Blanca Mountains or in the Mimbres Mountains (Thomas 1932:312).

On May 26 a Comanche man, possibly Cuetaninaveni—he was called "the same Comanche who had been [in Santa Fe in January] with Paraginanchi"—and a woman arrived seeking asylum. According to Anza, the man had been caught in adultery with the wife of one of the other chiefs and was now threatened with death, a punishment "irremissably imposed" (Thomas 1932:313). The report is probably a confused third-hand interpretation; that is, unless Comanche custom changed over the years, the penalty for adultery would have been *nanawokʉ* 'damages'; death would be imposed only on the woman.

Two days later, Paraginanchi came to Santa Fe, bringing with him Ecueracapa's third son, Tahuchimpia—Anza gave the name as Father-in-law, but it seems to be *ta huutsipia* 'one's daughter-in-law'. The chief asked that Anza treat him as if he were his own child and teach him the language and customs of the Spaniards. Anza respectfully acknowledged the trust but noted that since the son was twenty years of age, it might not be possible to "make such progress as his father desired" (Thomas 1932:314).

Paraginanchi also reported that in mid-May Comanches had killed two Apaches and captured fifteen mules. Of probably greater immediate interest, however, was that he had stopped first at Pecos, where his village of fifty-seven lodges awaited trade. Moreover, three Yamparika rancherías whose chiefs "desired to know Anza" had come with him. Their names and translations were later given as Pajabipo (given as Basin Paunch, probably *paha* 'mortar', *bihpoa* 'paunch', a rawhide mortar), Cunabunit (given as He Saw the Fire, *kuna* 'fire' *puni* 'to see', *tu* nominalizer[18]) and Quahuacante (given as Dead Hide, possibly *kwaharu* 'antelope', *katu* 'possessor').

Thus, on May 30 Anza traveled to Pecos for another meeting with Comanche chiefs. There he met with a total of "forty authorized persons," including chiefs Paraginanchi, the recently arrived Pajabipo, Cunabunit, and Quahuacante, as well as Hicipat, Quihuaneantime, and Pisimampat, who had been at the first Pecos conference in February. The meeting was as much to conduct the formalities as to break new ground: the chiefs said that the peace was the talk of the rancherías, and they gave all credit for it to Ecueracapa. Anza, in return, praised them for deferring to that chief. They then adjourned for a trade fair; the secretary in Mexico City who summarized Anza's report noted that "the number of men and women and children, that of their mounts, and the statement of the quantity and kinds of effects they exchanged are found in writing in the report of that chief [Anza]. Accordingly, they are not placed in this account" (Thomas 1932:315). Unfortunately, Anza's original has not been found, and the details of that trade are unknown.

During the visits that summer Anza had made two requests of the Comanches. The first was that they should, "by means of lines and signs" on a blank card, send him detailed information on their campaign against the Apaches, their detachments, their effective forces, and their successes. It was returned in July by Ecueracapa's eldest son, Ohamaquea (*oha makwa* 'yellow back of the hand', 'he has something yellow on his hands', or simply 'yellow hand' [Hultkrantz 1968]). The tarja, or tally sheet, showed five "detachments," an advance party of 31 under Quetaninaveni—probably the same as Cuetaninaveni—114 under Ecueracapa, 88 under Salambipit (*isa papi* 'wolf head'), 50 under Encajive (*ehka* 'those', *hibi* 'drink'), and 64 under Piaquegipe (*pia kwahipU* 'big back'), a total of almost 350 warriors (Thomas 1929a; 1932:324). The chiefs were noted, carrying insignia of their rank, Ecueracapa with the sword he had received from Anza, the others with crooked lances —*patso?ikowe kwitubi*—held point down, in front of their men.[19] That Apache campaign was a modest success: they killed six Apaches and captured eighty-five horses; one Comanche was killed, and Ecueracapa and seven others were wounded.

Anza's other request to the Comanches had been that they provide eight warriors to assist on a joint campaign with Navajos against Apaches along the lower Rio Grande. Ohamaquea brought with him not eight, but twenty-two Comanches (table 3.2).[20] Their expedition was again only a modest success. The party attacked one small ranchería, but the Navajos and Comanches were disappointed in the meager spoils; the prisoners were sent back to Santa Fe with the Navajos. Moving on, the Comanches, acting as advance scouts, found a number of rancherías, probably meaning tents. Disregarding the disparity in numbers, they attacked, killing three and taking the "whole horse herd," with only four Comanches wounded. However, the Spaniard commanding the expedition was put off by their impetuosity and sent them back to Santa Fe (Thomas 1932:32).

In all, almost six hundred Comanche lodges had visited Pecos that summer (table 3.3). With Ortiz's estimate of "3 men of arms and 7 or 8 women and children in each lodge," approximately 6,000 Comanches had been present. They included some 200 lodges of Kotsotekas (about a third of the total number of the Kotsotekas as given by Ortiz), 100 of Yamparikas, and 200 of Jupes; the Yamparikas and Jupes may have been the 300 lodges reported looking for Ecueracapa in May. Anza commented that the actual number probably "exceeds at least by a third part that computed by this statement" (Thomas 1932:327).

In July Anza sent the treaty to Mexico, and in October Jacobo Ugarte y Loyola, newly appointed comandante general of the Provincias Internas, returned it, expressing his pleasure with Anza's success; he generally approved of the proposed peace (Ugarte 1786b; Thomas 1932:332). He did, however, have a number of suggestions and modifications. Rather than having multiple intermediaries between the Comanches and the Spaniards, such as would happen if the governors of both New Mexico and Texas continued independent relations, New Mexico should have the principal responsibility for dealing with Comanches. Agreeing to the recognition of a principal chief for the whole Comanche nation, he authorized an annual salary of 200 pesos worth of "effects and entertainment" to be paid from the fund for "extraordinary expenses," and he advised Anza to "take much care . . . so that the . . . election may fall upon Ecueracapa." Once that was accomplished, Ecueracapa should nominate a "lieutenant general" for the Jupes and Yamparikas and, if necessary, one for the eastern Kotsotekas of Texas, each with an annual salary of 100 pesos. Anza was authorized to consult with the Comanches about new trade tariffs, trading sites, and more equitable trade regulations, but he was warned not to interfere in internal Comanche affairs, and especially not to offer sanctuary for refugees from Comanche justice, as that would undermine the authority of the chiefs.

Ugarte also wanted the treaty expanded to include a number of features of general Spanish policy. Apache captives under the age of fourteen were to be ransomed, both as part of the Spaniard's policy of ransoming children and to encourage the Comanches to continue the war against the Apaches; Christian captives held by the Comanches, either Spaniards or other Indians, were to be returned without reward. Although authorizing official interpreters to be assigned to the Comanche chiefs, Ugarte suggested that Comanche children, preferably sons of chiefs, be sent to Mexico City to be instructed in Spanish

Table 3.2

Participants in the 1786 Comanche-Spaniard Expedition against the Apaches

NAME	ANZA'S TRANSLATION	MODERN RETRANSCRIPTION
Ohamaquea		
Tomanaguene	He raises his hands	possibly *tohima* 'raise', *makwe* 'hand' *nih* 'dual'
Tahuchimpia	Father-in-Law	*ta* 'one's', *huutsipia* 'daughter-in-law'
Tosaparua		
Camquenacavite	Red House	*kahne* 'house', *ekavit* 'red'
Quemanacare	He who is far away	[*ke* negative, *manakwʉ* 'far away', *tʉ* nominalizing suffix]
Quetampunique	He whom they have not seen shot	*ke* 'not,' *tam* 'one', *puni* 'saw'
Nomasonasallo	He who made his sack	[*noo* 'to carry on back', *sona* 'cloth', *surʉ* 'that one']
Huillome	The Awl	*widyu* 'awl'
Ancachuate	Without Purpose	. . . *waa tʉ* 'without'
Tampiallanenque	Great Laugh	*tam* 'one', *pia* 'big', *yahne* 'laugh', *nky* causative
Sucaque	What is it	*suhka* 'that', *haki* 'where'
Tanansimu	Small Rake	
Amabate	Without a Head	[*ama* 'chest', *waa tʉ* 'without']
Tanticanque	One who eats	*tan* 'one', *tʉhka* 'eat', *nky* causative
Ybienca	Red Woman	*hubi* 'woman', *eka* 'red'
Ecopisura	Scraping Spoon	
Parnaquibitiste	Very Small Bear	*parua* 'bear', *ʉkʉbitsI* 'new, young'
Taoinan	Flute	*ta* 'one's', *woinu* 'flute'
Humanvaenvite	Red Sparrow Hawk	*humara* 'hawk', *ekavit* 'red'
Tamacencaniguay	Questioned because of the Ring	*ta* 'one', *manika* 'ring', *niwai* to ask for
Cageneigueuate	Without a Sash	*nyʔynehki* 'sash', *wa* without, *tʉ* nominalizing

SOURCE: Armagost 1989; glosses in brackets provided by Jean O. Charney

Table 3.3
Comanche Visitors to Pecos Pueblo, Summer 1786

CHIEFS	LODGES
Kotsotekas with Ecueracapa	
Ecueracapa	100
Tosacondata	10
Tosapoy	80
Hichipat	10
Paraginanchi	30
Cuetaninaveni	20
Quihuaneantime	11
Sonocat	20
Canaguipe	40
Pisimanpat	10
Toyamancare	15
Ticinalla	20
Second [Jupes]	
El Chama	50
Querenilla	6
Third Led by Tosacondata	
Huanacoruco, Kotsoteka[a]	10
Tosaparua, Yamparika	8
Pasahuoques, Yamparika	20
Fourth Led by Tosapoy	
Ysaquebara, Jupe	80
Tucuparua, Jupe	9
Encantime, Jupe	11
Fifth Led by Paraginachi	
Pajabipo, Yamparika	15
Cunabunit, Yamparika	10
Quahuacante	8
Total	593

[a]Huanacoruco's divisional affiliation is unclear. Earlier he had been explicitly identified as a Kotsoteka, and while here so labeled, as later, he was associated with Yamparikas.

SOURCE: Thomas 1932:325–27

and in the Roman Catholic religion, and Anza was urged to persuade the Comanches to make permanent settlements.

Finally, Ugarte noted a matter of continuing confusion. After Anza reported the results of his first meetings with Comanches, Ugarte had suspected that the New Mexican Ecueracapa, allegedly also known as Cota de Malla, and the Texan Camisa de Hierro, were the same man. In August, when he wrote to Cabello in Texas summarizing the events in New Mexico, he noted that the five sessions were "presided over by the principal of them all, Ecueracapa or Contatanacapara, known by the nickname of Cota de Malla, whom I deduce is possibly the same that you call Camisa de Fierro [sic]" and asked the governor to confirm his deduction (Ugarte 1786a). In reply Cabello stated:

> The Great Captain Cota de Malla . . . is the same which in my reports I have as Camisa de Fierro, the derivation of which is Cota de Malla, whose name Pedro Vial, Francisco Xavier de Chaves, and the two brother Captains of whom I told you when they were here, is Guaquangas. All in all, there is no doubt that he is the Captain with the greatest credibility the Comanches have. [Cabello 1786e]

That is, Cabello did exactly as Ugarte asked; he confirmed that Cota de Malla had been called Camisa de Hierro by Pedro Vial and that his own name was Guaquangas. Unfortunately, he did not state whether either was Ecueracapa. To further confuse matters, in his reply to Ugarte the previous spring, Cabello had attributed the name Guaquangas to a chief "of the second class."

It is not clear whether Ugarte had yet received Cabello's report when he wrote back to Anza in October. By then he had also received other reports— their source is unknown—that suggested to him that rather than being a single man, there were two Comanche chiefs with very similar names. He thus asked Anza "to establish the truth with the greatest certainty" and also to check on a report that Cabeza Rapada had been killed (Thomas 1932:341). Unfortunately for historians, there is no record that Anza ever replied.

However, as recommended by Ugarte, Anza held a second council with the Comanches in their own territory (Anza 1786). There Ecueracapa was "elected" general, although the details of the process are unknown, and Tosacondata was named as his lieutenant. The revised treaty was ratified, and in November twelve Comanches, including Tosacondata, Ohamaquea, his brothers Tahuchimpia and Tomanaquena, the Jupe "war chief" Encantine, and five other men and two women, traveled south with the treaty.

Arriving in Chihuahua on December 30, 1786, the Comanche delegation was received with honor. The comandante general was particularly impressed with their appearance: the men wore clothes of skins, their faces were painted with red ocher and other earth colors, their eyelids colored with vermilion; imitation gold buttons, beads, and ribbons bedecked their hair. In contrast to the men, the women appeared unkempt, with short hair (Ugarte 1787a). Each man was presented with a medal, although smaller than that given to Ecueracapa, and a musket.

But they did not receive the "staffs of office" promised by Anza, nor was one sent to Ecueracapa: Ugarte had received word that the Texas Comanches feared the power of such insignia and that if they were lost or broken, their owners would soon die; several chiefs of the eastern Comanches were said to have returned their batons. Thus before issuing any staffs to his visitors, Ugarte wanted assurances that no such superstition existed among the New Mexican Comanches (Ugarte 1787b). Anza's response is unknown, but it must have been positive, for "bastones con puño de plata" 'canes with silver heads', became common symbols of Comanche chiefs' authority for the next four decades.

Ugarte was also having second thoughts about the recognition of lieutenants general for the Jupes and Yamparikas. Given the independence of those northern Comanche divisions, he was afraid that making their chiefs subordinate to Ecueracapa would result in much jealousy. Moreover, he had heard that Encantine was the son of a chief of great popularity who would not look kindly upon receiving only half the salary of the principal chief. Therefore, Ugarte told Anza that only if it appeared advantageous, "superior" chiefs of the Jupes and Yamparikas should be recognized as independent of the Kotsotekas and that all should be given special gifts rather than a fixed salary (Ugarte 1787b; Moorhead 1968:157–58).

During those conversations Ugarte again raised the question of the identity of Camisa de Hierro, Cota de Malla, and Ecueracapa. The reason for that renewed interest was a recently received report of a battle at the junction of the Pecos and Rio Grande rivers in early November, only two months before. According to the report, a force of some two hundred Spaniards under Don José Menchaca, lieutenant commander of the presidio at Aguaverde, engaged a party of about three hundred Comanches. The Comanche chief—who was identified as "Camisa de Hierro, also known as Cota de Malla, one of the principal chiefs of the Eastern Cuchanecs who made the peace in Béxar"— and five others were killed. After those losses, the Comanches raised a white flag with a Burgundian cross, and with many protestations of peace, they said that Cota de Malla had been the only chief in favor of attacking the Spaniards—it was said he wanted their horses—and now that he was dead they preferred to continue friendly relations (Navarro García 1964).[21]

To clarify the report of the battle, Ugarte questioned the Comanche messengers about the identity of the chief who was killed. Was he the Texan principal chief Camisa de Hierro, also known as Cota de Malla, and was this the same individual as the New Mexican principal chief Ecueracapa? The messengers—among whom were Ecueracapa's sons and an unnamed interpreter, possibly Alejandro Martin—argued that the name Cota de Malla had been wrongly attributed to Ecueracapa. Rather, they said, the name Cota de Malla referred only to a chief of equal rank and following among the eastern Comanches of Texas, who had recently died in battle (Ugarte 1787a). That seemed to corroborate the report of Menchaca's battle. Moreover, whereas Ecueracapa had been given a Spanish flag, the Texas chiefs had been specifically given Burgundian cross flags. That a flag of the latter type was present in that encounter suggests that some of the participants who had been in Béxar in September were along the lower Pecos River in November, and it seems likely that Camisa de Hierro was among them; the reason for his apparent change of attitude from the time of Vial's council is unexplained.

Despite the reservations about the identity of the principal chiefs, the concern with subordinate chiefs and symbols of authority was quickly resolved, and that spring Anza again traveled to Comanchería to meet with the chiefs. On April 21, 1787, the treaty was finalized and Ecueracapa and Tosacondata were formally recognized as general and lieutenant general of the Kotsotekas; Paruanarimuco (*parua narumuku* 'bear harness'), apparently Encatine's father, was installed as lieutenant general for the Jupes and the Yamparikas (Moorhead 1968:159). Those formalities inaugurated a new era of Comanche-Euroamerican interaction.

Comanche Political Organizations, 1706–86

In the eight decades between the earliest reported contact and the establishment of the 1785–86 peace in Texas and New Mexico, Comanches dealt with a variety of Euroamericans in a variety of interactions. These included Frenchmen from Louisiana, Illinois, and Canada, and Englishmen from the thirteen Atlantic colonies. By far the most interaction was with the Spaniards of New Mexico and Texas.

The records of those eight decades document an increasing knowledge of the Comanches on the part of the Spaniards. Although through the 1740s New Mexicans made no distinctions among them, there seem to have been two groups of Comanches near New Mexico. One, east of Pecos and Galisteo, was particularly hostile toward those pueblos and against any Euroamericans they met. The other, northeast of Taos, maintained trade with that pueblo and peacefully passed along French traders. By the 1750s the Span-

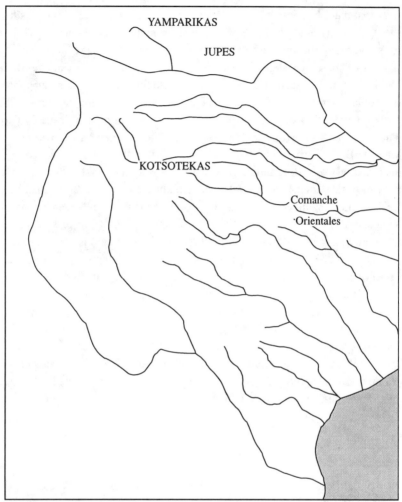

YAMPARIKAS

JUPES

KOTSOTEKAS

Comanche
·Orientales

Map 3. Comanchería, ca. 1785.

iards had begun to note greater political differentiation within the Comanche ethnic category. New Mexico governor Marín was the earliest Euroamerican to record Comanche language ethnonyms: Pibian and Yamparica. In the 1770s de Mézières implied that there were several groups, but he named only two, Naitane and Yarambica. His assistant, Gaignard, noted that there were four groups, but similarly named only two, again Naytane and Yamparika. Governor Mendinueta named three "congregations," Yamparika, Come Civolos, and Gente de Palo, whereas Miera mapped four, the Comanche language equivalents of Medinueta's three—Yamparika, Cuchan Marica [Kotsoteka], Jupe, and the Pivianes, a probable reappearance of Marín's Pibian.

By the mid-1780s two of those names, Naitane and Pibian, had disappeared from the documentary records of Spanish New Mexico and Texas, leaving Jupe, Yamparika, and Kotsoteka as the named Comanche political groups. The reasons for those disappearances are unclear. On the one hand, it is possible that inasmuch as Naitane was a Wichita language ethnonym generic for all Comanches, and that it appeared only in documents from the east, as Wallace and Hoebel suggested (1952:24), as Euroamerican contacts with Comanches from that direction increased, it was superseded by more specific ethnonyms. Pibian, a Comanche language ethnonym appearing only twice in the west, presents a more difficult problem. Since the last appearance of the name was in the late 1770s, one possibility is that its people may have been scattered by the 1780 smallpox epidemic.

The other three names, Kotsoteka, Jupe and Yamparika, allow a closer processual analysis. Beginning in the 1780s there is a general documentary agreement about the geographical distribution of Comanche groups, best exemplified by Anza's description:

> the Jupes and Yamparicas extending from the Rio Napestle to the north a little beyond the Sierra de Almagre. Many others . . . are farther along in the same direction. The Cuchanecs [Kotsotekas] extend from the cited river south as far as the Colorado which is distant a few days from New Mexico. Both are separated on the east . . . from another group of [Kotsotekas] living in the direction of the Jumanos or Taguayaces. [Thomas 1932:295]

There are, however, several problematic aspects to those descriptions that must be noted. Miera mapped the Yamparika far to the north and west; Anza brought them closer to New Mexico, but still north of the Arkansas River. But at that same time, the 1780 Tejas Indian report blamed two "Namborika" villages on the Guadalupe River for raids on Béxar; if that ethnonym is Yamparika, it placed otherwise northern Comanches in the far south. Given that the ethnonym Yamparika appeared on all eighteenth-century lists, both east and west, one possibility is that some Yamparikas were among the first Comanches to come south, taking up a southern Plains location and becoming known far and wide before returning to the north. John (1975:620) suggested another possibility, that they were refugees from Cuerno Verde's defeat of the year before; however, as noted above, given the data on Miera's maps, Cuerno Verde may have been Jupe. A third possibility is suggested by Vial's lumping of the Comanches into two groups, "Eastern" and "Western," the latter "who are known by the name of Yambarika"; indeed, later Texas Spaniards tended to refer to all Comanches beyond the immediate vicinity of Béxar as Yamparikas. Thus, the identification of the Indians on the Guadalupe may be a similar example from among the southern Indians. In any case, it does point out the indeterminacy—but does not negate the potential value —of provisionally equating geographic location and divisional identification.

If Anza's listing of rancherías and chiefs who visited Pecos can be read as local bands, in 1786 there were at least eight, and possibly nine, Kotsoteka local bands, totaling at least seven hundred lodges northeast of New Mexico. Other Kotsotekas were far to the east, but their internal composition is unclear; at one point Vial implied that there were 10 rancherías of the Orientales, but it is also tempting to suggest that Vial's "12 other little captains" refer to chiefs of local bands, implying that there were 12 eastern rancherías. However, a hard and fast limitation of only one "principal man" per local band is probably too strict.

Also unclear are the political relations between those two branches of Kotsotekas. One key to the latter question—and the reason for the continued focus on it—lies in whether Ecueracapa in New Mexico and Camisa de Hierro in Texas were one and the same person. A determination that they were the same would lead to the implication that in the 1780s one man held significant power and authority among the Comanches both in New Mexico and "near the Taovayas"; at most it would imply that there was a single Kotsoteka organization recognizing a single leader; at least it would explain the absence of the principal chief from Texas from the fall of 1785 through 1786: he was in New Mexico negotiating with Anza. Conversely, a determination that they were not the same individual would suggest that there was at least a minimal political separation, that a new—or at least separate—organization existed among the Texas Kotsotekas and that no one individual had authority in both New Mexico and Texas.

Unfortunately, the available evidence supports only the Scots verdict of not proven in either direction.[22] In the absence of more definitive documentation, the only historically justified position is that in the late 1780s there were three individuals with similar Spanish nicknames. Two of them were of high standing, Ecueracapa (possibly also called Cotatanacapara) in New Mexico, and Camisa de Hierro in Texas; the latter was indeed probably killed in the fall of 1786, for there is no further mention of him in the Texas records. The third was the man also called Guaquangas, a chief of the "second class."

Although Anza's Yamparika and Jupe lists are unclear about certain divisional affiliations, there were perhaps six Yamparika local bands, with a total of 108 lodges, and five Jupe local bands, with a total of 223 lodges, all north of the Arkansas River. The relative numbers suggest the reason why Parua-narimuco, a Jupe, was chosen as lieutenant general for the then-combined Jupes and Yamparikas: he had the greatest following.

During those same eight decades, the Spaniards portrayed Comanche political leadership in two contradictory modes. On the one hand, some observers noted a lack of overall political authority. According to Felipe Sandoval in 1750, they were "very disorganized . . . obeying no head." Governor Vélez Cachupín noted, "Each chief proceeds according to his personal inclination," and complained that they "excuse themselves by blaming others of their nation, saying that among them are warlike captains who commit outrages and those who are well disposed are unable to prevent them." Governor Marín said, "Some obey him, others do not." Similarly, de Mézières argued that chiefs could neither prevent damages nor redress any committed by others. On the other hand, several Comanche leaders were portrayed as having significant power and authority. Several were labeled "little king" (the elder Cuerno Verde) or "great chief" (Evea, and others unnamed). Cuerno Verde was reported as having heralds and assistants to help in mounting and dismounting; the "great chief" with whom Gaignard negotiated in 1774 ordered his own people to stop mourning for raiders killed by the Spaniards. Ultimately, Ecueracapa, the "most celebrated and distinguished chieftain," may have arranged the assassination of Toro Blanco.

It is tempting to argue that one or the other of those observations is true, the other biased, and that chiefly power resulted directly from Euroamerican intervention in the Comanche polities. Dealing with the latter point first, except for Ugarte's instructions to Anza to "take care that the election may fall on Ecueracapa" (Thomas 1932:332), there is no evidence of the direct involvement of Spaniards in Comanche political processes. Indeed, when the named chiefs first appeared in the historical documents, they were already endowed with the power and authority that made them noteworthy: they were definitely not the creations of Spanish intervention, however much the Spaniards would have liked to co-opt them.

At the same time, those apparently contradictory observations on Comanche leadership are not inconsistent, but are in fact complementary: they describe the limits of political power—the ability to direct action—from different perspectives. The subjects of Vélez's and de Mézières's generalizations on the lack of power were demonstrably involved in multipolity situations in which no single chief exercised paramount authority. That was, indeed, de Mézières's point: he explicitly noted that chiefs had little power outside their own groups; but within them, they were supreme. The several cases of individuals or small groups who "had broken away from . . . authority, separating themselves from the main body of the nation," or of individuals by whose actions "they would not be considered part of . . . [the] people" clearly indicate that the Comanches themselves recognized those limits to their political power. Conversely, in each case of a chief specifically portrayed as exercising power (Nimiricante, all the Cuerno Verdes, and Ecueracapa), the context of that power was within defined political boundaries.

In the first part of the eighteenth century, Comanche economic power and the political organizations built on it were based on three primary resources: hunting, warfare, and trade. There was a geographical component to the distribution of those resources, and thus they were differentially available to Comanche leaders.

Although there continues to be debate about the specific spatial and temporal distribution of the buffalo within what became Comanchería (Wallace and Hoebel 1952; Colson 1954; Dillehay 1974; Turpin 1987, 1988; W. R. Brown 1987; Bamforth 1988; Huebner 1991; Baugh 1991), there seems to have been a general north-south differential in the buffalo populations corresponding to the general differential in the biotic communities, which were themselves subject to climatic variations. Thus, as the Comanches advanced into Texas—out of the Kansan biotic province and into the Texan and Balconian provinces (Blair 1950)—there were fewer buffalo, and the direct political-economic organizational impact of their exploitation decreased. At the same time, access to other resources, particularly horses and Euroamerican goods, increased in that same southerly direction. On the east, access was mediated by such other tribes as the Osages, the Wichitas, and the Pawnees; only on the south and southwest did Comanches have direct contact with the sources of supply.

R. N. Richardson (1933:19) suggested that the initial impetus for the Comanche move south may have been a desire to obtain horses, but the details of the horse in the early Comanche economy are unclear. The earliest documents do not say whether the Comanches were mounted or not. In one of the earliest ethnographic descriptions of the Comanches, written in 1726, Brigadier Pedro de Rivera noted that they still used dogs for transport: "They are always on the move and in battle array, for they war with all tribes. They halt at any camp site and set up their campaign tents which are made of buffalo hides and transported by large dogs which they raise for this purpose" (Rivera 1946:78); he did not say that they had no horses, and it is not clear if his comments were based on first hand observation. Some fifty years later, the cartographer Bernardo de Miera y Pacheco noted that when Comanches first came to Taos, they had a "multitude of dogs loaded with their hides and tents." But by the 1730s Comanches were reported "scattered about, caring for the many horses which they get from New Mexico" (Hackett 1931–46, 3:348). In 1749 Comanches were said to be "dispersed, with their large droves of horses, for which reason they could not live together, having to seek sufficient pasturage and water for their horses" (Hackett 1931–46, 3:317).

There are no descriptions of Comanche hunting until the nineteenth century, but there is indirect information on the economic and political roles of hunting in the form of data on trade. Trade between the Plains and the Southwest is aboriginal (Swagerty 1988:352; Baugh 1991); after driving the Apaches from the Plains, the Comanches took over their role in the trade with both New Mexico on the west, and the riverine Prairie-Plains groups to the east. By the 1720s the Comanche trade had become a necessary part of the New Mexico economy. Much of that trade was conducted in the pueblos and other towns, both as informal barter and in formal trade fairs; peaceful Comanche trading visits to the towns were such a normal occurrence that they were rarely recorded, and the main evidence for them comes from indirect statements such as the trial testimony in the case against Diego de Torres.

The earliest trade regulations came in 1725, when because of some unstated "embarrassment" at a fair at Taos—whose Indian participants were not identified—Governor Bustamente ordered the local authorities at Taos, San Juan, and Pecos to supervise the fairs but not to interfere in the free trade between settlers and Indians (J. D. Bustamente 1725). In 1737, newly appointed governor Henrrique de Olavide y Michelena published another set of regulations, principally that trade or ransoming with the Gentiles—non-Christian Indians—was not to be conducted without first notifying the proper authorities (Olavide y Micheleña 1737). Although never explicitly identified as such, it is possible that the pre-trade visits such as Panfito's 1749 visit to Taos were as much to comply with those regulations as to solicit tobacco and other gifts. As late as 1775, a party came to Taos seeking trade, but because they had not gone to Santa Fe first to make peace with the governor, their trading petition was refused. At the same time, the trade regulations seem to have had minimal effect on the Comanches. That is particularly evident in the various efforts to ban the Comanche trade altogether: Panfito's 1749 visit was in the midst of one such ban. Later that year some six hundred Comanches were trading at Taos. Faced with that blatant disregard for regulations, the New Mexico authorities had to admit that the trade in hides, meat, and horses was necessary to the well-being of the province.

According to Brigadier Rivera, Comanche trade was "confined to tanned skins, buffalo hides, and the Indian children they capture (because they kill the adults)" (Rivera 1946:78). According to Father Domínguez in 1776, "When the Comanches are at peace and come to trade, they bring a thousand or more animals" (E. Adams and Chavez 1956:111). Conversely, the Euroamerican trade brought the Comanches valuable and desired goods. In 1750

Father Andrés Varo noted:

> Here is collected all the ironware possible, such as axes, hoes, wedges,
> picks, bridles, machetes, belduques, and knives . . . here in short is
> gathered everything possible for trade and barter with these barbarians, in
> exchange for deer and buffalo hides, and what is saddest, in exchange for
> Indian slaves, men and women, small and large, a great multitude of both
> sexes. [Hackett 1931–46, 3:486–7]

In 1785 Viceroy Gálvez authorized trade fair items of "sugar loaves, maize,
tobacco, brandy, guns, ammunition, knives, clothing or coarse cloth, vermillion, mirrors, glass beads, and other trifles" (Gálvez 1951:49).

The extent of direct Comanche contact with Euroamericans in the east is
less clear. The confusion between the ethnonyms Comanche, Apache, Padouca, and Ietan—and the latter's homophones Aliatan, Halitane, Lalitane, and
Naitane, in various spellings—makes identification difficult and suggests that
high-level diplomatic contact did not often occur. The Mallet brother's 1739
use of the Wichita ethnonym Lalitane suggests that by the second quarter of
the eighteenth century Comanches had extended their range far enough to
contact the Wichitas, but not beyond.

On the other hand, local-level contact certainly did take place. By 1739 a
French trader had already lived with some Comanches, and by 1747 Frenchmen were welcome if irregular visitors in Comanche villages. But when the
Spaniards closed the Louisiana trade, direct Comanche-Euroamerican contacts diminished markedly. For example, Manbaricas told Gaignard that it had
been eight years since they had seen Frenchmen. Again, although Pedro Vial
had spent eight years among the Wichitas, he admitted that his contacts with
the Comanches were limited. And though French and Anglo-American
traders from Illinois and contrabandistas from Louisiana had set up trading
stations on the middle Arkansas River and were trading guns and ammunition
through Wichita middlemen for Comanche horses, the extent of the contact is
uncertain.

The eastern trade, as described by Felipe Sandoval in 1750, included
muskets and ammunition, hatchets, and beads in return for horses, hides, and
tallow. In the one example of the exchange rate, a young Comanche traded
three horses for a musket and a hatchet. In 1774 Gaignard reported that their
commerce was in slaves and buffalo hides, which they traded for "trifles," including tobacco, knives, axes, and beads (Bolton 1914, 2:88–95). Gaignard
left out one major part of the Comanche trade: horses. Indeed, while Gaignard was at the Taovaya village, six Frenchmen came in from the Arkansas
River to trade for "horses, mules, and slaves" (Bolton 1914, 2:89). By the
1780s, however, no traders were reaching the Comanches from the east;

indeed, Comanches envied the Taovayas' trade with the Spaniards (Cabello 1786a). Such an emotion could have been a strong motivation for peace.

Of all the French trade goods, the quantity of muskets reaching Comanchería has caused the greatest confusion among later researchers. Hyde stated, "At this period [the 1750s] every Comanche who came to Taos had a new French musket, two pounds of powder, and a pouch filled with musket balls" (Hyde 1959:107). However, the specific context of the reference Hyde cited was Panfito's visit, and referred to all of six Comanche visitors. Moreover, although Panfito said the French had traded them "plenty" of muskets, the Frenchmen who passed through Comanchería during that same period saw only five muskets in Comanche hands and noted a lack of ammunition for them. In 1751 the 300 Comanches attacking Pecos had only sixteen guns. The conclusion is inevitable: Comanches had only a few guns.

The actual politico-economic mechanics of the early trade, both eastern and western, are obscure. Several sources imply that the early trade was monopolized by governmental officials. In 1750 Father Varo had noted that "the governor, alcaldes, and lieutenants gather as many horses as they can" for the trade (Hackett 1931–46, 3:486). E. Adams and Chavez (1956:252) note, citing F. Ocaranza (1934:185–89) that "earlier in the century it was the practice of some governors and officials to reserve this trading for themselves, punishing the ordinary people who sought to gain some profit at these fairs," but there is apparently no other evidence, direct or indirect, for such a monopoly. On the other hand, later references imply a freer trade, and that the later regulations can be seen as efforts as much to protect the Comanches from the New Mexicans as to protect the settlers from the Comanches. Father Domínguez noted, "As soon as they buy anything, they usually sell exactly what they bought; and usually keep losing, the occasion being very rare, because our people ordinarily play infamous tricks on them" (E. Adams and Chavez 1956:252). Ten years later Viceroy Bernardo de Gálvez suggested that "trading should not be permitted unless the commandant of the post is present . . . to avoid disturbances which carry fatal consequences as usually are experienced with the Comanches in Taos" (Gálvez 1951:51).

From the other side, several examples show the chiefs' roles in facilitating trade and in establishing other resource domains derived from the trading context. Delegations such as Panfito's arrived several days in advance, as much to announce their upcoming arrival as to obtain gifts of tobacco for redistribution. In 1754 Governor Vélez instructed his successor that when Comanches arrived for the Taos fair, the chiefs were to be called together for a smoke and a council, clearly necessary rituals (Thomas 1940:129).

There may have been a tariff charged for trading; in 1786 Anza abolished the "contribution required from the pagans as a fee for permission to trade"

(Thomas 1932:306); there is, however, no other evidence of the rate. Prices in New Mexico seem to have been relatively stable; in 1735 Diego de Torres traded ten cuchillo knives for ten buffalo robes. Since at least 1754, prices were set by annual decree (Kessell 1979:406). According to Father Domín-guez in 1776

> The Comanches usually sell to our people at this rate: a buffalo hide for a belduque, or broad knife made entirely of iron which they call a trading knife here; "white elkskin" (it is the same hide [i.e. buffalo] but softened like deerskin), the same; for a very poor bridle two buffalo skins or a vessel like those mentioned; the meat for maize or corn flour; an Indian slave according to the individual, because if it is an Indian girl from twelve to twenty years old, two good horses and some trifles in addition, such as a short cloak, a horse cloth, a red lapel are given; or a she-mule and scarlet cover, or other things are given for her.
>
> If the slave is male, he is worth less and the amount is arranged in the manner described. If they sell a she-mule, either a cover or a short cloak or a good horse is given; if they sell a horse, a poor bridle, but gar-nished with red rags, is given for it; if they sell a pistol, its price is a bridle; if both together, a horse is given for them. This is the usual, and a prudent judgement of how everything must go can be based on it. [E. Adams and Chavez 1956:252]

Anza reiterated those rates in 1786, with two exceptions: the Comanches could now get two belduques for a buffalo hide, and a horse could now bring thirteen knives. At the 1786 fair the Comanches traded about "six hundred hides, many loads of meat and tallow, fifteen riding beasts, and three guns to their entire satisfaction" (Thomas 1932:306). At Anza's rates, they must have received the equivalent of more than thirteen hundred knives, plus other goods.

The fairs must have been colorful spectacles. In 1750 Father Vara wrote:

> When the Indian trading embassy come to these governors and their alcaldes, here all prudence forsakes them, or rather I should say that they do not guess how completely they lose their bearing because the fleet is in. The fleet being, in this case, some two hundred, or at the very least fifty, tents of barbarous heathen Indians, Comanches, as well as other na-tions, of whom the multitude is so great that it is impossible to enumer-ate it. [Hackett 1931–46, 3:486]

According to Father Domínguez, "The trading day resembles a second-hand market in Mexico, the way people mill about" (E. Adams and Chavez 1956: 252). That chaos was amended at the fair after the 1786 Pecos peace confer-ence, when Governor Anza "marked off two lines so that the contracting parties, placed on the outside of both could exhibit and deliver to each other in the intermediate space the effects which they had to exchange" (Thomas 1932:306). New Mexicans, both Pueblo Indians and Spaniards, also visited Comanche villages, but other than the evidence of bureaucratic efforts to limit such visits, there is there is no information on their extent.

In contrast to New Mexico, there is only minimal evidence for formal trade fairs in Texas. In January 1786 Governor Cabello reported that sixteen Comanche visitors to Béxar held a "fair," but they only traded two Apache captives and some hides and meat for three horses, some knives, candy, and piloncillos of brown sugar. Although Cabello called the prices "well regu-lated," he did not elaborate (Cabello 1786a). In any event, the Texas trade did not match the scale of the New Mexico fairs.

The Béxar and Santa Fe treaties inaugurated a new era in Comanche-Euroamerican relations and established a new Comanche political resource: political gifts from Euroamerican governments. Although they had their ante-cedents in the pretrade gifts, the Euroamerican nations with whom the Comanches dealt were well aware of the relationship between politics and gifts. The Spaniards were the most open about the possibilities. Thus, in 1786 Viceroy Bernardo de Gálvez noted, "We shall benefit by satisfying their desires. It will cost us less than what is now spent in considerable and useless reinforcements of troops. The Indians cannot live without our aid" (Gálvez 1951:41). So he authorized the governors to present the chiefs with the value of fifteen to twenty pesos in goods, tobacco, and provisions and each warrior with goods worth one or two pesos for himself and his family (1951:50).

Flags had long been used as symbols of alliance between Euroamericans and Comanches and other Indians. In 1724 Étienne Véniard de Bourgmont presented a white French flag to a Padouca (Apache) chief and exhorted him to keep it "always as white as I give it to you, without spots" (Folmer 1942: 294). In 1759 Parilla claimed that there was a French flag flying at the Tao-vaya village on the Red River. At the same village some fifteen years later, after concluding a peace with the Comanches, Gaignard gave the chief a Spanish flag, which the chief promised to place over his door "so that all Co-manches might see it and know that henceforth they must not harm a Span-iard" (Bolton 1914, 2:94). In 1784 Pedro Vial took "seven . . . flags made in New Orleans" costing 7.5 pesos; in 1785 Cabello described the common flags as of "platilla or other ordinary white linen . . . with a staff two and a half varas long, painted with the Burgundian cross" (Cabello 1785e). The princi-pal signer of the 1785 Texas treaty received such a flag (Cabello 1785c).

Other gifts were specifically designed as prestige items indicative of pol-itical status and as carriers of symbolic meaning. In 1773 Gaignard gave blankets "to cover the blood," knives "to stop up the crooked trail," and tobacco "so that the war may be at an end" (Bolton 1914, 2:88-95). As in much of Spanish America, the principal chiefs were given silver-headed canes as insignia of office. Finally, there were political gifts of subsistence goods. In 1785 Pedro Vial had carried some one hundred pesos worth of gifts to the Comanche chiefs. The various messengers to Santa Fe were "received with pleasure . . . and presented with some tokens of esteem" (Thomas 1932:296); unfortunately, no list of those gifts has been found.

4

Comanche-Euroamerican Relations, 1786–1820

Along the Canadian, 1786–88

After the formalization of the 1785–86 treaties, the Spaniards attempted to open direct communication between Santa Fe and Béxar. As it was, communication between the two capitals had to travel a roundabout route of some seventeen hundred miles through Saltillo, Chihuahua, and El Paso to reach Santa Fe, whereas the direct route would be only about seven hundred miles (Loomis and Nasatir 1967:262). Thus, during the years 1786–90 several overland journeys were made to map and explore the best route between Santa Fe and Béxar. Although the Spaniards' motives were imperialistic, the records of their efforts provide a unique view of the geographical distribution of Comanche villages across the southern Plains in the late eighteenth century (map 4).

In the fall of 1786 Pedro Vial and one companion, Cristóbal de los Santos, left Béxar on an overland journey to Santa Fe (Loomis and Nasatir 1967:262–87).[1] Unfortunately, the exact route they took is not clear; during much of the first part of the journey Vial was sick and apparently delirious; the rest of his diary is vague as to locations and distances. Several scholars have attempted to travel Vial's route, but their results have yet to be published (Loomis and Nasatir 1967:270).

In January 1787, after spending two months at the Tawakoni village on the Brazos River, Vial moved on to the Taovayas on the Red River. Two days' journey upriver he arrived at a Comanche village under chief Zoquiné (possibly *tso* 'with the head', *kwi* 'smoke', *na* nominalizing suffix) where he spent ten days.

At a council at the chief's lodge, where many assembled to "smoke the pipe," Vial reported the "captain at San Antonio" had sent him to open the road to Santa Fe so that both Comanches and Spaniards could "travel from one part of the country to another." The Comanches, politely taking no notice of the absurdity of that proposition, replied that they were very pleased, but since it was now too cold to travel, he should spend the winter with them, after which they would accompany him to Santa Fe (Loomis and Nasatir 1967:278).

During his stay, Vial had several such meetings. At one, the chiefs discussed with Vial the politics of southern Plains trade. They complained that Béxar was too distant from them and was too close to the Apaches, and they suggested that the old mission at San Sabá be reactivated as a trading center. Unfortunately, Vial recorded few other details of their conversations.

At another meeting, the Comanches gave their version of a recent fight with some Spaniards. According to one version of Vial's diary, "They asked me if I knew anything about the news they had heard; I said 'no', and they told me that the chief who had gone with me to San Antonio when I made peace had been killed by Spaniards." It seemed that a war party had come upon a noisy camp which they took for Apaches, and they prepared to attack at dawn. In the midst of their preparations a chief named Patuarus arrived, and saying that their targets were Spaniards and were friends, he placed himself between the opposing forces. The "foolish boys" called the chief a coward and would no longer recognize him as captain; the chief retorted that "not even all the Comanches could stop the Spaniards." When the Spaniards returned the Comanches' fire, the captain and another fell dead; the Comanches retreated, and finding a place of refuge, Tanicón (meaning unknown), brother of Zoquiné and Guaquangas, raised their flag in surrender (Vial 1787).

At that point in his journal, and outside the flow of his report of the Comanches' narrative, Vial identified the Spanish commander as José Menchaca; indeed, several details—the killing of a chief and the use of a flag in surrender—parallel Menchaca's report of his fight with Comanches in November 1786 (Navarro García 1964). While there is little reason to doubt that the two reports refer to the same fight, there are problems with the implications of Vial's identification of the participants. For instance, while it is possible that the Comanches had told Vial the commander's name, there is no other historical evidence that Comanches ever used the proper names of Euroamerican officials; indeed, other than the 1753 reference to Governor Vélez Cachupín as the "boy captain," there are no other reports of Comanche nicknames for Euroamerican officials. It is therefore unlikely that in January 1787, in a Comanche village along the Red River, Vial could have learned the identity of the commander of a Spanish force operating out of Agua Verde on the Rio Grande, some five hundred miles away, only two months earlier. Therefore, the commander's name was probably added to the account later.

A more significant problem arises from comparison of the identifications of the deceased chief in the Comanches' report as given by Vial and in Menchaca's report. Vial wrote that that chief had gone with him to Béxar the previous summer to make peace," and gave his name as Patuarus; thus he may have been the chief listed by Anza as Paruatuosacante. However, Menchaca gave the name of the chief he killed as "Camisa de Hierro, also known as Cota de Malla, one of the principal chiefs of the Eastern Cuchanecs who made the peace in Béxar." Combining the two reports creates a conundrum: although it is possible that the Texan principal chief Camisa de Hierro's Comanche name was Paruatuosacante, both Vial's and Menchaca's reports stated that the deceased chief had gone to Béxar with Vial. But Governor Cabello was still waiting to meet Camisa de Hierro. Since it is inconceivable that a principal chief had gone to Béxar with Vial but had not been recognized, or that one of the Comanches who had gone to Béxar with Vial was indeed Camisa de Hierro and that Vial did not note it, it is unlikely that the deceased chief Patuarus was one of the principal chiefs. This conclusion does not rule out the possibility that the deceased chief was Camisa de Hierro, only that his Comanche name was not Paturarus; nor does it rule out the possibility that Patuarus—or Paruatuosacante—had indeed gone with Vial to Béxar, only that he was not the principal chief Camisa de Hierro. Moreover, the Comanches said that "the captain and one other" fell dead, while Menchaca claimed five dead. It is possible that both Camisa de Hierro and Patuarus—who had gone to Béxar with Vial—may have been killed in the fight.

To further confuse matters, at a later meeting at Zoquiné's village, a chief Vial called "Camisa de Malla, whom they call Guaquangas" (Vial 1787) told Vial that he was "waiting to go to San Antonio with me and would take along many persons to see the great captain," the governor (Loomis and Nasatir 1967:279-80). A number of writers (e.g., Loomis and Nasatir 1967: 280; John 1975:716) have suggested that this chief was not only the Texan Camisa de Hierro, with whom Vial had negotiated the year before, but that he was also the principal chief of all the Kotsoteka Comanches, known in New

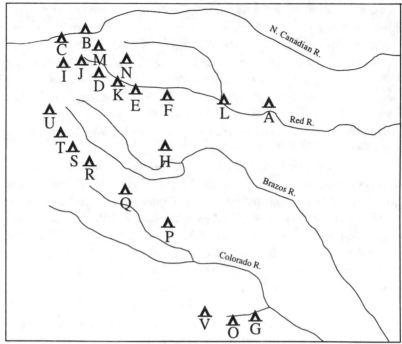

Map 4. Location of Comanche villages, 1786–1808. See table 4.1.

Mexico as Ecueracapa. However, that conclusion calls into question the identification of the chief killed by Menchaca: the deceased could not have been principal chief Camisa de Hierro if he was meeting with Vial two months later.

I believe the answer to this problem lies in the recognition, noted above, that in the mid-1780s there were three Comanche individuals with similar Spanish nicknames. Two of these men were of high standing, Ecueracapa in New Mexico and Camisa de Hierro in Texas. The latter may indeed have been killed in the fall of 1786, for there is no further direct mention of him in the Texas records. The third individual was called Guaquangas, characterized earlier by Cabello as a chief of the "second class." It was with him that Vial now discussed trade, and it was his brother Tanicón who had surrendered to Menchaca.[2]

In March Zoquiné, Guaquangas's other brother, along with three other chiefs—unnamed—two warriors, and several women and children, guided Vial to Santa Fe. Heading northwest from the Red River, they skirted the Llano Estacado and passed to the North Canadian River. In May, in what is

Table 4.1

Travelers through Comanchería and Their Comanche Hosts, 1786-1808

Vial, 1786–87	**Vial, Fragoso, Fernández, July 1788**
A Zoquiné, Jan. 9, 1787	J Naisaras/Naisare, July 1, 1788
B Paruanarimuco, May 14, 1787	K Pochinaquente/Pachiacazen, July 8,
C Unnamed Yamparika, May 16, 1787	1788
	L July 15, 1788
Mares, 1787	Zoquacante/Chobacante
D Aug. 9, 1787	Cohli/Quipuniputimi
Zoquinatoya	Pisimampat
El Tazaquipe	
Anagama	**Fragoso, 1788**
Sofais	M Maya, 3 others nearby, July 1, 1788
E Nocay, Aug. 11, 1787	N "Comanches and unattached
F Aug. 22, 1787	Comanches," July 5, 1788
Tocinaquinte	
Ychap	**Amangual, 1808**
	O Cordero, Apr. 12, 1808
Mares, 1788	P Sofais [Chiojas], Apr. 23, 1808
G Tocinaquinte, Jan. 7, 1788	Q Yamparika, May 3, 1808
H Sofais, Quenarecante, Mar. 1788	R Ysapampi, May 8, 1808
I Mar. 24, 1788	S Village under Ysapampa, May 11, 1808
Comquitansaran	T Yamparika village, May 14, 1808
Paruamupes	U Quegüe, May 17, 1808
Tanchaguare	V Cordero, Dec. 4, 1808

SOURCE: Loomis and Nasatir 1967

now New Mexico, they encountered Paruanarimuco's ranchería. That chief, fresh from his recognition as Comanche lieutenant general, "immediately . . . brought out the Spanish flag and took us to his lodge." Unfortunately, Vial recorded little about their conversations, noting only that Paruanarimuco was pleased with the "Captain" in Santa Fe. The next day Vial passed a ranchería that he identified as Yamparika. However, considering his earlier identification of all western Comanches as "Yambericas," it is not clear that was their proper identification; indeed he did not give a divisional identification for Paruanarimuco. Once having passed them, Vial gave no notice of other novelties on his trip to Santa Fe (Loomis and Nasatir 1967:281–85).

Paruanarimuco was also on his way to Santa Fe with a most interesting proposition: he wanted to establish a permanent village on the Arkansas River. Anza jumped at the chance to accomplish the permanent settlement of

Comanches. That fall a master builder and thirty laborers were sent from Taos, and by October nineteen houses were completed. But the settlement, to be called San Carlos de los Jupes, was begun in inauspicious times. When Anza retired in the fall of 1787, the Jupes took it as the end of Spanish support; they returned the tools and sent the overseer home. The new governor, Fernando de la Concha, managed to regain their confidence, and they stayed until January 1788, when they abandoned the settlement, allegedly due to the death of a woman "whom Paruanarimuco especially esteemed" (Thomas 1929c). There was also rethinking about the project in Mexico City, and when Concha sought authorization to try again, the whole project was deemed too costly (Moorhead 1968:163).

During the next two years several other Spaniards traveled between Béxar and Santa Fe, visiting the Comanche rancherías on their way and reporting their findings. On July 31, 1787, José Mares, Cristóbal de los Santos and Alejandro Martín, the New Mexican interpreter, left Santa Fe for Béxar. On August 9, beyond the edge of the Llano Estacado, they encountered the rancherías of chiefs Zoquinatoya, El Taraquipe, Anagana, and Sofais (Loomis and Nasatir 1967:293). The first name was probably derived from *tsokwina toya* 'smoke mountain', but it is not clear whether he was the same man as the one called Zoquiné. The meanings of the other names are unknown. There were a number of citations in the 1780s and later to the names Sofais, Soguayes, Chojais, and Soxas, none of which can be translated, but since it seems likely that only one individual was meant, the spelling Sofais will be used.

Sofais and several other Comanches joined Mares's entourage, which on August 11 arrived at the camp of chief Nocay (meaning unknown). On August 22 they met two other rancherías led by Tociniquente (possibly *tutsu kwita* 'bad excrement') and Ychape (possibly *isapʉ* 'liar'), the latter perhaps the Hichapat who attended the 1785 Pecos meeting. Thus, with a retinue of eighty-one Comanche men, women, and children, Mares, de los Santos, and Martín passed the rest of the trip to Béxar (Loomis and Nasatir 1967:294–302).

Accompanied by Sofais and Tociniquente, Mares began a return trip to Santa Fe in late January 1788. In February they found Sofais's ranchería on the Double Mountain Fork of the Brazos River, where they spent several weeks. During that time, another ranchería, led by Quenaracara (*kwina na karʉ* 'eagle sitting down'), joined them. In early March, accompanied by Sofais and Quenaracara, Mares set out again. On the twenty-fourth they met the Kotsoteka rancherías of Comquitanquesaran, Paruamumpes, and Tanqueyaran. The meaning of the first name is unknown; the second appears to be *parua muupitsI* 'bear owl'; the third may be *tah kweʔya na* 'he takes off his shoe'. On April 6 Sofais turned back, but Tanqueyaran's two sons continued into Santa Fe with Mares (Loomis and Nasatir 1967:314).

Vial returned to Texas in June 1788, accompanied by several young New Mexicans as companions and chroniclers. On July 1, three leagues east of modern Tucumcari, New Mexico—the origin of that place name has been suggested as either *tu makaru* 'black sitting on it', referring to the belief that there was always a cloud over it, or as *tukamuru* 'ambush'—they met a ranchería of fifty-six lodges under Naisaras (meaning unknown). Several other rancherías were reported to be nearby, including that of Maya, possibly Ecueracapa, although the chroniclers took no special notice of his presence (Loomis and Nasatir 1967:330). On July 5, beyond Palo Duro Canyon, they found "Comanches and unattached Comanches everywhere." Four days later they met Pochinaquina, probably Tociniquente, with fourteen lodges. The next day Vial went off to look for "Yamparicas" (Loomis and Nasatir 1967:334), but since he did not keep a separate journal, it is unknown whether he was successful; moreover, considering his earlier usage of "Yamberica" to refer to "western Comanches," it is not clear whether Vial was similarly confused here, or whether indeed there were Yamparikas beyond the Palo Duro.

The other two parties, although separated, met a large Comanche camp of 372 lodges under three chiefs. One of the chroniclers, Santiago Fernández, reported their chiefs as Zoquacante, Cochi, and Visimaxe (Loomis and Nasatir 1967:321). The other, Francisco Xavier Fragoso, gave their names as Chobacante, Quibuniputimi, and Pisimanpat (Loomis and Nasatir 1967:337). Both versions of the first name are not interpretable beyond the element 'cante', that is, *katu* 'possessor'. The second, at least as given by Fragoso, may be based on the element *puni* 'to see'. The third individual was present at the 1786 Pecos conference with Anza; according to one later citation, which gives his name as "Pisinamp ó Tuerto," he was also known as One Eye (Nava 1798). Sofais, who was also present, accompanied them as far as the Taovaya village. While Vial and Fragoso went on to Natchitoches, Fernández returned to Santa Fe by way of Sofais's village, where some horses borrowed on the outward trip were returned (Loomis and Nasatir 1967:332–37).

The following summer Fragoso, with five Comanches as guides, returned to Santa Fe. That time, however, they met few other Indians. In July they passed "17 Comanches—strapping youths without a chief" on campaign against the Apaches; in early August near Palo Duro Canyon they met Ecueracapa's ranchería. A small trading party of thirteen had just left for Pecos; Ecueracapa recalled them to serve as guides (Loomis and Nasatir 1967:366).

New Mexico, 1786-1806

Cooperative military affairs accounted for many Comanche-New Mexican interactions during the two decades 1786-1806, but the course of events was not always smooth. Ecueracapa and a number of Comanches planned to join in campaigns projected for the fall of 1787 against Apaches south of the Hopi villages. But in May some Jupe youths—the new governor, Fernando de la Concha called their division "the most perverse of the Nation," a strange denomination for a group whose principal leader was at that time attempting to settle at San Carlos—stole eighteen horses from a Spanish trading party. Word was sent to Ecueracapa, then some seventy leagues from Santa Fe, finalizing plans for the expeditions. Over the objections of his fellow chiefs, he came into the capital. There he apologized for the youths, who he said had "little or no judgment" and who had "no appreciation for his counsels or those of the principal men of the nation." An indirect cause of the theft may have been a lingering drought that drove the buffalo from their usual range: by the fall of 1787 the buffalo had been gone from Kotsoteka country for seven months, and the people had no robes to trade (Concha 1788).

The two campaigns that fall were not successful. In the first, the Spaniards hastily retreated after an ambush, while the Comanches held their position. The second, under the direct command of Comandante Inspector Joseph Antonio Rengel, fared slightly better, but Rengel disparaged the Comanches' fighting abilities and suggested that in the future, although Spain would supply arms and ammunition, the Comanches should campaign on their own (Moorhead 1968:167).

In March 1788 Ysampampi (*isa paapi* 'wolf head', possibly the Salambipit who led eighty men against the Apaches in 1786)[3] led ninety-five warriors against the Faraone Apaches, taking thirty-five prisoners (Simmons 1967:23).

In the summer of 1790, possibly as the result of a request by Paruanarimuco made during a visit to Santa Fe in May, Juan de Dios Peña led a group of about twenty New Mexican soldiers and "auxiliaries"—vecinos from San Juan, the Rio Arriba, and Taos—in a joint campaign against Pawnees. The Comanches were armed in part by firearms from the armory in Santa Fe, but like the 1787 joint campaign against Apaches in Arizona, cooperation between the Comanches and the Spaniards proved to be a difficult task.

Near San Juan Spring in northeastern New Mexico, Paruanarimuco passed the Spaniards, saying he was headed for his own village. The Spaniards lagged behind, traveling until late that night looking for him. Two days later, at the Rio Salado, they met Pujavara (*puhaparua* 'medicine bear') with seventy-two lodges, but that chief did not wish to participate in the proposed campaign because of the distance to the Pawnees and the dangers to his horses.

After spending five days with Pujavara, the Spaniards and Comanches moved on to the Trinchera River in southern Colorado, where they spent another five days. One of the New Mexicans, while searching for lost animals, found not only a herd of mustangs but also four Pawnees, who fired at him, hitting his horse in a leg. He made it back to the camp that night, but when Peña tried to organize a foray against the Pawnees, the Comanches were uncooperative.

The next day the whole party moved on, and after traveling about three leagues they came upon a ranchería under Tanquesuana (possibly *ta kesua na* 'the mean one') and Onacama (possibly the Anagana who met José Mares in 1787). There they were told that Chama (possibly the man Chama or Chamanada from 1786) had come with the news that Ecueracapa would soon arrive. Indeed, within two days four other rancherías were camped nearby, and within a week there were 340 lodges present, under Ecueracapa, Paruanarimuco, Tanquesuana, Naisaras, Ysampampi, Onacama, and Achacata (meaning unknown).

The chiefs met to discuss their route, where there might be buffalo, and how to carry out the campaign. After ten days of resting their horses, the whole camp moved on. A week and several stops later they came upon a number of Pawnee "ranchos," probably tents. Peña again tried to organize a foray but again was unable to convince the Comanches of the urgency. Ultimately, Ecueracapa, Paruanarimuco, and Pujavara sent him off, saying that he was holding them up. They returned the borrowed firearms, and Peña returned to Santa Fe (Peña 1790).

The source of the difficulty between Peña and the Comanches is unclear, but was probably due in part to the fact that the Comanches were organized not as a war party, but as local bands, with their families, and thus had concerns besides the direct military focus of Peña's force. A month later the Comanches attacked a Pawnee ranchería, killing thirty, with the loss of only three (Concha 1790).

In early December a Kotsoteka village on the upper reaches of the Nueces River in Texas was attacked by Mescalero buffalo hunters accompanied by "auxiliaries" from El Paso. According to the report, there were only nine Comanche men in the village to fend off the almost two hundred Apaches; they were holding their own until the Spaniards joined on the side of the Apaches. The men, and many women and children, were killed in the fight, including the capitancillo Sojuacante (possibly the Zoquacante met by Fernández and Fragoso in 1787), Tosaparua (one of the volunteers in the 1786 campaign), and the interpreter, Francisco Peres. Thirty-nine Comanches "of all sexes and ages," including Ecueracapa's own daughter, were taken captive (Concha 1791).

Two Comanches escaped and made their way to Santa Fe, where they told Governor Concha of the battle. He was reluctant to believe their report but kept them in Santa Fe to prevent their alarming the Yamparikas and Jupes while he wrote for advice to Comandante General Pedro de Nava. Meanwhile, the hunting party returned to El Paso with their captives and reported to Domingo Diaz, commander of the presidio, who also reported to Nava. Nava and Concha were particularly upset that the carefully arranged Comanche alliance might falter on the actions of a subaltern. The corporal who had charge of the escort—his name has not been uncovered—was severely reprimanded for failing to take the necessary precautions, which "were required to contain a very improper insult against the Comanches"; Diaz was instructed not to send any more escorts with the Mescalero hunters, and the captives were released and sent north to Santa Fe with the mail caravan (Nava 1791).

In March, after the caravan arrived in Santa Fe, one of the official interpreters was sent out to find Ecueracapa. In the interim one of the first two refugees died from his exertions. At his own request he was baptized and was buried with much ceremony, apparently satisfying not only the ten captives but also five other Comanches who were visiting the capital.

On April 18 Ecueracapa, along with eight of the "most respected captains," Chama, Pujavara, Hachaca (possibly the man called Achacata), Onacama, Guaxacante (*waha katɯ* 'he has two'), Piacuitara (*pia kwitarai* 'big anus', i.e., 'big Pawnee'), Quecuarapate (meaning unknown), and Ecueracapa's son Ohamaquea, and forty-six others arrived in Santa Fe. Concha gave them assurances that he understood their desire for revenge upon the Spaniards who had assisted in the attack; with the return of the refugees, he hoped that their feelings were assuaged.

The Comanches were reconciled to the Spaniards, but they did not have the same sentiments toward the Mescalero and Llanero Apaches, who had been attacking them all spring; an estimated one thousand Comanche "men of arms" were reported in the Wichita Mountains planning a campaign (Nava 1791). They wished to make another joint campaign with the Spaniards—they had, it was claimed, more than twelve hundred men—and asked for both men and munitions. However, Concha could not, or would not, accede to either request (Concha 1791).

Thus, the Comanches again went campaigning on their own. In June 1792 Ecueracapa and Paruanarimuco, with five captains, including Quenaracara and Hachaca, led an expedition against the Pawnees. They found three small and one "considerable" ranchería, killed a captain and ten warriors, and took eight women and nine children captive (Concha 1792).

In the late winter 1792–93—the exact date is unclear—Utes and Navajos attacked a Comanche village whose men were out buffalo hunting, "destroying it completely." The Comanches paid a similar visit to a Ute village (Simmons 1967:25). Later in 1793 Hachaca was killed and Ecueracapa "grievously wounded" on a campaign against Pawnees (Nava 1793a); Ecueracapa must have died sometime that fall. In November 1793, at a meeting along the Colorado River, Encanguane (*eka wahne* 'red fox') was elected Kotsoteka general "with the universal applause of the rancherías" (Nava 1793b; Simmons 1967:31).

Comanches continued to visit Santa Fe for trade and gifts but the New Mexico records contain few details of the encounters. In July 1797 Pisinampe[4]—that time called the "Captain of the Eastern Comanche"—reported that the "Comanche General" had died and that he—Pisinampe—should be recognized as the new principal chief. Instead of immediately investing him, however, the new governor, Fernando de Chacón, waited until the Kotsotekas could convene at Pecos. There they elected another, Canaguaipe, "by a plurality of votes," to be the new general. Canaguaipe had attended the 1786 Pecos conference, and in 1787 he was the leader of the second-largest Kotsoteka ranchería with 155 lodges. Chacón gave him the insignia of leadership, a silver-headed cane and medal, and a scarlet cape, as well as "two fanegas [2.5 bushels] of corn, one arroba [11.5 kilos] of punche—native tobacco—and a tercio [burro load] of sugar . . . to pass along to his brothers" (Chacón 1797a).

By the following October Pedro de Nava was growing frustrated at continuing Mescalero attacks on El Paso, and he instructed Chacón to "call in one or two of the principal Comanche captains" to ask them to join in a campaign against both the Mescaleros and the Lipan Apaches (Nava 1797). On November 19 the Comanche general, presumably Canaguaipe, and five of his principals—all unnamed—visited Santa Fe for a conference. Chacón promised to supply such rations, arms and ammunition, and assistance in soldiers and auxiliary vecinos as he could spare. But the chiefs said that most of their young men were about to set out on one campaign, and the rigors of two would be too much for their horses (Chacón 1797b). Although Nava and Chacón discussed the proposed operation during the course of the winter, there is no confirmation that it actually took place, and there is nothing more known of Canaguaipe or of his tenure as Kotsoteka chief. An August 1801 "Summary of Events" noted that Comanches were arriving at Pecos to trade and to hold "election of the general's post now vacant" (Chacón 1801), but there is no mention of who was elected or other details.

A confused series of events began in 1803 when Huanacoruco—last mentioned in 1786—visited Nemesio Salcedo, the comandante general of the

Provincias Internas, to claim that Quegüe—the meaning of the name is unknown; it was once given as "Tanquegüe," 'the one . . . ' (Cónde 1818)—
had refused the "baton" as the Yamparika principal chief and that the insignia
should be given to one of Huanacoruco's own sons. Further, he charged that
the interpreter at San Miguel was incompetent and demanded that he should
be replaced by another of his son (N. Salcedo 1804).

Salcedo passed Huanacoruco's request along to Governor Chacón, who
responded that the charges were "false in all parts." First, "the election of the
General of the Comanches does not depend on the Governor of the province,
who only approves the one who has been elected by all of the Captains." Furthermore, the suggested general was "in actuality only 14 or 15 years old."
Finally, Chacón noted that the proposed interpreter was in fact not even
Huanacoruco's own son (Chacón 1804). A further confusion concerns the
divisional identities of the players. In 1786 Huanacoruco was called a Kotsoteka; here he was claiming the Yamparika leadership. Conversely, in all other
documents, Quegüe was identified as a Kotsoteka; why he should have been
offered—let alone refused—the Yamparika chiefship is unclear.

One possibility is that those confusions emanated from Huanacoruco
himself in an attempt to improve his own political position. In 1803 rumor of
a fabulous Hill of Gold located in Comanchería sent a case of gold fever
through New Mexico. The source of the rumor is unknown; in May Huanacoruco said he knew where the Hill of Gold was and offered his services as
guide (N. Salcedo 1803a). In August "Cuerno Verde, alias El Caricortado,"
that is, "alias Cut Face"—not to be confused with the three Cuerno Verdes of
1767–79—came to Santa Fe with news of its discovery (Chacón 1803). In
September Huanacoruco and a Spaniard, Bernardo Castro, set out but were
hindered by a Comanche-Pawnee war (N. Salcedo 1803b). In early 1804
Huanacoruco and Castro again set out, but this time Huanacoruco said the
place was in Pawnee territory and it was too dangerous to proceed (Chacón
1804). Later, after Castro was killed by Apaches, the Spaniards dropped both
the search and Huanacoruco.

Although Huanacoruco's claim is the only direct indication of a change
in Yamparika leadership, there are other indications of political transition.
The Santa Fe daily diary indicated that an unnamed "Comanche General"
made several visits during 1803 (Anonymous 1803), but it is unknown
whether he was either the Yamparika chief Paruanarimuco or the unnamed
Kotsoteka chief elected in 1801.

In November 1805 several Yamparikas, unnamed, visited the new governor, Joachín del Real Alencaster, to solicit several favors. Primary among
those was that he ratify Somiquaso (possibly *so?me?* 'tanned buffalo hide',

kwasu²u 'jacket'—a name interestingly reminiscent of the Spanish name Ecueracapa 'leather cape'—called Carlos by Alencaster) as Yamparika general, "asi como el Quegüe para los Cuchanticas."

Linguistic and orthographic interpretations of the latter Spanish phrase have significant implications for understanding the political situation. I believe it to be "like Quegüe for the Kotsotekas." Simmons, however, perhaps reading the indistinct word that I read *como* as *otro*, gave it as "and another from among the Cuchanticas called Quegüe" (1967:33). While Simmons's interpretation would suggest that Quegüe was recognized as Kotsoteka chief at the same time Somiquaso was recognized as Yamparika chief (that is, in 1805), my interpretation implies that Quegüe's succession to the Kotsoteka leadership had taken place at an earlier, but so far undocumented, occasion. Moreover, Alencaster gave only a single silver-headed cane and medal, again evidence of only a single recognition. All he asked in return was that the Comanches come every year to trade, as a "good way to avoid unpleasantness" (Alencaster 1805).

Finally, in a move reminiscent of Paruanarimuco twenty years earlier, the Comanches also requested that "houses of wood forming a plaza" be built for them. Alencaster offered to send workers to "construct their houses if they would return for them in the spring," but there is no evidence that the Comanches returned or that the houses were ever built.

In his report on the encounter, Alencaster noted that the Yamparikas, who had "formerly lived to the north," were now to be found on the Rio Colorado "near . . . the Conchos." That located Somiquaso far to the south of Yamparika territory above the Arkansas River. Simmons suggested that Alencaster meant the Canadian River (1967:33); Loomis and Nasatir suggested the Red River (1967:441). However, later reports show that some Yamparikas were indeed as far south as the Colorado River of Texas; as early as 1787, Paruanarimuco, the Jupe and Yamparika "lieutenant general" was on the Canadian. Furthermore, although it is possible that they were related to the "Namboricas" reported in the same general area twenty-five years earlier, the intervening years provide no direct evidence of the presence of any but Kotsoteka Comanches in the area.

But those Yamparikas of 1805 had not moved into a profitable country. Upon leaving Santa Fe, they promised to return at the first of the year to trade what few hides they had, and Alencaster offered to license traders to visit their camps (N. Salcedo 1805). Thus, in December 1805 Alencaster sent Alejandro Martin to visit and trade at the new settlement. He returned after less than month to report that although the Yamparikas were "well supplied" with Spanish manufactures obtained from the New Mexican settlements, they would trade only a little buffalo meat and fewer than twenty furs of "little value." Moreover, Martin and his party had their own trade goods stolen and could not persuade Somiquaso to effect their return (Alencaster 1806).

The movement of those Yamparikas from the Arkansas River may have resulted from pressures exerted by the arrival of several new groups from the north, including Kiowas, whose advance the Yamparikas and Jupes had long resisted, Cheyennes—called by the Spaniards Flecha Rayada 'striped arrows', in Comanche the *paka naboo* 'painted arrows'—and Cuampes. The latter ethnonym had been used in the sixteenth century to refer to the Faraone Apaches (Hodge 1907–10, 1:369; Schroeder 1974), but it had been obsolete for almost a century. Although that new group on the Arkansas River may thus have been Plains Apaches, they may also have been a different group altogether: Arapahos (Ewers 1969:102 n118; John 1985). Whoever they were, Comanches fought several major battles with the Nations of the North, particularly with Kiowas, between 1801 and 1806 (Chacón 1801; John 1985). A truce between some Yamparika Comanches and some Kiowas was arranged in 1806, and the Kiowa chief El Ronco 'the hoarse one' married the daughter of Somiquaso and joined his group (Alencaster 1806; Loomis and Nasatir 1967:450).

There are some important points of comparison among the documentary records of that truce, the oral history of Kiowas as given by James Mooney (1898), and the oral history of Comanches as recorded by Joe Attocknie (1965). According to Mooney, after an accidental initial contact at a Spaniard's house, a Kiowa named Guik'ate 'wolf lying down' and a Comanche named Pareiya *paa* 'water' *tɨʔɨya* 'be afraid' 'afraid of water' agreed that peace would be beneficial to both groups. However, since the matter should be considered "by the whole tribe," Guik'ate accompanied Pareiya to the main Comanche camp on the Double Mountain Fork of the Brazos River, where peace was celebrated.

There are three general points of present concern: the location of the Comanche village, the identity of the Comanche participants, and the date. Mooney implied that the Comanche village on the Brazos was that of "the whole tribe," implying all of the Comanches, but that is improbable. From his own information, Joe Attocknie stated that the Comanche was Yamparika; thus Mooney's location of the village on the Brazos closely accords with Somiquaso's Yamparika village on the Conchos or the Colorado rivers.[5] However, the equation of Somiquaso and Pareiya is probably not warranted.

The beginning of Joe Attocknie's Comanche account paralleled Mooney —a chance meeting at a trading post—but contained significant detail on the internal Comanche political process. To begin, Attocknie—who spelled the protagonist's name as Patuhuhyah, closer to the phonemics than Mooney's spelling—noted that Patuhuhyah was only a village member; the chief was

Tutsayatuhovit (Attocknie glossed the name as 'black prairie dog') a man "not only . . . of gigantic stature but also of great breadth" (Attocknie 1965). Initially, Patuhuhyah, along with other village members, conducted private negotiations with the Kiowas in his own lodge. Then, persuading his fellow villagers of the benefits to be gained from friendship with the Kiowas, he sent a messenger asking the village chief to come to the meeting. The chief told the messenger that the Comanches at the meeting should make their own decision; it was their idea and it was up to them to decide. Three times he was called; finally, on the fourth call, he came to "just take a look." Upon entering the tipi and looking at each person, he said,

> "Did I not tell you people to make a decision yourselves? I told you I would agree to any decision that you made at this meeting." As he took another look around the tipi, he continued, "Where are they? Where are the strangers? As I look through the people in here, you all look alike, there is no one who looks different, you are all my children. Will some one point out and tell me which ones are my other children who have come to visit us? Show them to me so I can touch them and take their hand in friendship." [Attocknie 1965]

Attocknie's account concluded, "Peace had been decided by the huge head-man."

That final attribution of credit to the headman may seem misplaced in light of the description of Patuhuhyah's private negotiations. However, in the context of the separation of the public and the political from the domestic and the private it may become clearer. As presented by Attocknie, the proposed truce began as Patuhuyah's private matter into which Tutsayatuhovit as village chief would not intrude. Only when the entire village had been persuaded of its merits did he arrive to set his, and their, seal on the matter by his irony, "Where are the strangers?" implying that now there were none. It remains a question as to how often actions thus initiated on the private level moved to the public political arena.

The final point to consider is the date of the Kiowa peace. The Spanish records are specific: Somiquaso's peace with El Ronco occurred in 1806. On the other hand, by "balancing" a sequence of relative dates, births, deaths, and lengths of generations, Mooney arrived at 1790 "as the most probable approximate date" of the Comanche-Kiowa peace (Mooney 1898:164). Meanwhile, Attocknie (1965) brought it forward in time. First, from his own information, he noted that Paruasemena was a "past prime warrior about age 35 or 40" when the truce was made (Attocknie 1965). Then, from Thomas Battey's conclusion that Paruasemena was "probably upwards of eighty years old" when he died at Fort Sill in 1872 (1877:90), he concluded that Paruasemena must have been born about 1790. From those two facts he would put the date of the truce well into the 1820s.

Perhaps the best resolution is to acknowledge that the Comanche-Kiowa peace was a process, not an event, and that there may have been many such truces, each involving a different set of participants, villages, and divisions,. However, the result was that by the 1820s most Comanches and Kiowas were peacefully interacting.

Meanwhile, in May 1807 Flechas Rayadas 'striped arrows', that is Cheyennes, and Cuampes, probably Arapahos, camping on Almagre Creek sent word to Santa Fe that they wanted to trade "because they needed some things." Governor Alencaster sent them a flag and 100 pesos worth of goods and told them that if they made a formal request for peace he would give each chief a certificate of chieftainship, canes of office, and medals (Loomis and Nasatir 1967:452). In September the Cuampes chief sent word to Santa Fe that he was seeking to open trade with New Mexico "on the same terms as with the Comanche" (N. Salcedo 1807); it is not known whether there was any further contact.

Texas, 1786–1808

Although the Spanish-Comanche alliance worked passably well in New Mexico, conditions in Texas were much less stable, and a variety of circumstances worked against peaceful interaction. Not the least of them was a difference in the Spanish governmental approach to the two provinces. The viceroy in Mexico took notice of Texas only when it was threatened from the east, first by the French, later by the fledgling American republic. At other times Texas was considered a backwater of the empire, even more so than New Mexico. In the early nineteenth century, New Mexico had a Spanish population of almost thirty thousand, while Texas barely numbered three thousand.

A further complication was the loss of Comanche leadership in Texas. Several leading Texas Comanches were killed in 1786: both Cabeza Rapada and Camisa de Hierro were reported killed, the former by Apaches, the latter by Spaniards, as was Patuarus, or Paruatuosacante. An election for a successor to Cabeza Rapada was held, but there was confusion in the Comanche camps, and the Béxar records do not explicitly record the outcome. Thus, for the last fourteen years of the eighteenth century there does not seem to have been a single Texas Comanche with sufficient prestige, power, or authority to warrant the status of principal chief. Sofais and Zoquiné, both of whom had helped Vial in 1786, are the most prominent Texas Comanches in the documents. They led expeditions against the Mescalero Apaches—Sofais in 1788 (Martínez Pacheco 1788), Zoquiné in 1789—and they were supported with gifts and presents by the Spanish. In the fall of 1789 Zoquiné had a large flag inscribed "Given by Ugalde to the Chief of the Comanche" (Castañeda 1936, 5:17). In 1790 Sofais and Ojos Azules 'blue eyes' helped recover stolen horses (Muñoz 1791), and in 1792 they received gifts of tobacco and other supplies (Muñoz 1792a, 1792b, 1792c).

Besides Sofais and Zoquiné, the Texas Spaniards supported a number of lesser chiefs, one of whom revived an old confusion. In February 1794 a Comanche, who was called by the governor "Malla, ó Camisa de Hierro," visited Béxar with seventy-four followers, bringing word of Encanguane's election in New Mexico to replace Ecueracapa, who some called Cota de Malla. When that was reported to Pedro de Nava, the comandante general was as confused as Ugarte had been in 1786: here was Iron Shirt reporting that Iron Shirt had died and had been replaced. He asked the Texas governor to "inform me if the said Malla . . . is known by other names among the Comanche or has other names in their language" (Nava 1794); although there is no record of a reply, he was possibly the chief of the "second class" Guaquangas. Whoever he was, he, together with his son, called simply "son of Malla," often acted as intermediaries between the Texas Comanches and the Spaniards.

Despite those positive interactions, a series of incidents kept the Comanches on the verge of war with the Texans. In May 1795 a Comanche identified as Chamanquequena—the meaning is unknown, he was possibly one of the Chamas from 1786—came to Laredo, and after paying his respects, left with thirty Spanish horses (Nava 1795). In 1801, when the son of the Yamparika local band chief Blanco 'white' was killed by some unidentified Spaniards, his father cried for vengeance (Nava 1802). In 1803 Spanish soldiers caught and killed nine Taovaya horse thieves. The Taovayas cried for revenge and called upon their Comanche allies for help. Later that year, through a case of mistaken identity, a capitancillo known as El Sordo 'the deaf one' and twenty-seven others were arrested for horse theft and murder (N. Salcedo 1803c)—he was possibly the El Surdo named by Vial in 1786 as a chief of the third class; his Comanche name may have been Sanarico or Esanarico (possibly *esa na tuhka* 'wolves eating together') (M. Salcedo 1812). They admitted the theft but denied the murder; the mistake was caught in time and they were released (N. Salcedo 1803d).

In each of those cases several Comanche leaders worked to prevent the outbreak of hostilities. Although some Comanches sympathized with Chief

Blanco, others—including Pisinampe, Zoquiné, Sofais, and Yzazat, the latter
"not known before in these territories" (J. B. Elguézabal 1802a)—refused to
join. Sofais and Yzazat moved their camps to the Rio Llano so that they
could keep an eye on events in the opposition camps, promising to keep the
governor informed and suggesting that they travel to Chihuahua to meet
personally with the comandante general. When Blanco's followers killed a
Spaniard and the Texans in turn demanded satisfaction, the Texas Comanche
leaders argued that the incident was Blanco's private revenge (J. B. Elguézabal 1802c). Later that summer, when a previously neutral (and unidentified)
faction threatened to upset the delicate balance, the New Mexico Comanche
leadership stepped in to end the dispute, saying that if war broke out it would
not only be with Texas but with New Mexico as well, and would "result in
the loss of the many benefits" to all (J. B. Elguézabal 1802d). In November
Blanco himself came to Béxar, saying that at a "junta general," a 'general
meeting' of the nation, they had determined to forget their differences" (J. B.
Elguézabal 1802e).

Prominent in settling the Blanco affair was a chief called Chihuahua. He
was previously unnamed in either the Texas or the New Mexico records,
although it is possible that he was the unnamed Kotsoteka principal chief
elected in 1801. It is obvious that he had sufficient authority, both with the
Comanches and with the Spaniards, to prevent the outbreak of active hostilities. At the junta general he suggested that the Comanches form a police
force to ensure compliance with the treaties, and he brought thirty warriors to
Governor Juan Bautista de Elguézabal requesting uniforms for them (J. B.
Elguézabal 1802c). In 1803 he, Yzazat, and Sargento 'sergeant' received
permission to visit Governor Manuel Antonio Cordero at Monclova in search
of a permanent trader for the Comanches (J. B. Elguézabal 1803). In the
outcry over the excessive Spanish response to the Taovaya horse thieves,
Chihuahua declared for peace; during the interrogation of El Sordo he
scolded the prisoners, vowing to punish anyone who should repeat such
crimes, even to kill them at the cost of his own life. It was at Chihuahua's
request, and after a personal interrogation, that El Sordo was released (N.
Salcedo 1803d). In 1805, together with Yzazat and Sargento, he welcomed
Manuel Antonio Cordero, transferred from Monclova to Béxar.

But Chihuahua's presence in Texas did not stop all raiding. In an attempt
to put a stop to those raids, Governor Cordero sent Captain Francisco Amangual to visit the rancherías. Amangual had almost twenty years' experience
dealing with the Comanches; in 1785, as corporal, Amangual had escorted the
Comanche chiefs from the treaty council in Béxar (Cabello 1785c). Now he
was ordered "to make the chiefs understand that they were obligated to con-

front the individuals of their nation who were warring in our territory." Furthermore, he was instructed, "With the goal of easing trade and arranging the best relations . . . it is proper that the said Captains elect and propose to you a Chief of all their division" (N. Salcedo 1806a). On his return Amangual reported that they had named Sargento as the Kotsoteka "gefe principal" 'principal chief' (N. Salcedo 1806b), and that he had taken the governor's name as his own. It is not clear why Chihuahua was not elected; he had not died and in fact remained in and around Texas until at least 1816.

Sargento-Cordero acted quickly. As Ecueracapa's emissaries had done in 1787, he visited the rancherías of the Texas Kotsotekas, as well as some neighboring Yamparikas, to establish his authority. He identified the primary source of "little robberies and extortions" as coming from Pisinampe's ranchería, noting that that chief was the "only one who had not come to present himself" to the governor upon his arrival in Texas. When confronted, Pisinampe excused himself, saying that he had been ill and not able to control his . people, and anyway, the culprits had already gone on to Yamparika rancherías farther away (M. A. Cordero 1806).

In March 1808, in an attempt to increase Comanche awareness of Spanish power, as well as to counter increased Anglo-American presence and influence, Amangual was again sent to Comanchería with a force of about two hundred men, a large herd of horses and mules, and several wheeled vehicles, possibly including cannon. Like Pedro Vial's record of travels in 1785, Amangual's reports give much information on the distribution of and political relations among the local Comanche groups between Béxar and Santa Fe (map 4).

Approximately twelve leagues west of the old San Sabá mission, Amangual visited Cordero's ranchería. There the Spaniards were met by "a multitude of Indians . . . painted with red ochre and dressed in various costumes." In return, the Spaniards "received them with our troops in column formation, and with our drums beating a march." After "ceremonies of politeness and friendly relations," Cordero and "the most important Indians" assigned the Spaniards a camping area near their village. That afternoon "two chiefs and an assistant" came to accompany Amangual to Cordero's lodge, where he was received "with much jubilation." Later Amangual gave the chief a "walking cane and rifle sent by our Governor . . . to govern and protect his people" (Loomis and Nasatir 1967:467–68).

For the next week Cordero and his people traveled with the Spaniards. There were many buffalo on the Colorado River, and they spent much time drying the meat. While they were so occupied, Sofais—Amangual spelled it Chiojas—and his family visited from his village of more than two hundred tents about three leagues distant in the valley of Almagre Creek. Chief Cordero, with an escort of four soldiers, returned the visit, and Amangual followed later.

While at Sofais's, Amangual made a "long and clear speech" reminding them of the "loyalty and fidelity we bear them, and that they should observe the same, that they should not trade with any other nation that may come to induce them, for their object is none other than that of afterward turning them from their loyalty to us" (Loomis and Nasatir 1967:473). The chiefs responded by saying that they considered themselves as Spaniards, and that they did not accept anything from other nations; they particularly denied knowledge of any Anglo-Americans trading in their country.

There is, however, some question of the chiefs' wholehearted cooperation. There was evidently some animosity between Cordero and Sofais, and Cordero may have tried to intimidate Sofais; their meeting had been "called . . . by order of General Cordero." Amangual also effected a power differential: gifts for Sofais's ranchería were delivered to Cordero "in order that they be distributed through him." That animosity was also directed against the Spaniards. In marked contrast to the welcome given by Cordero, at Sofais's village "not one Indian came out to receive us"; later, after the Spaniards had moved their camp nearer to Sofais's, "all kinds of Indians swarmed out to visit us . . . they were more discourteous . . . than the people of Cordero" (Loomis and Nasatir 1967:472-74).

When Amangual set out again, Cordero apparently remained behind for there is no further reference to him in the report. Beyond modern Abilene the Spaniards stopped near an old Comanche village. While there, an armed and mounted Comanche came into their camp. He identified himself as being from the ranchería of El Tuerto 'one eye', "one of those who were in our company with Cordero." The next day another Comanche arrived, saying that the first had stolen both his horse and his gun. Apparently those items were recovered, for the first was "left on foot." Moreover, he "turned out to be Yamparica and not one of El Tuerto's band, as he claimed yesterday " (Loomis and Nasator 1967:477-78).

The identity of El Tuerto and the divisional affiliation of the visitor are unclear and present some difficulties. In 1798 Pisinampe had been called Tuerto (Nava 1798), but Amangual made no mention that Pisinampe might be with him. Moreover, there is no other mention of a chief named Tuerto. The identification of the visitor as Yamparika is interesting, for the Spaniards were now near the location of Somiquaso's transplanted Yamparikas, suggesting that the visitor may have been from his ranchería.

In any case, however, from that point on Amangual referred to all the Comanches he met as Yamparikas, suggesting that, like Vial in 1785, as far

as the Spaniards in Béxar were concerned, all Comanches beyond an undefined line were Yamparikas.

Several days later, about fourteen leagues beyond modern Snyder, Texas,
two more Comanches, again identified as Yamparikas, including the son of
the *gefe grande*, the 'big chief' came to visit. Their own village camp was
nearby, and Amangual sent a squad of soldiers to get acquainted with the
chief. The next day Ysampampi and two others came to visit Amangual;
Ysampampi was last mentioned in 1790 on Peña's expedition against the
Pawnees. Loomis and Nasatir's translation indicated that two chiefs were
present, "the big chief and Sanbanbi" (1967:481). However, that is probably
a misreading of the orthography, reading "el gefe grande y sambanbi" 'the
big chief and Sambambi' for "el gefe grande ysambambi," 'the big chief
Ysampampi'.[6]

According to Amangual, when the Spaniards returned the visit,

> the big chief and the other chiefs of the tribe came out to meet [them].
> They were well dressed, but they wore very unusual clothes: long red
> coats with blue collars and cuffs, white buttons, yellow galloons [braid];
> one was dressed in ancient Spanish style: a short red coat, blue trousers,
> white stockings, English spurs, an ordinary cornered hat worn cocked, a
> cane with a silver handle shaped like a hyssop. Others wore red neckties;
> they wore sashes made out of otter skin, adorned with beads and shells.
> [Loomis and Nasatir 1967:482]

It is obvious from their attire that those were individuals highly regarded by
some Spaniards, but Amangual did not recognize the symbolism. The cane
marked the presence of a principal chief; since he was unknown to the Béxar
Spaniards, they must have been from New Mexico. However, his identity is
unknown. There is no record that Ysampampi received a cane of office. The
chief was not Quegüe, for Amangual met him later. Thus Somiquaso, the
Yamparika, and the only other chief known to have a cane, may indeed have
been present but unrecognized and unnamed by the Texans.

Amangual spent the next two days conferring with the chiefs. He said
that the king wished them to live at peace and that they had a right to expect
loyalty and honest dealings from the Spaniards. The chiefs in turn "displayed
a deep understanding and promised to be faithful in their friendship." They
also "set us right concerning the Indian settlements as far as the Red river"
and about the lay of the land upcoming, for "the land is very different from
what I had imagined, there is a great difference" (Loomis and Nasatir 1967:
483).

Near modern Post, Texas, they passed two rancherías, one of fifteen
tents, the other of twenty-seven, "under the jurisdiction of . . . Ysampampi."

When the horses of one company stampeded, they were found in a nearby Yamparika ranchería of twenty-nine tents. Near the modern town of Quitaque (*kwita ku?e* 'excrement hill'), Quegüe, the Kotsoteka principal chief— although Amangual called him a Yamparika—arrived bearing "a cane, and a medal with the picture of our king around his neck" (Loomis and Nasatir 1967:489)

After three days in conference the Spaniards set out again. Because their own guides were ill, Amangual tried to hire new ones, but none wished to go, saying the proposed route was too difficult. Frustrated, Amangual demanded that Quegüe "compel" some of the Indians to go with them. The chief, however, demurred, saying that he had no such authority. Ultimately, one of their own guides revived enough to continue, although he left his wife behind. With the exception of a war party of seven men and one woman from Quegüe's ranchería, armed with spears and four muskets, and another group of three Yamparikas (two women and a man), they encountered no more Comanches on their trip to Santa Fe.

Amangual's trip had been intended to impress the Comanches, but it was not a particular success. He did meet all the principal chiefs, Cordero, Quegüe, and probably Somiquaso, but he recorded little to suggest he recognized their status, and the meetings did little to bind the Comanches to the alliance. Twice he had to be put on the correct road, betraying the Béxar Spaniards' ignorance of the territory. Once, only Comanche forbearance allowed them to suffer Amangual's demands to be guided through impassable country.

When Amangual returned to Béxar that fall, the itinerary was determined by exploration rather than diplomacy. He went down the Rio Grande to San Elisario, southeast of El Paso, and cross-country to the Pecos River near the present Texas town of that name. On November 29, several days east of the river, he met a war party from Cordero's ranchería who provided guides. On December 4, on the banks of Almagre Creek, forty leagues west of the old San Sabá mission, and perhaps thirty leagues from where they had met the previous spring, he again visited Cordero's ranchería. He stayed there for two days, resting the horses; when twenty-one of them could not recover in time, they were exchanged for Comanche horses. On December 7 they continued, and except for small parties of Cordero's people, they met no other Comanches.

Texas and New Mexico, 1809-20

The period 1809-20 was filled with attacks on the Spanish political regime. The 1810 Hidalgo Revolt in Mexico was paralleled by a coup d'état in Texas, crushed in 1811. In 1812 Texas was invaded by the Magee-Gutierrez adventurers from Louisiana, who, although decisively defeated in 1813, initiated a period of unrest that lasted for the rest of the decade. There were also worries that French revolutionary agents would try to foment unrest (M. Salcedo, Bonavia, and Herrera 1810).

Comanche relations with the Spaniards started positively. In August 1809 Chimal Colorado ('red shield') and Pasagogo (meaning unknown) visited Santa Fe and told Governor Josef Manrrique the news of the summer: a Comanche woman held captive by the Kansas had escaped and returned to them, the Pananas—possibly Pawnees, although also possibly Wichitas—had abandoned their towns, and the Kiowas and Come Perros—it is not clear whether Arapahos or Plains Apaches were meant by the latter term—were making war on Texas. They also said that reports that Anglo-Americans from the Missouri River were trading with them were "absolutely false" (Manrrique 1809). But in mid-February 1810 Corporal Juan Lucero, visiting chief Quegüe at his village near the Colorado River, heard from Pasagogo that six Anglo-Americans were near the Salt Lakes. A few days later Lucero tracked the Anglo-Americans back to Pasagogo's and Quibiguaipe's (meaning unknown; the second part of the name is possibly *wa?ipʉ* 'woman') ranchería. There they found the so-called McLanahan party—Joseph McLanahan, Rueben Smith, James Pattison, and three slaves. They were arrested, tried in Santa Fe, and sent to Mexico (Manrrique 1810b, c).

Later that summer Manrrique proposed another joint Comanche-Spaniard expedition against the Apaches. After spending the winter in the Wichita Mountains considering the proposed campaign, chiefs Quegüe and Cordero, along with Calles (meaning unknown) and twenty-seven others—including fifteen warriors, six women, and six children—arrived in Santa Fe to discuss it (Manrrique 1810b). Although Manrrique called them "insatiably greedy," the Comanches agreed to participate (Manrrique 1810a). A meeting with Quegüe and Cordero at the Bosque Redondo in June finalized plans (Manrrique 1810c).

Setting out that summer, Manrrique found Pasagogo, Quibiguaipe, and El Higado ('liver') at Alamo Gordo Creek on the Pecos River. Quegüe and Cordero joined them at La Espia Hill on the lower Pecos, along with five other unnamed chiefs and a total of 258 warriors, 108 of whom came from Texas. The ensuing campaign encountered "ten or twelve Apache rancherías," killed four enemies, wounded others, and took eleven horses (Manrrique 1810a, 1810d; M. de Salcedo 1810).

While Chief Cordero was in New Mexico, other Comanches were raiding in Texas. Some of the raiding was acceptable to the Spaniards: Chimal Colorado came from New Mexico to raid the Lipans and the Tonkawas for horses. However, other Comanches continued to raid Spanish haciendas. In May there were raids in the San Saba valley; on July 13 there were raids near San Marcos and Laredo. Yamparikas and Quichalaricas—the latter an unknown ethnonym—raided Monclova. In August there were robberies at Rio Grande, Rio Frio, and Ranchos de la Nueces. Three hundred horses were taken from La Bahia (M. Salcedo 1810).

Texas Governor Manuel Antonio Cordero, knowing that Chief Cordero was in New Mexico, sent word of the raids through Manrrique, who passed it to the chief. In turn, the chief dispatched his son and forty warriors to Béxar to deal with the problem. In early August those warriors plus 150 Spanish soldiers "to cause respect" were sent "to investigate the transfer of stolen horses to Pisinampe and then to the Anglo-Americans" (Bonavia 1810a).

When Chief Cordero returned to Béxar in August, he accused both Chihuahua and Pisinampe of being directly involved in fomenting the raids. That was corroborated by a captive, said to be the son of Chief Manco—possibly the chief of the third class reported by Cabello in 1786—who was captured in the raid on San Marcos. He reported that Chihuahua's ranchería was "restless" and that the raiders were from Pisinampe's ranchería. He also said that they were stealing horses "to trade with the Americans, who were maintaining an establishment on the Colorado" (M. Salcedo 1810).

Other evidence implicated El Sordo (Arrambide 1810). In early 1810 he and Chihuahua had visited Governor Manuel de Salcedo in Béxar and with "expressions which marked a refined malice," told him that it was because "we wouldn't give them guns, nor permit trade with the Americans, that we were not friends" (M. Salcedo, Bonavia, and Herrera 1810). By the summer El Sordo had split from "his proper nation" and had drawn together a mixed band of Comanches, Wichitas, and Tawakonis who raided far into Texas. Still further evidence pointed to the Yamparikas: under interrogation, a prisoner said he came from the Yamparika ranchería of Yama Yupine (meaning unclear), now camped near the Taovayas, with seven other Yamparika rancherías (Arrambide 1812). It is not clear whether those Yamparikas were Somiquaso's people moved from the Colorado, or whether another group had moved south. Whatever their origin, in October they "declared war" against the Spaniards (Bonavia 1810b).

That same month Paruaquita (*parua kwita* 'bear excrement'), said to be the Yamparika principal chief in New Mexico, came to Texas to meet with

Chief Cordero (Cordero 1810). Governor Cordero said his name meant Oso Ballo 'red bear' and that he was known in New Mexico as Oso Amarillo 'yellow bear', but neither of the latter names appears in New Mexico records. Since Somiquaso, the last known Yamparika principal chief, had not been heard of directly since 1805, nor indirectly since 1808, there may have been a change in the Yamparika leadership, but there are no other indications.

Cordero and Paruaquita reported that Anglo-Americans were trading with the Tawakonis; further, the Anglo-Americans had contacted Cordero himself and had tried to persuade him to break his Spanish friendship. The Comanches said they had refused the offer and promised support for improved relations with the Texas Spaniards; to underscore their pro-Spanish posture, they stated that "if any Comanche [stole from] or [killed] any Spaniard, the same would be killed." Finally, to cement relations between the two chiefs, Cordero gave his daughter to Paruaquita.

In the summer of 1811 Paruaquita, with 152 warriors, 160 women, and 85 children, returned to Texas to "establish a solid peace like that in New Mexico" (Herrera 1811b). He recovered horses stolen both by Taovayas and by El Sordo's people. On August 7 Cordero and Yzazat came to Béxar, along with the "hopes of Oso Ballo . . . to treat with the Government for a Peace like that known in New Mexico" (Herrera 1811a).

In September, possibly at the instigation of Paruaquita, El Sordo himself visited Béxar to report that Taovayas and Tawakonis were planning extended raids. Despite being unarmed and with women and children, he was arrested and sent to jail in Coahuila. The breach of diplomatic etiquette sent shock waves throughout all of Comanchería. Paruaquita was reported gathering a party on the Colorado to demand his release. Others, however, notably Hoyoso (previously unmentioned), said they would support the Spaniards (N. Salcedo 1812a).

There were also rumors that the Mexican Hidalgo revolutionaries were trying to win over the Comanches, that the revolution was being fought to "liberate the Comanche from Europeans" (Aranda 1811), and it was feared that Paruaquita's gathering was part of a revolutionary conspiracy (M. Salcedo 1812). Although it is not known whether there was a connection between those rumors, on April 8, 1812, a powerful party of Comanche warriors, including Cordero, Paruaquita, Pisinampe, and Yzazat, appeared at Béxar to demand an explanation for El Sordo's arrest. Governor Salcedo met them with more than six hundred men, the largest Spanish force ever faced by the Comanches. Although the Comanches dispersed without a fight, the previous good relations could not be restored (Domínguez 1812).

Peace prevailed, but El Sordo remained in jail, and Comanche relations with Spanish Texas were never quite the same. Chief Cordero virtually disappeared from the Béxar records after 1812. In August, when the Magee-Gutierrez adventurers invaded from Louisiana, few if any Texas Comanches rallied to the support of the loyalists (Castañeda 1936, 5:155), and when the invaders were repulsed in 1813, many took refuge with Comanche groups, carrying out a war of attrition against the Spaniards (John 1984:366). After Governor Salcedo was assassinated by the Filibusterers, Béxar itself was virtually abandoned for the rest of the decade.

In the southwest, the Spaniards in El Paso complained,

> Under the pretext of pursuing Mescaleros and other Apaches on the frontiers of this province, different parties of Comanches have approached and entered the Presidios of San Elizario and del Norte where . . . they have been attended, helped with their maintenance, and given gifts to their respective captains. [N. Salcedo 1811]

But "outrages" continued, and the Comanche captains were urged to "respect the frontiers, to refrain from all manner of war," and "to refrain from passing the left bank of the Rio Grande" (N. Salcedo 1811).

Reciprocal raiding continued. In January 1814, after continued attacks, the ranches near Béxar were ordered abandoned (Arredondo 1814). By June the supply convoy to Béxar had been attacked repeatedly, and in August it was reported that the Comanches had almost completely destroyed "the livestock of the province" (Armiñan 1814). According to Governor Antonio María Martínez, since 1813, because of both Indian raids and the dissatisfaction of unpaid soldiers, Texas had "advanced at an amazing rate towards ruin and destruction" (McElhannon 1949:120). One notable Spanish success occurred in January 1818, when a raid on a Comanche camp in the Agua Negra recovered twelve horses and fourteen mules worth 386 pesos (Pérez 1818a).

New Mexico, 1812–21

In 1810, due in part to the influences of revolutionary France, Spain reconstituted a liberal Cortes, or parliament, to include for the first time representatives from the overseas colonies. In 1812 Pedro Bautista Pino of Santa Fe was selected as the delegate from New Mexico. In preparation for his representation, he wrote a long account of his home province, including a lengthy exposition on the "Gentile Nations which Surround the Province" (Carroll and Haggard 1942:246).[7] Although Pino was from an old New Mexican family, the extent of his contacts with Indians is unknown; however, he includes more identifiably Comanche words in his discussion than words from any other Indian language, suggesting that he had at least a consultant, if not a personal familiarity with the language. Nonetheless, it is unclear whether Pino's association with the relatively liberal Cortes, or with a liberal political philosophy, may have influenced his descriptions of the Indian polities.

In his descriptions, Pino began by noting, "It is impossible to enumerate the different tribes . . . that surround the territory of New Mexico" (Carroll and Haggard 1942:128)—foreshadowing Hoebel's comment, "It is not possible to state precisely how many Comanche bands there were" (1940:12)— and, again foreshadowing Hoebel, he listed those tribes, which he gave in order of "discovery." Beginning with the Pueblos, whom he listed by language—Piros, Queres, Tiguas, and so forth—he passed to the Gileños, Llaneros, and Lipanes, all of which "are Apaches but have different provincial names." He then listed fifteen ethnonyms, the

> *llamparicas*, which means in their language, the "grass eaters." The *ancavistis*, which means the "red people." The *cuchunticas*, the "eaters of buffalo." The *jupis*, "men of the woods." The *muares*, "big chiefs." The *chaguaguanos*—I don't know what it means. The *pasuchis* : *cahiguas* : *aas-orejones* : *cuampes* : *panana* : *canseres* : *guasachis*. [Carroll and Haggard 1942:128][8]

Pino finished off his survey with the "Yutas; the Navajoes; and the honorable Comanches" (Carroll and Haggard 1942:128).

It is obvious that the reason Pino had difficulty enumerating the peoples around New Mexico was that his list embodied several of the problems of differentiating tribal groups. For the Pueblos, he confused language and political organization. He also confused levels of integration: the first, third, and fourth names on his list are clearly the Comanche ethonyms Yamparika, Kotsoteka, and Jupe; the second name is the Comanche word *ekapitsʉ* 'red person', otherwise unrecorded as an ethnonym. However, he separated those groups from "the honorable Comanches."

After comments on Comanche clothing and religion, Pino commented on Comanche political culture:

> Their government is republican in form and is unified, because of necessity rather than through law. If they were not united, they would be attacked by all neighboring tribes because they never have sought to make peace or to enter into an alliance with them. Authority is vested in subordinate chiefs, while one among them, because of his intelligence and courage, is elected general chief; he administers a military form of government. [Carroll and Haggard 1942:130]

Although the connotations of Pino's description of Comanche political organization as arising from "necessity rather than through law" and as a "military form of government" are unclear, they suggest voluntary association as the basis of political organization—a theory of social contract rather than a Hobbesian coercive imposition of force or a primordial tribal identity.

Pino continued with a discussion of the relations between the Comanches and New Mexico:

> At the time peace was made with the Comanche, a system of giving presents to the tribes was established. We would never have believed the benefit that has accrued to the province from this practice if we had not seen it. A continued state of peace and friendship of the greatest importance in checking other tribes has been the result of the small number of presents given them. . . . To these presents, which may seem but trifles to use, we owe the preservation of our province and perhaps our lives. . . . Every day these Indians give proof of their loyalty to Spain. When they observe the least movement on the part of the United States, they punctually report the matter to the province. As soon as they heard of the revolution in the viceroyalty of Mexico in 1810, they presented themselves to Commandant Salcedo and offered to destroy Hidalgo and all who opposed the general chief [*capitan grande*]. [Carroll and Haggard 1942:135-36]

Although perhaps an exaggeration, it sketches in outline form the relationship between Comanches and New Mexico.

Finally, in a footnote, Pino noted,

> About twenty years ago . . . one these chiefs, named Maya, placed his son in school in the capital in the care of Lieutenant Vicente Troncoso. When Maya died, his tribe recalled the youth to teach him the art of war. He was sent to them, knowing how to read. Today he holds his father's position, holding the Spaniards in highest regard. [Carroll and Haggard 1942:130]

The chief Maya of whom Pino spoke was obviously Ecueracapa, also called Malla, and the incident seems to parallel Anza's report that Ecueracapa had sent his son Tahuchimpia to Santa Fe to be educated. However, any relationship between Ecueracapa and the chiefs of the early 1800s is unknown.

During the decade beginning in 1810 the New Mexican Comanches were often held up to their Texan relatives as exemplars of peaceful relations. On at least one occasion a peace offer to the Texan Comanches was made through their New Mexican cousins. In December 1814 a group of Comanches, including Capitancillo Vicente (previously unmentioned), two sons of Ysampampi—named Ysacoroco (*isa korohkO* 'wolf scarf') and Tanqueuji (possibly *tahkweyu?i* 'he takes off his shoes', but probably not the Tanque-yaran mentioned in 1788)—six warriors, eight women, and four children, came to Santa Fe with a plan to make peace with the eastern Kotsotekas "who make war in Coahuila." In a possible reference to El Sordo, the messengers said that the easterners made war on Coahuila because of the prisoners held there. Governor Ysidro Rey sent Pedro Pino—it is not clear if he was Pedro Bautista Pino, the delegate, or one of his cousins—to meet with them at the Cañon de Resgate—Yellow House Canyon, near Lubbock, Texas. A second meeting was arranged, but it is not known whether it took place (Rey 1814).

Although nothing came of that effort, Comanches continued contacts and visits with Santa Fe. In 1814 Vicente sent word to Santa Fe that twenty of his horses had been stolen by Spaniards. Two New Mexicans were arrested, tried, and found guilty of the crime (J. M. González and J. D. Cordero 1814). In 1815, 242 Comanches, including the Yamparika chief Soguare (meaning unknown; he was probably not Somiquaso) and the Kotsoteka chiefs Ysapampa, Quegüe, Calles, Chimal Colorado, and Canabuci (*kana* 'slender', *putsi* emphatic, 'skinny') came to visit and receive gifts. During the same time trading expeditions went to Comanchería and returned "without news" (Maynez 1815). In 1816 Calles "informed the governor of bad conduct of the Orientales seduced by the Spanish rebels," referring to the eastern Comanches trading with the refugees from the Magee-Gutierrez filibusters (Bonavia 1816).

In the late summer of 1818 the interpreter Juan Lucero spent a month traveling through Comanchería, finding all quiet. Soguare and more than a thousand other Comanches returned with him to trade (Cónde 1818; Thomas 1929a:156). They also brought word that Quegüe, the principal chief of the Kotsotekas in New Mexico, had died "on the road." Governor Facundo Melgares sent word to the chiefs that as soon as they had chosen a successor they should let him know (Thomas 1929a:156), but there is no direct report of a successor.

The New Mexico Spaniards were so concerned about maintaining good relations with the Comanches that in 1819, when a punitive expedition was sent against the warring Indians in Texas, they forewarned the Comanche leaders (Cónde 1819; Simmons 1967:35–36).

First Anglo-American Contacts

The close proximity of the new United States offered the Comanches a new political-economic resource in the form of markets for horses and sources for guns. However, those markets were also a threat to continued Comanche-Spaniard relations. The Spaniards perceived several aspects to that threat: that the Americans would try to export their revolution, that the Americans would try to annex Texas, or that the Americans would try to seduce the Indians away from their Spanish allegiance. The immediate problem was that the Anglo-American horse traders did not care where their Indian suppliers got their horses, thus encouraging the theft of horses from Texas and the provinces farther south.

The threats came together in the persons of James Wilkinson and his protégé, Philip Nolan. Wilkinson was an accomplished schemer. During the Revolutionary War he was said to have been involved in the so-called Conway Cabal, an attempt to replace George Washington as commander in chief of the Revolutionary Army. He had resigned from the army in 1787 and moved to New Orleans as a land speculator and tobacco trader. He later reentered the army, and on the death of George Rogers Clark he became the senior officer in the army. In 1805 he was appointed governor of Louisiana Territory. Even before that appointment he was, it has been alleged, Aaron Burr's military accomplice. It has also been alleged that since his days in New Orleans he had been in the pay of the Spaniards (DeConde 1976:51). Nolan had a long acquaintance with Texas. By 1791, if not earlier, he was in Texas gathering horses for the New Orleans market (Loomis and Nasatir 1967:205; Weems 1969:53). In the next decade he made several extended trips, trading particularly with Taovayas and Comanches. The business was profitable: in 1796 alone he brought 250 horses to Natchez (Loomis and Nasatir 1967:207).

There were also larger goals at stake. President Thomas Jefferson had long been convinced that the undefined limits of Louisiana extended to the Rio Grande and had launched an extensive effort to establish the claim. Besides mainstream diplomatic efforts, he also supported attempts to undermine the Spanish-Indian alliances. Apparently Wilkinson had interested Jefferson in Nolan and in 1799 had provided a letter of introduction for Nolan saying that he could provide "details of the country, the soil, clime, populations, improvements, and productions" (Loomis and Nasatir 1967:214). It is not clear, however, whether Nolan and Jefferson ever actually met (D. L. Flores 1985:103 n. 19). That same year the governor of Spanish Louisiana, Manuel Gayoso de Lemos, wrote to the viceroy in Mexico City that "a group of Americans planned to enter Texas to win support of the Indians and to brew a revolution" and that he would "keep an eye on Nolan" (Weems 1969:95). Gayoso also thought that Nolan had an explicit "commission from General Wilkinson to make an expert reconnaissance of the country" (Loomis and Nasatir 1967:213).

In October 1800, although he knew an order had been issued for his arrest, Nolan and about eighteen others entered Texas without passports (Loomis and Nasatir 1967:220). Beyond the Red River they built a corral and spent several months capturing wild horses and trading with a Comanche band led by Nicoroco—possibly Huanacoruco. In March 1801 a troop of soldiers from Nacogdoches caught up with the Anglo-Americans. They were surrounded, and in the fight that followed Nolan and many others were killed, and the rest were captured and sent to Mexican prisons (Yoakum 1855, 1: 405).

To be sure, there were other Anglo-American traders in Comanchería; Spanish and Anglo-American records indicate that there were other travelers and traders on the fringes of Comanchería, but whether they contacted Comanches is unknown.

Official Anglo-American interest in the Comanches increased in 1805. Early that year General Wilkinson wrote to Secretary of War Henry Dearborn, "The Ietans [Comanches] . . . constitute the most powerful nation of savages on this continent, and have it in their power to facilitate or impede our march to New Mexico, should such movement ever become necessary" (D. Jackson 1966:229). His use of the Wichita ethnonym suggests that his information came from French traders and contrabandistas rather than from personal experience; in a December letter to Jefferson he referred to the "Cammanches or Ya-i-tans" (Wilkinson 1805). His goal was simple: "to extend the name and influence of the United States." But that, he continued, would "require considerable disbursements" (D. Jackson 1966:229). In the fall Wilkinson again wrote Dearborn, "I think no time should be lost in preparing for a convention of the Ietans, Panis, Osages, at the Arkansas . . . to make acquaintance between these nations and to establish peace among them . . . and if possible to attach and bind the whole to our interests" (D. Jackson 1966:251).

The Anglo-American government had already acted upon those premises. In December 1804 Dearborn had asked Dr. John Sibley, surgeon at Fort Claiborne, Louisiana, to "act occasionally as Indian agent in the vicinity of Natchitoches" (Dearborn 1804). Specifically, Sibley was requested to hold "such conferences with the chiefs and others of the several Indian Tribes in the vicinity of Natchitoches as you shall deem necessary for securing the friendship of the Indians generally in that quarter" and to tell them that

> if they expect to be treated as the Children of their Great Father, the President of the United States, they must break off all connection with any other power and rely on their father for such friendly aid as he extends to all his other red children within our extensive territories. [Dearborn 1805]

Moreover, he was ordered to

> use all the means in your power to conciliate the esteem and friendship
> of the Indians generally, and more especially of such nations as might, in
> case of a rupture with Spain, be either useful or mischievous to us,
> according to the side they might be induced to take. [Dearborn 1805]

Sibley had an initial budget of $3,000 "to be distributed in the most useful
manner" and could call upon the traders for further credit if necessary (C.
Carter 1934–62, 20:352–53). The Spaniards soon became aware of Sibley's
efforts. In August 1805 Comandante General Nemesio Salcedo wrote to warn
Governor Cordero, "Dr. Sibley . . . has been commissioned to attempt to seduce all the nations of the borderlands from their obedience to us" (N.
Salcedo 1805).

Zebulon Pike's 1806 expedition was ostensibly intended to explore the
southern boundaries of Louisiana and the Arkansas and Red rivers; Pike was
also under instructions from General Wilkinson to attempt to meet Comanches and if possible to win their friendship. Meanwhile, the Spaniards, in an
attempt to intercept Pike, or at least head off his influence, sent Lieutenant
Facundo Melgares down the Arkansas. Pike was later to report that Melgares
had counseled with Ietans before moving to the Pawnees; unfortunately, it is
not known if Melgares kept a journal of his trip. Pike himself was intercepted
and sent to Mexico City. After an informal detention he was released and
made a leisurely return to Louisiana. Despite his specific commission to meet
with Comanches, Pike admitted to meeting only a single "Camanche," at the
Tonkawa village some thirty miles east of the Colorado River in Texas, on
his return. He gave him a silk handkerchief and a "Commission to the commandant at Natchitoches" (Coues 1895:706). Back in Natchitoches, he gave
John Sibley some second- and third-hand accounts about the Comanches.
Those, together with other scraps of information about the "Hietans, or
Comanches . . . likewise called by both names," were transmitted to
Washington, where they were published in the congressional journal (Sibley
1805).

Among other comments of greater or lesser reliability, Sibley noted
several aspects of political and economic significance:

> [They] have neither towns nor villages; divided into so many different
> hordes or tribes, that they have scarcely any knowledge of one another.
> No estimate of their number can be made. They never remain in the
> same place more than a few days, but follow the buffalo, the flesh of
> which is their principal food. Some of them occasionally purchase of the
> Panis [Wichitas], corn, beans, and pumpkins. . . . Their horses they never
> turn loose to graze, but always keep them tied with a long cabras or

halter; and every two or three days they are obliged to move on account of all the grass near them being eaten up, they have such numbers of horses. They are good horsemen and have good horses, most of which are bred by themselves. . . . They hunt down the buffalo on horseback, and kill them either with the bow or a sharp stick like a spear which they carry in their hands. They are generally at war with the Spaniards of Santa Fe and St. Antoine [*sic*]; but have always been friendly and civil to any French or Americans who have been amongst them. [Sibley 1805]

Sibley's description of Comanche political organization as "so many hordes or tribes" is apt, although "horde" has probably as many negative connotations as does "tribe." Sibley offered both the requirements of buffalo hunting and of horse herding as reasons why they "never remain in the same place more than a few days"; ironically, as a secondhand report, Sibley's one-sentence description of Comanche buffalo hunting provides the greatest contemporary detail of that activity yet given, but his comment that they bred most of their horses is probably an exaggeration. Finally, his comment that Comanches were "generally at war with the Spaniards," while friendly with the French—that is, Louisianans—and Americans—with whom little interaction had been yet documented—is so out of line with contemporary events in Santa Fe and Béxar that it can best be interpreted as both wishful thinking on Sibley's part and as attempts by some Comanches to reopen contacts with the east.

It was not until 1807 that Sibley actually met any Comanches. In the fall of 1806 a small party consisting of six or seven men went up the Red River to trade with the "Panis," that is, Wichitas.[9] They included John S. Lewis, William Alexander, Jeremiah Downs, John Litton, Berimon Watkins, Joseph Lucas, and a Mr. Lusk, local Natchitoches residents with a variety of connections with the Indians; Lucas was of mixed Caddo-French ancestry and was apparently fluent in the sign language (D. L. Flores 1985:23, 106 n. 42). In June 1807 Lewis, Downs, and Watkins returned to Natchitoches (Sibley 1807b:40); Lewis reported that during the winter he had spent spent several days in a Comanche village

about 40 miles from the [Wichita] towns, by the invitation of a Hietan chief who came to the [Wichitas]. He believes the camp contained not less than two thousand persons[10] and that they had not less than five thousand horses and mules. [Sibley 1807b:41]

They had some "remarkable fine animals," but Lewis had only "a few trifling articles of goods with him," so there was no commerce (Sibley 1807b:41). Despite that lack of trade, the "great chief" of the village, unfortunately unnamed, said that he intended to come to Natchitoches in a short time;

moreover, he had recently "been to S^t. Antonio and received some presents from Gov. Cordero" (Sibley 1807b:42). D. L. Flores (1985:127 n. 16) suggested that one of the chiefs was "Visinampa," i.e. Pisinampe, but he gave no citation; moreover, Pisinampe had not visited Béxar for several years.

In early August the "great Caddo chief" arrived in Natchitoches and reported that some three hundred Indians—Caddos, Wichitas, and "Hietans," that is, Comanches—were on their way to visit him (Sibley 1807a:48). The first to arrive were four "great chiefs" and eighty Comanches; they were only a detachment: "some thousand of the Hietans came as far as the Trinity River where they would remain until those that came here returned" (Sibley 1807a). On their arrival Sibley gave them "provisions and cooking utensils, some tobacco." To the chiefs he gave

> 4 hats, 4 plumes, 4 calico shirts, 4 parcels of paint, 4 braggys (britch clouts) [sic], 4 looking glasses, 4 knives, 4 black silk handkerchiefs, 4 combs.

Sibley then invited the Comanche chiefs to his house. There he

> entertained them, gave them tobacco, smoked with them, etc. Offered them spirits, which they refused but were fond of a sweet drink made from honey or molasses and water. Sent for a Taylor [sic] and had them measured for a scarlet coat faced with black velvet and trimmed with white buttons. [Sibley 1807b:49]

A week later, after other delegations arrived and had been received, he again "received at my house the whole of the Hietan party" and gave them presents:

> for the 4 Chiefs & their wives 4 Scarlet coats, faced with Black Velvet & trim'd with Large Plated Buttons, 4 Scarlet Blankets, 4 Bells, 4^{lb} Vermilion, 4 white III^{pt} Blankets,[11] 4 Tommehawk Pipes, 4^{lb} Beeds, 4 Tin Cups, 4 Pieces Binding, 4 Pair Scissors, 2^{oz} Thread, 4 doz. Needles, 2 doz. Knives, 8 fire Steels, 3 doz. flints, 4^{lb} Powder, 8^{lb} Lead, 2 Guns, 1 Pair Bullet Molds, one United States flag. And for the Party divided amongst them by the interpreter, 40 stroud and white Blankets, 52 flaps and Braggys, 52 Knives, 40 Tin Cups, 8^{lb} beeds, 4 Pieces Binding, 20 Hatchets, 20 fire steels, 4 doz. flints, 14 Horse Bells, 52 [Handkerchiefs], 1^{lb} thread, 4 doz Needles, 14 Pair Scissors. [Sibley 1807b:54]

Then, as the Comanches were leaving,

> the Principal Chief produced a Spanish Flag and lay'd it down at my feet, and desired the Interpreter to tell me, "that he received the flag from

Govr Cordero of St Antonio, & wish'd now to exchange it for a flag of the United States, that it might be known in their nation.

I told him we were not at War with Spain and had no disposition to offend them, Otherwise I should have Anticipated his request by Presenting him with a United States flag before, but it might offend the Spanish Gov^t and be in the end disadvantageous to them; he said "they were very desirous of having our flag and it was the Same to them whether Spain was pleas'd or displeas'd and If I would give him One it should wave through all the Hietan Nation and they would all die in defence of it before they would part with it, I had a flag brought . . . I first rap'd it round Myself, gave it to him he did the same, & embraced it with Great earnestness in the presence of all his people. [Sibley 1807b:55]

The identity of the "Principal Chief" is unknown. That he had a Spanish flag suggests that he was at least a captain, and possibly a principal chief, but there is no record of a Comanche receiving a flag from Texas since the 1780s; indeed, apparently the most recent presentation of flags to Indians in northern New Spain was that of New Mexican governor Alencaster to the Flecha Rayadas (Cheyennes) and Cuampes the previous May.

The next day, Aug. 18, 1807, Sibley met the Indians in formal session, with "calumet and council fire lighted." He began his speech by noting that "by Arrangements between France and Spain two Nations beyond the great Water," the United States now owned Louisiana, and the president wanted to continue the friendship of the Indians as long as they continued friendship. Indeed, the people of the United States were now natives:

It is now so long since our Ancestors came from beyond the great Water that we have no remembrance of it. We ourselves are Natives of the Same land that you are, in other words, white Indians, we therefore should feel and live together like brothers and good neighbors, we Should do no harm to one another but all the good in our power.

However, since the western boundary of Louisiana was not yet fixed, he continued, "whether the country you inhabit falls in our Boundaries . . . it will always be Our wish to be at peace and friendship with you. . . . The World is wide enough for all." He finished by inviting them to

rest yourselves a few days, and accept of our hospitality in such as we have to offer you, and a few presents which I shall present you in the name of your great Father the President of the United States . . . and as you have now found the way here you will be enclin'd to come again and that we shall find we can trade together for our mutual advantage.

You will always find here such articles of merchandise as you may want, for which you can exchange your horses, mules, robes and silver ore. I should be glad that some of you would go some days journey farther into our country, that you may know more of it and be better acquainted with our people, and your father the President would be glad to see you. [Sibley 1807b:57–59]

The "silver ore" reference is interesting, and it is not clear where Sibley heard that the Indians might have silver; back in 1784 Louisiana trader Juan Baptista Bousquet had said he had seen a piece of "silver ore" in the Wichita villages some years before (Cabello 1784b), and rumor of it may have continued in the Lousiana border communities ever since, but whatever its source, the possible presence of silver mines in the Indian country would be a continuing undercurrent in and around Comanchería for many years to come.

There were short responses by the Indians. Prophetically, the Tawakoni chief said, "time will determine whether this days talk will prove true." One of the Comanches—apparently not the "great Chief"—said their best speaker was absent; he had gone out to look after the horses. But, he continued,

From the Moment we heard of the Americans being Arriv'd at this place we were determined to come & see them our New Neighbours; and we are all now all of us highly pleas'd that we have Come. On our way, we fell in with Some of Our friends who came Along to Accompany us, we are in want of merchandize and shall always be glad to trade with you on friendly terms and now we have found the way & see that you have everything we want we shall probably visit you again. [Sibley 1807b:61–62]

Finally, Sibley raised the possibility of some of the Indians visiting the United States; the Tawakoni and Comanche chiefs said they were interested, but their people were waiting for them on the Trinity and they must return.

The following October seventy-four more Comanches, including again four unnamed chiefs, visited Sibley. He gave the chiefs "4 Scarlet Blankets, 4 shirts, 4 hats & plumes, 4 braggys, 8 oz vermilion, 4 combs, 4 looking glasses." Several days later he entertained the "whole Hietan party" at his own house. There he

presented the Chief with a Medal, on which was engrav'd a representation of the Eagle Encircled in the words "United States of America." I met them with it Suspended with a Broad Ribbon to my own Neck, took it off myselfe hung it on the Chief—it had a good effect.

Again he made presents:

for the four chiefs 4 stroud blankets, 4 White Ditto. 4 guns, 8^{lb} powder. 16^{lb} Balls, 16 flints, 4 fire Steels, 8 knives, 4 Tomehawk Pipes, 1^{lb} Vermilion,. 4 braggys. 4 Pieces of Binding, 4 bells, 4 Tin Cups, and for seven great Men of the Nation, 7 Blankets, 14 knives, 2^{lb} Vermilion, 7 Handkerchiefs, 7 tin cups, 7 fire Steels, 7 braggys, 7 Pieces binding, & 7 combs, and the Remaining Articles divided Amongst the remainder of the party—12 Knives, 10 Hatchets, 10 Pair scissors, 1^{lb} Thread, 100 Needles, 2^{lb} Vermilion, 2 $1/4^{lb}$ Beeds, 12 Blankets, 17 Yards Calico, 10 Flaps, 10 Handkfs, 2 pieces & 6 Y^{ds} Binding—10 looking glasses, 10 combs, & 2 Tin Cups. [Sibley 1807b:70-71]

The council that followed was held in Spanish; one of the Comanches could speak it "tolerable well . . . he learn'd it in Mexico when he was young where he liv'd several years." The Comanche chief—the same one with whom John Lewis had spent time the previous winter, but again unnamed— said that they "did not bring anything to trade for they did not know what we wanted." Rather, they "came Just to see & Satisfy themselves if it was true what they had heard of us." They would welcome traders, as "Horses & Mules were to them like grass they had them in such plenty, they had likewise dress'd Buffalo Skins and knew where there was Silver Ore plenty" (Sibley 1807b:74-75).

Sibley concluded his 1807 report with another extended discussion of the Comanches; since he had no other contacts with Comanches, most of those comments must be seen as elaborations on his 1805 comments:

when they hear of a flock of buffalo, [they] strike their tents and travel after them and to discover them always have reconoitering parties out. They use fire Arms only in War. They kill the buffalo with the Spear or the Bow & Arrow & mostly the latter. they are dexterous Horse men, they ride in amongst a flock of buffalo with their bow in their hand, single out the one they intend to kill, ride along side of him and drive the arrow through him, the animal bellows, runs a short distance and falls. They catch and drink the blood as it flows, tear the liver and eat it raw while it is yet warm. and it is said they eat the gall with it by way of condiment which they esteem a Luxury. . . . It is impossible to form an estimation of how numerous the whole nation is that can have any pre- tention to accuracy they are divided into many hordes or bands con- taining from two to four or five thousand souls, they may not exceed thirty or forty thousand souls and they may exceed half a million.

However, he did make several comments which were probably based on his recent experiences with them:

They seem subservient to the commands of their chiefs as though they [the chiefs] had a right to expect obedience. . . . The trade of this nation is Horses, Mules, dress'd buffalo skins and Silver ore. . . . They seem indifferent about those common articles of finery that other Indians are fond of, blue and red stroud, vermilion, blankets, blue beeds and knives are almost the only articles they seem anxious to obtain. Jewelry, calico, hand-kfs, binding, ribbands, they care nothing about. [Sibley 1807b:76–82]

The next year Sibley licensed Anthony Glass to trade for Comanche horses at the Wichita villages (D. L. Flores 1985). Glass spent most of his time with the Wichitas. He had some success trading with them, noting that "English goods are brought to this nation by a tribe of trading Indians who live on the waters of the Missouri called *Owaheys* who bring their goods from English traders from the Lakes of Canada" (D. L. Flores 1985:56); Owahey may be *awahe:i,* the pan-Caddoan term for the Skiri Pawnees, and the claim of a trade to the north is reminiscent of Vial's comment twenty years earlier. However, not only is it unclear how the Pawnees would have obtained English goods, but given the continuing hostility between Comanches and Pawnees, it is unclear why there would be trade.

During Glass's stay, a party of his men and Wichitas, "with a chief and the king's son," set off for the "Lower Hietans"; they returned two weeks later without success, and like Gaignard thirty years earlier, "suspected that the Indian guide they had with them had refused to guide them to the Hietan camp" (D. L. Flores 1985:52, 61).

During the fall and early winter of 1808 Glass traveled southwestward into Texas, possibly as far as the Colorado River, below the Concho (D. L. Flores 1985:62)—although John (1982:436) suggested that they went up the Colorado as far as Big Spring. They met and traded with a number of Comanche villages; at one point they were traveling with a party of "ten chiefs and near six hundred men with a large proportion of women and children" (D. L. Flores 1985:71). Included in the party were "some of those . . . who visited [Natchitoches] last year, and who are highly pleased with the treatment they received from Doctor Sibley"; the "Chief of the Lower Hietans who visited [Natchitoches] last fall . . . joined us and says that the Spaniards have treated him very civil since he made that visit. He is a great friend of the Americans" (D. L. Flores 1985:73). A number of visitors passed through the village; two Lipan Apaches arrived with word that the Spanish governor had called for the heads of the traders, but they were sent packing; a Comanche from "one of the upper Hordes" came through saying some of his people had recently stolen horses and mules from around Béxar. Some other Comanches stole some of Glass's horses, but they were quickly recovered "by means of the exertions of the Chiefs and I believe they did all in their power to prevent their people from stealing" (D. L. Flores 1985:79).

They also sought out a rumored "mass of metal" they had heard about from the Indians (D. L. Flores 1985:61). No doubt their search was also inspired by the reports of silver ore given to Sibley the previous year. The metal turned out be "the colour of iron but no rust upon it . . . obedient to the magnet, very maleable would take a brilliant polish and give fire with a flint" (D. L. Flores 1985:69). It was one of several such pieces known by the Indians to be nearby.

For a number of reasons, Glass's journal is an important historical document. It is the earliest known account in English of a trading expedition among the Comanches, although unfortunately Glass gave no explicit discussion of the mechanisms of trade, prices, or deals. Again unfortunately, but typical of later Anglo-American observers, he did not identify most of the Indian individuals with whom he dealt; he named only a few of the Wichitas and none of the Comanches. Nevertheless, Glass was the earliest writer to make a geopolitical distinction between upper and lower Comanches. He probably borrowed the term "horde" from Sibley.

Perhaps the most important aspect of the journal is the evidence that it provides for a wider political-economic awareness and calculation by at least some Comanches. Only the previous spring Francisco Amangual had crossed some of the same country in an effort to impress Comanches with the Spaniards' authority; at least some of the Comanches met by Glass must have met Amangual. Moreover, while no doubt many of them had been to San Antonio, at least some of them had also been to visit Sibley the year before. Therefore, while Glass later reported that the Wichitas and Comanches "appear[ed] particularly attached to the government and people of the United States" (Garrett 1942–46, 47:323), that attachment must be considered in political, that is self-interested, terms.

In the following years other Anglo-American traders established contact with Comanches who acted both as suppliers of horses and as way stations to Santa Fe. It was the latter aspect that particularly worried the officials in New Mexico. In mid-February 1810 the McLanahan party was arrested at Pasagogo's ranchería (Manrrique 1810b, c).

The following November a party of ciboleros—buffalo hunters—from Taos heard from a combined Comanche-Kiowa ranchería on the Huerfano River that five "strangers"—Anglo-Americans—were with the Cuampes at the headwaters of the Arkansas. A search party was told that indeed there were five beaver hunters, but two other parties were unable to discover any more about them (Manrrique 1810a).

In the fall of 1815 Auguste Pierre Chouteau and Julius De Mun, both experienced traders with the Osages and other prairie tribes, obtained licenses from William Clark in St. Louis to trade with Arapahos on the upper Arkansas. The following February, leaving Chouteau and the rest of the party in the mountains, De Mun returned to St. Louis, where he obtained another license, this time to trade with Arapahos and Comanches. But there is no clear record that he in fact traded with either of those tribes for anything but enough horses "to bring in his furs" (De Mun 1817); the implication is that De Mun and Chouteau were themselves trappers, rather than traders.

The following summer Chouteau took the season's product, a reported 4,400 pounds of beaver fur, to market in St Louis. On the way, he was beseiged on an island in the Arkansas River, allegedly by Pawnees; some reports were more specific than others in either number—"150 Pawnees" (*Niles' Weekly Register*, Oct. 19, 1816), "150–200 Panis" (Lecompte 1969) —or tribe of attackers—"Republican [Chawi] Pawnees, Ottos [Otoes], and Rees [Arikaras]" (T. M. Marshall 1928:323). One thing is certain: their island fort was henceforth called Chouteau's Island.

A large but otherwise unidentified group of Anglo-Americans spent the winter of 1816–17 trading with the "Northern bands of Comanches"; on their return they were robbed by Omahas and Taweashes (Jamison 1817b). In the spring of 1817 the Chouteau-De Mun party were arrested by New Mexican Spaniards and all their goods were confiscated (De Mun 1817). In May 1818 rumors reached officials in Béxar that two Anglo-Americans were in the "center of the Comanche nation" selling "fusils, powder, shot, and buying horses and mules stolen from the province," but nothing further is known of their identity (Pérez 1818b).

Meanwhile, other Comanches reestablished diplomatic contacts with Anglo-American officials. In the summer of 1816 a Comanche called "Cordaro," said to be the "chief of the lower tribe of Comanches"—clearly Cordero—visited John Jamison, newly appointed agent at Natchitoches. He expressed a "great desire to cultivate the friendship of the American people" (Jamison 1817a). The next summer Chihuahua, "chief of the middle tribe of Comanches," visited with a small party. He was described as "a man of considerable urbanity of manner . . . amicable in temper . . . a determined warrior." Among other things, Chihuahua wanted to establish general principles to govern the trade between Comanches and Anglo-Americans; he promised to enforce such rules as far as possible.

According to Jamison, Chihuahua also reported that smallpox had made "dreadful havoc" with the Comanches during the previous winter, killing about four thousand people, including four chiefs and principal men. When told of the kine pox inoculation, Chihuahua said he would welcome its benefits, and Jamison suggested that the resident doctor be allowed to "perform these humanitarian services," but it is not known whether any Comanches were vaccinated at that time, and there are no other direct reports of the epidemic. As Chihuahua left, Jamison gave him some "useful articles of husbandry," clothing, and a full uniform (Jamison 1817a).

As had Anthony Glass a decade earlier, Jamison distinguished between "lower" and other Comanches, in this case "middle." That geopolitical differentiation was continued in a report by David G. Burnet, former mercenary, lawyer, and briefly a store manager in Natchitoches. About 1817, on his doctor's orders, Burnet had gone out to "live like an Indian" (Clarke 1969: 11). According to his memoirs, he wandered across northern Texas to the Colorado River, where, nearly delirious, he was found by a group of Comanches, with whom he lived for an unspecified time. By August 1818 he was in Nacogdoches, where he answered a questionnaire provided by Agent Jamison, whom he must have known in Natchitoches. Later, at Jamison's urging, he began a "more detailed account" as a series of letters describing the Comanches "or Ietans as they are sometimes called." Those letters were reprinted several times during his lifetime and later (Burnet 1824, 1840; Wallace 1954).[12]

According to Burnet, the "tribe known among us by the term Comanchees" was divided into three great "parties," the "Comanchees, Yamparacks and Tenaways." Ordering his discussion geographically, south to north, first were the "Comanchees, the lower or southern party." They were centered on the lower Colorado "or Red River of Texas," and numbered about fifteen hundred warriors. They were, according to Burnet, the principal aggressors against Texas and the provinces across the Rio Grande.

Next were the Yamparacks, numbering about eight hundred warriors. They were located on the headwaters of the Colorado, although they sometimes "extend[ed] their migrations to the tributary streams of the Rio del Norte." According to Burnet,

> [They] frequently intermingle with, and are found among the Comanchees and are, in no respect dissimilar to them, in manners, customs or appearance, but are virtually the same people, speak the same language, and are characterized by the same peculiarities. There is one exception, however, to the general resemblance. The Yamparacks are more honest and punctilious in their dealings, and much less addicted to thievery. [Wallace 1954:122-23]

Farthest away were the Tenaways, who lived in the "mountainous district that separates the waters of the Rio del Norte [Rio Grande] and the rivers of Texas, and they sometimes extend[ed] their perambulations to the head waters of the Red River of Natchitoches." Because of their distant location, they had little contact with Americans, although they did trade horses stolen in Texas to the Spaniards of Santa Fe.

Burnet's discussion of the Comanche groups parallels the general practice of the Texas Spaniards: those close to Béxar were called Comanches, those farther away were Yamparikas. His placement of the latter on the upper Colorado accords with Somiquaso's reported location of a decade earlier, and his inclusion of the "tributary streams of the Rio del Norte" can be read to mean the streams of the far upper Rio Grande in Colorado. Burnet's discussion of the Teneway—later usually spelled Tenewa—is the first documentary mention of that ethnonym, said to mean 'down stream'. But Burnet's geography is confused; his location of the Tenewa in a "mountainous district that separates the waters of the [Rio Grande] and the rivers of Texas" puts them either in the area of Raton Pass on the upper Canadian River—certainly mountainous—or on the Staked Plains—decidedly flat—both between the Rio Grande and the rivers of Texas. Virtually every later observer located them to the northeast, along the Red River, whence they carried on a horse trade to the east, not to the west as implied by Burnet. One solution to the problem is that Burnet simply did not know the Comanches' political geography.

Burnet devoted several paragraphs to political and legal organization. According to Burnet, those "three great national parties" were divided into villages, each with a chief, whose name could be used to refer to the village. There was a head or grand chief recognized by all three collectively. However, those chiefs were "rather in name than authority," possessing but little "positive official authority":

> They have but few traditionary laws, and these, they are seldom capable of enforcing. Compulsion is seldom exercised on a refractory culprit; and when imperious circumstances require it be done, it is effected by a convention of chiefs whose personal influences become auxiliary to an otherwise impotent authority. The pains and penalties of their criminal laws are almost confined exclusively to the weaker sex. . . . If one man wantonly kills another, the nearest friend of the deceased is permitted . . . to revenge his death by taking the life of the murderer. But the price of blood, may be commuted for articles of more value and convenience than blood, and murder may be atoned for, and the spirit of revenge appeased. [Wallace 1954:124–25]

Here Burnet discovered that Comanches made a distinction between public and private spheres of politics and law, but he phrased that difference in terms of his own political-legal culture.

In August 1818, the same month Burnet was answering Jamison's questionnaire, W. A. Trimble, commander of the western section of the 8th Mil-

itary Department, forwarded to Secretary of War John C. Calhoun a short
"account of the Indians residing between Red and Rio del Norte rivers"
(Morse 1822:256–60). Beyond information procured in 1817 from "Americans, Frenchmen and Spaniards"—presumably traders—Trimble's sources are
unknown. After brief comments about Caddos, Delawares, and Cherokees, he
noted:

> the Comauch [*sic*] Indians are the largest and most warlike nation in this
> country. They have always been at war with the Spaniards, upon whom
> they commit the most horrible depredations. The whole nation moves
> with the Buffaloe, from south to north in the Spring; and from north to
> south in Autumn. During the winter they occupy the country on the
> sources of the Brassos and Colerado [*sic*]. They spend their summers on
> the sources of the Arkansaw and Missouri, among the eastern spurs of
> the Rocky mountains. They carry on, with traders from Red River, an
> extensive traffic, in horses and mules, which they catch in the plains or
> capture from the Spaniards. . . . It would perhaps be practicable to effect
> a peace between the Comauches and Spaniards. Such a measure would
> harmonize with the general policy of the government. . . . The smallpox
> made dreadful ravages among the Indians of that country. The Comau-
> ches compute the loss which they sustained in 1816, from this horrible
> disease, at four thousand souls. The vaccine innoculation might be intro-
> duced among them as a trifling expense; such a course is dictated by
> humanity. [Trimble, in Morse 1822:259]

In contrast to Sibley, Burnet, and Jamieson, who spoke of geographic divisions, Trimble lumped the Comanches into a single group; indeed, according
to Trimble, the "whole nation" moved together. Again, the Comanches were
depicted as waging "incessant war" against the Spaniards, a charge becoming
increasingly common. Finally, Trimble echoed Jamison's report of a devastating smallpox epidemic in 1816; indeed, the parallels between their accounts
in wording, number, and appeal to humanitarian goals suggests that Trimble
had spoken to Jamison, if not seen his report. Through its publication in
Morse (1822), Trimble's report on the effects of the disease has become
widely cited (Stearn and Stearn 1945:61; Ewers 1973:108; Swagerty 1988:
360), but as noted above in connection with Jamison's account, there is no
other evidence for such a major loss by the Comanches.

After Cordero's and Chihuahua's visits to Jamison in Natchitoches, Comanche contacts with Anglo-American officials again declined. Meanwhile,
since the early 1800s, the westward movement of eastern Indians had increased to a flood. By the early 1820s, groups of Cherokees, Chickasaws,
Creeks, and others had moved into western Arkansas Territory, lands for-

merly occupied by various Caddoan groups and more recently held by Clermont's Osages. That movement initiated a complex process of reorganization of intertribal relations in the west.

Unfortunately, the history of that period is clouded by conflicting rumors of alliances and wars. In 1817 it was reported that various eastern Indians had allied with western groups, including Comanches, for an attack on the Osages (*Niles' Weekly Register*, Sept. 17, 1817). In 1819 Major William Bradford at Fort Smith reported the rumor of a council of the Plains tribes—said to include Osages, Pawnees, Sioux, Foxes, and Arapahos—to be held at the Salt Plains between the Red and the Arkansas rivers. Although the purpose of the meeting was unknown, the rumored attendance of the "Iotans," the "most numerous tribe" west of the Mississippi, was held to be of great portent (Bradford 1819).

Using an argument similar to John Sibley's a decade earlier, Bradford suggested that the chiefs be brought to Washington to impress upon them the strength of the government. Otherwise, "should a war occur with Spain, they might prove the same auxiliary force . . . as did the Northwestern Indians to the British during the late War" (Bradford 1819). Secretary of War John C. Calhoun, however, in a circular to all Indian agents, declared that such visits caused more confusion in the daily activities of the offices of the bureaucracy than support in the Indian country (Calhoun 1820a). In May 1820 Calhoun wrote to Jamison's successor, George Gray, that considering the positive relations between the United States and Spain, it would be improper to give presents to Indians from Spanish Texas. Should any such Indians visit, they were to be treated civilly, but were to be made to understand the reasons why presents could not be made (Calhoun 1820b).

In 1819, the Adams-Onis Treaty between the United States and Spain attempted to settle the continuing debate about the limits of Lousiana. The newly established boundary extended from the Gulf of Mexico up the Sabine and Red rivers to the 100° west longitude, then north to the head of the Arkansas River, north to the 42d parallel, and then due west to California (Weber 1982:12). Stephen Long's 1819-20 exploring expedition visited the headwaters of the Arkansas and met Cheyennes, Arapahos, Kiowas, and Apaches, but no Comanches (Thwaites 1904-7, 14:16). At the Big Bend of the Arkansas, Captain Bell's detached party did encounter an "Ietan" war party that had been ambushed by Otoes, but they were in no mood to discuss diplomacy (Thwaites 1904-7, 16:233).

One result of his expedition, however, was a report in the *Washington, D.C., National Intelligencer* for September 15, 1820, based on "accounts recently received from a very respectable source in the territory of Arkansas."[13] After briefly discussing various Caddoans, Pawnees, Cherokees, and

Tonkawas, the anonymous writer devoted his longest paragraph to the "Comanchees":

> [There are] a number of tribes under this name. They are strolling savages, and ramble the plains of Santa Fee [*sic*] southeasterly, across Red River, the Colerado [*sic*], Brasos, and Trinity, and are at perpetual war with the Spanish provinces. The Spaniards say they are 30,000 strong. It was stated last fall by the Spanish officers at the Sabine, who were attached to the Spanish expedition against Gen. Long and his followers, that those Indians had, within the last season, destroyed upwards of 1000 families on the Rio del Norte, and in parts of the Spanish provinces. These Indians are becoming quite expert in fire-arms within a few years, having been furnished by traders from the United States, by way of exchange, for horses and mules, which these Indians would, from time to time, plunder the Spanish settlements of. These Indians consider themselves the most powerful nation in the world, and, next to them, the Americans, (as they call the people of the United States.) But since Long's defeat, they rank Spain before America, considering Long to have the command of all the United States.

Although most of the details of that report, particularly the claim of "perpetual war," were misrepresentations taken out of context, the description of the Comanches as comprised of "a number of tribes" is interesting, for it recognized the multiple nature of Comanche tribality. It was also the first notice in English of the trade in stolen horses and mules in return for guns and ammunition. Unfortunately, the identities of those traders are unknown.

Comanche Resource Domains, 1786–1820

The thirty-five years from 1786 to 1820 began as the most prosperous in modern Comanche history. They ranged far and wide, rounding up available horses and captives to supply their growing trade east and west. Traders visited their camps, and they were welcomed in Santa Fe and San Antonio. Some Comanches went as far east as Natchitoches and as far south as Chihuahua. By the end of the period, however, the chaos of the collapse of the Spanish empire and the advance of the Anglo-Americans brought major changes to Comanche political and economic organization.

Hunting continued to be a basic resource domain. However, as before, there is little direct evidence of its role in either the domestic or the political economy. The only documentation of hunting during that period were two mentions of the lack of animals. The first, in 1787, noted that the buffalo had been absent from Kotsoteka country for seven months (Concha 1788); the second was the implication that Somiquaso's move to the Concho River was not particularly profitable, such that his people had few hides or meat for the traders who visited them (Alencaster 1806).

In addition, there is little direct evidence for the role of war honors in Comanche politics. There are some indirect indications: Ecueracapa was "most distinguished . . . by his skill and valor in war" (Thomas 1932:295) and "Francisco does not have credit or standing whatever in his nation" (N. Salcedo 1812b).

Beyond the ideological role of military prestige in politics was the more pragmatic aspect of warfare and raiding: the spoils of war constituted a resource domain under the control of the war leader. Between 1786 and 1820 Comanches fought with Pawnees, Osages, Apaches, Kiowas, Cheyennes, Arapahos, and Navajos, and hostilities were implied with many others. Comanches also participated in joint expeditions with the Spaniards. In 1786 Ohamaquea led a Comanche contingent against the Apaches; later that summer twenty-two Comanches volunteered for a campaign against Apaches near the Hopi villages. Sofais led an expedition against Texas Apaches in 1788, and Zoquiné led another in 1789. In 1790 there was the troubled combined campaign of Comanches under Ecueracapa, Paruanarimuco, and Tanqueyaran and Spaniards under Juan de Dios Peña against the Pawnees. In July 1791 "over 1000 men of arms" were reported meeting in the Wichita Mountains planning to go against Lipans, Mescaleros, and Lipayanes. In July and November 1792 Ecueracapa, Quenaracara, and Hachaca campaigned against the Lipans and the next year against Pawnees. In 1810 the principal chiefs Quegüe and Cordero joined Governor Manrrique of New Mexico in another Apache campaign. Those joint Comanche-Spaniard enterprises were not particularly profitable. Ecueracapa's 1786 Apache campaign netted eighty-five horses. In the 1792 Pawnee campaign they attacked three small rancherías, killing a captain and four warriors, and capturing four women and nine children. The 1810 campaign gained eleven horses "which were given to the Comanches."

Ironically, as a focus of military campaigns, the Spaniards themselves provided much of Comanche political capital, for despite the 1785-86 treaties, many Comanches felt they were not bound to the peace and freely raided the Spanish settlements in New Mexico, Texas, and the provinces farther south. Besides, there were other Europeans who would gladly give guns, metal, blankets, and other goods for any and all horses offered by Comanches.

Indeed, the political-economic importance of Comanche war booty was probably greater after its conversion into trade items at the trade fairs. In

1787, only a year after the Pecos peace conference, Governor Concha reported, "Seven fairs have been held at the pueblo of Taos, a very considerable one at that of Pecos, and another at Picuris" (Concha 1787). The fairs do not appear to have coincided with New Mexico calendrical events or Pueblo feast days (table 4.2) but occurred whenever the Comanches arrived. As before, the chiefs first sent word to announce their impending arrival and to solicit gifts; the governor, or his local representatives, attended to ensure that "the greatest harmony is preserved" (Concha 1794:246).

By the late 1780s trade conducted in the Comanche camps began to play an increased role in the Comache economy, although it is not clear how old that practice was. In 1789 Governor Concha permitted "the residents and [Pueblo] Indians who solicited their [the Comanches'] commerce to go to their lands" (Concha 1794:249). Concha placed two stipulations on the trade. Trips were to be limited to licensed traders, and then only at the request of the Comanches themselves. Licensing did not always prevent unauthorized visits to the Plains, and unlicensed traders were often arrested and their goods confiscated. Governor Real Alencaster's attempts to enforce those regulations in 1805-8 led to a rebellion in the Pecos valley (Levine and Freeman 1982:6). The traders were initially known as "viageros" 'travelers' (John 1984:346); by 1813 some were being called "Comancheros" (M. Baca 1813).

Concha also established official interpreters in the Comanche camps "to observe them and to give an account of their movements" (Concha 1794:240). As Gálvez stated, "I granted this liberty with the idea of acquiring a complete knowledge of the water holes and lands in which they are situated, in order to wage war with this advantage in case they suffer some alteration in the established peace" (Concha 1794:246). The policy of using traders and interpreters as informants on affairs in Comanchería was officially sanctioned in 1805 (N. Salcedo 1805) and again in 1810, when Governor Manrrique issued conditional licenses to traders (Manrrique 1810d).

Although some Comancheros relied upon chance meetings with Comanches (Haley 1935:163), others went to specified rendezvous. There were several more or less permanent trading sites in Texas: Muchoque (*motso ku?e* 'mustache hill'), in Borden County; Las Tecovas, northwest of Amarillo; Cañon del Resgate, near Lubbock; and at Quitaque (Levine and Freeman 1982).

On the east, traders from Nacogdoches, Natchitoches, and Saint Louis, both legal and contraband, followed the roving pattern, going directly to the Comanche villages. There is little information on the easterners, and the names of only a few are known. In the 1780s Pedro Vial traded with the groups along the Red River. Philip Nolan visited Comanchería after 1790

Table 4.2

Comanche Visitors to Santa Fe, 1790–1815, by Month

	J	F	M	A	M	J	J	A	S	O	N	D
1790		1	41	18	22	5	1	17	5	1	13	1
1792			3	7	49	17	16	2	24		9	
1794				9	4	19	7	45	21	2	1	
1797	2		15	20			32	7	69		10	
1798	9		1		26		2	11	50	38	20	8
1800			24		1				23	17	18	
1801	2	12						34	32			42
1802	3		27				50	65	25	30		
1803						6	25	51	44			
1806								37				
1807	6						4	10	18	97		17
1810							23					
1815				9	2		15	12	14			
Totals	22	13	111	63	104	47	175	291	325	185	71	68

SOURCE: Kavanagh 1986

(Loomis and Nasatir 1967:207). James Purseley was said to have spent the year 1802–3 trading with Kiowas and Padoucas—from the context, the latter probably meant Comanches rather than Apaches (Coues 1895). In the winter of 1806–7, seven men from Natchitoches spent the winter with the Wichitas, and at least one visited nearby Comanches (Abel 1922). Anthony Glass visited Comanches in 1808 (John 1982; D. L. Flores 1985), as did William Becknell in 1811 (Inman 1898:38). Along with other refugees from the Magee-Gutierrez revolt, José Francisco Ruíz lived with the Comanches along the Red River, 1813–20. It is probable that David Burnet visited Comanche camps along the Red River or the Colorado River, or both, in 1818–19, and Alexander LeGrand may have, but there is no direct evidence for his presence. In May 1818 it was reported that two Americans were in the "center of the Comanche nation" selling "fusils, powder, shot, and buying horses and mules stolen from the province" (Pérez 1818b). That same year Benjamin Rush Milam began trading at the headwaters of the Colorado; by 1819 several men in Natchitoches were known as "old Comanche traders," and there was an established "Camino Comanche" from Nacogdoches to Comanchería (McLean 1974–93, 2:210).

It is probable that much of the trade with New Mexico was conducted in the Comanche language. Not only were many Pueblo Indians of Comanche extraction, but there were also many Genizaros, baptized Plains Indians, in the general population. As former captives, other New Mexicans—such as Alejandro Martín and Juan Cristóbal Tenorío—spoke Comanche and often served long terms as official interpreters. In the east, however, many of those conditions did not apply, or at least there is little documentary record of them. Instead, they may have used sign language; as James Wilkinson noted in an 1805 letter to President Jefferson, Philip Nolan had "acquired a perfect knowledge" of sign language while trading with the Comanches (Wilkinson 1805). That is the earliest reference to the use of sign language among the Comanches, and possibly the earliest on the Plains.[14]

The extent of Comanche contacts to the north, particularly to the northeast, is problematic. There is no reason to doubt that Yamparikas attended the Shoshone rendezvous west of South Pass. However, whether there was direct Comanche involvement in the Black Hills rendezvous or in the trade with the Missouri River villages is unknown. Although documents such as Tabeau's 1803-5 narrative (Abel 1939) contain references to "Padaucas" (1939:154), and to "[Têtes] Pelés, the Alitanes, the Serpents . . . these last three have the same language" (1939:160) as involved in the trade, it is problematic whether those references are to Comanches. Also puzzling is Tabeau's report, "The Spaniards whom they see at St. Antonio or Santa Fe make light of their peltries and offer them only some hardware in exchange" (Abel 1939:158), the "they" being the tribes of the northern Plains, Caninabiches [Arapahos?], Squihitanes [Arapahos?], Nimousissines [?], Padaucas, Catarkas [Plains Apaches], Datamis [Kiowas?], Tchiwaks [Chawi Pawnees?], and Cayowas [Kiowas?]). With the possible exception of "Padauca" meaning Comanche, there is no definitive mention of any of those peoples visiting the Spaniards in either of their provincial capitals at that time—the Flecha Rayadas (Cheyennes) and Cuampes did not show up on the Arkansas asking for trade "on the same terms as with the Comanche" until 1807 (N. Salcedo 1807). Moreover, if those "Padaucas" were Comanches, the claim that they had only minimal trade with San Antonio or Santa Fe is demonstrably false.

A major source of Comanche political capital came from political gifts from Euroamericans. New Mexico funds for presents were budgeted under several accounts, the Gastos Extraordinarío de Paz y Guerra, the Fondo de Aliadas, and the Fondo de Gratificación. According to Simmons:

> In 1788, . . . only 60 pesos were directly set aside for Indian expenses in New Mexico. . . . At this time, the supply of goods was in the hands of private contractors and included in the manufactured goods destined for the colony but within a short time, the contract was terminated and the king himself authorized 4000 pesos. This means that gifts were now procured directly from the presidial supply master. [Simmons 1968:145]

By 1789 the fund had been supplied, and between 1789 and 1820 the Gastos Extraordinarío de Paz y Guerra totaled approximately 55,000 pesos. Table 4.3 shows the Comanche share (48 percent) of the total amounts distributed from Santa Fe in the years for which both figures are available. Similarly, between 1794 and 1799 approximately 8,849 pesos' worth of gifts and supplies were distributed to Texas Indians (Gutierrez 1800). Some of those gifts were distributed from Béxar; others, particularly for the "Naciones del Norte," the Wichita and allied groups, were distributed from Nacogdoches. Unfortunately, the Béxar records are less complete than those of New Mexico, and comparable totals are not available. Except for the income derived from the sale of wild horses, the Fondo de Mesteñas, which between 1795 and 1799 contributed 3,100 pesos to the Fondo de Gratificacíon (Gutierrez 1799), Texas funds came from the Royal Treasury. The gifts included both subsistence and prestige goods. Between 1787 and 1789 Governor Concha sent almost 300 bushels of corn to Comanchería, ostensibly to alleviate the effects of drought, but also to foster a political relation (Moorhead 1968:168). Table 4.4 gives the items received "for the Northern Indians and Comanches" in Béxar in 1795, and table 4.5 gives an inventory of the Santa Fe warehouses from 1811.

A large part of the Spanish gift budget was taken up by the elite items necessary for the recognition and legitimation of the Comanche leaders. According to Pedro Pino, the possession of those symbols of authority was important to the Comanche leadership: "In order to get an idea of the esteem in which they hold the king, one need only to note that any appointments they received are ignored unless they are confirmed by our officers" (Carroll and Haggard 1942:135–36). Although that statement represents the Spanish perspective, the efforts by Somiquaso and Huanacoruco to be recognized as chiefs suggests that Comanches themselves were aware of the relation and of the power of the symbols. At the same time, it must also be noted that Amangual's apparent failure to recognize the wearers of such symbols as important men belies their symbolic value to Euroamericans.

The 1801 accounts list 113 pesos to "confirm [the unnamed chief] in the name of General of the Nation." That confirmation included the presentation of definite and specific articles. In 1786 Anza gave Ecueracapa a saber, a Spanish flag, and a "staff of office which must be exhibited in all the rancherías as notice of having been admitted to peace" (Thomas 1932:76). When Canaguaipe was elected in 1797, Chacón recognized him in the name of the king "by turning over to him the symbols: a cane with silver head, a medal of the same and . . . a scarlet cloak" (Chacón 1797a). The accounts for 1797 list 573 pesos to cover the expenses of that election, plus another 82 pesos for the

Table 4.3
Comanche Share of Gifts, Santa Fe, 1789–1804

YEAR	COMANCHE SHARE	TOTAL [a]
1789	4,248.0.00	5,906.0.00
1790	1,769.7.10	5,712.2.02 1/2
1791		
1792	1,248.8.11	3,882.7.11
1793		
1794	1,110.4.07 3/4	3,286.1.09
1795		
1796		
1797	2,602.8.07 3/4	4,216.4.03 1/8
1798	1,366.6.03 3/4	3,327.9.09 7/8
1799		
1800	537.9.07 3/4	1,072.4.04 1/2
1801	992.3.03	1,924.1.00
1802	1,833.5.10	2,826.0.07
1803		
1804	1,436.0.00	3,599.5.07
Totals	±18,683	±39,110

[a]In *pesos*, *reales*, and *granos*. There were 12 *reales* to a *peso*, 12 *granos* to a *real*.

SOURCE: Kavanagh 1986

Table 4.4
Gifts Intended for "Northern Indians and Comanches," Santa Fe, 1795

3 bolts red and blue cloth	42 doz jingles
18 blankets	4 bundles beads
4 uniforms, 2 red 2 blue	7 lbs steel wire
1 lb gold wire	147 varas ribbon
100 combs	8 "hands" of tobacco (@ 50 lbs)
8 lbs vermillion	150 lbs lead
12 rifles	75 lbs powder
6 doz knives	100 flints
1000 needles	100 gun rods
108 scissors	7 bundles burlap
24 small bells	54 mirrors

SOURCES: Muñoz 1795; Castañeda 1936, 5:126

Table 4.5
Articles Purchased for the Allied Nations, Santa Fe, 1811

12 doz high crown sombrero	288.0	2 Canes with silver heads	16.2
1900 piloncillos	129.0	23 1/2 doz large Belduques	105.6
1 lb gold braid	32.0	6 1/2 doz small Belduques	29.2
24 1/2 lb thread	98.0	12 Black sombreros	21.0
20 oz. Vermillion	10.0	42 varas red bayeta in spools	131.2
220 varas scarlet cloth	88.0	6 Doz large metal buttons	3.0
60 varas false gold braid	19.0	12 gross small metal buttons	36.0
60 varas silver braid	19.0	14 pcs ribbon No. 40	70.0
160 1/2 varas Tlascalan bayeta	361.1	90 pcs blanketing	656.2
873 varas blue Querétaro cloth[a]	1969.3		

[a]A type of stroud or trade cloth. As early as 1789 Comanches expressed a desire for "Querétaro cloth" (Martínez Pacheco 1789).

SOURCE: Rey 1810–11

general. In 1808 Amangual gave Sargento-Cordero a "walking cane and rifle sent by our governor . . . to Govern and protect his people" (Loomis and Nasatir 1967:468). An 1803 invoice of gifts for the northern Indians and Comanches included "one package with twelve bastoncitos with marked wooden handles" costing 12 pesos (J. Martínez 1803). The 1810 inventory of goods in the Santa Fe warehouses intended for the Comanches includes a "baston con puño de plata" 'cane with silver head' valued at 8 pesos (Rey 1810–11).

Two sizes of medals were given, large ones for principal captains or generals, smaller ones for the capitancillos. Burgundian-cross flags of one and one-half varas—about a yard—square were also reported in the 1803 Béxar invoices (J. Martínez 1803). Patuarus had such a flag, as did Paruanarimuco (Loomis and Nasatir 1967). In 1789 Zoquiné had a flag "bearing the royal arms of the King and an inscription 'given . . . to the Chief of the Comanche'" (Castañeda 1936, 5:17).

Another major prestige gift was cloth or clothing. Canaguaipe received an embroidered scarlet cloak at his installation in 1797. The 1803 Béxar invoice listed "10 complete suits of clothing of blue Querétaro" costing 126.4 pesos and "15 sombreros with false gold trimming" for 26.2 pesos. Francisco Amangual described chiefs wearing "long red coats with blue collars and cuffs" (Loomis and Nasatir 1967:482). Pedro Pino reversed the colors, noting "coats and capes made of blue Querétaro, with red lapels for the big chiefs, three-cornered hats, and some medals struck by the commandant general" (Carroll and Haggard 1942:135).

Firearms were important prestige gifts. Most firearms were apparently channeled through Béxar, as there are few references in the Santa Fe invoices to firearms, powder, ball, and related items. In 1795 the Texas gifts included 12 fusils, 75 pounds of powder, 150 pounds of lead, 100 flints, and 100 gun rods (Muñoz 1795); in addition, a gunsmith was hired to repair Indian guns (Orandain 1796). In 1798, 8 rifles and a musket were given (Gutierrez 1800); in 1800, at least 6 rifles (Curbelo 1800a, 1800b). Castañeda (1936, 5:128) reported that in 1800, 100 English rifles at eight pesos each were ordered from Gilbert Leonard, a trader at New Orleans. Apparently the Comanches preferred a specific caliber: shipments of guns in both 1806 and 1808 were of the wrong size and were not accepted by the Indians (John 1984:359).

The gifts were distributed at the "regalos anuales," the annual distributions, and by provisioning the periodic visitors to the various capitals. In the years between 1790 and 1815 almost 1,500 Comanche visits to Santa Fe were recorded (table 4.2). During that same time more than 4,000 Comanche visits to Béxar were recorded, along with some 3,000 combined Comanche and other Norteño visits (table 4.6). Those occurred in all months of the year, although mostly in the late summer. The most complete year recorded in Béxar was 1810 (Luna 1810). That year 3,905.6 pesos were reported spent on 3,172 visitors, of whom 1,374 (43 percent) were Comanches (table 4.7).[15]

Gifts were given according to the importance of the visitor. The daily diaries recorded visitors in five classes: general, captain or capitancillo, gandul—the term literally meant 'loafer', the Spaniards used it to refer to warriors—muger 'woman', and muchacho/muchacha 'male/female child'. An 1807 memorandum (table 4.8) showed the ideal amount of gifts to be given each class of visitor (Villanueva 1807).

Although individuals or small groups of Comanches might show up at Santa Fe or Béxar (table 4.9), most Comanches obtained access to political gifts through their chiefs. Governor Chacón, for example, gave Canaguaipe gifts "to pass along to his brothers" (Chacón 1797a). Table 4.10 shows the gifts given to Sofais on three occasions, 1800-01; the first was in March 1800 when he, two other "capitancillos," fifty-five warriors, forty women, and eleven children visited Béxar (Curbelo 1800a). In May of that year Zoquiné, Sofais, two "Yamparikas," and 190 others visited Béxar and received gifts (Curbelo 1800b). In July 1802 Sofais came to Béxar asking for gifts "to distribute to the other capitancillos of his division" (J. B. Elguézabal 1802b). In 1808 gifts for his ranchería were given to Cordero "in order that they be distributed through him" (Loomis and Nasatir 1967:473).

Table 4.6

Comanche Visitors to Béxar and Nacogdoches, 1794–1810, by Month

	J	F	M	A	M	J	J	A	S	O	N	D
1794							1,262[a]					
1796		843[a]										
1798					97							
1799										42		
1800			109		194							
1801	88	29									134	49
1801							19[b]					
1802							65	129	1	13	34	
1803						132	719	293				
1806	76	248	286	169	7	74	376	306	224	239	30	17

[a] Not further distinguished by month.
[b] In Nacogdoches.

SOURCE: Kavanagh 1986

Table 4.7

Comanche Visitors to Béxar, 1810

MONTH	COMANCHE VISITORS			TOTAL VISITORS	GIFTS IN PESOS
	MALE	FEMALE	TOTAL		
January	56	4	60	122	394.2.11
February	131	68	199	230	342.7.10
March	229	179	408	422	708.3.06
April	7	1	8	133	139.4.07
May	1	1	2	22	37.4.03
June	2	3	5	129	97.0.00
July	64	53	117	495	430.5.06
August	0	0	0	9	294.2.05
September	51	38	89	329	137.5.01
October	302	18	486	1,239	394.5.70
November	0	0	0	50	147.7.04
Total	843	531	1,374	3,172	3,905.6.04

The figures are as given by Miguel Diaz de Luna.

SOURCE: Luna 1810

Table 4.8

"Statement which Shows in Resumé the Quantity or Number of Gifts and Effects Consumed in the Regaling of Each Indian according to Their Class," October 1807

	GENERAL CON CASACAS ESCARLATA[a]	CAPITAN CON CAPA[b]	CAPITAN SIN CAPA	GANDUL	MUGER
Paño[c] (woolen cloth)	7 1/2	8 3/8	2 3/8	2 3/8	2 3/8
Bayeta Azul (blue bayeta)				1 1/2	
Bayeta Tlascala (Tlascalan bayeta)	1	1 1/2	1/2	1/8	
Escarlata (scarlet cloth)	7				
Manta (blankets)	13 1/2	9 5/8	9 3/8	4 1/2	
Sombreros (hats)	1	1	1		
Belduques (knives)	1	1	1	1	1
Piloncillos (hard sugar cones)	1	1	1	1	1
Botones [dozens] (Bottons)	3	11	11		
Liston N°.40 (ribbon)	1	2	2		
Abalorio (beads)					10
Chalona Azul (blue cloth)	3/4	3/4	3/4	3/4	3/4
Atornillos (screws?)					1
Zigarros (cigars)	1	2	1	1	1
Pontibi (?)	8				

[a] The *General con Casacas Escarlata* 'General with Scarlet Military Coat' presumably refers to the style of coat described by Amangual in 1808 as "long red coats with blue collars and cuffs."
[b] It is not clear what is meant by the difference between *Capitan con Capa* and *Capitan sin Capa* 'captain with/without cape' as this is the only such usage so far found.
[c] No measurements were included in the statement. Presumably cloth was measured in *varas*.

SOURCE: Villanueva 1807

Table 4.9

Comanche Visitors to Santa Fe, 1790–1815, by Class

	GENERAL	CAPTAIN	GANDUL	MUJER	MUCHACHO/A	UNSPECIFIED
1790	3	9				113
1792	2	20				105
1794	5	15	2	2	2	83
1797	3	80	40	37	2	4
1798	4	56	63	33	10	1
1800	22	24	29	7	1	
1801	1	7	9	12	2	91
1802	1	17	3	11		169
1803	1					125
1804	1				3	
1806	2	18	15	2		
1807	2	81	41	11	17	
1810	2	18	3			
1815	6	22	5	3	15	
Total	55	367	210	118	52	691

SOURCE: Kavanagh 1986

Table 4.10

Gifts to Sofais, 1800–1801

	MARCH 12, 1800	MAY 1, 1800	JULY 28, 1801[a]
Fusils	3	3	
Gun worms	55		
Cartridges	29		
Tobacco (hands)	8	3	12
Vermillon	2 lbs 11 1/2 oz	7	
Copper Pot	1		
Frying Pan	1		
Beads	6 1/2	12	
Yellow Wire	3 lbs 9 oz		
Iron	3 lbs 9 oz		
Estabones (knife steel)	50	20	
Awls	30	21	24
Combs		14	
Mirrors	9	4	2

Table 4.10, *continued*

	MARCH 12, 1800	MAY 1, 1800	JULY 28, 1801[a]
Perines (?)	14	13	
Bells	1		
Knives	39	21	2
Scissors	6		
Axes	2		
Varas Paño	16	10 1/4	
Shirts			3
Breech Cloths			2
			Meat
			Corn
			Salt

[a] In Nacogdoches

SOURCES: Curbelo 1800a, b; M. Músquiz 1801

Although Anglo-Americans were aware of the power of political gifts, they were somewhat more reticent about acknowledging it. Perhaps the only direct mention of political gifts was Wilkinson's 1805 comment that "to extend the name and influence of the United States . . . will require considerable disbursements" (D. Jackson 1966:229). In 1805 John Sibley had a budget of three thousand dollars; in August 1807 he gave a medal to the principal Comanche chief and had the others measured for suits of "scarlet faced with black velvet and trimmed with white buttons." Later that year he gave Comanche visitors "some useful articles of husbandry" (Sibley 1807). Cordero received a full uniform in 1816; Chihuahua received one in 1817.

Comanche Divisions and Divisional Politics, 1786–1820

The political gifts from the Spaniards and the trade with Anglo-Americans formed equal and therefore conflicting resource domains that Comanche chiefs attempted to manipulate and control. Conversely, both the Spaniards and the Anglo-Americans attempted to force exclusive loyalty from their clients. Although the Comanches often professed loyalty to one or the other, it is probable that most followed a middle road, trying to maintain good relations with Spaniards while still profiting from the horse trade with Anglo-Americans.

In New Mexico there was an apparently easy succession of chiefs following Ecueracapa: Canaguaipe, Encanguane, one whose name was not re-

corded, and Quegüe. There was, however, also some attempted political manipulation, as in 1797 when Pisinape tried to get himself appointed chief, and
in 1803, when Huanacoruco claimed that Quegüe—a Kotsoteka—had "rejected the cane of the Yamparikas."

Although the Kotsotekas in New Mexico were able to maintain a political organization with a succession of chiefs, the situation in Texas was
cloudy. There is evidence that the Texas Comanches still considered themselves to be Kotsotekas. For instance, Zoquiné and Sofais were supported by
political gifts from Béxar, but neither claimed to be a principal chief in
opposition to a New Mexican. Similarly, Encanguane's election in New Mexico in 1794 was reported to the Texas governor by a Comanche, suggesting
that a political connection still existed.

The arrival of Chihuahua in 1802 signaled an important change in Texas.
That he held some authority is clear, but the basis of that authority is not. He
may have been the unnamed individual elected Kotsoteka chief in New
Mexico in 1801, or at least a rival of Quegüe for that position in 1801–3. But
when Governor Cordero demanded a single Comanche representative, Sargento-Cordero was elected instead. Governor Cordero's demand and Sargento-Cordero's election seem to have been the trigger leading to the ultimate
political separation of the Texas and New Mexico Kotsotekas.

During the two decades after 1786 most of the Yamparikas apparently
remained north of the Arkansas River, as there are few direct references to
them in the New Mexico records. Initially, their affairs were handled by the
Jupe chief Paruanarimuco, who was recognized as Comanche lieutenant
general in 1787. Despite Ugarte's suggestion that a Yamparika might also be
made lieutenant general, that was not done. Perhaps they were still too far
north to be a power in New Mexico, and according to Anza's census, they
had far fewer lodges than had the Kotsotekas. It is possible that the "Padaucas," referred to by Tabeau (Abel 1939) as being involved in the Missouri
River trade and having only minimal trade with Santa Fe, were Yamparikas,
and that their apparent relative lack of Spanish goods was indicative of their
position north of the Arkansas. That also raises the possibility that from the
northeast, "Padouca" meant Yamparika while "Comanche" meant Kotsoteka.

As for Paruanarimuco, except for Pedro Vial's meeting with him along
the Canadian River in the spring of 1787, he was usually found along the
Arkansas River, where he attempted to establish San Carlos de los Jupes later
that year. By 1794 he was referred to explicitly as a Yamparika lieutenant
general (J. R. Sarracino 1795), implying that the relative positions of the
Jupes and the Yamparikas, and his own position within them, had reversed.

Huanacoruco's abortive 1803 attempt to claim recognition as Yamparika
chief and Somiquaso's more successful 1805 bid suggest that, first, Parua-

narimuco had died before 1803, and second, that the succession was disputed. That is, Huanacoruco's and Somiquaso's actions were political strategies that used access to the New Mexico Spaniards as a major political resource, perhaps even as the legitimating action. It may be noted that Joachín del Real Alencaster, the governor who recognized Somiquaso in 1805, was himself new to the job, and the Comanche may have taken advantage of the Spaniard's inexperience to resolve his own political problems; indeed, Alencaster's action was the only recognition by the Spaniards of a Comanche chief not accompanied by an "election." Somiquaso's coincident move to the headwaters of the Concho River may have been related to such a context, but details are unknown.

Although some Yamparikas may have been in that southern vicinity as early as the turn of the century (chief Blanco and—if Paruaquita's interest in him was based on divisional affiliation—possibly El Sordo), within a few years those southern Yamparikas had been implicated in the horse trade with Anglo-Americans through a trade route extending to other Yamparikas "farther away"; "farther away" may have been to the northeast, rather than to the northwest. Indeed, in 1810 eight Yamparika rancherías were reported near the Taovayas on Red River, possibly including El Sordo's new group. Unfortunately, the Texans' tendency to call any distant Comanches Yamparika makes evaluation of those reports difficult.

That same year El Sordo had split from his "proper nation" and, together with assorted Wichitas and other Indians, was leading horse raids into Texas. Meanwhile, the Texas officials reported that Paruaquita, said to be the Yamparika principal chief in New Mexico, had visited Béxar, affirming a pro-Spaniard stance. Those events probably reflect a widening split in the ranks of the Yamparikas, with each group following different resource domains. On the west, north of the Arkansas River, were those generally allied with the Spaniards of Santa Fe. Their chiefs used access to Spanish goods, both trade and political gifts, as the basis of their political power. On the east were others, exemplified by El Sordo, who combined a warfare and raiding domain with trade with Anglo-Americans.

After 1811 and the failure to obtain El Sordo's release from jail, the defeat of the Magee-Gutierrez filibusterers, and the ensuing abandonment of Béxar, Comanche involvement with official Texas ceased for the rest of the decade. There was a concomitant collapse of those resource domains based on access to political gifts and prestige and subsistence goods, as well as an apparent collapse of trade.

The Texas Comanches made two adjustments to that changing political environment. One was to seek out a new source of prestige goods: the Americans in Natchitoches. Unfortunately, Sibley did not name the chiefs who visited him in 1807. A decade later both Chihuahua and Cordero visited John Jamison and received uniforms and other gifts. The second adjustment was to increase contacts with the traders along the Red River, who included many refugees from the Magee-Gutierrez forces. By 1818 that trade had resulted in the establishment of a new political organization, the Tenewas, who, if not the genealogical descendants, were the political and economic descendants of El Sordo's people and their horse trade to the east.

5

Changes in Comanchería,

1820–46

War and Peace in Mexican Texas, 1820–29

In the winter of 1820 members of the Béxar *ayuntamiento,* the local council, complained to their provincial delegates about their strained circumstances, about requisitioned supplies unpaid for, about property illegally confiscated in the 1813 revolt, and particularly about the continued incursions of the Lipans and Comanches who had "made away with cattle, horses, and other property . . . killing and capturing a considerable number of persons of all ages, conditions, and sexes." They pleaded for a "well-organized campaign" against the Indians and for the reestablishment of the presidios (Hatcher 1919:62–63).

In response to an official inquiry apparently based on those complaints, Juan Antonio Padilla, an army officer stationed at Béxar, submitted a report on the "Barbarous Indians of the Province of Texas" (Hatcher 1919:47). Padilla had been paymaster for various military companies in and around Béxar and was often in trouble with his supervisors for insubordination and other problems (A. Benavides 1989:757–59); it is unknown whether he had any direct contact with the Comanches. It is apparent, however, both from his official position and from his own often inconsistent comments, that he had been a Loyalist during the 1811–13 revolt. For instance, he blamed the recent raids on "the foreigners and rebel Spaniards who escaped from the victorious army at Medina" (Hatcher 1919:55). He had little good to say about the

Comanches, calling them "treacherous, revengeful, sly, untrustworthy, ferocious, and cruel, when victorious; cowardly and low, when conquered."
Further, "They are inconstant in their friendships and break their contracts for
any cause. . . . Their sole occupation is idleness and crime" (Hatcher 1919:
53–54). Although they were "governed by the person most noted for bravery,
intrepidity, and ferocity," Padilla belittled their political motivations, saying
that "they obey him when they wish, without noting him. And if they follow
him to war, it is because of the love they have for murder and theft" (Hatcher
1919:55).

But beneath his vituperation, his comments do hold a degree of information about the Comanches in Texas, or at least about the state of knowledge
about the Comanches current in Texas in 1821. Padilla made three comments
relevant to political organization. Like Texas Spaniards of the previous half-
century, Padilla divided the Comanche "nation" into two parts. To the northwest toward New Mexico were the "Yambaricas," of whom he had no further
information. But unlike his Texan predecessors, who referred to those nearby
as Comanches, Padilla used the ethnonym "Yucantica." According to Padilla,
they were composed of ten or twelve smaller groups—Padilla used the term
pueblos—that is, local bands. Their wealth was in "good horses and arms,"
which they sold to "certain foreigners and perverse Spaniards" who had
"introduced munitions and other things . . . making a well worn road through
the unsettled regions towards Natchitoches."

As an ethnonym, Yucantica is previously unrecorded; it occurs in only
one other document—Jean Louis Berlandier's report on the Indians of Texas
in 1830 (see below, p. 224)—and that usage was itself probably derived from
Padilla. Moreover, rather than representing a new group, the term Yucantica
was probably a faulty transmission of Cuchantica, the Spanish rendering of
kuhtsutuhka. If that evaluation is valid, it suggests that as late as 1820, Texas
Comanches were still known to some as Kotsotekas. Padilla's count of "ten
or twelve" local groups is somewhat more difficult to evaluate. Since there is
no evidence that he had personal knowledge of the Texas Comanches, the
number is suspect. At one point in his 1786 report, Pedro Vial had implied
that there were ten rancherías of the Orientales, at another, he referred to "12
other little captains" (Vial and Chavez 1786); Padilla may have combined
these into the single phrase "ten or twelve." Finally, his comment about the
"well worn road . . . towards Natchitoches" indicates that the eastern horse
trade was still extant.

Meanwhile, in April 1821 the Spanish government in Mexico City
accepted a peace plan proposed by Juan Cortés (Arredondo 1821). A resident
of Natchitoches, Cortés had been paymaster at the La Bahía presidio in the
1790s; in that capacity he may have had some contact with Comanches, but

details are unknown (A. Benavides 1989:229–31). His proposed plan had three goals, motivated as much by what he said were "humanitarian sentiments" as by "patriotism": to persuade the Comanches of the benefits of peace, to persuade them to give up their captives, and to get them to visit the capital (Ruíz 1821). He believed that he could pacify the Comanches "with a few gifts," although the only gifts he specifically mentioned were twelve military coats of scarlet with blue cuffs and lapel facings for the principal chiefs (Cortés 1821a). He also believed it would be possible to free captives "without paying any ransom" (Cortés 1821b).

Cortés suggested that three men—José Francisco Ruíz, Vicente Tarin, and Julio Estrada, each of whom "had spent several years with the tribes"— should be sent out to confer with the Comanches (Arredondo 1821). Of the three, only Ruíz's experience with Comanches is known. He had been an officer in the royal army but had joined the insurgents in 1812. After their defeat he lived with Comanches for several years. At Cortés's suggestion, in the spring of 1821 he was granted a pardon to facilitate his assistance with the peace proposal (Ewers 1972:2). But before the plan could begin there was a change of government—the coup that installed Augustín de Iturbide as Mexican emperor—and action on the Comanche peace was postponed until the fall (Vivero 1821).

While Cortés was planning his "humanitarian" approach, others were following different tactics, leading to complications and conflicts. One had rather farcical overtones. In the spring of 1822 José Raphael Guadalupe del Espiritu Santu Iglesias y Parra, also known as Botón de Fierro ('iron button'), said to be a Comanche chief, had persuaded Emperor Iturbide that he could bring about peace with the Indians on the borders (J. P. García 1822). But by August doubts arose about him; there were comments that instead of advancing to the frontier, all he had done was to "take the opposite direction, and to fall back to Chihuahua" (López 1822d). In October it was discovered that he was not Comanche at all; he was, in fact, a native of Alta California, and a carpenter by trade (Trespalacios 1822). He was tried and convicted of "scandalous conduct" (Bolton 1913:173).

At the same time the Béxar ayuntamiento, in contrast to its belligerent attitude of the year before, commissioned Juan Manuel Barrera—a former army officer, alcalde of Béxar, and cattle trader—and three others, to seek peace with the Comanches. The other three were Miguel Delgado, Miguel Castro, and Pedro Gallardo, and except for Barrera's 1814 report that Comanches had almost completely destroyed "the livestock of the province" (Armiñan 1814), none had any known contact with Comanches. They visited the Tawakoni villages on the Brazos River, where they met with Varvaquiste, Pisinampe, and Quenoc (Barrera 1821). Of the three, Pisinampe was well known to the Spaniards of the previous three decades, but the other names are apparently previously unrecorded. The third name is possibly *kwina* 'eagle'. Although the Texas Spaniards spelled the first name in several ways (e.g., Barbaquista, Varvaquiste, etc.), by keeping close track of the various spellings and of the individual's movements, including a later trip to New Mexico, the name can be established as Paruakevitsi *parua ukubitsI* 'little bear'. He was also probably the Tenewa principal chief, circa 1818, whom David Burnet later remembered as Parrow-a-kifty, which he also translated as Little Bear (Burnet 1847). A man called Paruaquibitste, given as "Very Small Bear," had been one of the twenty-two Comanches who participated in the 1786 Comanche expedition against the Apaches (Thomas 1932:328), but he was probably not the same individual. More contemporaneously, Ruíz later remarked of him, "No one knows him in Béxar" (Ruíz 1823).

In early 1822 Barrera was on his way to Béxar with a Comanche delegation when he realized that he had promised more presents than he could supply. He offered Ruíz's presents as security, but Ruíz did not yet have any to give (Cortés 1821b). In March, when Yncoroy arrived in Béxar to find that there were no presents for him, he turned around and left (Lopez 1822a, 1822b, 1822c).

Meanwhile, in the fall of 1821 José Francisco Ruíz had received authorization to contact the Comanches and had gone to Pisinampe's village to argue for peace, meeting with that chief, Paruakevitsi, Guonique, and Temanca (Ruíz 1822), the latter two previously unnamed. At a three-day council, later reported to have consisted of the "principal chiefs, captains, and elders . . . attended by five thousand persons," Ruíz argued that the new government was no longer Spanish, but was native Mexican. According to the report, after Pisinampe, "whom they venerate as a father," spoke in favor of peace, the assemblage resolved, "by unanimous vote," to send one of their principal chiefs

> to negotiate for peace under the terms that he might find most appropriate and useful for the Comanche nation, and principally so that they, united with the Mexican Nation, would not permit Spain, or any other power whatsoever, to take any part of the territories which they now occupy. [McLean 1974-93, 4:428]

In July Pisinampe led a group of chiefs to Béxar to negotiate a truce. At first they objected to a provision that all prisoners would be surrendered without ransom, but agreement was reached and a truce signed August 11, 1822 (Lopez 1822d); a delegation went to Mexico City to sign a formal treaty.

It is not clear who went; other than Ruíz, the passport gives no names and specifies only "one captain, eight warriors, and four women" (Trespalacios 1822). According to the January 1823 *Gaceta del Gobierno Imperial de Méjico,*

> The chief named Guonique, a subject who deserves the general applause of the Comanche because he is enterprising, truthful, observant, prudent, and resolute, and with the plentipoteniary power conferred upon him by his nation, . . . presented himself in this Court, where he was liberally entertained with his retinue. [translated in McLean 1974-93, 4:428]

Lucas Alamán, then minister of foreign affairs and later historian, described their meetings:

> There came to Mexico, sent by the Comandante of the Provincias Internas, a captain of the Comanche Nation named Guonique to treat for peace with the government. . . . The influence of the respectable elder Pitnipampa [Pisinampe?] whose eloquence . . . had prevailed in the counsels and meetings of the Comanches. Guonique, among whose qualities is counted voraciousness, . . . was received as an envoy of a civilized nation. . . . They celebrated a treaty in which they established the rules which must be observed in commerce between the two nations. [Alamán 1942:650]

The treaty called for peace and friendship between the two nations, forgetting all that had occurred under the Spanish government. All prisoners would be returned except those who wished to remain. The Comanches would recognize the boundaries of the United States and Mexico as stated in the 1819 Adams-Onis treaty formalizing the Louisiana Purchase, defend those borders against barbarian invasions, and report any invasions they heard of; they would not allow hostile nations to pass through their lands, nor allow any Euroamerican exploration. They were to trade only at Béxar, traveling on public roads and under the direction of a chief, with a medal as passport, and the chief would be responsible for any damages they might commit. Mexicans would use the same precautions when entering Comanche country. Trade, to consist of manufactured materials on the one side and the products of the hunt on the other, would for the time being be free from any duty. However, a portion of all mustangs caught must be turned over to the government; shod horses would be paid for. Twelve youths would be sent each year to Mexico City for schooling, and a tribal envoy and interpreter would reside in Béxar to deal directly with the Mexican government. The agreement was reached December 13 and ratified by the emperor the next day (Mexico 1878: 617-19).

The Comanches stayed in Mexico City through January 14, 1823. When several members of the imperial government deserted to the Spaniards, Guonique sent word to the emperor that, if needed to prevent a return of the Spaniards, he and Paruakevitsi would station 4,000 armed warriors on the border and in six months could raise 27,000 men. Those figures are clearly exaggerations, but whether the exaggeration is due to Guonique waxing eloquent, faulty interpretation by Ruíz, or inflation by the imperial gazetteer, is unknown. Swearing "by the sun and by the earth"—*tabebehkatɬ* 'sun killing', the traditional Comanche oath (Wallace and Hoebel 1952:195)—Guonique said that the "Comanche Nation of the East" would destroy its enemies with "the rifle, the lance and the arrow" (McLean 1974-93, 4:431-33).

Besides the concessions for peace contained in the treaty of 1822, the Mexicans promised 2,000 pesos to be made available for gifts, but the course of their accounting is not clear. Apparently, the officials in Texas assumed that because the treaty had been approved in Mexico City, the money would be forthcoming. When after two years no money had appeared, Governor Rafael González complained that its delay threatened a "total breakdown of the peace" (J. R. González 1824). However, the officials in Mexico City had a different understanding of affairs: because the agreement was not approved by the Congress before Iturbide's ouster in 1821, there was no money for gifts (Alamán 1824a). By October 1824 money was made available for presents (Alamán 1824b), and Ruíz was appointed distributor (Ruíz 1824).

Comanches were again welcomed in Texas towns. In October 1824 Ysachene (possibly *isa* 'wolf', *tseena* 'fox'), "one of the principal chiefs," ten chiefs, and other warriors were welcomed to Béxar with a three-gun salute (G. Flores 1824). The next February Hoyoso—last mentioned in 1812—visited Monclova and was given a Mexican tricolor flag as a personal gift from the president of the republic (Pedraga 1825), as well as a hat and other presents, and a military escort to the presidio at Rio Grande (Elozúa 1825). In March several chiefs were given ranks in the militia forces: Hoyoso, "Alias El Vicho" ('the insignificant one'), was made lieutenant colonel; Terequena (*tue kwina* 'young eagle') "Alias El Americano," was made lieutenant; and Huaquenajavi (*waha kwina habi* 'two eagles lying down'), also called Ygnacio Perez, was made sub-lieutenant (R. González 1825).

Ruíz continued to visit the Comanches. According to Jean Louis Berlandier, writing in the early 1830s, in the mid-1820s, possibly 1824, Ruíz was present at a meeting of Comanches and other tribes, including Yamparikas and Chariticas, planning to go to war against the Osages. Berlandier's distinction between Comanches and Yamparikas parallels the distinctions made a generation earlier between Comanches close to Béxar and Yamparikas farther off, but it is unclear whether Chariticas meant Plains Apaches or Arapahos. Ruíz counted 2,300 tents arranged along the banks of a stream, covering four leagues and housing some 2,500 warriors. The Osage campaign was not a success; the advance scouting party was ambushed, and the main party of Osages was found to be aided by fourteen white men (Berlandier 1969:73).

Despite those efforts at attaining peaceful relations, Comanche raiding in Texas continued, particularly in the northeastern part of the province near the Red River and in the south along the Rio Grande. By 1825 a virtual state of war existed between Comanches and Mexicans (R. González 1825). In March Comanches raided along the Coahuila border; many horses and mules were stolen at both San Fernando de Nava and the presidio at Rio Grande; and a soldier was killed at Santa Rosa. There were raids in October near San Fernando, La Bahia, and Atascosa, and again in November near Santa Rosa, San Juan de Allende, and San Fernando de Nava (McLean 1974-93, 1:260).

A rescued captive said the attack on the Villa de Nava was by Yamparikas from the upper Colorado who were also planning to take the horse herd from the presidio at Rio Grande (Andrade 1825). Again the divisional attribution is unclear; those raiders could have been descendants of Somiquaso's people, or the term Yamparikas could have been simply a generic identification of Comanches far away. In a celebrated incident in June 1825, Ysachene, Bonique ("alias El Negro"), and Hoyoso, along with 226 warriors and 104 women and children, came to Béxar. Discontented with the quantity of gifts, and "with the freedom and impudence that has become customary because there is not sufficient troops to contain them," they robbed three houses, took three horses, and killed nineteen cows (Ahumada 1825a).[1] Hoyoso was later captured while trying to steal horses from Béxar. Ysachene tried to negotiate for his release but was rebuffed (Ahumada 1825b); Hoyoso's fate is unknown.

The new Anglo-American colonies in Texas and their horses offered inviting targets for Indian raids (Bastrop 1823). The impresario, Stephen Austin, was well aware of the causes of the raids, and he wrote to the Mexican government that as long as there was a market in the United States for horses stolen in Mexico, there could be no lasting peace with the Comanches. By trading guns for horses, traders north of the Arkansas were, in effect, "sending an army into foreign territory" (Barker 1926:54). It was not until 1826 that the Mexican secretary of state asked the American minister to Mexico to stop the "traders in blood who put instruments of death into the hands of those barbarians" (Weber 1982:95), but there is no record of any action on the part of American officials.

The colonists harbored a general fear that the Indians were uniting against them. The primary instigators were held to be Wacos and Wichitas, but the rumors said that Comanches had been invited to join. Several expeditions against the Indians were attempted, but none got off the ground. The motives involved in those expeditions were not all military; in the summer of

1825 several traders from Austin's colony who claimed to have been robbed by Indians began agitating for retaliation. Austin however, wrote to the governor, "Their real purpose is to kill Indians and steal their horses" (McLean 1974–93, 1:528).

In the summer of 1827 the Freedonian revolt broke out in eastern Texas; it was quickly repressed, and General Anastacio Bustamente, vice president of Mexico, at the head of the forces already called out, turned his attention to the Indians. He issued a proclamation offering peace but promising warfare until peace was achieved (Berlandier 1980:343 n. 1). In July, after Captain Nicasio Sanchez defeated a Comanche war party on the Agua Fria River, the leaders of the local groups around Béxar—Yncoroy, Quelluna (keyena 'turkey', from the Spanish gallina), and Quellucare (meaning unknown)—came in, saying that although the principal chiefs were off fighting Osages, they would agree to a "suspension of arms" until the chiefs could be summoned home. In the interim Comanches promised to refrain from "hurting or insulting" Mexicans, and Mexicans would not visit the Comanches without a civil passport and notifying the military (A. Bustamente et al. 1827).

After a year of tension, in August 1828 Paruakevitsi came to Béxar and was "showered with gifts" (Berlandier 1844:177). He returned in October with thirty-six men, fourteen women, and many children, saying he had spent the year "examining the intentions of the different tribes of his nation" and had determined that all wanted peace (Elozúa 1828). On one of those two occasions the Comanche chiefs and the Mexican officials ritually ended hostilities. As described by Berlandier:

> The chiefs were drawn up in a circle. First they swore, in the presence of the sun and earth, that they would do no more harm to the inhabitants of Mexico. Then they dug a hole in the ground in the center of the circle, and into it they placed some of their gunpowder, several arrows (which they broke before placing them in the hole), some daggers, and a quantity of the standard ammunition issued to the troops. They then covered them with dirt and filled the hole to signify that henceforth weapons would be buried forever between their people and the Mexican nation. [Berlandier 1969:66]

That description parallels the ceremony performed by Governor Anza some forty years earlier to symbolize peace with Ecueracapa.

In March 1829 Paruakevitsi told Governor José María Viesca that he was going to New Mexico to "present himself as a friend to the Comandante General of that territory" (Elozúa 1829a). During his absence Paruakevitsi "entrusted the care of the good order" to his subordinates Quelluna, Toyoros (toya 'mountain') and El Ronco, possibly the Kiowa who married Somiquaso's daughter in 1805 (Elozúa 1829b).

New Mexico and Northern Mexico, 1821–45

In 1821 in New Mexico, Chimal Colorado—last mentioned in 1815—was given a silver medal as Comanche general (Griego 1822), but the circumstances of his claim to the position are unknown. During the early 1820s Comanche relations with New Mexico changed for the worse. Those changes are nowhere more evident than in the decline in Comanche visitors to Santa Fe and in the amount of gifts available for them. Between 1820 and 1822 officials in Santa Fe ran up debts of over 6,600 pesos for gifts to all of the Allied Nations, yet they received no funds from Mexico (Cavallero 1823). In August 1821 a group of Comanches, angered at the lack of annual gifts at Santa Fe, killed several cows and sheep at San Miguel (Duran 1821). The governor, aware that gifts were the mainstay of good relations, called for a public subscription to raise funds for the annuity goods (Melgares 1821).

Moreover, instead of the constant stream of visitors carrying news and messages between Comanchería and the capital, now the New Mexicans had to send out word when an interview was desired, and that did not always produce results. In July 1824 Governor Bartolomé Baca invited the principal chiefs to a meeting on the Canadian River. When only a small party showed up, messengers were again sent out, searching eight days without success. With only the leader of the small party to talk to, Baca made a long speech, complaining that they had all deceived him (B. Baca 1824).

In January 1825, when Comanches raided near El Paso and San Elizario, Comandante General Manuel Ochoa wrote to Baca that he would no longer tolerate the killing and robbery "prejudicial to the common interests" (Ochoa 1825a). The governor sent word out to the Comanches, requesting that the principal chief come to Santa Fe. Apparently he did, although the Comanches were reported to be "insolent as they have become accustomed to be" (B. Baca 1825a).

In March Indians raided into Chihuahua, with many "grievous injuries to the lives and houses of the people." There were rumors that they had actually intended to attack Apaches but had found the haciendas too inviting. Ochoa asked Baca to tell the Comanche leaders that

> it was not necessary for them to attack our people . . . since they [the Comanches] could whip them [the Apaches] without our taking part in favor or against one or the other, respecting that both nations were friends and allies of our government, and we would maintain our neutrality in their debates. [Ochoa 1825b]

In May Chimal Colorado came to Santa Fe to deliver five captives taken from El Paso. He admitted that Comanches had guided the party, but he blamed the raids on Kiowas and noted that on their return the Comanche chiefs made them give up the captives. He offered to join with the Mexicans to castigate the Kiowas (B. Baca 1825b).

In midsummer the alcalde at San Miguel del Bado reported that traders returning from the "Comanches Pelones" said the Kiowas had two captives from El Paso, who had agreed to guide them back and show them where the cattle were herded (Twitchell 1914, 1:347). That group, the 'bald' or 'shaven' Comanches, are previously unmentioned in the New Mexico records. Hyde (1959:202) argued that in the eighteenth century a group called in French Tête Pelée 'bald head' were an ethnically mixed group of Trading Indians who traveled between the southern Plains and the village tribes of the Missouri. There is, however, no firm link with those Comanches.

Several days later another party of traders reported that some Comanches had admitted firing on Mexicans, but they said that the Kiowas were the real instigators and that the Kiowas were angry because "twelve Kiowas and a Chief had been killed." They were gathering the various Nations of the North, including Wichitas and Come Perros 'dog eaters'—either Arapahos or Apaches—in the Wichita Mountains to plan a counterstroke against El Paso (Twitchell 1914, 1:346). Although there was no major attack on El Paso that year, it is possible that that was the war-planning meeting attended by José Francisco Ruíz about 1824–25 at which a campaign against the Osages was discussed. It is also possible that intertribal meetings such as that were the basis of the Anglo-Texan fears of an intertribal alliance against them.

On September 8 Chimal Colorado, Vicente, and Genizaro[2] visited San Miguel del Bado on the Pecos River (T. Sena 1825a). Ten days later El Baston ('the cane') arrived (T. Sena 1825b), but because there were insufficient funds for gifts in the provincial treasury, the people of San Miguel were urged to contribute to the "regaling" of the visitors (Narbona 1825). On December 30 Chimal Colorado, Vicente, and Genizaro again visited San Miguel and were fed without incident (T. Sena 1825c).

Raids into Chihuahua continued into 1826, and diplomatic efforts to curb them were accelerated. That summer, messengers went back and forth between Santa Fe and the Comanche camps (Narbona 1826a). In August Chief Cordero and two other chiefs, including Ysacoroco, possibly the son of Ysapampa noted in 1812, Estrellas 'stars', and a number of men visited Santa Fe and laid the groundwork for a further meeting (Narbona 1826b). The resulting treaty, "with the motive of removing all unpleasantness," set the Pecos River as the limit of "the lands which the Comanches inhabit." The Comanches would not "pass its right bank without previously telling the Comandante General." It allowed that "subsistence commerce under the established laws" would continue, and the Comanches promised not to interfere with the Santa Fe Trail and to help the caravans when necessary. The annual presentation of gifts would be reestablished in Santa Fe and in Béxar, and Cordero and Paruaquita would be recognized "with the character of Generals on the part of the Republic of Mexico." They were given medals "with the Arms of the Republic on the obverse and an emblem representing peace on the reverse" and canes "as insignia" (Elias et al. 1826).

In October Chief Cordero and the Yamparika chief Paruaquita, not heard from since the contretemps in Béxar in 1810, traveled to Chihuahua City for formal treaty talks, where they claimed to speak for the Jupes, the Tanemas, and the Kiowas. This is one of the last references to the Jupes and one of the few contemporary uses of the Tanema ethnonym; the claim to be the Kiowa representative is uncertain. Vice Governor José Antonio de Arce of Chihuahua was not sanguine about the treaty's abilities to ensure the peace. He warned the state legislature that although "for 20 years they have not passed within 200 leagues of us, now they make war against San Elizario. . . . If we allow them to destroy this second post they can penetrate into the most populated part of the state" (Arce 1826); his fears for Chihuahua were realistic, but possibly premature.

In April 1827 interpreter Juan Cristóbal Tenorío was sent in search of the Comanches with instructions to seek an interview with the "Principales de la parcialidad Comanche" (the "principals of the Comanche division") to discuss "our friendship" and the "treaties which were celebrated in Chihuahua by Cordero and Paruaquita," but it is not known whether he actually met any Comanches (Anonymous 1827). The following October several hundred otherwise unidentified Comanches were reported raiding between Taos and Abiquiu (Martín 1827); forty men were sent north to stop them, but there was no contact (Manuel Martínez 1827). At the same time a small body of Comanches under Samparillena and Molote, both previously unmentioned, were "soliciting trade" at the Punto de Salinas on the eastern slope of the Manzano Mountains southeast of Albuquerque (Arocha 1827a, b).

The next spring Tenorío went with a party of traders to discuss "important matters in the national service" with the Comanches (Arocha 1828a). He returned on June 28, bringing with him a chief named Panchoconuque, previously unmentioned. The object of the visit was to persuade Governor Arocha to give Panchoconuque the title of "general," together with a cane of office, because "it is not of hard wood [*palo duro*]" (Maese 1828); the allusion to "hard wood" may refer to the cane as a physical symbol of the title of general. Rather than immediately invest the chief, Arocha postponed the matter until when he could meet with all the Kotsotekas (Maese 1828).

Thus, on August 29 Arocha and several others, including José Francisco Ruíz from Texas, met with some "600 souls" on the Gallinas River beyond San Miguel. After Tenorío translated the 1826 treaty, Arocha asked the assembled people if they would conform to it: "The answer by the whole ranchería: that the Kotsotekas would conform with the treaties of peace and friendship which they had just heard, and would ratify them anew." They also promised not to permit the Nations of the North to continue their hostilities against El Paso and San Elizario. The people then selected Toro Echicero 'sorcerer bull' to "lead and protect their welfare." It is not clear why Panchoconuque was not elected, or even whether he was present; his name does not reappear in the records. Arocha presented the new chief with a medal and a silver-headed cane "as insignia of his commission" and "such presents as I could and was permitted by the scarcity which existed in the warehouse of the Allied Nations" (Arocha, Ruíz, and Cavallero 1828).

In March 1829, Paruakevitsi had left Texas to "present himself as a friend" to the Comandante General of New Mexico. He arrived in New Mexico in July and sent word to Arocha that "with the end of realizing a lasting treaty" with the Republic of Mexico, he proposed to meet at Alamo Gordo on the Pecos (Arocha 1829). Samparillena again acted as messenger and intermediary, traveling back and forth between Santa Fe and Comanchería to arrange for the upcoming meeting (J. A. Chávez 1829a). Although there was confusion about getting enough money for presents, Governor Arocha, Jefe Politico José Antonio Chávez, and Samparillena and his party set out for the Bosque Redondo (Arocha 1829; Chávez 1829b). On July 25, after a brief delay at the Cañada de Juan de Dios, they met Paruakevitsi, his captains, "and more than a hundred warriors." The next day the two groups met in a formal session. Arocha read General Bustamente's 1827 truce proclamation, and all agreed that it was "bueno" (Arocha 1829). The chiefs promised to try to prevent raids in the eastern states (Texas, Coahuila, and Nuevo Leon) and at El Paso. Paruakevitsi was to travel as quickly as possible to Béxar and deliver to José Francisco Ruíz a communiqué covering the events of their meeting (Chávez, Arocha, and Ruíz 1829). Then, in contrast to the poverty of the 1828 meeting, there were plenty of gifts for the chiefs, "jackets, gunpowder, tobacco, corn meal, serapes, scissors, and other things" (Chávez 1829b).

On December 30, 1829, Captain Namayajipe (possibly *nama* reflexive, *yahipu* an in-law, 'my in-law') of the "Comanche tribe and Yamparica division" visited Santa Fe hoping to persuade Chávez to join in a campaign against the Nations of the North. It is also possible that the captain may have been Shoshone: six days later, on January 5, 1830, a party of "Sonsores" under Chief Namaya visited Anton Chico (M. A. Baca 1830a); the similarity of the names suggests they were the same man. The governor denied Namayajipe's request, saying Mexican arms could not be used as auxiliaries in a war between "gentiles." While the Comanches spent three days looking for lost horses, the Mexicans scrambled for goods with which to regale them "as was the custom." However, when Namayajipe saw the poor quality of the goods, he sent interpreter Tenorío to return his cane and medal. After a "humiliating" explanation of conditions in New Mexico, Chávez finally persuaded the chief to reclaim the insignia and take the gifts (J. A. Chávez 1830a). It is unknown, however, how Namayajipe came into possession of the prestige items, since there is no mention of a change in the Yamparika leadership since Paruaquita's visit in 1828, and absolutely no evidence that Shoshones were ever presented with medals or canes in New Mexico.

In the 1830s official relations between Comanches and Mexicans alternated between active hostilities and attempts at reconciliation. Few Comanches visited Santa Fe, or at least their visits were not recorded. On January 2, 1830, seven Comanches were given gifts of punche (native tobacco), gunpowder, and mirrors. On the fifth, Samparillena and fifteen others arrived and two cows were killed for them, but there is no record of other gifts (Anonymous 1830). In August parties of Comanches, Utes, and Navajos came to Santa Fe to get "gifts as usual," but there were not enough gifts for all, and some left unhappy (J. A. Chávez 1830b). After three New Mexicans were killed at Anton Chico on the Pecos, possibly by "Pananas," an auxiliary force tracked the Indians as far as the Rio Colorado, but never made contact (M. A. Baca 1830b).

In 1831 both the Comanchero trade and the hunting of buffalo by ciboleros—professional New Mexican buffalo hunters—were again prohibited (J. A. Chávez 1831). Although that did not stop the traffic, it made it illegal and thus not something to be reported. The possibility of hostilities did not stop traders, some of whom traveled far out onto the Plains. In January 1832 a Texan force campaigning against the Comanches met a party of Taoseños at the head of the Rio Florida, and another between Vibora and Albanas in southern Texas (Barragán 1833).

However, when the two situations conflicted—when illegal traders met with Indian hostilities—the ambivalent nature of the relations between Comanches and local New Mexicans was highlighted. For instance, in early September, 1831, a group of twenty Comanches, Kiowas, and Pawnees, with two captives, came to Cuesta in the Pecos valley. Their leader was "one of the sons of Huacoruco (alias Viscarra)"; it is not clear to whom the alias applies, father or son; the father might be the Huanacoruco of the period 1780–1800. They had eight horses, two of which were branded, and were asking for powder, clothing, and serapes. One man bought a branded horse for two serapes and six charges of powder; another gave a fringed blanket for the other marked horse. A widow exchanged a gun for a horse, and her son bought a colt of one or two years with a blanket, two hands of tobacco, and a three charges of powder. A man bought a young mare for a bit of powder and a serape; another bought a mare for two hands of tobacco, and a third bought two horses (Ronquillo and Vigil 1831).

Meanwhile, a party of traders from the Rio Arriba, Santa Cruz de la Cañada, and the Rio Chama were traveling toward the Plains. At Agua del Toro, near Tierra Blanca below Anton Chico, they were attacked by Indians who took all their horses and trade goods. Four New Mexicans were killed and two wounded—one of whom had eleven wounds from lance, arrow, fire-arm, and knife, and had been scalped—but two men escaped and brought the news to Cuesta. Although some said the party was comprised of Pawnees and Kiowas, others said there were Comanches present also because they had found moccasin prints, several of which had the 'crossed foot' ("el pie crusado") and others of which had 'rounded toes' ("la punta de la tegua redonda") (Ronquillo and Vigil 1831). The meaning of these descriptive expressions is unknown.

It was never clarified whether the attacking Indians were those who had traded in Cuesta, but all Comanches were now suspect. When six Coman-ches—five men and a woman—came to San Miguel, they were kept at a dis-tance until they could explain themselves and their relationship to the recent attackers. They argued that the tracks could have been made by Cuampes (Arapahos or Apaches) or even Shoshones (Ronquillo and Vigil 1831). Then Toro Echicero himself came in, hoping to reestablish trade and to obtain the return of prisoners held in Chihuahua. He said that when they were released, hostilities would stop (Vizcarra 1831); the identity of those prisoners is unknown. Governor Chávez rejected the offer, saying that the Comanches had not proposed "anything in our favor." He then reversed the offer, sug-gesting that if the chief would stop the hostilities and release Mexicans held captive, then the comandante general might release the prisoners. Toro Echi-cero grudgingly acceded and asked that the propositions be forwarded, but apparently no action was taken (Chávez 1831).

In October other Comanches "declared war" on Chihuahua (Chávez 1831; Creel 1928:11), attacking the army horse herd and killing two soldiers. In response José Ronquillo, captain of the northern frontier, was sent against the Indians (Calvo 1831), but little was actually done. In June 1833 there was a report of a "considerable gathering at the Cañada de Trujillo, Ojo Medan-oso, and Monte Rebuelto"—the latter place also known as the Round Mound on the Canadian. The governor took the opportunity of that report to complain about his situation. Although he thought their "arguments could be reduced to venegeance for the deaths of five men of their nation in the Rio Pecos," he noted that the Comanches made promises of peace "in the security of not being inconvenienced by us." Moreover, the Comanches had a pragmatic, "machiavellian" policy of

> war against the frontiers of Chihuahua . . . trading in New Mexico . . . warring against the Jicarillas and Navajos . . . and watching to see if the Anglo-Americans return to their country in September . . . to see if they can accomplish a favorable outcome. [Ronquillo 1833]

In their encounters the Comanches usually had the upper hand, a fact the New Mexican authorities knew only too well. A recurrent problem was the bad shape of the military and auxiliary forces, caused in part by the difficulty in obtaining remounts. In October 1832 a unique solution for that problem was suggested:

> Notwithstanding the disapproval of the commerce which is here customary, and which it is impossible to avoid with the Comanche, and in view of the deplorable state of the remounts, it occurred to me to commission the interpreter Juan Cristóbal Tenorío, a Corporal, and six soldiers, who with four hundred pesos, more or less, in goods . . . to buy horses from the Comanche. [Ronquillo 1832]

The outcome of the proposal is not known. In 1834 the entire military force of New Mexico consisted of 900 men "all vecinos, badly armed, poorly equipped, and without instructions in handling arms" (Abreú 1834).

In May 1834 Ronquillo again led an expedition against the Comanches, killing two, capturing fourteen, and retaking forty-five horses (Rodriguez 1833-39). Although it is not known whether there was a connection with that defeat, by July 23 an agreement had been signed at El Paso by the Comanche leaders Ysacoruco, called "General of the Two Palominos," and four others— Coyote Griton 'shouting coyote', Tecolote Cabezon 'owl head', Zorra Alta 'high fox', and Aguilla del Aire 'eagle of the air' (Sonnichsen 1968). The first is possibly the man who visited Santa Fe in 1826, a son of Ysampampi, although the significance of "the Two Palominos" is not known; none of the others were previously named.

Needless to say, that agreement did not stop the raids. On February 3, 1835, a group of Comanches arrived in Béxar with a herd of horses stolen in Chihuahua (Jenkins 1973, 1:18); in May six or seven hundred Comanches crossed the Rio Grande at the Big Bend (R. A. Smith 1960:99), and in June the Mexican government wrote to the Texas governor urging him to stop his people from buying branded horses obviously stolen in Chihuahua (Jenkins 1973, 1:149). The authorities were constantly reprimanding Texas citizens for buying branded horses and mules (Músquiz 1834; Ugartechea 1835b; Navarro 1835). A proclamation against that practice was read at two feast-day celebrations and was posted in a public place (J. M. Flores 1835).

Realizing that the central government of Mexico would offer no assistance, the state of Sonora revived the old scalp–hunting laws. Chihuahua followed suit in 1837. The scalp of a male, fourteen years and older, was to bring 100 pesos; that of a female 50 pesos; and that of a child under fourteen, 25 pesos (R. A. Smith 1960:102). The first priority was to be Apaches, second Comanches and Kiowas, and third Navajos. Durango's 1840 scalp law required hacienda owners to organize militia companies for defense; the state government would pay a per diem allowance for time spent in the field as well as a share in the booty. However, Durango required full proof (that is, heads), for there had been rumors that Mexicans were also being scalped.

In 1839, because of the deaths of twenty-five citizens "who went to look for trade," another attempt was made to license traders from New Mexico (M. Armijo 1839) as well as to limit the ciboleros. But in 1840, although many New Mexicans had solicited licenses to trade with the Comanches "as they [had] always done" (Archuleta 1840), the governor had to admit, "the territory is so easy to leave that if we tried to enforce the order, it would take a force of no less than one thousand men to man the military points on the frontier" (M. Armijo 1840). In January 1841 five men were caught on an illegal buffalo hunt; they were fined twenty-five pesos and spent a month in jail (Salazar 1841).

In the fall and winter of 1840–41 three major Comanche war parties crossed the Rio Grande into Mexico. The first party hit in September 1840, passing through Guerrero, Tamaulipas, and Nuevo Leon. The second party began in October, crossing the Rio Grande above Lampozos and continuing to Salinas Victoria and San Nicolas de los Garza, finally recrossing the Rio Grande in November. The third party hit Coahuila in December, passing to San Luis Potosi and into Zacatecas (Vizcaya-Canales 1968:51). In May 1842 an estimated 300 Comanches raced down the north bank of the Rio Grande almost to the coast; the local population fled into Mexico (*Houston Telegraph and Texas Register* May 4, 1842).

In July 1844 a group of "Comanches Llaneros," a previously unrecorded ethnonym, appeared at Santa Fe (B. Baca 1844) under "Generals" Caballero and Quilluea and eleven capitancillos. Both generals are previously unmentioned and the names of the capitancillos as given in the manuscript are so garbled that translations or even transcriptions are nearly impossible. They reported that 300 men were on their way to raid in Chihuahua (Anonymous 1844). Later that year a Comanche party was "whipped by the Mexicans in a fight near Matamoros" (Winfrey and Day 1959–66, 2:172). It is possible that this was the "battle with the Mexicans about 1845" that Mooney recorded as having "practically exterminated" the Tenewas (Mooney 1910).

In May 1845 a large Comanche party, said to be 1,000 lodges, was reported to be making preparations to cross the Rio Grande to take revenge for an "unfortunate Expedition" made sometime earlier. They returned in July "with a large drove of animals which they got from the Mexicans near Laredo on the Rio Grande" (Winfrey and Day 1959-66, 2:299). Later that year a group of Comanches met with Francisco García Conde, commander of the Mexican Fifth Military Division. They said that although they were in favor of peace, "very many" warriors were already on their way south. Two parties of more than 100 each traveled as far south as Zacatecas City and spent more than six weeks in north-central Mexico, some staying as long as three months (R. A. Smith 1960).

Thus, Comanche relations with Mexican New Mexico in the 1840s involved a serious contradiction. Trade relations were relatively peaceful, a peace "which the Supreme Being has miraculously preserved for a long series of years" (Mariano Martínez 1845b). However, that trade was often in horses and cattle stolen from farther south. Try as they might, neither the local New Mexican government nor the national Mexican government could halt the trade in stolen horses. In June 1845 the governor wrote to the state legislature that the Comanches had "provoked a war by their repeated incursions in Chihuahua, Durango and Zacatecas," and that it might become necessary to prevent them from visiting the New Mexican settlements altogether (Mariano Martínez 1845b). Moreover, the governor often complained that the Comanches continued to maintain relations with the Nations of the North, "who are reputed to be enemies of the Spaniards" (Mariano Martínez 1845a).

But there were also incidents of positive interaction between Comanches and New Mexicans. By the Treaty of Velasco after the Battle of San Jacinto, the Republic of Texas claimed all the land north and east of the Rio Grande, including eastern New Mexico. In 1841, in an effort to establish political sovereignty over that territory, to divert the profitable Santa Fe Trail trade through Texas, and to overawe the Comanches with military power, Texas president Mirabeau Buonaparte Lamar authorized a military expedition to capture Santa Fe. Poorly organized and lacking guides, the so-called Texan-Santa Fe Expedition wandered aimlessly on the Llano Estacado. Their horses were stolen by Kiowas, and both Comanches and viageros sent news of their advance to Santa Fe (Kendall 1844:208). The Texans were captured at San Miguel del Bado; they were tried, several were summarily executed, and the rest were sent to Mexico City in chains. In 1843 the Texans tried again with the so-called Warfield-Snively Expedition, which also considered attacking the Santa Fe Trail. They had even less success, with Comanches and viageros again sending word of their advance (M. Armijo 1843a); Governor Manuel Armijo reluctantly admitted that although "these pirates [the Comanches] have made assaults on both the territory and myself . . . they must be given the credit for bringing the news" (M. Armijo 1843b). To conclude the venture, in a clearly illegal move Captain Phillip St. George Cooke, of the U.S. Army, crossed the international border into Mexican territory, arrested the Texans, and confiscated all their guns. They were then set loose to straggle back to Texas.

The Santa Fe Trail through Comanchería, 1821–34

In 1821 Saint Louis trader William Becknell heard about the Mexican Revolution and decided to try his luck in Santa Fe (Becknell 1823). His profits lured others into the trade, and while there is no record that Becknell met any Comanches or other Plains peoples on his trip west, others were more fortunate. About the same time that Becknell began his trip, former militia general Thomas James organized a party of traders to visit Santa Fe. Although his account is undoubtedly biased in favor of his own role in events, and of Anglo-American views of Spaniards and Mexicans, there seems little reason to doubt most of the events.

On the North Fork of the Canadian River James's party was stopped by a party of Comanches under two chiefs, a "friendly" chief and an unfriendly "one-eyed Chief" (James 1846:68); both of the chiefs are otherwise unidentified, although the latter may be Pisinampe, also called El Tuerto 'one eye' (Nava 1798). After distributing approximately three thousand dollars worth of gifts, the party was allowed to continue. About three weeks later they came to a large Comanche encampment, according to James a thousand lodges under a "little vicious looking old man" (1846:69). Here James again distributed gifts, and was about to lose his entire stock to looters when the "principal chief named Big Star" arrived and dispersed the crowd; at another place in his narrative, James called that chief "Big Star Chief of the Ampireka Band" (1846:138). The ethnonym is clearly Yamparika, but "Big Star" is otherwise unidentified. The next day the one-eyed chief reappeared, and a dispute erupted about what to do with the Americans. At a council, from which young men were barred, it was decided to put the traders to death. Only the timely arrival of a Spanish officer and a chief James called Cordaro— clearly Cordero—saved James and his party. James described the chief as "a tall Indian of about seventy years of age, dressed in the complete regimentals of an American colonel" (James 1846:75–76). The chief presented credentials, probably received during his 1816 visit to Natchitoches:

This is to certify that Cordaro, a Chief of the Comanches has visited the Fort at Nacotoche with fifteen of his tribe; that he remained here two weeks, and during the whole time behaved very well. It is my request that all Americans who meet him or any of his tribe should treat him and them with great respect and kindness, as they are true friends of the United States. (signed) John Jameson; U.S. Agent at Nacotoche on Red River. [James 1846:75–76]

With Cordero's assistance the Americans were allowed to proceed.

According to James's account he reached Santa Fe in December 1821; in mid-January 1822 Chief Cordero arrived, "dressed in his full regimentals." At the chief's request a council with the governor was held, "attended by the Spanish officers, magistrates and principal citizens." Here Cordero

> expressed his pleasure that we and the Spaniards were friends, that he would be pleased to see us living together like brothers and he hoped that the American trade would come to his country as well as to the Spaniards. He complained that we traded with their enemies, the Osages, and furnished them with powder, guns, and lead, but had no intercourse with the Comanches. He hoped the government of the United States would interfere and stop the depredations of the Osage upon his nation. "They steal our horses and murder our people," said he, "and the Americans sell them the arms and ammunition which they use in war on us." [James 1846:85]

There is, however, no record of that meeting in the New Mexico archives.

There are other confusions in James's account. For instance, he claimed that Chief Cordero had James write a letter to Agent Jamison and that on arriving at "Nacatoche" the chief received three horses loaded with presents (1846:86). However, there is no record of a later visit by Cordero to Natchitoches; moreover, Agent Jamieson had died in 1819 and had been succeeded by William Bradford—indeed, James should have known that, for he admitted having stopped at Bradford's house at Fort Smith on his outward journey (1846:63). Finally, although James said Cordero died "soon after" 1824, Cordero was alive two years later, at the 1826 council at the Bosque Redondo.

Arriving in New Mexico at about the same time was the Hugh Glenn–Jacob Fowler party (J. Fowler 1898). While James went to Santa Fe, the Glenn-Fowler party spent the winter on the upper Arkansas River, near modern Pueblo, Colorado, trading with about seven hundred lodges of Indians, including Kiowas, Cheyennes, Arapahos, and Ietans (J. Fowler 1898: 57–59). The latter may have been Comanches, for the upper Arkansas had long been Comanche country. However, their chief had understood Stephen Long the year before to have promised to send gifts, and inasmuch as Long had met only one bedraggled party of Ietans, and apparently made no promises of presents to them, the identification of the Indians who traded with the Glenn-Fowler party as Comanches is uncertain. Hyde (1959:202) speculated that they were "Trading Indians," a composite group of Utes and Apaches who traveled between New Mexico and the northeastern Plains. Although it is an intriguing possibility, there is no conclusive evidence for the existence of such a group.

In 1822 Thomas James and the brothers Robert and John McKnight led another expedition to the Comanches. Proceeding up the North Fork of the Canadian River, they built a "fort," probably no more than a stockade, below the confluence of Wolf Creek. John McKnight and three other traders volunteered to visit a nearby Indian village to persuade the inhabitants to come to the new post; James identified the village as Comanche, but since it soon emerged that none of McKnight's party could speak either the Indians' language or Spanish, the basis for the identification is uncertain. By signs, Mc-Knight told the Indians that there was an interpreter back at the trading post. Then, leaving two of his men as hostages, McKnight and one other trader returned to find James. Meanwhile, the post on the Canadian had washed away, and James and the rest of the party had moved about a hundred miles upstream (apparently inside Mexican territory), and built a second post. But they had failed to leave any notice of their move at the former site. McKnight and his companion were never heard from again. James accused the Comanches of having killed them but offered no evidence to support his accusation.[3]

Despite that initial disquietude, James apparently did a thriving business with a Comanche village under a chief named "Alasarea the Towash."[4] As before, the Comanches complained about the lack of American trade:

> They . . . united in requesting me to encourage my countrymen to visit them with goods and trade with them. Trade with the Spaniards they said, was unprofitable; they had nothing to give them for their horses except ammunition, and this they refused to sell to the Indians. They wished the Americans to be friendly and intimate with them, and complained bitterly that we supplied their enemies, the Osages, with arms and ammunition. "The Osages," they say, "get their powder, balls and guns from the Americans, but we can get none, or very few of them. This is wrong, very wrong. . . . Tell our Great Father . . . to protect us and send his people to trade with us." [James 1846:150]

Later, James's old adversary, the one-eyed chief, appeared in the village. In place of his antagonism of the year before, he was now friendly. He excused his former attitude by saying that the year before he was seeking revenge for a brother killed by Osages. Since James had just come from the Osages, he would have made a proper substitute. But now he would take James as a brother in place of his own, and he would be safe in the whole nation.

Once, when some of James's horses were stolen, the chief mounted his horse,

> whip in hand and in about two hours returned with two of the stolen horses. In the afternoon he brought back a third, and at night came up with the fourth. His whip was bloody and his face contorted with rage. He was in a mood to make men tremble before him, when none but the boldest spirits would dare to cross his path or oppose his will. After he left the last horse with me I heard his voice in every part of the camp, proclaiming, what the interpreter told me was a warning for the protection of my property. "Your horses are yours," said he, "to sell or keep as you please; but when you once sell them you cannot take them back." [James 1846:143]

It is not clear, however, whether the denunciation of "Indian giving" was that of the one-eyed chief or whether James put those words into his mouth.

The new St. Louis-Santa Fe (and beyond to Chihuahua) trade was said to be lucrative; in 1825, produce worth $18,000 were said to have returned profits of $190,000 in "gold and silver bullion, and coin, and precious furs," although the profit margin was reduced by exorbitant Mexican tariffs (Storrs 1825; Benton 1825, 1:109). It is, however, unclear how the province of New Mexico, long reported to be proverty-stricken—even with the addition of the northern Mexican state of Chihuahua—could have afforded the continued export of the large amounts of hard currency such as was reported in the initial reports of the Santa Fe trade. Nevertheless, with the advent of the Santa Fe trade, American interests and policy toward Comanches changed. In place of the earlier efforts, as in John Sibley's time, to have the Comanches join the Anglo-Americans against the Spaniards, the new policy was an effort to get them out of the way, and the rhetoric used to describe the Comanches changed accordingly.

For instance, in reporting John McKnight's death, *Niles' Weekly Register*, reprinting an article from the *St. Louis Enquirer* included a brief description of the Comanches; they were

> a numerous and warlike nation, bordering on the heads of the Arkansas, and spreading through a great portion of Texas. It is supposed they could bring into the field at least 15,000 warriors. The Spaniards have never been able to do anything with them, and have almost relinquished the country to their possession. From St. Antonio, in Texas, to Santa Fe, in New Mexico, the Camanches roam at large, the undisputed masters of the soil. All the early frontier establishments of the Spaniards have long

since been cut off by those Indians, and the further ingress of the Europeans entirely checked by the fears which they inspired. But the Americans they have heretofore viewed in the most friendly manner, between between whom and themselves there has always been kept up a kind and mutual intercourse.

Although much of the article paralleled other contemporary American newspaper accounts of the Comanches, territory, population, and the Spaniards' (i.e., Mexicans') inability to control them, it added a new feature: the Comanches now viewed to be standing in the way of "European ingress" and had even forced the Spaniards to retreat.

In 1824 Sen. Thomas Hart Benton of the new state of Missouri, eastern terminus of the trade, began an effort to secure federal protection from both the New Mexican tariffs and from Indian attacks; one of his key arguments was that the Indians—especially Pawnees and Comanches—posed a serious and continuing threat to the trade. In Benton's rhetoric, the Comanches were no longer a valuable and potential ally; they were a savage foe. Moreover, the 1819 Adams-Onis treaty establishing the borders of Louisiana was "a protecting barrier to the cruel Comanches, who kill and rob our citizens" (Benton 1825, 1:347). In the Senate he compared the situation to another contemporary issue, the suppresion of piracy in the Carribean:

> Will you lavish your sympathy upon a citizen hung by a pirate, and deny your compassion to a citizen shot and butchered by an Indian? The story of piratical murders has been told to you in language which harrows up the soul; now listen to a plain statement of robberies and murders committed upon our citizens on their way to Mexico. [Benton 1825, 1:344]

Then, quoting from a report on the trade he had requested from the Santa Fe trader Augustus Storrs (Storrs 1825), Benton continued with a chronology of aggression along the route:

> Mr. Chouteau was attacked upon an island in the Arkansas River, by 300 Pawnees. They were repulsed with the loss of thirty killed and wounded, and declared it to be the most bloody affair in which they had ever been engaged. This was their first acquaintance with American arms. In 1822, Mr. Maxwell was killed and another American wounded, by the Camanchas, near the mountains. In 1823, the Pawnees killed a Spaniard, on the Arkansas, and forcibly took from him thirteen mules. The company which went out last summer had upwards of forty horses and mules stolen, about fifteen miles south of the Arkansas, by the Camanches.[5] The same company, thirty–two in number, encountered, on their return, a war party of eighty Pawnees. The war whoop was raised, and both parties drew up for action, but the enemy agreed to a compromise when

they found they could not rob without losing the lives of their warriors. In the winter of 1822-'23, Mr. John McKnight, of St. Louis, was killed by the Camanches, at some distance south of the Arkansas. [Benton 1825, 1:344]

Benton's and Storrs's rhetoric was to have lasting consequences on the historiography of the Santa Fe trade, but the validity of their claims is questionable. The first incident in Storrs's account was the Chouteau's Island fight of 1817; but the defenders of Chouteau's Island were not calico and gewgaw traders from St. Louis to Santa Fe; rather, they were fur traders on the upper Arkansas River, and the fight occurred five years before the Santa Fe trade had even begun. Benton's second, third, and fourth incidents are otherwise unreported in the literature on the Santa Fe Trail. The final incident was the killing of John McKnight, but again in a context unrelated to the direct Santa Fe trade. Indeed, by 1825, although there were indeed killings and stock thefts on the Santa Fe Trail, only a few incidents could be attributed to the western Indians, and none specifically to Comanches.

Nonetheless, Benton, on behalf of the citizens of Missouri, pushed through a bill authorizing $10,000 for building a road—actually simply marking the trace—"from the frontier of Missouri to the Confines of New Mexico," and another $20,000 to defray the costs of obtaining the "consent of the intervening tribes of Indians" (Benton 1825, 1:341). George C. Sibley, eldest son of John Sibley, headed the road commission (K. C. Gregg 1952:5). Agreements were made with the tribes on the eastern end of the new trail, but apparently the commissioners did not meet with any western Indians.

In 1826, because of the alleged trouble from Indians on the western end of the trail, the Missouri state legislature petitioned Congress for a military post at the crossing of the Arkansas into Mexico (Stephens 1916:246). Jacob Brown, the ranking general in the Army, argued that "the nature of the service required . . . a different character from a fixed garrison of infantry. A post could not be established without incurring all the difficulties of access and communication," and it was not built (Brown 1827). Shortly thereafter, although the exact date is unclear, the brothers Charles and William Bent and Ceran St. Vrain established a series of trading posts on the upper Arkansas River. The first was the so-called Stockade Post near the mouth of Fountain Creek. Later the more familiar adobe Fort William was built some miles below, between the Timpas and Purgatoire rivers, near present La Junta, Colorado (Grinnell 1923:31; Hyde 1968:61; Lecompte 1972). Although the Bents' posts were located in what had been important Comanche territory during the previous century, by the late 1820s it had become Cheyenne and Arapaho country, and Comanches were rare visitors. In one widely repeated but probably only semihistorical account, a Comanche party led by Bull Hump—otherwise unknown and probably a Cheyenne name for a Comanche individual—on a horse-stealing expedition against the Cheyennes, stopped at the stockade. There they saw Cheyenne moccasin tracks but were persuaded that those Indians had already left, thus avoiding a fight. For the next decade Comanches and Cheyennes exchanged raids, each stopping at the stockade for supplies, often just missing each other, and the Bents had to smooth things over between alternating groups (Grinnell 1923:31; Hyde 1968:42–43).

Meanwhile, because of the series of reported incidents, Anglo-Americans increasingly thought of Comanches as war-like raiders. However, as with Storrs's and Benton's rhetoric, it is often difficult to substantiate those reports. For instance, in 1831, at President Andrew Jackson's request, the famed mountain man Jedediah Smith compiled a list of more than two hundred incidents of killings or robberies in the western Indian and fur trade recorded between 1816 and 1831. Of those, only ten were attributed to Comanches; during the same period Osages were blamed for forty-three incidents, Blackfeet for eighteen, Kansas for seven, and Sioux for five (A. Jackson 1831). Ironically, Smith would become the eleventh Comanche victim, although even that attribution is uncertain.

According to Smith, the ten Comanche incidents were, after John McKnight, in 1826: Simo and Adamoso (killed); 1828: Means and Lamb (killed, lost 300 mules); 1829: Samuel C. Lamb, George Gordon, Samuel Arrison, and William Nation (killed). There seems to be nothing further recorded about "Simo and Adamoso" except that they were in the employ of "Pratte & Co." (A. Jackson 1831:89).

Details of the 1828 incident are confused and it is not clear whether they form part of a single historical stream or refered to separate incidents that have become combined. According to an article in the November 29, 1828 *Niles' Weekly Register*, copied from the *St. Louis Intelligencer*,[6]

> [an eastbound] party of twenty-five . . . were met by a party of Indians who drove off all of their mules and horses not leaving them any with which to travel. . . . Capt. John Means . . . being at a distance from the main body of the company, had his gun taken from him by the Indians, and with it shot dead. . . . The party then pursued their journey on foot, leaving behind them several wagons in some of which were large sums of money. Having considerable specie, they were obliged, we understand, to bury it until they could reach the settlements [a distance of several hundred miles], and procure horses on which to bring it.

According to Josiah Gregg, writing a decade later, the incident had begun with the preceding caravan. Two young members had wandered off from the main party and had gone to sleep on the banks of a stream where they were shot by parties unknown, presumably Indians. One of the unfortunates, Mc-Nees, was immediately killed; the other, Monroe, died later at the Cimarron Crossing. While the party was burying him, several Indians were noticed nearby; although they were likely unaware of the events, they were fired upon and one was killed. The traders were then pursued to the Arkansas River, where they were robbed of nearly a thousand head of mules and horses. Meanwhile, Indians

> beset a company of about twenty men, who followed shortly after—they killed one of their number, and subsequently took from them all the animals they had in their possession. The unfortunate band were now not only compelled to advance on foot, but were even constrained to carry nearly a thousand dollars each upon their backs to the Arkansas river where it was cached . . . till a conveyance was procured to transfer it to the United States. [Gregg 1844, 1:27-29]

Although Captain John Means was clearly the Means referred to by Smith as "Means and Lamb," the *Intelligencer* article cited above made no mention of Mr. Lamb. On the other hand, Smith made no mention of the McNees and Monroe incident, and no mention of it has been located in the St. Louis newspapers, a strange omission for an event so memorable that the crossing of the Cimarron was thereafter called McNee's Crossing.

In later years the story was embellished further. According to the reminiscences of Milton E. Bryan, probably written around 1890, at the Upper Cimarron Crossing, his party found "a large camp of Comanches, evidently there for the purpose of robbery and murder." Unable to turn around "because of the mountainous character of the country"—in fact, the nearest mountains are about one hundred miles west—the party rode right through the village. The chief "met us with a smile of welcome, and said, in Spanish: 'you must stay with us to night.'" The traders refused, and as they hurried on, Captain Means in the rear guard, "was ruthlessly shot and cruelly scalped." The traders were harassed to the Arkansas, losing all their horses. They deciding to bury their money on an island in the river—possibly Chouteau's Island—in order to lighten their loads. According to Bryan, they returned the next year with an army escort and recovered their money (Inman 1897:69-73).

Another set of reminiscences on the incident was written by William Y. Hitt, again many years after the events (Inman 1897:77-85). According to Hitt, their party of about thirty-five men was first attacked less than three days out of Santa Fe by "Mexicans and Indians" who stampeded all their stock—an incident unmentioned by Bryan or Gregg. The traders returned to Santa Fe but could not persuade the officials to recover their animals, and they were forced to buy back their own horses. Starting out again, they had made three hundred miles when early one morning their camp was suddenly attacked by Indians; Hitt did not identify the attackers. Moreover, he made no mention of a village camped across the trace, nor of burying the money.

However, because of the reports of the attack on Means, the first west-bound caravan of 1829, under Charles Bent, was escorted to the international boundary on the Arkansas River by four companies of mounted infantry, with one cannon, under Major Bennett Riley (Perrine 1927, 1928; Young 1952). The outward trip had few incidents of consequence. At Chouteau's Island, while the traders continued on, the escort halted to await their return in the fall. Interestingly, although Milton Bryan described in great detail how he recovered the money from the island and turned it over to Riley for safekeeping, Riley's journal—actually kept by the adjutant, James Izard (Perrine 1928)—makes no mention of it.

Soon after crossing the Arkansas the traders were attacked by unidentified Indians, and Samuel C. Lamme—clearly Smith's Samuel C. Lamb—was killed (Perrine 1928:281). Alerted by riders from the besieged caravan, Riley disregarded the international boundary and went to their aid, firing the cannon with some effect. Although the attackers were beaten off, the traders were harassed all the way to Santa Fe.

After they reached Santa Fe, the traders had "ascertained from the most respectable Mexicans trading with the Camanchies and Kiawas," that is, from Comancheros, that the movement both of the military column and of the traders' caravan since they passed Council Grove on the Neosho River in far eastern Kansas had been known and reported in Santa Fe. Moreover, the Indians had brought details of the fight on the Arkansas to Santa Fe even before the traders' arrival; according to those reports, it was indeed Comanches who had attacked the traders, and they had lost at least eight men (Perrine 1928:293). There is, however, no direct confirmation in the New Mexico archives of such Indian or Comanchero reports; indeed, there is no direct confirmation that Comanches ever brought in reports of the approach of the caravans.

Meanwhile, Riley spent the rest of the summer camped at Chouteau's Island, engaging in several skirmishes with Indians, losing five men, including at least two of those counted by Smith: George Gordon, a discharged soldier who had decided to walk back to the settlements, and William Nation, a mail rider from Leavenworth. Riley did not specifically identify their attackers. One other man, unnamed, was killed during an attack "probably Kiawas, Camanches, and Aripahoes, & perhaps Pawnee Picts" (Perrine 1928:286), and a fifth, Bugler King, who was caught alone while hunting buffalo.

Therefore, of Smith's ten Comanche incidents, all but Simo, Adamoso,

and the first Lamb can be independently confirmed, and Arrison was probably the unnamed soldier with Major Riley. However, Smith mentioned neither
the McNees and Monroe incident, Hitt's Mexican and Indian theft, nor the
Bugler King incident. Of those, only the Bugler King incident, recorded in
the Riley-Izard journal, has any authority; Gregg's report of the McNees-
Monroe incident was based on hearsay, while Bryan's and Hitt's reports were
reminiscences of long past events. At the same time, the identity of the
attackers in Smith's ten incidents remains problematic: only the McKnight,
the second Lamb (Lamme), and the unnamed soldier with Major Riley
incidents were attributed to Comanches by contemporaries; even then the
Lamb (Lamme) attribution was based on rumor in Santa Fe, and the unnamed
soldier attribution was "probably Kiawas, Camanches, and Aripahoes, &
perhaps Pawnee Picts"; like Hitt, the attribution of the Means incident to
Comanches came some sixty years later by Milton Bryan. Thus, although the
reports of Comanche hostilities were generally unsubstantiated, the Comanches were quickly gaining a reputation among Anglo-Americans.

In 1831 Albert Pike, a young Bostonian looking for adventure, came to
Santa Fe. In the fall of 1832 he enlisted with a group of fur trappers, in-
cluding the mountain man Bill Williams, to go to the Red and Washita rivers.
His accounts of that trip—a letter written two years later (Pike 1833), his
Prose Sketches and Poems (Pike 1843), and an unpublished autobiography
(Pike 1886)—are somewhat contradictory, and it is difficult to reconcile
them.

While Pike and his group were camped at the Bosque Redondo on the
Pecos River,

> a small party came into the camp from the Staked Plains with a very
> discouraging story of their experiences. They told our people that they
> had been down there trading with the Comanche and that the Comanche
> had learned that we were going into their country. They said that the Co-
> manche declared that if the Mexicans came in and brought any Amer-
> icans with them they would kill every one of them [the Americans]. . . .
> They stated that the Comanche would trade very fairly with a party of
> traders and let them go off with everything they had bought and then
> follow them and take it all away. [Pike 1886:16]

That message did not discourage the party, and near the edge of the Llano Estacado they came upon a Comanche village. According to Pike's contemporary account, the camp was of twenty lodges, and the people were extremely
poor; they had no blankets, no buffalo robes, no meat, and were shabbily
dressed (Pike 1843). In contrast, his later autobiography stated that there were
"about 5,000 horses and mules" and that "the Comanche had fed us on

buffalo meat. . . . The American Indian is pretty generous when you trust to his generosity" (1886:21).

The "old chief" said they had just been to Santa Fe—possibly one of the group that had visited San Miguel in September—and "they had shaken hands with the Americans and were friends" (Pike 1843:59). However, the trappers had a different interpretation:

> As we all knew that part of the Comanches living to the south along the Presidio del Norte and bordering on the Indians of Texas, were . . . entirely distinct from the Northern Comanches, we took great pains to find out to which our present acquaintances belonged. We knew that those in the South were more friendly to the Americans and less treacherous than those in the north who are allied with the Kiowas. They uniformly asserted that they were from the Del Norte and were friendly. In corroboration of this they had a few red and green American blankets which we thought they must have obtained in San Antonio. . . . [But] on the whole we concluded to believe them to be hostile and northern Comanches, whom fear and not their own good will had forced to keep peace with us. [Pike 1843:59]

The trappers were invited to camp near the village, but they declined. When the Indians crowded around, the chief was "directed . . . to order them to keep their distance." Finally, Pike ordered the chief, in Spanish, to send back his men or they would open fire on them. The next day Pike and his party moved on, apparently passing near four other Comanche villages whose warriors were out with some Kiowas (Pike 1833). Those were apparently Pike's only contacts with Indians on the western Plains. The source of his two-part division of the Comanches into northern and southern groups is unknown, as is his evaluation of their relative friendship and hostility.

In December 1832 a party of traders left New Mexico by way of the Canadian River. In the Texas panhandle they were attacked by Indians, who killed several, and in their escape they left their baggage and several sacks of silver coins. From that episode came the Kiowa year name, the "winter they captured the money" (Mooney 1898:254). Although Mooney gave the credit wholly to Kiowas, *Niles' Weekly Register* for March 23, 1833, said the attackers were Comanches, as did Pike (1833). Josiah Gregg said they were both Comanches and Kiowas (1844, 2:49–53).

In 1834 a second military escort, Company A of the newly organized United States Dragoons under Captain Clifton Wharton, was sent along with the caravans from the Neosho River to the Arkansas River border with Mexico. In mid-June, near the Arkansas they received a report that several of the traders in advance of the caravan were being chased by about forty Comanches; Wharton said they were "Camanches (known to the Indians generally as Patoka)" (Perrine 1927:275)—one of the few nineteenth-century documentary uses of Padouca in reference to Comanches. When the Indians came in view, Captain Wharton formed the command into a line, intending to charge. At that the Comanches unfurled a "Spanish" flag, fired their guns into the air, shouted "buenos amigos, buenos amigos," and came forward to shake hands. When they had left, the caravan moved forward again. At the Arkansas itself they were met by about a hundred warriors on both sides of the river. After further protestations of friendship from the Indians, again under cover of a flag, Wharton arranged for a council with the "principal Chief." In the interim between that preliminary and the actual meeting, some of the traders were discovered mounting a cannon to overlook the council site, apparently intending to open fire on the Indians. They were only restrained from attacking the army officer sent to remove them by the captain of the caravan, Josiah Gregg; when Gregg later told a group of Indians waiting at the appointed spot to keep away or they would be fired on, the entire Comanche party left the scene (Perrine 1927:278–79).

It is not clear who those Comanches were. That they had a flag suggests they were associated with an important chief, but whether the flag was in fact Spanish rather than Mexican is unknown; several flags had been given in New Mexico since 1821 (see below). The location on the Arkansas River suggests that they may have been Yamparikas, but few identities of Comanches who frequented the Arkansas in the 1830s are known. It seems clear, however, that their hostility—if hostility it was—was negotiable and that Gregg's actions in securing the council site, although not exacerbating the situation, did not improve it.

Observers of the Comanches, 1828–40

From earliest contact, many Euroamericans encountered the Comanches. However, relatively few committed their observations to paper in any extended manner. That is not the case with five observers in the late 1820s and 1830s: José Francisco Ruíz and José María Sánchez y Tapia (Mexican), Jean Louis Berlandier (Swiss), and John Cameron and George W. Bonnell (Anglo-Texan).

Three of those observers—Ruíz, Berlandier and Sanchez y Tapia—were associated with the Mexican Comisión de Límites, under the direction of General Manuel Mier y Terán, examining the boundary line between Mexico and the United States. José Francisco Ruíz was the most knowledgeable Mexican Texan about the Comanches, having been in almost constant contact with them since 1812. Sometime in early 1828 he wrote a "Report of Observations" on the Indians of Texas for General Mier y Terán (Ruíz 1828:4).

The report dealt primarily with war practices and spoke only briefly on topics related to politics and political organization. Echoing earlier Texan usage, Ruíz distinguished the Comanches from the Yamparikas, who, although they "speak the same language and have the same customs . . . are hostile to [our] people when at war" (1828:14). Ruíz also commented on Comanche economics:

> The Comanche are provided with arms and ammunition by trade in horses and mares with other Indians of the United States of North America known on these frontiers by the name of Aguayes, and in New Mexico by the name of Pananes, who trade English-made muskets, which are preferred by the Comanches, and are obtained from Anglo Americans. . . . The Aguayes come to trade with the Comanches as far as the Brazos, but the Comanches do not visit them. [Ruíz 1828:14, 17]

Sometime before his death in 1840, Ruíz drafted a short report, "Comanches—Customs and Characteristics" (Lamar 1921, 4:221–22). As published with M. B. Lamar's papers, that undated report is credited only to "Ruis, a Mexican at Bexar," but since it is unlikely that another of that name could have quality knowledge of the Comanches, it could only have been done by José Francisco. The report is in English, but it is not clear whether the random punctuation and spelling result from Ruíz's unfamiliarity with English or from the preliminary nature of the document.

In the short report he noted that although the Comanches were the "most numerous" of the Texas Indians, they were composed of

> various small tribes . . . such as the Orientals or Eastern Comanches who are generally friendly and frequently visit Bexar and other parts of Texas for the purpose of trading; Yamparicus, who occupy the western parts of Texas, and frequently visit N Mexico—Júez and, Tanémaez, Cuschu-Texca (,Buffalo eaters)[,] Zonzori[,] all of whom are wandering and live in tents of a conical form. [Lamar 1921, 4:221–22]

After the first name, clearly Yamparika, the next ethnonym is derived from *hu* 'timber', the same root as the earlier ethnonym Jupe, but the people were probably not related; it was later spelled Hois by Anglo-Texans. The third ethnonym is clearly Tanema; Ruíz's reference here is, like the 1826 New Mexico treaty citation, one of the few contemporary uses of that form. The fourth and fifth ethnonyms are Kotsoteka and Shoshone. Unfortunately, because of the inconsistencies in punctuation, it is not clear whether Ruíz meant to separate the "Orientals" from the Yamparikas, subdivide either into Hois,

Tanema, Kotsoteka, and Shoshone, or consider them all on the same level of organization.

In early November 1828 the Comisión de Límites arranged to spend several days hunting with José Francisco Ruíz (Berlandier 1844). As they were about to leave, a group of sixty Comanches under El Ronco and Quelluna—Berlandier spelled the latter name Keyuna—arrived at Béxar. As an authority on the Comanches, Ruíz was detained to serve as interpreter. When the Comanches left, Ruíz, the Comisión, and thirty soldiers and civilians who had licenses to hunt buffalo, accompanied them for a five-day journey up the Guadalupe River.

Berlandier's journal (Ohlendorf et al. 1980) and his later reports of the hunt (Berlandier 1844, 1980:341-66) are among the few eyewitness accounts of a Comanche party on the move. Moreover, that hunting expedition was apparently Berlandier's most extensive personal contact with any of the Indians of Texas and possibly the source of his collection of ethnographic materials now in the Smithsonian.[7] However, some of his statements are of such a specific nature that they could only have been derived from Ruíz's wide experience; but it is not always clear which of Berlandier's comments are from his personal observation and which from another's report.

According to Berlandier,

> [when the Comanches] form encampment, and having put up their cone-shaped leather tents, made by their women, the man goes hunting, or he may lay down over some furs which his women spread out for him. Shortly before nightfall, many smoke a pipe in a distant corner of the camp. The ones in charge of the ceremony do not sit down until they have asked permission to do so, and not until all the proper ceremonies have been carried out. It is at these meetings that they exchange their deepest secrets and it is here that an adulteress is usually discovered. The guilty man is almost never killed; the aggrieved husband usually thrashes him and takes some of his horses and mules. [Berlandier 1844:178][8]

That description may be compared to Ruíz's description—see above, chapter 2—but is otherwise the earliest ethnographic description of the smoke lodge, informal village council, and the collection of *nanawokʉ* 'damages' from an adulterer (Hoebel 1940:40; Wallace and Hoebel 1952:147).

Besides direct observations, Berlandier's research on the native peoples of Texas utilized other official reports and records from the Provincias Internas del Oriente and from Béxar; summarizing their quality, he noted ruefully, "Often a presidio or garrison captain will be commissioned by the government to furnish information on the country. The Captain rarely leaves his fort and usually gathers data from his soldiers and then sends along reports studded with inaccuracies" (1844:177). Since there were but few extended reports on Comanches in the archives, it is likely that Berlandier had access to Juan Antonio Padilla's 1820 report and possibly to General Rivera's report from a century before. He also had access to Ruíz's 1828 report, which he quoted both with and without citation; he also had access to Ruíz himself.

Sometime after 1834 Berlandier wrote his report, *The Indians of Texas in 1830* (Berlandier 1969). It was much more comprehensive than either Padilla's or Ruíz's; but that is sometimes a mixed blessing, for he often presented his information as a synthesis covering several groups, and it is not always clear whether the synthesis is justified for any specific group.

Berlandier began by voicing dissatisfaction with the terms nation and tribe—nation because "that term evokes the idea of a people with limited territorial boundaries"—preferring the term people instead:

> By people I mean a group of individuals who speak the same tongue, have the same customs, and usually spring from a common origin, who are known by the same name, and who live in peace, usually together. Peoples may be fairly large ones, like the Lipans or the Comanches, and may be subdivided into tribes, which form rancherías or villages, each with its own chief. [1969:42]

That is a close approximation, in descending order, of the levels of sociopolitical integration recognized by modern ethnographers, and although Berlandier was not consistent in application of those terms, the concept is inherent in his work.

In contrast to other Texans who divided the Comanches into two groups, Berlandier divided them into three: western, central, and eastern (1969:121). However, his conclusions were probably not based on observation, but were an attempt to synthesize two separate reports. According to Berlandier, on the east were the Comanches proper, to whom most of Berlandier's discussion applied, and with whom Berlandier traveled. On the west were the Yamparikas, who were described in much the same language as in Ruíz's 1828 report, suggesting that Berlandier had access to it. Between them were the Yucanticas, who "form ten or twelve rancherías" (1969:151). Since that ethnonym otherwise appears only in Padilla's 1820 report, where their numbers were reported in the same words, it is likely that Berlandier's three groups resulted from an attempt to synthesize Padilla's two names (the correct Yamparika and the incorrect Yucantica) with Ruiz's two names (Comanche and Yamparika), concluding logically, but incorrectly, that the three names referred to three distinct groups.

Almost in passing, Berlandier provided a brief but important discussion of Comanche economics. Concerning trade between Indians, he repeated

Ruíz's 1828 discussion of the Comanche gun trade with the Pawnees, although in contrast to Ruíz (1828:14), who merely stated that the Pawnees sold "guns made in Great Britain," Berlandier explicitly stated that the Pawnees "bring their guns in from Canada" (1969:120). Of the Euroamerican trade:

> During the period of peace more or less numerous tribes of Comanche come in to trade with the presidios. They bring bear grease, buffalo meat and various furs. They used to go to Santa Fe in New Mexico each year to do their trading, and they have been known there for over a century. From the villages and presidios they get shot and powder, loaves of sugar called piloncillos, silver ornaments for themselves and their horses and sometimes weapons such as swords which they use to make their lances, or cheap cloth ornaments. [1969:120]

And again, "In time of peace, the Comanche come to Béxar to sell buffalo hides and deerskins, meat, and bear grease to the inhabitants, who, particularly the soldiers, give them ammunition in exchange as well as weapons" (Berlandier 1969:31 n. 3). When a trading party approached a settlement they would stop

> [a] league away and send a courier with notice of their arrival and request for permission to enter. Sometimes the garrison troops mount and go out to escort them. The formal entry is something quite singular. As the bugles sound, you can see all the natives, holding themselves very proudly, riding in between the ranks of cavalry drawn up with sabres flashing in salute. I have seen one such group of Comanches take umbrage because no escort went to meet them. This slight was enough to make them decide not to enter the presidio at all. [1969:31]

That much was probably first-hand knowledge. However, in discussing the alternative, Berlandier's information is somewhat less reliable. He stated that when there were hostilities with the presidios, the tribes who have "no place to trade" turn to

> the Anglo-Americans who bring their merchandise right into the rancherías, and who get from them not only the furs they have to sell, but also the mules and horses they have stolen from the townspeople with whom they are at war. These tratans ['traders'] keep them stirred up to a state of hostility for their own advantage, giving them an abundance of cloth, cinnabar, guns, powder and shot, in order to put their rivals in the trade out of competition. This trade, in which the inhabitants of both sides of the borders were engaged, has dropped off recently since a few of these traders were killed a few years ago by some Comanches and Chariticas in whose rancherías they had visited. [1969:48]

Although it is certainly likely that traders would always attempt to keep their customers "stirred up . . . for their own advantage," it is also certainly likely that competing traders would blame the opposition, also "for their own advantage." There is, unfortunately, as yet no clear evidence for the practices of Anglo-American trade during that period. Similarly, there is no evidence with which to confirm Berlandier's mention of the killing of traders in the rancherías.

Another member of the Comisión de Límites also made comments about the Comanches. José María Sánchez y Tapia was sublieutenant of artillery and served as the expedition's cartographer and draftsman (Berlandier 1969: 4). Sánchez kept a diary—not published in English until 1926 (Sánchez 1926), in Spanish not until 1939 (Sánchez 1939)—but other than his experiences on that trip, Sánchez had no known contacts with Indians in general or Comanches in particular.

The diary entry headed "Bejar," apparently written between February 28 and April 13, 1828, contained all of Sánchez's comments about Comanches. However, since according to Berlandier's diary, the party had as yet not met any Comanches, the information was probably based on conversations with Ruíz. According to Sánchez, "Ever since the discovery of Texas, this nation [the Comanche] has occupied the same lands where it is found today, from the city of Bejar to Santa Fé in New Mexico. The Yamparicas and Tanemues were included as part of the same nation." Here, following usual Spanish Texan practice, he called the local groups Comanches, distinguishing them from the groups—Yamparikas—farther away. Interestingly, he also used the ethnonym Tanemues—that is, Tanema, i.e. Tenewa—which is, except for its use in the 1827 treaty and by Ruíz, as noted above, about 1840, the only use of that term from Spanish or Mexican Texas. Sánchez's account then passed to a series of comments about continuing Comanche campaigns against the Osages, their aversion to alcohol, penalties for female adultery, female drudgery, prisoner torture and war ceremonies, and the difficulties in making peace.

However, together with Berlandier, José María Sánchez made one other set of observations about Comanches. Those were visual: both Berlandier and Sánchez made sketches of Comanches, which were transformed into watercolors by a probable kinsman, Lino Sánchez y Tapia (Berlandier 1969).[9] Except for Miera y Pacheco's use of tipis as Comanche icons on his maps of New Mexico, those were the apparently the earliest visual representations of Comanches. It is beyond the scope of this study to examine in detail the ethnographic content of those paintings, but as representations of Comanches they deserve some comment. The three sketches were entitled—in French—

"Comanches du Texas Occidental, vêtement lorsqu'ils sont en paix" (Comanches of western Texas, dressed as when they are at peace) after an original by José María Sánchez y Tapia, "Comanches du Texas Occidental, vont à la guerre" (Comanches of western Texas, going to war) after an original by Berlandier, and an unattributed "Yamparicas." John C. Ewers attempted some attribution of dates for the sketches, suggesting that the first "may have been made no later that the spring of 1828," that Berlandier "could have made [the second] of Comanche visitors to Bexar or of two of the Comanche with whom he traveled . . . in November 1828." Of the one depicting Yamparikas, Ewers was "inclined to believe that this drawing was based upon verbal descriptions rather than upon field sketches" (Berlandier 1969:156). Since Berlandier and his party never got above the Pedernales River, I would suggest that that is true of them all.

In 1836 Dr. John Cameron wrote a report entitled "Comanche Indians: The Country West of the Colorado" (Lamar 1921, 1:475). Although Cameron had earlier served as commissioner to the Texas Cherokees, nothing is known of his connections, if any, with Comanches. Based on the quality of his information, he had contact either with them or with knowledgeable intermediaries.

He began by noting that "The Comanche Indians are descendants of the Nation called sonsori who occupy a very northern territory distant from those in Texas about what they estimate two months travel" (Lamar 1921, 1:475). That is apparently the earliest explicit notice of the cultural and linguistic relationship of Comanches and Shoshones. Interestingly, it was based on Texas Comanche statements, and their estimate of the distance between them suggests that they still maintained a connection with the Shoshones.[10] Cameron divided the Comanche "nation" into two broad groups. Like Ruíz, he further noted that they were "subdivided into various minor ones," but in contrast to Ruíz, he was somewhat more specific: on the west were "the Occidental tribes . . . Yamparícos & cuschutéscas." Those names are clearly Yamparika and the Kotsoteka. On the east were "the oriental tribes . . . called júes—tenemás—tapisu." The first is Hois, the second clearly Tanema—that is, Tenewa—but the third is an otherwise unknown ethnonym.[11]

Although it is not known whether any of the observations of Ruíz, Berlandier, Sánchez y Tapia, or Cameron were used in the development of policy, they are important to a historical understanding of the Comanches. All four clearly describe multilevel political integration from village through tribe to people. Like Cameron, Ruíz distinguished the eastern Comanches from the Yamparikas, but the significance of his inclusion of the Shoshones with the Hois, Tenewas, and Kotsotekas is unclear. While Cameron made clear the distinction between Hois and Tenewas as orientales and Yamparikas and

Kotsotekas as occidentales, Berlandier's tripartite division of Comanchería was a significant departure from earlier Texan representations which had simply distinguished between the Comanches near Béxar and the Yamparikas farther away. As noted, that may have been Berlandier's attempt to make sense out of the three different ethnonyms reported by Padilla (Comanche and Yucantica) and Ruíz (Comanche and Yamparika).

In contrast to the factual observations of Berlandier, Ruíz, and Cameron, George W. Bonnell's comments were polemical. Bonnell came to Texas from New York in 1836 to fight in the Texan war of independence. Although he had apparently no prior knowledge of Indians, he was appointed to be Sam Houston's commissioner of Indian affairs. His only known direct contact with Indians was during a trading expedition to Esawakony's (probably *isa wakaré?ee* 'wolf turtle') village in the spring of 1838. However, that lack of direct experience did not prevent him from writing two short papers and one book section detailing the Indians of Texas, particularly the Comanches.

Shortly after returning from the Comanches in May 1838, Bonnell wrote a letter to the *Houston Telegraph and Texas Register*, published on June 16. The letter was signed "X. Y." but the similarity of wording between it and the other Bonnell documents suggests the identity of the author. Bonnell's letter painted a broad portrait of the Comanches and of their lands:

> We had heard much of the nobility of this race, and expected to meet the noble savages in all the pride and lofty bearing which we had heard imputed to them by travelers from the far west. Judge our astonishment when we found the village of the Principal Chief to be filled with half-starved savages of the very lowest order of the human species. They appeared to be but one remove from the brute creatures and infinitely inferior to any other nation of Indians which has come within our knowledge. . . .
>
> We learned from them that the Nation consisted of about 20,000 souls and could raise about 5,000 warriors. They never cultivate any grounds, and depend entirely upon hunting for support. Consequently, they cannot live except in small parties. This would render indigent a much more formidable people than themselves. Without commissaries, a body of 1,000 Indians cannot be kept together for one week. . . .
>
> Their wealth principally consisted of horses and mules; those raised by themselves were generally of superior order. . . . Their fine horses they could scarecely be induced to sell, but those which they had stolen from the Mexicans they would dispose of at almost any price. . . .
>
> We are induced to think, from this specimen of degradation, that the *"noble savage"* about which so much has been said and sung, have been only in fancy, and that they are not to be found in any portion of our western prairies. . . .

From this race of Indians, Texas has nothing to fear: first on account of their inability to do us any injury, and next, *it is in their interest to be our friends.*—They manifested much more anxiety to form a treaty than the Mexicans, and declared that they had never shed the blood of a white man, and that the Mexicans were their natural enemies. Three of our company remained after the rest had departed, and were treated with the same kind of cordiality which we experienced before the company was divided; and were furnished with provisions and guides to return. . . .

Their language consists of about 300 words of the most uncouth and incoherent sounds. They have, however, improved it, by ingrafting upon it many Spanish and some English words. But their language is still too poor to convey their meaning without many gestures and grimaces and it must undergo many improvements before it can be committeed to paper.

The country they inhabit is one of surpassing beauty, and will undoubtedly, at no distant period, become the seat of civilization and opulence. The land is of the first quality—with water so clear and transparent that you may see the bright pebbles at the bottom of a stream twenty feet deep; and the large proportion of aged Indians is an undoubted proof of the healthiness of the climate. The country is well supplied with timber, and has an abundance of iron ore, lead and copper, and perhaps some of the more precious metals. [*Houston Telegraph and Texas Register*, letter dated May 12, published June 16, 1838, emphasis in original; McLean 1974-93, 16:499-502]

Bonnell's comments are a mixture of fact and folklore, more reflective of Anglo-Texan preconceptions about Comanches than objective personal observations. Like observers of the Comanches since the eighteenth century, Bonnell argued that the hunting lifestyle precluded lengthy concentrations of population; however, the conclusions he drew from that observation are naive. In the coming years, while individuals, Comanches as well as Anglo-Texans, would argue that their best interests would be served by maintaining good relations, others on both sides would argue the opposite. Bonnell's estimate of the Comanche population, and the size of its fighting force, is interesting as much for its apparent source—the only "fact" in his article that he attributed to the Comanches themselves—as for the variations that would be played upon on it in the later articles. Bonnell was the only observer to suggest a difference in value of Comanche-raised horses and those stolen from Mexico. The comment about the poverty of the Comanche language and its necessary reliance upon sign language to convey meaning is one of the earliest occurences of that piece of folklore. Bonnell's final paragraph contains all the elements of proper boosterism: a beautiful country with a healthy climate; abundant natural resources—clear water, timber, minerals— perhaps even including precious metals; it is destined to be a "seat of civilization." However, that portrait clashed with his earlier observation: although there were apparently many healthy "aged Indians," they were, nonetheless, still "half-starved savages of the very lowest order of the human species."

Bonnell's second and third documents closely parallel each other. The second was his 1838 report as commissioner of Indian affairs (Bonnell 1838). The third was a section of his book, *Topographical Description of Texas to Which Is Added, An Account of the Indian Tribes* (1840). Both documents touched on a number of topics; however, three sets of parallel quotations merit some discussion.

The first of these parallel sets echoes the discussion of Comanche population in Bonnell's May 12 letter:

> In May last . . . I heard from [Esawacany] the principal chief . . . that the nation amounted to about twenty thousand souls, and that it could probably raise a force of five thousand warriors. About one-third of this number reside north of the Arkansas river, in the territory of the United States. [1838:42]

In 1840, this was given as

> The whole tribe number about twenty thousand souls: of these not more than five thousand ever visit the territory of Texas; and not more than fifteen hundred reside south of the Red river. Of the latter, there are about four hundred warriors—the rest are women, children, and old men. [1840:130]

In the second parallel set Bonnell commented on Comanche government. In 1838 he noted:

> The Camanche nation is, perhaps, the most perfect democracy on the face of the globe; everything is managed by primary assemblies, and the people have a right to displace a chief and elect a successor at pleasure. Even male children have a right to rebel against their parents, and the parents have no right to punish them but by consent of the tribe. But any warrior claims and exercises the right of *punishing a woman* with the utmost rigor, for the most trifling offense. With such a state of things it cannot be expected that there would be much harmony in their councils; and their war councils not infrequently terminate with a battle between the different tribes. This sometimes produces permanent enmities, and the chief of the disaffected tribe as in the instance of Tawacony, separates from the nations and sets up for himself. [Bonnell 1838:42; emphasis in original]

In 1840 this was given as:

> Their system of government is the most perfect democracy on the face of the earth. A chief is created or deposed at pleasure: even children may rebel against their parents, who have no right to punish them without a vote of the tribe. A mother forfeits her life if she strikes her male child, however young he may be; because a *warrior* or *brave* must be bred up in all the savage ferocity of his nature. But a male may beat a woman or even take her life with impunity. They in turn beat their female childrens with utmost severity, and are the cruelest tormentors of the unhappy prisoners who may chance to fall into their hands. [1840:136-37; emphasis in original]

Except for the slight differences in wording, the first several lines parallel each other. But Bonnell's goal was irony, not description or analysis; indeed, after those first few lines, where the first document continued with a description of alleged disorderly council meetings, the second document expanded on the theme of domestic violence.

In the third set of parallel quotations, Bonnell expounded upon the history of Comanche relations with Euroamericans:

> They have made many treaties with Mexico, all of which have been violated; and not unfrequently, within twenty-four hours after their signature; insomuch, that the remark, "as faithless as a Camanche treaty" has become proverbial in Mexico. [1838:43-44]

> They have made hundreds of of treaties with the Mexican government which have not been observed as long as the parties were signing the instruments. In the year 1829 or '30, four treaties were made and violated, at San Antonio, by the Comanches in one week's time, and the expression "As faithless as a Comanche treaty" has passed into a proverb in that country. [1840:132]

These statements are of minimal accuracy; however, in propaganda, repetition is the key to success. Thus, despite such knowledgable observers as Jean Louis Berlandier, José Francisco Ruíz, and John Cameron, preconceptions and prejudices such as those expressed by George Bonnell continued to influence and reinforce the Anglo-Texan attitudes about Comanches.

Texas, 1828–35

In the fall of 1829 Paruakevitsi returned to Béxar from his meeting with the New Mexican officials, inaugurating a short period of good relations. By 1831 several Comanches were working as scouts for the Mexicans, primarily

chasing Tawakoni horse thieves (Moreno 1831; McLean 1974–93, 6:316).
But there were also hostile incidents. In August Quellune and El Collote, the
latter previously unidentified, were accused of involvement in raids near
Béxar (Cosio 1831; McLean 1974–93, 6:356). Later that month Yncoroy sent
his son, Chato 'Pug Nose', to report that a small group of Comanches was
planning to raid Goliad (Elozúa 1831a; McLean 1974–93, 6:362). However,
the commander at Goliad received the warning too late; a Spaniard and a
Tonkawa chief were killed in the raid. One report said the leaders were
Mueracuita, Nacazari, and Yamparika Castro (Elozúa 1831b; McLean 1974–
93, 6:365); another gave two names, Mueracuita, and Barba Cortada (Elozúa
1831c; McLean 1974–93, 6:400). The first name on both lists is *mura
kwitapʉ* 'mule excrement';[12] the second name is *nakI* 'ear', *sarʔi*, 'dog', i.e.,
'hound dog'; the third is Spanish, 'short' or 'cut beard'; all are previously
unnamed.

Other chiefs attempted to maintain good relations. Paruakevitsi returned
some horses stolen by Tawaconis (Viesca 1831); in October Yncoroy came to
Matamoros with forty-six animals taken in August (Elozúa 1831d; McLean
1974–93, 6:459). Also in October Tasuniqua (previously unmentioned), and
other Comanches visited Aguaverde to trade. The commandant, although
blaming Yamparikas for recent hostilities, entertained them as best he could
while trying not to give motive for resentment (J. M. García 1831). In December 1831 Yzazona (previously unnamed) returned sixteen horses stolen
from Goliad (Elozúa 1831d; McLean 1974–93, 6:459); Yncoroy and Quellune retrieved others (Elozúa 1831e; McLean 1974–93, 6:464).

Whenever possible, the Mexicans retaliated against raiders. Early in the
morning of November 13, at the Arroyo de los Vacas, they attacked a Tawakoni village. Unfortunately, Paruakevitsi and other Comanches were visiting
the village, trying "to make his voice heard for peace and friendship." When
the attack hit, the chief shouted "Comanches, Amigos, Amigos Españoles,"
but he and a son were among those killed (Lafuente 1831; McLean 1974–93,
6:557). Despite his death, some Comanches tried to continue peaceful relations: in January Yzazona sent word that the Comanches did not hold ill
feelings against the Mexicans; later one of Paruakevitsi's sons, described as
"a young boy," came to Béxar carrying the "best sentiments of Peace"
(Elozúa 1832b).

A further blow came when Yncoroy's ranchería was attacked by Shawnees, and many Comanches were killed (Lafuente 1832), including Yzazona
and one of Yncoroy's parents (Cos 1832). Details of the incident are scanty;
in M. B. Lamar's papers is a synopsis of an 1840 newspaper story that
reported:

There was . . . a party of Shawnees encamped [within] 35 miles of San Antonio with 25 warriors. The chief of this party was Linia, second Chief of the Tribe. His wife being in the city . . . was insulted grossly by a Comanchee chief, who endeavored to abduct her by force to his camp. She however, succeeded in resisting his attempts; and . . . succeeded in ascertaining when the Comanches would leave the city and by what route they would take in returning. . . . When the Comanches arrived at the pass . . . laden with the valuable goods they had extorted from the cowardly Mexicans, they were suddenly fired upon. . . . 20 of the Comanches fell dead. [Lamar 1921, 3:461]

Still, many Comanches attempted to maintain peace. On April 8, 1832, Chato, with twenty-six others, came to Béxar, saying that his people wanted to continue the peace (Elozúa 1832a). Another party came to the Paraje de San Felipe to trade furs (J. M. García 1832a). Comanches also visited San Fernando on the Rio Grande. On April 6 two men and two women arrived and left three days later. On April 15 Tasuniqua and three others visited; a week later Astoria (previously unmentioned) arrived with six men and four women. On May 2 seven captains, including Yncoroy, Quellune, Astoria, Muraequa (previously unnamed, possibly *mura eka* 'red mule'), Muraquitap, and Quina, with more than two hundred men, women, and children, came to trade, but they stayed for only three days because there were no presents (J. M. García 1832b).[13]

But relations deteriorated. Since "it was not possible to know if the entire nation [had] declared war," and although "there [was] no reason to believe" that it had, local officials were warned to take care (J. J. Elguézabal 1831). On April 19, 1832, when Tasuniqua came to the Paraje de San Felipe to trade furs as usual, the commander at Rio Grande attempted, unsuccessfully, to lure him into a trap (J. M. García 1832a). On the 28th a party under Cara Cortada ('cut face', possibly the man most recently called Cuerno Verde), was in the Arroya de Rosales "with bad intentions" (Barragan 1832a). Another party of seven or eight was near the Paraje de Rosita (Barragan 1832b). In October Comanches killed two soldiers between Leona and Buena Vista. On the eighteenth, after two herders were killed, troops were sent out "without success." On the thirtieth Comanches stole the horse herd from Villa de Rosas. This time they were overtaken, three Indians were killed, and 125 horses were retaken (Elozúa 1832c). The same day troops from Bahia killed two of the raiders and recaptured three horses (Elozúa 1832d).

In the summer of 1833 Tasuniqua offered a general peace (J. J. Elguézabal 1833), but there is no evidence that it was seriously considered. In April of 1834 Casimero (*kasamaahru* 'bushy, uncombed hair') came to confer with the authorities in Béxar (Seguín 1834). He said one of the main reasons for the Yamparika hostilities was that some of their children were held hostage at Rio Grande—their identities are unknown and they are otherwise unidentified. They would, however, bring one of their captives as proof of friendship, and Cojo ('lame') promised that depredations would cease. But the next month Comanches overran several haciendas near Béxar; others crossed the Rio Grande and hit several haciendas in Nuevo Leon. Later that year Quelluna told Berlandier not to travel to the west, "as a few hotheads were causing trouble there" (Berlandier 1969:122). In August 1834 Comanches and Tawaconis took the entire horse herd of Goliad (P. Benavides 1834).

Although earlier Spanish policy had been to remain neutral in intertribal wars (Guerra 1832), in 1832 it was decided to encourage the Shawnees in their Comanche war (Piedras 1832). The project languished for two years, but by 1835 Peter Ellis Bean—who had been with Nolan's 1801 expedition, was now one of Austin's colonists, and served as Mexican agent for the Shawnees—was placed in charge and was urging Shawnees, Cherokees, and others to make war on the Comanches, promising them all the booty (Jenkins 1973, 1:44). The various municipalities in Texas were urged to make contributions for ammunition to friendly Indians (Jenkins 1973, 1:47). In May Bean reported that the Indians were not willing to wage war on the Comanches, even for stock (Jenkins 1973, 1:118), but by June 15 he reported that 500 Indians were ready to take the field (Jenkins 1973, 1:152). However, it is not known whether they actually left.

In spite of the new Spanish policy, in May General Martín Perfecto de Cos ordered the renewal of presents for the Indians, and particularly for the Comanches (Jenkins 1973, 1:102). In August 300 Comanches came to Béxar and then continued on to Matamoros to arrange a treaty with the general (Jenkins 1973, 1:321). Casimero reported that while they were en route, other Comanches were raiding near Laredo (Jenkins 1973, 1:365). However, the peace process was cut off by the rebellion of the Anglo-Texan settlers.

Along the Canadian and the Arkansas, 1830–42

The early 1830s brought great changes to political relations on the southern Plains as various peoples moved into Comanchería. The Kiowas increased their interactions with the Comanches, and the Cheyennes and Arapahos, who had been on the Arkansas River since at least 1805, were now permanently attached to the Bents' traders. In 1829 two Cheyennes, whose names were recorded as Painted Bird and White Bear, visited Santa Fe and were given clothing and other gifts (García 1829). There were also reports of Patas Negras (Blackfeet), Arikaras, and Pawnees below the Arkansas River (F. Sarracino 1833; Abreú 1834).[14]

Meanwhile, throughout the 1820s and early 1830s, groups of eastern Indians, Cherokees, Chickasaws, Creeks, Shawnees, and others, in the face of growing hostility from their Anglo-American neighbors, had begun moving into Arkansas Territory and beyond, and clashes with various Plains groups were becoming increasingly common. In 1833 Comanches and Wichitas attacked and robbed a party of Cherokee hunters. In revenge a Cherokee party attacked a small group of Wacos, killing three and capturing two (Foreman 1933:113). Finally, there were the Osages, who were rapidly expanding their own sphere of influence south of the Arkansas River. Their tactics were epitomized in the so-called Cut Throat Massacre of 1833, in which an entire Kiowa village was attacked and many inhabitants killed; their heads were cut off and stuffed in the brass camp buckets.

In early 1830 Sam Houston, then a trader with the Cherokees, proposed that he, Osage agent Auguste P. Chouteau, and Colonel Matthew Arbuckle be commissioned to make peace among the Osages, Pawnees, and Comanches, but his offer was ignored (Foreman 1926:200). Houston tried again in 1832, offering to try to persuade Comanches and "Pawnee of the South," that is, Wichitas, to meet with treaty commissioners at Fort Gibson (Wisehart 1962: 108). That time his offer was accepted.

Houston traveled to Texas by way of Fort Towson, Indian Territory, where he picked up some scraps of information about the Comanches. The information was, he noted, of necessity imperfect: although the first contacts between Americans and Comanches had been friendly, unscrupulous traders had taken advantage of the Indians, and it was now difficult to get "authentic" information (A. W. Williams and Barker 1938-43, 1:267). According to Houston's informants, the Comanches were divided into four bands, Kimanchies, Sotoes, Amparacs, and Jatans (A. W. Williams and Barker 1938-43, 1:268). Of those ethnonyms, Kimanchies and Amparacs are obviously Comanche and Yamparika, Jatan is probably Ietan, and Sotoe is probably the Caddo term *suahto* 'Comanche' (Mooney 1896:1043). In a later report Houston used the phrase "both tribes of the Comanche," implying only two groups (A. W. Williams and Barker 1938-43, 2:16).[15] Each was governed by a chief with a "National Chief . . . superior . . . to the Chiefs of the bands and whose authority is much respected." Then, in contrast to the implication of the comment that because of "unscrupulous traders" contact with Comanches had been broken, he noted that Fort Towson traders regularly visited the Comanches, who were "friendly with the citizens of Texas and trade with the American population of that Province" (A. W. Williams and Barker 1938-43, 1: 267).

Houston's Fort Towson informants also reported that "some knives, guns, and blankets such as the 'N.West fur company' furnish, have been seen among the Pawnees and [Comanches], but to no considerable extent" (A. W. Williams and Barker 1938–43, 1:269), that is, there was some indication of trade with the north. But in a later report, he noted that the "intercourse between the Northwest Fur Company and the Pawnees is much more direct and general than I supposed," with their "influence" extending as far as the Brazos and Colorado rivers in Texas (A. W. Williams and Barker 1938–43, 1:273).

The identification of the Pawnees of the North, and specifically of the "Northwest Fur Company," as the source of the northern trade is interesting, for it parallels Ruíz and Berlandier's contemporary discussions of Pawnees trading English guns obtained via Canada. However, while the North West Company was indeed Canadian, it had merged with the Hudson's Bay Company in 1821; thus, by the early 1830s there was no longer such an enterprise. The occurrence of the same story on opposite sides of an unfriendly international border suggests that there was more to it than contemporary political rumor-mongering; unfortunately, there is at present no further information.

Houston reached Béxar in January 1833 where, together with several Mexican officials and using their interpreter, he met with a number of Comanches. Houston found them "well disposed" to make a treaty with the United States; the chiefs entertained "a high regard for the Americans while they cherish the most supreme contempt for the Mexicans." But, "it was necessary for them to return to their people and counsel before they could send a delegation." Houston gave the Comanches a medal of President Jackson "to be conveyed to the Principal Chief (who was not present)" (A. W. Williams and Barker 1938–43, 1:272). Unfortunately, their identities are not known, and the Béxar archives do not record any visits by Comanches during that month.

The Comanches had agreed to visit the commissioners in three months, and Houston made preparations to escort them to Fort Gibson. However, other circumstances intervened. The Mexican authorities in Texas had reconsidered the advisability of assisting in an American treaty. Meanwhile, the other Indians of Texas were preparing their joint campaign against the Comanches with Peter Ellis Bean. Since a treaty delegation must pass through their territory, any misfortune would rebound upon the United States. Houston ultimately suggested that if it was "really the wish of the President" that the Comanches should be contacted, then the goal should be pursued through official channels (A. W. Williams and Barker 1938–43, 2:17). Therefore, there was no conference with the Comanches in 1833.

Meanwhile, young Albert Pike thought so highly of his Comanche experiences and knowledge that when he heard of Houston's mission he sent a letter to Secretary of War Lewis Cass criticizing it. Echoing his earlier distinction, he argued that there were two "distinct and entirely separate portions" of Comanches. The southern group, which lived near San Antonio and wintered on the Del Norte (Rio Grande) River, was friendly with Americans. The northern Comanches, who ranged between the Arkansas and the Red rivers, wintering on the Canadian and the Pecos rivers, were allied with the Kiowas and the Arapahos, and "took every opportunity of injury." Since Houston's meetings had been with the southern Comanches, who were already friendly with Americans, his mission would "effect nothing." On the other hand, should the government wish to make peace with the northern Comanches, Pike would guide a treaty party and serve as interpreter (Pike 1833). Cass did not take up his offer.

That same year, a force of mounted rangers and other troops was sent out from Fort Gibson on the Arkansas River in Indian Territory to drive the Comanches and the Wichitas westward in order to make room for the now forcibly removed eastern Indians. The expedition was a complete failure. Among other disasters, below the Washita River on the Red River, they were attacked by unidentified Indians, and one ranger was taken captive (Foreman 1926).

The next year, because the "war parties of the Comanche and Kiowa have annoyed our citizens in their intercourse with the Mexican states" (Cass 1834)—except for the incident with Major Riley in 1829, an otherwise unsubstantiated statement, but clearly echoing Senator Benton's rhetoric of the late 1820s—a more organized expedition was sent out to attempt to meet the Comanches and if possible to recover the ranger and a young boy captured the previous spring. The expedition was composed of the main body of the United States Dragoons under Colonel Henry Leavenworth; Company A was on detached duty that summer escorting the caravan to Santa Fe. The dragoons had only slightly better luck than the rangers; Leavenworth died less than a month out, and many of the troopers came down with an unidentified illness, as did the artist George Catlin, who accompanied the expedition.

On July 16 the dragoons, now under Henry Dodge, arrived at a large Comanche village along Cache Creek near the Wichita Mountains (Wheelock 1835). According to Catlin, they were met first by a Comanche horseman who carried a piece of white buffalo skin on the point of his lance in answer to a white flag shown by the dragoons (Catlin 1841, 2:55). Catlin gave that Comanche's name alternatively as The Little Spaniard, the name he was known by in other records of the expedition, and as *He-su San-chees*. The latter is clearly the Spanish name Jesus Sanchez, but although Catlin noted that the man was half Mexican, he apparently did not recognize the linguistic origins of his name.

The divisional affiliation of those Comanches is unclear. In his official report of the expedition, Lieutenant T. B. Wheelock noted only that "the Comanches of Texas are a much more powerful tribe than those on this side of the Red River; they are called the Hoishe Comanche" (Wheelock 1835:87). From the syntax, it is not clear which side of the river the Hois were on, although it is probable that they were the "Comanches of Texas."

The principal leaders were not present, so the dragoons moved west to a Wichita village on the North Fork of the Red River. After they had spent two days talking with the Wichita leaders, the Comanche principal chief, Tabequena, arrived. His name is *tabe kwina* 'sun eagle'; Curtis (1907–30, 18:231) translated it as Golden Eagle; Catlin gave Ta-wa-que-na as "Mountain of Rocks," a typically unreliable translation. After some persuasion he returned the Martin boy, but he said that the ranger had been killed by other Indians. When he reported that a group of Mexican traders had recently departed, Dodge seized the occasion to argue that Americans would give better goods and better prices and that they should come to Fort Gibson, and possibly even to Washington, for a treaty. That ended the official meeting. Several Comanches, a group of recently arrived Kiowas, and a number of Wichitas and Wacos, returned to Fort Gibson with the troops. Most of the Comanches turned back when one of the women fell sick, but The Spaniard accompanied the dragoons back to Fort Gibson.

Despite the historic importance of that meeting, there are serious discrepancies between the military accounts and Catlin's account, and between those accounts and later commentaries. The official report was by Wheelock (1835). It, and a book by one of the dragoons (Hildreth 1836), were based on the journal kept by Hugh Evans, Dodge's orderly (Perrine and Foreman 1925). George Catlin's account (Catlin 1841), however, is very different. It is not a first-hand account; indeed, he was sick most of the time and was not even present at the meetings.

The differences between the military accounts and Catlin's account are significant. The official report states that Tabequena was the principal chief and mentions no other Comanche chief by name, but Catlin says that Ta-wah-que-na was only the "second" chief and that after several days of negotiation, another chief—Catlin gave his name as Ee-sha-conee, "the bow and quiver" (1841:67); it is *isa koni* 'returning wolf', usually spelled Esacony—showed up and Tabequena deferred to him. Since the expedition was attempting to bring the Comanches to a treaty council, it would be important to know who was principal chief, and if such a deference occurred, to report it.

To complicate modern interpretations, Wilbur S. Nye—who began his account of the meeting by noting that "at this early date they believed what the white man told them" (1969:8), thus ignoring more than a century of Comanche-Euroamerican interaction—wrote,

> The two head chiefs of the village were Sequi-to-tori (Splashing the Mud) and Poy-weh-ne-parai (Buffalo Lean Fat). Catlin, Wheelock, and other contemporary accounts give the name of the chief as Ishacoly (Isaconee—Wandering Wolf). . . . The Kiowas and Comanches, because of an old superstitious custom, frequently changed the name of deceased tribesmen. [Nye 1969:8 n. 6]

That account is misleading in several respects. First, according to Joe Attock-nie, Seguitotori—possibly *sekwipu* 'mud', *tohto?itu* 'they exit forcibly'—was the Comanche name of Jesus Sanchez, the Spaniard, who was not a chief. The name Poy-weh-ne-parai is not Buffalo Lean Fat; although it seems to include *puhihwi* 'metal' it is otherwise unknown. Then, of the "contemporary accounts" only Catlin mentioned Ishacoly—in the form Ee-sha-conee—in the context of the dragoons, but he gave the name as "the bow and quiver." Finally, although it is not known what other names the village chiefs might have had, the naming taboo itself does not account for the differences in the names as reported. The custom of avoiding the name of the dead, seems to have occurred under two circumstances: when immediate relatives were present and might became upset, and when the name was associated with bad luck. But the response to either condition was for the living to change their own names, not to change the names of the deceased; those would remain unspoken, and they would be referred to by teknonymy—father of so-and-so, for example. Conversely, the name of a particularly powerful man was often kept and given to others.

At Fort Gibson the delegation of Plains Indians met in council with representatives of the immigrant tribes, Cherokees, Choctaws, Creeks, and Senecas, as well the local Osages. There was some discussion about the propriety of recognizing The Spaniard as a Comanche representative, and after initial suspicion on all sides, a general consensus emerged. Colonel Dodge and Western Superintendent Francis Armstrong made symbolic presents, including flags and medals, to the visiting westerners, and the eastern Indians gave them white beads and tobacco:

> The white beads are an emblem of peace and purity. . . . When you smoke the tobacco of friendship, all evil will go off with the smoke. . . . The beads and tobacco, you must take home to your people . . . tell them,

"The beads show the road is clean," and let them smoke the tobacco in remembrance of us who send it. . . . These white beads are the white path that leads from your door to our door. [Foreman 1933:134-36]

At Fort Gibson, the Americans said that they had no authority to enter into formal treaty relations with the westerners but hoped to meet again in the buffalo country to arrange for a formal treaty. Thus, in 1835 Cherokee agent Montford Stokes, General Matthew Arbuckle, and Supterintendant Francis Armstrong were appointed to meet with the tribes and conclude a treaty. In a statement typical of American understanding of the motivations of Indian warfare, the commission was told:

It is believed that hereditary feuds have existed there for a long succession of years and that many of the tribes have received as an
inheritance that state of hostility in which they are placed. Our efforts
must be used to inspire confidence between them and us, and then to
introduce among them permanent pacific relations. [Cass 1835]

That contemporary economic or political motives might be involved seems not to have been considered.

Meanwhile, the Comanches and the Kiowas had been contacted by trader Holland Coffee, who had established a post at the west edge of the Cross Timbers. While reporting that the Comanches were attacking "Chewawa and the Pass"—Chihuahua and El Paso—he noted that they were said to be looking forward to the meeting with the Americans (Stewart 1835). Their "Great Chief," unfortunately unnamed, who claimed to be the "chief and great captain of all these tribes," was particularly anxious to meet the president (F. W. Armstrong 1835).

In order to meet with the Indians in their own country, a military post, later called Camp Holmes and Camp Mason, was established on the western edge of the Cross Timbers on the South Fork of the Canadian River, near modern Purcell, Oklahoma. By July there were about seven thousand Indians, mostly Comanches, camped about ten miles away. However, the commissioners did not arrive for another month, and by then the game and grass had become scarce and many of the Indians had left.

The meeting finally got under way in late August with several days of speeches by the commissioners; on August 23 Esacony, called the "first chief of the Comanches," spoke. He was the only Comanche whose speech was recorded, and although short, it gave hints of the Comanche political climate. As reported in its entirety, he said:

I will tell you the same thing that I have told you before. I am the only head chief of my nation. I have been waiting here for you a long time, and when you have done with me I will go. When my people all started away from here I told them I intended waiting for the commissioners. They all wished nothing but peace and friendship, and I have staid here to represent them all. What more can I ask, than to be at peace with my red Brothers. It was your wish, and that of my great father that I have staid here a long time, and I wish you to give me something. Being sick, I cannot talk more. Half my body belongs to the Osages and half to the Comanches and all the rest I will hold close to my heart. [Foreman 1936: 412]

That is, Esacony began by noting that he had spoken to some Anglo-American officials ("I . . . told you before") to whom he had asserted his status as "head chief"—apparently in opposition to another chief. It is not clear who those other Anglo-Americans might have been; the 1835 Camp Holmes treaty council is the earliest contemporary mention of Esacony; Catlin's account of the meetings with the dragoons was not published until 1841. The other claimant to the position of head chief was probably Tabequena, who was apparently not present at this meeting. Thus it is probable that the dispute between Esacony and Tabequena reported by Catlin took place during the wait for the commissioners in 1835, and not the year before.

Esacony continued that he had been waiting for quite some time; indeed many of his people had already left. In one sentence—"What more can I ask, than to be at peace with my red Brothers"—Esacony agreed to the stated purpose of the treaty. Then he asked for presents; approximately ten thousand dollars in gifts were distributed at the council. The implication that Esacony was half Osage is unclear.

The treaty was signed on August 24, 1835 (Kappler 1903:435). Although it expressed the usual American interests in "establishing and perpetuating peace and friendship" and required "nothing . . . from these nations except to remain at peace," the fourth article, a single sentence, was to have lasting repercussions. It stated:

It is understood and agreed by all the nations or tribes of Indians party to this treaty that each and all of the said Indians or tribes have free permission to hunt and trap in the Grand Prairie west of the CrossTimbers, to the western limits of the United States.

The treaty was signed by nineteen Comanches (table 5.1), but their divisional affiliations were not given.

Table 5.1

Signers of the Camp Holmes Treaty, 1835

NAME	GIVEN AS	MODERN RETRANSCRIPTION
Ishacoly	The Wolf	*isa* 'wolf,' *koni* 'to turn' or 'return'
Queenashano	The War Eagle	*kwina* 'eagle'
Tabaqueena	The Big Eagle	*tabe kwina* 'sun eagle'
Pohowetoshah	The Brass Man	*puhiwi* 'metal,' *tosa* 'white'
Shabbakasha	The Roving Wolf	*isa* 'wolf'
Neraquassi	The Yellow Horse	*nura* 'to run off' *kwasi* 'tail'
Toshapappy	The White Hare	*tosa* 'white,' *papI* 'hair'
Pahosareya	The Broken Arm	
Pahkah	The Man who draws the Bow	*paka* 'arrow'
Witsitony	He who sucks quick	*pitsi* 'suckle' *toni* 'put (in mouth?)'
Leahwiddikah	One who stirs up	
Esharotsiki	The Sleeping Wolf	*isa* 'wolf'
Pahtrisula	The Dog	Patricio ?
Ettah	The Gun	*eta* 'bow'
Tennowikkah	The Boy who become a Man	*tena* 'man' *puhka* 'become'
Kumaquoi	The Woman who cuts buffalo meat	*kuhma* 'male', *koo?itu* 'cut up'
Taqquanno	The Amorous Man	
Kowa	The Stinking Tobacco Box	
Soko	The Old Man	*tsocopU* 'old'

SOURCE: Kappler 1904:435–39.

Some time after the treaty was signed, Auguste Chouteau built a trading post at Camp Holmes and was soon conducting a brisk business with the nearby Indians.

As the Kiowas were not party to the Camp Holmes treaty, Major Paul Legeste Chouteau, Auguste's younger brother, was sent to persuade them to attend a meeting. In the winter of 1835 he found a combined camp of Comanches, Kiowas, and Apaches on Cache Creek. He was unable to persuade the Kiowas to come in for a meeting, but he did discover that the Comanches had become dissatisfied with the treaty. Not only had there been insufficient goods, but they now realized that they had opened their country to the eastern Indians; they were so angry that they had torn up their copy of the treaty (Stokes and F. W. Armstrong 1835).

Meanwhile, in September 1836, David G. Burnet, former lawyer, merchant, reporter on the Comanches, and now the first president of the Republic of Texas, appointed Alexander LeGrand to visit the Comanches and if possible to negotiate a treaty with them (Jenkins 1973, 7:427).[16] Details of LeGrand's journey are unclear; he later claimed that Houston had "suppressed" his original report (Estep 1950:177); in an unofficial account he said he met Chicony, possibly meaning Esacony, at the confluence of the "Big and Little Washita" rivers (Yoakum 1855). If the name of those rivers is read as Washita, the meeting took place near modern Chickasha, Oklahoma, and only some thirty miles west of Camp Holmes. However, if it is read as Wichita, the meeting took place near modern Wichita Falls, a more likely location.

According to LeGrand, the chief expressed much antagonism toward the Texans, saying that

> so long as he saw the gradual approach of whites and their habitations to the hunting grounds of the Comanches, so long he would believe to be true what the Mexicans had told him, viz, that the ultimate intention of the white man was to deprive them of their country; and so long would he continue to be the enemy of whites. [Yoakum 1855, 2:228]

Later that winter Paul Chouteau, returning to Camp Holmes after an absence, found that Esacony and a small party of Comanches had just left, having waited several days for him. The chief was again reported to be very angry at the whites for "injuries received since and commencing at the time of the council . . . in 1835" and was threatening to destroy the post and all of its inhabitants. Wanting confirmation, Auguste Chouteau sent his son, Edward, with four other men south into Texas to find the chief on his "wintering grounds." They got to within fourteen miles of Esacony's village when a group of Wichitas and Wacos persuaded them to turn back; the Wichitas claimed that there were a number of white captives at Esacony's village, including at least two English women, one a Mrs. Mathew, who had resided for a considerable time in the United States (P. L. Chouteau 1837). Nothing further is known of those captives.

Throughout the 1830s the Yamparikas were involved in a war with Cheyennes and Arapahos over occupation of the Arkansas valley; the war probably exacerbated by the competition between the Bents along the upper stretches of the river and the Chouteaus along the lower. In the summer of 1837 the Cheyenne Bow String warriors attacked Kiowa and Comanche villages on *isahunuʔubi* 'wolf creek'; they were wiped out (Mooney 1898: 271; Hyde 1968:73; Powell 1981:38-41). According to Joe Attocknie,

Comanches named the battle Utah Hookne (yuʔa 'robe', hora 'dig a hole', kahni 'house'), the Robe Entrenchments, after the robe-draped entrenchments dug by the Cheyennes.

Meanwhile, Captain Benjamin L. E. Bonneville[17] at Fort Gibson offered to negotiate a peace with the western Indians. He had recently returned from an exploring expedition through the Rocky Mountains (Irving 1851) and thought of himself as an expert on Indians. He argued that the Comanches were divided into two groups, the "Comanches of the Woods" and the "Comanches of the Prairies or Yamparicoes," who together numbered about 2,700; 'Comanches of the Woods' is an adequate translation gloss of hois, but 'Comanches of the Prairies' is not a translation of yamparika. Bonneville's proposal was not acted on.

A greater problem was the growing presence of the relocated eastern Indians. In 1837 Auguste Chouteau was commissioned to "travel among them [the Comanches], and by making proper explanations and representations, and by other means, to endeavor to effect a reconciliation" (C. A. Harris 1837: 567). He was instructed to argue that "the United States, having purchased these lands from the tribes possessing the occupant title, has guaranteed the exclusive right in it to the emigrating tribes. They [the Comanches] cannot therefore be permitted to hunt upon it, after the latter [the eastern Indians] are prepared to settle upon it and cultivate it" (C. A. Harris 1837:568). Exactly how the otherwise unidentified tribes who had "occupant title" gained that title from the clearly occupant Comanches was unstated. Although Commissioner of Indian Affairs Carey Harris reported, "It is believed that [Chouteau's] exertions have been productive of much good" (C. A. Harris 1837: 567), it is doubtful whether the Comanches understood the legalities of the argument.

In December 1837 Tabequena visited the Chouteaus' post on the Canadian River and voiced several complaints. Of foremost concern were some Osages, who, while visiting the Comanches under the pretext of trading, had stolen horses. Although the two peoples had been on "amicable terms," the Comanches would not "suffer these injuries to go unnoticed." Tabequena also complained that in all their previous negotiations with Mexican officials, Comanches had been presented with flags and medals, and he was much disappointed that none had been given by the United States at the treaty council. Chouteau was "convinced that they conceive them to be a great honor and pledge of faith" and that presenting them would facilitate peace (A. P. Chouteau 1837).

Chouteau had also been asked to persuade some of the western chiefs to visit Washington. To that end, Chouteau had asked Tabequena, whom he called "one of the chiefs of the Padokah Indians," went to visit the Plains tribes, Comanches and others, and to organize a delegation. Chouteau's use of "Padokah" is interesting: he seemed to use the term as a specific rather than a general ethnonym; it refered to Tabequena and his people rather than to the Comanches as a whole.

In early May 1838 Esacony was reported to have been near Camp Holmes but had been scared off by rumors of Pawnees; that was apparently the last documentary mention of him. Later that month Tabequena came into Camp Holmes with twenty-two "principal chiefs," including those of the Kiowas, Katakas (Kiowa Apaches), Padokahs, Yamparikas or Comanches, Shoshones, Hois, Kotsotekas, and Wichitas; unfortunately, none were named. Chouteau said he would have made a treaty with the Hois and the others, but "a sufficient number of chiefs were not present." Ultimately, the government decided to postpone the trip, and Chouteau gave them presents to assuage their disappointment; the chiefs promised to return the following year (A. P. Chouteau 1838).

Chouteau's list of tribal names is one of the few band-list views of the Comanches from the east. As he had done earlier, in reference to Tabequena, Chouteau used Padokah as a specific rather than a generic ethnonym, in contrast to the whole of the Comanches. But in contrast to the established Texan duality between Comanches *and* Yamparikas, Chouteau combined the two, Yamparikas *or* Comanches; that is, the Tenewas were Padokahs, and the Yamparikas were Comanches. Chouteau included the name Hois, and, in one of the few uses of the ethnonym in the 1830s, he also included the name Kotsoteka. He did not include the name Tenewa, probably because those people were known to him as Padokahs. But he did include Shoshones, one of the latest indications that links between those linguistic cousins had not yet been broken.

Tabequena also reported that the Comanches and the Kiowas were preparing to return the Cheyennes' hostile visit of the previous year. Chouteau tried to dissuade them; he sent his nephew, Edward, and a small escort from Fort Gibson to accompany Tabequena to his village 175 miles away, to ask the Indians to hold back for a while. They arrived three days after another Cheyenne and Arapaho attack had been driven off; the enemies lost thirteen killed and many wounded (A. P. Chouteau 1838).[18]

In early May 1839, while Josiah Gregg was visiting Camp Holmes, Comanches were reported to be coming in to meet Chouteau as previously promised and to continue on to Washington (Rogers 1839). A week later Tabequena—called by Gregg "Big Eagle"—and some sixty others, including a few Kiowas, arrived from their village on the Washita River. The chief was described by Gregg as "a corpulent, squint-eyed fellow . . . familiar to all the Comanche traders, . . . [He] boasted in no measured terms of friendship with

Americans" (Gregg 1844, 2:19–21). Tabequena was greatly disappointed to learn that trader-agent Auguste Chouteau had died during the winter, but he promised to use his influence to protect the traders at Camp Holmes. After trading some mules, Tabequena and a small group of his people went on to Fort Gibson.

Chouteau's replacement, William Armstrong, unsure of how to proceed, argued that the season was far too advanced to start for Washington, and he again postponed the trip, giving the chiefs about six hundred dollars in presents, including red, blue, and checked prints, knives, paints, combs, powder, scarlet cloth, bar lead, handkerchiefs, tin cups, tobacco, binding, gun flints, needles, linen thread, calico, bridles, brass kettles, sugar, coffee, blankets, hatchets, painted buckets, beef, corn, and bacon (W. Armstrong 1839); Gregg commented that it was "a handsome reward from the government for their visit" (Gregg 1844, 2:22).

Meanwhile, unaware that the trip to Washington had been canceled, Gregg traveled up the Canadian River in company with another party of dragoons sent to try to persuade other Comanches to accompany the delegation. In present Lipscomb County, Texas, beyond the international boundary, they met a group of Comanches whose unnamed leader wore

> the usual Comanche dress, but instead of mocassins, he had on a pair of long white cotton hose, while on his bare head waved a tall red plume, a mark of distinction which proclaimed at once a capitan major or principal chief. [1844, 2:38]

The plume is an otherwise unnoted prestige symbol. Gregg continued,

> In a short time we had ten chiefs sitting in a circle within our tent, when the pipe, the Indian token of peace, was produced, but doubting the sincerity of our profession, they at first refused to smoke. The interpreter however, remarked as an excuse for their conduct that it was not their custom to smoke until they had received some presents: but a few Mexican cigaritos being produced, most of them took a whiff, as if under the impression that to smoke cigars was no pledge of friendship. [Gregg 1844, 2:39]

Lieutenant Bowman of the dragoons—his first name is unknown—wanted to discuss peace and amity and to invite the chiefs to visit Washington. The chiefs, however, thought the dragoons were Texan troops, and since they were then in the midst of a series of clashes with the Texas Rangers, hesitated before meeting the soldiers. After explaining that the United States was distinct from Texas and was at peace with the Comanches, and giving "as an earnest of our friendly disposition . . . some scarlet cloth with a small quantity of vermillion," the talk proceeded (Gregg 1844, 2:39–41). But they would not go with the dragoons.

Gregg was later to publish what has become a classic account of the Santa Fe trade. Although he devoted several chapters to a discussion of the various Indian groups, and he is often cited as an authority on the Comanches, he had only a few comments that bear directly on them. Most of his relevant comments are contained in a single paragraph:

> The Comanches are divided into numerous petty bands, each under the control of its own particular chief. When a chief becomes old and careworn, he exercises but the "civil authority" of his clan; while his son, if deemed worthy, otherwise some distinguished brave, assumes by "common consent," the functions of war chief. As is the case with all barbarous tribes, their chiefs assume every judicial and executive authority. Complaints are made to [the chief] and sentence summarily pronounced and often as summarily executed. For most offenses, the chief, if he considers his authority sufficiently well established, freely uses the rod upon his subjects. He rarely attempts this, however, upon noted warriors or "braves," whose influence and resentment he may have reason to fear. The punishment of murder . . . devolves upon the bereaved relatives, who are free to pursue and punish the perpetrators according to their own liking, which is seldom short of death. But the offended party, if disposed to compromise, has also the privilege of accepting a commutation and releasing the murderer. [Gregg 1844, 2: 308]

In contrast to Ruíz, Berlandier, and Cameron—and indeed, in contrast to several generations of Spanish and Mexican officials—Gregg limited Comanche political organization to the "petty band," the autonomous local residential group. Although logically out of order, and almost in passing, Gregg then noted a distinction between a chief's war and civil "duties."[19] Then, in contrast to the numerous deprecations that Comanche chiefs held little or no authority in internal matters, Gregg stated that chiefs assumed "every judicial and executive authority," although that authority was not only situational, dependent upon the nature of the complaint—murder was not a public matter —but was subject to pragmatic calculations of relative power.

Except for that last observation, Gregg's comments contrast strongly those other observers. It is worth noting that although he had been in the Santa Fe trade for at least a decade, his 1834 and 1839 encounters are his only documented contacts with Comanches, and neither apparently gave much opportunity to observe political processes. It is therefore probable that much of his information on the Comanches came from the talk of his fellow freighters around the campfires at night.

Following the death of Auguste Chouteau in 1839, his trading post at Camp Holmes was abandoned. By that same year Holland Coffee had sold his interest in the post on Cache Creek, and although it was still referred to as Coffee's, it is not known whether he maintained any connection with it (Middlebrooks and Middlebrooks 1965). About that same time Abel Warren opened another trading post in the same vicinity (Clift 1924). Despite those efforts there was a major decline in the availability of American goods along the Canadian. Bent's Fort on the Arkansas remained a trade center, but it was in Cheyenne and Arapaho territory, and the Comanches were still at war with them. Therefore it was probably not coincidental, although the details are unknown, that in the summer of 1840 a general truce was arranged between the Cheyennes and Arapahos north of the Arkansas and the Comanches and Kiowas south of that river. Again, probably not coincidentally, the peace was formalized during an encampment of the tribes below Bent's Fort; it was said that the Comanches gave away so many horses that the Cheyenne people lacked enough halter ropes to lead them all away.

Soon thereafter, the Bents obtained licenses to trade with Comanches (LeCompte 1972:278), and Comanches were again welcome on the Arkansas. Indeed, in January 1841, Charles Bent wrote to the governor of New Mexico that he expected 1,500 Comanches, and an equal number of Arapahos, Cheyennes, and Sioux to be near his post. In March, he reported that "thirty-one Comanche and Kiowa chiefs . . . 'have made peas [sic] with us'" (Lecompte 1972:280); they are, unfortunately, unnamed. Following that arrangement, traders were sent southward into Comanchería in the winter of 1841–42, and in the summer of 1842, a more permanent horizontal log post—apparently called the "wood post" by Mexicans (Kenner 1969:132 n. 61)—was built on the north side of the Canadian in what later became Hutchinson County, Texas (Lecompte 1972:281).[20]

According to Grinnell (1923:42), Tohausen and Eagle Tail Feathers, speaking for the Kiowas, Shaved Head for the Comanches, and Poor Bull for the Apaches had asked that traders be sent to their country. The name of the Comanche chief involved in that arrangement, Shaved Head, is reminiscent of the Texan Comanche chief of 1785, Cabeza Rapada. Grinnell, without further citation although probably based on George Bent's letters, reported that he "had the left side of his head shaved close, while on the right side the hair was long, hanging down to his waist or below. His left ear was perforated with many holes . . . and was adorned with many brass rings" (1923:42). Unfortunately, he cannot be linked to any contemporary Comanche leader.

Comanche Relations with the Texas Republic, 1836–40

In the summer of 1835 the Anglo-American colonists in Texas revolted against the centralization plans of Mexican president Antonio López de Santa Anna. The Comanches played an ambivalent role in the ensuing conflict. On the one hand, there were constant rumors that Mexican agents were stirring up the Indians against the revolutionaries. For instance, on September 20, 1835, B. T. Archer, chairman of a Committee of Safety at Columbia, Texas, published a handbill addressed "to the Public," denouncing the then recent Matamoros meeting between Comanches and General Martín Perfecto de Cos: "The military, the tools of the despot, have made a treaty with the Comanches and other tribes of savages and have engaged them to fight against us" (Jenkins 1973, 1:467). In early 1836 several western newspapers reported, the "Comanches have declared against Texas and will second the operations of General Santa Anna" (*Little Rock [Arkansas] Gazette*, March 22, 1836). Stephen Austin himself wrote to President Andrew Jackson charging that "Santa Anna is . . . exciting the Comanche and other Indians who know nothing of law or political division of territory, and massacres have been committed on Red River within the United States" (Jenkins 1973, 5:477). There is no evidence of either Santa Anna's influence or of the alleged actions.

Although Jackson chose not to involve the United States in the affair, saying that neutrality would be maintained (Jenkins 1973, 5:477), the special fear of pan-Indian alliances continued. General Edmund P. Gaines, commander of American forces along the Sabine River, wrote to Secretary of War Lewis Cass that should the Caddos and Texas Cherokees become involved in the war, their "perfect knowledge of the territory could lead Comanches, Pawnees, Delawares, and Shawnees to every plantation, cabin, and camp" (Jenkins 1973, 7:228). Spy Buck, a Shawnee scout, reported to Lieutenant Joseph Bonnell, who in turn reported to Gaines, that the "Comanche, Waco, Tawacony, Towash and Kichee have made peace with each other and have combined against the whites." Further, the "Indians watch the road from Nacogdoches to San Antonio" and at least "twelve tribes have sent their women to the Trinity River for safety." Bonnell added, "This report is believed here, and *whether true or not,* I consider it my duty to tell you of it" (Jenkins 1973, 7:484).

Often those two rumors were combined. Chief Bowles of the Cherokees was reported as saying that he was a friend of Mexico, that he had "tried for 12 months to join all tribes together," and that the Texans were "just like the Americans, always stealing piece by piece" (Jenkins 1973, 7:179). In April 1837 an envoy to the Cherokees reported that they were preparing for war against the settlements and expected the Comanches to join them (Jenkins 1973, 5:429). In March 1838 it was reported:

> [Colonel Henry Karnes] believes that their suspicions with respect to our motives have been occasioned by false representation made by the Mexicans at Matamoros and by the North American Indians now among them, who tell the Comanche that our object is to acquire lands unjustly.
> The Shawnee traders who are now with the Comanche, are disposing of articles so very cheap that Col. [Karnes] is confident the object of their visit is entirely political, that they are endeavoring to influence their minds against the Texians, and form combinations which will enable the whole of the Indian tribes near our border to act in concert against us. [Winfrey and Day 1959–66, 1:42]

Some Comanches did take advantage of the unrest to raid the settlements. On October 30, 1835, a party of about thirty Comanches was reported in the vicinity of Guadalupe Victoria (Jenkins 1973, 2:266). On December 25 raiders near Colonel Edward Burleson's camp on the Gonzalez River were repulsed with the loss of one Comanche captured (Jenkins 1973, 2:317). In the spring of 1836 the settlers of the La Villa de Dolores Colony on Las Moras Creek decided to abandon the colony because of rumors of the approach of both Mexicans and Comanches. In mid-April the caravan carrying the retreating settlers was attacked by Comanches. Two women, Sarah Ann Horn and a Mrs. Harris, were taken captive and held for over a year, finally being ransomed in San Miguel, New Mexico (Rister 1955). On May 1 the Hibbons family was attacked on the Guadalupe River; two men were killed and Mrs. Hibbons and two of her children were taken captive. She managed to escape and by chance stumbled on Captain Peter Tumlinson's company of the Texas Army, which backtracked and attacked the Comanche camp, rescuing the children (Smithwick 1899:82). Parker's Fort on the Navasota River was hit on May 19, 1836. Five persons, including Rachel Plummer and Cynthia Ann Parker, were taken captive.

But other Comanches attempted to establish peaceful relations with the new government. On January 8, 1836, an unnamed Comanche "ambassador" sent word to J. C. Neill, the commander at San Antonio, that although the Comanches remained hostile, they would honor a truce for twenty days and asked for a commissioner to come and treat for peace. On January 17, J. W. Robinson, the acting governor of Texas, appointed Neill, José Francisco Ruíz, Edward Burleson, Byrd Lockhart, and J. W. Smith as commissioners to the Comanches (Winfrey and Day 1959–66, 1:13); of the five, only Ruíz's experience with the Comanches is known. They were instructed to avoid as far as may be consistent with the situation of Texas, the direct acknowledgement of any national rights existing in the Comanche Indians and make and fix no definite boundary between them and the free people of Texas, but you may give the consent of the Government to the said Indians to hunt, fish, etc., in certain areas for and during the pleasure of the government of Texas. [Jenkins 1973, 4:48]

It is not known whether that commission attempted any contact with the Comanches, but the Texans, being good Jacksonian Democrats, denied from the start any legitimacy to aboriginal land rights or limits.

Meanwhile, on March 7, 1836, Sam Houston wrote to Congressman James Collinsworth, "If any plan can be devised by which the Comanche can be approached by headwaters of Brazos and they induced to fall down and range upon the Laredo route to Bexar and steal horses, it will be important" (Jenkins 1973, 5:17). Ten days later Houston again wrote Collinsworth, saying, "Let the Comanche be approached" (Jenkins 1973, 5:122). By August it was reported that the "Comanche and Lipatlan can be enlisted" (Jenkins 1973, 7:182), and that they had "intimated a wish to take part in the present contest" (Jenkins 1973, 7:385). In September Henry Morfit, sent by the United States government to investigate conditions in Texas, wrote to Secretary of State John Forsyth that

the Comanches are looked to by the Texans as ready auxiliaries as they have immemorially been opposed to the Gachupines or Spanish, and are not less so to their successors, the Mexicans. If these warriors are enlisted in the cause, the pretensions of Texas may assume a stronger form (Jenkins 1973, 4:419)

In December Houston wrote to the Comanche chiefs:

Your enemies and ours are the same. I send you my friends to talk to you—to give presents and to make peace with you and your people. . . . You have many things to trade and swap with us. You need many things that we can let you have cheaper than you have ever been able to get them from the Mexicans. You can let us have horses, mules and buffalo robes in change for our paints, tobacco, blankets and other things which will make you happy. . . . I wish you to have a smooth path, that shall lead from your camp to my house, that we can meet each other and that it shall never become bloody. I do not wish that your women and children should be scared or unhappy. You may believe the words that my friends speak to you for me. . . . When the grass rises in the Spring, you must come with your chiefs and I will make you and them presents. I am the chief who sent the silver medal to the Great Comanche Chief from San Antonio in 1833. [A. W. Williams and Barker 1938-43, 7:5]

Ultimately, General Thomas Rusk wrote to the secretary of war, "I am well satisfied a treaty can be effected with Comanches on the most favorable terms" (Jenkins 1973, 7:153). However, the nature of the contacts made with them are not known. As late as October, 1837, the Standing Committee on Indian Affairs of the Texan Congress reported that the Comanches

> are the natural enemies of the Mexican whom they contemptuously discriminate their "stock-keepers" and out of which nation they procure slaves . . . Your committee had not any evidence of hostile feelings on the part of these Indians towards the people of this Republick and do not entertain a doubt but that a treaty of amity between this Govt and those Indians might be effected if presents and energetic measures were adopted for that purpose by the Executive and the Congress of this Republick. [Winfrey and Day 1959–66, 1:24]

It is possible that a "treaty"—probably more of a cease-fire—was made with some Comanches in April 1837 (Johnston 1878:84), but nothing more is known of it.

That summer, despite his earlier antagonism, chief Bowles accepted a commission to visit the Comanches. At a village of southern Comanches he was advised "not to think to conciliate the great northern villages, for they hate the white man," and the southerners advised him to go no farther. On the headwaters of the Wichita River he found sixteen villages, "known as those who trade with [Holland] Coffee," but the "Principal Chief" was still farther off, and no one present would listen to Bowles. Moreover, there were war parties returning daily with large droves of mules, horses, and prisoners. Growing fearful, Bowles returned south without having contacted the leaders (*Houston Telegraph and Texas Register*, June 12, 1837).

Later that month Quinaseico (*kwina si?a* 'eagle feathers'), Puestia (meaning unknown), and six warriors appeared at Coleman's Fort on Walnut Creek in Bastrop County, south of Austin, saying that "their tribe was desirous of entering into a treaty with the whites and to that end requested that a commissioner be sent to their camp to talk the matter over with the head men." Noah Smithwick, being the only one present who could speak Spanish, was selected, and he travelled with them to their village thirty miles east on Brushy Creek in Burleson County (Smithwick 1899:124).

Some sixty years later when he dictated his memoirs,[21] Smithwick recalled the village as being headed by Muguara. The closest name in the archival documents is the man called Muraequa, possibly *mula eka* 'red mule', by the Mexicans (J. M. García 1832b). Based on *mu* 'nose', Joe Attocknie (1965) suggested the name was Moo-wa-ta 'to browse with the nose', a reference to coyotes. Possibly basing his drivation on *tekwaru* 'talk to someone', Fehrenbach (1974:329) gave the name as Mukewarrah 'Spirit

Talker'; but there is nothing in either the phonetics or the phonemics which suggests spirits (*nanisuwʉkaitʉ*).

Smithwick also recalled that there were four other chiefs present, Paha-yuko (*paha yuko* 'he has intercourse with his aunt'), Potsanaquahip (*potsana* 'male buffalo', *kwahipʉ* 'back'),[22] later called Buffalo Hump, Esanap (either *isa* 'wolf' or as later *esi* gray, *napʉ* 'gray shoe'), and Catanaipa (possibly *ke* 'not', *tenahpʉ?* 'man'). The first two would be prominent chiefs in later years, but their names would not be mentioned in direct contemporary documents for several years and there is no evidence that they played active roles in events in the intervening years; thus it is probable that Smithwick was reading these names back upon his memories.

Smithwick was surprised by the camp's small size: it was "not nearly so large as I had expected, there being only about fifty lodges and not over one hundred warriors" (Smithwick 1899:124). R. N. Richardson (1933:113) interprets the small size as an indication that Muguara was not the "head chief" of the southern Comanches. Although it is unlikely that Muguara was a principal chief of the stature of Ecueracapa, the size of the village itself does not necessarily reflect his status; a divisional principal chief would also be a local band chief, as well as head of a *nemenahkahni;* thus even a divisional chief might sometimes camp only with his own local band or *nemenahkahni.*

Smithwick stayed three months with Muguara, during which time he "had many long, earnest talks with the old Comanche chiefs." In one, Muguara complained about the encroaching settlements:

> We have set up our lodges in these groves and swung our children from these boughs from time immemorial. When game beats away from us we pull down our lodges and move away, leaving no trace to frighten it, and in a little while it comes back. But the white man comes and cuts down the trees, building houses and fences, and the buffalos get frightened and leave and never come back, and the Indians are left to starve, or if we follow the game we trespass on the hunting ground of other tribes and war ensues. . . . If the white men would draw a line defining their claims and keep on their side of it the red men would not molest them. [Smithwick 1899:134]

Although it is not clear whether the idea of a line separating Indian and White was indeed Muguara's, it was soon to become a major point in Comanche-Texan politics.

In February 1838 about 150 Comanches came into Béxar, requesting a "deputation of citizens to go meet with them." Those sentiments of peace were shared by many Texans, both for the immediate benefits of trade and for the indirect benefit of access to rumored silver mines on the San Saba River—probably survivals of the rumors of silver ore in Comanchería dating back to at least 1785—and the possibility of diverting the wealth of the Santa Fe trade to Texas (*Houston Telegraph and Texas Register*, Feb. 24, 1838).

Meanwhile, General Albert Sidney Johnston, commander of the Texas Army, Colonel Lysander Wells, and Colonel Henry Karnes were appointed commissioners to meet with the Comanches. They were empowered to

> assure them of our friendly feelings . . . and of our earnest desire to cultivate with them a trade for our mutual advantage, and to this end, trading houses shall be established for their convenience by which means they would find a market for their mules, buffalo robes, etc. [DeShields 1912:243]

Some Texans may also have been considering the necessity of a line. General Johnston apparently felt that "there could be no satisfactory peace until the limits of the two races were definitely settled, and each was restrained within its own territory." The problem for Texas was, Johnston felt, first, that Spain had recognized no Indian "right to the soil," a doctrine maintained by Texas,[23] and second, that he had no clear authority to discuss the matter with the Comanches. He sent a note to President Houston asking advice, but receiving no reply, he "determined . . . merely to hold a friendly talk with the Indians, avoiding all disputed points" (Johnston 1878:88).

Together with a delegation of citizens, the commission went to the Comanche camp. At the council that followed, as reported in the *Houston Telegraph and Texas Register*,

> fifteen chiefs met them in council . . . and were anxious to secure the friendship of our government, but would listen to no terms unless the government would guarantee to them the full and undisturbed possession of the country north of the Guadalupe Mountains. [Mar. 17, 1838]

Thus, despite Johnston's efforts to avoid it, the Comanches "made a positive declaration as regards their territorial limits"; indeed, they claimed

> the finest country in Texas lying on the waters of the Colorado extending as low down as the upper line of Bastrop county. . . . They claim all the territory North and West of the Guadalupe Mountains, extending from Red River to the Rio Grande, the area of which is nearly equal to one fourth of the domain of Texas. [Winfrey and Day 1959-66, 1:42-43]

As an explanation for the Comanches' intransigence, it was suggested that several "Mexicans and Shawnees had visited them and endeavored to instigate the commencement of hostilities" (*Houston Telegraph and Texas Register*, Mar. 17, 1838).

Since the commissioners were not "authorized to accede" to such stipulations, the Comanches were asked to send a deputation to San Antonio. Arrangements were made to meet again, at which time it was hoped they would "conclude the most favorable treaty practicable, without indicating the precise limits of the territory which will be secured to them, assuring them at the same time, that the Government has no disposition to injure or take from them any rights which they may possess" (Winfrey and Day 1959-66, 1:44).

The question of a line separating Comanches and Texans was the focus of much concern to the Comanches, while the Anglo-Texans carefully avoided it. In April Karnes was instructed to "say to [the Comanches] that they will continue to hunt where they have game, and if they find our people in their hunting grounds with the passwords, to treat them kindly, as our people will do should the Comanche come into our settlements" (DeShields 1912:243). Later that month, Essowakkenny (Esawacany) and Essomanny (probably *isa nahnia* 'wolf's name'), along with 150 others, arrived in San Antonio (Johnston 1878). General Johnston later described the two as "about twenty-seven or twenty-eight years old, and about five feet eight inches in height. Essomanny was rather a bull-headed fellow, with a firm and sensible expression; Essowakkenny had a more intelligent countenance" (Johnston 1878:88). Some accounts also mention another name, Esananaka (*isa nanaka* 'wolf's noise'), but it is not clear whether that was a third individual or a confusion with the other two names.

General Johnston began by speaking of the advantages of peace, to which the Comanches agreed. Johnston then suggested that "if they were better acquainted with the white people, they might like them better"—conveniently ignoring the previous century's contacts between Comanches and Euroamericans—and suggested that if they desired, trading posts would be built in their country. Esawacany replied that trading posts seemed to scare away the buffalo; he did not want posts in their country, but would not object to them at the borders. On an improvised map on the palm of his hand, he drew those borders only about three miles from San Antonio.

Johnston, again avoiding the question of boundaries, expounded on the benefits of peace. Esawacany said his people were at peace with the Mexicans. Johnston said although his people were not at peace with the Mexicans, it would be good for the Comanches to be at peace with everybody. Esawacany replied that he would not make peace with the Mexicans until he had taken all their horses. Finally, Johnston asked them to visit President Houston; Esawacany declined but said that the other, Essomanny, who was braver, would go. Johnston then distributed presents "of considerable value" and the Comanches left "well pleased" (Johnston 1878:89).

On the strength of the Comanches' promises to Johnston, a number of trading parties visited the Comanche villages that spring. Colonel Karnes took a load of goods to a Comanche camp, where he was "well treated and made much money" (Johnston 1878:89). Similarly, Comanche trading parties visited Texan settlements. In early April, a party of one hundred Comanches came into the new town of Bastrop, each with "two or three horses or mules loaded down with peltries," saying that they desired peace and asking that traders be sent to them (*Houston Telegraph and Texas Register*, Apr. 28, 1838); Noah Smithwick may have accompanied one or more such trading expeditions (Smithwick 1899:136).

Later that month, another party of Comanches went to visit President Houston. They included Muguara and some of his people, but apparently did not include Essomanny; again Noah Smithwick accompanied them (Smithwick 1899:138), as did a Mr. Miles, but nothing more is known of the latter (*Houston Telegraph and Texas Register*, Sept. 15, 1838). They stopped for a few days at Austin; while there, Frédérick Leclerc, a young French medical doctor passing through Texas, described them:

> some one hundred Comanche Indians . . . heading towards Houston to make a peace treaty. . . . A Texan officer was serving as their guide. The Comanche tribe has remained powerful; it is still feared in Texas, where Spanish legends have given it a reputation for bravery and ferocity which is all too accurate. . . . But of all these Indians the one whose costume was the most bizarre was unquestionably the old chieftain. He wore a narrow red belt around the waist, a blue uniform with a red collar, the remains of epaulets and metal buttons, the sort of uniform worn by our [French] National Guard or our infantry soldier, and a hat covered with oil-cloth like our postillions [carriage drivers] . . . This hat was a Mexican's, whom he had killed a short time previously during a skirmish in the Rio Grande valley . . . At first we had a great deal of trouble making these Indians understand us; only the young Texas officer spoke a few words of their tongue. Fortunately, there was among them a poor Mexican boy of about twelve years of age who could serve as interpreter. . . . One day [the chief] had several Indian children brought forth and showed me their arms which bore the scars of an expert vaccination. Whatever may be the origin of such a blessing, it is certain that these savages had mastered and put to use this means of preventing the most dreadful curse which confronts the Indians. [McLean 1974-93, 16:446-49]

The "young Texan officer" was either Noah Smithwick or Mr. Miles; but if the former, there would have been no need for the captive boy to act as interpreter. The description of the uniforms is interesting; the last uniforms documented to have been given to Comanches by Euroamericans were those presented by John Jamison to Chief Cordero in 1816 and Chief Chihuahua in 1817. As a medical doctor, Leclerc easily recognized vaccination scars, but their source is unknown; in 1817, John Jamison had explained vaccination to Chief Chihuahua and although he reported that the chief was very interested in the process, it is highly improbable that the Comanches practiced vaccination themselves.[24]

In late May the Comanche delegation arrived at Houston. The citizens thronged to see them, but were disappointed:

> All expected to meet a band of fierce, athletic warriors with sinewy limbs and gigantic frames, but what was their astonishment on arriving at the President's House, to behold paraded there about twenty-five diminutive, squalid, half-naked, poverty stricken savages, armed with bows and arrows, and mounted on wretched horses and mules! Every feeling of admiration was dispelled at once, and our citizens viewed them with mingled feelings of city and contempt. . . . The day after their arrival, their squaws and children were scattered in all directions through the city picking up old tin plates, iron hoops, clippings of tin, glass bottles, and similar rubbish which they appeared to consider extremely valuable. They have evidently been less affected by the arts of civilized life than any other tribes within the limits of Texas. . . .
>
> Mr. Legrand, who has resided several years among the Comanches states that this party belongs to a portion of the tribe called "Comanches of the Woods"—who inhabit the hilly country north east of Bexar. They are a poor, degraded, sorry race and hardly have any resemblance to the Comanches of the prairie. [*Houston Telegraph and Texas Register*, May 30 [June 2], 1838; McLean 1974-93, 16:559-60]

This clash of symbolic images with the reality of Comanche life, as reported by Bonnell on May 12, 1838 (see above, pp. 228-29), and by the citizens of Houston later that month, has engendered over a century of commentary. In his letter Bonnell had begun by denying the "noble savage" image altogether, or at least suggesting that "they are not to be found in any portion of our western prairies." LeGrand was not quite so willing to discard the image: while the Indians in Houston were "Comanches of the Woods," there were others, "Comanches of the Prairies," who were, he implied, more nearly in line with the ideal. In the twentieth century, Texas historian Rupert Richardson commented—in contrast to the analysis given in the *Telegraph and Texas Register,* which said that the Comanches visiting Houston "have evidently been less affected by the arts of civilized life"—that "apparently the many decades of contact with the Spanish and with the Anglo-American colonists of recent years had proven to be demoralizing" (Richardson 1933:

101). More recently, anthropologist C. Symmes Oliver argued—without direct citation but apparently referring to these documents—that the Hois were "poverty stricken" and that they "knew times of great hardship" (Oliver 1962:72). However, such explanations for the contrast between the noble savage stereotype and the realities of the hunting lifestyle offer only minimal insight into the Comanches' behavior in the trash dumps of Houston: the Texans' discarded manufactured goods—specifically hoop iron, tin, and glass—were the raw materials from which to make arrowheads.

During their talks with President Houston that May, the Comanches spoke of their desire for a line demarcating Indian territory in Texas. According to Smithwick, Houston replied, "If I could build a wall from the Red River to the Rio Grande, so high that no Indian could scale it, the white people would go crazy trying to devise means to get beyond it" (Smithwick 1899:138). Although no line was forthcoming, a "Treaty of Peace and Amity" (Winfrey and Day 1959-66, 1:50) was signed on May 29, 1838, by R. A. Irion and Dr. Ashbel Smith for the Texans, and Muguara, Muestyah (probably the man Smithwick called Puestia), and Muhy (previously unmentioned) for the Comanches.

The first nine articles of the treaty represented Texan concerns. As so often happened in treaties, the Comanches were to surrender their sovereignty over legal redress of offenses against them. The Comanches would "bring to just punishment"—presumably Texan punishment—anyone who committed depredations. If any Texan property "should . . . fall into the hands of any of the Comanche Tribe, the Chiefs shall be bound to see that it is restored to the owner or Agent of the Government." If any stock were stolen by Comanches, "the offender shall be punished according to his crime by the whites." On the other hand, Texas—not the Comanches—would punish any citizen of the republic who might infringe on the rights of the Comanches, but only so long as "the Comanche shall comply with the stipulations of this treaty." There would be an agent to "superintend their business and protect their rights . . . so that they may not be cheated by bad men." There would be traders authorized by the president who would have a monopoly on the Comanche trade, and the Comanches promised in turn to "make war on all tribes of Indians at war with traders appointed by the President . . . because such conduct would throw trouble in the way of their trading." Finally, the chiefs were to visit the Texas capital on the second Monday in October of ever year, "that they may talk to the president."

In contrast to those businesslike procedures were articles 10 and 11, which clearly reflect generalized Indian—if not Comanche—words and concepts:

Art. 10. The Comanche promise that they will stand by the white man and be his friend against all his enemies while he has a *star* to show and will not kill their men or steal their property.

Art. 11. Peace is never to die between the parties that make this agreement that having shaken their hands upon it and the Great Spirit had looked down and seen their actions. He will curse all chiefs that tell a lie before his eyes their women and children cannot be happy. [Winfrey and Day 1959-66, 1:50-52; emphasis in original]

The meaning of the reference to the star is unknown; the curse is perhaps a reference to *tabebehkatɬ* 'sun killing', the traditional Comanche oath.

Upon their leaving, Houston gave the chiefs gifts, including a white flag as a symbol of peace, and a passport that read:

I, Sam Houston, President of the Republic of Texas, do hereby request, all who may meet with the bearers: Muguarrah, Muestayah, and Muhy, chiefs of the Comanche Nation, who are the friends and brothers of the Texians, freely to permit them to pass through the country so long as they conduct themselves with peace and friendship towards the whites, and to treat them with kindness and attention. . . . If any trader or other person authorized by the Government should visit the Comanche Nation, he is to have free and safe conduct, and in case of need to be protected. [A. W. Williams and Barker 1938-43, 2:242]

Despite those attempts at peace, relations remained uneasy. While it is clear that the truces and the peace treaty arranged in May 1838 between the Anglo-Texan government and the Texas Comanches would have had little effect upon other Comanches, it is also clear that they did not stop aggressive actions by other Anglo-Texans against Comanches. Moreover, there were a number of rumors about Comanche hostilties circulating through Texas, and sorting out the details remains difficult. For instance, according to Leclerc in Austin,

Ten days [after the Comanches had passed through on their way to Houston for the treaty, i.e. early June] the Comanches had returned . . . Our old chief . . . carried in his hand a long pole of sugar cane at the top of which was strung the Texas flag. . . . The flag which the old chief bore was evidence enough of the success of the peace-treaty mission, but the Comanches were not to keep it long. This same band which was welcomed in San Felipe [Austin] was, a few days later, to steal every horse it could find in the vicinity of San Antonio. Three Texians lured by the spirit of adventure, the desire to make money, and to open new lanes of commerce, had accompanied the Indians to their savage strongholds. These unlucky souls were never to return; it was learned that one of them had been murdered long before the Comanches reached their wigwams, and nothing more was heard of the other two. [McLean 1974-93, 16: 448-49]

Leclerc was the only observer to specify that the delegation had received a Texas flag rather than a simple white flag, and he was apparently the only reporter of an immediate raid on San Antonio. On a wider scale, Leclerc was the first to use the motif of the traders to the Comanches who never returned.

According to notes in M. B. Lamar's papers, while Bonnell's party was at Esawacany's village, word came that another chief had been killed on the Colorado River. In retaliation, some of the Indians threatened to kill the traders, but Esawacany said they would have to kill him first; the Texans, "Bonnell, Alsbury, and others 13 in number returned to Bexar in safety" (Lamar 1921, 4:230). Oddly, Bonnell never mentioned the incident. However, that reported number of traders reappeared at least once, and in combination with the motif of the traders who never returned. According to William Johnston, after Colonel Karnes was well treated, a party of thirteen men followed: "they were never heard from again, it was supposed they were treacherously murdered by the Comanches" (Johnston 1878:89).

On August 10 Colonel Karnes attacked a party of 200 Comanches at Arroyo Seco, reportedly killing Essomanny (*Houston Telegraph and Texas Register*, Sept. 1, 1838), but according to a note in Lamar's papers, Captain Jack Hayes of the Rangers reported that

> Asa Minor the leader, a chief of some note . . . had been shot thro [sic] by two balls, and lay as dead for three days when he was found with life still in him. His countrymen revived him and he was soon restored to health. He afterwards came to Bexar and there related his fate. [1921, 4:232]

In that same fight, "another named Casimeri"—possibly the Casimero known from Mexican Texas—"was dangerously wounded" (*Houston Telegraph and Texas Register*, Sept. 1, 1838).

On September 8, a group about 70 Comanches visited Bastrop. They "manifested much dissatisfaction on account of the late engagement with Col. Karnes, on the Arroyo Seco." Mr. Miles—who had accompanied the Comanches on their visit to Houston in May—reported that he had attended a "big talk" on the Colorado River in which "all the principal chiefs of the various tribes" participated, and all were said to have been in favor of peace (*Houston Telegraph and Texas Register*, Sept. 15, 1838.)

On October 20 a group of surveyors outside San Antonio was attacked by Comanches. When a party of thirteen Texans responded, they were quickly surrounded; eight men were killed outright, and four of the five others were wounded. That day the Comanches also captured six Mexicans (*Houston Telegraph and Texas Register*, Nov. 3, 1838). Five days later there was a battle at the Anadarko village near the site of modern Fort Graham (Yoakum 1855, 2:247), and Esawacany was reported killed (Lamar 1921, 4:230). At the end of November, several of the Mexican captives were released with an apology; their detainment had been a misunderstanding:

> One of the chiefs, who visited Houston last spring, recognized them as belonging to the settlements on the Colorado and Brazos. It appears that the Indians imagine that the people of Texas are divided into tribes and that as they have made a treaty of peace with the tribes east of the Colorado, they are obliged to release any captives . . . belonging to the settlements east of that stream. The Comanches . . . manifested the greatest hostility for the citizens of Bexar, and spoke of them as a people entirely distinct from the citizens of Eastern Texas. [*Houston Telegraph and Texas Register*, Nov. 24, 1838].

President Houston still hoped to establish peace with the Comanches by creating a line separating them from the Texans. But he complained that the Texas Congress had taken away his ability to act (*Houston Telegraph and Texas Register*, Nov. 28, 1838). Then in December 1838 the election of Mirabeau B. Lamar to the presidency of the republic presented a more difficult obstacle to peaceful relations. Lamar brought a radically different approach to the Comanches. In place of Houston's policy of peace, he would wage war; Texas had been "too easy on the Indians who committed depredations" (Weaver 1980:25).

In January 1839 a Lipan hunting party reported a Comanche camp on a tributary of the San Saba River. Fearing that "if the Comanches were allowed to remain they would soon be making predatory incursions into the settlements," Colonel John H. Moore, with about sixty Texans and sixteen Lipans, attacked the village (Smithwick 1899:154). The initial surprise attack almost passed through the village, but when the Texans retreated to reload, most of their horses were run off, and they were then surrounded by several hundred Comanches. At a pause in the firing, the Comanches approached under a white flag, said to have been the one given by Houston the previous May (Winfrey and Day 1959-66, 1:57). During the truce, the Comanches proposed to trade their white prisoners, possibly including Matilda Lockhart, a young girl taken on the Guadalupe River the previous fall, for the Comanches captured in the initial attack. Unfortunately, those Comanches had already been "killed or otherwise disposed of without advice from us" by the Lipan auxiliaries, and the exchange fell through.

During the winter of 1839–40 a number of captives were ransomed. Texas historian John Henry Brown (1899:3) suggested that those transactions were the result of a treaty, but details are unknown. One of those ransomed was Matilda Lockhart. As reported later by Colonel Hugh McLeod, the girl said that there were more captives at the "principal camp" and that the Comanches' plan was that if they could get a good price for her, the others would be brought in one at a time (J. H. Brown 1899:778).

On January 9, 1840, three Comanches, one of whom "appeared to be a Priest," came to San Antonio and "cried loudly" for Colonel Karnes. The spokesmen said that his nation had met in general council and, rejecting offers from the Cherokees and from Mexican Centrists, had elected a "distinguished chief" to treat for peace; their party had been sent ahead to open the negotiations. Karnes sent them back with the message that the Texas government would not enter into any treaty without the release of all captives and the return of all stolen property. Karnes reported that the messenger promised to return in about a month with their principal men and all the captives they held (Winfrey and Day 1959–66 1:101).

General Johnston, informed of the messenger, ordered that their delivery of the captives would be "regarded as an evidence of their sincere desire for peace, and they [would] therefore be received with kindness and permitted to depart without molestation." But, he went on:

> You will state to them that this government assumes the right with regard to all Indian tribes within the limits of the Republic, to dictate the conditions of such residence; and that their own happiness depends upon their good or bad conduct towards our citizens: that their remaining within such limits as may be prescribed and an entire abstinence from acts of hostility or annoyance to the inhabitants of the frontier, are the only conditions for the privilege of occupancy that the government believes it is at this time necessary to impose: that the observance of these conditions will secure to them the peace they profess to seek. You will further say, that under the sanction of the Law, our citizens have a right to occupy any vacant lands of the Government, and that they must not be interfered with by the Comanche. To prevent any further difficulty between our people and theirs, they must be made clearly to understand that they are prohibited from entering our settlements. Should the Comanche come in without bringing with them the Prisoners, as it is understood that they have agreed to do, you will detain them. Some of their number will be dispatched as messengers to the tribe, to inform them that those retained will be held as hostages until the Prisoners are delivered up, when the

hostages will be released. It has been usual heretofore to give presents; for the future such custom will be dispensed with. [Winfrey and Day 1959–66, 1:105]

On March 19 Muguara and about sixty-five men, women and children—Johnston (1878:116) said thirty-two men, thirty-three women and children—walked into the trap. Apparently thinking the meeting was for general trade, they brought a large amount of furs and horses, but only one captive. That captive is unidentified; a number of writers (e.g., Bonnell 1840:134; Johnston 1878:116; J. H. Brown 1899:76; R. N. Richardson 1933:110) imply that it was Matilda Lockhart. However, since she is credited with giving the details about captives held by Comanches in other villages—that is, the details used by the Texans to conspire to hold the Comanches hostage for their return—she must have been recovered earlier.

Twelve Comanche men, variously described as "chiefs" or "principal men," and a number of others met with the Texans in the Council House on the plaza. When the Texans demanded the other captives, Muguara denied that his group held any more, although he admitted that "other tribes" did. At that, a detachment of soldiers were marched in and the Comanches were told that they were now "prisoners and would be kept as hostages for the safety of our people." Panicked by the change of events, one man drew his knife and stabbed a solder. In the general melee, thirty-five Comanches were killed and twenty-seven women and children and two old men were taken prisoner (McLeod 1840).

One woman was sent back to the Comanche camps with the demand that the rest of the captives be released. She soon returned with two Texan and five Mexican captives whom she was willing to trade for her relatives, making up the difference in horses. Colonel William S. Fisher declined the horse trade but did release an equal number of Comanches for the captives she brought in ("Later from the West," *Houston Telegraph and Texas Register*, Apr. 5, 1840). Mary Maverick Green said that the remaining captives at the Comanche villages were killed and that a chief named Isimanica (apparently Essomanny, who had incorrectly been reported killed in 1838) and about 300 warriors appeared at San Antonio to demand the release of their relatives. After getting no response, they moved off to the San José mission, where the prisoners were being kept, but with no better luck (Green 1952: 117). As late as September 1843 William Bollaert reported, "There are a few Comanche children in San Antonio; on asking one, a boy who was assisting a stone mason, how and when he came to be there, he replied, pointing to the council house, 'My father was killed there', but he appeared gay and happy" (Bollaert 1956:229).

In August a large Comanche war party, reportedly 500 men, made a sweep through southern Texas. They attacked Victoria and then moved on to the coastal village of Linnville. On their return north the Comanches were intercepted at Plum Creek, near modern Lockhart, Texas, and were routed, losing 50 or more (Wilbarger 1889:28). In October Colonel Moore, with 90 Texans and 12 Lipan Apaches, went up the Colorado on a search-and-destroy mission against any Comanches who might have escaped. About three hundred miles upriver, possibly above the junction with the Concho River, the Lipans reported a village of sixty families, with 125 warriors. Attacking at first light, the Texans achieved complete surprise, claiming 48 killed outright, 80 drowned in the river, and 34 captured, along with 500 horses (Yoakum 1855; Wilbarger 1889:185).

Some contemporary accounts played on fears of Mexican involvement in the Victoria-Linnville raid. According to Yoakum, "It is probable that they were directed in this incursion by the Mexicans at Matamoros. It is well known that large amounts of goods had been brought to the two points attacked for the purpose of trading with the Federalists on the Rio Grande. The Centrists thought it a good move thus to break up the depots" (Yoakum 1855, 2:298). John Smith, a Texas officer, allegedly found a letter from a Mexican officer at Plum Creek suggesting that the raid would be profitable. A variation on that theme stated that an Arkansas trader had inspired the raiders with information on the Linnville and Victoria warehouses (R. N. Richardson 1933:114).

There was little evidence to implicate the Comanches involved in either the Council House fight or the fight on the Colorado in raids on Texas settlements. In fact, upon the return of the Texas forces from the Colorado, it was learned from the prisoners that Essomanny had been "visiting the several lodges of the tribes to induce them for peace" (*Houston Telegraph and Texas Register*, Apr. 15, 1840). For much of the next year there was no contact, although Texas continued to send military expeditions into Comanche country. In fall 1840, there were other reports of Indian raids in and around San Antonio, but none were clearly identified as Comanche.

Sam Houston's Peace, 1841–44

In December 1841 Sam Houston again became president of the Texas Republic. Almost at once he sent out messengers to some of the Indian groups telling of his desire for peace. Many of those Indians were also seeking peace, but it was not until the summer of 1843 that an attempt was made to contact the Comanches. Meanwhile, there were other encounters. In May

1842 an estimated 300 Comanches raced down the north bank of the Rio Grande almost to the coast (*Houston Telegraph and Texas Register* May 4, 1842). That raid and similar encounters, rumored and actual, coming in the midst of the second Texas-Mexican war, 1841–42, raised fears that Mexican agents were aggitating the Indians against the Texans.

In 1843 the government of Texas sent representatives in search of a chief named Pahayuko, hoping that he could be persuaded to come to a conference at Bird's Fort, west of Fort Worth. Why they were sent explicitly to Pahayuko, rather than to other Comanches leaders living closer to the settlements, was unrecorded. Indeed, there were other Comanches with equal or greater influence in Texas. Moreover, this is the earliest mention of Pahayuko in contemporary documents (Noah Smithwick, writing some sixty years later, reported that Pahayuko had been present at Muguara's village on Brushy Creek in 1836; however, his name was otherwise unreported in the intervening seven years.) Pahayuko's divisional affiliation is unclear. Anglo-Texans usually referred to him as a southern Comanche; however, since he was often found along or above the Red River, he was probably a Tenewa.

The expedition consisted of J. C. Eldredge, the new superintendent of Indian affairs; General Hamilton Bee; trader Thomas Torrey; the Waco chief Acahquash and his wife; several Delaware guides and interpreters; two Comanche children (possibly captives from the Council House fight);[25] and a number of unidentified individuals. All was not well organized in the party. Besides guiding, the Delawares John Conner and James Shaw were also itinerant traders, and their other interests managed to delay the expedition for at least a month along the way. It was not until July that they reached the Wichita villages on Cache Creek. There they heard that the Comanches might be on Pecan Creek, on the south side of the Red River, west of the Wichita Mountains.

But at Pecan Creek they found no sign of Comanches. One of the children was sick, so they spent ten days in encampment, sending out scouts and runners to find the Comanches, but without success. Moving back across the Red River, they happened on an old blind Comanche man and a young boy picking wild plums, who led them to their village. Pahayuko had that morning gone to visit the Wichita village on Cache Creek. While runners went to find Pahayuko, the "second chief," unfortunately unnamed, invited the Texans to move within the bounds of the village.

Eldredge described the camp:

> The encampment was in the open prairie on the bank of a small creek and covered a surface of about half a mile, the chief's tent was at one end of it and to the tents in its immediate vicinity we had access if we

desired, but the Chief would not permit me to visit the other end of the village saying "it was not good" making at the same time the action of scalping—I observed also that the Warriors occupying those lodges did not come near us while the others thronged our quarters from morning til night. [Winfrey and Day 1959–66, 1:266]

Several days later Pahayuko returned; he was "large and portly, weighing . . . upwards of two hundred pounds with a pleasing expression of countenance, full of good humor and joviality." After a brief introduction and meeting with Eldredge, he went into council with "his chiefs and warriors and remained in earnest debate until nearly sunset." Eldredge's tent was only a short distance from the council, and he reported:

> [I was] enabled to see and hear all that passed. Many of the warriors in their speeches were much excited and violent in their gesticulations and manner, I learned from an interpreter that these had relations slain at San Antonio when their chiefs went in to make a treaty [the Council House fight] and were strongly advocating a retaliation upon us, after which they were willing to listen to terms of peace. [Winfrey and Day 1959–66, 1:267]

Based on those comments, it seems that Eldredge was visiting a composite village made up of two groups of Comanches, each localized within the whole. One group, affiliated with Pahayuko and the "second chief," was open to contact with Texans; the other, whose leadership was unknown to Eldredge, claimed to have had close relations with Muguara's people and demanded revenge for the Council House fight. Unfortunately, further details are unknown.

The debate was touch and go. Acahquash made a "long and animated speech," emphasizing that "our head chief was not the same chief who ruled in Texas at the time of the massacre but was the friend of the red man." In the afternoon the "second chief," a Wichita, and a Tawakoni arrived to say that since the expedition had left their village, several people had taken sick and died and that they too might be poisoned if they attended the council. Ultimately, the council decided to let Eldredge speak the next day. That night, when the council adjourned, Pahayuko "mounted his horse and rode through and around the encampment giving commands in a loud tone of voice, the import of which was that no one should trouble us during the night or interfere with our horses or other property" (Winfrey and Day 1959–66 1:268).

The next day Eldredge met the council. He presented the "Alamo Council pipe"—an otherwise unknown artifact—but Pahayuko refused to smoke with him then or during his whole stay with the Comanches. He presented the two children and addressed the council. He reiterated, "The chief Houston is not the same who was Chief in Texas when your people were slain." Further, "Houston . . . has sent me with two others to you having in our hands this white flag, an emblem of peace . . . and these presents— they are not the offerings of fear but the gifts of friendship—as such you will receive them for no more will be given until a firm treaty of peace is made" (Winfrey and Day 1959-66, 1:268-69).

Eldredge, or perhaps other circumstances, must have been persuasive. On August 9 Pahayuko addressed the Texan:

> My brother . . . I have heard your talk and the words of your great chief Houston. . . . When we make a treaty I want it to be a strong treaty, one that shall last as long as this world exists. All the chiefs of my several bands must be present and there is no time to collect them together. I want them present that there may be no lies spoken on my side. [Winfrey and Day 1959-66, 1:271-72]

They agreed to meet again on the Clear Fork of the Brazos River at the full moon in December to make what was hoped to be a firm and lasting peace; Pahayuko would visit the different bands and induce the chiefs to attend (Winfrey and Day 1959-66, 1:228, 251-75). But for reasons that remain unknown, there was no meeting on the Brazos that December.[26]

In early 1844 messengers were again sent out to find the Comanche leaders, read them a message from Houston, and bring them to a council. Although they did not find the Comanche camps, they did meet four men who took word to the chiefs. Several days later two Comanches, who identified themselves as Mopechucope and Potsanaquahip, came into their camp. The first name is *mupi* 'owl' *tsukupu* 'old'; Potsanaquahip was named by Smithwick as present at the Brushy Creek village in 1836, but this meeting with the Texan messengers was the earliest documentary mention of both chiefs.

Houston's message to Pahayuko was read to them, and Mopechucope dictated a reply, saying:

> My Brother
> I received and heard your letter . . . [which] you sent to Pahayuco. . . . although I am not known to you, I am looked up to by all my tribe for council, even Pahayuco himself looks to me for council. . . . Pahayuco with some of his band have gone to the Salt Plain on Arkansas some have gone over to the Pecos and the Rio Grande but it is known and understood by all the Comanche that we are at peace with Texas and has been ever since the Treaty with Eldredge. . . . I will do all I can for peace, and I know I can manage my own people. You want some of us

to come to the council in April, but it is impossible for me or any of my tribe to come at this time, we are too scattered, only myself and one or two more men left here with all the women and children.

Mopechucope then came to the heart of his concerns:

[I] want . . . a line run between our countries . . . to commence on Brazos river passing over the Comanche Peak from thare direct to the mouth of the first large creek running in the Colorado on the west side below the mouth of the San Saba; from thence in a direct line to the Rio Grande, all above that line is Comanche Country as ever has been. I myself have never left it nor never intend to; at this treaty with the Indian if you wish to designate the line . . . the aforesaid line will satisfy the Comanche; if you do not choose to make it until you see us I hope it will be all right. [Winfrey and Day 1959–66, 2:6–9]

Thus, the matter of the line again became central to Comanche-Texan relations.

In May Texas commissioners met with delegates from a number of Indian groups to discuss "establishing a nominal line . . . between the Upper and lower Cross Timbers," but until a treaty could be arranged the chiefs were advised that "it would be best for no Indians to come below that line" without a letter from their agent explaining their presence (Winfrey and Day 1959–66, 2:38). In essence, that created a de facto line.

In June a group of Comanches encountered a small patrol of Texas Rangers under Captain Jack Hays on Walker's Creek near the Guadalupe River. The Comanches dismounted and, forming a defense, shouted taunts at the Texans. The Texans, attempting to slip around to attack from the rear, found themselves surrounded but managed to fight their way out. Taking refuge in the woods, they held off another attack. Captain Hays was reported to have asked if there were any loaded weapons, and the sole loaded weapon was directed at the chief, who "tumbled dead from his saddle." Remounting, the rangers pursued the Indians, "powder burning" them from their revolvers as they caught up (Neighbours 1965).

The Walker's Creek fight has been the subject of much Texan folklore. As historian Kenneth Neighbours noted, "many accounts of the battle exist, but unfortunately few are primary" (1965:122). Indeed, there is confusion about almost every element of the story. Wilbarger (1889:78) and DeShields (1912:329) cite it as occurring in 1841. Foster-Harris, although echoing the motif of the death of the Comanche chief, placed it "about 1840" at Bandera Pass (1955:125). Fehrenbach (1974:316ff) cited it as taking place in 1840 on the Pedernales River. Wilbarger (1889:78) and Neighbours (1965:123) reported that the chief who was killed was Yellow Wolf, a name previously un-recorded.

Other aspects of the battle reports have more mythic proportions, for the action on Walker's Creek was the first combat test of the Colt revolver; indeed, for years afterwards, the battle was commemorated on the cylinder engravings of the Dragoon models of Colt's pistols. Some versions of the story would have it that the battle was also the Comanches' introduction to the weapon and that it was so effective that the Comanches were routed.

While Walker's Creek may have been the revolver's first combat test, it was not the Comanche's introduction to the weapon: according to Josiah Gregg, while traveling up the Canadian River in 1839—five years before the battle on Walker's Creek—he had demonstrated a Colt revolver to a Coman-che who responded with an equally rapid and more accurate volume of arrows (Gregg 1844, 2:36). Moreover, the combat effectiveness of the early Colt revolvers may have been somewhat less than the mythmakers would have it. For instance, the rate of fire was sometimes held to be a significant element in the outcome of the battle, but while rapidity of fire may have had an initial psychological advantage, that advantage was decreased by the technological problems of reloading. Each Ranger had two pistols, each with four preloaded five-shot cylinders, thus each Ranger had forty shots available. However, replacing the cylinders involved several steps, none of which could be easily done on horseback—nor while marching down a sun-drenched street in a dramatic showdown—and since those first Colts had no reloading lever, once the forty rounds were expended, each Ranger was disarmed. That point was attested to by Captain Hays's asking if anyone was *still* loaded, a meaningless question in an era when guns could be reloaded, but now meaningful in the absence of reloading levers. Indeed, the first part of the battle may have been over in less than a minute, while the replacing and firing of the other cylinders may have prolonged the fight another half hour. Nor would the weapon's accuracy have been decisive; although the motif of the powder burns could be held to demonstrate the daring heroism of the Rangers, it was also a mark of the poor accuracy of the weapons: they were effective only at a range that would produce powder burns.

Meanwhile, Robert S. Neighbors, Texas agent to the Lipan and the Tonkawa Indians, found a camp of some thirty Comanches "of Santa Anna's party" under "Ta.na.cio quache or Bear's Tail" on Boregas Creek; Santa Anna's Comanche name is unknown; the latter name includes the element *kwasi* 'tail', but the element "ta.na.cio" is unrecognizable. They said they had been "whipped by the Mexicans in a fight they had near Matamoros" and were going to Laredo to get more horses before returning to the Brazos River.

They were, however, interested in peace, and one of the party, the "son of Tas-sha-ro-she, one of the great chiefs of the nation," wanted a passport and would come to Torreys' trading house on the Brazos for that purpose (Winfrey and Day 1959-66, 2:172); both the father and the son are otherwise unidentified.

In preparation for the fall meeting, the Delaware scouts John Conner and Jim Shaw were sent out to the Comanches, whom they found on the Clear Fork of the Brazos River, 200 miles above the Kitsai villages. During their presentation Mopechucope sat silent while the "young man," Potsanaquahip, "was rather put at the head of affairs." At first he said he would not go; his people were not ready; Houston should go first to the council grounds and let them know he was there and then they would come. Only when the messengers replied in exasperation that they would not come again did Mopechucope finally speak, saying he had promised to be at the meeting and that he would go. It was only as they were leaving that Potsanaquahip came along (Winfrey and Day 1959-66, 2:102).

The meeting got under way in October and included all the peoples of Texas. Potsanaquahip and Mopechucope were the principal Comanches present; Pahayuko, in mourning for a son "killed in the Spanish war," was reported to have "killed his horses, destroyed his lodges and taken new skins to the Salt Plains there to erect new lodges and make a new home" (Winfrey and Day 1959-66, 2:64). The artist John Mix Stanley, who was present at the meeting, reported his words, "I mourn the loss of my only boy, who met his death on the war-path. I must cry and mourn till green grass grows; I have burnt my lodges, killed my mules and horses, and scattered ashes on my head" (J. M. Stanley 1852:52). How Stanley learned those words is unclear.

According to the official report, Potsanaquahip was the primary Comanche speaker. After apologizing for Pahayuko's absence, he began:

> The Great Spirit above is looking down and sees and hears my talk; the ground is my mother and sees and hears that I tell the truth. When I first heard the words of your chief I felt glad; and I was uneasy until I struck the white path and came here to see him. That is all I want to say, what I came here for was to hear the words of peace I have heard them and all is right; peace is peace—I have no more to say. [Winfrey and Day 1959-66, 2:106]

Stanley, however, reported that after giving Pahayuko's apology, Potsanaquahip—described by Stanley as the "second chief of the Hoesh End of Comanches and War-Chief of all the Comanches"—repeated that chief's instructions to him:

I send you afar off to meet in council the captain from the white nations
of the east. You must make peace with all nations and tribes, for I am
sick of hearing the cry of my people mourning the loss of some relative
killed in battle. Should you meet any captain from Texas, tell him that
we have heard that the people of Texas believe that we still hold many
prisoners taken from their country; but such is not the case, there is but
one, and he, a young man, has been raised among us from his infancy,
and is now absent on a war-party against the Spaniards. If they believe
not this statement, they have permission to come among us and examine
for themselves; they shall come and go freely, safely, and unmolested. . . . We want permission to travel among the white settlements in the
east to learn the white man's method of planting corn, and also to seek
for some of our people whom we have lost. I want the chiefs and headmen of all nations and tribes to hear my talk and know that it is a good
one. [J. M. Stanley 1852:53-54]

Those words are not in the official transcript, and it is not clear whether they
represent a lacuna in the record, an unofficial statement, or the workings of
Stanley's imagination.

Houston had written a draft treaty that was read to the assembly, initiating an extended discussion of boundaries and the line. Following Mopechucope's advice from the year before, the treaty proposed a line from the Cross
Timbers to Comanche Peak and on to the San Saba River. However, Potsanaquahip did not like that line and wanted one farther south; "when the
buffalo come below there is nothing for us to eat above. . . . The buffalo
come down and it is them that I want" (Winfrey and Day 1959-66, 2:112).

But in arguing for a lower line the Comanches may have done themselves out of any line at all. In response to Potsanaquahip's objections,
Houston said "You are pleased with the Treaty and call it all good but that
part about the line; we will sign all but that part, which we will rub out and
go on as before." In September 1845 Supterintendent Thomas Western wrote,
"The Indians in Council last October (especially the Comanche) refused their
assent to a permanent divisory line, as proposed by the then president, General Houston. They were then satisfied that the line of Trading Houses should
be considered as the line" (Winfrey and Day 1959-66, 2:113). If the latter
discussion occurred during the council, it was not recorded in the minutes.

On October 9 the treaty was signed by Houston and by Potsanaquahip,
Mopechucope, and Chomopardua (*tsomo parua* 'bead bear'?) for the Comanches. It began with the usual statements of friendship, for example, "The
tomahawk shall be buried." Although no line was actually defined, the treaty
stated that the "Government of Texas [would] permit no bad men to cross the

line into the hunting grounds of the Indians," and if any were found by the
Indians, "they [would] bring him to one of the agents, but not do any harm to
his person or property." The Indians would make no treaty with any other
nations at war with Texas and would tell the agents if other Indians were
planning to make war on Texas. They would not steal horses or other property, but if any stealing were done they would punish the culprits and return
the property.[27]

Several articles dealt with trade: the Comanches would trade only with
Texas, and then only with licensed traders at established trading houses; if
trading houses were established "below the line," the Indians would be
permitted to go to them. No alcohol would be sold to the Indians. Powder,
shot, "and other arms" would be provided as well as blacksmiths, mechanics,
schoolmasters to "instruct them in a knowledge of the English language and
Christian Religion," and farmers to "teach them how to cultivate the soil and
raise corn." Two articles dealt with "conventions of war": no women and
children would be hurt, the white flag would be honored, and prisoners would
be exchanged. Finally, a general council would be held once a year at which
presents would be given to the chiefs; other presents could be given "as the
President from time to time [should] deem proper" (Winfrey and Day 1959–
66, 2:114–19). The treaty was ratified by the Texas Senate January 24, 1845,
becoming one of the few Texas Indian treaties ever to be so confirmed.

The meeting concluded with a short but interesting discussion of ethno-
political differences as viewed by the Hois and by the Texans. When Potsanaquahip said his people would not visit some of the trading houses because
they were so close to the Kiowas, Houston, surprised, replied, "We thought
you were all one people." Potsanaquahip then stated, "There are nine different tribes who have not yet made peace [with Comanches, i.e. Hois]: the
Kiowa, Lipan, Chian, Arapaho, Charatahar or Dog Eaters, Yamparika or Root
Diggers, Ceanaro, Shoshoni or Snake Indians, and the Pornemohaws" (Winfrey and Day 1959–66, 2:113). This is a confusing list and may represent a
garbled interpretation. However, it may also suggest some of the political
relations of the time. The term Pornemohaws is probably "Pawnee Maha"
and refers to the Skiris. The inclusion of the Yamparikas among the enemies
suggests that the Hois chiefs of Texas were speaking only for themselves.
Similarly, the inclusion of the Chians [Cheyennes?] and Arapahos as enemies
implies that the 1840 peace on the Arkansas River included only the Yamparikas. But if "Chian" is Cheyenne, the reason for the distinction between the
Cheyennes and the Ceanaros (*si?a naboo* 'painted feather'), one of the Comanche names for the Cheyennes, is unclear. Likewise, unless Charatahar
(*sari?i tuhka* 'dog eater') meant Plains Apaches, the reason for the separate
listing of Arapahos, also called Dog Eaters by Comanches, is unclear. Of the

Kiowas, Potsanaquahip noted, "They are more powerful than the Comanches and we fear them" (Winfrey and Day 1959-66, 2:113).

During that council John Mix Stanley painted portraits of seven of the Comanche participants. In a catalog published several years later (Stanley 1852), Stanley gave their titles as Potsanaquahip, Potsanasanaco and his wife, O-hah-ah-wah-kee, Nah-moo-su-kah, a Comanche Mother and Her Child, and a Group of Women Playing a Stick Game. Stanley gave the name Potsana-sanaco as "The Eater of the Black Buffalo Heart"; it is possibly *potsana* 'male buffalo', *sanaco* either 'gum' or 'sap', or 'flanks'; Stanley called him "One of the principal warriors of the Hoesh Band, or Honey-Eaters." However, since 'honey eater' is not a translation of Hoesh (Hois), and since the otherwise earliest use of the ethnonym Honey Eater (Penateka, *pihna-tuhka*) dates from 1848, it is probable that those captions were not written at the time of painting but after 1848. Stanley gave the name O-hah-ah-wah-kee as "The Yellow Paint Hunter" (*oha* 'yellow', *wehkinitu* 'to look around for'), and he called him the "Head Chief of the Ta-nah-wee Band of Comanches." Although Ohahahwahkee was indeed probably a Tenewa, he was later to describe himself as "not a great man" (Duval 1849). The meaning of the other name is unclear. Unfortunately, all of those paintings were destroyed in the fire at the Smithsonian, January 24, 1865.

Although Pahayuko had not signed the treaty, he later said he felt himself obligated by it. In January, while visiting Torreys' trading house to return two captives—a young boy taken the previous June from near Austin, and a runaway slave—he said, "When I was a young man, I was accustomed to go among the white people and trade, and I am anxious that time should return as we wish to be at peace with all and raise our children in peace." Continuing his peace theme, he said, "My war chief Tuna-woora-quashi—given as Bear with a Short Tail, that is *tuna* 'straight' *wura* 'bear' *kwasi* 'tail', 'bear with a straight tail,' possibly the Bear's Tail mentioned above—is brave but prefers peace to war and has come in to see that the peace is good. . . . Whenever any of my people come in you must give them presents" (Winfrey and Day 1959-66, 2:422). It is not known whether he received any presents at that time; it was later reported that he had left angry because there were none.

A week later Anson Jones, the new president of the Texas Republic, wrote to Pahayuko, saying, "No more war shall be between your people and mine." He proposed a council for the following fall at which Pierce M. Butler, former governor of South Carolina and at that time with the United States Indian Office, would be present and would "make good words of peace for his people" (Winfrey and Day 1959-66, 2:180). Santa Anna was also contacted, and he promised to go to San Antonio to enter into the treaty provisions (Winfrey and Day 1959-66, 2:268).

But in February a group of Delawares from the United States killed three Comanches on the San Marcos River. The Comanches swore revenge, and Pahayuko warned that no white man or Delaware would be safe in Comanche country. Texas Superintendent of Indian Affairs Thomas Western thought "the excitement [would] soon subside," but his agents were warned to be on guard (Winfrey and Day 1959-66, 2:216). Comanche Agent Benjamin Sloat told Pahayuko that the guilty parties had been "demanded of the United States to which they appertain" (Winfrey and Day 1959-66, 2:219).

By May the difficulties between the Comanches and the Delawares were settled, and a large Comanche war party, said to be 1,000 lodges, was camped on the Little River above Torreys' trading house making preparations to cross the Rio Grande into Mexico. Some time before, they had made an "unfortunate Expedition to Mexico and [were] returning there in force to take revenge." Western's comment—"the misfortune of Potsanaquahip by the treacherous Mexicans" (Winfrey and Day 1959-66, 2:238)—implies that Potsanaquahip had been the leader of a party that had met with disaster, but the details of that incident are not recorded.

Since the revenge expedition was going to pass by Austin and San Antonio, they wanted the Texans to know that they meant no harm and were at peace with Texas. Superintendent Western authorized Agent Sloat to give them a passport (Winfrey and Day 1959-66, 2:239) and requested the Travis County Rangers to furnish them with provisions "should they call at Austin on their way out" (Winfrey and Day 1959-66, 2:237). They would be allowed to pass "no nearer than five leagues" from San Antonio, but "so long as the chiefs did not permit their people to go into the settlements to scare the women and trouble our citizens, they would not be molested." When they returned "with a large drove of animals which they got from the Mexicans near Laredo on the Rio Grande," they passed right through the settlements and presented their passport along the way. Superintendent Western ordered Robert S. Neighbors, "Please order off the Comanche who have introduced themselves in to the settled parts of the country. . . . They must be given to understand that by the Treaty they have made with us, they are not permitted to come below the line of trading houses" (Winfrey and Day 1959-66, 2: 293).

At about the same time other Comanches were raiding the Texas settlements. In June two young men were killed below Austin, a ranch near Seguin was attacked and one man was killed, and horses were stolen from the new German colonies (Winfrey and Day 1959-66, 2:262, 279). Agent Sloat, two other Whites, and the Delaware Jim Shaw were sent to the Comanche villages to investigate and to persuade the chiefs to come to the annual council in

September. They were received "very friendly" at Mopechucope's camp on the San Saba River.

Sloat heard that there had been a recent disturbance in the camp. The leader of the party that had raided near Austin the previous June was trying to raise another party. When a chief named Cut Arm (otherwise unidentified) confronted him, telling him he must not go, the "outlaw shot him dead on the spot." In the ensuing fray, both the young war leader and his father were killed, and another was wounded (Winfrey and Day 1959-66, 2:284). Sloat commented that Cut Arm could not take action earlier "owing to his [the young warrior's] party being the strongest" (Winfrey and Day 1959-66, 2: 298).

Sloat and his party spent several days searching for a lost horse. When they decided it must have returned home, and they themselves might be thought to have been killed, Sloat sent Shaw back to the Torreys with a positive report. Several days later, when Sloat told Mopechucope that he was leaving for Pahayuko's village, the chief insisted he should wait until Shaw returned, and a guard was placed over their lodge "to prevent our escaping." Shaw finally returned with a load of trade goods. Considering Shaw's actions during Eldredge's mission to Pahayuko in 1843, it is possible that Shaw thought that was a good trading opportunity and had asked Mopechucope to keep Sloat there until he came back.

Later Potsanaquahip arrived, and the Delaware problem was discussed again. Since relatives of the three Comanches who were killed were now present, Sloat was told that if they were not given presents, they might kill the Whites. Using Shaw's goods, which would be replaced out of presents at the next council, those relatives were presented with cloth, tobacco, powder, and paint. Sloat wrote, "Now we thought our troubles was over," but the next day's council was confused. When Sloat tried to persuade the chiefs to come to the fall council, they refused, saying that it was all a trap; one of the Delaware interpreters had told them that "We was telling lies on purpose to get them down to the council . . . to kill them." Potsanaquahip then announced that he was going to war across the Rio Grande and that Captain Jack Hays of the Texas Rangers had not only told them to come to San Antonio but that he would go with them to Mexico. Potsanaquahip had all the warriors from his own and Pahayuko's local bands and was trying to get more from Mopechucope's (Winfrey and Day 1959-66, 2:325). Although Sloat protested that he should go on to Pahayuko's, he was forced to accompany them to San Antonio (Winfrey and Day 1959-66, 2:286), where the Comanches received two "beeves and other provisions" and then left for Mexico (Winfrey and Day 1959-66, 2:325).

The council at Tehuacana Creek that fall was something of an anti-
climax, although it had its excitement. When the Indians began to gather in
September, Mopechucope was the only prominent Comanche chief present;
Potsanaquahip was still in Mexico (Winfrey and Day 1959-66, 2:299) and
Pahayuko was nowhere to be found. Superintendent Western and several of
the other commissioners were also not present, so no business could be conducted. The Comanches were concerned about the rumors that they would be
killed at the council. The commissioners assured them that "they need not be
the least uneasy, for the white people would not harm them, and if they heard
any bad news, to come to the Commissioners, and all would be explained."
The next night, when several other Texans arrived, the Comanches again
became uneasy. Finally, when the commissioners learned that the presents to
be distributed to the Indians had not yet arrived, they "deemed it advisable to
hold no further councils until it was known that they [the presents] were
near" (Winfrey and Day 1959-66, 2:335).

When the council finally reconvened a week later, besides Mopechucope,
the Comanches present were "war chiefs" Saviah and Quaharapoah, "chief"
Sakoyahkah—given as Cry for Water, possibly *saa* 'broth', *yake* 'cry' —and
"captains" Akachuata—possibly *eka* 'red'—and Quahana—given as After a
Wife, possibly *kwʉhʉ* 'wife'. The name Saviah is given on one list as Little
Wolf and on another as Yellow Wolf; it is either *isapia* 'big wolf' or *isa
paʔatʉ* 'long wolf'. The name Yellow Wolf seems to have been fairly
popular: a chief named Yellow Wolf was allegedly killed at Walker's Creek
in 1844; early in 1846 "the Yellow Wolf . . . had killed the Mexican at San
Antonio" (Winfrey and Day 1959-66, 2:284), but any connections between
them are unknown. The other four names are previously unmentioned.

The first day was spent in speeches praising the peace of the previous
year. Saviah was the only Comanche to speak:

> I have come here because Mopechucope told me to come, for I would
> see that the white men were friends, and would treat me well, and I
> brought my warriors to be satisfied of the fact. I am glad that all I heard
> was true, that the white people were friendly, and that a treaty had been
> made. . . . I have come to listen and not to talk, for our chief does all of
> that . . . but it makes my heart glad to see all at peace with the white
> people and I hope it will last always. [Winfrey and Day 1959-66, 2:338]

If that is an accurate interpretation of Saviah's words, it provides an important perspective on the sets of reciprocal relationships that comprised Comanche politics. On the one hand, Saviah was in a subordinate position to Mopechucope—he was present "because Mopechucope told [him] to come";
indeed, he did not come to talk—"our chief does all of that." In turn, he was

in a dominant position to his warriors, whom he "brought to be satisfied" of the good will of the Whites. Unfortunately, further details of those relationships are unknown.

After rain forced a delay, General Edwin Morehouse complained that Wacos, Tawakonis, and Wichitas, who were not present at the council, were stealing horses. Mopechucope said, "I have frequently told them to stop, but they would not listen. But if any come near my villages I will make my warriors take any stolen property they may have and will bring it in to my white brothers" (Winfrey and Day 1959-66, 2:339). A day later the presents finally arrived, and the next three days were spent distributing them; after that the Indians left.

In their instructions, the commissioners were asked to talk to the Indians about the line because "it is rumored, they have changed their minds" (Winfrey and Day 1959-66, 2:354). However, there is no mention of any such discussion in the minutes of the council. Moreover, the commissioners later reported that the Comanches had given permission for Lipans and Tonkawas to live "within the limits" of the Comanches (Winfrey and Day 1959-66, 2:370). That matter is not mentioned in the minutes either.

In November Mopechucope and Santa Anna finally came to the council grounds, along with twelve other chiefs and forty warriors (Winfrey and Day 1959-66, 2:411). The chiefs' names were given as Ahkatsica, Wabeoukeac, Nouishawipe, Tosawecut, Cuardepoa, Pardewa-lecua, Chieseppiti, Paveceawoofpa, Parowrea, Wadacanapsa, Satar Pransewa, and Kanauma. Except for Cuardepoa, possibly the man identified above as Quaharapoah (*kwaharʉ* 'antelope', *puʔe* 'road', 'antelope road'), and Tosawecut (*tosa wi katʉ* 'he has a white [or silver] knife') none of the names are readily identifiable.

They were uneasy and came to the council armed with knives, guns, and bows (Winfrey and Day 1959-66, 2:414). However, after some serious talk by Mopechucope, in which he "counselled the young men to peace," he "asked the young men each and singly if they were for peace. Some of them replied that it was a matter of very little consequence whether they were or not as they should abide by the advice of the old men" (Winfrey and Day 1959-66, 2:415).

There was also some discussion about the Lipans. Mopechucope said:

[The great cause of difficulty] between his people and the white was the Lipan tribe of Indians which he said must be immediately removed from the white settlements to the Comanche range. He said this to our chief at the last treaty but it has not yet been done. . . . It was impossible for him to hinder his young men from going among the Lipan, and he insists upon their immediate removal. [Winfrey and Day 1959-66, 2:412]

That is, Mopechucope seemed to demand that the Lipans be forcibly moved into Comanchería so that they would be close to the Comanches; put another way, the young men were going to raid the Lipans anyway, and if the Lipans were not moved, the settlements would be in the line of fire. Those comments conflict with the report that Comanches might allow Lipans to live peacefully within their lines (Winfrey and Day 1959–66, 2:270).

At the conclusion of the meeting Santa Anna asked for a passport so he could go to war on the Mexicans, who had broken a treaty "that was made some years since." The reference to a treaty is not clear; it could refer to the formal treaties of the late 1820s or to the more informal "partial treaties" constantly negotiated between specific towns and specific Comanche local groups. Finally, presents were distributed and the Comanches left "well satisfied" (Winfrey and Day 1959–66, 2:415).

It was to be an anxious winter at Torreys' trading house. Pahayuko was said to be coming in to visit, but there were no presents for him, and "it [would] be highly important to furnish him with presents in proportion to those made to other tribes. . . . It will be recalled that this chief on his last visit left very much dissatisfied because no presents had been provided for him." The new agent, Paul Richardson, was authorized to purchase gifts from the Torreys in case Pahayuko should come in, but he stayed away for the season (Winfrey and Day 1959–66, 2:423).

Comanche Resource Domains, 1820–46

The twenty-five years 1820–46 brought major changes to the organization of Comanche resource domains. Hunting continued to be a major factor in the domestic econmy, although Berlandier's 1828 account of a "bear and bison hunt" is the only first-hand description of a Comanche hunt, but it gives only a few details about its organization and internal dynamics. The 1822 Mexico City treaty called for the establishment of a duty-free trade in the "products of the hunt," which, according to Berlandier, included bear grease, buffalo meat, buffalo hides, deer skins, and various furs. To Warren's trading post Comanches brought "furs of all kinds, dressed buffalo robes, dressed and raw deer skins, dried buffalo tongues, beeswax" (Clift 1924:139). Mexican General Manuel Mier y Terán reported that in less than a year various Indians, including Comanches, brought to Nacogdoches the skins of some 40,000 deers, 1,500 bears, 1,200 otters, and 600 beavers (Morton 1948:68).

The other major Comanche trade items—horses and captives—were the products of raids. As a means of replacing population after a military defeat or epidemic, the taking of captives was probably aboriginal (Magnaghi 1970), and captives continued to be a significant part of the Comanche domestic economy well into the nineteenth century. It is not clear, however, whether expeditions were made specifically with the intention of taking captives for population replacement or for sale to others, that is, whether the taking of captives was a conscious part of the political economy.

It was, however, a profitable business. In 1837 the Texas legislature appropriated $691 to reimburse Holland Coffee for Texans ransomed from the Indians (Rister 1955:163n). The identities of many of those captives are unknown; Coffee's traders had attempted to ransom Sarah Ann Horn and her friend Mrs. Harris, taken the year before, but the Comanches refused. Horn was ultimately ransomed by an American living in San Miguel who paid a horse, four bridles, two blankets, two mirrors, two knives, some tobacco, and powder and ball, "something less than eighty dollars" (Rister 1955:171).

Above all, the trading economy—both the inter-Indian trade, for which there are scanty records, and the Indian-European trade—was based on horses. As early as 1795 Anglo-American horse traders such as Philip Nolan were buying Comanche horses. In the 1830s the Bents offered to buy all the horses the Comanches could supply. However, because the Comanches obtained their horses by raiding rather than by natural increase, the Comanches were caught up in a larger web of connections. Many Spanish, Mexican, and Anglo-American communities were in the middle of the Comanches' supply network. When the settlements lost horses to raiders, Comanches or others, they turned to the Comanches for resupply from horses that were, in turn, stolen from farther south. There was thus a piratical transfer of horses from south to north. The Spanish and Mexican governments periodically issued orders prohibiting the purchase of branded horses from the Comanches, but the orders had little effect.

A major force impelling the trade was the demand for horses and mules by the developing Anglo-American South. That Anglo-Americans were ultimately responsible for sponsoring large-scale stock thefts was not lost on various Spanish and Mexican officials. Juan Antonio Padilla blamed "certain foreigners and perverse Spaniards" who had "introduced munitions and other things to exchange for animals" (Hatcher 1919:54–55). Stephen Austin noted that by trading guns for horses, traders north of the Arkansas River were in effect sending an army into Mexican territory (Barker 1926:54). In 1826 the Mexican secretary of state asked the American minister to Mexico to stop the "traders in blood who put instruments of death into the hands of those barbarians" (Weber 1982:95), but there is no record of any action by American officials.

During that period there is no evidence of the formal trade fairs such as had existed in New Mexico in the eighteenth century, but there was informal trade. Berlandier noted that "during periods of peace . . . Comanches came in to trade with the presidios" (1969:12). In New Mexico details of Comanchero-style trade are scarce. At least one reason for the lack of direct evidence of the trade was that by the 1830s both the Comanchero trade and the hunting of buffalo by ciboleros were again prohibited and not something to be reported (J. A. Chávez 1831). But traders continued to travel far out onto the Plains. In January 1832 a Texan force campaigning against the Comanches met Taoseños at the head of the Rio Florida; another group was found between Vibora and Albanas in southern Texas (Barragán 1833). And small-scale local trade continued. In the fall of 1831 eight horses, powder, guns, and clothing were exchanged at Cuesta in the Pecos valley (Ronquillo and Vigil 1831.) Indeed, the role of trade was so great that when plans were made for a counterstroke against Apaches and Comanches, a commission of Taoseños wrote to the governor that "they had no intention of making war on the Comanches, who had guarded . . . the most faithful friendship . . . and true peace in this territory" (Ortiz, Ulibarri, Garcia 1835).

Other traders came from the northeast. William Becknell, who opened the Santa Fe trade, had originally intended to trade with the Comanches. Both Thomas James and the Glenn-Fowler parties did extensive trading with Comanches as well as with the New Mexicans. After the establishment of the Santa Fe Trail, however, there was little direct positive contact between the freighters and the Indians along the route. Although much of the folklore of the Santa Fe Trail revolves around the peoples at the western end, the Comanches, Kiowas, Cheyennes, and Arapahos, the initial hostilities came on the eastern end, from the Kansas and Osages, whose territories had been compressed by the increasing local Anglo-American populations. That hostility, combined with the Anglo-American tendency to see all Indians as alike, made the freighters wary of any contact along the trail. Conversely, the unwillingness of the freighters to engage in the civilities of visitors, combined with the perceived decline in the buffalo herds—blamed on the freighters but also due, at least in part, to changes in the broader climatic cycle known as the Little Ice Age—caused the western peoples to become increasing hostile toward Anglo-Americans.

There were other northerners in Comanchería as well. Ruíz commented, as quoted by Berlandier (1969:120), that the "Aguayes or Pananes," that is, Pawnees, traveled as far south as the Brazos River to trade English muskets for Comanche horses and mules (Ruíz 1828:14, 17), Berlandier adding that the Pawnees "brought their guns in from Canada" (1969:120). Sam Houston noted that besides the traders at Fort Towson in Indian Territory, the "influence of the Northwest Fur Company" extended as far as the Brazos (A. W. Williams and Barker 1938–43, 1:268–71). Details of that alleged Canadian connection are unclear, but it is possible that the American fur traders, operating out of Saint Louis, were buying Comanche horses through Pawnee middlemen and that their identity became garbled by the time word got back to Texas.

During his stay with the Comanches in 1836, Noah Smithwick accompanied several trading trips to the new town of Bastrop (Smithwick 1899: 136). Conversely, Texas traders visited Comanchería, although few names are known. As early as 1825 several men from Austin's colony were visiting the Comanches (McLean 1974–93, 1:528). During the time of the Texas Republic, other Texans visited Comanche camps in seasons of peace. Those traders included both Euroamericans and other Indians. In the spring of 1838 several parties visited Comanche camps to trade; that same month there were Shawnee traders among the Comanches (Winfrey and Day 1959–66, 1:42). In 1843 J. C. Eldredge's Delaware guide, Jim Shaw, used that diplomatic mission as an opportunity to trade with the Comanches and Wichitas but found that all their hides had already been traded to the Cheyennes. In July 1844 a trader named Cavanaugh—no apparent relation to the present author— traveled to the Comanche camps with Shaw (Winfrey and Day 1959–66, 2: 84).

The Camp Holmes treaty marked a formalization in trade relations between the Comanches and the tribes of eastern Oklahoma. Those included the Osages, who, although often straining the relationship, remained trading partners. In 1836, when Esacony threatened to destroy Camp Holmes, he also warned the Osages to stay away (Folsom 1836), although that was probably not to keep them out of Comanchería, but to keep them out of possible harm. In December 1837 a party of Cherokees piloted by Kitsais traveled to the Brazos River to trade powder and lead for mules and horses (Foreman 1933:151). By 1840 several Chickasaws had substantial trade with Comanches (Foreman 1933:95, 172). In 1841 a party of Cherokees was rumored to be preparing to trade ammunition to the "hostile tribes on the Brazos" (Winfrey and Day 1959–66, 1:128). In 1843 "the whole body of the Comanche" was reported to be on the Big Salt River "in expectation of a visit from the Osage with whom they were to make peace and trade" (Winfrey and Day 1959–66, 1:259). That year fifteen Omahas traded in Comanchería so successfully that they had traded even their own guns and ammunition; vulnerable on their return, they were attacked and robbed (Foreman 1933:215). By 1845 Delawares and Shawnees were reported to be carrying on a regular trade with the Comanches (W. Armstrong 1845:508). That same year some Osages, while on their fall hunt, fell in with a party of Camanches, who appeared very friendly and invited them to eat with them and with whom a considerable trade took place. The Osages say they saw a great many white prisoners among them (Camanches) of both sexes, old and young; that they could have bought numbers of them if they had the means to pay for them. The Camanches offered to exchange them for horses but they had none to give. [Cruttenden 1845:545]

In the Comanchero mode of trade, chiefs exercised two types of political control. On the one hand, they controlled the access of their people to the traders; on the other, they protected the traders from their people. Only after the chief approved of the traders did he allow the others to come to trade. Years later Comanchero Juan José Montoya of Cochiti told Adolf Bandelier, "The Comanche fix a certain day and place, at which the Pueblos appear, and the trading is preceded by a council and presents. The rules of trading are fixed then" (Lange and Riley 1966:163). Although published some forty years after the start of that period, M. C. Fisher's report is probably characteristic of the early trade as well:

When a trader arrives at a village where he is known, he proceeds at once to the lodge of the head chief, where he receives him as his guest, and commands his squaws to unpack his ponies, and convey all his goods, blankets, and cooking kit to the lodge set apart for his reception. The chief, after giving him a feast and a smoke, begs from him anything that he may fancy and then proceeds to harangue the village in words saying . . . the trader had arrived in their village for the purpose of trading with them. [Fisher 1869:284]

According to Thomas James, "We arrived in the evening and were met by the head chief about two miles from the town. He appeared friendly and took the goods and deposited them in his lodge" (1846:131-2).

[Later that day] the old Chief in whose lodge I staid, entered my tent with five old Indians, and all with a grave and solemn air sat themselves down in silence. . . . as I sat on a tobacco keg, I broke off twelve plugs and took out of a box six wampums, variously colored, and greatly prized by the Indians. . . . The Chief hesitated long, but at last slowly raised his hand, took my presents and smoked the pipe. . . . The chief then went out into the village and proclaimed in a loud voice that all should prepare to go next morning, over to the Canadian, to trade with the Tabbahoes [Europeans]. . . . The proclamation was continued by the herald on horseback till late at night "Get up your horses and make ready to go over to the white man's and trade with the Tabbahoes. They have come a great way and brought us many good things—the Tabbahoes are good. [James 1846:134-35]

According to Josiah Gregg, prices were fixed by the chiefs at the beginning of the trading session: "In Comanche trade the main trouble consists of fixing the price of the first animal. This being settled by the chiefs, it often happens that mule after mule is led up and the price received without further cavil" (Gregg 1844, 2:45). James noted that sometimes that led to problems:

They claimed twelve articles for a horse. I made four yards of British strouding at $5.50 per yard and two yards of calico at 62 1/2 cents per yards and a knife, flints, tobacco, looking glass and other small articles made up the compliment. They brought to me some horses for which I refused the stipulated price. They then produced others which were really fine animals, worth at least $100 each in St. Louis. I bought seventeen of these, but would not take any more at the same price, the rest being inferior. The refusal enraged the chief, who said I must buy them, and on my persisting in my course, drove away the Indians from around me, and left me alone . . . No Indian came near me for the rest of the day. [1846: 131-32]

Conversely, inasmuch as each village was under a specific chief, as were the major trading stations, the ability of the chiefs to ensure a degree of order and security at those trading sites greatly increased the willingness of traders to venture across the Plains to their sites. There are several specific references to chiefs honoring the peace of the market place, sometimes extending beyond the actual context of trade. According to Fisher, "After the trade, (or as we would call it, the fair) is over, the chief delivers up everything he had received and guarded over to the trader, and often send out a few young men with him to help him on his road with his accumulated herd of animals" (1869:284). Adoph Bandelier reported that once Juan José Montoya's father, of Cochiti Pueblo,

was leading a party to the Comanche when he was stopped by the Kiowa on the way with the request to trade with them. Although he had been cited by the Comanche for a certain day and to a certain date, he still complied with the request. After trading, the Kiowa surrounded the camp at night, and under pretext that the Queres [Keres, i.e., Cochiti] had introduced Texans who had killed Kiowas, demanded return of the goods in expiation for the murder. Then the Queres refused and while they were disputing, even ready to come to blows, the Comanche dashed into the camp. The chief ascertaining the cause of the trouble, had the Kiowas whipped out and thus delivered the Pueblos. [Lange and Riley 1966:163]

In Texas, the presidios and settlements continued to be points of contact and trade. According to Berlandier, when a trading party approached a settlement they would stop some distance away, and send in a courier announcing their visit; there were also formal ceremonies at their arrival, with " "the natives, holding themselves very proudly, riding in between the ranks of cavalry drawn up with sabres flashing in salute" (1969:31). That description paralleled the practice of a century before when a trading party would send in a messanger for pre-trade talks and price fixing.

The major change in Comanche trade patterns was the establishment of more or less permanent European trading posts in and near Comanchería, posts controlled by Europeans rather than by Comanches. The earliest post seems to have been Thomas James's 1823 fort on the North Canadian River, from which he traded for about a year (James 1846:123ff.). The various Bent's Forts—the Stockade, built about 1825, and the Old Fort, built about 1832—monopolized the upper Arkansas trade. In the 1830s the Bents sent several trading expeditions into Comanchería, and in 1842, after the Cheyenne-Arapaho peace, they built the so-called wood post on the South Canadian River in the Texas Panhandle. In 1834 Holland Coffee established a post near the old Taovaya village on the Red River (Stewart 1835; Foreman 1926:157); that post flourished until about 1840. In 1835 Auguste Chouteau founded a post at Camp Holmes on the South Canadian and in 1837 built another on Cache Creek near modern Fort Sill (Mooney 1898:172). Another Cache Creek post was established about 1840 by Abel Warren at the confluence with the Red River (Clift 1924). It flourished until about 1846.

Mooney placed Chouteau's Cache Creek post "on the west bank of Cache Creek, about three miles below the present Fort Sill" (1898:172), and included a brief discussion of political geography: "Chouteau's fort on the Canadian was considered to be in Comanche territory. Shortly after the treaty with the Kiowa in 1837, he established what they [the Kiowas] regard as the first trading post in their own country" (1898:172). That is, of course, from the Kiowa perspective, and the basis of the attribution of Camp Holmes to the Comanches and the Cache Creek area to the Kiowas would have been subject to Comanche dispute.

The Texas Republic attempted to license permanent post traders. Under article 3 of the unratified treaty of May 28, 1838, Texas traders would have monopolies on the Comanche trade. In the early 1840s Thomas, John and David Torrey established a series of trading houses. The first was at New Braunfels. The second was on Tehuacana Creek, 8 miles below Waco; it was authorized as an Indian trading house in January 1843. Under the 1844 Treaty of Tehuacana Creek, which was signed four miles from the trading house, the Comanches agreed "not to trade with any people other than the people of

Texas," and then only with government licensed traders at established trading posts. Ultimately, the line of posts became the primary dividing line between Texas and Comanchería. Comanches also visited posts outside their normal range. By 1839 a "well-used trail" reached Edwards' trading settlement on the Little River in the Cherokee country of eastern Indian Territory. Part of Edwards' success was due to his enterprising son-in-law, Jesse Chisholm, who was half Cherokee.

There were large amounts of goods available at the posts; table 5.2 shows the kinds of goods sent to the Torreys' trading house between February 1844 and May 1845. Warren's Cache Creek trading post in the mid-1840s stocked

> red and blue blankets, strips of blue cloth, bright colored gingham handkerchiefs, hoop iron (for arrow and lance heads), glass beads, heavy brass wire, which they twisted around the left wrist to protect it from the recoil of the bow-string, vermillion, red and yellow ochre for face paint, bright hued calico and wampum beads, which they wore around their necks in great quantities. These beads were from two to four inches long, pure white, and resembled clay pipe stems in size. They were highly esteemed and served the part of currency in their dealings. They wanted guns but the government forbade the sale of firearms at the time to the wild Indians. [Clift 1924:139]

The trading posts soon became major points of interaction with the Comanches. The northern Comanches visited by the Cherokee Chief Bowles in 1837 included "sixteen villages known as those who trade with Coffee" (*Houston Telegraph and Texas Register*, June 12, 1837). That interaction at the posts was not only economic, but also diplomatic. Holland Coffee assisted in gathering the Comanches for the 1835 Camp Holmes Treaty; in the 1840s the Torreys' trading house and adjacent council grounds on Tehuacano Creek were the sites of numerous councils and treaties, not only with Comanches, but also with the other tribes on the Texas frontier.

Control of trade at the posts was different from that in the camps. W. J. Weaver, remembering trade at Warren's post on Cache Creek in the mid-1840s, described the trading procedures:

> the gates were closed and secured, and presently they came in crowds to the fort to trade with bundles on their back. After much wrangling with our interpreter, they were admitted, three or four at a time, after leaving their belt knives and hatchets outside. The chief of the band was there. He said nothing but looked at the trader. The trader looked at him a moment, then took down a bridle richly ornamented with red woolen

Table 5.2

Goods Sent to the Torrey Brothers' Trading House, 1844–45

brown domestic	binding	powder
brown drilling	ribbons	lead
bleached shirtings	sundry ornaments	rice
ticking	Indian bells	soap
blue drilling	spool thread	beads
calico	buttons	brass wire
cottonades	pants stuff	percussion caps
brass kettles	broad cloth	brass nails
vermillion	strouding	combs
drugs and medicines	blankets	awls
hair pipes	files	hats and bonnets
shawls	pocket knives	crockery ware
sugar	butcher knives	boots and shoes
coffee	pipes	assorted axes
tobacco	shaving boxes	jews harps
flour	coffee mills	gun tubes
salt	tin ware	needles
fishhooks	nails	steels
hoes	skillets and pans	flints
pins	looking glasses	

Gross amount sent: $14,300.13

SOURCE: Winfrey and Day 1959–66, 2:242

> fringe and tin stars, and gave it to him with a plug of tobacco. The chief
> grunted, nodded, lit his pipe, and the trading went on and lasted for
> several days. [Clift 1924:139]

Here, although the trader attempted to control the context of the trade, it did not start until the chief approved.

After the 1820 revolution, Mexico attempted to maintain the Spaniards' Comanche policies; unfortunately, few documentary records survive from that period. Although there are reports of diplomatic efforts, visits, and political gifts, there are few financial records that would allow an adequate quantitative analysis of Mexican-Comanche political-economic relations, and such records as exist are difficult to reconcile with each other.

One thing is certain: in the early 1820s Comanche-Mexican relations were often hampered by a lack of cash. In the year 1820–21 the New Mexico

Indian Fund had accrued a debt of 2,066 pesos (Griego 1822), and public subscriptions were held to raise money for Comanche visitors (Melgares 1821). In 1822 expenditures of 3,138 pesos for gifts and food for the Indians who visited Santa Fe, plus the 270 pesos for the interpreters, increased the debt to 5,475 pesos. The 891 pesos spent in 1823 on gifts and food, plus another 270 pesos for the interpreters, brought the total Indian Fund debt to 6,639 pesos (Cavallero 1823; Kavanagh 1986:320). It is not clear whether that debt was repaid. In August 1825 Chimal Colorado visited Santa Fe and received some 1,021 pesos worth of gifts (table 5.3).

But a month later there was again a lack of funds for gifts, and the citizens of San Miguel were urged to contribute "for the important service of the nation" (Narbona 1825). That fall a visiting party received 160 pesos worth of gifts. In mid-December two cows and 16 pesos worth of goods were given to six visitors (Vigil 1825). In 1826 one group of visitors received gifts worth only 32 pesos, and five groups between April and August received gifts worth a total of only 45 pesos (Hinojas 1826b; Narbona 1827). Later that month Cordero, Estrellas, and Ysacoruco were regaled with 498 pesos worth of goods (table 5.4). Cordero and Paruaquita were recognized as "Generals" and given medals "with the Arms of the Republic on the obverse and an emblem representing peace on the reverse" and canes as insignia of rank.

The 1826 treaty promised the reestablishment of the annual gifts. In the summer of 1827 Captain Juan José Arocha bought about 2,500 pesos worth of goods in Chihuahua for gifts for the allied nations (table 5.5), although it is not clear how he paid for them. However, few Comanches visited Santa Fe that year. In early 1828 twenty-four animals had been killed for some two hundred Comanches west of the Rio Grande in New Mexico, but by the summer there was again a lack of goods for regaling the Comanches (Arocha 1828a, b). Only 38 pesos worth of goods were given to Samparillena in 1830 (Anonymous 1830), and in 1832 there were only 24 pesos worth of gifts for the Indian allies (Hinojas 1826a). In 1840 the Fondo de Aliadas contained only 109 pesos, of which the largest share (78.4) was spent on food and gifts for an otherwise unidentified leader called Capitancillo Arocha, eight warriors, and four women (A. Sena 1840).

A similar situation existed in Mexican Texas. In 1822 the imperial government promised 2,000 pesos for Texas Indians. However, that money did not arrive until 1825. Whereas some Comanches were regaled with prestige gifts on their visits below the Rio Grande—for instance, at Monclova in 1825 Hoyoso was given a Mexican tricolor flag, a sombrero, and other gifts (Elozúa 1825)—for the next decade there are few records of gifts in Texas, and complaints were common (e.g., Ugartechea 1835a). In May 1835 General

Table 5.3

Gifts for Chimal Colorado and Other Comanches, August 1, 1825

48 varas blue cloth	283[a]
49 varas red cloth	343
55 pesos for Chimal Colorado	55
115 small knives	75
50 white linen shirts	15
9 packets vermillion	54
25 pesos for food	25
1 gross mirrors	72
3 bushels flour	9
1 gross painted mirrors	90
6 gross yellow gilded metal buttons	36

[a] Value in *pesos*.

SOURCE: Vigil 1825

Table 5.4

"Gifts for the Comanche Captains, Cordero, Ysacoruco, Estrellas, and the Warriors Who Accompanied Them," April 1827

29 1/2 varas blue cloth (for capes, jackets, and breeches)	153.0[a]
30 mirrors	18.6
26 shirts	78.0
134 knives	21.3
16 3/4 varas scarlet cloth	117.2
16 ounces vermillon	8.1
15 1/2 doz buttons	7.6
1 hat	8.0
7 1/2 vara linen	9.3.6
6 common blankets	60.0
6 1/2 varas wide manta	3.2
4 varas *coquillo*	2.4
Meat, flour, corn	48.3
3 kilos thread	3.0
9 hand tobaco	6.4
2 bushels of bread (for the 2 chiefs going to Chihuahua)	7.0
1 vara cotton cloth	.4
Total	498.6.6

[a] Value in *pesos*, *reales*, and *granos*.

SOURCE: Narbona 1827

Table 5.5
"List of Goods Bought by Capt. Juan José Arocha Destined to Regale the Allied Nations of the Territory of New Mexico," June 11, 1827

6 bales paño Gueretaro	882.0	2 bales each with 70 sombreros	61.2
6 3/4 doz mirrors	50.0	22 hanks large polished beads	50.0
22 3/12 gross scissors	50.0	11 gross anillos de piedra	50.0
6 gross yellow metal buttons	[ ]	3 gross white metal buttons	19.4
1 gross mirrors	9.0	40 bridles	90.0
6 4/12 gross rings	28.4	33 1/2 doz belduques	100.0
29 packets vermillon	100.0	1 piece Castillan Bayeta	110.0
27 varas sacrlet casimira	128.2	1000 varas English manta	914.0
40 varas scarlet bayeta	90.0	12 1/2 varas bayeta	13.6
12 varas cloth	9.0	2 calzones	7.0
36 hatchets	108.0		
		Total	2,473.7[a]

[a] The total is as given by Arocha; values are in *pesos* and *reales*.

SOURCE: Arocha 1827a

Cos issued instructions for reestablishing Comanche gifts because "their quietude depends for a major part" upon them (Cos 1835), but action was cut off by the Anglo-Texan Revolution.

By 1820 there had been no official contact with Anglo-Americans for three years and thus no political or prestige gifts. Major Stephen Long had apparently promised the Indians he met at the head of the Arkansas River that presents would be sent; thus, when the Glenn-Fowler party spent the next winter in that region, they were thought to be the promised representatives and were accused of stealing the presents. In 1826 the mere rumor that a Comanche chief wanted to talk had the agent at the Red River Agency at Caddo Prairie asking Washington for "instruction from the government on how I am to receive him" (Carter 1934-62, 20:484). Beyond that, there was apparently no official contact for the rest of the decade.

Although they provided no gifts, the Americans were easily upset when they perceived the Spaniards tampering with the Indians in American territory. In December 1824 Superintendent Benjamin O'Fallon of the Saint Louis Superintendency wrote to the Mexican governor of New Mexico, complaining:

> I understand you have inadvertently placed on the breast of a young Pawnee who recently visited your country a Spanish Medal. From my good feelings towards you, I am in hopes that you will act in relation to the Pawnee and other Indians from our territory with more discretion in

Table 5.6

Goods Bought for the Texas Comanches, March 4, 1838

Goods bought from W. M. Cook

6 lbs paint	6.00	5 string beads	6.25
4 pr ear drops	3.00	5 string beads	3.75
5 budalim [?]	3.75	2 string beads	3.00
88 pr ear drops	10.00	5 bead bags	25.00
2 ditto	8.00	3 bead pums [?]	3.00

Total $71.75

Goods bought from W. N. Bronaugh

12 Pr Blankets	96.00
12 Doz Bells	9.00
9 Lbs Beads	22.50

Total $127.00

Total Purchase $198.75

SOURCE: Winfrey and Day 1959-66, 1:36

Table 5.7

Gifts for the Comanches, 1843

Bought from Torrey & Bros., May 5, 1843

3 pieces end prints, 84 yds	21.00	1 piece endprints, 28 yds	5.60
1 doz fringed shawls	7.50	1 1/4 doz fringe shawls	10.63
1 White and yellow	7.50	1 piece broad cloth	46.68
1 piece bed ticking, 45 3/4yds	11.43	3 piece Twilled, 92 1/2	15.68
1,000 percussion caps	1.25	7 lbs brass wire	4.20
1/2 box fancy handkerchiefs	2.25	1 piece brown bagging	7.50
25 lbs powder (Duponts)	12.50	50 lbs lead	5.00
3 box butcher knives	12.00	4,000 brass nails	6.00
2 doz combs	4.00		

Total $90.00

Bought from John Conner for presents to Comanche Indians, Aug. 12, 1843

12 1/2 lbs tobacco	12.50	3 1/2 box Knives	21.75
2 doz glasses	6.00	2 hatchets	3.00
93 3/4 yds strouding	11.25		

Total $54.59

Total Purchase $144.59

SOURCE: Winfrey and Day 1959-66, 1:179, 230

the future. It would be considered unfriendly and improper . . . to give or sell to them any uniform clothing other than that of the United States, or medals, flag, arm bands or other ornaments or dress bearing the figures, devices or emblems of any other nation. [O'Fallon 1824]

Similar statements referred to the Comanches. In 1842 Charles Bent complained that "many of the Chiefs had sent to them by the [Mexican] authorities collars and staffs," constituting an illegal tampering with the loyalties of "American" Indians (Lavender 1954:214). There is, however, no confirmation of such gifts from the New Mexican government to Comanches or other Plains Indians.

In the early 1830s, because of both the increased traffic on the Santa Fe Trail and the implications of the impending removal of the eastern Indians, the Anglo-American government attempted to draw Comanches into treaty relations with the United States. That included the use of presents. Sam Houston sent a Jackson medal to the "principal chief." At the 1834 Fort Gibson meeting with the eastern tribes, white beads and tobacco were sent to the chiefs. A year later at the Camp Holmes treaty conference, about ten thousand dollars in gifts were distributed; Tabequena—although he was apparently not present—later complained that they did not include prestige gifts of medals or flags. In 1839 Comanches arriving at Fort Gibson hoping to go to Washington were given some six hundred dollars in gifts.

In its early years the Texas Republic provided political gifts. The delegates to the 1838 San Antonio treaty council received $198.75 worth of presents, mostly blankets (table 5.6). But with the collapse of relations in 1839 there were no gifts for five years. In 1843 J. C. Eldredge took only $144 in gifts to Pahayuko's village (table 5.7). While Eldredge was there, Pahayuko asked for a silver medal in the shape of a double cross, a spear, a uniform, and a sword; indeed, he insisted on having Eldredge's sword. The 1844 Texas treaty called for an annual general council with presents for the chiefs, "as the President from time to time may deem proper." Thus, after 1845 the Torreys' trading house on Tehuacana Creek was stocked with a great variety of manufactured goods, and political gifts again flowed into Texan Comanchería.

Changes in Comanche Divisional Organization, 1820–46

Unraveling the changes in Comanche political organization during the period 1820–46 is difficult. Although men such as José Francisco Ruíz, David Burnet, and others, had first-hand experience with Comanches, general knowledge of the Comanches continued to be limited, and few observers had access to information from the sweep of Comanchería. Many continued to view the Comanches as comprising two groups, for example, Yamparikas and Yucanticas (Padilla); Yamparikas and Comanches (Ruíz in 1828); Northern and Southern Comanches (Pike); "both tribes of the Comanche" (Houston); "Comanches of the Woods" and "Comanches of the Prairie" (Bonneville, LeGrand); Comanches "on this side" and on "the other side" of the Red River (Wheelock). A few observers noted internal organization. Thus, the 1826 New Mexico treaty included the Kotsotekas, the Yamparikas, the Tanemas, and the Jupes; Houston once divided them into four bands, Kimanchies, Sotoes, Amparacs, and Jatans, although two of those (Sotoe and Jatan) are probably ethnonymic synonyms; Sanchez noted the Comanches, Yamparicas, and Tanemues. Both Ruíz and Cameron generally grouped them as oriental and occidental, but they also noted internal divisions: Ruíz included the Juez, the Tanemas, the Yamparikas, and the Kotsotekas; Cameron mentioned the Juez, the Tanimas, the Tapisus, the Yamparikas, and the Kotsotekas.

In New Mexico, and along the Arkansas River, the Kotsotekas and the Yamparikas maintained their organizations through a succession of successful leaders, although details of their histories are unclear. In 1821 Chimal Colorado was given a silver medal and acted as the Kotsoteka principal chief for several years. By 1826 Cordero again held the principal leadership role after being absent from the records for most of the decade.

The succession in 1829 by Toro Echicero was marked by an apparent rivalry with Panchoconuque, although details are unknown. For the Yamparikas, Paruaquita retained his position, held since at least 1810. In 1826 he and Cordero signed the 1826 New Mexico treaty for themselves and the Tenewas (Tanemas), the Jupes, and the Kiowas, although their authority to speak for the latter is unlikely. By 1830 Paruaquita seems to have been replaced by Namayajipe. For the rest of that decade, although Comanches are mentioned, no divisional ethnonyms are given; the political history of the Comanches Llaneros and the Comanches Pelones, who appeared in 1844 and 1845, is unknown.

Comanche political organization in Mexican Texas barely recovered after the debacle of the period 1800–1810, and well into the period of the Texas Republic, no Texas Comanche leader held sufficient authority to catch the notice of Euroamerican observers, Mexican or Anglo-Texan. It was not until the mid-1840s, in a context of renewed political relations between Comanches and Euroamericans, that Mopechucope and Potsanaquahip emerged as principal leaders.

The Tenewas alternated their focus back and forth between Texas to the south and the United States to the east, an alternation that was probably linked to political relations with those Euroamerican groups and with the Texas Comanches, as well as with other Indian groups. Relations between the Hois and the Tenewas were often close, with personnel moving back and forth between them. Indeed, the most prominent Comanche chief in Mexican Texas was Paruakevitsi, a Tenewa, to whom the local Texas Comanches deferred. But in the aftermath of Paruakevitsi's death in 1832 and the collapse of Mexican Texas from 1834 to 1836, the Tenewas shifted their focus to the east.

The contrasting political stances taken by Esacony and Tabequena vis-à-vis the Anglo-Americans to the east represent alternative strategies. Although the basis of Esacony's enmity is unclear—the presence of the removed eastern Indians was certainly involved—Tabequena was more explicitly concerned with countering the commercial competition from the Osages. In the 1840s Tenewa focus again shifted to the south; Pahayuko was probably Tenewa, frequenting the Salt Plains of the Arkansas River, but his stature was such that in later years (see chapter 6) he was often called the principal chief of the southern Comanches, and sometimes explicitly of the Hois. That may also have led to a degree of rivalry with Mopechucope, who once noted, "I am looked up to by all my tribe for council, even Pahayuco himself looks to me for council" (Winfrey and Day 1959-66, 2:6). The comment made several years later by Texas agent John Rollins probably best summarizes Pahayuko's position: he "occupie[d] a kind of middle ground being sometimes in the north and sometimes in the south" (Rollins 1850a).

6

Comanchería at Midcentury,

1846–60

Texas, 1846–48

The United States annexed Texas on January 1, 1846. That action was not unexpected, and preparations for informing the Texas Indians, particularly the Comanches, of the transfer of authority had been under way since the previous fall; in September 1845 President James K. Polk noted in his diary, "This was deemed important at this time, especially if Mexico should declare war against the U.S. or invade Texas" (Polk 1910, 1:26). There were other reasons as well, including the desire to recover Anglo-American captives, "variously represented to be in number from 15 to 100 and upwards, women and children" (Foreman 1948:315). That upper number may well be an exaggeration, but the possibility of any recovery was sufficient to motivate action. Thus, in September 1845 Cherokee agent, and former South Carolina governor, Pierce M. Butler, and M. G. Lewis of Tennessee were appointed as joint commissioners to visit the Comanches and to "make them some small presents, and if possible secure their friendship" (Polk 1910, 1: 26).

In December Butler and Lewis, and a party of upwards of fifty persons, including several representatives of the relocated eastern Indians, set out from Indian Territory to renew the Camp Holmes Treaty with the Texas Indians. The party spent the next six weeks searching alternatively for the Comanches and for Comanche Peak, where they hoped to meet the Indians; when they finally found the latter in early March, they were disappointed at its size, a mere "brushy hill" (Foreman 1948:322).

Near that brushy hill the commissioners held a brief preliminary meeting with Potsanaquahip, Mopechucope, seventeen captains, and thirty-three warriors (P. M. Butler 1846). At that council "the Comanche formed themselves into a large circle in the open prairie . . . [Potsanaquahip] at its head, and next [Mopechucope], and filled out with the captains and warriors" (Foreman 1948:323). After a series of speeches by the commissioners and the Cherokee delegates, the Comanches asked for an adjournment in order to bring their people together.

Butler and Lewis reported that the Indians wanted the postponement because,

> they say, treaties have heretofore been entered into and promises made to the chiefs in council and passed by them to their people which have not been fulfilled, and the consequence has been [that] their veracity has been brought into question and their influence to some extent curtailed. They wish therefore that their people in masses should attend and hear for themselves what the Great Father the president has to say to them. [Lewis and P. M. Butler 1846]

If that is a valid representation of the views of the Comanche chiefs, it provides a unique commentary on their perception of their political situation, its causes, and their solutions to it. That is, on the basis of promises made by earlier treaty commissioners—although it is not clear whether they referred to Anglo-Texans (as recently as Sam Houston's treaty of 1844, or as far back as the various treaties and truces of 1838), Mexican-Texans (as far back as 1828), or even more ancient—they had attempted to steer their people in particular directions; the failure of those earlier treaty commissions to keep their promises had brought the chiefs into disrepute. The chief's solution was to bring all their people to the council, as much to shame the commissioners into making promises in front of all the people as to allow all the people to hear what was said. It remains unknown whether that also meant that under normal circumstances the chiefs would have preferred to negotiate alone.

Another comment on the slow start of the meetings came from Sam Houston, who, several years later, charged that during his administration as president of the Texas Republic, relations between Texans and Indians had improved to such a point that by 1846 the Indians had refused to meet with the Federal commissioners until they had the "sanction of the Government of Texas." Moreover, he claimed, it was not until Robert S. Neighbors was sent among them "with good talks" and carrying the "symbols of confidence" that they came in to the council grounds (Williams and Barker 1938–43, 6:120,

155). Historian Kenneth F. Neighbours (1975:29) described those symbols as "the ring and casket" but gave no further details. The ritual use of symbolic objects was frequent in United States–Indian diplomacy, especially by such sympathetic individuals as Sam Houston, and indeed, in 1843 the Republic of Texas bought a "large council pipe for Indian purposes" (Winfrey and Day 1959–66, 1:210), and there is one pictured in Neighbours (1975:55), but there is no documentary evidence for the use of such a pipe with Comanches.

It was not until early May the Butler and Lewis finally met with the Texas Indians at the council grove on Tehuacana Creek. At about the same time, a few hundred miles south, General Zachary Taylor's army on the Rio Grande was thought to be nearly surrounded by the Mexican army. Since the fear of Mexican-Indian alliances was still prevalent, the commissioners, believing the Indians aware of those circumstances, "had to make many promises and make many profuse presents and resort to unusual expenditures of money to secure both themselves and to divert and detain the Indians" (P. M. Butler and Lewis 1846:5).

The Comanches present included Pahayuko, Mopechucope, Santa Anna, Potsanaquahip, and Saviah. There is some confusion about the relative statuses of the Comanches present. Mopechucope was usually called the "principal chief" of the Texas Comanches, but in his diary, Elijah Hicks, the Cherokee delegate, recorded that "Buffalow Hump [Potsanaquahip] the Principal chief is here" (Foreman 1935:83); then, in an article for the Cherokee Advocate published two months later, Hicks said that Potsanaquahip "exercised the powers of principal chief" while Mopechucope was his "second chief" (Foreman 1948:323). Meanwhile, the council minutes called Saviah the war chief, a title often applied to Potsanaquahip.

After some discussion, unfortunately unrecorded, a treaty was concluded and signed on May 15, 1846. In article 1 the Indians "acknowledge[d] themselves to be under the protection of the United States . . . and no other sovereignty." Article 2 stipulated that the United States had exclusive right to regulate trade. Article 3 reserved to the United States any mines that might be found in the Indian territory; all miners would be licensed by the president.[1] Article 4 required all parties to deliver up prisoners, but should Indians refuse to give up their captives, force could be used to take them. Article 5 noted that the tribes would be allowed to send representatives to Washington whenever they thought their interests required it. Article 6 stated that the Indians would inform the agent if they heard of any conspiracy "against the peace and interests of the United States." Article 7 specified that Indian raiders would be delivered and bad men—citizens of the United States—would be punished "according to law." Article 8 dealt with the suppression of horse stealing. Article 9 covered the licensing of traders and the establishment of trading houses. Articles 10, 11, and 12 covered "perpetual peace between the United States and said tribes," peace between Indians at peace with the United States, and that there would be penalties for trade in liquor.

As submitted to the Senate, article 9 included a blank,

> In consideration of the friendly disposition of said tribes, evidenced by the stipulations in the present treaty, the comissioners of the United States, in behalf of the said states, agree to give to the said tribes or nations goods, as presents, at this time, and agree to give presents in goods to them, to the amount of ____, next fall at the Council Springs, on the Brazos . . . or at some other point to be designated, and of which due notice shall be given to said tribes. [Winfrey and Day 1959-66, 3: 43-51]

Presumably the blank would be filled in later.

Of all Comanche treaties up to the time, the Butler and Lewis treaty had the most signers: besides Pahayuko, Mopechucope, Santa Anna, and Potsana-quahip, nineteen others affixed their marks to it (table 6.1). It is not clear whether there is any significance to the order of names on the list, and many of the translations as given cannot be corroborated. Mulaquetop—as Mura-quetap—was last mentioned in 1832. Kanaumahka ('nearly dead') was possibly the man called Kanauma who visited the Torreys' trading house with Mopechucope in November 1844—although there seems to be little about the name that fits the translation—along with Quaharapoe (as Quaharapoah or Cuardepoa). There were two individuals called Blind Man; while one, Ka-henabone, seems clearly to be *kehena* 'nothing', *puni* 'to see', the other, Kaihenamonra, seems equally unclear: the element "monra" is unidentifiable. Ishameaqui is 'traveling wolf', but should not be confused with Returning Wolf, Isacony—also called Traveling Wolf—the Tenewa of the 1830s.

In their letters and final report on their treaty, Butler and Lewis listed "the tribes with whom we were in negotiations," but because the information is much confused, it merits some discussion. In a March 1846 letter to the commissioner of Indian affairs, Butler said that the Comanches,

> regarded as the mother tribe and the controlling spirits of all the prairies, are represented only in part [at the council]. Though all Comanches are known on the prairie under the appellation of Patocahs, they are divided into five distinct bands, each headed by their chiefs and captains, to wit the Nonahs and Yamparickas, Tenawish, Penatecas and Hooish. The three former range more north, the two latter more south and which are now in attendence. . . . From the best information, each band of Comanches number about 500 lodges, and each lodge 5 souls will make 12,500 Comanches. [P. M. Butler 1846]

Table 6.1
Signers of the Butler-Lewis Treaty, 1846

NAME	GIVEN AS	MODERN RETRANSCRIPTION
Pahayuca	The Amorous Man	
Mopechucope	Old Owl	
Cushunaraha	Ravisher	
Okaartsu	Rope Cutter	*o* objective prefix *ki?a* 'cuts' *tsa* topic marker, 'he cuts it'
Mulaquetop	Nasty Mule	
Tabupuata	The Winner	
Kaitaita	Little	
Kaihenamonra	Blind Man	*kehena* 'nothing'
Hochuca	Birdhouse	*hotsúú* 'bird', *kahni* 'house'
Pahmoowata	No Tobacco	*pahmu* 'tobacco', *wah tɨ* 'without'
Monecanahheh	Ring	*ma?nika?* 'ring'
Pochanaquarhip	Buffalo Hump	
Santa Anna		
Saviah	Little Wolf	
Quarhahapoe	Antelope Road	
Kanaumahka	Nearly Dead	*kana* 'thin'
Ishameaqui	Traveling Wolf	*isa* 'wolf', *mia* 'go', *ki* 'motion towards'
Moheka	Polecat	possibly based on *muhbi* 'nose'
A Kachuata	No Horn	*aa* 'horn, *wahtɨ* 'without'
Kahenabone	Blind Man	*kehena* 'nothing', *puni* 'to see'
Mawara	The Lost	
Kewiddawippa	Tall Woman	possibly based on *kanaba?aitɨ* 'tall', *wa?ihpɨ?* 'woman'
Panache	Mistletoe	*puhi turɨhka?* 'mistletoe'

SOURCE: Winfrey and Day 1959-55, 3:49-50

Butler's letter contains an interesting assortment of ethnonyms and associated data. He admitted that the Comanches were only partially represented at the council; later documents would suggest that all groups were represented. The basis for the assertion that the Comanches were generally known as Patocah is uncertain: there are only a few English-language documents that use that ethnonym in clear reference to the Comanches. There are two previously un-recorded ethnonyms: Nonah and Penateca. The meaning of the former is un-known, the latter is clearly *pihnatɨhka* 'honey eater'; Butler's letter is the earliest documentary appearance of that latter ethnonym. Meanwhile, in paral-lel with Ruíz's and Cameron's observations of a decade earlier, Butler made two broad geographical groupings, linking the Tenewas, Nonahs, and Yamparikas as northerners and the Penatekas and Hois as southerners. Although Butler made each band roughly equal in size, the average number of inhabitants per lodge was only five, down from Ortiz's 1786 estimate of twelve per lodge: either lodges were getting smaller, Comanches were getting wealthier, or observers were getting more accurate.

By July, when their final report was submitted, probably penned by Lewis alone, those words were modified. In place of Butler's "all Comanches are known on the prairie under the appellation of Patocahs," the report gave "the Comanches of the Prairies are known under the general appelation of Pahtocahs"; the change was minor, but it implied that there were other Comanches besides those "of the Prairies." Of more consequence, in place of Butler's five bands, the report described the Comanches as "subdivided into six distinct bands":

> 1st, the Yampeuccoes, or "Root Diggers." They number about 500 lodges average about 7 to the lodge making in all about 3500 souls. They range generally on the headwaters of the Canadian and Red Rivers;
>
> 2nd, the Hooish or "Honey Eaters" who number about 400 lodges, averaging about seven to the lodge making about 2800 souls. They inhabit the southernmost part of Comanche country bordering the settlements of Texas. Their principal chief, [Pahayuko], is an excellent man, and quite friendly with the whites;
>
> 3d, the Cochetakers, "Buffalo Eaters." They have something upwards of 300 lodges and number about 2000 souls and are located principally on the headwaters of the Brazos;
>
> 4th, the Noonah or "People of the Desert." They have about 250 lodges, in all about 2750 souls; are located between the Colorado and the Rio Grande;
>
> 5th, the Nocoonee or "People in a Circle." They number about 250 lodges, in all 1750 souls, and are located between the Colorado and the Rio Grande;
>
> 6th, the [T]enaywoosh, or "People of the Timber." They have about 400 lodges and number about 2800 souls. These people command the prairies and are the principal ones to be treated with and conciliated. [P. M. Butler and Lewis 1846:6]

Although giving more specific numbers and distribution of the population than Butler's earlier list—and estimating the number of individuals per lodge as seven—the Butler and Lewis report is equally problematical. It, too, includes a previously unrecorded ethnonym, Nocoonee, but the translation "People in a Circle" is incorrect; since *koni* refers to 'turning' or 'returning', the translation 'returners' would more nearly convey the meaning. Moreover, the names Tenaywoosh, Hooish, and Penateka, and the translations 'downstream', 'people of the people', and 'honey eaters' are thoroughly confused. That is, the Butler and Lewis report transposed the name Hooish (*hupe* 'wood people') with the gloss 'honey eater'—the proper gloss for *pihnatʉka*—and the name Tenaywoosh (*tenewa*) with the gloss 'timber people'—the proper gloss for *hupe;* at the same time it omitted both the name Penateka and the gloss 'downstream' altogether. To further confuse matters, the original manuscript gives the form as "Tenaywoosh," but all printed versions of the report have it as "Lenaywoosh." Finally, although Butler clearly stated that only the "southern" bands were in attendance at the councils, the Butler and Lewis report's extended description of the six "bands" implied that all of them were represented at the meeting.

As part of its appropriation for the treaty, Congress had allocated fifty thousand dollars to bring a delegation to Washington (Viola 1981:55). Although Mopechucope, Potsanaquahip, and Santa Anna were selected to travel, Santa Anna was the only Comanche who was actually named as having made the trip to Washington. On July 1, 1846, they met President James K. Polk. According to Polk's personal diary

> At 5 O'Clock P.M. Between 40 & 50 chiefs and warriors of the Comanche and other bands and tribes of wild Indians from the prairies in the North of Texas,[2] were presented to me by M. G. Lewis, Esq'r, who had been sent with Gov. Butler last fall to visit these tribes. I received them in the Ladies Parlour above stairs, in the presence of a few ladies and other persons. I had a friendly talk with them through an interpreter, assuring them that they might rely upon the friendship and protection of the U.S. as long as they would remain peaceable and friendly. Their orator made a speech in which he said they had made [a] Treaty of peace and friendship and they would keep it. The interview was a very interesting one. Santa Ana [sic], their principal chief, is fine looking man of good size and middle age, and is evidently a man of talents. . . . I was informed that the Chief, Santa Anna, had said that he thought before he came to the U.S. that his nation could whip any nation in the world, but that since he came here he found the white men more numerous than the stars, and that he could not count them. [Polk 1910, 2:3]

The political roles implied in that description are unclear. The "orator" was clearly a *tekwawapI* but his identity is unknown. Santa Anna was called the "principal chief," but here it must be read as the "principal chief of those present," not as "principal chief of the Comanches"; whether Polk himself believed he was meeting with the overall principal chief is unknown.

But all was not well with Butler and Lewis's treaty. Governor Butler had been seriously ill and had not accompanied the delegation. Then, relations between Lewis and Sam Houston, the latter now a senator, suffered a major breach. Although many details are unknown, the trouble came to a head in mid-July, when Houston invited the Indians to a late-night, private council at his hotel. Lewis vehemently objected to that meeting as having a "sinister" purpose; upon learning that the commissioner of Indian affairs had also been present, Lewis abruptly resigned (Lewis 1846b). Thus, the treaty had no direct sponsor in Washington.

An even more serious problem was that by the time the delegation had reached Washington, the Senate had adjourned without considering the treaty. When the senators reconvened in the fall, after the return of the delegation, several criticisms and amendments were made. The article providing for regular representatives to Washington was struck out entirely; as explained to Robert Neighbors, "it cannot be of much consequence to the Indians as there will always be among them [persons] through whom all their wishes and wants can be made known" (Medill 1847a:2). The immediate problem was the matter of political gifts, presents, and annuities. First, by the time the Senate reconvened it was too late to get any goods to the council grounds. In October 1846 Lt. Governor Albert C. Horton wrote to President Polk that the Indians "suspect[ed] that [the] provision . . . (and to them the most important of any) [would] not be fulfilled" (Winfrey and Day 1959–66, 3:77). According to Thomas Torrey,

> Since the treaty, the Comanches ask, "how is it that our great father has a forked tongue—his young men told us we could have presents twice a year and plenty of them—our good friend Sam Houston had given us our presents in the spring and fall, our Great Father has not done so. . . . Why is it that you people are in our country, when they never came before that treaty and it is broken by you? They must come no more. . . . we want the blankets for our squaws and old men. Our Father sends word he had no money to buy presents, and we must wait until the big captains agree to our treaty. . . . we know that our father is strong, we want to please him, but he does not keep his word. We want to see our friend Sam Houston, he never told us lies." [Torrey 1847]

When the chiefs told the Torreys that, as white men, they would be responsible for the promises of the white man's government, the traders took the hint and advanced $10,000 worth of goods on credit, and Neighbors made presents to twenty-five hundred Indians that fall (Neighbours 1975:35).

In March 1847, when the Senate approved the treaty, the blank in Article 9 was filled in with the amount of $10,000; later that month $20,000 was appropriated for the Texas Indians, of which not more than $10,000 was to pay the Torreys for the goods advanced the previous year, with the remainder for presents for 1847. But it was stipulated that that was to be a one-time pay-

ment, not a continuing annuity; Commissioner of Indian Affairs William
Medill wrote to Neighbors:

> It must be clearly understood that presents are only given in fulfillment
> of stipulations in the treaty which, in fact, provides for only one delivery
> of goods. The idea must not be permitted, that presents to the amount of
> ten thousand dollars annually are to be made to them. To make them
> presents to so large an amount without an equivalent, except their
> promises to remain peaceable would be bad policy. [Medill 1847b:6]

Then the Senate struck out Article 3, the provision reserving mines "in
the Indian territory" to the United States. Although apparently only a small
matter, it was to have long-lasting effects, for the political motivation behind
the article and its cancelation was not one of mineral rights; rather, as
Commissioner Medill explained to Neighbors,

> the striking out of the third article has, it is believed, no material bearing
> upon the interests or welfare of the Indians at this particular time. It was
> probably supposed to involve the question of relative jurisdiction of the
> United States and Texas which there was not sufficient time to examine
> into and define. This must, ere long, be settled, when no doubt, proper
> safeguards will be established to prevent the intrusion of improper
> persons among the Indians. Prior to that time, it is presumed, this will
> not take place to any injurous extent. [Medill 1847a:2]

But it was exactly the question of jurisdiction over Indian territory in Texas,
indeed the existence of Indian territory in Texas, that caused the greatest
problem.

The problem was basic: What was the nature of Indian-occupied lands
within the (albeit disputed) boundaries of Texas? Were they to be considered
as public lands and transferred to the jurisdiction of the federal government,
or, following the Republic of Texas's denial of Indian land rights, would they
remain under state jurisdiction? During the negotiations leading to Texas
annexation, James Buchanan, U.S. secretary of state, argued that "the public
lands of Texas ought unquestionably to belong to the United States. . . . This
government alone should possess the power of extinguishing the Indian title
with her limits" (Buchanan 1845). Similarly, several prominent Texans, including former president Burnet, advocated "that the Federal government
should become the proprietor of the vacant domains of Texas" (Burnet 1847:
8). But nothing more was done to resolve the issue.

In April 1846, during the negotiations, Butler and Lewis had written to
Medill:

> We are rather novely and delicately situated with regard to the boundary to be established with the Indians. Texas has the legal right of soil while the United States has the political jurisdiction. Texas has set no limit to her claim of territory above us and her warrants, according to their face are subject to location anywhere upon her unappropriated soil. Many have been located above the highest point where there is any possibility of establishing the boundary line. This will necessarily bring us in collision with a few individual interests. We will avoid this if possible. We are assured by intelligent gentlemen of Texas that the disturbance of a few of these greedy entries will not be sufficient cause for objection. The establishment of a line between the white and red men is indispensable to the future peace and safety of the frontier. [Lewis and P. M. Butler 1846]

But by the time the treaty was concluded, "nothing [was] done directly upon the subject of a boundary line between the red and white men" (Lewis 1846a). The wording of the Article 3 implied that there was to be a line dividing Indian territory from the rest of Texas, and although the treaty contained no description of it, Lewis thought "all the advantages of a definite line [had] been secured by the discretion secured to the President in the establishment of military posts, trading houses, etc." (Lewis 1846a). When the Indian delegation came to Washington, one of the items they wanted to discuss was a "definite adjustment of a boundary line between the several tribes and the settlements" (Winfrey and Day 1959-66, 3:62). In the interim, citizens of Texas were asked to "refrain from trespassing on the lands that are debateable . . . until some definite action of the Federal Government shall be known" (Medill 1847).

Meanwhile, in early 1847 the Society of German Noblemen purchased the Fisher-Miller land grant between the Llano and Colorado rivers and began settling a colony in the midst of Comanche hunting grounds. Since by the conditions of the purchase contract, surveying had to be completed by September 1847 or the grant would be forfeited, an intense program was begun that spring. Believing that it might be necessary to use force to complete the survey, the Germans were organized in quasi-military companies. Governor James Pinckney Henderson, fearing that the appearance of armed troops in Comanche country might spark a general war, sent Neighbors to dissuade them, or, if that were not possible, to assist them in coming to an agreement with the Comanches. The first option was negated; by the time Neighbors arrived, Baron von Meusebach—Ottfried Hans, the Freiherr von Meusebach, known in English as John O. Meusebach—and forty surveyors had already left. Neighbors, Jim Shaw, and Dr. Ferdinand Roemer, a German scientist traveling in America, caught up with them at Ketumsee's village on the San

Saba. The name Ketumsee is usually translated as "he pays no attention to happenings," but that meaning cannot be confirmed.

On March 1 they met with the chiefs; Biesele (1930:186) reported that twenty chiefs participated, but he did not name them. Roemer described the principal participants:

> Mope-tshoko-pe, the political chief, was a small old man who in his dirty cotton jacket looked undistinguished and only his diplomatic crafty face marked him. The war chief, Santa Anna, presented an altogether different appearance. He was a powerfully built man with a benevolent and lively countenace. The third, Buffalo Hump, was the genuine, unadulterated picture of a North American Indian. Unlike the majority of his tribe, he scorned all European dress. [Roemer 1935:269]

That is the only documentary occurrence of the phrase "political chief" in reference to a Comanche chief. Santa Anna was here called war chief, and Potsanaquahip was given no title.

Meusebach presented three points: that the Germans had "permission to go where they please [and] the Comanche can come to our wigwams and cities without fear and can go wherever they please and be protected"; that each side would keep the other informed about possible attacks; and that Meusebach would send men to survey the San Saba at least as far as the Concho, if not beyond, "so that we may know the boundaries where we may go and till the soil" (Tiling 1913:100).

In return for those concessions, Meusebach said "If you are willing, after consultation with your warriors, to make this treaty, then I will give . . . many presents or equal them with the white pieces of metal, that we call dollars . . . as many as one thousand and more of them" to be given later in Fredericksburg. In addition, while they were visiting Fredericksurg the Germans would supply the Comanches with another thousand dollars in provisions. Meusebach later said he had promised the Comanches three thousand dollars in gifts (Biesele 1930:186).

The Comanches wanted to discuss the matter among themselves, and the meeting was adjourned until the next morning, when Mopechucope spoke. He said he had consulted "the warriors and the old men. We shall abandon the war path and travel on the white path of peace, as my father proposed yesterday, and I will do my utmost that we remain forever on this path, after the treaty has been made." But he was concerned:

> I perceive something that is not dear to my heart, when you now are going to build your wigwams at the water called the Llano. I know that

the people that calls itself Texans want to erect a barrier between us and the palefaces, and I must speak first with the Comanches farther away, because I do not want to promise anything and break my word afterwards. When the grass is growing again, the Comanches will meet and I hope that I can remove all difficulties. [Tiling 1913:102-4]

Ultimately, Santa Anna and Potsanaquahip agreed, and the German-Comanche Treaty was signed May 9, 1847. There is some confusion in the literature about who signed the treaty for the Comanches. King's copy of the treaty (King 1967:176) listed only Santa Anna, Potsanasanaco (painted by Stanley at Houston's 1844 treaty council), Mulaquetop, Matasane (previously unmentioned), Toshaw-wheschke (possibly the Tosawecut who attended the 1846 council with General Morehouse; it is also possibly *tosa wesikitu* 'white curly'), and Nokakwhek (previously unmentioned).[3] R. N. Richardson (1933: 147) added Mopechucope and Ketumsee. They were certainly present at the beginning of the council, but Mopechucope said that he would not sign until he had consulted with his own people—he did not want to make promises he could not keep—and the records are not clear that he returned to sign it. The absence of Ketumsee's name from the signatories is also unexplained; it was at his village that the council took place.

In March 1847, after settling the German Treaty, Neighbors was appointed federal special agent for the Texas tribes. In sending word of the appointment, Commissioner Medill noted, "it will be your duty to see the different bands as often, and be as much among them, as may appear to be necessary" (Medill 1847a:2). Thus, he began an active field program of visiting the various tribes in their own camps.

In April Neighbors reported that the Comanches wanted trading houses, and he wondered whether he had the authority to grant licenses (Neighbors 1847a). In late May he visited a camp of 250 lodges, said to be the principal village of the Comanches, about a hundred miles north of Austin; there he met with Pahayuko, Mopechucope, and Potsanaquahip. The Butler and Lewis Treaty and its Senatorial revision was read and interpreted to the council. All were satisfied until the amendments were read. Potsanaquahip objected strenuously to striking out the line:

I cannot agree that the third article shall be striken out, for that article was put in at my request. For a long time a great many people have been passing through my country; they kill all the game, and burn the country, and trouble me very much. The commissioners of our great father promised to keep these people out of our country. I believe our white brothers do not wish to run a line between us, because they wish to settle in this country. I object to any more settlements. I want this country to hunt in. [Neighbors 1847b]

But ultimately, he agreed to the changes, or at least he dropped his objections.

Meanwhile, in spite of their treaty, the Germans were sending surveyors above their line; Santa Anna was reported to have told them to "leave the country, as his tribe would not permit further surveys to be made" (Neighbors 1847c). Moreover, the Germans were slow in producing their promised presents, and in July, when a party of surveyors was attacked by Indians—although it later turned out that the perpetrators were Wacos—the Germans thought it was by Comanches retaliating for the lack of payment (Neighbours 1975:38).

The Comanches too were nervous. In mid-July Santa Anna and Mopechucope moved their camps far to the north. As Neighbors explained:

> The Comanches, being at all times jealous of any encroachments by the white man and much opposed to the extension of our settlements . . . they have been induced to believe that the whites intend to deprive them of their whole country, and were preparing to make an attack upon them. Our friendly relations cannot be maintained permanently with them until [the boundary question] is finally settled. [Neighbors 1847c]

In September, meeting Neighbors at the Kitsai village on the Brazos River, Mopechucope reported rumors heard from Mexican and German traders that a military expedition was being sent against them. Neighbors persuaded him that no such expedition was being planned and that that year's presents had arrived and would be distributed at the next full moon (Neighbors 1847d).

On September 25 Pahayuko, Mopechucope, and Santa Anna, with about 2,200 other Indians—Caddos, Anadarkos, and Wichitas—received their goods. Labiarte (probably Saviah) came in November. In December Potsanaquahip returned from Mexico with "many horses, mules, and a number of prisoners"; along with twenty-five "principal warriors and under-captains," he stopped at the Torreys' trading house (Neighbors 1847e, 1847f). At each meeting the Indians raised the question of the line, and each time Neighbors persuaded them to "leave the matter to the future." He did, however, comment that although the "Indians evinced disposition to adhere to the treaty, the citizens . . . show a disposition to violate the agreement" (Neighbors 1847g).

At Neighbors's urging, in November 1847, Governor Henderson, arguing that the Indian Intercourse law of the Republic of Texas was still in effect (Henderson 1847), established a line "30 miles above the highest settlements above which no white person should be allowed to go" (Neighbors 1847f).

For the time being, there was peace; in December Neighbors reported that "since the line, the frontier has enjoyed a tranquility heretofore unknown" (Neighbors 1847g). But it was not to last long.

That month several Texas Ranger companies lost horses to Indian raiders. In January 1848 Mopechucope returned six of the horses to the Torreys' trading house but quickly left. Later that month Neighbors heard of a great assembly of Yamparikas, Tenewas, Kotsotekas, and others on the upper Brazos River, whose "avowed intention was to make preparations for a descent upon the southern provinces of Mexico, Chihuahua, and others early in the spring. They [were] proposing to unite and send several thousand warriors" (Neighbors 1848a).

In late January, Neighbors received word that Comanches wished to meet with him; at Mopechucope's village of the "Penetekas or Hois" on the Salt Fork of the Brazos he found "all the principal chiefs and councilors of the lower bands" (Neighbors 1848b). The first evening "all the chiefs assembled for a smoke at the lodge of Mopechucope, where all matters appertaining to their affairs were freely discussed, as well as the subject of the depredations lately committed." Mopechucope blamed the Tenewa and Nokoni Comanches for the raids on the Rangers; he explained that the Tenewas had been returning from Mexico when some Lipans told them that Comanches and whites were at war, and they then "decided to steal some horses from the Rangers." Upon arriving at the Penateka camp, the chiefs confiscated the horses. At that, the Tenewas "sent out their warriors to steal more," saying "they wanted to see how long before the old chiefs of the Penetekas would get tired of returning stolen horses" (Neighbors 1848b).

The next day Mopechucope sent runners to call on Pahayuko to control his men. The latter's camp must have been nearby, for he arrived the following day, bringing along five Tenewas, including one identified as Puhacawakis (*puha* 'medicine', *wehkinitu* 'to look around for', 'looking for medicine'), a Nokoni called Ohois, given as Naked Head, and a Kotsoteka, Chipeseah, given as Growing Chief. While the element "-seah" in the latter name seems to be *sua* 'grow', the full translations of those names cannot be confirmed.

The following day they met in a brief council. In his talk Puhacawakis noted, probably in reference to those who signed the Camp Holmes Treaty, that "all the chiefs who had counciled with the whites are now dead. I have never counciled before and don't know much." That night they conducted a smoke lodge, feasting and discussing "war and women" (Neighbors 1848b).

The next morning they met in formal council. The chiefs reported that there had been several Kickapoos, Seminoles—including Cooacoochee 'Wild Cat' and Alligator—and Creeks traveling among them "representing them-

selves as emissaries" who told the Comanches that the "whites were decidedly hostile and were preparing to make a campaign and that they had lied at
every council." When those emissaries reported that the presents were intended as payment for land, Pahayuko replied, "If I had known that I would
not have taken them." Despite those rumors, Neighbors reported that the Tenewas, Nokonis, and Kotsotekas were all willing to come under the same
agreements as the Penetekas (Neighbors 1848b).

The chiefs blamed the problems on young men beyond their control. In a
brief comment, Neighbors highlighted the pragmatic differences between Comanche and Anglo-American politics. Of his meeting at Mopechucope's
camp, Neighbors noted:

> I used every exertion to induce the chiefs to restore the stolen property,
> and notified them that they would be held by the government to a strict
> account, and be made to pay for each horse stolen; but found myself
> unable to effect that object, the chiefs assuring me that they were unable
> to exercise sufficient control over those who had stolen them, for their
> recovery, but would still do their utmost to preserve peace, and induce
> those disposed to depredate to remain quiet, and if they could recover
> any of the stolen horses, they should be immediately returned. I am
> decidedly of the opinion that, had I sufficient force to sustain the chiefs
> in their good intentions, I should have been able to settle all matters of
> difference. . . . each chief appearing to act for himself, I could affect no
> concert of action by which I hoped to recover the stolen property.
> [Neighbors 1848b]

In stating the problem in those terms, Neighbors showed full acceptance of
the basic tenets of his own political culture: society was held in check by
coercion; lack of coercive power meant anarchy. In contrast, for the chiefs,
the far greater problem was the conflict between the resource domains derived from raiding, of principal importance for young men trying to establish
a social standing, and their own domains based on political relations with
Euroamericans.

Other problems with the line were surfacing as settlers moved above it;
indeed, even the council grounds at the Torreys' trading house had been
fenced off as private property by a lawyer; the squatter threatened to "shoot
the first Indian that came on the land" (Neighbors 1847f). The problem was
exemplified by the Texas Emigration Company, which had obtained the
Peter's Colony grant to "all the lands" above a line running from the Brazos
River through Comanche Peak to the Red River. Henry Hedgcoxe, agent for
the colony, wrote to Neighbors asking him whether he had

either by law or instruction from the proper authorities of the United States or the State of Texas, any authority or right to hinder any citizen of this state, or of the United States from going into or prosecuting his lawful business in any part of the state of Texas, whether the country is occupied by Indians or not. [Hedgcoxe 1848]

Although Neighbors argued that if the company intended to survey the area, it would lead to hostility, he was forced to admit that he had no authority to restrain them: "the subject was a matter for the authorities of Texas, and not an Indian Agent of the United States" (Neighbors 1848). But the authorities of Texas were not about to take action. Lt. Colonel Peter H. Bell, chief of the Texas Rangers, ordered his men not to interfere with any settler going beyond the line. When told of that, Mopechucope complained:

You told me that the troops were placed there for our protection as well as the whites; that I know is not so. They told me also that if I wished to go below the line, if I would go to the captains of the stations they would give me permission to go down below to hunt. Soon after the council, I wanted to go down below the station on the Colorado, as I heard that there were some buffalo down in the lower prairies. I applied to Captain [Henry E.] McCulloch with a party of eight old men and their women and children; he would not let me go down. I told him that I did not wish to go to the settlements, had no warriors with me, but merely wanted to hunt where there were no houses and kill some meat for my women and children as there were no buffalo above his station. He said he would not permit me under any circumstances to go down. This made me angry and I quarrelled with him. I told him that I was an old man, and had hunted on these prairies before he was born. . . . We have been at peace for a long time, and I do not see why you keep so many soldiers on the line if you wish to keep peace. [Neighbors 1848b]

Neighbors himself complained to the commissioner that since no one was to pass the line without a passport, "I would respectfully ask . . . who is to grant [them]?" (Neighbors 1848b).

In late May, when Santa Anna visited San Antonio to have a "friendly talk" with the governor, a number of citizens became alarmed and the Indians were told to go back above the line. When they asked for a permit to hunt below it, Neighbors, claiming no authority to "force the Indians above any given line," referred them to Captain Shapley P. Ross of the Texas Rangers. Ross, in turn, refused permission. The Comanches angrily responded, "When we made a treaty, we believed the white people wished to be friendly. If they are not friendly, and the Comanches cannot go to their [the Texan's] houses, there is no use in making treaties" (Neighbors 1848d).

That fall, as he had information that some of their men had stolen horses from the Rangers for which Lipans had been blamed, Neighbors, later joined by Ketumsee, went out to Santa Anna's and Potsanaquahip's village on the Clear Fork of the Brazos. There the leader of the horse raiders, "Kar-wa-be-bo-we-bit," was pointed out. The name was translated as "Can See Nothing" and he was said to have been a signer of the Butler and Lewis Treaty. Thus he may have been one of the two men named Blind Man who signed that treaty. He admitted taking the horses but said it was the troops' fault; they had attacked Comanches who were going south. He also admitted that he had taken the horses to the Lipan camp, causing them to be blamed for the theft, but said he did not care if the Lipans got blamed as Lipans had often acted as guides for the Rangers. When Neighbors explained that by the Treaty of Guadalupe Hidalgo the United States had promised to stop raiders from crossing into Mexico, Karwabebowebit said that the Comanches had made peace with Texas but not with Mexico. For his part, Potsanaquahip also declined to stop raiding, saying that his daughter was a captive in Mexico—there is no further information on her captivity—but he would stay away from settlements or get a pass (Neighbors 1848).

The United States Takes Over on the Arkansas, 1845–49

In the summer of 1845 Captain John C. Frémont of the Topographical Engineers was sent on an exploring expedition up the Arkansas River. At Bent's Fort, while Frémont went filibustering to California, Lieutenant James W. Abert was detached to make a reconnaissance down the Canadian River. They apparently ignored the fact that Abert's trip would take him through what was still Mexican territory. Neither Frémont's expedition from St. Louis to Bent's Fort, nor Abert's return met many Comanches, although a 1970 reprint of Abert's 1846 report would be entitled *Through the Country of the Comanche Indians*. Nonetheless their reports and other accounts are significant for the attitudes toward and knowledge of Comanches expressed by the members of the expedition.

Besides the official report, there is one other account of the exploring expedition. Written by a civilian member of Abert's party, Isaac Cooper, it was published under the pseudonym of François de Montaignes (1852–56). As might be expected, there are differences between the accounts, several of which are noted below. Frequently the accounts are off chronologically, Abert reporting events on one day, Montaignes on another. While it seems likely that Montaignes's memoirs were based on an original journal, it is not known whether he also utilized Frémont's or Abert's offical published reports in writing his own.

The outward journey from St. Louis was relatively uneventful. They met Kaws and Kickapoos, Shawnees, and Osages; they would later meet Arapahos and Cheyennes. They also heard from incoming travelers "awful tales and yarns about Camanches and Pawnees" (Montaignes 1852-56:30). At Bent's Fort, there were Cheyennes, Kiowas, and even a group of Brule Sioux. Frémont and Abert tried to get a Kiowa, "a man of great influence among all the Indians in that region, particularly the Comanches, who were greatly to be feared," to be his guide (Abert 1846:2), but the Indian demurred.

Before he left Bent's Fort, Abert was told that "recent difficulties with the Texans, in which the Comanches had suffered the loss of forty of their bravest men and chiefs, had so incensed them that matters appeared quite serious" (Abert 1846:5). Montaignes was specific about those difficulties: "the Massacre at San Antonio de Bejar . . . has infused a panic into the Camanches and their allies, which will make them forever shun the too intimate society of such men as Texian Americans" (1852-56:73); at another place he noted, "The Camanches have received a grievous panic at the slaughter of their 60 chiefs at San Antonio de Bejar" (1852-56:114).

But the Council House fight was five years in the past, and although there had been periodic skirmishes between Comanches and Texans, including the recent (1844) battle of Walker's Creek, the Hois Comanches had just signed Sam Houston's treaty, and relations in Texas were turning positive again. It is probable that, on the one hand, the reactions of the Indians to any mention of Texans, and on the other, the reported number of casualties at the Council House fight, reflect the inflation of rumor with distance from source.

On August 14, 1845, Abert and his party left the vicinity of Bent's Fort. There were thirty-seven men in the party—Montaignes counted thirty-five, but may not have included the two "colored men" (Abert 1846:6)—including the mountain men Thomas Fitzpatrick as guide and John Hatcher as hunter; they were to guide Abert to Bent's post on the Canadian River. Frémont regretted that they had been forced to leave a howitzer at St. Louis, "particularly as we had no one who understood the Comanche language" (Abert 1846:5).

Crossing Raton Pass, they traveled down the Canadian River. On September 7 they passed the site of an "old"—the embers were still warm— Indian camp. According to Abert, the singular ring of stones heaped in the center marked the site of the "medicine lodge" also showed that it had been occupied by the Comanches. As there were few traces of lodges having been used, but principally rude wigwams, Hatcher pronounced that they had belonged to the Buffalo eaters, one of the most ferocious bands of the Comanche nation. This band follow the migratory herds of the buffaloes, eat their flesh and cloth themselves in their skins. [Abert 1846:32]

According to Montaignes, Hatcher identified them as "100 lodges or 200 men . . . the band of old Bald-Head, as this is the only one having regular lodges. The balance makes use but of temporary shelter formed of brush or bark" (1852–56:107).

The basis for attributing the camp to Comanches, and specifically to "Buffalo eaters" of "old Bald-Head" is unknown. The first evidence—the "singular ring of stones"—was not further described; depending upon how big it was, it could have been anything from a sweat lodge to a Sun Dance lodge, although the former seems more likely. Of the specific attribution to "Buffalo eaters," presumably Kotsotekas, Abert gave no further details beyond Hatcher's description of them as "one of the most ferocious bands of the Comanche nation." Bald Head is previously unmentioned; he could be the Shaved Head who, ca. 1841, allegedly asked the Bents to build their post along the Canadian, but there is no secure linkage. Finally, Hatcher's comments about lodges are contradictory: depending upon reporter, there were either a "few" lodges or "100." Similarly, depending upon reporter, it was either the presence or absence of lodges that marked the Indians as Buffalo eaters. Although there are other descriptions of Comanche use of wikiups— e.g., Leclerc in 1838 (McLean 1974–93, 16:446)—that there was a differential of domestic architecture along divisional lines is unattested elsewhere.

For the next several days a group of Indians trailed along at the fringes of Abert's party. On September 9 Thomas Fitzpatrick persuaded several of them to come into the camp; he proclaimed them to be Buffalo Eaters (Abert 1846:35). Because of the lack of a competant interpreter, the conversation was in broken Spanish and "the manual signs which consitute the standard language among all the prairie tribes" (Montagnes 1852–56:111). Nevertheless, Fitzpatrick was able to glean the information that their village was 6 or 7 miles distant, while the Bents' Canadian River post was 2 or 3 days farther downriver—elsewhere Hatcher said it would be a week's travel—with Kiowas "and the tribe of old Red Shirt the Camanche" beyond (Montaignes 1852–56: 111, 113). Red Shirt is previously unmentioned.

At this point in his memoirs, Montaignes added the footnote:

> The Camanches are divided into several bands or clans. as for example:
> Buffaloe Eaters.—horse Eaters.—Hoes etc.—Root Eaters. They all eat
> Buffaloe meat, & those known by the distinctive cognomen of Buffaloe
> Eaters, follow this animal in his march North and South, & whilst he
> feeds on the green prairies of Mexico, the villages of these Camanches
> are not far distant. [Montaignes 1852–56:111 n. 4]

That information must have come from either Fitzpatrick or Hatcher, but
there are problems. The first, third, and fourth ethnonyms are clearly Kotsoteka, Hois, and Yamparika; the second, however, is otherwise unknown. The
near contemporaneity of Montaignes's—or Hatcher's—"Horse Eaters" in
1845 with William Bollaert's description of Comanches eating horses in 1844
(1956:361) (see above, chap. 1, note 2) suggests that the belief that Comanches regularly ate horses was part of the same rumor tradition.

On September 11, two more Buffalo Eaters visited the camp, and the
next day, a group of Kiowas, along with a few Crows, visited. In return,
Abert and party attached themselves to the Kiowa village. Abert was surprised by the demenor of the Kiowas:

> These people, contrary to the general opinion, appeared to be gay,
> cheerful, and fond of frolic; they laughed, chatted, and joked, much to
> the astonishment of some of us, who possessed of preconceived notions
> which were, doubtless, obtained from the popular writers of the day.
> [Abert 1846:40]

There was an initial concern among the Kiowas; apparently that first
group of Buffalo Eaters had told the Kiowas that Abert's party were Texans.
But, according to Abert,

> [the Kiowas] laughed heartily at a party of Comanches they had pre-
> viously met, who had been frightened at our approach and fled, leaving
> their mules and furniture scattered over the prairie, and meeting these
> Kioways, advised them to fly, as they reported us to be as numerous as
> the blades of grass on the prairie. These however, were determined to
> satisfy themselves, and striking our trail, had followed until last evening.
> [Abert 1946:39]

Montaignes gave a slightly different version:

> Their village was about 8 or 10 miles distant on a small creek. They had
> been roused by some Camanches (Old Foxes), who had seen us en route
> across the prairies & who reported our numbers to exceed a thousand.
> (Camanches will lie)—and that we were all Texians,—that we were

invading their region . . . they had been following our trail . . . and were almost sure of our being Tejanos or Texians—they didn't desire to injure Americans. [Montaignes 1852–56:123]

On September 15, Abert encountered a party of Pueblo Comancheros, twenty days out from Taos, "seeking the band of Camanches under old Bald Head for the purpose of traffic" (Abert 1846:42; Montaignes 1852–56:133). Abert noted that

> they are badly armed, and presented a shabby and poor appearance . . . They are called "Comancheros" and make frequent trading expeditions into the country of the Indians with whom they exchange their stock for horses and mules, which the Indians frequently retake before they reach their homes. Their defenceless state gives the Indians little to fear. They suffer them to traverse the country even whilst they are at war with the Mexicans. [Abert 1846:43]

That is, of course, an Anglo-American perspective, and as such it would have been distinct from both the Comanche—or Kiowa—and the Comanchero perspectives. In particular, the notion that the Comancheros lack of defense— and the implicit opposite, incapability of offense—was very much in line with the then-current image of Mexicans as indeed defenseless. That the apparent lack of an armed posture might have resulted from a mutually understood political-economic modus vivendi was lost on the Anglo-Americans.

The next day they camped "on the south side of the Rio Rojo [Canadian], one mile distant from its water, and about three miles above the point whereat formerly stood the trading post of which we were in search" (Montaignes 1852–56:133).[4] They had hoped—or at least were prepared—to meet a large gathering of Indians at the Canadian River awaiting the Bents' annual wagons, but

> Red Jacket, one of the Comanche chiefs, who had been highly enraged with the Texans on account of their late difficulties, had gone with his party to the Antelope Buttes, and that most of the other tribes had exhausted their supply of meat while awaiting the arrival of Bent's wagons and were scattered around in search of buffaloes. [Abert 1846:44]

Red Jacket was the probably Red Shirt mentioned by Montaignes, but, as with the "recent difficulties" described to Abert at Bent's Fort (the Texas Council House fight), any relation between Red Jacket/Shirt and Muguara's Hois Comanches is unknown. At another place, Montaignes described the post, probably from Hatcher:

> The post . . . was but a species of rude log or block house into which, the trader, at certain periods of the year, conveyed his goods, and at which all the trading for robes and furs, was carried on untill the Indians' stock of robes was exhausted. Then, after burning the house or fort, in order to prevent other traders from making use of it, he would return to the states with his robes, to exchange for money and more goods. To this fort would the Camanches and Kiowas annually resort to traffick their hunting spoils, for beads, bells, wire, vermillion, cotton handkerchiefs, tobacco, and trinkets. [Montaignes 1852–56:113]

This is apparently the earliest contemporary description of the activities of the Bents' first Canadian River post; however, there is no other mention of its annual burning. Soon thereafter, the party left the Canadian River for the Washita River; although they met Tohausan's Kiowas a short distance down the Washita, they met no more Comanches.

It seems clear that although most of Abert's party had no prior experience with Indians in general, and with Comanches in particular, they all had preconceived notions of Indian demeanor, originating as much in "the popular writers of the day" (Abert 1846:40) as in the rhetoric of Thomas Hart Benton and Augustus Storrs a decade and a half earlier. Moreover, they were reinforced by the "awful tales and yarns" told around the campfires. It also seems clear that neither Fitzpatrick and Hatcher had wide experience with the Kiowas or Comanches; although Hatcher had been Bent's trader among both the Kiowas and Comanches for about ten years (J. Carter 1966), he did not know the Comanche language, and despite his connections with the Kiowas,[5] as indicated by his continued use of signs, he probably did not know that language either. The stock of historical knowledge held by the party was out-of-date, and their ethnographic knowledge was minimal. It also seems clear that the campaign of rumor and innuendo about the Comanches begun by Senator Benton in the 1820s was now self-supporting.

Although Abert did not meet the large group of Comanches and Kiowas at the Bents' Canadian River post—he thought it was because the caravan was late and the Indians had scattered to resupply—the traders must have arrived soon afterward. However, they did not have good business that winter; Charles Bent reported that because of rumors that there were troops at the post, the Comanches stayed away. By the end of the winter Ceran St. Vrain reported receiving 750 robes, a "fair" return (Lecompte 1972:285). It was probably during that winter that the Bents built their more famous adobe post on the Canadian, which apparently was only used during the years 1845–46 (Lecompte 1972:285).[6]

Meanwhile, General Stephen Watts Kearny's Army of the West had invaded Mexican New Mexico. One of Kearny's first acts after his relatively bloodless occupation was the appointment of Charles Bent as governor and ex-officio superintendent of Indian affairs. In November Bent reported on the Indians in the new territory. After discussing the various groups, he noted that although the Comanches

> [had] been at peace for many years with the New Mexicans, [they had] carried on an incessant and destructive war with the Departments of Chihuahua, Durango and Coahuila from which they [had] carried off and still [held] as slaves a large number of women and children and immense herds of horses, mules, and asses. [Abel 1915b:7]

He concluded:

> You are doubtless aware that presents of goods are indispensible in all friendly communications with Indians. I would respectfuly suggest the necessity of goods of that kind or the means wherewith to purchase them, being placed at the disposition of the Superintendent of Indian Affairs for this territory. [Abel 1915b:7]

But nothing was done on his recommendations. In January 1847 Bent was killed in an uprising in Taos (Garrard 1955).

Soon after serving as Abert's guide, Fitzpatrick was appointed agent for the Indians of the western Plains to be headquartered at Bent's Fort. In recommending him, Senator Benton called him "a man of character and experience, who [had] been above twenty years acquainted with these Indians" (Hafen 1931:230). While Fitzpatrick may have been acquainted with other Indians, except for the fact that he was nearby when Jedediah Smith was killed, allegedly by Comanches in 1831, and that he had served as Abert's guide the previous fall, no other details of Fitzpatrick's experience with Comanches are known; he certainly did not know the language.

Although the sources of Fitzpatrick's knowledge of the Comanches are unclear, he did have strong opinions. In the fall of 1847, replying to a questionnaire from the ethnologist Henry Rowe Schoolcraft that asked for information on the Indians, he suggested that it would take "years of close application" to complete such a study and that the result would be futile, for

> I fear the real character of the Indians can never be ascertained, because it is altogether unnatural for a Christian man to comprehend how so much depravity and wickedness could possibly belong to human beings apparently endowed with a reasonable share of understanding. . . . I am not one of those who expect and look for the immediate improvement and civilization of the Indians. [Fitzpatrick 1847a]

He was later to write, "I consider treaties less than useless. . . . I have never

been fully convinced of the propriety or good policy of admitting and acknowledging the right of Indians to the soil" (Fitzpatrick 1847b).

After the Frémont-Abert party traveled up the Santa Fe Trail in 1845
there seems to have been little interaction between the Indians of the Western
Plains and travelers for almost a year. Apparently the next hostile incident
was not until May 28, 1846, when one man in an eastbound Bent, St. Vrain
and Company caravan was killed at Pawnee Fork (Barry 1972:589). By then,
the Mexican War was two weeks old; the existence of a state of war was proclaimed by President Polk on May 13—the news did not reach Santa Fe until
at least June 13—and the Santa Fe Trail became a major highway for army
units traveling to Mexico, New Mexico, and California.

While there was only a single hostile incident reported along the Santa
Fe Trail in 1845, and another in 1846, the record for 1847 was very different,
if somewhat confused. In October 1847 Thomas Fitzpatrick claimed:

> In all the skirmishing and 'scrapes' on the Santa Fe road last summer
> and spring, I cannot make out more than twenty-seven white men killed;
> but an Arapahoe has told me that the Camanche and Kioway, together
> count sixty and can produce that number of scalps; but I am disposed to
> think it much exaggerated. [Fitzpatrick 1847a]

The following August, Lt. Colonel William Gilpin, commanding a force sent
to overawe the Indians along the route, reported that during the summer of
1847, forty-seven Americans were killed, 330 wagons were destroyed, and
6,500 animals were stolen by Pawnees, Comanches, Kiowas, and Apaches
(Gilpin 1848:136-7). Tabulation of contemporary reports (table 6.2) supports
Fitzpatrick's rather than Gilpin's tally.[7]

Moreover, although the reports blamed only Comanches, Arapahos, and
Pawnees, the basis for those identifications are unknown, and it is probable
that others were also involved. The specific Comanches are also unknown;
with the exception of one case, detailed below, no individuals were named. In
February 1848 some Arapahos told Fitzpatrick that only two bands of Comanches were involved in the war (Fitzpatrick 1848b). Moreover, the causes
of the hostilities are unclear. There were several reports that Mexicans had
been stirring up antagonism against the Americans, and indeed were fighting
with them. There were also rumors that the Comanches were upset that
soldiers had brought disease to their camps (Lavender 1954:278).

It may also be noted that by the summer of 1847 the Comanches—and
Kiowas?—along the Arkansas River had been without Euroamerican supplies
for at least a year; the Bents' Canadian River post was not resupplied after
the 1845-46 season and the Comanches stayed away from the main post on
the Arkansas. Their only apparent source of supply was through the Osages;

Table 6.2

Incidents on the Santa Fe Trail, 1847

DATE	PLACE	INCIDENT
Feb 6	Jackson's Grove	Pawnees stole mules.
Mar	?	Norris Colburn killed by Sacs.
Apr 30	?	1 man of Aubrey's wagon train reported killed.
Apr	Caches/Fort Mann	90 Comanches attacked Carson-Beale-Talbot party; 49 head of stock taken; Williams killed.
May 9	?	Comanches killed 1 teamster.
May 11	?	Indians stampeded 15 yoke of oxen.
May 12	Pawnee Fork	100 Comanches and Arapahos attacked American and Mexican wagon train; Comanche leader [Red Sleeve?] killed.
May 28	Mann's Fort	Eastbound Bent, St. Vrain wagon train attacked by Arapahos at Walnut Creek; Tharp killed[?];40 head of stock taken.
[late May]	Mann's Fort	Westbound party harrassed for 3 days by Comanches and Arapahos; several Indians killed.
June 3	Walnut Creek	2 travelers killed.
June 9-21	Mann's Fort	400 Indians made several attacks; 3 travelers killed; 15 Comanches killed with cannon.
June 17-21	Caches	2 fights with Comanches and Arapahos.
June 23	Pawnee Fork	50 Comanches attacked; 160 head of stock taken.
June 24-26	Coon Creek	"Love's Defeat"; 250-300 Comanches and Mexicans attacked; 5 travelers killed; 320 head of stock taken; 12-15 Comanches killed.
July 4	Cimarron	Comanches and renegade Mexicans attacked; 1 mule and 17 oxen taken.
July 13-14	Pawnee Fork	2 or 3 travelers killed.
July 13	?	1 negro killed.
July 20	Fort Mann	Unarmed firewood party attacked; 8 killed.
July 25-Aug 1	Pawnee Fork	3d Reg. Mo.Vol.; 26 horses and all the cattle taken; 6-8 Comanches killed.
Sept 11-30	2d Reg., Mo.Vol.	1 man "lost."

SOURCE: Barry 1972:661-716

in 1848, Kiowas reported that "for two years, the Comanches [had] been meeting Osages for trade, by which the Comanches receive[d] their necessary supplies in barter for horses" (Fitzpatrick 1848b). That commerce was later seen as evidence of a widespread conspiracy between the Comanches and the Osages. On the other hand, Cheyennes had no immediate economic reason for involvement; they still had access to the Bents' trade. The Arapaho position is unclear. They were often specifically identified as among the attack-

ers, but in February 1848 the Arapaho chief Coho denied having anything to
do with the war, except to buy Comanche horses; Coho also said he was
present when a Mexican "delegation"—Comancheros?—urged that the Comanches attack the caravans (Fitzpatrick 1848a).

Only one incident from the summer of 1847 has a surviving Indian account. According to Mooney, the Kiowas called 1847 "Summer that Red
Sleeve was killed" (1898:286), possibly referring to the May 12 fight on Pawnee Fork. But even that account denies that the travelers on the trail were the
primary target. According to the Kiowas, they and some Comanches were out
hunting Pawnees when they came to Pawnee Fork and found the caravan.
Red Sleeve[8]—Mooney gave it as Îkämosa *(ekamakwɨsaʔ)*—wanted to attack
immediately, but when Setängya (Satank) demurred, saying the Americans
were friends, Red Sleeve called him a coward. In the charge Red Sleeve's
horse was killed, pinning him under it. Because Red Sleeve had called him a
coward, Setängya refused to come to his aid. Although different in Comanche, the similarity of the names Red Sleeve *ekamakwɨsa* and Red Arm
ekapuura with the names Red Jacket/Red Shirt *ekakwasuʔu* given by Abert
and Montaignes in 1845 suggests their identity, and that those names may
have been American descriptive nicknames rather than personal names.[9]

In the late summer of 1847, the five companies of Missouri Volunteers,
two mounted, two infantry, and one unmounted artillery, under Lt. Colonel
William Gilpin, were assigned to protect the trail. Variously called Gilpin's
battalion, the Indian battalion, or the Arkansas battalion, in September they
marched up the Santa Fe Trail. While two companies went on to Bent's Fort,
three encamped at Fort Mann.[10]

The record of the battalion during its one year of existence was uneven.
In November at Fort Mann, after smoking with a Pawnee chief, the captain in
charge allowed about sixty Pawnees inside the gates apparently intending to
detain the whole party. A melee ensued when the Indians realized what was
happening; four were killed, two taken prisoner, and fifteen or twenty
wounded (Barry 1972:727). In March, having spent most of the winter in garrison due to lack of provisions, especially mules, Gilpin set out on a tour.
Crossing Raton Pass, he stopped at Mora, New Mexico for provisions, and
then went down the Canadian. The region was "burned for many hundred
miles"; Gilpin later learned from captives—he did not further identify them—
that "the Indians, informed in advance of the movements of my command by
renegade Mexicans, had thus devasted their country with fire, and retired"
(Gilpin 1848:137). But if the Indians did set the fires, it was probably more to
encourage the spring grass than to escape Gilpin. He traveled as far as the
Antelope Buttes before turning north to the Arkansas; he met no other
Indians.

Gilpin's troops reported four engagements with Indians. On June 7, Lieutenant Phillip Stremmel's Company C was attacked at Pawnee Fork by about 200 Indians, "mostly" Comanches; Stemmel claimed five Indians killed, ten wounded (Stemmel 1848:146). On June 18, while camped along the Arkansas River, Stemmel's Company C and part of another were attacked by between 600 and 1,000 Indians; the attackers lost twenty-three and an "emmense number wounded." Of the attackers, Lieutenant William B. Royall stated, "from all we can hear, the Indians are a combination of various tribes, principally Camanches and Osages" (Royall 1848:144). On July 8, a detachment under Captain John C. Griffen, scouting the Cimarron River, found a deserted village; Griffen estimated "from the signs . . . there may have been thousands of them." Early the next day they found a Mexican boy who said the party was less than three leagues from the Comanche village—the first indication that they knew who they were tracking. Several hours later they "came in sight of their warriors, about six hundred strong, posted on a well chosen piece of ground." The ensuing battle lasted three hours, with charges and counter charges on both sides; only the canister rounds of the artillery were decisive. Griffen claimed the Indians to have lost "not less than thirty of their best men, and may have lost many more" (Griffen 1848:149); other reports stated that only a few Indians had been killed, and that the village was broken up "without serious fighting" (Barry 1972:764). On July 20, Captain Thomas Jones following on Griffen's trail, found a party of forty-one Indians believed to be Pawnees in a grove of trees. They "refused to make themselves known and began the fight." Jones believed that at least twenty-one were killed (Jones 1848:150).

There is one other report of an encounter between Indians and the battalion: in December, Thomas Fitzpatrick reported, "last summer a party of Comanches, 30 in number, killed and scalped 8 men in front and in the very face of a battalion of 500 mounted men and then marched off" (Fitzpatrick 1847b). Nothing further is known of the incident.

It has since been claimed that the battalion killed 250 Indians, including Comanches, Pawnees, Prairie Apaches, and Osages, along the Canadian, Cimarron, and middle Arkansas rivers (Lavender 1954:328). The sources of that conclusion are unknown; from the counts given by Gilpin's officers, only 79 Indian deaths were claimed, not counting the four Pawnees killed in the melee at Fort Mann in November. Moreover, except for the village attacked by Griffen—if the testimony of the Mexican boy is accepted—the identifications of all the Indian opponents are uncertain.

Gilpin claimed the success of his campaign went beyond the battlefield. His encampment in the midst of the Cheyenne and Arapaho "winter residences" was sufficient to "overawe" those Indians, and they had abandoned all intercourse with the southern tribes [Comanches and Apaches] and invited the Kiowas to withdraw from the Camanche alliance [and to] unite with them (the Arapahoes and Cheyennes) in pacific relations with the Americans. This has accordingly been effected, and the Kiowa Indians, long the scourge of the borders of Mexico, Taos and this road, have since then been, and are now awaiting peace, and residing with the Cheyennes upon the upper Arkansas, near Bent's Fort [Gilpin 1858:137]

All of Gilpin's conclusions are invalid. Still, Gilpin understood that the mere passage of troops through Indian country would have no lasting value, and he recommended the establishment of a series of forts and military posts along the Arkansas, including the purchase of Bent's Fort to be used by the army.

There was little contact between travelers on the Santa Fe road and Indians in the summer of 1848; Fitzpatrick suggested that the lull was due to "the Indians having, in 1846 and 1847, secured so much booty by their daring outrages upon travelers [that they were] . . . luxuriating in and enjoying the spoils" (Fitzpatrick 1848c); that claim, however, is not fully supported by the chronicles of caravans for those years, at least not for 1846 during which there were no attacks, and only minimally for 1847. But despite the relative peace, Fitzpatrick reported that the Santa Fe road was "at the present time . . . in most need of special measures for its protection." Echoing Gilpin, Fitzpatrick proposed that the United States buy Bent's Fort for use as a depot; his reasoning was simple: "by taking care of stock in the winter," the army would

be able to make early campaign against the Comanche and carry war into their own country, at a season of the year when the horses of the enemy are almost unfit for any service, and without the service of the horse (it is well known) the Comanche are by no means formidable, and therefore easily subdued. [Fitzpatrick 1848b]

He also argued, ironically in the face of one possible cause for the 1847 hostilities, that trade "has been the great civilizer of mankind" and so ought to be extended to the Indians (Fitzpatrick 1848b).

In the fall some six hundred lodges of Comanches, Kiowas, Apaches, Cheyennes, and Arapahos were encamped at the Big Timbers, thirty miles below Bent's Fort. Fitzpatrick entertained the assembled multitude with feasts and gifts (Bigelow 1856:359). It is not clear where Fitzpatrick got the authority for such distributions, there having been no congressional appropriation for presents to the Comanches or other southern Plains tribes.

In the euphoric aftermath of his meetings, Fitzpatrick visualized a mammoth peace council to which all the Indians of the Plains would be invited, and where proper boundaries between tribes and boundaries with the United States would be marked out. Fitzpatrick returned to Saint Louis in the spring of 1849 and quickly persuaded Superintendent David D. Mitchell of the potentials of the plan. Mitchell sent him on to Washington, where he received permission for the treaty meeting and a preliminary five thousand dollars for presents (Lavender 1954:318).

Fitzpatrick was so sure that his plan would be approved that before he left he had told the Indians to gather at the Big Timbers in mid-July, when he would have presents for them. But at the appointed time Fitzpatrick was still in Washington. James S. Calhoun, newly appointed Indian agent for New Mexico, passing through Bent's Fort, noted:

> At and near the Arkansas crossing, we found several thousand Indians of various tribes assembled, awaiting the return of Mr. Fitzpatrick from Washington. Their expectations in relation to presents to be received by them on the return of Mr. F. were so extravagent as to cause emigrants and others to have fearful apprehensions. . . . being ignorant of Mr. F.'s authority to enter into stipulations with these Indians, and his means to quiet their expectation, I did not feel at liberty to communicate to them my official capacity. [Abel 1915b:18]

Fitzpatrick finally arrived that fall, but without the authority to conduct negotiations. Although discussions were postponed, he did distribute presents, but again, the basis of his authority to do so is unclear.

Along the Canadian, 1847–53

One of the Indians who had accompanied Butler and Lewis on their 1846 trip to the Comanches was the Seminole called Cooacoochee, also known as Wild Cat. After that treaty he took the opportunity to learn the wealth of the western country, and later that summer, with a party estimated at 250 Seminoles, and carrying a large amount of goods, he went out to trade for furs and mules. The return on their investment was small, and he did not repeat the venture (Foreman 1934:245). That same year a party of Osages had better success, trading "tobacco, lead, powder, blankets, blue cloth, strouding, and fire arms" for 1,500 mules valued at between $50,000 and $75,000. Moreover, two Osages decided to stay with the Comanches, one marrying a Comanche (Richardson 1847). It seems probable that they were the source of the rumors of Osage involvement in the raids along the Arkansas that summer.

There were many rumors flying around the Plains in 1847. A group of Kickapoos told some Comanches that the whites and Osages had formed a coalition against them. At the same time, the Osages reported that the Comanches were in a "much better condition to attack the trains and traders than they were [the previous] summer, and much stronger in numbers having recruited from other tribes." More ominously, they were said to be "exasperated" about the "intention . . . of the goverment in sending troops across the plains," a fact the Osage agent blamed on the "erroneous representations" of Mexican emissaries. The Comanches sent their Osage in-law back to his people to spy out the truth of the rumor. As reported by the Osage agent,

> Had this report reached . . . any other tribe, it is like they would have put confidence in it and have given it full credit and acted accordingly. But they have great confidence in the Osages, being very reluctant to lose the benefits of the trade with them. [Richardson 1847]

Two years later—there was apparently no reference to Comanches along the Canadian River during the interim—in the spring of 1849, Jesse Chisholm, the Cherokee trader, visited the Seminole agency with a party of Comanches headed by the Tenewa Ohawakin—last mentioned as being painted by Stanley at the Butler and Lewis Treaty—who said that the Kickapoos had said that Wild Cat wanted to see him. The actual state of affairs is somewhat unclear, for in turn Wild Cat said that the Kickapoos had told him that the Comanches wanted him to come out to them.

In the formal council that followed, the Seminoles, saying that they had had a war with the Whites but had quit it and now wanted to remain at peace, hoped that the "unfortunate troubles" on the Santa Fe Trail could be halted so that "peace may be made all over the world again." In reply, Ohawakin said he

> was not a great captain, but was a man his people believed would tell the truth, and they had confidence in him. . . . he was not calling himself a greater chief than he was, there were many above him. The people wanted others to go but they were afraid, but he remembered the words of his uncle [Tabequena] who told him to be a peace man with the white and not to be afraid of them. [Duval 1849]

He said the "Southern" Comanches had met in council and had sent him to seek peace from some of the other agents of the Great Father. If they were friendly, he was "authorized to say that all whites going out on prairies would be safe." Furthermore, the "Northern" Comanches had asked whether they should also "come in and be friends with the whites" (Duval 1849). Although there was no immediate result of that meeting, it does suggest that some Comanches were actively looking for positive relations with the eastern peoples.

Gold Rush through Comanchería

News of the California gold strike reached the eastern United States in the fall of 1848. By early 1849 streams of gold-seeking "argonauts" had set out across the plains. Two established routes passed through Comanche country: the Santa Fe Trail on the north and the less frequently used Canadian River route on the south.

Meanwhile, the Texans, still hoping to derive income from the transcontinental trade, planned a new route through El Paso, southern New Mexico, and Arizona. Because it was felt that "the Indians through whose hunting grounds the trains to El Paso had to go should be advised of the movements and intentions" of the surveyors, Robert Neighbors was asked to head an expedition to determine the most practical route (Neighbours 1954). Captain John S. Ford of the Texas Rangers was second in command. It was also hoped that because they often traversed the area on their way to Mexico, the Comanches would furnish guides.

Starting in mid-March from the Torreys' trading house on Tehuacana Creek, and accompanied by most of Potsanaquahip's local band, they headed for Mopechucope's village on Leon Creek. There it was decided that Potsanaquahip would be hired as guide. At Spring Creek, a tributary of the Colorado River, they found the village of Saviah and Sanaco. The latter name is *sanaco* 'gum' or 'sap'; unless he was the man called Potsanasanaco, he is previously unmentioned. John Ford, based on information from Neighbors, reported that Sanaco's father had been killed in the Council House fight and that at one time he had thought he would never make peace with the Texans: "They killed my father, I did all I could to avenge him. I have buried the hatchet" (Ford 1963:119). As will be seen, that was not quite the case.

Problems with the expedition soon developed. Major Collinson Gates, commander at nearby Fort Martin Scott, had told Sanaco—details of Sanaco's visit to that fort are unknown—that settlements would soon follow the new road and that a railroad would soon be built through to Chihuahua. With that news, the Comanches now objected to the road, and Potsanaquahip returned part of his pay, refusing to go farther (Neighbours 1975:74). After three days Neighbors persuaded a captain named Guadalupe, apparently also called Tall Tree, to be the guide. With his assistance the expedition passed relatively uneventfully through to El Paso (Ford 1963:121).

Their route through Texas became known as the California Trail, later called the Butterfield Trail. Although it was a popular route, there are relatively few narratives of travel on it and even fewer reports of contacts with Comanches. William Evans crossed by that route in May 1849, but his only contact with Comanches was to the south, in Chihuahua City, when an Indian

called Santana was attempting to make a partial peace with the city author-
ities; it is not clear whether he was the Comanche Santa Anna of Texas.
Another Santa Anna—again it is not clear which man of that name was
referred to—was later accused of attacking an emigrant party near Santa Rosa
(Neighbors 1849b). In late May, while traveling along the Llano toward the
San Saba, Cornelius C. Cox recorded in his diary:

> Some member of [the Thompson company, five days ahead] has written
> in Pencil mark upon a Tree near the road, a thrilling account of an
> engagement the Company have had with the Comanches—The Indians
> numbered fifteen hundred and fought desparately but lost the battle. It
> being a bad day for fighting the Whites only took about two hundred and
> fifty scalps—this a right hard story, but still it has made some of our
> company very vigilant. [Martin 1925-26:43]

There is no confirmation of that engagement.

Travelers on the central (Canadian River) and northern (Santa Fe Trail)
routes had more contacts with Comanches. In May 1849, after Ohawakin's
visit to the Seminoles of the previous March, travelers on the Canadian route
met a "good many Comanches, with whom they had talked and smoked, and
from whom they had parted in peace." Other immigrant parties on the Canadian route noted Comanches watching from neighboring hills, and there were
rumors that the Comanches and Pawnees had "united for the purpose of plun-
dering" (Bieber 1937:308), but there were few reports of incidents. In one, in
late July, near modern Tulsa, four Germans fell in with a party of Indians,
said to have been Comanches, who appeared friendly. The two groups traveled together for several days. One night, after those Indians had left, the
Germans were attacked by other Indians; one was killed outright, and the
others, wounded, managed to get to Aird's trading post on the Arkansas
River, whose trader, Thomas Aird, confusedly suspected "the Kiowa band of
Comanches" (Foreman 1939:90).[11] In early August Pahayuko brought news
of the fight to Fort Washita. He reported that he and his people had spent the
last six months on the Salt Plains of the Arkansas; while returning southward
they met other Comanches, possibly those with whom the Germans had
traveled, who reported that the wounded Germans had straggled into their
camp. Pahayuko thought the attack was committed by Quapaws; Colonel
Dixon S. Miles, commander at Fort Washita, however, suspected the Comanches (Foreman 1939:90).

At about the same time, Captain Randolph B. Marcy of the Fifth Infantry
and Lieutenant J. H. Simpson of the Topographical Engineers stationed at
Fort Smith were assigned to map the Canadian River route from Fort Smith
to Santa Fe. The impetus for that expedition was as much to help the gold

seekers as it was to establish a central railroad route to the Pacific (Goetzmann 1966:272). A company of emigrants joined them for protection.

Traveling up the Canadian, they saw plenty of Indian signs but had no
encounters until they reached the Cerro Tucumcari in New Mexico. There
they found a Comanche village; Marcy said the camp numbered about three
hundred persons with twenty-five hundred horses (Marcy 1849:188); Simpson
said one hundred lodges and fifteen hundred horses (Simpson 1849). According to Simpson, the chief presented a paper that read:

> Bent's Fort, February 26, 1849
>
> The bearer of this paper is one of a delegation of Comanche chiefs who
> have arrived here to offer the pipe of peace. I have therefore accepted the
> offer and they promise on their part that their nation shall never again
> war on the Americans. It is the opinion of the Indians of this country that
> the Comanche are now serious and it would be well for all white men
> who may meet the bearer of this paper to treat him in a civil manner, so
> long as himself and his nation deserve it. It is well known that the Co-
> manche have been warring on us for a long time, and we have, so far, no
> surety that they will desist, except their own profession. The name of the
> chief is Issakiep or the Wolf's Shoulder.
>   [signed]
>   T. Fitzpatrick
>   Indian Agent, Upper Platte [Simpson 1849:15]

As given in Comanche, the name seems to be *isa kiipu* 'wolf's elbow'; it was
later spelled Esakeep; 'wolf's shoulder' would be *isa kwahipu*. According to
Joe Attocknie (1965), there were two men with similar names living along the
Canadian River about 1850. One, Esakwahip, was a young man killed in
Mexico within a year or two of 1850. The other, Esakeep, was an older man,
chief of a Yamparika local band. Thus, it was probably the village of the
latter man that Marcy visited; indeed, Marcy later (1856:97) called him a
"Northern Comanche." There are, however, no reports of a visit to Bent's
Fort. Moreover, Marcy did not mention the passport.

Marcy did, however, attempt to explain to the Comanches the great
migration:

> The Great Father, the President, having such a multitude of white
> children in the country to the east that there was not room sufficient for
> all of them, had purchased another country far towards the setting sun,
> and that he was now sending, and would continue to send, many of his
> children through their country to occupy the new purchase. He hoped and
> expected the Comanche would not molest these people in their journey
> through their country. [Marcy 1849:188]

He also said that "General Arbuckle (their father at Fort Smith) remembered well the treaty he had made with Tabequena . . . wherein they stipulated that our people should be allowed a free and uninterrupted passage through their country, and he hoped they had not forgotten it." Interestingly, Marcy made no mention of the more recent Butler and Lewis Treaty, perhaps because the arguments for the Texan line raised in that treaty were antithetical to the arguments now being raised for free passage.

According to Marcy, Esakeep replied that he was a "firm friend of the Americans . . . not one of those who took a friend by the hand and let him go whenever it suited his purposes." He liked all that he heard here and at Bent's Fort except two things, that the government would not permit any more war parties to go to Mexico, and that he should give up his Mexican prisoners. "These two things . . . gave him much pain" (Marcy 1849:189).

That is the only time Marcy mentioned having met Esakeep. Therefore, it must have been at that time that Esakeep told Marcy that his four sons were a "great source of comfort to him in his old age, and could steal more horses than any young men in his band" (Marcy 1866:23). Marcy retold that story several times in his later books.

The Marcy-Simpson expedition reached Santa Fe without further encounters with Comanches. In October they returned from New Mexico by way of El Paso and the Llano Estacado. One foolhardy lieutenant was killed by Kiowas, but they met no Comanches until they reached the Clear Fork of the Brazos River. There they found Sanaco's village, which in the spring had been on the San Saba. Sanaco showed testimonials of good faith from many Texans, including one from Robert Neighbors saying, "he is Principal War Chief of the southern Comanche and appears to be sincere in his profession of friendship for us" (Foreman 1939:379). It is not known when he received those credentials.

In early May 1850 Esakeep, now said to have some fifteen hundred people, met the Black River California Company along the Canadian River twenty days out from Little River (Bieber 1937:302). The chief must have again presented Fitzpatrick's passport, for he was again described as "Issakeep or Wolf Shoulder." The village was prosperous; as described by the journalist of the party:

> The women pitched and struck the lodges, saddled and unsaddled the horses, gathered wood or fuel, and performed the drudgery of the camp; they wore their hair short and were very plain in their dress. . . . The men were the reverse, all painted, some of a single color, some with many colors, with queues six or seven feet long braided with great nicety, and wreathed with beaded or silver ornaments which tapered to about the size of a dime or half dime. Many of the exquisites carried umbrellas to pro-

tect them from the sun, and nearly all the young men had new and brilliant blankets of blue or red cloth. They were excellently mounted and had with them probably five thousand horses. [Bieber 1937:305]

Another emigrant party, the Knickerbocker Company, came upon a Comanche encampment of

> some 800 old men, women and children. The war and hunting party being off. They had about 1500 horses and mules, a few of which we bought. But while we were giving the chiefs a dinner, and making them presents at the expense of the company, an order came from a detachment of U.S. Dragoons, encamped near here, forbidding each mutually from trading. . . . We subsequently learned that a treaty was in progress between them and the United States, and that officer was escorting the Chiefs to Santa Fe for this purpose. [quoted in Foreman 1939:254]

The identities of those Comanches and their escort are unknown, and there is no report from New Mexico of such a meeting. The Comanches may have been Esakeep's people, or at least Yamparikas: in February 1849 Pahayuko told Robert Neighbors that he had met with a New Mexican official who invited the Comanches to visit a "post in that country . . . [and] the Yamparikas have gone" (Neighbors 1849a). There are, however, no records from New Mexico covering that period.

In the fall of 1851 Marcy reported, on word from Creeks, that Comanches had attended a council with them; two years later, in the spring of 1853,[12] about two hundred lodges of Comanches were reported to be in the Wichita Mountains. After exchanging messages with the Creeks, in July, together with other "Prairie Indians," they sent delegates to a "Grand Council" on the Salt Plains (Foreman 1934:203–4). The identity of those Comanches is unknown, but their location in the Wichita Mountains, as well as their relations with the eastern tribes, suggests that they were Tenewas.

More Comanche Raids South of the Rio Grande, 1849–53

Although the itinerary of Comanche raids in Northern Mexico can be traced through the newspaper and government dispatches (R. A. Smith 1959; Vizcaya-Canales 1968), relatively little is known about the Comanches involved. That is not the case with a series of interactions between Mexicans and Comanches in the years 1850–53.

Sometime in 1849 or 1850, officials in Chihuahua and other northern states encountered a group of Comanches headed by a woman named Tave Peté—according to the German traveler Julius Froebel, she was the Comanches "generaless and prophetess" (Froebel 1859:22)—and her sons or grandsons, Tave Tuk and Mawve or Magüe, who quickly established a series of varied relationships with the states of northern Mexico.

According to Mexican newspapers, her name in Spanish was Arriba el Sol; R. A. Smith (1970:26) gave it as Above the Sun. It was probably, as in the Spanish, *tabe* 'sun', *pitu* 'to arrive'. The name Tave Tuk was given by Froebel (1859:381) as Bajo el Sol, literally 'under the sun' but figuratively 'sundown' or 'sunset'; R. A. Smith said it was "there was no one like to him under the sun" (1970:26). After *tabe*, the second element was probably *tuhka* 'under'. Smith (1970:26) translated the second son or grandson's name as Valiant; it is probably *mo?o* 'hand'. Indeed, M. T. W. Chandler, on Emory's exploring expedition, who encountered him in 1852, called him Mano 'hand' (Emory 1857:81).

In interviews with Mexican officials they gave several reasons for being in Mexico: they came to avenge the death of a "son of the general" killed in 1849, to make a treaty with the Hacienda de la Zarca, and because the Texans had "declared war, . . . thrown them out and pursued them with great numbers" (R. A. Smith 1970:40). But above all they were there to make a living, and they were very creative about how they did it.

They had several armed clashes with the Mexican army. In February 1850 a large Comanche party attacked the Hacienda del Carmen, 110 miles northwest of Chihuahua City. After a six-hour fight a truce was called. Tabe Tuk, Estrella (possibly the Estrellas from Mexican Texas), and Miramontes went to talk. When the truce was broken and the Mexicans fired, both Estrella and Miramontes were killed. But that unfortunate occurrence did not sour the Comanches on relations with the Mexicans. In July they were back in northern Chihuahua, where Tabe Tuk warned a military judge at San Carlos that they made war on Chihuahua "because we [the Mexicans] do not celebrate peace with them, and because they must destroy us to save their race." By August the Comanches were raiding in southern Chihuahua; by September they were in Durango (R. A. Smith 1970:40). In response, a "war of extermination against the savages" was proclaimed by the Mexican government, and federal officers were charged with "strict responsibility to grant no peace and to wage vigorous war" (R. A. Smith 1970:36), but that order did little to mobilize either the national or state forces or to deter the Comanches.

However, the various scalp laws were still in effect. In 1849 both Durango and Chihuahua authorized paying 200 pesos per scalp, represented by hair, head, or ears. Several groups of Mexicans, both regular army and "irregular" scalp hunters, took to the field against the various groups of Indians. Included among those irregulars were Americans James Kirker and James Box, Seminoles under Wild Cat and John Horse, and Kickapoos under Papiquan. In 1851 another old tradition was reestablished: Emilio Lamberg, sub-inspector of the Military Colonies of Chihuahua, suggested that although Comanches and Kiowas were raiding in Chihuahua, Apaches had already devastated a much larger part of the state. It would therefore be a "lesser evil" to use the Comanches against the Apaches (R. A. Smith 1970:45). On April 15 the old woman Tabe Peté, Tabe Tuk, Magüe, and one other, unnamed, arrived at Chihuahua City. After proper protocols and gifts they agreed to "stop raiding and start delivering Apache scalps" (R. A. Smith 1970:47). But they would do it later; meanwhile, assured that Chihuahua would not attack from the rear, the Comanches raided into Durango and Coahuila, with side trips into Sonora and Sinaloa.

Mucho Toro 'many bulls', described as "evidently an escaped Mexican peon" (Emory 1857:86), and Magüe took the booty north across the Rio Grande, to pass along to various traders, including Benjamin Leaton at El Paso, the Barnard and Torrey posts in Texas, the Chouteau and Warren posts in Indian Territory, and the Bents' posts on the Arkansas and Canadian rivers (R. A. Smith 1970:33). At Comanche Spring in southwest Texas, Major William H. Emory met Mucho Toro with thirty or forty men driving a thousand horses that he claimed had been "purchased" in Mexico (Emory 1857: 87). While at El Paso Emory also received "authentic reports of the unmolested march through Chihuahua of 400 Comanches under Bajo el Sol" (Emory 1857:86).

Although the Comanches had delivered no Apache scalps in 1851, the new governor of Chihuahua, José Cordero, felt that the scalp laws were the "cheapest, most effective, and surest way of getting rid of Indians," and he renewed the contract. He also admitted that his real goal was to see Apaches and Comanches at war with each other so that the "two tribes might devour each other before devouring us" (R. A. Smith 1970:51). He gave "military coats with the Governor's seal on the collar" to both Tabe Tuk and Magüe and special presents to Tabe Peté (R. A. Smith 1970:50). This time, instead of raiding, the Comanches went after the Apaches. By May 1852 they had been paid at least 18,000 pesos for scalps and other trophies of Apaches (R. A. Smith 1970:51).

While Comanches were selling scalps in Chihuahua, they were also raiding in other states. The year 1852 marked the all-time high in Mexican raids, and no month passed without a report of actions (R. A. Smith 1970:62, n. 61). In February two large parties crossed the Rio Grande, one at Las Jitas, below the Conchos River, traversing the western Bolson de Mapimi to

Durango; the other crossed slightly downstream at El Vado de Chisos, just above the Big Bend, passing to Laguna de Jaco and approaching Durango from the northeast. There they broke up into smaller parties. In March Americans at Bellville on the Rio Grande reported, "Indians have been at the Capitania Ranch three miles above this place, three times this month." In April a party of fifty Comanches stayed in the vicinity for about two hours and gave a Lieutenant Tyler a "fight." A rescued captive recognized them as the party that had attacked the Capitania Ranch a few weeks before (Winfrey and Day 1959–66, 3:158). By May and June Comanches reached Tepic in Jalisco before they turned back. It was on that raid, or one similar, that Comanches saw the *kwasi taivo* 'men with tails'—monkeys—living in the trees (ten Kate 1885a:123).

On July 14 Tabe Tuk was intercepted in southern Durango by a troop of Mexican cavalry. The Comanches were driven back with some loss. The next morning they counterattacked but were repulsed. During a truce the Comanches said they were expecting the arrival of reinforcements, and they were allowed to escape (R. A. Smith 1970:53). After Tabe Tuk was killed in an attack on an Apache ranchería, Magüe took over active leadership of the group (Froebel 1859:351).

The Comanches had several encounters with the Mexican forces in 1853. On October 17 Paquemacote (possibly *pekwi* 'fish', *makotse* 'to wash with the hands') was killed in the Sierra de Gamon. On November 20 a camp at the Mesa de las Godornices was hit, with a loss of ten, including Kiowa allies. On December 7 Comanches defeated the First Squadron of San Luis Potosi at Arenal, in Durango. Later that month four other Comanche leaders were killed in a fight with the Mexican army—Cohiste (given by Smith as Stomach Ache; *kohi* 'intestine, belly area'), Ojatevichi (given as Braggart but probably *oha* 'yellow', *tubitsi* 'real'), Tosachique (given as Blond, possibly including *tosa* 'white'), and his brother Tane (given as Pox Marked). The fatal blow came at dawn of February 13, 1854, at the spring of Espiritu Santu in southern Chihuahua, when more than one hundred Comanches were reported killed, including Tabe Peté and Magüe (R. A. Smith 1970:60).

Texas, 1848–51

Smallpox had hit the Texas Comanche camps in 1848. More serious was the cholera that came soon after the Neighbors-Ford El Paso expedition passed through their villages. It was said that Santa Anna and Mopechucope, along with "about 300 of their people who had camped on the Brazos near the Caddo village" had died (L. H. Williams 1849); Mopechucope must have died soon after Neighbors and Ford visited his camp on their way to El Paso. Foreman (1939:162 n. 19) reported that Santa Anna died of cholera in January 1849; however, Neighbors made several other references to the chief later that year, suggesting that he was still alive in June. Luckily, Pahayuko had spent the first part of the year on the Salt Plains of the Arkansas River (Foreman 1939:90), thus escaping the disease.

The full toll of the epidemics is not known. The only pre-epidemic count is Butler and Lewis's 1846 estimate for the Hois as having 2,800 people; although it was probably based on estimates by Robert Neighbors, given the other uncertainties in their report, it is unreliable. The number of Penatekas left after the epidemic is somewhat clearer. In 1851 Jesse Stem, agent for the Comanches, reported:

> of the number of the Comanches, it is difficult if not impossible, to get any accurate knowledge. The southern bands, who are the only Comanches that remain in Texas continuously, are not numerous. . . their chiefs are Catumsie [Ketumsee], Buffalo Hump, and Yellow Wolf. . . . Catumsie estimated the number . . . at about 600, including Lipans. The Northern Comanches come into Texas only in the winters, . . . from the best information I could get . . . Pahahyuko's band consists of about 200 lodges and 1000 persons, and Shanico's [Sanaco's] of about 200 persons. I could learn nothing [from the intrepreters John Conner, Jim Shaw, and Bill Shaw] . . . of any other prominent chief or band of the northern Comanches. [Stem 1851]

A somewhat more accurate, if still crude method was used by Lt. Colonel William J. Hardee in 1852:

> the chiefs have been induced to bring in bundles of sticks to make the number of men, women, and children in their respective tribes . . . the lower [bands] represented by Buffalo Hump, Yellow Wolf, and Ketumsee, number 700 souls or 140 warriors, the upper [bands] represented by Pahayuko and Ichonako [Sanaco], number 1500 souls or 300 warriors. [Hardee 1852]

Stem's and Hardee's numbers were close: Stem gave 600 for Ketumsee, Buffalo Hump, and Yellow Wolf; a year later, Hardee gave 700. Stem gave 1,200 for Pahayuko—although Pahayuko may have been Tenewa—and Sanaco; Hardee, although admitting that his numbers were based on hearsay, gave 1,500. The combined total for the Texas Comanches was between 1,800 (Stem) and 2,200 (Hardee).

In the fall of 1849, the Penatekas met in general council on the Brazos River to elect a new principal chief. One report said Sanaco was elected (L. H. Williams 1849), another said that Potsanaquahip and Ketumsee had come to Fredericksburg to report that "the election resulted in the choice of Buffalo-hump [Potsanaquahip]" (Steele 1849). However, as late as 1852, neither had the support from either the Comanches or from the Americans to consolidate his authority. This is not to say they did not try. In 1852, Special Agent Horace Capron reported:

> There is evidently a great want of proper governmental organization amongst these bands of Comanches. Although originally from the same tribe (the Honey Eaters) they are now divided into small parties under different leaders. Each one considering himself entitled to equal respect and requiring a separate audience. They are convinced however of the necessity of having one responsible chief and each one is aspiring to the dignity. . . . The most prominent amongst them are Ketumsee, Shanaco, Yellow Wolf, Buffalo Hump and Kearivo [previously unnamed], each urging his claim with a becoming modesty and expressing a willingness to submit to an election, yet all are evidently afraid to bring the matter to the test. I was solicited to point out one from amongst the number, the one in my opinion best qualified to fill the office, but I declined the honor doubting the sincerity of their promise to abide by the decision. And further, were I to select one I might not take either, but rather a compromise candidate in Tosawa, a war chief of great influence and daily becoming more popular. [Capron 1852]

In the late 1840s Texas began building a line of forts to protect its settlements; after annexation the forts were transferred to the U.S. Army. Almost immediately they had Comanche visitors. Several incidents were reported years later by Richard I. Dodge, but his military career in the West, and particularly his experiences with Comanches, are difficult to evaluate. Of the former, practically the only details he gave are in the comment "in 1849, I commenced my 'Plains Life' at Fort Lincoln, Texas" (Dodge 1883:566). Of the latter, most of the information he gave is in the form of anecdotes.

In one incident, some Comanches demonstrated that they had found a new way to make a living:

> A band of Indians under Mulaquetop [last heard from as a signer of the Butler and Lewis Treaty] once camped near Fort Chadbourne in Texas and were frequent visitors and great nuisances as beggars at that post. Some of the officers were decidedly "horsey," several owning blooded horses, the relative speed of each being known, by repeated trials, almost to a foot. Mulaquetop was bantering for a race, and after several days of manoeuvering, a race was made against the third best horse of the garrison, distance four hundred yards. The Indians betted [sic] robes and plunder of various kinds, to the value of sixty or seventy dollars against money, sugar, etc., to a like amount. At the appointed time, all the

Indians and most of the garrison were assembled at the track. The
Indians "showed" a miserable sheep of a pony, with legs like churns; a
three inch coat of rough hair stuck out all over the body and a general
expression of neglect, helplessness and patient suffering struck pity into
the hearts of all beholders. The rider was a stalwart buck of one hundred
seventy pounds, looking big and strong enough to carry the poor beast on
his shoulders. He was armed with a huge club, with which after the word
was given, he belabored the miserable animal from start to finish. To the
astonishment of all the whites, the Indian won by a neck.

Another race was proposed by the officers, and after much dicker-
ing, accepted by the Indians, against the next best horse of the garrison.
The bets were doubled; and in less than an hour the second race was run
by the same pony, with the same apparent exertion and with exactly the
same result.

The officers, thoroughly disgusted, proposed a third race, and
brought to the ground a magnificent Kentucky mare, of the true Lexing-
ton blood, and known to beat the best of the others at least forty yards in
four hundred. The Indians accepted the race, and not only doubled bets
as before, but piled up everything they could raise, seemingly almost
crazed with the excitement of their previous success. The riders mounted;
the word was given. Throwing away his club, the Indian rider gave a
whoop, at which the sheep-like pony pricked up his ears and went away
like the wind, almost two feet to the mare's one. The last fifty yards of
the course was run by the pony with the rider sitting face to his tail, making hideous grimaces and beckoning the rider of the mare to come on.

It afterwards transpired that the old sheep was a trick and straight
race pony, celebrated among all the tribes of the south, and that
Mulaquetop had only just returned from a visit to the Kickapoos in the
Indian nation, whom he had easily cleaned out of six hundred ponies.
[Dodge 1883:341]

Those classic hustles did not always work; on another occasion, Dodge
reported:

A party of Comanches came into a military fort where I was stationed
and after knocking down sticks holding money, and performing various
feats with their bows, challenged any white man to shoot against them.
The challenge was accepted by a young officer, who though he had had
no experience with bows and arrows since boyhood, easily beat them out
of all they cared to lose, and sent them away thoroughly disgusted.
[Dodge 1883:419]

Not all of his encounters were so friendly. According to Dodge, soon
after its construction in 1849, Fort Lincoln's horse corral, made of "thorny

chaparral brush, tightly pressed between upright posts . . . impassible for whiteman or horse," was breached by the Indians (Dodge 1883:544). In May 1850 Captain John S. Ford's company of Texas Rangers met a party of seventy-five Comanches at Amargosa near the Comanche Crossing. On the twenty-ninth they attacked another, killing its chief (Ford gave his name as Otto Cuero; previously unmentioned, its meaning is unknown) and capturing a young man named Carne Muerte ('dead meat'), said to be the son, or brother, of Santa Anna. He was sent first to Fort Mackintosh and later to San Antonio (Ford 1963:161; Brooke 1850); his ultimate fate is unknown.

In 1849, in the change of officers following the national elections, Robert Neighbors was replaced as Texas agent by J. H. Rollins. Rollins had been present at the Butler and Lewis Treaty council, but what further experience he may have had with the Comanches is unknown. He was more frank in recognizing his lack of knowledge about the Comanches than were many others who had dealt with them. In May 1850 he noted:

> When I speak of the Comanche, I mean the Southern Comanche. I have no knowledge of the Northern Comanche, they have never attended any treaty with the U.S. in Texas. One chief Pahayuko, occupies a kind of middle ground being sometimes in the north and sometimes in the south. He is presently in the Salt Plains hunting buffalo. [Rollins 1850a]

Rollins's ill health, together with the fact that Congress had provided no money for presents, forced a radically different approach to Indian affairs; he apparently felt it was better to leave the Indians alone than to disappoint them (R. N. Richardson 1933:161). Thus, for almost a year there was no official contact with the Texas Comanches.

In September 1850 Rollins finally went traveling. On the Clear Fork of the Brazos River he met with Ketumsee, Saviah, Potsanaquahip, and Sanaco. In a "hard talk" he said that he came "not to make accusation or to adjust difficulties, but to advise them of their true position and interest, and to invite them *once more* and for the *last time* to meet me in council" (Rollins 1850b, emphasis in original). Potsanaquahip admitted that there were violations of the treaty on both sides, but he laid the primary blame on others. They agreed to meet again in December on the San Saba River, where a new agreement was signed by Potsanaquahip and nine other Comanches, as well as by representatives of other Texas Indians (table 6.3) (Winfrey and Day 1959-66, 3: 130-36).

For the most part, the Rollins agreement was simply a restatement of the 1846 Butler and Lewis Treaty. In one respect, however, it went beyond the earlier document: the Indians agreed

Table 6.3

Comanche Signers of the Rollins Agreement, 1850

NAME	GIVEN AS	MODERN RETRANSCRIPTION
Po-cha-na-quar-hip	Buffalo Hump	
Sa-va-ah	Small Wolf	
Ka-tumpsa		
Toshwa[a]	White	*tosa* 'white' *wi* 'knife'
Car-a-wah	Never Stops	probably *ke* negative suffix *karu* 'sit' *wah* 'without'
Ceacheneca	Feather	*si²a* 'feather' *tsinika* 'to stick into'
Guadalupe		
Weit-che-ki	Humming Bird	*wu²ku buu* 'humming bird'; possibly *wesikitu* 'curly'
Ka-ba-ha-mo[b]	Never Smokes	*ke pahmu* 'no tobacco'
Quahano		
Pe-ah-tie-quosh	Rifle Breech	*pia² eetɇ kwasi* 'rifle's tail'
Mo-he-ka	Pole Cat	

[a] It is usually spelled Tosawa and translated as either White Knife or Silver Broach.

[b] Possibly the Pahmoowata 'no tobacco' who signed the Butler–Lewis Treaty.

SOURCE: Winfrey and Day 1959–66, 3:135–36

> not to go below the present line of Military Posts on the east side of the Colorado River, or below the Llano River, and a line running West from its headwaters on the West side of said Colorado, without express permission from the Indian Agent or some Officer Commanding a Military Post in Texas, in writing; and they will give immediate notice to the nearest Military Post should other Indians attempt to do so. [Winfrey and Day 1959–66, 3:134]

Thus, one-half of the line problem was formalized.

The agreement also tried to deal with the other half of the problem: "The United States shall, within the year 1851 . . . treat with said Indians as to a definite line between them and the white, so that the Indian country may be known and respected." But the Rollins agreement was never submitted to the Senate, and the line provisions were ignored. Thus, the agreement did nothing to stop the conflicts between Texans and Comanches. A newspaper debate about the extent of Comanche raids soon developed. Some newspapers reported numerous raids, but others claimed that the reports were exaggerations.

In late 1851 Rollins died and was replaced by his assistant, John Rogers. In October Rogers met with the "head men and warriors of the southern Comanche, Lipan and Mescalero Apaches" on the San Saba River (Winfrey and Day 1959-66, 3:143). He reiterated that the United States and Mexico were at peace and that the Indians "must not cross the Rio Grande for the purpose of robing and steeling" [sic] and reminded them that under the Treaty of Guadalupe Hidalgo the Indians were to give up all Mexicans who were held captive. Furthermore, he argued that they "must go to work, the Buffalo is gone the deer there is not any" (Winfrey and Day 1959-66, 3:144).

Ketumsee, now called the "principle chief of the Comanche of the South"—although his claim to the position is unclear—after apologizing for not having "some one to speak and reply for him," brought up the matter of the line. He said:

> [My people] have wandered about for seven years and [have been] driven from their homes where their parents are buried and where they raised corn and [are] still driven back by the white man and have no home or resting place. We do not wish to . . . take another person's land as the white men have done. We want land and homes of our own to raise corn and other things for our women and children we know how to do it. The great Chief of the United States of America is all powerful and can do anything he may wish. If he will set apart a section or piece of country to settle on and cultivate that we can call our own and place us under the protection of the laws of the United States and the great chief and appoint some person to assist and instruct us . . . we will go to work and feel happy. [Winfrey and Day 1959-66, 3:145]

Except for the statement of Pahayuko, given by Potsanaquahip at the 1844 treaty council, that is the earliest notice of possible Comanche interest in agriculture.

On October 28, 1851, the assembled Indians signed the so-called Rogers agreement (Winfrey and Day 1959-66, 149-54). Although it made provision for neither land nor line, it did acknowledge both the Butler and Lewis Treaty and the Treaty of Guadalupe Hidalgo. The Comanche signers were Ketumsee, Tosawa, Carawa, Ceachinika, and Peahtiequash—all of whom had signed the Rollins agreement of the year before—the previously unmentioned Jack the Cripple, Mowery (given as End of the Track) and Pemon Soco (given as Old Wild Bull, *pemoróó* 'cattle', *tsuku* 'old'). As with the Rollins agreement, the Rogers agreement was not submitted to the Senate but was considered an extension of the Butler and Lewis Treaty.

New Mexico, 1849–52

In July 1849 James S. Calhoun arrived in Santa Fe to take up his duties as Indian agent. One of his first assignments was the collection of "statistical and other information as will give every particular" relating to his charges (Abel 1915b:3). Calhoun viewed the Indians of New Mexico as two groups, the peaceful Pueblos and the "wandering tribes, who have never cultivated the soil and have supported themselves alone by depredations" (Abel 1915b:18). Of the latter, he could offer no clear solution to their raiding; on the one hand, "the thought of annihilating these Indians can not be entertained by an American public," but neither could

> the Indians abandon their predatory incursions and live and learn to support themselves by the sweat of their own brows by liberal philanthropy. This subject I humbly conceive, should engage the earnest and early consideration of the Congress . . . for it is respectfully submitted that no earthly power can prevent robberies and murders unless the hungry wants of these people are provided for, both physically and mentally. [Abel 1915b:19]

Later he would say,

> The wild Indians of this country have been so much more successful in their robberies since Genl Kearny took possession of the country, they do not believe we have the power to chastise them. Is it not time to enlighten them on the subject and to put an end to their ceaseless depredations[?] [Abel 1915b:32]

At the very least, he argued, the Comanches and others should be "located and confined within fixed limits and compelled to remain there" (Abel 1915b: 178). For the moment, however, neither alternative would be attempted.

Calhoun was especially concerned about regulating trade with the "wandering" Indians. He noted that the "constant and unrestrained intercourse of traders with the Indians of this territory is perhaps the greatest curse upon it." Since the Congress had as yet not formalized the relations between New Mexico and the Union, there was no statutory authority for Indian agents to regulate "Indian Trade and Intercourse." Thus, at Calhoun's suggestion, military governor John Munroe gave him authority to issue licenses and Calhoun published the following notice:

> Licenses to trade with Indians, will be granted . . . upon the following conditions. . . . Applicants must be citizens of the United States, provide satisfactory testimonials of good character and give bond on a penal sum

not exceeding five thousand dollars, with one or more sureties, that he will faithfully observe all the laws and regulations made for the government of trade and intercourse with the Indian tribes of the United States and in no respect violate the same, and they will not trade in firearms, powder, lead or other munitions of war. Applicants will distinctly state what tribe they wish to trade with and under a license granted, they will not be authorized to trade with others. . . . For the present no license will be granted authorizing trade or intercourse with the Apaches, Navajos or Utes. [Abel 1915b:105]

A fee of ten dollars would be charged for each permit, although there would be no charge for the licenses issued to the Pueblos to trade with the Comanches—a practice, Calhoun noted, that "ought to be gently and quietly stopped."

Although Calhoun reported to have received a large number of applications to trade with the Kiowas and Comanches (Abel 1915b:104), by June he had issued only thirteen licenses (table 6.4). Meanwhile, the local military commanders were ordered to:

Keep a strict watch on all trading parties. If any are found without licenses you can use your discretion as to retaining them in confinement keeping their Goods or merely turning them back with orders not to proceed. In both cases you will report the facts to these Headquarters. If persons or parties even with licenses to trade should be found to have contraband articles for traffic in their possession such as arms or ammunition of any kind or liquors of any sort you will arrest and confine the parties and seize and hold their goods until the decision of the Col Comdg upon each case is known. [Abel 1915b:107–8]

Calhoun was particularly concerned with ending the trade in captives. That was not easy, as the trade was lucrative; Calhoun reported Apache prices for captives depended "upon age, sex, beauty, and usefulness. Good looking females, not having passed the 'sear and yellow leaf' are valued from 50 to 150 dollars each. Males, as they may be useful, one half less, never more" (Abel 1915b:162). But Calhoun was authorized to spend a total of only $300 for "the release of such Mexican captives as may be found among the Indians and for which demands may be made on the Government of the United States" (Abel 1915b:4).

In March 1850 Calhoun reimbursed a number of New Mexicans for captives they had recently ransomed from the Comanches (table 6.5); their history offers an interesting glimpse of the captive trade. Three were taken from places deep in Mexico; Santiago Papasquiaro, Durango is some 700 miles south of El Paso, and is deep in the Sierra Madre Occidental; Monclova

Table 6.4

Licenses Issued from New Mexico for Trade with the Comanches

TO WHOM ISSUED	WHEN GIVEN	DURATION
Jesus Derara	Nov. 23, 1849	3 months
Anto. Leroux	Dec. 29, 1849	May 1, 1850
Jas. V. Smith	Jan. 6, 1850	Ap. 8, 1850
Appel H. Birboan	Jan. 11, 1850	3 months
Wm. H. Moore	Jan. 31, 1850	Ap. 8, 1850
Miguel Griego of Taos	June 3, 1850	Aug. 20, 1850
Juan Antonio of Jemez	June 3, 1850	July 15, 1850
Carlos Vigil, Gov. of Tesuque	June 5, 1850	July 25, 1850
Juan Vaxara of Sandia	Oct. 25, 1849	2 months
Lorenzo Aquilo of Santo Domingo	Jan. 6, 1850	No time limit
Jose Quintana of Cochiti	Jan. 12, 1850	2 months
Jose Suazo of Tesuque	Feb. 13, 1850	May 1, 1850
Carlos Vigil, Gov. of Tesuque	May 19, 1850	No time limit

SOURCE: McLaws 1850b

Table 6.5

James Calhoun's List of Ransomed Mexican Captives

Refugio Picaros, age 12, taken from the rancho called Papascal, near Santiago [probably Santiago Papasquiaro], Durango, by Comanches, sold to Apaches; bought by José Francisco Lucero of Moro for 4 knives, 1 plug of tobacco, 2 fanegas corn, 4 blankets, 6 yards red Indian cloth.

Theodoro Martel, age 10 or 12, taken from service of Jose Alvardo, at La Pops near Saltillo, by Apaches; bought by Powler Sandoval of Moro for 1 mare, 1 rifle, 1 shirt, pair drawers, 30 small packages of powder, some bullets, and a buffalo robe.

Caudalaus Galope, age 12, Apaches, taken near rancho Fernandez near Santa Cruz, state unknown, bought by Vincent Romero of Moro, for corn, tobacco, knife, shirt, mule, small package powder, and balls.

Rosalie Taveres, age 25, taken from Monclova by Apaches and Comanches; her husband and daughter killed; bought by Powler Sandoval for 2 striped blankets, 10 yards blue cotton drilling, 10 yards calico, 10 yards shirting, 2 handkerchiefs, 4 plugs tobacco, 1 bag corn, 1 knife.

SOURCE: Abel 1915b:183

and Saltillo in Nuevo Leon are fairly close to Nuevo Laredo and the Rio Grande, but both are still some thousand miles from Moro, New Mexico, where they were ransomed. By the time of their ransoming, several had already been traded at least once between Apaches and Comanches. The prices paid were relatively small, the most valuable item was possibly the rifle given for Teodoro Martel. Although three of the four were ransomed by residents of Moro, near Las Vegas, New Mexico, it is not known if their motives were humantarian or economic.

It was intended that redeemed captives would be turned over to Mexican agents. However, Calhoun was "without specific instruction in relation to the proposed disposition of captives, nor . . . advised of the appointment of an Agent by Mexico," as was promised in the treaty (Abel 1915b:183). In July 1851 Calhoun redeemed five more captives; by that time, the arrangements for repatriation had been worked out, and they were sent to El Paso and delivered to a Mexican agent (Abel 1915b:390).

Calhoun's direct contacts with Comanches were limited, and his first— albeit indirect—contact is puzzling. In early June 1850 a "package of papers were found attached to the top of a pole that had been planted on a mound in the prairies, near or within the borders of the Comanche country." The package included:

1) A letter from President Houston, dated May 4, 1843 to Pahayuko inviting the Comanche to visit Bent's Fort [probably Bird's Fort, i.e., Fort Worth] for the purpose of making peace.
2) A treaty of peace signed by J.C. Eldide [Eldredge] and Pahayuko dated "Comanche encampment Aug. 9, 1843."
3) A letter from President [Anson] Jones of Texas to Pahayuko inviting the Comanche chiefs to meet his chiefs at the Council grounds at Tahuacano Creek—dated July 14, 1845.
4) A "Talk sent to Pahauko, Head chief of the Comanche nation by P. M. Butler, US Commissioner 11th Decr. 1843."
5) A ratified treaty in print "concluded at Council Springs, in the country of Robinson, Texas, near the Brazos river, this 15th day of May, A. D. 1846, P. M. Butler and M.G. Lewis, Commissioners" &c &c. and the chiefs and others of the Comanche and other tribes of Indians.

In reporting the package to Commissioner Orlando Brown, Calhoun suggested that

The manner in which these papers have been disposed of by the Indians is significant of dissatisfaction if not mischief. The Comanche and other Indians are to hold a council at the full moon of this month somewhere

near the Rio Colorado, at a place known as Sutton's Fort, 12 days travel
from Santa Fe. I have procurred an old Indian trader and the governor of
Tesuque to be there on that occasion. [Abel 1915b:211]

The purpose of the papers is unknown. All except the copy of the Butler and
Lewis Treaty were addressed to Pahayuko, whose normal range was several
hundred miles from New Mexico, and all were at least four years old. They
may have been messages for Pahayuko, or, conversely, they may have been
placed there as symbols of Pahayuko's formal acceptance of peaceful relations. Unfortunately, no further description was given of their "disposition"
nor further explanation of how it might have signified dissatisfaction on the
part of the Comanches. "Sutton's Fort" is otherwise unidentified; it was possibly the Bents' old Canadian River post.

Although there is no record of meetings with the governor of Tesuque—
apparently Carlos Vigil—later that month, Calhoun wrote that "a large body
of Comanche who are represented as being friendly are now collected on the
Pecos at the Bosque Redondo" (Abel 1915b:108); a week later it was reported that "the Captains of the Comanche tribes," Yraquipa (probably Esakeep)
and Quisaqueca (previously unmentioned) had joined with the Jicarillas and
the Mescaleros "for the purpose of making a treaty" (Abel 1915b:212). A
large amount of goods was bought and distributed to the assembled tribes, but
there is no official record of a treaty.

Some weeks later twenty Comanches were reported at Santo Domingo,
hoping to recruit a party to go against the Navajos. In contrast to the Spanish
and Mexican policy of remaining neutral or actively encouraging such affairs,
the Americans felt it was necessary to have "sufficient troops to defeat any
combination between the pueblo and Comanches, or to put down any war
between tribes which would seriously injure this territory" (Abel 1915b:215).
But again there was no direct contact.

The next year a delegation of Comanches, consisting of Eagle Feathers
("the principal chief,"), five other men, five women, and a child, came to
Santa Fe (Abel 1915b:343). That chief is previously unmentioned under that
name, although the name Quisaqueca of the year before may be a mutilation
of kwina si?a 'eagle feather'. They had a long talk with Calhoun, now the
governor, during which "professions of friendship were made by both sides,
and various propositions were made in regard to preserving peaceable relations . . . and on other matters connected with their own welfare" (Abel
1915b:345).

The Comanches were put up for the night; around midnight some "evil-
disposed person" called on the chief and said that they would be killed if they
stayed. The party left in great haste, leaving all of their possessions behind,

including a Mexican captive. Scouts finally caught up with them and tried to explain that as long as they were visiting with the governor, they had a safe passage and no one would harm them; they could pick up their belongings at San Miguel. In their flight they had killed some cattle at Anton Chico; Eagle Feathers did it because he "had not forgotten nor forgiven the loss of his captive." It is not known whether he returned for any of his goods.

In early July Calhoun reported a rumor that a party of 300 Comanches en route to the Navajo country were in the Pecos Valley, where "they wantonly committed depredations by killing stock for which they had no use and driving off others" (Abel 1915b:379). At about the same time former governor Munroe, resuming his army rank of colonel, reported a rumor that a large body of Comanches were raiding near Cuesta. When Munroe sent a company of dragoons to investigate, they found nothing amiss and even talked to several Comanche chiefs "who all professed peace and seem peaceable." On July 29 the Comanches crossed the river, passing Cebolleta; although they promised to pay a return call on that post, because of scarcity of water and grass they returned by way of Albuquerque (Abel 1915b:347).

Although it was reported that "the Comanche continue to send us friendly greetings" (Abel 1915b:260), no further contact was detailed until the next year. The reasons for the Comanches' absence are unknown. There are no direct reports of disease in the New Mexico Comanche camps, but there were in other areas, which may have kept them away. In April 1852 it was reported that they were gathering on the Arkansas River to trade and hunt buffalo "as is their usual practice in the spring" (Abel 1915b:529). In May, when a party came to Anton Chico, Calhoun went to meet them, but two days before he arrived "they suddenly left. Some Mexicans had told them we intended to kill them all so soon as I arrived" (Abel 1915b:363). For the next year Comanches were seldom seen or heard from in New Mexico.

The Treaty of Fort Atkinson, 1853

In 1850 Congress refused to appropriate funds to support Fitzpatrick's treaty meeting, and it was again postponed. Then cholera hit the northern Comanche camps, and the Comanches stayed away from the Santa Fe Trail for a season (Mooney 1898:190). In February 1851, after Congress appropriated $100,000 for the purpose of "holding treaties with the wild tribes of the prairie," Fitzpatrick sent out runners to gather the tribes at the site of the new Fort Atkinson, near modern Dodge City, Kansas. There Fitzpatrick announced that the long-delayed council would be held at Fort Laramie, on the Platte River. Although Cheyennes, Arapahos, and Sioux readily agreed,

Kiowas and Comanches refused outright, saying "they had too many horses to risk . . . among such notorious horse thieves as the Sioux and Crow" (Hafen 1931:280).

Comanche discontent was based in part on a lack of goods at Fort Atkinson. In November the post's commander, Lieutenant Simon Bolivar Buckner, complained that

> the Superintendent [Fitzpatrick] has entirely failed to comply with the assurances given to the Commander of the Department on the subject of sending to this post a supply of presents for distribution amongst the Indians who might visit the post with a friendly intent. . . . Even the Comanche have been actuated to visit the Fort during the past summer by the hope of receiving some token of friendship from the white men. A very favorable impression might doubtless have been made upon them during their visit by a judicious distribution of presents amongst them. The effect however, has been quite the reverse; they having left the post very much incensed against the Americans for what appeared to them a violation of faith. [Buckner 1851]

As spring 1852 approached, the Indian groups along the Arkansas River began moving toward Fort Atkinson in anticipation of another distribution, and Buckner again became apprehensive about the coming summer. In February, based on information from Tohasan the Kiowa, he reported, "it is very likely that there will be . . . several thousand of these wild Indians within a very short distant of the post. . . . under the circumstances the most that could be expected of the present garrison would be to protect the post and its vicinity" (Buckner 1852a). On March 10 he reported:

> It is very certain that the Kansas, Osages, Cheyenne, Arapaho, Kiowa and Comanche will be here in large force very early in the spring. The Cheyenne and one band of Kiowa with few Apache are between 30 and 40 miles above here. The remaining portion of the Kiowa and the mass of the Comanche Nation are journeying from Red River in this direction and will probably reach this vicinity early in April. At the last of that month there will probably not be less than 3,000 lodges of the various nations in the immediate vicinity of the post. [Buckner 1852b]

He again complained about Fitzpatrick's absence from the field, saying, "It would be advisable to have an agent here as early as practicable with presents for distribution" (Buckner 1852c).

In early May Buckner again wrote that there was a "great probability that a large number of Comanches would visit this vicinity in a short time." Already "a large portion of the nation [was] encamped with in two or three days journey" of the fort awaiting Fitzpatrick (Buckner 1852e). By the end of the month some Comanches had returned to the south, but others remained in the vicinity of Fort Atkinson waiting for Fitzpatrick (Buckner 1852g). The situation was such that Buckner sent Lieutenant Henry Heth out in search of the agent (Buckner 1852g).

While their people were camped fifty miles to the south, the Comanche chiefs "Sis-ko-tah"—called Shaved Head, although that is apparently not a translation of the Comanche—and The Tall Crow arrived at Fort Atkinson for interviews with Buckner. Buckner called them "two of the most influential chiefs of the Comanche," but both are previously unmentioned. Of Shaved Head, he noted, "none has a greater influence than he over almost the whole of the Comanche Nation," and although he had formerly been an inveterate enemy, he now professed a desire to make peace (Buckner 1852f). There is no known relation between the Shaved Head of 1852 and the Shaved Head who allegedly requested the Bents' Canadian River post or the later Bald Head, reported in the same vicinity ca. 1845.

The Indians came anticipating Fitzpatrick; however, they also had complaints. In early April the Kiowas complained about the ciboleros, buffalo hunters from New Mexico (Buckner 1852d). The Comanches made the same complaint; Siskotah told Buckner, "Buffalo are as essential to the Comanche as corn is to the Mexicans," and he promised "not to molest the fields if they refrain from killing the buffalo" (Buckner 1852f). In late May, when a party of sixty ciboleros were found near the fort and their leader, Felipe Martinez of Taos, could produce "no paper to show by what authority they were in the Indian country," they were sent back to New Mexico (Buckner 1852h). By the first of June another party of Pueblo ciboleros had a permit signed by John Greiner, interim superintendent in New Mexico, granting them the right to kill buffalo and forbidding anyone to molest them while so engaged. Buckner was especially upset with the latter provision, arguing that the agent had exceeded his authority, was in conflict with the laws regulating trade with the Indians, and was "utterly at variance with government policy and the whole principle of justice" (Buckner 1852i). Although he arrested the leaders of the party, Antonio Lopez, Felipe Martinez, and Thomas Garcia, the rest of the party went up the Arkansas River, where they resumed hunting (Buckner 1852j).

In early June the Comanche camps were spread out along the Arkansas River, about "10–18 miles below the fort." They included 100 lodges with Siskotah and Yellow Beads—the latter a "distinguished chief," but he is previously unmentioned. In an interview with Buckner they said that they would wait until they heard of the movements of Major Fitzpatrick. Although they did "profess a friendly attitude," Buckner also noted, "None of them attempt to conceal . . . that a large portion of the people are still disposed to be hostile." It was mainly through the exertions of the Arapahos, "by far the best disposed Indians on the Plains," that the peace was maintained (Buckner 1852k).

There were 6,000 to 9,000 Indians near Fort Atkinson. The Comanches were in three groups. Three hundred lodges were in the Arkansas Valley, some near the fort. The rest were in two villages forty miles to the south. Reports indicated, "There cannot be less than 1,000 lodges all together and probably there are 1,500" of all tribes in the vicinity of the fort; Buckner estimated that for all tribes there were two warriors for each lodge (Buckner 1852l).

Kiowas reported that the Comanches had "been very unsuccessful in their war with the Texans, that they [had] been deprived by the white people of many of their horses and prisoners" and had lost many of their people (Buckner 1852b). Lieutenant Henry Heth reported that those Indians had been "driven from Texas and its vicinity by successful attacks by Texians upon their camps during the past winter" (Heth 1852); although details of those Texan "successes" are unknown, they may be related to the actions with Ford and Dodge in 1849–50. Buckner was not sure how much credence to give the reports, but Heth noted that they had "withheld from committing hostilities by the hope of obtaining presents" (Heth 1852).

Tensions continued to mount as summer advanced. Some Comanches tried to run off the stock of a small wagon train near the fort. William Bent, hearing of the threatened attack, rode back and with "bawdy gestures and Indian style boasting," escorted the train to his fort. He then treated the chiefs to sweets out of a sugar keg. With the arrival of two more companies of riflemen, the Indian camps moved farther away from the fort (Lavender 1954: 323). Thus, Buckner reported that although "no actual depredations have yet been committed by any of them . . . on several occasions they have employed a species of obstinate begging not a little assimilated to robbery" (Buckner 1852l).

When Lame Chief—although said to be Comanche, he was probably the Arapaho Coho—came in to hear news about Fitzpatrick, Captain R. W. Chilton, new commander at Atkinson, tried to impress upon him the distinction between the Indian Department, "which alone was responsible for the promises under which they assembled," and the military's obligation to suppress any difficulties occurring on the Santa Fe Trail (Chilton 1852a). In his report Chilton complained about the policy of giving presents:

Admitting the value of making presents is a good one, the character of the presents are bad. Instead of purchasing in toto articles which would add to their comfort and prove serviceable to men, women, and children, such as blankets, strouding, etc., and such horse equipments as they could use as bridles, halters, and stirrups . . . a large portion of the fund is generally used in purchasing gewgaws of no earthly use, guns, powder, and ball with which to operate against us more effectively, almonds and raisins and numerous other trifles of the same character. . . . The presents are rarely made to the well-behaved and peaceable but to those most troublesome to us, who have sense enough to know as well as ourselves that these presents are intended as bribes to forbearance and in their ignorance of our strength regard them as extorted from ourselves. . . . Following this train of thought they say, "our good peaceable neighbors who profess such warm friendship for the whites get nothing while we are especially favored therefore the more troublesome we prove, the larger and more frequent our bribes." [Chilton 1852b]

Julius Froebel, the German traveler, visited Fort Atkinson at about that time and described the scene:

During the summer there had been an assembly of several thousand Indians for receiving presents. The agent had not yet made his appearance and the Indians threatened attack. Fortunately a short time before our passing this way, the presents had arrived. . . . The distribution of these gifts is a wise stroke of policy . . . as the savages become gradually dependent on the wants of civilized life. [Froebel 1859:265]

The Comanche chiefs Tohopetecane and Wayabatosha visited their camp, showing passports from which Froebel got their names. The first name was given by Froebel as White Tent; it appears closer to the ungrammatical *tuhu-vitʉ* 'black', *kahni* 'tent'. The second name was given as White Eagle, from *tosa* 'white', but the referent cannot be identified. According to Froebel, those Comanches belonged to "the Tribe which the Mexicans call Cibolero, that is Buffalo Hunters." If that was intended as Kotsoteka, it is one of the few uses of that ethnonym in the 1850s. The two were dressed

in the full attire of Comanche warriors, clothed in leather, with richly-ornamented moccasins, their faces daubed with red paint, and their heads ornamented with eagle's feathers; their thick and long plaited hair hanging down their backs, loaded with silver plates growing smaller downward—in the neck the size of a saucer, at the end of the plait as large as a half a dollar. These silver plates are made in Mexico expressly for Comanches, and are an important article in the trade with these savages, which is carried on at the Presidio del Rio Grande. [Froebel 1859: 266]

Later, an older man, Okháhktzomo (possibly *oha* 'yellow', *tsomo* 'bead', and thus possibly the Yellow Beads who visited Buckner earlier in the summer), said to be the "Great Chief," visited Froebel. He was dressed in a blue woolen blanket wrapped around his body; his hair was cropped short in mourning for his son killed by Pawnees. A fourth chief, unnamed, also visited. He wore "over his Indian nether garments made of leather, the blue blanket-coat of a North American from the west. A pair of gilt epaulets were attached to the coat, one on his breast, the other dangling at his back between his shoulders—by which the old Comanche prince (for such was his rank) was distinguished." He presented a certificate stating that he "had formerly been one of the most dangerous and cruel enemies of the whites, but that he had latterly altered his disposition, and from his influence with the Comanche tribes, was entitled to be treated with respect, but at the same time with great precaution." Since the description paralleled Buckner's description of Shaved Head, Froebel's unnamed chief may have been Shaved Head. That evening "Okháhktzomo exhibited his authority by ordering our Indian visitors to leave the camp and return home. To some, who did not obey immediately, he applied his horsewhip" (Froebel 1859:266–68).

Although the Indians had been waiting all summer for Major Fitzpatrick and his goods, in reality Fitzpatrick had no authority to make any distributions. Since he had as yet signed no treaty with the Arkansas River tribes, no money had been appropriated for them. But on his own responsibility, Fitzpatrick obtained $9,000 worth of goods for the Platte and Arkansas Indians (Mitchell 1852a, b). He arrived in early fall, deposited the goods at the fort, and immediately returned to Saint Louis.

Thus, the army was left with the responsibility of distributing the goods. Throughout the fall, groups came in to receive the presents left by Fitzpatrick (Heth 1852), but there was little contact between the Comanches and the army during the winter. By February 1853 they were reported to be moving north again, "agreeable to an understanding had with Fitzpatrick last summer," and with "a large number of stolen animals and persons" (Heth 1853).

In May Fitzpatrick received authorization to conduct negotiations with the Arkansas River Indians (Clelland 1853), and in August Congress appropriated $20,000 for the treaty and presents. By July Fitzpatrick had gathered 280 lodges of Comanches, Kiowas, and Apaches at Fort Atkinson (Beckwith 1855). When no competent interpreter could be found, a Mexican captive was put into service and the discussions were conducted in Spanish, assisted by sign language, which Fitzpatrick claimed enabled him to "perfectly . . . comprehend the remarks and feelings of the Indians" (Fitzpatrick 1853:361).

The several days of meetings were filled with "most protracted negotiation" marked by "hesitation on the part of one or two of the more southern bands of the Comanches." Although the "acknowledgement of right of way was readily conceded . . . upon the subjects of military posts, reservations of land, and hostilities against Mexico, they were found to be far more tenacious." There was a "decided aversion" to the location of military posts and reservations because "they destroy timber, drive off the game, interrupt their ranges, excite hostile feelings, and but too often frequently afford a rendezvous for worthless or trifling characters." Fitzpatrick himself noted that because the military establishment itself was minimal, the forces available for any one post were "so small . . . that they maintain their own position in the country more by the courtesy of the Indians than from any ability to cope with the numbers that surround them. Instead of serving to intimidate the red man, they rather create a belief in the feebleness of the white man" (Fitzpatrick 1853:362).

But the "chief difficulty" concerned hostilities in Mexico and the keeping of captives, who were "so intermingled" with the population that the chiefs "refused positively and distinctly" to entertain any proposals for their delivery. Ultimately, they agreed to give up any captives "that may hereafter be taken" and to "refrain from warlike incursions into the Mexican provinces." Fitzpatrick was convinced that because "this provision was not consented to without much deliberation, so it is believed that it will be honestly carried out, at least if any true inference can be drawn from their subsequent conduct." For its part, and "in consideration of the foregoing agreements," the United States would "protect and defend the Indian tribes . . . against the committal of depredations upon them . . . by the people of the United States" and would provide an annuity "for the better support and the improvement of the social condition of the said tribes" for a period of ten years, extendable to fifteen. Fitzpatrick drove a hard bargain; the amount of the annuity, $18,000, was "as low as a sense of justice would authorize." Moreover, it was "only about one third the sum provided for like purposes by the treaty concluded with the Sioux, Cheyenne, Crow and other tribes of the north" (Fitzpatrick 1853:363–64).

The treaty was signed on July 27, 1853, by six Comanches, six Kiowas, and three Apaches. The Comanches were Wuleaboo, Wayabatosa, Hainickseu, Parosawano, Warakonalta, and Kanaretah. The first name was given as Shaved Head, but the difference between that name and Buckner's Siskotah is unknown. The second was the man described by Froebel earlier that summer. The third name was given as The Crow, and thus possibly Buckner's Tall Crow. The name is possibly *hai* 'crow', *naki* 'ear', *siʔa* 'feather'; Joe Attocknie translated the name as 'raven ear-ornament', and described him as having white patches over his ears in his otherwise black hair. The fourth name was given as Ten Sticks; it is Paruasemena *paruasumarunu* 'ten bears'. The name

Ten Sticks probably comes from a confusion of *pariabɪ* 'dogwood' with *parua* 'bear'. The fifth name was given as Poor Coyote Wolf; it is possibly *wɯra* 'mountain lion', *kana* 'poor'. The last name was given as One That Rides the Clouds, but that cannot be confirmed.

The divisional affiliations of two are unclear: Froebel called Wayabatosa a "Buffalo Hunter," possibly meaning Kotsoteka, and the treaty called Kana-retah a "Southern Comanche," but details are unknown. Paruasemena and Hainickseu were Yamparika, and the rest were probably Yamparika as well. The other Comanche groups were apparently uninformed about the treaty council. Indeed, while the council was going on, Tenewas were meeting with Creeks and other eastern groups on the Salt Plains, and Penatekas remained in Texas.

The signing was followed by the distribution of goods. As he had done the year before, Major Chilton commented on their content, noting, "A large portion . . . consist in arms and ammunition with which to operate against us more effectively . . . as they use the bow and arrow alone for hunting purposes (a fact well known to Indian agents) and guns only on their war expeditions" (Chilton 1853). Then the chiefs "sent out runners to recall all the war parties that had recently started in that direction," and they asked for letters of safe conduct for one or two chiefs "who departed immediately for the neighboring States of Mexico, in order to confirm friendly relations, and to give assurances . . . that they were no longer enemies" (Fitzpatrick 1853).

Despite Fitzpatrick's certainty that the Comanches would not raid into Mexico, in September Tohasan the Kiowa told Major Edward Johnson, new commander at Fort Atkinson, that immediately after the treaty the Comanches went south to raid in Mexico and Texas, losing eight men (E. Johnson 1853). The Comanches themselves "denied having consented not to war on Mexico, they say there is no other place to get horses and mules" (Whitfield 1854: 299).

Agent Fitzpatrick died while lobbying for the treaty in Washington. His replacement, retired general John A. Whitfield, was given the responsibility of explaining to the Indians that the Senate had added amendments to the treaty, including one that allowed the diversion of annuities to a fund to "establish farms among and for the benefit of said Indians." Whitfield arrived at Pawnee Fork to find what "old prairie hands" described as the largest assembly ever of Indians on the plains, with an estimated twelve thousand to fifteen thousand lodges of Comanches, Kiowas, Cheyennes, and Osages. They were not in a peaceful mood. Two days before Whitfield arrived, a large war party departed, intending to wipe out "all the frontier tribes found on the plains" (Whitfield 1854:297). They attacked a party of Sacs and Foxes, but after a three-hour fight they were driven from the field by the superior firearms of the easterners.

On their return to Fort Atkinson, Whitfield called them to a council, where he explained the amended treaty. Shaved Head said although he had been raised to be an enemy of the Whites, now the hatchet was buried; he was willing to consent to just about anything the Great Father wanted, but for the present he did not want farms; so great a change could not be brought about in a short time. Ultimately, the Indians agreed to the change, but only five Comanches and three Kiowas signed. Of the original signers, Shaved Head—given that time as Tochranabo, although that name seems closer to *tosa* 'white' *naboo* 'striped, or marked'—Hainickseu, Wayabatosa, and Paruasemena—spelled that time Parasaramano—were present. Warakonalta was not present, and there was a new signer, Tyharrety, given as One Who Runs after Women, possibly *tai* 'vagina', *ho?aitʉ* 'to hunt'.

Observers of the Comanches, 1847–55

In March 1847 the pioneer ethnologist Henry Rowe Schoolcraft was commissioned to "collect and digest such statistics and materials as may illustrate the history, the present condition, and future prospects of the Indian tribes of the United States" (Schoolcraft 1851–57, 1:vi). Schoolcraft sent a long questionnaire to selected knowledgeable correspondents, covering tribal organization, religion, manners and customs, intellectual capacity, and language. For the Comanches, Schoolcraft had four primary correspondents, Thomas Fitzpatrick, William B. Parker, Robert S. Neighbors, and David G. Burnet. Their comments range from hearsay to the informed and thereby reflect the range of public knowledge about the Comanches. There is little of substance in Fitzpatrick's account (see above). He called the Indians "depraved" and the project futile, and most of his account was a comparison between the "wild tribes of the whole western territory" and the "ancient history of the Jews or Israelites after their liberation from Egyptian bondage" (Fitzpatrick 1847b). Similarly, Parker, whose only known contact with the Comanches was as supernumerary on the Neighbors-Marcy survey of the Texas reservations (see below), provided little substantive information.

More responsive was Robert S. Neighbors, who had more experience with the Comanches than any other Texan of his generation. But there are problems with his discussion. According to Neighbors, the Comanches called themselves "naüni, which signifies—first alive, or live people" (Neighbors

1852:126). It is not clear where Neighbors got the word, it does not occur in any of his reports from the field. It is possible that he meant *nʉmʉnʉʉ* 'people', the Comanche word for themselves. It is also possible that he was using the word given in Butler's report as Nonah and in Lewis's report as Noonah, but in neither of those references did the term refer to the Comanches as a whole.[13]

According to Neighbors, the Comanches were divided into "eight distinct bands each ruled by their own chiefs" (table 6.6). He was not consistent about the terminology for those units; in parts of his discussion he impled a single tribe divided into bands, but elsewhere he referred to those political divisions themselves as tribes. Nonetheless, his list is interesting as much for what it leaves out as for what it contains. The ethnonyms Hois, Pinetaker (Penateka), Noconi (Nokoni), Tenawish (Tenawa), and Koochetaker (Kotsoteka) had appeared before, although Hois had not appeared in a direct reference for almost a decade. The translation of Tenawish as 'Liver Eaters' is erroneous —'liver eaters' would be *nʉmʉ tʉhka*; Neighbors thus added to the confusion surrounding that ethnonym. Nonaum is reminiscent of both Naüni and the terms Nonah and Noonah used by Butler and Lewis, but Neighbors provided no direct translation; however, his discussion of them living "where there is no timber or running water" could be seen as a description of Lewis's "People of the Desert." The other ethnonyms (Itchitabudah, Hainenaune, and Parkenaum) were not only new, but Neighbors was the only documentary appearance of them. Itchitabudah is *utsuʔitʉ* 'cold'. Hainenaune seems to be based on *hani* 'corn', *nʉmʉ* 'people'. Parkenaum seems to be based on *paa* 'water'; it may be *paki nʉmʉ*. Conversely, the ethnonym Yamparika is not on Neighbors's list, thus paralleling the earlier Texas Spaniard practice of distinguishing between the local Comanches and the distant Yamparikas.

Neighbors also gave a list of the "principal chiefs that are known" (table 6.7), but despite his claim that they were "principal chiefs," aside from Pahayuko, it is rather a list of men who had some dealings with the Texans, regardless of their capacity in those dealings. Except for Ohawakin, the Tenewa, Kotsoteka, and Nokoni "chiefs" were the men who had visited Neighbors in 1848, none of whom were mentioned again. The name Ohawakin appeared only once in a direct Texan context: a picture of him had been painted by Stanley at the 1844 Texas treaty. Thus, unless Neighbors knew of that reference, he probably obtained the name from Seminole agent Duval's 1849 letter reporting his visit to that agency in 1849, a letter filed with Texas Agency correspondence in the National Archives. Conversely, as he consistently did, Neighbors included Pahayuko with the Hois, although he was probably Tenewa. Again, Neighbors named no Yamparikas. Thus,

Table 6.6
Robert S. Neighbors's List of Comanche Bands

1st "Hois" or Timber people, because they live in a timbered country. They are also called "Pine-Takers" or honey-eaters, being fond of honey.

2d "No-co-nies," because they always live and travel in a circle; their country that they claim being circular.

3d "Teu-a-wish," [an obvious typographical error for Tenawish] or Liver-eaters, because they eat the liver of all game they kill in its raw state.

4th "No-na-um," because they live in the high prairie where there is no timber or running water, and never leave that kind of country.

5th "It-chit-a-bud-ah," Cold people, or the northern band, because they live in a cold country.

6th "Hai-ne-na-une," or Corn-eaters, being fond of corn.

7th "Koo-che-ta-kers," or Buffalo-eaters.

8th "Par-ke-na-um," or Water people; because they always camp as near the waters of lakes or creeks as they can get.

SOURCE: Neighbors 1852

Table 6.7
Robert S. Neighbors's List of Comanche "Principal Chiefs"

Hois Chiefs:
Pahayuca, or 'One who has connexion with his uncle's wife'
Mopechucope, or 'Old Owl'
Pochanaqwuhiep or 'Bull Hump, commonly known as Buffalo Hump'
Santa Anna
Saviartee, or 'Small Wolf'
Tunaciowuasha, or 'Bear's Tail'
Mooraketoph, or 'Mule Dung'

Tenawish Chiefs:
Pohucawakit, or 'Medicine Hunter'
Ohawakit, or 'Yellow Hunter'

Koochitaku Chief:
Chipeseah, or 'Growing Chief'

Nokonie Chief:
Ohois, or 'Naked Head'

SOURCE: Neighbors 1852

Neighbors's report must not be seen as representing all the Comanches, but as the title suggests, and like the reports of Spanish and Mexican Texans, it was restricted to the Comanches known to Anglo-American Texans.

Much of the rest of Neighbors's comments are in the form of single sentences arbitrarily grouped into paragraphs. In summary, Neighbors reported the following: A man's ambition was the primary motivation to social position; prominence was not hereditary, but was primarily based on a war record as well as political skills. There was no fixed number of either chiefs or political units; those were dependent upon the ability of men to attract and maintain followers. Conversely, they could lose prominence by a reversal in luck and fortunes, but not for private matters unconnected to the public political arena. Such matters were the concern only of the parties involved. Similarly, warfare was the concern of the individual "tribes."

Principal chiefs might call general councils of their own people or "intertribal" councils. Councils were opened and closed with a pipe ritual, the pipe being filled by the *tekwawapI* 'speaker'. Important questions were discussed, often at great length, until apparent unanimity was achieved, and although the discussion was open to all, except women, the chiefs took the major part in the discussion. They did consult the warriors, but the mass of the population followed their decisions. Good judgment rather than rhetorical skills were valued. Councils called by the Whites had no legitimacy unless they coincided with the Indian's own interests; in such cases they had private consultations and the chief presented the consensus. Significantly, and symbolic of the changed political relations between Comanches—and indeed other Indians—and Anglo-Americans, Neighbors noted, almost in passing, that the symbolism of the medal and the position of the medal chief, so prominent in earlier times, were no longer important; rather than a recognition of an indigenous political position, the medal had become merely a symbol of friendship with Euroamericans. All in all, and despite the problems with some of Neighbors's specific data, his was a good summary of what was known of Comanche political culture.

The same cannot be said of Schoolcraft's fourth correspondent. Upon receipt of Schoolcraft's questionnaire, Neighbors passed it along to former Texas president David G. Burnet, who wrote an independent report, dated August 1847. Although he noted that during the years 1818-19 he had "spent a considerable time with, or in the vicinity of the Comanche Indians of Texas," he also admitted, "[My] information is entirely too limited and imperfect for me to attempt a specific answer to the several queries." Moreover, lacking notes, his comments were of necessity based on the "recollection of near thirty years." Indeed, his 1847 report echoes his earlier report (1818) with only minor amplification of selected points.

In contrast to Neighbors's eight bands, Burnet divided the Comanches into three "principal bands," as he had done before:

> The Comanche, with whom we have most intercourse . . . occupy the region between the Rivers Colorado of Texas and the Red River of Louisiana, ranging from the sources of the Colorado . . . down to the Llano Bayou, and from the vicinity of the Pawnees of the Red River [the Wichitas] to the American settlements in that stream. They are frequently at war with the Pawnees and sometimes make hostile incursion upon the Osages. . . . The Yamparack range the country north and west of the Comanches, and the Tenawa are . . . again interior from the latter. They are essentially one people, speak the same language, and have the same peculiar habits, and the same tribal interests. [1851:230]

As with his earlier report, it is difficult to reconcile Burnet's geographical distribution, particularly of the Yamparikas and the Tenewas, with their otherwise known locations. At best, Burnet's term "interior" for the Tenewa must be understood as "northeast."

In 1818 Burnet had argued that there was a "head or grand chief" recognized by all three parties collectively; now, although noting, "In 1819 [sic] their principal chief, who was generally recognized as the head of the three bands, was called Parrow-a-kifty" [that is, Paruakevitsi], he was more forceful, whether intentionally or not, in distinguishing politics from law, that is, intergroup from intragroup relations. Thus, he argued that the three "cognate tribes cannot be said to have any common tribal government," with the result that "one captain will lead his followers to robbery and carnage while another and perhaps the big chief of all, will eschew the foray and profess friendship for the victims of the assault." That was particularly evident in the various relations with Mexicans: "The Tenawa and Yamparacks trade with the Mexicans of Santa Fe [his earlier report had given only the Tenewas in that trade] while the Lower [Comanches] war upon the Mexicans of Chihuahua and all the lower provinces." From that fact Burnet drew the conclusion, "Treaties made with these untutored savages are a mere nullity unless enforced by a sense of fear pervading the whole tribe, and it is somewhat difficult to impress this sentiment upon them for they have a cherished notion . . . that they are the most powerful of nations" (Burnet 1851:232).

On the subject of chiefly internal legal authority, he repeated his earlier comments: "Their authority . . . is rather nominal than positive; more advisory than compulsive; and relies more upon personal influence than investment of office," and he added a comment on the process of becoming a chief:

They have a number, altogether indefinite, of minor chiefs or captains, who lead their small predatory bands and are selected for their known or pretended prowess in war. Anyone who finds and avails himself of an opportunity for distinction in robbing horses or scalps may aspire to the honors of chieftaincy, and is gradually inducted by a tacit popular consent, no such thing as a formal election being known among them. [Burnet 1851:231]

These processual comments are a valid, if crude, way of describing a warrior's ascent to social standing. However, Burnet's observation that elections were unknown probably reflects the fact that the last recorded election prior to his time was that of Cordero in 1805.

Fear and Coercion on the Texas Reservation, 1854–60

Between 1849 and 1852 Robert S. Neighbors held a number of public positions. He served as commissioner to organize Texas counties in the areas of New Mexico east of the Rio Grande, although he only succeeded in organizing El Paso County; he was surveyor for Peter's Colony; and he served as representative in the state legislature. In the latter capacity he introduced several bills and resolutions dealing with Indian affairs, particularly in relation to the establishment of an Indian territory in the northern part of the state, but no immediate action was taken (Neighbours 1975:104). Following the election of Franklin Pierce in 1852, Neighbors was appointed supervising Indian agent, with responsibility for all the Indians in Texas.

In February 1854 the Texas legislature granted twelve leagues of land—approximately 23,040 acres—to the United States for the use of the Texas Indians. Neighbors and Captain Randolph B. Marcy were assigned the task of selecting the lands. After a brief tour of the Brazos River drainage, they selected three plots of four leagues each. One, below the junction of the Clear and Salt Forks of the Brazos, to be called the Brazos or Lower Reserve, was for the Wichitas, Caddos, Tawakonis, and Anadarkos. Adjacent was one for the Apaches of western Texas, although it was doubted they would ever accept it. The third plot was for the Texas Comanches, to be called the Clear Fork or Upper Reserve. It was located on the Clear Fork of the Brazos in modern Throckmorton County. In January, 1856, a military post, Camp Cooper, was established within the boundaries of the reserve, but was removed in early 1858.

While Neighbors and Marcy were surveying the plots, they had a chance to observe at first hand Comanche politics at work. On August 9 Ketumsee visited their camp, saying he had been trying to get the other "principal men to accompany him, but they all made objections." He reiterated his earlier desire to settle down, and although he noted that other chiefs had often said the same, he was not sure that they were sincere. William B. Parker, a geologist friend of Marcy's who was along as supernumerary, observed:

> After a smoke he commenced, holding in his hand a bundle of short stalks of grass. Handing these one by one to the Captain [Marcy], he made his remarks on each, representing by each, one of the chiefs or war captains of his band, and giving his disposition towards the whites. After remarking upon four of high standing, and three of mediocrity, he bundled the balance, 8 in number, in a bundle, and handed them together, with a grunt and remark, "no count." [W. B. Parker 1856:181]

There is unfortunately no record of which chiefs he so evaluated.

Several days after Ketumsee left, Neighbors sent out messengers to the chiefs, asking them to come in for a visit. Two "sub-chiefs of Sanaco's band," Quahawetah and Oti, came in to visit. Parker gave the former's name in English as Tall Tree; he was possibly Neighbors's guide to El Paso in 1849 as well as a signer of the Rollins agreement, but if so there is no indication of recognition on either side. The other was given as Hunting a Wife, said to be a Tonkawa by birth, captured by the Comanches. As given, neither translation seems to be correct, but if reversed, at least *kwuhu* 'wife' fits the first name.

They called Ketumsee a liar and a scoundrel, warned that he was not to be believed, and claimed that Sanaco "alone was authorized to speak for the tribe." After staying for several days, the two went out to get Sanaco; they came back with the chief, two other "war captains," and a large party of warriors, women, and children (W. B. Parker 1856:188).

That was apparently the first time Marcy had met Sanaco. He later reported that during those meetings he attempted to buy the chief's horse, but the chief demurred, saying that

> the animal was one of the fleetest in their possession; and if he were to sell him, it would prove a calamity to his whole band, as it often required all the speed of this animal to insure success in the buffalo chase; that his loss would be felt by all his people, and he would be regarded as very foolish; moreover, he said, (patting his favorite on the neck), "I love him very much." [Marcy 1854:97]

That is a significant commentary, open to several interpretations. Although Marcy later recounted the story in the context of Comanche horsemanship, it also suggests that since only one man had a hunting horse, those Comanches

were horse-poor and that Sanaco held a horse owner's resource-power
domain.

However, it could also reflect Marcy's tendency to misappropriate anecdotes, which is shown more clearly in another incident, apparently also from
that time period. The women with Sanaco included Santa Anna's widow. According to Parker:

> she still mourned her loss, going out every evening in the neighborhood
> of the camp, to howl and cry and cut herself with knives. . . . She had
> separated herself in a measure from the tribe, and formed a band of
> women, seven in number, like herself widows. She owned a large herd of
> mules and horses, and was a most successful hunter, having alone shot
> with her rifle fifteen deer in a morning's hunt. She was a fine looking
> woman, an Amazon in size and haughty bearing, rode astride, and dres-
> sed in deep black. [W. B. Parker 1856:193]

In retelling the story in 1866, Marcy said, "in 1849 I met the widow of . . .
'Santa Anna' who had been dead about *three years*" (1866:57, my emphasis);
in fact, Santa Anna died in 1849. Moreover, Parker's story of a rich woman,
owner of many horses and mules, conflicts with Marcy's implication that
Sanaco's people were horse-poor.

After several days Ketumsee returned, saying that he had been trying to
persuade his followers to come in, but again "without success." That night,
when the chiefs assembled in council, Sanaco, reiterating his authority, said,
"The chiefs and headmen of the Southern Comanches have authorized me to
reply"; during the whole of the proceedings "Ketumsee sat like a statue, glum
and silent, evidently displeased at not having been spokesman" (W. B. Parker
1856:201).

In his presentation Marcy said that he had been sent by Washington to
locate lands for them on which to build homes and cultivate the soil so they
might

> no longer lead the uncertain life they did; the buffalo had disappear-
> ed . . . and other game were fast disappearing; that in a few years they
> and their children would have to resort to some other means than the
> chase for a subsistence; that they would not be permitted to depredate on
> the white settlements, and there was no alternative—they must learn to
> cultivate the soil. [W. B. Parker 1856:199]

Unfortunately, only part of Sanaco's reply was recorded, in which he
invoked the memory of "our former chief Mokochucope"—that is, Mopechucope—and said,

We endeavor to carry out his wishes after he is gone. He told us to take the advice and example of the whites, and it would make us happy and benefit us. We are glad to hear the talk which has been sent us. . . . we accept this talk and will endeavor to accede to all our Great Father requires of us. [W. B. Parker 1856:201]

Both Marcy and Parker reported that the ensuing discussion was free and frank. "We asked them many questions, the answers to which satisfied us that a majority of them were disposed to make a trial of the experiment in farming" (Marcy 1866:212); "many questions were put to him, which he answered freely and favorably" (W. B. Parker 1856:201). Those comments seem to imply that the Comanches were positively inclined toward the reservation, or at least that Sanaco was.

However, in another book Marcy quoted a speech, said to have been made during that conference, that casts doubt on Sanaco's full cooperation: Marcy had asked pointedly if they were going to settle on the reservation but received only a roundabout answer. When he again pressed the point, Sanaco replied, "You have my talk what more do you want." Again, Marcy pressed him. Finally, Sanaco said:

You come into our country and select a small patch of ground, around which you run a line, and tell us the President will make us a present of this to live on, when every body knows that the whole of this entire country, from the Red River to the Colorado, is ours, and always has been from time immemorial. I suppose however, if the President tells us to confine ourselves to these narrow limits, we shall be forced to do so whether we desire it or not. [Marcy 1859:218]

That incident appears only in Marcy's *Prairie Traveler*, a handbook for overland travelers, and then only in the context of the reticence of Indians to "get to the point." It was noted neither in Marcy and Neighbors's report nor by Parker. It does, however, seem in keeping with Sanaco's later actions and is a telling commentary on the deficiencies of the official record of the meetings.

Upon the conclusion of the council, various presents, including printed cottons, blankets, knives, strouding for leggings, silver armlets, and "wampum"—probably bone hair pipes—were given directly to the chiefs, who distributed them to the people (W. B. Parker 1856:201).

During the fall and early winter of 1854 "the whole Southern Band," some twelve hundred people, was on the Clear Fork awaiting the final preparations for the reservation. However, settlement was not going to be easy. In January 1855 John Leyendecker, trader at Fort Chadbourne, sixty miles away on the Concho River, passed word that an expedition was being planned against "all Comanches." Although Ketumsee "did not credit the report," Sanaco and Potsanaquahip fled from the Clear Fork with their people (R. N. Richardson 1929:46).

Only about one hundred people remained after the scare; the composition of that group, whether it was Ketumsee's own *numunahkahni* or a local band composed of the remnants of a number of *numunahkahni* cannot now be determined. Because there were initially so few, they were first located on the Brazos Reserve with the Wichitas and the Caddos. Gradually, more people returned, and by March Ketumsee had 180 followers. In May, when they were finally transferred to the Clear Fork, he had 226. The population soared to 500 in 1857, settling to 350 in 1858. That fluctuation was due primarily to the comings and goings of a variety of other Comanches. In late September 1856, 24 of Sanaco's people came in. In the winter of 1855–56 Sanaco came in with most of his people, saying he was ready to settle, but he soon left. He was later reported as saying that if he could get "as much whiskey as he and his people could drink, he would come in and bring all his people with him, and remain until whiskey gave out, and then would leave" (Leeper, Sr., 1858b). Potsanaquahip also visited several times, usually to replenish supplies.

There were other, more exotic Comanche visitors, as well as unfulfilled promises to take up residence. In May 1857 a visiting Tenewa promised to bring in his people. Historian Kenneth F. Neighbours, without citation, identified him as "Chief Ironsides (Pah-hah-yuca) of the Tenawish" (1975:168); Neighbours later (1975:172) attributed the identification of Iron Sides with Pahayuko to John S. Ford, but again without direct citation. If that indeed was Pahayuko, it was his only visit to the reservation and was the last mention of him.

Meanwhile, in 1857 A. H. McKisick, agent for the Wichitas at Fort Smith, noted that a group of Kotsotekas was in the Indian Territory near the hundredth meridian (McKisick 1857:261); in early 1858 a delegation from them arrived at the Clear Fork Reserve "to ascertain upon what terms they would be allowed to settle here"; they later left saying "the agent up there had made propositions more to their taste" (Leeper, Sr., 1858f:177); it is not clear if they meant McKisick or the Agent on the Arkansas. In November 1858 Ketumsee's brother and ten others visited the Comanche camp. He said about eighty more were approaching and might be expected in several days. Still more were near the Arkansas River, and they were sent for (Leeper, Sr., 1858i), but if they came in, they did not stay long enough to be counted.

The civilization programs of the reservation achieved modest successes, but they were slow to get under way. While on the Brazos Reserve the Comanches were asked to help establish farms, but they said they wanted to wait until they were on their own reservation; in the meantime they would watch and see how it was done (Neighbours 1975:158). By September 1856, now on their own reserve, they fenced and cultivated two hundred acres (Manypenny 1856:14), and the agents reported a start toward self-sufficiency. How valid that claim was is unknown.

Ketumsee was the recognized chief of the reservation Comanches, but his claim was not secure, and others attempted to usurp his position. One reason Sanaco left the reservation, at least according to Agent John R. Baylor, was that he could not supersede Ketumsee. Potsanaquahip was more successful, albeit for a brief period. In the fall of 1857 he persuaded Ketumsee and about seventy-five armed warriors to go to the nearby Brazos Reserve, intending to force the Caddos and the Delawares to stop furnishing scouts for the army. But José María, the Anadarko chief, was ready for them with armed men of his own. Realizing that discretion was the better part of valor, the Comanches left (R. N. Richardson 1929:48).

Ketumsee was paid thirty dollars a month "so he could devote his time to his duties and not have to hunt" (Neighbours 1975:182), and he had other perquisites. He had a permanent house: after the army abandoned Camp Cooper, Ketumsee moved into one of the cabins formerly used as barracks, while most Comanches still lived in tents. He controlled the distribution of goods to the people through his "sub-chiefs" and headmen, Tosawa, Kakaraway,[14] and Pianachamon (*pianahotsaʔmaʔ* 'big saddle blanket'; Joe Attocknie 1965 translated the first part of his name as 'blood vessel', and said that he was uncle to Tosawa). Ketumsee also used his access to the reservation officials to effect a modicum of political control over the leading men on the reservation. At his suggestion, captains and headmen were recognized, and apparently he could withdraw their commissions at will. In January 1858 Agent Matthew Leeper wrote to Neighbors,

> Ketemsee appears to be dissatisfied with his 2 chiefs Kakaraway and Toshawa, to whom clothing had been promised upon condition that they would faithfully use their best exertions in carrying out your wishes with regard to recovery of stolen horses from the wild tribes. He says they have not yet done this and therefore do not deserve any clothing. [Leeper, Sr., 1858a]

By April Leeper reported, "Ketumsee has taken into his service two of his former chiefs [Tosawa and Pianachamon] to whom he had made presents of clothing. They appear to be well satisfied and perfectly willing to aid and be governed by Ketumsee" (Leeper, Sr., 1858d).

Although they were in a new situation, Comanche political culture continued. Ketumsee and his headmen exercised a limited authority in public external affairs. In 1856, when two men, possibly of Sanaco's band, came in with some horses taken on a raid in Mexico, Ketumsee took them and turned them in to the agent (Winfrey and Day 1959–66, 3:252). When an Indian named Jack Porter, otherwise unidentified, returned from a raid into Mexico with twelve horses, a council of chiefs informed him that if he repeated the act he would be shot; Agent Leeper reported that since that time no parties had left the reserve (Leeper, Sr., 1858f:176).

On the other hand, the chiefs did not involve themselves in private domestic affairs. When one headman stabbed his wife, her brothers vowed revenge, but neither the agent nor the chiefs became involved (Baylor 1856). In 1858 there was this report:

> one of the old men recently appointed Captain by chief Ketumsee seems to have been engaged in an intrigue with the wife of another old fellow in the camp, who agreeable to their custom made application for remuneration [nanawokʉ]. The Captain, unwilling to dispose of his property for so trivial an offense was instantly slain by two sons of the injured party, and together with the old man, and another son immediately fled. . . . They returned at night for belongings, women and children, etc. (4 men, 5 women, 4 children) and fled again. [Leeper, Sr., 1858c]

In that case, the first old man, apparently trusting in his own social standing as *paraibo*, rejected the *nanawokʉ* claim. The other took the next step, and killed him. Had not the murderer and his family fled, Ketumsee, as divisional *paraibo*, might have stepped in to prevent a continuing feud, but only in order to avoid a threat to public peace.

During that same time there was a constant friction among the Comanches, the reservation officials, and the army at nearby Fort Belknap and later at Camp Cooper, located on the reservation. In April 1856 Lieutenant Colonel Robert E. Lee, commander at Camp Cooper, wrote to his wife that "Catumseh has been to see me. We have had a talk, very tedious on his part and very sententious on mine. I hailed him as a friend, so long as his conduct and that of his band entitled him to it, but would meet him as an enemy, the first moment he deserved it." Lee visited the Indian camps and found the "whole race . . . extremely uninteresting" (F. R. Adams 1955: 114).[15]

In December 1857 Captain George Stoneman of the Second Cavalry, questioning the validity of the censuses, came on the reservation to take one of his own, upsetting the Indians in the process. When Agent Leeper heard about it, he asked the officer on what authority he was there. Stoneman, however, "refused to answer to someone to whom he [was] not subordinate" (Leeper, Sr., 1857). By 1858 Agent Baylor had so alienated Ketumsee that the chief was not even speaking to him.

The most serious incident occurred in August 1858. Two Indians, an unnamed Nokoni and another named Santa Anna, stopped at Tosawa's house—formerly "occupied as quarters by one of the companies at Camp Cooper" (Van Camp 1858)—to rest their horses. Leeper called the latter a "notoriously bad Indian," but without elaboration. He is otherwise unidentified; he was obviously not the Penateka chief Santa Anna, who had died in 1849, although he was possibly the man of that name who had attempted a partial peace in Chihuahua in 1852. Ketumsee called on Leeper to have them removed, and in turn, Leeper called on Lieutenant Cornelius Van Camp to do the deed. Van Camp took a detachment of about twenty men to arrest them, but when the soldiers suddenly appeared on the scene, "the whole camp was alarmed, dogs barking, women screaming, and warriors yelling, stringing their bows." Ketumsee said the two men were at Tosawa's house; there, when Van Camp explained their business, Tosawa apparently thought they meant to kill the two, and he replied "that he, and every man, woman and child who could fight would die rather than see them killed." At that point, Ketumsee thrust himself through the crowd, saying "too much talk no good," but was restrained by some of the women (Van Camp 1858). There were then about seventy men around Tosawa's house. Ketumsee, saying that many of them were "of his own party," called his supporters to rally around him. But only his brother, his nephew, a man named Hawk, and a few others joined him. It was then discovered that the soldiers had only one bullet apiece—they were going to be transferred the next day and had used up all their ammunition in target practice. A debacle was avoided by Tosawa, who sent several of his men to escort the two off the reservation (Leeper, Sr., 1858g).

Several explanations were offered for the hostility. The visitors were entitled to hospitality; the people on the reserve had been "repeatedly threatened with extermination and were apprehensive that the troops surrounded the house for that purpose." They were also upset at Leeper, and he had heard rumors that before the "belligerent party" came in to explain, they had made "threats that if I did not talk to please them, they would kill myself and my family" (Leeper, Sr., 1858g).

The friction caused by the incident did not end there. That night Tosawa lost some horses to raiders, but when he asked Van Camp to follow them, that officer refused, noting that it was suspicious that none of the "friendly" chiefs of the day before had lost horses, and anyway, "by their actions they had forfeited any right of protection" (Van Camp 1858).

As Tosawa found out, the establishment of the reservations did not stop Indian raids in Texas. Blame for the raids was placed not only on the northern Comanches—Yamparikas, Nokonis, and Tenawas—but also on San-aco's people. In October 1855, when a number of horses were stolen from Caddos on the Brazos Reserve, a party of a dozen Delawares and Caddos pursued the raiders across the Red River. There they met a party of ten Yamparikas who gave them all the details. The Yamparikas also said that northern Indians, including the Sioux, had declared war on all people south of the Red River, Indian and White alike. That night each party attempted to ambush the other, but the Delawares managed to cut the Yamparikas's bowstrings. Seven Yamparikas were killed, but the others escaped to tell the news (Winfrey and Day 1959–66, 3:250).

In June 1856 Colonel Lee led an expedition against Sanaco's people, "who had been committing depredations on the settlements about San Antonio, but they had received notice of our movements from the Indians in our vicinity, scatter[ed] his people and fled to the North." With four companies of cavalry, Lee tracked the Indians 1,600 miles to the Red River; Lee later reported, "We caught as many Indians as bears" (F. R. Adams 1955:149). In December of that year Agent Baylor blamed "Ocha's band of Kansas Comanches," for raiding in Texas (Winfrey and Day 1959–1966, 5:200). The chief is unknown, as is the designation Kansas Comanches; although Yamparikas did frequent the area north of the Arkansas River, none were ever directly called Kansas Comanches. Moreover, in the years immediately before the Civil War, there were rumors throughout the Texas frontier that red-haired white men from Kansas were leading Comanches on horse raids to Texas (Marshall 1985). It is therefore not at all clear that Baylor knew what he was talking about—that those were Yamparikas from Kansas—or perhaps he had thoroughly confused fact and rumor.

In January 1858 Nokoni and Tenawa Comanches were said to be lurking around the Comanche reservation (Neighbors 1858a), and in June a captured Nokoni woman, reported to be the wife of the son of Mohee (possibly the Muhy who signed the 1838 Texas treaty), said that they had been down to the settlements on the Pedernales River stealing horses (Leeper, Sr., 1858e). Mohee himself was later captured by Lieutenant Van Camp but escaped; in November he was reported to be still in the vicinity of the reservations (Leeper, Sr., 1858h).

In early 1858 Pianachamon went out to Sanaco to recover a stolen horse; he returned in February, saying Sanaco was camped with Nokonis near Cedar Mountain on the headwaters of the Red River. One chief gave him nine horses, but the rest refused to give up any, calling him a fool for working with the Whites. Ketumsee himself doubted the story of the nine horses, as they were reported as having died or given out on the way (Leeper, Sr., 1858b).

That same month Wacos from the Brazos Reserve recovered sixty-seven horses from a party of northern Comanches. They later captured two other Comanches with stolen horses. The Brazos Reserve chiefs met in council to try them, and they sentenced them to be shot. Before the execution occurred, they implicated one of Sanaco's sons as being leader of the raids; it is not clear if the execution took place (Ross 1858a).

In May a party of approximately one hundred Texas Rangers under Captain John S. Ford, with another hundred Caddo, Wichita, and Tonkawa scouts under Lawrence S. Ross, crossed the Red River into Indian Territory, where they found the trail of a large party of Comanches. On May 12, 1858, they attacked a camp on Little Robe Creek, on the north side of the Canadian River near the Antelope Hills; in the fight, according to reports, seventy-six Comanches were killed, including "the two principal chiefs," with a loss of only two Texans killed and three wounded (Ross 1858b). Survivors of the attack, identified as Kotsotekas, were later reported as seeking refuge on the Clear Fork Reserve (Neighbors 1858b). The Rangers' attack had only minimal justification. Not only did they cross into territory beyond their jurisdiction, but there were no American horses among the three hundred captured, indicating that that camp was not directly involved in any immediately preceding raids into Texas.

Several dimensions of ethnohistorical problems surround the accounts of the fight on Little Robe Creek, ranging from contrasting conclusions based on contradictory observations, through erroneous conclusions based on the misinterretation or even absence of data, to what may charitably be called wishful thinking. One of the immediate problems is a possible confusion of incidents between the 1858 fight on Little Robe Creek and an 1860 fight in western Kansas; the latter will be discussed below.

Two accounts of the 1858 fight on Little Robe Creek provide comparisons. According to the memoirs of John S. Ford, commander of the Rangers—originally written about 1885 and edited and published by Stephen B. Oates in 1963, with Oates noting that Ford's manuscript account of the battle was often "disconnected and in places wholly obscure" (1963:232 n. 8)—a small camp of five tents was encountered first. All but two inhabitants were taken prisoner, but those two escaped and were seen riding towards a much larger encampment north of the Canadian. The Caddo and Wichita scouts were put out as skirmishers "to make the Comanches believe they had only Indians and bows and arrows to contend against." Several Comanches made feints between the lines, including the "head chief," called by Ford "Po-bishe-quash-o—Iron Jacket" (*puhihwi kwasu²u* 'iron shirt'), but they were killed.

The camp was then attacked and when the "second in command" was killed, the Indians "fled in every direction." Soon warriors from another even larger encampment arrived, but they too were repulsed. The Rangers finally broke off the fight when a woman captured in the fight told them that Buffalo Hump's (Potsanaquahip's) village was nearby (Ford 1963:236). To the Texans, it was a "gallant fight and glorious victory" (Winfrey and Day 1959–66; 3:287).

Joe Attocknie's (1965) account of the fight, based on Indian testimony from both sides, focused primarily on the efforts of an abortive decoy party that managed only to wipe out the Tonkawa rear guard—an action unmentioned by Ford—in which a Comanche named Tosahwhekot (*tosawikutʉ* 'white knife possessor') was killed, and on the Texans as timid warriors. Indeed, according to Attocknie, the Texans cowered behind the "the calico breech-cloths of their motley, many-tongued, bronze allies." In a secondary focus, Attocknie recorded that a young warrior named Moopuh 'mustache',[16] nicknamed Poohewe Quasoo 'iron shirt', had recently returned from Mexico, so recently in fact that his own war horse was jaded and he had to borrow another in order to join the battle. But it was a poor horse, unable to gallop. His father, upon seeing his situation, galloped to join him; "having the faster mount, he soon passed Moopuh, thereby getting killed even before his iron-jacketed son." Finally, Attocknie noted that rather than a great and glorious victory, in Comanche tradition the Texans were so badly treated that they lost all their supplies and rations, were forced to retreat, deserted by Caddo and Wichita scouts—although the Penateka scouts remained loyal—and ultimately even forced to eat their horses.

Those two accounts offer a range of comparisons. First, there is outright contradiction: events in one account—such as the annihilation of the Tonkawa scouts and the defeat of the Texans and their subsequent starvation during retreat in Attocknie's account—are, by lack of mention, implictly if not explicitly denied by the other. Second, there is point of view: the Comanche view of the timid Texans hiding behind the breechcloths of their allies may be a reference to the Texans' strategic use of the Wichitas and Caddos as skirmishers. Finally, there is elaboration: to Ford, the casualties included two chiefs, the famous Iron Jacket and one other; in Attocknie's account, those same casualties were only a young warrior and his father.

At the same time, the identification of Puhiwiquasso is problematical. Although he has been called "widely known" (R. N. Richardson 1933:235), the earliest documentary appearance of the name in the context of the 1858 fight, as Po-bish-e-quash-o, was not until some twenty-seven years later, in John Ford's manuscript notes for his autobiography—that is, if the date of 1885 is accepted as the date of their writing. A year later, in his biography of Cynthia

Ann Parker, James DeShields (1886:36) gave the name as Pohebits Quasho, but he provided no citations for it. Joe Attocknie's discussion of Poohewe Quasoo, albeit as a mere warrior rather than a chief, lends credence to his existence in 1858. Still, Attocknie's acknowledged awareness of those other sources has implications for his argument, and it is not possible to know the extent to which his presentation was influenced by the writings of those other historians.

Meanwhile, there is one other dimension of uncertainty in the accounts of the fight on Little Robe Creek. According to Joe Attocknie (1965), the Rangers were led to the Comanche camp by Caddo, Wichita, Tonkawa, and, worst of all, by Penateka scouts. Indeed, Attocknie named as leader Kooehwhoe Tosavtuh *(ku?ewoo? tosabitʉ* 'white dove'), who he said was also known as Tosawa, and by Nehke Wupahe, later spelled Neithkawoofpi *(nehki wʉpah?itʉ* 'belt whip'). Indeed, the latter was cited as the ultimate source for some of Attocknie's information. But while it is documented that Ford had Caddo, Wichita, and Tonkawa scouts, no documentary evidence has been found directly stating that he had Penateka scouts.

In partial confirmation that Tosawa and White Dove were the same person, in 1869, agent Lawrie Tatum said of him

> The name that he had when he was a boy was Silver Handled Knife, which he owned, translated Silver Broach. The name he has now assumed is Turtle Dove. [Tatum 1869b]

Tatum's comment is ambiguous about the date of the name change. On the one hand, it could have occurred in 1869, and Attocknie projected it onto accounts of earlier events. On the other hand, it could have occurred at some unstated time in the past, including as far back as 1858, and was related to the unfortunate situation in which a Comanche named Tosawa led scouts into a battle in which a Comanche named Tosawecut was killed; because of the similarities of names, and the custom of name-changing in the face of inauspicious conditions, Tosawa changed his own name, and while it was accepted by Comanches, Anglo-Americans persisted in using his old name. At present, both possibilities remain.

The most serious threat to the reservation Comanches came from former agent John R. Baylor. He blamed the reservation Indians for the raids, or for providing a refuge for the northerners, and he was rabidly pursuing an anti-Neighbors policy. Charges of rapine and depredations were laid at the door of the reservations, but when a commission was convened to investigate them, not one witness came forward with positive evidence (Neighbours 1975:217).

By that time Neighbors had given up hope of success for the Texas reservations. He had been recommending for at least a year that they be abandoned and the Indians be moved out of Texas to the Indian Territory north of the Red River near the Wichita Mountains, there to be consolidated with the other prairie tribes (Neighbors 1857).[17]

In April 1858 he received authority for that move, and in late June he traveled north with the headmen of both reserves to meet with Elias Rector, superintendent of the Central Superintendency, based in Saint Louis, and to pick out a site for their new agency. Rector did not like the area along Cache Creek, near the Wichita Mountains, preferring instead the Washita River valley to the north.

The preparations for the evacuation of the Texas Indians did not stop Baylor. In the spring of 1859 he raised a party of 250 men and camped near the Clear Fork Brazos Reserve with the purpose of taking scalps. In late May they attacked the new Camp Cooper, six miles away off the Reserve, trying to take the artillery piece there, but they were driven off by fifty Anadarkos under José María (Neighbours 1975:240).

In Texas 1860 was to be an election year. The incumbent governor, Harold R. Runnels, hoped to win reelection against Sam Houston by supporting the anti-Indian factions, which were of greater importance than the question of secession from the Union. In June 1859 he established a board of commissioners to investigate conditions on the reservations. One of its first acts was to authorize a force to police the reservations, that is, to keep the Indians in, rather than to protect them from Baylor's raiders. On July 24, when they tried to arrest Kakaraway for being off reservation, a short fight ensued in which one Indian was killed and another wounded; two of the police were also wounded.

A week later Neighbors, 1,100 Indians from the Brazos Reserve, and 384 from the Clear Fork Reserve, together with Agents Leeper and Ross and the various agency personnel, started north, arriving at the valley of the Washita River on August 16, 1859. Turning his charges over to Samuel Blain of the Wichita (Indian Territory) Agency, Neighbors returned to Texas. He may have intended to move his own family to the Washita River and continue in the Indian service, but upon reaching the town of Belknap he was ambushed and shot from behind (Neighbours 1975:279).

New Mexico, 1852–60

There were few reported Comanche interactions with Americans in New Mexico in the early 1850s, and most information came second-hand from Comanchero traders. In 1852 the governor of Tesuque Pueblo, himself a prominent Comanchero, reported meeting with Eagle (possibly Eagle Feathers),

Esakeep, and Tecube (previously unmentioned). The governor had heard rumors that Bajo Sol, "one of their principal chiefs," had made an alliance with the Mexican government to regain the territory lost in the Mexican War, but there was little action beyond those rumors; indeed, that was one of the only mentions of Bajo Sol north of the Rio Grande (Greiner 1852a; Abel 1916:191). If anything, the rumors probably referred to one of the various scalp-hunting agreements between Comanches and the northern Mexican states. In midsummer a Pueblo Comanchero reported that a large number of Comanches and Mescaleros were at the Bosque Redondo "for the purpose of trading" and wanted the agent to meet with them; the traders were particularly apprehensive about the Comanches because "they complain[ed] the government [had] not kept their promises to give presents" (Greiner 1852b). Early the next year Governor William Carr Lane suggested that the "wandering tribes" be removed from the Rio Grande to the eastern borders of the territory. He was particularly concerned about the "unwelcome presence of the Comanches and other Texas Indians who haven in New Mexico, [who] in their marauding excursions to the Republic of Mexico . . . are not always regardful of the right of property in this territory" (Lane 1853).

In the summer of 1855 Comanches again visited New Mexico. In May Pahayuko visited Governor David Meriweather in Santa Fe, while Sanaco, who had fled Texas the previous January, visited settlements along the Pecos River; there they reportedly "broke up the ranch of Messers Beck and Giddings" (Meriweather 1855a, 1855b). In July Sanaco was reported at the head of a war party of "Hoes and Coetoeteka" going after Apaches. A small group of Indians was trailed to Lucien Maxwell's ranch on the Rayado River, where they were found to be Yamparikas (Blake 1855). In September frantic rumors of 250 Comanches attacking Hatch's ranch northeast of Anton Chico on the Gallinas River, the "Easternmost settlement in New Mexico," were received at Santa Fe, but upon investigation it was found that the total damage was one cow and some green corn (Fauntleroy 1855; R. Johnson 1855). Maxwell attempted to call that a raid in order to get reimbursement from the government (Kenner 1969:121).

In September 1856 Esakeep visited Hatch's ranch and was given an ox and other foodstuffs (A. Hatch 1856). Later that month a party of some two hundred Comanches and Kiowas passed between Albuquerque and Santa Fe on their way to Navajo country, but details of the expedition are somewhat confused. According to one later account by General James H. Carleton, "I myself was in command of the troops in Albuquerque in 1856 when the Comanche and Kiowa visited that town. . . . I gave them an ox and some flour and coffee, and had a talk with them" (Carleton 1864b). However, in another account he stated:

I am advised that in the year 1856 the Comanches, in connection with a few Kiowas, made a raid through the settlements in the direction of the Navajo country, and it is said that on their return from the Rio Grande, they robbed houses, violated women, and killed the stock of the citizens. [Carleton 1864a:321]

Thus, it is not clear whether there were two expeditions, or whether Carleton was purposely obfuscating.

Meanwhile, Anglo settlement was spreading out along the Canadian River into the Indian country, and there were rumors of Comanche discontent but no incidents until March 1858, when Samuel Watrous's new ranch was burned to the ground and the foreman killed. The Comanches sent word that they wanted no further settlements east of Hatch's. In November the east-bound mail carrier was attacked, closing the mail route from Missouri to California. The next spring a party of surveyors along the Canadian River was captured but later released after a four-hour debate (Kenner 1969:126). In early 1859 a group of Comanches visited Hatch's and stated that they wanted to negotiate terms of peace (G. Thompson 1983:115). J. H. Collins, New Mexico superintendent of Indian affairs, hoping to reopen the mail line, went to meet them, taking along an escort of 130 soldiers. But the Indians, apparently frightened by the military, fled. Later that autumn the Indians returned to the settlements in force. A Creek Indian cattle drover was killed at Hatch's. By December the citizens of San Miguel County were complaining of destroyed ranches and saying that they expected more attacks any day (Greenwood 1859). Other raids on ranches along the Pecos River and on the Santa Fe Trail were blamed on the Comanches (Carleton 1864a).

In the summer of 1860 the army launched a three-prong punitive expedition against Comanches and Kiowas. Major John Sedgwick, leading one column from Fort Riley, Kansas, found no Indians at all. Another, under Major C. F. Ruff, spent June wandering around eastern New Mexico and northern Texas. Then after a mysterious horse disease, they had to walk back to his base on the Canadian River. In July he set out again. He burned a village on the Canadian—its identity is unknown—and chased its inhabitants as far as the Bents' old Canadian River post before he turned back. Both Ruff and his officers blamed their Comanchero guides for being none too eager to guide them to their clients (Kenner 1969:129–32).

In late July, the third column, six companies of the First Cavalry under Captain Samuel D. Sturgis, operating from Forts Washita, Arbuckle, and Cobb, found traces of an Indian village some distance north of the Arkansas River. After a four-day chase northward, they caught up with some Indians on the Solomon Fork of the Kansas River. Those Indians abandoned their camp equipment, and there was another four-day chase. Some distance north of Beaver Creek the Indians turned to fight, but, according to Strugis, after a brief stand they fled the fifteen miles north to the Republican River and dispersed. In all, he claimed twenty-nine Indians killed with a loss of two Indian guides killed, three soldiers wounded, and one missing (Hafen and Hafen 1959:245–254). The identity of the Indians Sturgis attacked is uncertain; indeed, he reported it as "Kioways, Comanches, and (I think) Cheyennes" (Hafen and Hafen 1959:246).

Of all of the military activities that summer, only Sturgis's campaign has information from the Indian side; indeed, there are two Indian accounts, one Kiowa, one Cheyenne. Unfortunately, there are problems reconciling those accounts. On the one hand, it was probably Sturgis's running fight that Mooney's Kiowa consultants described for the summer of 1860 (1898:308):

> [a part of the Kiowa tribe] with the Kwahadi and other western Comanche, under the chiefs Tabananaka (Hears the Sun) and Isahabit (Wolf Lying Down), were camped north [of the Arkansas] when one day the latter party discovered a large body of people crossing the river. Tabananaka went out to reconnoiter, and returned with the report that there were a great many of them and that they were probably enemies. The Kiowa and Comanche at once broke camp and fled northward, and on their way met the Cheyenne and Arapaho, to whom they told the news, whereupon the latter also fled with them. By this time it had been discovered that the pursuers were white soldiers, accompanied by a large body of Caddo, Wichita, Tonkawa, and Penateka Comanche. As they fled the Kiowa and their allies kept spies on the lookout who one night reported their enemies asleep, when they turned and attacked their enemies at daylight, killing a soldier but losing a Comanche named Silver Knife (properly Tin Knife) who was shot through the neck with an arrow. [Mooney 1898:308]

The other primary Indian source of the 1860 battle was a 1905 letter written by George Bent to George Hyde. Bent mentioned Comanches only in passing:

> Gen'l Sturgis with 5 companies of Dragoons from Ft. Gibson., Atk. Came up Washita River to Fort Cobb and employed as scouts Wichitas, Caddoes, Delawares, and Penetethka[18] Comanches, who always lived with these tribes and not with other Comanches. Called Quahadas who lived on Stake Plains and raided into Texas and Mexico. Asahavey was chief of Penetethka Comanches and Tabananeka was chief of the Quahadas of Stake Plains . . . Gen'l Sturgis was hunting for Kiowas Comanches & Apaches who had been raiding in Texas and chased them across the Arkansas River. Had three fights had one fight on Smoky Hill River with Kiowas he Killed chief named 'Hat' in this fight. Next day had fight with Arapahoes young Cheyenne called White Fool was killed in this

fight only three Cheyennes was with the Arapahoes they were Just returning from war party and were in camp with Arapahoes and told them that they had seen big party of soldiers coming towards the village so the Arapahoes went out and met Sturgis and had fight with him. Several days after this Sturgis had big fight on Solomons River with Cheyennes Arapahoes and Kiowas. They all got together and waited for Sturgis to come up. [Bent 1905]

A great deal of confusion surrounds Comanche participation in Sturgis's fight, including the probable conflation of elements from the 1858 fight on Little Robe Creek. The identity of the Indians Sturgis pursued is at issue. Sturgis himself wrote that they were "Kioways, Comanches, and (I think) Cheyennes." Mooney characterized the village as comprised primarily of Comanches, specifically Kwahadas, and a few Kiowas, but no Cheyennes or Arapahos; although Mooney was referring to a battle in 1860, the ethnonym *kwahada* 'antelope' did not appear in a direct reference until 1862, two years later. On the other hand, Bent claimed that the only Comanches in that fight were the Penateka scouts.

The specific identification of Comanche individuals provides little help in locating the battle. According to Mooney's Kiowa consultants, the Comanche village was led by Tabenanaka and Isahabit (Mooney 1898:308). Bent also gave those names, and also associated Tabenanaka with the Kwahadas, but he gave Asahavy as chief of the Penateka scouts, not as the second chief of the village. However, Tabenanaka was Yamparika (see fig. 2.3). Moreover, a great deal of confusion surrounds the other individual, for there were two men with very similar names in the 1860s and early 1870s. One was *isa habitʉ* 'wolf lying down'. His divisional affiliation is unclear, although he was apparently associated with the Nokonis; he played a relatively minor part in public affairs. The other man was *esi habitʉ* 'grey object lying down'. His name has been spelled in various ways (Asahabit, Esa-Havey, etc.; I will use Esihabit) and has been given several free translations (Grey Streak, Wolf's Road, Milky Way). He was a Penateka, but according to Joe Attocknie, had married a Yamparika woman and was living with her people (i.e., following uxorilical residence).

Both Mooney (for 1860) and Joe Attocknie (for 1858) mention the death of Silver Knife. All three, Mooney, Bent, and Attocknie mention the Penateka scouts, and all three mention Tabenanaka and Esihabit.[19] The death of Silver Knife cannot be independently verified as occurring at one or the other event. As in the case of the Wichita and Caddo scouts in 1858, there is documentary evidence that in 1860 Sturgis received permission to take six Delaware scouts—he had asked for twelve—and may have had as many as twenty Kansa Indian scouts as well (Hafen and Hafen 1959:196–97, 213), but there is apparently no documentary evidence that he had any Penateka scouts. According to Attocknie, the abortive scouting party included Tabenanaka's brother Pohocsucut (*puha kwasuʔu kutU* 'he has a medicine shirt'), as well as Paruasemena's son Esananaka, and his grandson Cheevers. Moreover, Esihabit was present when the village was attacked; indeed, he used his own exploits in the fight both when publically recounting his war exploits and when bestowing personal names.

While it is possible that it was the same village—that Tabenanaka and Esihabit were on Little Robe Creek in 1858 and were north of the Arkansas in 1860, and that both John Ford in 1858 and Samuel Sturgis in 1860 had undocumented Penatekas along (although Silver Knife could only have been killed once)—the chances of that coincidence would be very small. However, which incidents belong to which fight cannot now be sorted out.

In the fall of 1860, after the troops at Camp Radziminski were withdrawn to the new Fort Cobb on the Washita, the camp was taken over by Texas Rangers. In December another party of Rangers attacked a Comanche village on the Pease River in Texas, recapturing Cynthia Ann Parker. In October the entire army cattle herd in the Canadian valley was taken by unidentified Indians. In January 1861 an otherwise unidentified Comanche village of 150 lodges on the Cimarron River was burned.

Then in April 1861 the situation changed again. Two new threats took strength away from renewed army actions against the Comanches. On the one hand, there was a threatened war with the Mescalero Apaches; on the other, the impending American Civil War. Alexander Hatch (of Hatch's Ranch) attempted to negotiate a separate peace with the Comanches, but was squelched by Colonel W. W. Loring, a Confederate sympathizer, who was afraid that a peace with New Mexico would exclude the possibility of Comanche peace with Texas (Kenner 1969:135 n. 76). Finally, in May 1861, Superintendent Collins and Captain R. A. Wainwright met with Esakeep, Pluma de Aguilar (Eagle Feathers), and several others "known to be the principal chiefs of the band of Comanches which occupies the country along the Canadian," at Alamo Gordo Creek and agreed on "stipulations of peace" (J. H. Carleton 1864a:321). Besides Eagle Feathers and Esakeep, the other signers were Guagunc, Paracasqua, Parawausca, and Pehores; the latter are all previously unnamed, and the meanings of all the names are unknown. One stipulation was that Comanches would "not return to the settlements unless permitted to do so by the authorities of the Government." But the truce was broken several days later when a party led by Esakeep coming into Hatch's was warned off and a Comanche was killed (Kenner 1969:136).

Although that ended any official peace, it did not mean that all relations between Comanches and New Mexicans were ended. In 1862 Agent Lorenzo

Labadi reported, "Comanche have occasionally visited Anton Chico; they profess a desire for peace, and so far as I am advised, have behaved well during the year" (Labadi 1862). More importantly, Comanchero activity continued.

Along the Arkansas, 1854–60

For a year after the ratification of the Fort Atkinson Treaty, the Santa Fe trade was relatively quiet, at least as far as the Comanches were concerned. Although Agent Whitfield reported that conditions on the trail were generally "intolerable," he also said he had received no reports that Comanches or Kiowas were involved. On the other hand, he reported the rumor that "Mexicans" had set up "toll stations" on the trail. Moreover, hoping to keep the Indian trade for themselves, they had told the Comanches that the treaty goods were "bad medicine" (Whitfield 1854). Richardson (1933:187), although citing Whitfield's annual report, attributed the rumor of bad medicine to Osages. However, Whitfield's attribution of the rumor to Mexicans is clear and unequivocal. Although Osages may have realized that the treaty would take away their trade, as well as turn the Kiowas and Comanches against them, in 1854 the three tribes were friendly, even going to war together.

In 1856 the new agent, Robert C. Miller, reported that Shaved Head continued his "peaceful countenance." But the chief predicted that "when he should pass away from among his people they would no longer respect the treaty, but would, like the Kiowas, depredate upon his white brothers" (Miller 1857c). When the chief died in 1857, Miller reported that "so far, his apprehensions appear groundless, for his influence is still felt, as their days of mourning for him are not yet over" (Miller 1857c). Indeed, when Miller delayed distributing that year's annuities because some of the principal men were not yet present, some Kiowas threatened to "help themselves." At that, some Comanches,

> always reasonable, and ever ready to show friendship for the whites, stepped forward and offered their services to protect the train. The conduct of the Commanche on this occasion deserves all praise, manifesting as it did, a sincerity in the profession of friendship, and exhibiting a real anxiety to maintain peace and amity with the government. [Miller 1857c]

But by 1858, the Comanches' disposition had changed. When Agent Miller met the Upper Arkansas tribes at Pawnee Fork, the Cheyennes (remembering a fight with the army the summer before), the Arapahos, and the Apaches expressed a desire for a new treaty. The Comanches, however, "expressed an utter unwillingness to treat. Truly they have forgotten the teachings and influence of their good old chief Shaved Head" (Miller 1858b). In contrast to the attitude of the Cheyennes, who were chastised by their defeat, Miller blamed the Comanche's beligerence on the presence of Potsanaquahip and "many Comanches of the south" who had fled from the attack on the Little Robe Creek village less than two months before. According to Miller, Potsanaquahip

> exerts a controlling influence over the Comanches of the north . . . He boldly boasted of hostility towards the Texans, stating they had surprised him, and thereby obtained a temporary triumph, but as soon as the distribution of annuities was over, it was his determination to lead not only his own band but a portion of the Comanches of the north, against the white man of the south. [Miller 1858b]

When the distribution was over, a portion of the Comanches went hunting with the Arapahos—Miller said they were "Shaved Head's band" but gave no indication who had succeeded that chief; indeed he said the they had "joined the latter tribe" (Miller 1858). Another group joined some Kiowas going against the Osages. A third group, led by Potsanaquahip, went southward looking for Texans.

Potsanaquahip did not have to look far. In September an expedition under the command of Captain Earl Van Dorn got under way from Fort Belknap. Lawrence Ross, son of the agent on the Brazos Reserve, led a force of 135 Indians from that reservation. They established a base camp on Otter Creek, at the west end of the Wichita Mountains, calling it Camp Radziminski after a recently deceased officer. In October Van Dorn attacked a Comanche camp near the Wichita village at Rush Springs on the Washita River, killing 58 Comanches, burning 120 lodges, and capturing 300 horses. Richardson (1933:240) says the village was under Potsanaquahip; Nye, however (1969:19), said that although Potsanaquahip was present, the leaders were Quahateme, which he gave as Hair Bobbed on One Side, and Hotoyokowat (*hu* 'wood' *toya katU* 'hill' sometimes called Over the Buttes), a Yamparika. Nye (1969:22) also reported that another fatality was Mohee, but by the following November a Comanche named Mohee was still reported to be near the Texas Reservation. Two other casualties were Lieutenant Cornelius Van Camp, killed, and Major Earl Van Dorn, seriously wounded.

In the spring Van Dorn led another expedition against the northern Comanches. In early May 1859 they passed a two-week-old village said to have 2,000 fires. A day later they attacked another camp, later said to have been Potsanaquahip's, driving away its inhabitants, killing forty-nine, and taking thirty prisoners. It was from those prisoners that it was learned that the first

camp was under Ola Mocohopie (meaning unknown) and Mulaquetop (Richardson 1933:242). The prisoners were first sent to Camp Radziminski and
then to San Antonio. Their fate is unknown.

Thus, the Comanches were sullen when their new agent, William Bent,
met them in September at Walnut Creek. There he found 2,500 Kiowas and
Comanches who "signified a desire for peace," but at the withdrawal of the
troops accompanying Bent, they "assumed a threatening attitude" (Bent 1859:
138). Not the least of the problems Bent faced was that he brought no treaty
goods (Robinson 1859). The reason for the lack of presents is unknown.

Comanche Political Resources at Midcentury

The period 1846–60 brought a number of major changes in the relative
importance of Comanche resource domains. Several long-standing domains,
most obviously those derived from the distribution of subsistence and prestige political gifts, declined in importance, while others, such as those
derived from the trade in horses, buffalo products, and captives, took on
new value.

One aspect of the distribution of political gifts in that period differs from
previous distributions: they all came from Anglo-Americans. That is, the Comanches had lost any political capital they may have had from being able to
play on their position between the Spaniards and the Mexicans on the south
and west, and the Anglo-Americans on the east. However, there was still a
geographic differential in the distribution of political gifts.

Beginning in 1849 Thomas Fitzpatrick made distributions to the upper
Arkansas Comanches, although he had no treaty authority to do so, and there
is no account of the recipients or of the amounts given. In 1851 Fitzpatrick
was given authority to make distributions in conjunction with his Fort
Laramie Treaty, but since Comanches did not participate in that council, they
did not receive any of those distributions. They did, however, receive a small
portion of the gifts distributed at Fort Atkinson in 1851 and 1852. The 1853
Fort Atkinson Treaty specified $18,000 for annuities for ten years, but it is
not clear how the funds were actually spent, or whether they were spent at
all; the treaty monies had to be appropriated by Congress, and Congress was
not always willing to act. There were also several threats to "deduct from or
withhold" annuities to pay for depredations (Miller 1857c, 1858b); it is not
known, however, whether those deductions were ever made.

When they were available, however, the Arkansas River gifts ran the
gamut of American manufactures. Several companies specialized in goods for

the Indian trade, and there was extensive competition for the contracts to supply the treaty goods. Table 6.8 shows the annuity goods for the year 1858 by supplier. However, there were continual complaints about the quality, quantity, and selection of goods. In 1856 Agent Miller suggested:

> In lieu of fancy cover lids [coverlets ?], carbon umbrellas, rugs, coats, pantaloons, calico, and mosquito netting, I would suggest an increase in all kinds of provisions with the exception of coffee and rice which should be greatly decreased, being but little used (the latter the Indians scatter on the prairie). In place of common brown sugar, I recommend clarified. . . . there are too many fry pans, and not enough hoop iron. For want of latter, the pans are frequently made up into arrowpoints. [Miller 1856]

A year later he commented about the quality of other goods:

> As to the tobacco, I do not recall making use of the expression "rotten and worthless" as it is perhaps too strong. But it was really of an exceedingly inferior quality, not suitable to send even to Indians. It was very black and strong and so wet that it need but a gentle pressure to cause the moisture to ooze out upon your hand. . . I gave it the soldiers, but even the old and inveterate chewers . . . could scarcely make use of it. [Miller 1857b]

Prestige gifts included medals, flags, swords, and uniforms. In 1856 Agent Miller on the Arkansas wanted "18 coats and pantaloons . . . ornamented with the military buttons and lace which will serve as a mark of distinction for the head chief." Firearms and ammunition were also given, but there is little information about the numbers and calibers involved. In 1856 Agent Miller suggested to the supplier of the provisions, "Because of the smaller game, send flint lock rifles of 1/2 oz or 'trade ball' but not unless can supply all the soldiers, for the large tribes, 2-300 each" (Miller 1856).

In Texas the 1846 Butler and Lewis treaty called for a one-time distribution of provisions. Another $10,000 was appropriated in 1847, but by March 1849 R. S. Neighbors complained that "a sufficiency of means has not been provided for the purchase of necessary presents, tobacco, etc., required to carry on and maintain friendly intercourse with the Indians" (Neighbors 1849c). Neither the 1850 Rollins nor the 1851 Rogers agreements included provisions for annuities.

Although there was no clear treaty authority for subsistence and rations on the reservation, the residents were fed and clothed. In 1857 about $2,100 in cloth, clothing, and blankets were issued to the residents. Table 6.9 summarizes the resources available to the reservation population for those periods

Table 6.8

Annuity Goods for the Year 1858, by Supplier

Bought of Cronin, Hurxthal, and Sears, New York

350 prs 3 pt white blankets	2065.00	5952 1/2 yds calico	535.75
450 prs 2 1/2 pt white blankets	2070.00	4333 yds blue drill	476.63
40 prs 1 1/2 pt white blankets	48.00	3911 1/4 yds ticking	508.46
34 prs 1 pt white blankets	37.50	1781 1/4 yd plaid sundry	207.45
100 prs 3 pt scarlet blankets	700.00	33 lbs cotton thread	9.90
50 prs 2 1/2 pt scarlet blankets	250.00	216 lbs American vermillion	64.80
50 prs 3 pt green blankets	300.00	419 flannel shirts	471.38
50 prs 3 pt gentinillo	312.00	333 calico shirts	166.50
50 prs 2 1/2 pt gentinillo	235.00	8 doz Canadian bells	96.00
1033 1/4 yds blue cloth	1498.21	3672 yds brown drill	348.84
52 1/4 yds scarlet cloth	922.98	240 lbs black and white beads	120.00
82 lbs sewing thread	32.80	180 lbs ruby and blue beads	135.00
9 gross worsted gartering	11.25	46 prs wrappers	115.00
12 rugs	9.00		

Total $12,050.00

Bought of Ryan and Lantham

17,500 lbs flour	350.00	3611 1/9 lbs tobacco	650.00
7179 1/2 lbs rice	350.00	27 11/32 kegs powder	175.00
2608 1/3 lbs coffee	300.00	48 7/10 bags bullets	100.00
7948 1/2 lbs sugar	775.00	500 lbs hoop iron	25.00
8461 1/2 lbs pilot bread	275.00		

Total $3,000.00

Bought of J. Roche, Lancaster, Pa.

200 flint-lock guns	1300.00	200 gun covers	40.00
17 1/3 doz powder horns	65.98	packaging	36.75

Total $1,442.73

Bought of T. Poultney, Baltimore, Md.

511 brass kettles	189.07	25 gro fish hooks	7.50
90 tin kettles	67.50	96 doz fish lines	17.28
80 tin kettles	60.00	15 doz coarse combs	4.50
40,000 flints	52.00	10 doz fine combs	5.00
75 camp kettles	52.00	5 doz scissors	7.50
36 drawing knives	18.00	24 doz zinc mirrors	24.00
22 doz hack saw files	11.00	18 Japaned kettles	135.00
22 doz basting spoons	18.75	30 doz tin cups	30.00
84 doz table spoons	21.00	4 doz 6 qt pans	10.00
6 1/2 gro gun screws	13.00	8 doz 4 qt pans	16.00
8 1/2 fire steels	5.10	9 doz 2 qt pans	14.40
70 gro needles	3.50	40 camp kettles	60.00
22 doz squaw awls	22.00	26 half axes	208.00
48 doz butcher knives	76.80		

Total $1,303.50

Total purchase $17,796.23

SOURCE: Miller 1858

Table 6.9

Resources on the Texas Reservation, 1855-59

YEAR	MONTH	POPULATION	BEEF SUPPLIED(LBS.)	LBS./PERSON/MONTH
1855	March	180		
	May	226		
	June	249		
	Sept	277		
1856	Jan	450		
	May	507		
	Sept	557		
1857	Sept	424		
	Dec	350	79,800 (6 mos.)	38
1858	Jan	381	21,600	56.69
	Feb		20,400	[53.54][a]
	Mar		22,800	[59.84]
	June	380		
	July		27,387	[72.07]
	Aug		21,000	[56.75]
	Sept	371	24,600	63.78
	Oct	341	28,200	82.69
	Nov	374	25,025	66.91
1859	March	380		
	July	384		

[a]Per person totals in brackets based on previous month's population. Blank columns indicate that no data are available.

SOURCE: Kavanagh 1986:344-45

for which data are available. Meanwhile, the chiefs and headmen on the reservation received some $300 worth of cloth, vermilion, gun powder, and lead, as well as $124 in silver (Neighbors 1857). Ketumsee received a modest salary, "so he could devote his time to his duties and not have to hunt" (Neighbours 1975:182) and was the only Indian to live in a house, a former barracks at Camp Cooper.

In New Mexico apparently the only political gifts were "goods delivered to the Comanche and Apache by Benjamin Latz at Bosque Redondo, Canon de la Luna, Anton Chico, La Cuesta, Puertocillo, and San Miguel while on their way to Santa Fe for the purpose of making a treaty with Governor James S. Calhoun" in May 1851 (Messervy 1853). However, there is no information about which Indians, Comanche or Apache, may have received the goods.

There was another dimension to that geographical differential: each agency claimed the Comanches as "their" Indians. In July 1851, apparently in an attempt to get some of Fitzpatrick's appropriation, Calhoun of New Mexico claimed the Comanches as New Mexican Indians, saying, "[They] are principally within the limits of New Mexico" (Abel 1915b:393). Similarly, in 1853 Robert S. Neighbors objected to Fitzpatrick's treaty because the Comanches were "Texas Indians" and argued that "the state of Texas should be allowed the benefit of whatever Treaty is made" with them (Neighbors 1853).

Although the resource domains based on political gifts declined, other traditional domains continued. The Comanchero trading pattern continued after the Mexican War. Agent J. S. Calhoun issued licenses to New Mexico traders, many of whom were Pueblo Indians. Of the first fourteen licenses granted by Calhoun in 1850, seven were to Pueblos (see table 6.4). In 1850 Lieutenant John Buford at Cebolleta arrested six men from Isleta Pueblo for trading without licenses "of any kind" (McLaws 1850a). In 1853 Amiel W. Whipple's exploring expedition on the Canadian River met at least three parties of Pueblo traders from Santo Domingo and Tewa. While camping at Tucumcari, Whipple noted that there were several such parties in his vicinity, one of twenty-two persons "en route for the Comanche country" (Foreman 1941:95).

On the Arkansas, Agent Whitfield estimated that the Arkansas River Comanches had an annual income of $10,000, based on the consumption and sale of the meat and hides of 30,000 buffalo, 2,000 deer, 1,000 elk, and 500 bears—second only to the Cheyennes (table 6.10).

The horse trade continued to be the primary context for trade in Comanchería. Besides Anglo-Americans, other Indians also bought horses. In the summer of 1846 Wild Cat and a party of Seminoles went to Comanchería to trade for furs and mules (Foreman 1934:245). In 1847 Osages purchased "1500 head of mules worth $50-75,000," for which they traded "tobacco, lead, powder, blankets, blue cloth, strouding, and firearms," and they had already made arrangements for the next year's trade (J. M. Richardson 1847). In the same year 250 Seminoles trying for furs and mules met with little success (Foreman 1934:245). In February 1848 the Arapaho chief Coho told Thomas Fitzpatrick that he had nothing to do with the raiding along the Santa Fe Trail, "except to buy [their] horses" (Fitzpatrick 1848a). In 1848 Fitzpatrick reported, "For two years, the Comanche have been meeting Osages for trade, by which the Comanche receive their necessary supplies in barter for horses." In the spring of that year a party of sixteen Creeks and Cherokees headed by Unus Macintosh went out to buy horses: "Our mules were laden with tobacco, vermillion etc., which we expected to barter with the Comanches for mules" (Foreman 1939:165).

Table 6.10
Accounts on the Arkansas, 1856

	ADULT MEN	WOMEN (MEN + 50%)	TOTAL	HORSES	LODGES
Comanche	800	1200	3200	20,000	400
Kiowa	600	900	2400	15,000	300
Apache	80	120	320	2,000	40
Cheyenne	1080	1620	3150	17,500	350
Arapaho	600	900	2400	15,000	300

	EST. ANNUAL INCOME	EST. BUFFALOS KILLED	EST. ELKS KILLED	EST. DEER KILLED	EST. BEARS KILLED
Comanche	$10,000	30,000	1000	2000	500
Kiowa	7,000	20,000	600	1500	300
Apache	1,000	2,000	50	500	25
Cheyenne	15,000	40,000	3000	2500	2000
Arapaho	5,000	20,000	1000	1500	500

SOURCE: Whitfield 1856

Although the Comanches certainly raised horses, the scale of the horse trade emphasizes the significance of the translation of war booty into trade items. In 1853 Cuervo (Crow), a follower of Bajo Sol, told the *Durango, Mexico, Registro* that the Comanches sold the animals they stole "to tall white men with big feet, . . . Yankees who pay them with powder, bullets, rifles, swords, tobacco, and whiskey" (R. A. Smith 1970:32). Table 6.11 summarizes the reported losses due to Indian depredations in Refugio County, Texas, 1847–54, although not all of those were the result of Comanche action; table 6.12 summarizes the losses in Nueces and Montague counties in Texas, 1849–61.[20] It may be noted that the period of major horse raids in northern Mexico, 1848–52, corresponds to the period of major demand for horses during the California gold rush.

The trade in captives continued to be a significant part of the Comanche economy, and as before, it is not clear whether captives were an explicit or incidental object of raids. With the advance of Anglo-Americans into Comanchería, a new phase in the captive trade began as the Anglo-Americans placed an explicit cultural value on ransoming white captives, particularly women and children. A number of middlemen arose who bought captives from Indian owners with the expectation of being paid by the government. Of

Table 6.11

Losses in Refugio County due to Indian Depredations, 1847–54

WHO	WHEN	AMOUNT	WHO	WHEN	AMOUNT
M. Whalen	Mar 1847	$470.00	J. W. Byrn	Oct 1850	140.00
Thomas Welder	Mar 1847	760.00	John Welder	Oct 1850	2068.00
Wm. St. John	Apr 1847	120.00	John Wood	Mar 1851	125.00
John Wood	May 1847	270.00	Thomas Welder	Aug 1851	25.00
John Wood	Apr 1848	300.00	John Welder	Aug 1851	100.00
C. E. Dugat	Aug 1848	230.00	H. H. McGrew	Dec 1851	290.00
D. O'Driscoll	1850	210.00	John Wood	Dec 1851	150.00
Pablo Chaves	Jan 1850	425.00	John Wood	Dec 1851	210.00
John Welder	Jan 1850	1428.00	M. Simpson	Aug 1854	100.00
Thomas Welder	Jan 1850	450.00	S. Campbell	Aug 1854	90.00
Mary Doyle	Mar 1850	3971.00	M. Barlow	Aug 1854	320.00
John Wood	12 June 1850	1530.00	Juan Silveria	Aug 1854	350.00
Juan Silveria	June 1850	100.00	Jose Castillo	Aug 1854	2685.00
Thomas Welder	Aug 1850	300.00	Thomas Welder	Aug 1854	680.00
J. J. Thomas	19 Oct 1850	190.00	Mary Doyle	Aug 1854	120.00
H. Scott	Oct 1850	160.00	Pablo Chaves	Aug 1854	200.00
					Total: $18,107.00

SOURCE: Winfrey and Day 1959–66, 3:265

Table 6.12

Losses in Nueces and Montague Counties due to Indian Depredations, 1849–61

WHEN	COUNTY	HORSES	VALUE	CATTLE	VALUE
1849–1861	Nueces	506	$12,800.00	253	$1265.00
1857–1861	Montague	135	$22,090.00	18	$ 221.00

SOURCE: Winfrey and Day 1959–66, 4:56, 64

them, Calhoun noted, "The trading in captives has been so long tolerated in the territory that it has ceased to be regarded as a wrong, and purchasers are not prepared willingly to release captives without an adequate ransom" (Abel 1915b:183).

On the other side, the one item of trade that caused American officials the greatest concern was firearms. However, it must also be noted that the actual ease of obtaining weapons might be overblown. A common charge hurled at various traders was that they were arming the Indians with better weapons than those possessed by the army, however the validity of the charge is unclear.

Comanche Political Organizations, 1846–60

Many Anglo-Americans continued to refer to Comanches in geographical terms, for example, northern, middle, and southern. However, those terms were often inconsistently applied and generally did not correspond to the Comanche language ethnonyms and thus to Comanche divisional organizations. For instance, Marcy noted, "The Northern and Middle Comanches subsist almost entirely upon the flesh of the buffalo; they are known among other Indians as 'buffalo eaters'" (1856:94). The problem here is a confusion of native ethnonyms and their translations with the geographic names; although 'buffalo eaters' is a literal interpretation of Kotsoteka, the Kotsotekas were neither northern nor middle, but western Comanches. In 1851 Colonel Dixon S. Miles, commander at Fort Washita, called "Pa-yo-ho-kee," clearly the Tenewa Pahayuko, a "Northern" Comanche (Foreman 1934:128); others called the Tenewa middle, or even southern Comanches.

Those problems aside, the documentary record of Comanche political organizations in the period 1844–60 is primarily concerned with two divisions, the Hois and the Penatekas on the one hand, and the Yamparikas on the other. The Kotsotekas are virtually unmentioned in the historical record; there are but few references to them: the Buffalo Eaters who visited Abert's camp along the Canadian in 1845, Chipeseah's 1848 visit to Mopechucope, Fitzpatrick's 1852 reference to the Coosentickeras, the possible equivalence of Froebel's Ciboleros with Buffalo Eaters that same year, and the rumor that Sanaco was leading Hoes and Coetoekas against Apaches in 1855. One possible explanation for their absence may come with the equation of Magüe, one of the leaders of the northern Mexican raiders of 1848–52, with the later Kotsoteka called Mowway: it is possible, albeit unlikely, that many if not all

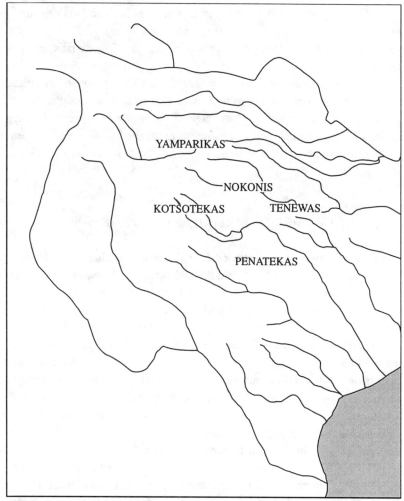

Map 5. Comanchería, ca. 1846.

Kotsotekas may have decamped from the plains of eastern New Mexico for
an extended five-year sojourn in northern Mexico.

The Tenewas and the newly named Nokonis have only a limited presence
in the historical records of the period 1844–60. Although in the first part of
the period, 1844–49, the Tenewas were "the principal ones to be treated with
and conciliated" (P. M. Butler and Lewis 1846:6), after the 1848–49 epidemics there was little direct mention of the Tenewas for many years. They
are indirectly noted in Colonel Miles's mention of Pahayuko as a "Northern"
Comanche in 1851, a possible visit by Pahayuko to New Mexico in 1855, and
another possible visit to the Texas reservation in 1857. However, based on

the references to the Comanches who frequented the Wichita Mountain area and who had continued interaction with the tribes of eastern Indian Territory, the Creeks, Seminoles, and Kickapoos, it can be inferred that the focus of the Tenewas was in that direction. Although the Nokonis were often suspected of raids on the Texas settlements, there is little definite information about them.

The most visible political change was the disintegration and reorganization of the Hois and the Penatekas of Texas. In 1846 Butler and Lewis, probably based on information from Robert Neighbors, and granting the confusion inherent in their list, estimated that they numbered 400 lodges with a population of 2,800; in 1851, although counting Pahayuko, who may have been Tenewa, they numbered between 1,800 and 2,200; in 1854 the "whole Southern Band," including Ketumsee, Potsanaquahip, and Sanaco consisted of 1,200 people. By 1859 there were only 384 people in that political organization. A variety of factors brought about the decrease. First there were the 1848-49 epidemics. Then the next few years brought a severe drought, and the buffalo stayed away from Texas (J. A. Allen 1877:525). In the power vacuum created by the loss of political leaders after 1849, the Hois Comanches—now called Penatekas—split into two, if not three, groups following different leaders. Initially, Potsanaquahip and Sanaco disputed the leadership, with Ketumsee apparently supporting Potsanaquahip. But by 1854 the Texas arena was divided between Sanaco and Ketumsee; the political overtones of their confrontation at the meeting with Neighbors and Marcy are obvious. During the years 1855-60 Sanaco was blamed for many raids about San Antonio (F. R. Adams 1955:149), and he spent much of his time to the west and north. His visit to New Mexico in 1855 was probably as much to dispose of goods to traders there as to go against the Apaches. Meanwhile, Potsanaquahip withdrew to the north; the 1855 rumor of war put a seal on his separation. That left only Ketumsee and his followers explicitly identified as Penatekas.

The political resources available on the Texas reservation were limited, and although there were apparently sufficient rations to support the residents, there were not enough to attract more. More importantly, there were no goods with which the political leaders could enhance their own prestige or that of their followers; Ketumsee's monthly thirty dollars probably did not go far in maintaining his people's support. Thus, the size of the population on the Texas reservation exemplifies the limits placed on a political organization by the availability of resources.

The Hois-Penateka organization was under great stress, but the Yamparikas to the north maintained a strong organization even in the interval between 1845-49 when trade was essentially shut off. If the Shaved Head of the 1850s was the same man who had asked for the establishment of the Bents'

Canadian River post in 1842, then he had maintained his position for at least fifteen years, if not longer. Both Simon Buckner and John Whitfield acknowledged that he had significant influence over the Comanches on the Arkansas River. During that period, except for the interval between 1845–49, the Yamparika connection with traders was secure. By 1855, according to Whitfield's accounting, the Comanche, that is, Yamparika, trade on the Arkansas was second only to that of William Bent's Southern Cheyenne relatives. Shaved Head's ability to maintain good relations between the traders and his people was of political as well as economic importance, and was ultimately expressed in the 1853 Fort Atkinson Treaty, four of the six signers of which were Yamparikas.

Another resource domain held by the Yamparikas along the Canadian River in New Mexico was personified by Esakeep and Eagle Feathers. Except for a possible trip to Bent's Fort by Esakeep, and Eagle Feathers's abortive 1851 trip to Santa Fe, all reports locate them along the river. There they acted as gatekeepers not only for Anglo-American parties traveling along the Canadian, but also for New Mexican ciboleros and Comancheros venturing out from the settlements, as well as for the various Comanche and Apache groups who had Mexican horses to trade.

7

Comanchería during and after the

Civil War, 1860–75

Confederate Fort Cobb, 1860–62

At the outbreak of the Civil War the Union garrison at Fort Cobb on the Washita River was withdrawn, and those officials who remained switched allegiance to the Confederacy; they were, of course, mostly Texans. Meanwhile, the new Confederate government at Richmond quickly moved to formalize relations with the residents of Indian Territory. There were a variety of reasons for that action, not the least of which was the attempt to persuade the slave-holding Indians of Indian Territory that their interests lay with the Confederates (Abel 1915a). In March Confederate president Jefferson Davis appointed Albert Pike, the Boston adventurer of the 1830s and later newspaper owner and publisher in Arkansas and Tennessee, to be "Commissioner to all the Indian tribes West of Arkansas and South of Kansas" (Davis 1861). After concluding treaties with the various nations in the eastern part of the territory, Pike arrived at Fort Cobb in early August. On August 12 he concluded two treaties, one with the "Peneteghca band of the Neum or Comanches" and other tribes of the Wichita Agency, the other with the "Noconi, Ta-ne-i-weh, Cochotihca and Yaparihca bands of the Neum, called by the white men, the Comanches of the Prairies and Staked Plains."

The Penateka treaty was signed by Kekarewa, called the "Principal Chief of the Peneteghca"; Tosawa, "the second chief"; and Pa-in-hot-sa-ma (prob-

Table 7.1

Signers of the Second Confederate Treaty, 1861

Nokonis:

Quenahewi; probably *kwina hibi* 'drinking eagle' although Joe Attocknie suggested *kwina hubi* 'middle aged woman'; previously unmentioned.

Kepahewa; probably *ke paa hibi* 'doesn't drink water'; previously unmentioned.

Cho-o-shi, no translation given. Said to be a "retired chief," he was possibly Chosewi, the Growing Chief who met with Neighbors in 1847.

Tenewas:

Pohowiquasso *puhihwitʉ kwasuʔu* 'iron shirt'. He was present during the negotiations but was absent at the signing and Quenahewi signed for him. The similarity of the name to the Iron Shirt allegedly killed in 1858 raises the possibility that the accounts of the latter's death were incorrect.

Ke-e-na-toh-pa, previously unmentioned, no translation given.

Yamparikas:

Bistevana, previously unmentioned, no translation given; said to be the "Principal Chief."

Tehiaquah, no translation given; probably *tuhʉya kwahipʉ* 'horse back'; in later years he was identified as Nokoni.

Pahaiechi, previously unmentioned, no translation given.

Kotsotekas:

Maawe 'Hand', probably 'shaking' or 'trembling hand.' Unless he was the man named Magüe or Mano of Tabe Tuk's group in Mexico, he was previously unmentioned. He was said to be the "Principal Chief." The name is usually spelled Mowway.

Chocora, previously unmentioned, no translation given.

Tecowewihpa, previously unmentioned, no translation given. The word is possibly *tekwawapu* 'speaker'

SOURCE: Pike 1861b

ably Pianachamon), called the "War Chief." The second treaty was signed by eleven Nokoni, Yamparika, Tenewa, and Kotsoteka chiefs (table 7.1).

Both treaties contained substantially the same provisions: that the various bands and tribes would be "good neighbors to each other"; that there would be "perpetual peace and brotherhood between the Comanches and the Cherokee, Creek, Seminole, Choctaw and Chickasaw Nations"; that the Penatekas would remain on their reservation; and that the others would settle on the reservation, which would be "their own property like their horses and cattle." The Confederacy agreed to furnish each warrior with a flintlock rifle and ammunition, as well as rations of sugar, coffee, salt, soap, and vinegar "for as long as necessary." They would also provide 20 cows and calves for each 50 persons, 1 bull for each 40 cows, and 250 hogs. In addition, farm equipment and other necessities would be provided. Particular emphasis was placed on the fact that Texas was now a part of the Confederacy and that Texas had "sign[ed] this convention when the Commissioner sign[ed] it. . . . all hostilities and enmities between it [Texas] and them [the Comanches] [were] now ended." There would be no Texas troops stationed within the limits of the reservation except for troops chasing Kiowas (Pike 1861a, 1861b). Pike also provided at least one "Letter of Safeguard" to a participant (table 7.2).

The treaties were presented to the Confederate Senate on December 12, 1861 (Davis 1861) and ratified by the end of the month. However, the Senate struck out the provisions for removing Texas troops and for supplying arms, the latter probably because the Confederacy needed all the guns it could get for the war. Although $64,862 was allocated to "comply with Treaty Stipulations" (Abel 1915a:322), in 1862 Albert Pike used the money to pay his Choctaw and Chickasaw troops (Gaines 1989:75); it is not known whether other moneys were ever appropriated for the Fort Cobb Indians, and if so, how they were distributed.

In later correspondence Pike reported that the Comanche chiefs promised to visit the other bands to induce them to come in, and he gave the names of those other bands as "Mocha, Ke-wih-chi-mah, Tich-aih-ken-e, and Pa-a-bo"; in an 1866 manuscript attributed to Pike the names and translations are given as Mooche 'Bluff on the Staked Plains'; Kewichchemah 'Who Never Gets Enough to Eat'; Tichakane 'The Sewers'; and Paabo 'Who Stays with the White People' (Pike 1866).[1] All are previously unrecorded as ethnonyms. The first probably refers to Muchoque (*motso ku?e* 'sharp hill' or 'moustache hill')[2], the prominent Comanchero trading location. The second is a personal name, usually spelled Kawertzeme and translated as Can't Fill Him Up or Long Hungry; it is possibly *kehewa* 'be all gone' *tsuma* 'used up'; he was Mowway's son-in-law, and said to have been Kotsoteka. The third is a previously unrecorded ethnonym, *tutsahkunuu* 'sewing people'; in later years they were said to be a local band of the Yamparikas. The fourth name is unknown.

On the Fort Cobb reservation the Penatekas were better housed than in Texas. In January 1862 Agent Matthew Leeper, who had served on the Texas Comanche reserve and was successor to S. A. Blain at the Wichita Agency in Indian Territory, noted that although on the Texas reserve there was but one house—Tosawa's, formerly used as a barracks at Camp Cooper—here there were "eight or ten neatly hewn log cabins with good chimneys, three double log hewn houses with good chimneys" for the chiefs, and a "number of warm comfortable picket houses which they partly built themselves and covered with grass" (Abel 1915a:340). Nye (1969:29) reported that Potsanaquahip

Table 7.2

Albert Pike's Letter of Safeguard for Bistevana

Letters of Safeguard

The Confederate States of America to all their officers, civil and military, and to all other persons to whom these presents shall come

The bearer of this is Bistevana, the principal chief of the Ya-pa-rih-ca band of the Ne-um, or the Comanches of the Prairie, and those who accompany him, and the headmen of that band; all of whom have this day concluded and signed on behalf of the whole Ya-pa-rih-ca band, articles of a convention of peace and friendship between that band and other bands of the Ne-um with us, and have thereby agreed to settle and live upon reserves in the country between Red river and the Canadian, leased by us from the Choctaws and Chickasaws; and the said chief has also agreed to visit the other bands of the Ne-um, not parties to the same convention, and now on the Staked Plain and elsewhere, and persuade them also to settle upon reserves in the same country. We have accordingly taken the said chief, and the said headmen, and all other persons, of both sexes and all ages, of the said Ya-pa-rih-ca band, from this day forward, under our protection, until they shall, for just cause, forfeit the same, and that forfeiture be declared by us; and we have therefore granted and do grant to them and to each of them these our letters of safeguard, for their protection, and to avail each and all of them as far as our authority and jurisdiction extends. You are, therefore, charged to respect these letters, and to give all the said persons protection and safe conduct, and any infraction by any of you of this safeguard will be visited by us with all the penalties due to those who violate the public faith and dishonor the confederacy.

In testimony whereof, Albert Pike, commissioner of the Confederate States to all the Indian nations and tribes west of those states, doth hereunto set his hand and affix the seal of his arms.

Done and granted at the agency of the Confederate States for the Comanches, Wichitas and other bands of Indians near the False Washita river, in the leased country aforesaid, this twelfth day of August, in the year of our Lord one thousand eight hundred and sixty-one.

SOURCE: Boone 1861c:106

asked Leeper to build him a house, but the agent refused, saying he "did not intend to built a house for any Indian." In addition to those houses, the Comanches had a number of Sibley tents taken from Fort Cobb after its abandonment by the Federals.

The Penateka chiefs worked closely with the new Confederate authorities. In mid-August, after Pike left, Horace P. Jones, former farmer on the Texas Reserve and now interpreter at Fort Cobb, formed a company of Indian

Table 7.3
The Comanche Police Force at Confederate Fort Cobb, 1861

NAME	MODERN RETRANSCRIPTION	COMMENT[a]
Pinahonchamon		Pianachamon, sergeant
Piveahope	*pibia huupi* 'big wood'	
Chickapoo		Kickapoo ?
Charley Chickapoo		
Jim Chickapoo		
Somo	*tsomo* 'bead'	
Booywysiska	*puhihwi* 'iron'	
Cuberawipo		
Canawith	*kana* 'poor'	
Arikapap	*aruka papI* ' deer head'	
Pithpawa		
Peahkoroh	*pia korohkO* 'big sash'	
Nanaquathteh		
Tonokah		
Athpah	possibly *ataputu* 'different'	
Pebarah	*pimoróó* 'cattle'	
Cursuah		
Cowandah		

[a]Except for Pianachamon and Arikapap (later known as Attacapap), none can be further identified.

SOURCE: Abel 1915b:344

soldiers to protect the agency in the absence of regular troops and to act as a spy company (table 7.3). But they were disbanded in May 1862 because "they would not remain at their encampment and their horses were never at hand when wanted" (Abel 1915a:350).

The Comanches were also involved in attempts to maintain peace in the Indian Territory, although the depth of their commitment to the effort is unclear. In mid-December, the chiefs of the reserve Indians sent a letter to the Seminole leaders in the east expressing regret that their "brothers in the Seminole Nation" were having internal difficulties, that they were "fighting one against the other, brothers against brothers, and friends against friends." They closed by saying that even though the Texans were up north fighting the"cold weather people"—a reference to the Federal forces, not to the Kiowa group of the same name—the Comanches would not fight unless the Northerners came down against them. The letter was signed by Potsanaquahip, Kikadawah (probably Kekarawa), the Anadarko chief José María, and Wichitas Tena,

Jim Pockmark, and George Washington. However, Potsanaquahip's involvement in such peace efforts is problematical, if for no other reason than his former antipathy toward Euroamericans.

In April Agent Leeper reported that some two thousand Indians from the "wild bands" of Comanches and Kiowas were camped within two days' travel of the reserve. They often visited the agency, where they shot the ration cattle in the pens and otherwise were "rather impudent and insolent in their demands." Although those antics disrupted the daily operations of the agency, of more long-term concern to Leeper was their influence on other young men:

> those wild fellows come in, hold war dances and scalp dances, speak of their agility in stealing horses and of their prowess in taking scalps of white men and Mexicans, and of the rapture with which they are received and amorous embraces of the young damsels on their return until the young men heretofore inclined to lead an idle but civil life on the Reserve are driven mad with excitement. Some of them have left, others are going today. [Abel 1915a:348]

Leeper sent interpreter Horace P. Jones to get Potsanaquahip to "check such outrages and reprove the boys for such improprieties," but "the old Indian . . . fiercely turned upon [him] . . . and abused [him] in the most unmeasured terms" (Abel 1915b:348).

Despite those incidents, Leeper jumped at the opportunity to meet with the "wild Comanches who have never been here before." In early May 1862 he reported that a group of chiefs had come in, wanting "to make a perpetual and everlasting peace." Leeper appointed July 4 for a

> general gathering in council of all the Chiefs and principal men belonging to the Comanches for the purpose of entering into a general and lasting peace upon the same terms and conditions which are offered those already settled. [Abel 1915a:347]

In reporting that, Leeper suggested that "three or four thousand dollars worth of goods furnished upon that occasion and distributed to them as presents would have a beneficial effect" (Abel 1915a:347).

Later that month General Pike reported—in words similar to those in Leeper's April report, suggesting that his report was based on it and other now lost reports—that "some two thousand [Comanches and Kiowas] are encamped about three days [Leeper said two days] from Fort Cobb." They asked if "they [could] be allowed to send a strong party and capture any trains on their way from Kansas to New Mexico." Pike had no objection: "To go on the war-path somewhere else is the best way to keep them from troubling Texas" (Pike 1862).

Some of those "wild" Comanches and Kiowas must have visited Fort Cobb during the next month. On May 31 Lone Wolf, the Kiowa chief, received a paper stating

> The bearer Esa Simmos ['one wolf' in Comanche] Kiowa Chief has visited and promised on the part of the tribe to be friendly with the people of Texas and ourselves. It is hoped that so long as they carry out that promise they will be treated kindly. [Signed] M. Leeper [Colley 1862]

However, there is no other documentary evidence of such visits.

In late June Leeper learned that "an annual festival or dance of the Kiowas and the wild Comanche bands is expected to be held about this time, which may detain them beyond the 4th of July"—according to Mooney (1898:310), the Kiowa Sun Dance that year was on upper Walnut Creek in Kansas—and he sent Tosawa and Pianachamon to "ascertain the precise time they may be expected here" (Abel 1915a:351). By July 11 they returned, apparently with the leaders of the Comanches and the Kiowas, for on that day Leeper reported that he had "entered into treaty stipulations with the Kioway Indians and all the Comanche bands with the exception of the Kua-hara-tet-sa-cono" (Abel 1915a:354). The latter name seems to be *kwaharu tutsahkunuu* 'antelope sewing people', a previously unrecorded ethnonym; it is similar to the form *tutsahkunuu* 'sewing people' mentioned by Pike in 1861, but the two groups were probably unrelated.

Leeper prepared to make a final treaty that fall, but on October 23, 1862, a party of Delawares and Shawnees from Federal Kansas attacked Fort Cobb. A number of whites were killed; the rest, including Agent Leeper, fled to Texas. Although the Wichitas and affiliated groups went north into Kansas, the whereabouts and activities of the Penatekas through the rest of the war are unknown. Nye (1969:33), based on informant statements, mentioned an incident in summer 1863 when a group of Kiowas attacked a Confederate force from Fort Arbuckle escorting a group of Caddos and Penatekas on a buffalo hunt. However, no confirmation of Confederate scouts in the vicinity, nor of how any Penatekas may have come to be at Fort Arbuckle, has been found. Confederate troops never reoccupied Fort Cobb, and for the time being the Fort Cobb Comanches had no official contact with Anglo-Americans.

The Arkansas River and New Mexico, 1861–67

Agent William Bent resigned in 1860 and was succeeded by Albert G. Boone, grandson of the pioneer. In March 1861 he reported that the chiefs of the Arapahos, Cheyennes, Kiowas, and Comanches were anxious for peace and wanted to go to Washington, even if they had to pay their own way (Boone 1861b). However, there is no other evidence that he had direct contact with Comanches until the following fall. In September 1861 Boone negotiated a truce agreement with Tapewinewah and Cocheaqwa at Fort Wise at the Big Timbers on the Arkansas River. Both Comanches are previously unnamed; Tapewinewah was given as Hard Metal, although the translation is doubtful. Cocheaqwa was given as Red Buffalo, probably *kuhtsu eka*; according to Joe Attocknie (1965), he was a son of Paruasemena (see fig. 2.1). They agreed to meet a year later at Fort Larned, Kansas, to sign a peace (Boone 1861a).

A month later eight unnamed "Texan Comanches" visited Fort Wise; a week after that Bistevana visited with five hundred or six hundred lodges. He brought with him a copy of the recently completed Confederate treaty and the safe conduct from General Pike. Instead of receiving a warm welcome, the Comanches were "much astonished" to find that they had made a treaty with the "enemies of [the United States] government" (Boone 1861c:104). They were probably also much confused by the Americans' actions; after twenty-five years of hearing that there were no differences between Texans and Americans, here were Americans saying that not only were there differences, but that Texans were now enemies.

The Comanches said they were anxious to "make [a] treaty and enter this agency." Probably a great incentive was the availability of annuity goods at Fort Wise and their absence at Fort Cobb. The Fort Atkinson Treaty goods for the previous two years had been withheld, although the exact reason is unknown, as is the reason why the distributions began again and how they came to be at Fort Wise. Boone suggested that a new treaty be made with the Comanches and that an annuity be set apart for them (Boone 1861c:105). Although the ensuing treaty was not formalized, it was the basis for the distribution of rations and annuities.

In February 1862 Little Raven, the Arapaho chief, brought news that smallpox was in the Kiowa and Comanche camps some fifteen miles below Fort Wise and that many were dying (Boone 1862). There is, however, no direct confirmation of this.

Meanwhile, in New Mexico, relations between Comanches and the Federals became friendly again. In October 1862 an army post, Camp Easton, was established on the Canadian River near the Cerro Tucumcari. Almost immediately there were Comanche visitors. In November Mowway, Little Buffalo (previously unmentioned), and other unnamed Comanches visited the post, even helping in the capture of some Confederate sympathizers. However, because it was "not consistent with our rules of war," post commander William Backus refused to divide the captured goods and arms with them

(Backus 1862). Backus also reported that the Comanches "wanted a captive for a war dance," but he did not elaborate; F. Stanley (1953:106) provided some details, but they are uncited and are probably more romantic than factual: he reported that the Comanches demanded that they be given a young girl who was with the party, saying they had just had a victory over Texas and needed a captive to burn. There is no other evidence of such practices among Comanches.

But Captain Backus did promise to pay for information about Confederate movements. Throughout the summer of 1863 Comanches visited the post, renamed Fort Bascom in August 1863. In contrast to the days of the Spaniards' gifts, however, they were given minimal provisions, food, and "old clothing" (Kenner 1969:142). Moreover, when Edward H. Bergmann, the new commander at Fort Bascom, presented the Indian Bureau a bill for $206.28 for Comanche subsistence, the Bureau refused to pay it, and the army, in turn, refused to provision Comanche visitors. Thus, in February 1864 Esakeep was turned away.

In early 1863 Agent Boone was replaced by S. G. Colley, who, in April, sent a delegation of Comanches, Kiowas, Apaches, and Caddos to Washington, D. C. According to the official record, the Comanches were Paruasemena and Prick in the Forehead; according to Joe Attocknie (1965) Paruasemena's companion on that trip was Painted Mouth *tupe naboo* 'painted lips', later spelled Tipenavon. Both Prick in the Forehead and Tipenavon were previously unrecorded names. The party stopped briefly at Fort Leavenworth where photographs were made of the two Comanches (plate 4), the earliest documented photographs of Comanches.[3]

In Washington they signed a treaty of perpetual "peace, friendship, and unity," agreeing that they would not "resort to or encamp upon" the Santa Fe Trail, nor "molest, annoy or disturb the travel, the emigration or the United States mail" on the trail; that they recognized the right of the postmaster general to build mail stations on the route; that except for article 6—the annuities article—the Fort Atkinson Treaty was "continued and made perpetual"; and finally, that "in consideration of the foregoing agreements . . . and of losses which they may sustain by reason of the travel of the people of the United States, and for the better support, and the improvement of the social condition," an annuity of $25,000 in "goods, merchandise, provisions or agricultural implements" would be made for five years, and for five additional years if deemed advisable by the president (Gorham 1869).[4]

Paruasemena was given a "certificate" proclaiming that he had "visited Washington, that he had behaved himself in a proper manner, and that he is a peaceful man." It further "direct[ed] all white men not to give him cause to break his word" (Taylor, et al. 1910:58). According to R. N. Richardson

Plate 4. Prick in the Forehead and Paruasemena. Photographed by Addis and Noel, Leavenworth, Kansas. 1863. Courtesy British Museum.

(1933:280), some time later medals were given to Hotoyokowat (*hu* 'wood', *toya* 'mountain', *kaweht* 'beyond', usually given as Over the Buttes), Mow-way, and Quenahewi, but there seems to be no official record of it.

Despite those efforts General James Carleton, commander of the Military Department of New Mexico, blamed Comanches for attacks at Walnut Creek on the Arkansas River, for taking horses from the troops between Forts Larned and Lyon, and for attacks on the upper and lower Cimarron crossings of the Santa Fe Trail. Carleton was particularly upset that on at least one occasion, when Comanches captured a group consisting both of Anglo-Americans and Mexicans, the Mexicans were set free, but the Americans were killed. He complained that "the discrimination which the Comanches have frequently made in favor of the people, natives to this Territory, and against Anglo-Americans, cannot be regarded in any other light than as an insult to the Government and to our people" (J. H. Carleton 1864a). Thus he declared the Comanches and the Kiowas in New Mexico "hostile" and began planning for an expedition against them.

However, New Mexico superintendent of Indian affairs Michael Steck, based on information from Comancheros, discounted the Comanches' participation in major raids. Carleton rejected the information as untrustworthy because of the commercial relations between Comancheros and Comanches. He did, however, note that since the abortive truce of Alamo Gordo in 1861, he had "not heard of their committing depredations upon the settlements of New Mexico." But, he said,

> If you will contemplate the record of their atrocities this year . . . I think you can hardly fail to see that I should be derelict in my duty if I should refrain from making at least one attempt to avenge our slaughtered and plundered citizens. [J. H. Carleton 1864a]

It may be noted that "the record of their atrocities" that year was exactly the point of debate.

In preparation for the upcoming campaign, in his role as ex-officio superintendent of Indian affairs in Colorado, Governor John Evans ordered the "friendly Indians" to collect at "places of safety." For the Comanches that was to be Fort Larned (Evans 1864). Although many Comanches did travel to Fort Larned, it is unlikely that all were there. Later, together with a "large number of Cheyennes, Arapahoes . . . Apaches, and Kiowas," they moved to the Pawnee Fork of the Arkansas River. There they spent a summer of relative inactivity, although Kiowa youths stole most of the fort's horse herd. By the fall, Agent Colley reported that "the Kiowas and Comanches have not committed any depredations for a long time, and it is supposed that they are now south of the Arkansas river, near the border of Texas" (Colley 1864).

Warned by Comancheros of the impending campaign, in September ten Kiowa and Comanche spokesmen went to Fort Bascom in an attempt to arrange a truce; the army reported the leader of the group as "F. M. Bears," probably Ten Bears, that is, Paruasemena (Kenner 1969:146). Carleton ordered the commanding officer at Fort Bascom to tell them,

> their people have attacked our trains, killed our people, and run off our stock; . . . we believe their hearts are bad, and that they talk with a forked tongue; . . . we put no confidence in what they say; they must go away, as we regard them not as friends; they need not come in with any more white flags until they are willing to give up the stock they have stolen this year from our people, and also the men among them who have killed our people without provocation or cause. [DeForrest 1864]

Needless to say, there was no further meeting.

Carleton had taken most of the summer to prepare for his campaign, and it did not get under way until the late fall. On November 10 a Kiowa village camped near the site of the Bent's old post on the Canadian River—now little more than weathering adobe brick walls—was attacked by the New Mexican forces and Ute and Apache auxiliaries under Kit Carson (Carson 1864). Carson said the village was 150 lodges; George H. Pettis, one of his officers, later reported it as 200 lodges (Pettis 1908). Carson's men succeeded in driving the Kiowas out of their village, but when Comanches from a nearby village of 350 lodges—Pettis said 500—counterattacked, the soldiers took up defensive positions inside the old adobe walls, escaping only by fighting their way back through the Kiowa village under the protection of their small cannon.

R. N. Richardson (1933:285) implied that the villages housed the Indians who had spent the summer on the Pawnee Fork and who later raided along the Santa Fe Trail and in Texas; indeed, Carson said he found in the Kiowa lodges "a number of women and children's dresses, bonnets, shoes, etc." (Carson 1864:943). But there is no direct evidence that the nearby Comanches were directly involved in any recent raids. According to his own statement three years later, Paruasemena was chief of the Comanche village (Sanborn et al. 1867:59); he had just been to Washington, and if he was the "F. M. Bears" who went to Fort Bascom two months before, he was indeed trying to maintain peace, while it was Carleton who was looking for war.

In the months following the Battle of Adobe Walls, there was considerable debate about its success. Much of the debate centered around a January 1865 visit to Fort Bascom by "Sheer-kee-na-kwaugh," said to be "principal chief of the whole Comanche Nation . . . because of the death of some other chief" (Bergmann 1865). No translation of that name was given, and it has not been identified by modern Comanche speakers. The "other chief" was un-named, and it is not clear who was meant. Sheerkenakwaugh's actions seem to indicate that he was a *tekwawapI* 'speaker' rather than a *paraibo* 'chief'. In reporting the visit Captain Bergmann said Sheerkenakwaugh was "the same who the general commanding saw at this place in May last" (Bergmann 1865), but no reference to a meeting between Carleton and any Comanche in May 1864 has been found.

Sheerkenakwaugh said he wanted peace and would do all he could to prevent further hostilities and would return in a month for Carleton's answer. That was viewed by some as proof that the Comanches had been taught a les-son by Carson's victory at the Adobe Walls. Others argued that the battle had pushed the Comanches to the edge of war and that Carleton was grasping at straws to prevent an outbreak. The former position was given strength when Sheerkenakwaugh failed to return to Fort Bascom in February (Kenner 1969: 152).

Meanwhile, in late May 1865 representatives of the "several bands of Comanches, the Noconies, Co-cho-te-as, Le-na-weets, Yampankas, and Mootchas" met with representatives of the "Confederate Indian tribes" at Camp Napoleon on the Washita River, near modern Vernon, Oklahoma, to establish an "Indian confederacy or band of brothers." The first four ethno-nyms are clearly Nokoni, Kotsoteka, Tenewa,[5] and Yamparika; the last, Mootcha, may be Pike's Mooche. Unfortunately, the representatives were un-named. With the smoking of the "pipe of peace" and the exchange of "tokens and emblems of peace and friendship peculiar to our race," the parties vowed that "the motto or great principle of the confederated Indian tribes shall be, 'An Indian shall not spill an Indian's blood'" (Veatch 1865). Then, in Sep-tember 1865, after the collapse of the Confederacy, representatives of the tribes in Indian Territory met with federal officials at Fort Smith, Arkansas, to acknowledge their error in signing treaties with the former Confederacy and to sign a new treaty with Washington; the "second chief" of the Coman-ches was present (Mix 1865), but his name and those of the rest of his dele-gation were not recorded. During the council he was asked if he had "power to sign for his tribe," and he responded, "not for the entire delegation." That was apparently his only role in the council.

The Treaty on the Little Arkansas River, 1865

In early 1865 General Grenville M. Dodge, arguing that it was time to follow up Carson's "victory" at the Adobe Walls and to "subjugate" the western Indians once and for all, organized a campaign (Nye 1969:38). However, at the same time the new agent for the Kiowas and the Comanches, Colonel Jesse H. Leavenworth—son of Henry Leavenworth, the first leader of the 1834 dragoon expedition—was arguing for a peaceful approach and was trying to assemble the chiefs for a council. He managed to get the military called back, and in August he arranged a truce with Comanche and Kiowa leaders along the Arkansas River, who agreed to meet in formal council in the fall (table 7.4).

In October a commission consisting of generals John B. Sanborn (retired) and William S. Harney, Kit Carson, William Bent, James Steele, and Central Superintendent Thomas Murphy met with Cheyennes, Arapahos, Kiowas, and Comanches on the Little Arkansas River in Kansas. According to the official record of speeches, during most of the council the only Comanches present were the Nokoni leaders Quenahewi and Terheryahquahip, and the Penateka, Potsanaquahip. Later, apparently after the principal meetings, three other Comanches showed up, Boyahwahtoyeh (*puhihwitoya* 'iron mountain', I will spell it Puhiwitoya, Yamparika), Puhiwiquasso (Tenewa), and Tosawa (Penateka) (Sanborn et al. 1865).

The discussions centered on three topics: (1) the release of captives, (2) the ceding of lands to the federal government, and (3) the removal of the Indians to reservations. Of the first, Tohausan, the Kiowa, said, "My people have four prisoners. I do not hide it. The Comanches speak for themselves." When asked about captives, Quenahewi said Comanches had three captive boys, two with one band, one with another, but neither of those bands were present. Then, implying one motive for taking captives, he asked the Kiowas, "Why do you keep prisoners, the white people will give you horses and property for them. You first turn over the prisoners, and they will give you blankets, calicoes, and make a treaty." Later Quenahewi, perhaps thinking of the necessity of reciprocity, reminded Sanborn, "down in Texas they have several Comanches prisoners. I think they and some Kiowas ought to be delivered up." Sanborn, misunderstanding the context, and thinking the reference was to Indians captured during the Civil War, replied, "Texas at that time was at war with us and not under our control. We are in power there now, and as soon as they can be obtained they shall be delivered up." But Quenahewi corrected him, "The prisoners were taken at Van Dorn's fight at the Wichita mountains"—the words were probably those of the interpreter; it is unlikely that the Comanches knew the English name of their attacker in 1858—"and are now being educated and don't wish to come back to the tribe, but the tribe wish to visit them." Sanborn answered, "They shall have that privilege"(Sanborn et al. 1865). Unfortunately, the identity of those captives in Texas is unknown.

Table 7.4

Comanches Meeting Colonel Leavenworth, 1865

NAME	GIVEN AS	MODERN RETRANSCRIPTION	DIVISION
Hotoyokowat[a]	Over the Buttes		Yamparika
Paruasemena	Ten Bears		Yamparika
Boyahwahtoyeh[b]	Iron Mountain	*puhihwi toya*	Yamparika
Quenahewi	Drinking Eagle		Nokoni
Terheryahquahip	Horse Back		Nokoni
Tokohnah[b]		*tu* 'black', *kahni* 'house', i.e., "Wichita"	
Parkakayoh[b]	Rawhide Blanket	*paka* 'rawhide'	
Potsanaquahip	Buffalo Hump		Penateka

[a] Hotoyokowat has been mentioned above but by later commentators; this meeting was apparently the first contemporary mention of him.

[b] Previously unmentioned.

SOURCE: Leavenworth 1865a

The more important issue was the reservation. In his opening speech Sanborn described a reservation encompassed by a line drawn from where the Canadian River crosses the New Mexico state line, south on the state line to the southeast corner of New Mexico, northeast to the headwaters of the Big Wichita River, down that river to the Red River, north to the Canadian and back to the starting point. For all the other lands the government was "willing to pay you more than you would ask or expect." Tohausan responded by claiming all the country from Fort Laramie to Texas, given to them by the Great Spirit, and he did not want it cut up and divided with other tribes or given to the whites. Quenahewi did not specifically comment to either that claim or to the reservation proposal, but simply said "I would like to have this county let alone for myself and my friends, the Kiowas, to roam over" (Sanborn et al. 1865)

The commission's published report recorded only minimal discussion, noting that "there was no ground for dispute" except for the specific reservation boundaries and the amount to be paid for the ceded lands. But clearly the Indians were not satisfied with the boundaries suggested by Sanborn. On the second day Quenahewi said, "I am fond of the land I was born on. The white man has land enough. I don't want to divide again." Sanborn responded, "We don't want any of the Comanche lands" (Sanborn et al. 1865). Sanborn did not press the Canadian as the northern boundary; he appointed

Leavenworth and Superintendent Murphy to meet with the chiefs in private to work out those details. During the private session the boundary line was modified to start at the northeast corner of New Mexico and proceed south to the southeast corner of the same, thence northeast to the junction of the North Fork of the Red River and the main flow of the Red, downstream to the ninety-eighth meridian, north to the Cimarron River, upstream to the Kansas line, and west to the beginning point. Thus the Comanche-Texas line was moved even farther to the northwest.

The final treaty called for "perpetual peace with the United States . . . and with all other Indians friendly with the United States"; it specified that grievances with other tribes or with the United States be submitted to the president for "impartial arbitration" and that crimes and other violations of the law be punished according to American law. The latter provision was not mentioned in the commission's report of the council, but it continued the tradition of the surrender of Indian sovereignty in treaties.

Although in the meantime the Indians could remain "in the country they claim as originally theirs," they agreed ultimately to "remove to and accept" a reservation and to give up all claims to land outside the reservation. They would have "absolute and undisturbed use" of the reservation land. No Anglo-Americans except government employees and individuals adopted into the tribes could reside there. Conversely, they agreed that they would not leave the reservation without "the consent in writing of their agent," and if they left they would refrain from committing depredations; they would not camp within ten miles of any of the main roads, nor visit army posts or settlements without the consent of the authorities.

On their part, the commissioners agreed to provide an annuity of ten dollars in goods per capita "until such time as [they] shall be removed to their reservations," after which the annuity would be fifteen dollars per capita. In order to calculate the annuity, the treaty authorized an annual census. The term of the treaty was to be forty years. Finally, the chiefs promised to use their "utmost endeavors" to gain the acceptance of the rest of the tribes not present (Kappler 1903:892–895).

The treaty was signed on October 18, 1865. That last step may have been somewhat hurried, as "the Comanche chiefs desired to leave." Following the signing, the council was adjourned so that the Kiowas could bring in their captives. It reconvened a week later when more signatures were added. The commission's report said that Puhiwitoya, Puhiwiquasso, and Tosawa were present at that reconvened session, but it is not clear whether they were at the principal meetings.

There were more speeches at the reconvened sessions. Puhiwitoya said, "We shiver in the wind," and he wanted the treaty goods delivered as soon as possible. Tosawa again complained bitterly about broken promises, and the lack of houses and farm equipment. He also noted that when he had made a treaty in Texas the previous winter, he "gave up five prisoners," but reiterating Quenahewi's complaint from the beginning of the council, "The Texans have prisoners still." The reference to a treaty in Texas is not clear; possibly Tosawa meant the meeting at Fort Smith the previous September, but there is no mention in the records of that meeting of the surrender of prisoners.

The goods were distributed on October 26; Puhiwiquasso was the only Comanche who acknowledged receipt (Murphy 1865). The whereabouts of the others are unknown, as is whether they received any goods.

There is some confusion about the signature list. Eleven Comanche names are on the document; in order they are Tabenanaka, Eshetaveparah (*esi tɯehpuʔrɄ* 'grey child', I will spell it Esiturepu. He was Tabenanaka's brother; see fig. 2.1), Esihabit, Quenahewi, Terheryahquahip, Potsanaquahip, Hotoyokowat, Paruasemena, Puhiwitoya, Puhiwiquasso, and Tosawa. However, that list includes the names of people who were not mentioned in the official report (i.e., Tabenanaka, Esiturepu, Esihabit, Hotoyokowat, and Paruasemena). Considering the stature of several of those individuals, particularly Paruasemena—a signer of the 1853 Fort Atkinson Treaty and its amendment—and Tabenanaka, it seems odd that they would have kept silent during such important negotiations. At the same time, other than Paruasemena, and except for their recent mention in Leavenworth's cease-fire, none of the signers had been mentioned previously in contemporary documents; indeed, except for Quenahewi, Potsanaquahip, Paruasemena, Tosawa, and possibly Puhiwiquasso, none of the signers had been previously mentioned by Anglo-Americans.

There were also proxy signatures: Tabenanaka "signed" for both Paruasemena and Hotoyokowat. It is not clear when the proxy signings took place, and, except for Albert Pike's treaty with the "Comanches of the Prairies and Staked Plains" in which Quenahewi signed for Puhiwiquasso, the Little Arkansas Treaty was the only example of such proxy signings.

Finally, there are questions about divisional representation. In summarizing the treaty, commission president Sanborn reported that "six of the nine bands of Comanches" were represented (Sanborn et al. 1865:711). That count however, was not of divisions, but of something approximating local bands. The evidence for that explanation comes from reports prepared a year later by special agents Charles Bogy and W. R. Irwin in November and December 1866. At Fort Zarah on the Arkansas River, they spoke to some Comanche chiefs, unfortunately unnamed, who told them that "this tribe at present embraces seven bands, there were formerly nine but two have merged with others" (Bogy and Irwin 1866b). For the Comanches, they listed:

3 bands of Yamparikas	(600 each)	1800
1 band of Cochetakers		700
1 band of Noconees		600
1 band of Penatekas		600
1 band of Quaradachokos		1000
[Bogy and Irwin 1866a]		

Unfortunately, they did not mention which bands had "merged," nor did the treaty give "band" identifications for the signers; thus it is not possible to link the signers with Bogy and Irwin's "bands." The last ethnonym on Bogy and Irwin's list is *kwaharʉ tsahkweʔarʉ* 'antelope skinner'; previously unmentioned in that form, it probably referred to the same people called *kwaharʉ tʉtsahkʉnʉʉ* 'antelope sewing people' in 1861.

The Kwahadas, Comancheros, and Captives, 1866–67

In the euphoria following the treaty on the Little Arkansas River, Agent Leavenworth and Commissioner of Indian Affairs Dennis N. Cooley insisted that the majority of the Comanches were friendly, with the exception of "a few outlying bands" (Cooley 1866), and that "a large number of Comanches were anxious to settle down." Although they may not have directly signed the Little Arkansas Treaty, Agent Leavenworth reported that the Yamparika chiefs Hotoyokowat and Paruasemana "traveled the same road I did"; they even helped gain the release of captives (Leavenworth 1865b). In September 1866 Paruasemena's 200 lodges were reported to be on the Salt Plains waiting for the fall distribution of presents, while "the chiefs and headmen [were] doing all in their power to keep the young men quiet" (McCusker 1866).

But those disclaimers did not stop the continued Comanche raiding. In late 1866 some Nokonis came back from Texas with two captives; Quenahewi sent word to Leavenworth that he was moving his camp "so as to restore as prompt as possible these children to their friends." Leavenworth passed that message along to the commissioner, but he also had Quenahewi's treaty goods placed in storage "subject to his good behavior" (Leavenworth 1866c). In early 1867 twenty-five of Mowway's Kotsotekas stole horses from Fort Arbuckle. Passing near old Fort Cobb, they chased Samuel Paul and J. J. Sturm; only Tosawa's intervention saved the two whites. In reporting the incidents, Captain E. L. Smith at Fort Arbuckle complained that "since the treaty, more depredations have been encouraged by the payment of liberal sums" (E. L. Smith 1867). When presented with evidence of widespread raiding, Leavenworth threatened to withhold annuities "until the parties guilty are properly punished," and the traders were ordered to sell no guns (Leavenworth 1867c). However, those threats carried little weight since there was no money available for Comanche goods. Indeed, in 1865 most of the Comanche money had been used for other tribes (Leavenworth 1867a).

Of particular concern were the reports of Comanche raids into Texas for cattle to be sold in New Mexico. In June McCusker returned from the Yamparika camps to report to Leavenworth that those Comanches had said the "only ones giving Americans any trouble" were the Antelope Skinners at the headwaters of the Red River (Leavenworth 1866a). At that time neither McCusker nor Leavenworth gave a Comanche form for Antelope Skinner, but by the end of the year the ethnonym Quaradachoko (*kwaharʉ tsahkweʔarʉ* 'antelope skinner') was being used to refer to a Comanche group (Bogy and Irwin 1866a); by 1868 Leavenworth had made the explicit equation "Quaradachokos or Antelope Skinners" (Leavenworth 1868a). Those Comanches, numbering about one thousand (Bogy and Irwin 1866a), were described by McCusker:

> [They] make their home on the head of the Red River and its tributaries and on the eastern border of the Staked Plains. These Indians are friendly with the traders in New Mexico who are constantly in their camps furnishing them with goods, arms, ammunition, and in fact anything they want. In return for this the Indians go to Texas and drive off large droves of cattle, horses, mules and the Mexicans encourage the Indians to do this, in many cases going with them, there is a large trading party among them this summer. [McCusker 1866]

At the other end of the trade, the New Mexico officials were well aware of the Comanches on their eastern borders, although they rarely gave a specific ethnonymic designation to them. In June 1866 an army beef contractor named Goldbaum (his first name is unknown) reported that while on a trading trip to Comanchería, he had "stayed with and traded with a ranchería of Comanches under Pahruacahiba . . . Puertas was chief of a neighboring ranchería" (Goldbaum 1866a). The first name is probably *parua kwahipʉ* 'bear's back'. The second name seems to be the Spanish 'doors'. Later that year, probably on information supplied by Goldbaum, New Mexico superintendent of Indian affairs A. B. Norton reported:

> There is a large body (about two thousand) continually occupying the eastern portion of this territory. The names of the different chiefs and the number of lodges . . . are as follows:

Puertas	30 lodges	150 souls
Paruacaiua	60 "	275 "
Quajipe	120 "	500 "
Maue	200 "	1075 "
total	410 "	2000 "

[Norton 1866]

As given, the list is in ascending order of population size, but it is not known whether that was intentional. Paruacaiua was probably Paruaquahip; Quajipe is *kwahipṵ* 'back'; Maue was probably Mowway, the Kotsoteka, although beginning about that time he was often linked with the emergent Quaradachokos. In January of 1867 General Carleton reported a slightly different total population for those four bands, 500 men, 550 women, and 550 children, with a total of 1,600, and he reported that they were "at times in the vicinity of Fort Bascom or the North East frontier of New Mexico" (J. H. Carleton 1867; DeForrest 1867).

The concern with the Quahadachokos was not just their cattle trade. In the summer of 1860 a young man, Rudolph Fisher, had been captured near Fredericksburg, Texas. For years thereafter his father attempted to recover him, writing letters to any official who might be able to help. In June 1866 the trader Goldbaum offered to return to Comanchería in an attempt to gain the boy's release (Goldbaum 1866b).

In July 1866, Comanches stole horses from the Navajos at the Bosque Redondo on the Pecos and from the army and nearby Americans at Fort Sumner. A force was sent in pursuit, and although the Comanches halted and raised a white flag, intending to say that they had only meant to take the Navajo horses, they were fired upon. Superintendent Norton argued that the Comanche raids had been instigated by Comancheros:

> these traders exchange goods for cattle and horses, thereby giving a market and encouraging the Comanches to steal from the inhabitants of Texas and Arkansas . . . and I have no doubt that these Mexican traders, being generally opposed to the Bosque [Navajo] reservation, have incited the Comanches to make these late raids upon the herds of the Navajoes, in order, not only to get their horses to sell and use, but also to make the Navajoes dissatisfied with their situation. [Norton 1866]

Left unstated were possible indigenous motives, for example, that the Comanches may have resented the loss of their traditional camping area, the site of their 1826 treaty with New Mexico.

Norton continued with a brief commentary on the role of licenses in the trade:

On my way back from the Bosque I met not less than sixty or seventy of these donkeys, loaded with goods, and about half that number of traders, and all claim to have permits to trade with the Comanches from General Carleton, and in one instance from General Pope. But when I ask for the permits, some other man ahead had it. In conferring with General Carleton, I find that he has, in some instances, granted such permits, and when a Mexican gets one, fifty will trade on the same license, claiming they are doing business for the man that has the permit. This trade has been immense of late. I know of one man here in Santa Fe who took about one hundred and fifty dollars worth of goods there, and came back with one hundred head of Texas cattle for his goods. [Norton 1866]

Unfortunately, no accounting of Carleton's licenses has surfaced.

Later that month Goldbaum and a New Mexican, Diego Morales, returned to Comanchería as interpreters for E. H. Bergmann, since promoted to lieutenant colonel and posted to Fort Bascom, to demand, upon threat of war, the stolen American horses (the Navajo stock was ignored), any American captives, and a cessation of raids. At the Arroyo de Nuez Bergmann met with Quahip, Parua-Kiowa (probably Paruaquahip), and Sheerkenakwaugh, and the Kiowas Toche and Pi-ti-tis-che (possibly the Kiowa known in Comanche as *pihitutsi* 'little heart'). After two days of often acrimonious discussion, Quahip, selected as spokesman for the assembly, stated that the chiefs had "no power to force their people to obedience." At that Bergmann walked out, saying, "You have made your bed, you shall sleep in it" (Bergmann 1866). There was no further contact for almost a year (DuBois 1867c).

By May 1867, in response to an order from the secretary of the interior to make a peremptory demand for Rudolph Fisher (Browning 1867a), Captain John DuBois at Fort Bascom was ordered to reestablish communication with the Quahadachokos (DuBois 1867a). DuBois sent messengers to their villages offering to ransom captives at "such a price in flour as they might consider proper"; because of a report that one of the captives could read Spanish, the offer was sent in writing. Two weeks later DuBois received a written reply dictated by Quahip and Paruaquahip; as with DuBois's letter, the reply was in Spanish, but the scribe's identity is unknown. Although admitting that they held two Texans—one white, one negro—and that others were held by Kiowas, the chiefs rejected DuBois's overture: they would give no credit to a messenger sent on a jackass. Thereafter, they said, if the "Captain wants to talk to us, let him and all his men come on good horses and well clothed" (DuBois 1867b).

New Mexico Superintendent of Indian Affairs A. B. Norton then sent Agent Lorenzo Labadi to the Llano Estacado, where he found 700 lodges of

Comanches and Kiowas. But their principal chiefs, Quahip and Mowway, had gone to Durango, and Paruaquahip with 300 Comanches and Kiowas had gone to attack the Navajos at the Bosque Redondo. Labadi managed to gather some 500 Indians at Quitaque, where he demanded an end to raids and the return "without ransom" of Rudolph Fisher and any other captives they held. That surprised the Comanches: they claimed that they had been encouraged to raid into Texas by "military officers of the government who told them to do all the damage they could against Texas, because Texas was fighting against our government"; they had not heard that the war was over. The Comanches probably understood the tribal politics of the Anglo-Americans—for twenty-five years they had been told that Texans and Americans were the same, then for four years they heard that Texans and Americans were enemies; and now they learned that Texans and Americans were friends again; those things happen in politics. But what may have been less understandable to them now was that they were being held accountable for their actions by the very people who had encouraged and benefited from those actions. The Comanches did, however, promise to stop their raids, but since there could be no treaty without Quajipe and Mowway, they postponed their meeting with Labadi until the full moon of October, when they would meet at the Cañon del Resgate (Labadi 1867a).

Meanwhile, to the east, Lieutenant Mark Walker of the 19th Infantry, temporarily in command at Fort Arbuckle in Indian Territory, met with Terheryahquahip about another captive, Theodore Adolphus "Dot" Babb, taken from Wise County, Texas. Walker reported that the boy had been "stolen by the young men of Horse Back's tribe"—but it is not clear if that specifically meant the Nokonis, or Comanches in general—that "it has cost [Terheryahquahip] considerable to get the child from his captors," and he wanted remuneration. Walker wrote up the chain of command for advice (Walker 1867). His letter quickly made it to the top: Lieutenant General William T. Sherman, commander of the Military Division of the Missouri, happened to be visiting Fort Leavenworth, where he saw the letter. He exploded:

> This paper happens to meet me here. It is now about as good a time as any for us to come to an understanding and rather than submit to this practice of paying for stolen children. It is better the Indian race be obliterated. I now have the power to call out the volunteer force of the frontier, and the commanding officer of Fort Arbuckle, may in his own way convey notice that this boy must be surrendered or else war to the death will be ordered. There must be no ransom paid. [Sherman 1867]

Although the government refused to pay ransom, Babb's father did, giving, according to Babb, both money and horses. All this was done solely and independently by my father, who was not assisted to the extent of one cent by the United States government. [Babb 1912:62]

On that latter point, G. Salmon—his first name is unknown—the clerk of Wise County, Texas, later noted that "Babb paid $535 for his children"— Babb's sister was taken captive at the same time but was held by a different group, and was ransomed a short time later (Winfrey and Day 1959-66, 4: 314).

There are six accounts of Babb's captivity and ransoming. The earliest is Lieutenant Walker's letter and the various endorsements it received as it moved up and down the chain of command (Walker 1867). Second is the mention by Clerk Salmon in 1870 (Winfrey and Day 1959-66, 4:314). The third and fourth accounts are by Lieutenant Richard H. Pratt of the 10th Cavalry; one is a brief reminiscence (Pratt 1905), the other is included in an edited memoir (Pratt 1964). The fifth account is Babb's own autobiography (1912). Finally, the incident is discussed in Wilbur Nye's history of Fort Sill (1968).

There are many inconsistencies among these accounts. For instance, in his autobiography Babb reported that he was taken in September *1865* (Babb 1912:20) and that he spent "about sixteen months" in captivity (1912:42). But both Walker and Salmon asserted that Babb was taken in September *1866*, and thus he would have spent only eight or nine months in captivity. Then, in contrast to Walker's account, which gave Terheryaquahip as the ransomer, Babb said that while he had been held by members of that chief's band, he was ransomed by "Esserhabey," that is Esihabit, for "several fine horses and numerous saddles, bridles, blankets, and other valuable gifts" (Babb 1912: 58).

Richard H. Pratt reported two slightly different scenarios. In his first account he said,

just before we arrived at Fort Arbuckle [summer 1867] the Comanches had captured a white girl of nine or ten years in Texas, and following the established custom, the commanding officer, through a white man living among the Indians, had negotiated to have her returned to her friends, by the government paying in goods, etc., what amounted to about $300.00. Subsequently Captain [J. W.] Walsh, as senior officer, had taken command and made me his adjutant, and it fell to me to write a letter to army headquarters, explaining about the arrangement for the return of the girl and to request authority to pay the Indians. This seemed to me a very strange method of dealing with these people, for it was plainly an incentive for them to continue raiding and stealing children. I gave Captain

Walsh my views, which he accepted and he instructed me to write a
letter giving these views, and remonstrate against making such payments.
This letter came back immediately endorsed by General Sherman in his
own handwriting. [Pratt 1905:204]

In this version, the captive was a girl (Babb's sister?), it was the government,
not Babb's father, who came up with the ransom, and it was Pratt not Lieutenant Mark Walker who wrote the letter.

Some years later, in dictating his memoirs, Pratt gave another version:

a white boy who had been captured . . . by the Kiowa Indians. The
previous commander had recommended that a bonus of a mule and
goods, amounting in all to about $300, be paid to the Indians for re-
turning the boy [Pratt 1964:14-15]

That time, the captive was a boy, but was held by Kiowas, and "a mule and
goods" is considerably different from Babb's "several fine horses and numerous saddles, bridles, blankets, and other valuable gifts" (Babb 1912:58).
Pratt continued much as his earlier account—that "buying his release was
government encouragement of this kind of lawlessness," and that his letter
brought a swift reply from Sherman. Pratt then exactly quoted Sherman's endorsement to Walker's May 14 letter; that quotation suggests that Pratt had
access to original records, but, again, he appropriated the credit to himself.

Wilbur Nye, without direct citation, also credited Esihabit as the ransomer. Nye was also more specific about the ransom, although again without citation, stating that "two hundred ten dollars in cash, and twenty dollars worth
of uniform clothing was turned over as ransom money" for Dot Babb, and
that later "Louella Babb, sister of Dot Babb, was ransomed . . . [for] $333
dollars" (Nye 1968:43-44). Although Nye's total was only two dollars less
than Salmon's 1870 accounting, suggesting its validity, there was no mention
of Pratt's "a mule and goods," or Babb's "several fine horses and numerous
saddles, bridles, blankets, and other valuable gifts." Moreover, as with Pratt,
Nye's presentation implied that it was the government who had paid the ransom rather than the children's father. Finally, according to Babb, his sister
was named Bianca, not Louella as given by Nye.

The Treaty of Medicine Lodge Creek, 1867

Since the abandonment of Fort Cobb by the Confederates there had been no
permanent Comanche agency; Agent Leavenworth had been operating from
Kansas, either at Fort Larned or from the town of Leavenworth. In February

1867 he asked for a specific agency site within the boundaries of the Little Arkansas reservation. By summer he was authorized to move to Fort Cobb and had persuaded Paruasemena with 300 lodges to come along (Hagan 1976:25).

However, other events caught up with them. In the fall of 1866 the Cheyennes and other Indians north of the Arkansas became involved in a war, instigated in part by the actions of various "designing persons," including the governor of Kansas, who claimed that a general Indian war was under way, thus provoking one. The claims were soon shown to be seriously overblown, but not before General Winfield S. Hancock led an expedition into Cheyenne country in a show of force. After burning one village, whose hostility was never proven, he returned to his headquarters to face a barrage of criticism.

By June 1867 reports from the field were of such a contradictory nature that Congress authorized another Peace Commission; it included John Sanborn and W. S. Harney from the 1865 commission, and Commissioner of Indian Affairs N. G. Taylor, Senators John B. Henderson and S. S. Tappan, and Generals William T. Sherman and Alfred S. Terry. Sherman was later recalled to Washington and was replaced by General C. C. Augur. They were to "ascertain the reasons for hostility" and to remove the causes of war, secure the frontier settlements and the railroads, and inaugurate some plan for civilizing the Indians. After meeting with various Northern Plains peoples, they made arrangements with Agent Leavenworth for the Comanches and the Kiowas, and Agent Edward Wynkoop for the southern Cheyennes and the Arapahos, to meet the tribes at the full moon of October on Medicine Lodge Creek in southern Kansas. The commission was primarily concerned with affairs north of the Arkansas and the supposed general war in Kansas; they took relatively little notice of Comanche and Kiowa relations with Texas and New Mexico. But their solution to all three was a policy of collecting the Indians on reservations.

The Medicine Lodge council was the best documented of the Comanche treaty councils. Besides the official report (Taylor et al. 1910), nine newspaper correspondents went along with the commission (D. C. Jones 1966), including Henry M. Stanley (1967). Nonetheless, questions remain about the timing of particular incidents.

Contacting the Yamparika Comanches along the Arkansas and the Penatekas at Fort Cobb was relatively easy. However, the Comanches of eastern New Mexico and western Texas were harder to reach. Ultimately, the Peace Commission attempted to kill two birds with one stone. Knowing that Agent Labadi was attempting to recover Rudolph Fisher, they instructed him to again visit the Comanches and persuade them to attend the Kansas meetings (Mix 1867). But when Labadi returned to Quitaque, he found that cholera had broken out in the villages, killing twenty to thirty people a day, and the Indians had fled; among the dead was Paruaquahip. Meanwhile, Quahip and Mowway were still in Mexico (Norton 1867).

The remaining chief, Puertas, wanted to visit Santa Fe, so Labadi, detained at Agua Negra by an eye infection, gave him a pass to visit the governor (Labadi 1867b). The chief apparently did make his journey, although confirmation in the New Mexican records of any official meetings with Comanches that year has not been found. On his return his party was attacked by other Indians, either Utes or Navajos, and the chief was killed (Norton 1867; Letterman 1867b). Labadi sent the chief's wife home with a small wagon, hoping that she would confirm that the attack was not the fault of the New Mexicans (Labadi 1867c). Whether she did or not is unrecorded; however, the result was the same: the Quahadachokos did not attend the Medicine Lodge councils that October.

When the commission arrived on Medicine Lodge Creek, they found several hundred lodges of various tribes waiting for them, including 100 lodges of Comanches. According to Stanley (1967:263) the Comanche chiefs present at the beginning were "Parry-wah-sahmer or Young Bear," that is, Paruasemena; "Tip-pah-pen-nav-aly or Painted Lips," Tipenavon; "Ponen-ewewe-tone-you or Iron Mountain," Puhiwitoya; "Para-er-ehve or Wise Shield"; and "Za-nah-weah or Without Wealth." The latter two were previously unmentioned; Zanaweah may be related to *tsanakatʉ* 'rich', *waa tʉ* 'without', but the other cannot be confirmed. All were apparently Yamparikas. More Indians continued to come in until there were close to 4,000 present.

At a preliminary meeting the question of when to get under way was raised. Black Eagle of the Kiowas proposed opening in four days, and Paruasemena agreed. When other Kiowas made other suggestions, Paruasemena commented, "What I say is law for the Comanches, but it takes a half a dozen to speak for the Kiowas" (H. M. Stanley 1967:267). When it was learned that most of the Cheyennes were still camped on the Cimarron River, some fifty miles to the south, and were "making medicine to restore the tribe's strength after the recent hostilities" (D. C. Jones 1966:81), it was decided to wait the four days.

During the break, while the commission held inconclusive hearings about the causes of the hostilities, a large party of unnamed Nokonis and Penatekas arrived. Although Leavenworth had said that he had sent word by way of Kotsotekas (Leavenworth 1866b)—and apparently no Kotsotekas attended the meeting—the newcomers said they had just heard of the council (D. C. Jones 1966:94), suggesting a serious lack of interdivisional communication.

When the council reopened, Senator Henderson outlined the mission. There had been contradictory reports about who commenced the recent hostilities, he said, and they wanted to "hear from your own lips" both grievances against the government and admissions of violence: "If we have harmed [the red man], we will correct it, if the red man has harmed us we believe he is brave and generous enough to acknowledge it." For the present, however, "we are greatly rejoiced to see our red brethern so well disposed toward peace." As individuals—that is, as private citizens, Henderson continued, the commission members desired the Indians to have "all the comforts of civilization, religion, and wealth"; now, as an official commission, they were

> authorized by the Great Father to provide . . . comfortable homes upon our richest agricultural lands . . . to build . . . school houses and church-es, and provide teachers to educate his children. We can furnish . . . agricultural implements to work, and domestic cattle, sheep, and hogs. [Taylor et al. 1910:57; H. M. Stanley 1967:281]

Satanta, the Kiowa, was the first to reply. According to Stanley, he began by rubbing sand over his hands and then shaking hands with all in the circle. He noted that it was the Cheyennes who had been fighting; "they did it in broad daylight . . . if I had been fighting I would have done so also"; indeed, the past spring, when soldiers came along on the Santa Fe Road, "I had not done anything, and therefore, was not afraid." He went on to claim all the land south of the Arkansas River for the Kiowas and the Comanches: "I don't want to give away any of it." He wanted no "medicine houses" built in his country, and he wanted his children "brought up exactly as I am" (Taylor et al. 1910:57-58; H. M. Stanley 1967:282).

Paruasemena, "putting on his spectacles," made a short speech in a "shrill voice" (Stanley 1967:283):

> I am glad to see see you all here today. I have been to Washington myself and I had a great talk with the President. I live by that talk. I have no wisdom, but expect some of you today. I will swallow it right down, and it will go wherever I go. I have the paper given to me at Washington ever since I received it. [Taylor et al. 1910:58]

The latter was a reference to the good conduct certificate he had received four years earlier in Washington. The spectacles are documented in an 1872 photograph but are otherwise unattested before then; the use of a "shrill voice" for oratorical style is also unattested elsewhere.

Then Tosawa, who was probably among the Penatekas who arrived on the seventeenth, in a "calm, argumentative voice" (H. M. Stanley 1967:283), repeated his complaints made earlier at the Little Arkansas:

> A long time ago the [Penateka] Comanches were the strongest band in the nation. The Great Father sent a big chief down to us, and promised medicines, houses and many other things. A great many years have gone by, but those things have never come. My band is dwindling away fast. My young men are a scoff and a by-word among the other nations. I shall wait till next spring to see if these things shall be given us; if they are not, I and my young men will return with our wild brothers to live on the prairie. I have tried the life the Great Father told me to follow. . . . I am tired of it. Do what you have promised us and all will be well. I have said it. [Taylor et al. 1910:58; H. M. Stanley 1967:283]

Tosawa's reference to the "Great Father . . . [promising] medicines, houses and many other things" is unclear, and might refer to any council from the 1846 Butler-Lewis Treaty to the 1865 Little Arkansas council. His claim that the Penatekas were once the "strongest band" is also unclear; it certainly had not been true for the previous three decades; Tosawa may have been tracing their lineage back beyond 1846, the earliest documentary mention of the ethnonym, to the Comanche Orientales and the Kotsotekas.

The next day the council got a late start; some Osages had showed up and needed to be settled. When the council reconvened, Paruasemena made a long and impassioned speech; indeed, it is the longest Comanche speech recorded.[6]

> My heart is filled with joy when I see you here, as the brooks fill with water when the snows melt in the spring; and I feel glad, as the ponies do when the fresh grass starts in the beginning of the year. I heard of your coming when I was many sleeps away, and I made but few camps before I met you. I knew that you had come to do good for me and to my people. I looked for benefits which would last forever, and so my face shines with joy as I look upon you. My people have never first drawn a bow or a gun against the whites. There has been trouble on the line between us, and my young men have danced the war dance. But it was not begun by us. It was you who sent out the first soldier and we who sent out the second. Two years ago I came up upon this road, following the buffalo, that my wives and children might have their cheeks plump and their bodies warm. But the soldiers fired on us and since that time there has been a noise like that of a thunderstorm, and we have not known which way to go. So it was upon the Canadian. Nor have we been made to cry once alone. The blue dressed soldiers and the Utes came out from the night when it was dark and still, and for camp fires they lit our lodges. Instead of hunting game, they killed my braves, and the warriors of the tribe cut short their hair for the dead. So it was in Texas. They made sorrow come in our camps, and we went out like the buffalo bulls

when the cows are attacked. When we found them we killed them and their scalps hang in our lodges. The Comanches are not weak and blind, like pups of a dog when seven sleeps old. They are strong and farsighted, like grown horses. We took their road and we went on it. The white women cried and our women laughed.

But there are things which you have said which I do not like. They are not sweet like sugar, but bitter like gourds. You said that you wanted to put us upon a reservation, to build us houses and make us medicine lodges. I do not want them. I was born upon the prairie, where the wind blew free and there was nothing to break the light of the sun. I was born where there are no inclosures [sic] and where everything drew a free breath. I want to die there and not within walls. I know every stream and every wood between the Rio Grande and the Arkansas. I have hunted and lived over that country. I lived like my fathers before me, and, like them I lived happily.

When I was in Washington the Great Father told me that all the Comanche land was ours and that no one should hinder us in living upon it. So, why do you ask us to leave the rivers and the sun and the wind and live in houses. Do not ask us to give up the buffalo for the sheep. The young men have heard talk of this, and it has made them sad and angry. Do not speak of it more. I love to carry out the talk I get from the Great Father. When I get goods and presents I and my people feel glad, since it shows that he holds us in his eye.

If the Texans had kept out of my country there might have been peace. But that which you now say we must live on is too small. The Texans have taken away the places where the grass grew the thickest and the timber was the best. Had we kept that, we might have done the things you ask. But it is too late. The white man has the country which we loved, and we only wish to wander on the prairie until we die. Any good things you say to me shall not be forgotten. I shall carry it as near to my heart as my children, and it shall be as often upon my tongue as the name of the Great Father. I want no more blood upon my land to stain the grass. I want it all clear and pure, and I wish it so that all who go through among my people may find peace when they come in and leave it when they go out. [Taylor et al. 1910:59–60]

If the official transcript is a valid record of Paruasemena's oratory, both the speech and the transcript are remarkable achievements; Satanta was often called the orator of the southern Plains, but a comparison of their speeches at the Medicine Lodge council shows that while Satanta may have had bombast, Paruasemena was more eloquent in his use of language. Practically every other sentence was a figure of speech, a metaphor, simile, personification, or metonymy, and each was appropriate to the context. But at this remove, it is difficult to evaluate Paruasemena's historical references: how many years

back did one count to determine who "sent out the first soldier"? Of more recent incidents, the reference "on the Canadian. . . . The blue dressed soldiers
and the Utes" clearly referred to Kit Carson's New Mexican militia and Ute
auxiliaries at the Battle of Adobe Walls. But the comment that "if the Texans
had kept out of my country there might have been peace," while understandable for a Penateka, is more difficult to understand for a Yamparika: in 1867
there were apparently still few "Texans" who were in Yamparika country,
even a Yamparika country defined as "between the Rio Grande and the Arkansas." There were, of course, other Anglo-Americans who were "taking
away the places where the grass grew the thickest and the timber was the
best," but they were not necessarily Texans.

After a brief speech by Satanta, Senator Henderson replied.[7] To some degree his comments addressed Satanta's and Paruasemena's concerns; for the
most part however, the commission had come with a pre-arranged agenda,
and Henderson merely tailored his words to that agenda. Both Satanta and
Paruasemena had said that they "did not like the medicine lodges of the
whites," but wanted to follow their own ways. The commision had no objection to that, Henderson said, but "the buffalo would not last forever . . . that
day would come when the Indian must leave his father's road, or suffer and
probably die." There was laughter from the Indians at this prediction. Then,
without commenting either on Satanta's or Paruasemena's claim to the lands
south of the Arkansas, or to Paruasemena's complaint that "the Texans have
taken away the places where the grass grew the thickest and the timber was
the best," Henderson continued:

> The whites are settling up all the good lands, and had reached the
> Arkansas. When they came, they drove out the buffalo. The whites are
> many and they few. They might kill some, but others would take their
> places. At last the red men will have been killed and the rest made
> homeless.

But despite this dire prediction, the commission was compassionate, "they
wanted [the Indians] to live." They were not being asked to stop hunting—
they could still hunt south of the Arkansas—"but they must have a place to
call their own." The commission offered to "give them good lands before the
whites should occupy them all." There

> a house would be built to hold the goods given them. Thither they could
> go when cold and hungry. Doctors would be sent to them, and black-
> smiths, as well as farmers to teach them to grow corn and mills to grind
> it. Each year everyone would be furnished a suit of clothing . . . There
> must be a place for the agent to live, . . . a spot to bury their dead. They

need not stay there except when they please. It did not hinder their hunting. It was proposed to make that home on the Red River and around the Wichita Mountains. [Taylor et al. 1910:61]

Henderson ended by saying the treaty papers would be ready to be signed the next day.

Articles 1 and 11 (and its 7 subsections) of the treaty dealt with questions of hostilities on the Plains: United States law was to be followed for the punishment of "bad men," and the Indians would not object to the construction of railroads, would not "attack, scalp nor carry off" any citizen of the United States, and would "withdraw all opposition to the military posts now established in the western Territories." The other articles dealt with questions of civilization. A reservation was to be established, bounded by a line starting where the Washita River crosses the 98th meridian, upriver to a point thirty miles west of Fort Cobb, then west to the North Fork of the Red River (or to the 100th meridian, whichever was easternmost), south to the main Red River, and downstream to the starting point; the reservation thus described would be about one-tenth the size of the reservation described in the Little Arkansas Treaty. Moreover, all of it would be located north and east of the Red River, that is, outside of Texas.[8] However, the Indians could continue to hunt within the bounds of the reservation established by the treaty of the Little Arkansas "so long as buffalo may range thereon in such numbers as to justify the chase." An agent would be appointed to reside on the reservation, and a number of buildings were to be constructed, including a warehouse, an agency building, a steam sawmill with a gristmill and a shingle machine attached, and residences for a physician, a carpenter, a blacksmith, a miller, and an engineer. A schoolhouse was to be built "so soon as a sufficient number of children can be induced to attend," and all children between ages six and sixteen would be compelled to attend. If any individual so desired, he could select up to 320 acres "for purposes of cultivation." Such farmers could obtain seed and implements not to exceed twenty-five dollars in value annually. If it were found that the reservation described did not contain enough land for such purposes, additional land would be set apart for them. Tosawa, "who [had] already commenced farming," was specifically named as the recipient of a house, and a fund was to be set up to provide an annual prize for the best crops. In place of annuities from the Little Arkansas Treaty, the government would provide a suit of clothes for each man, woman, and child and would provide $25,000 annually for thirty years for the "purchase of such articles as . . . from time to time the condition and necessities of the Indians may indicate to be proper." The treaty could be changed only with the approval of three-quarters of the adult population (Kappler 1903:977–84).

The proceedings ended with another short discussion. Satanta said: "This building of homes for us is all nonsense. We would all die. Look at the Penatekas. Formerly they were powerful, now they are weak and poor. . . . Why do you insist on this." Tosawa, perhaps smarting under Satanta's words about his people, but still echoing his argument of the past several years, replied, "For my tribe, the Comanches, I speak. I like those houses built, but if they are not completed before next summer, I don't want them" (H. M. Stanley 1967:289). Here Tosawa's use of the ethnonym Comanche to refer specifically to his people echoes the older Texan tendency to separate the southern Comanches from the Yamparikas and others.

Ten Comanches signed the treaty, the Yamparikas Paruasemena, Tipenavon, Puhiwitoya, Esananaka (*isa nanaka* 'wolf noise', given in the treaty as Wolf's Name; he was Paruasemana's son),[9] his brother Hitetse *hitutsi* 'little crow',[10] Howea (*huu wia* 'timber gap', also called Gap in the Woods), and Saddyo (*sari?i yuhu* 'dog fat'), the Penatekas Tosawa and Ceachinika, and the Nokoni Terheryaquahip.[11]

After the treaty was signed, the participants moved to the wagon train, where the presents were to be distributed.[12] Later that day the Plains Apaches, who had been confederated with the Cheyennes and Arapahos in the 1865 treaty, sent word that they wanted to join the Comanches and the Kiowas; thus, an appendix to the treaty to that effect was made and signed.

The Move to the Reservation

After signing the treaty, Agent Leavenworth went east with the Peace Commission; the Indians were left to their own devices. Leavenworth returned in the spring of 1868, intending to establish his agency along Cache Creek, near the Wichita Mountains. For the moment, however, he set up operations in the Eureka Valley, between the Keechi Hills and the Washita River, some ten miles southeast of Fort Cobb.

Leavenworth's major task was to get the Indians to move to the new agency. Unfortunately for him, he succeeded too well: in the first three months of 1868 several thousand Comanches and Kiowas visited him. Diplomacy required that they be fed and given presents, but the treaty had included no provisions for food rations. Desperate to keep the visitors happy, Leavenworth issued all his available goods, used the breeding stock for food, and purchased several thousand dollars worth of goods on unauthorized credit (Browning 1867b).

Some chiefs were relatively content with the new situation. Tosawa still argued for his promised house and complained that instead of flour, Leavenworth gave only cornmeal, which they could grow themselves (Tosawa 1868). Others tried to prevent raids. When a party of Nokonis and Penatekas from Terheryaquahip's and Esitoya's[13] bands persuaded two of Paruasemena's Yamparikas to go on a raid to Texas, other Comanches pursued them and compelled the party to return (McCusker 1867).

But raiding continued. One feature of the historical record from this period is the quality of detail on the personnel, itineraries, and results of the raiding expeditions; it is unclear however, how representative the period and these particular incidents are for a broader understanding of the political relations betwen a village or divisional *paraibo* and the young men as aspiring *tekwuniwapinuu* 'warriors'.

Soon after the Medicine Lodge council, Leavenworth reported that "a raiding party was gotten up . . . to raid the Chickasaws in Indian Territory" (Leavenworth 1868a). Leavenworth and interpreter Philip McCusker disputed the leadership of the raid. McCusker reported that there were

> ten Yamparikas from Ten Bears, Iron Mountain, and Tabenanaka's bands; on reaching the Nokoni camp, they were joined by one Nokoni and two Penatekas, 14 in all. Ten Bears' son [Esananaka?] was not in it, his brother Little Crow [Hitetsi] was, though not as leader. Little Crow crossed the Red, the others went on to the Chicaksaws. [McCusker 1868a]

However, Leavenworth countered,

> Mr. McCusker wants to let Little Crow off as easy as possible, and would attach leadership to others, Little Crow is a great chum of Mr. Mc. Little Crow is the leading brave of the Yamparika band of Comanche and is aiming at the head of his father's band. His father [Paruasemena], is always leaving him in charge of the band when he is absent, thereby showing conclusively to my mind, that he was the leader and should be held strictly responsible for these outrages. [Leavenworth 1868a]

If Agent Leavenworth was correct in his assessment of the relations between Paruasemena and Hitetsi, it is one of the few contemporary indications of possible lineal political succession from father to son.

In May 1868 a party of Yamparikas, Kwahadas—by that time, the short ethnonym *kwahada* was used in place of the longer 'Antelope Skinners' or 'Antelope Sewers'[14]—and Detsakanas (Pike's Tichakane) raided into Texas. In June a group of Kotsotekas from the bands of Mowway and Anahabit (*ana habitʉ* 'lying down for a vision') raided through Montgomery County, Texas.

In July at least two groups of Nokonis and Tenewas raided Texas (McCusker 1868c).

Leavenworth made several attempts to meet with the Kwahadas. In late April he sent Mowway and Queenahic (probably Quenahewi) to visit "the two leading chiefs of the wild tribes," Paruacoom (*parua kuhma* 'male bear', sometimes given as He Bear or Bull Bear) and Serotope (meaning unknown). The latter chiefs sent back word that they would come in and hoped that Leavenworth "would 'make their hearts glad.'" Leavenworth did so, giving them 26 uniform coats, 200 yards of blue cloth, and a small quantity of tobacco (Leavenworth 1868b). It is not known when that meeting took place; Leavenworth reported it in a letter dated June 30, 1868, but by then he had resigned his agency (see below). Whenever it took place, the Kwahadas did not stay, nor did they give up raiding.

In June McCusker reported that the Comanches would soon hold their Medicine Dance, followed by that of the Kiowas; the two tribes would then launch an attack against the new Navajo reservation at the Bosque Redondo on the Pecos River (McCusker 1868b), an area that had been a Comanche camp site for at least a century. This is one of the few contemporary mentions of a Comanche Medicine Dance. Interestingly, in his discussion of the Kiowa Sun Dance for that year, Mooney commented that "the Comanche had no Sun Dance of their own but sometimes joined with the Kiowa" (1898:322). However, McCusker, who had first-hand knowledge, clearly distinguished between the two ceremonies. According to Mooney, the Kiowa ceremony was on Medicine Lodge Creek, near the site of the treaty council; the location of the Comanche ceremony is unknown.

The trials and tribulations of his agency were too much for Leavenworth. On May 26 he left the agency in the charge of his clerk, S. T. Walkley, and went east. Although the Kiowas had earlier complained about Leavenworth, many of the Comanches were favorably impressed with him. By September they had gotten up a petition to keep him as agent (Tosawa and Others 1868); Walkley certified that "the petition originated and was dictated entirely by the Indians." The petition is interesting for several reasons. It represented the first active attempt by Comanches to influence the choice of the Anglo-American agent assigned to them, and it implied a wide consensus. Except for Yampa-rikas, it included representatives from all the divisions, including Kwahadas. It was signed by twenty-seven Comanches, including a number of "chiefs" and "headmen" of the Penatekas (Tosawa, Esitoya—who signed his own name, and Esihabit), Nokonis (Terheryahquahip), Kotsotekas (Mowway and Anahabit), Kwahadas (Efteyaha, Motseye, and Pakabee, all three previously unmentioned), and a Tenawa (Puhiwiquasso).

But the petition did no good. Leavenworth left and A. G. Boone, who had been agent in the 1860s, was reappointed. However, because of illness, he was unable to take the position until December. Meanwhile, Henry Shanklin of the Wichita agency also resigned, leaving Walkley as the only official of the Indian office at either agency.

The events of the summer were also giving Commissioner Taylor doubts about whether the Medicine Lodge Treaty itself should be ratified; in August he proposed to withhold annuities until peace was restored (Taylor 1868). That same month Tosawa's son-in-law organized a raid into Texas. He first "offered the war pipe" to some Caddos, and later to some Kotsotekas, but they refused to join him. He then went to one of Terheryaquahip's sons, who, along with ten other Nokonis, five Penatekas, twelve Yamparikas, and assorted other Kiowas, Kitsais, and Wichitas, attacked a number of homesteads near Spanish Fort on the Red River. They returned in early September with eight scalps and a large number of horses and mules (Walkley 1868).

By late summer other events were overtaking the Comanches. The Senate had ratified the 1867 treaties, including the Medicine Lodge Treaty, but appropriated only one-half the funds recommended for their provisions. Moreover, the Senate designated General William Tecumseh Sherman as administrator, rather than the Indian Office. Sherman organized two large administrative districts, separated by the Arkansas River, and placed Colonel W. B. Hazen in charge of the southern district, to include the Comanches.

By August several Kiowa and Comanche local bands—according to Nye (1969:51), the Comanches were mostly Yamparikas—had gathered at Fort Larned for the annuity distribution. It is not clear why they expected the distribution to be made at Fort Larned rather than at Fort Cobb, or some other place on the new reservation. Indeed, their presence at Fort Larned was the source of some unease for General Sherman, who blamed them for increased disturbances. Furthermore, another Cheyenne war was threatening, and the army was concerned that the Comanches and Kiowas would become involved. The army's immediate solution was to order all Indians out of Kansas; General Hazen was to escort all the Indians waiting at Fort Larned— Comanches and Kiowas, Cheyennes and Arapahos—to Fort Cobb.

As would be expected, there was confusion; the Indians, fearing treachery, did not meet Hazen for the escort but independently traveled south. Moreover, since the treaty gave no authorization for rations, there was no source of support for the Indians once they got to Fort Cobb; General Hazen argued that "by placing the Indian on prescribed reservations, we have assumed the obligation to feed him until we can teach him to feed himself in a new way" (Hazen 1869). Meanwhile, Clerk Walkley could get no further credit from the Fort Cobb traders to support those Comanches and Kiowas

already on the reservation. When two companies of cavalry arrived at Fort
Cobb, Walkley turned his charges over to the commander, a lieutenant, who
in turn passed them on to Captain Henry E. Alvord, sent ahead by Hazen.

When Hazen finally reached Fort Cobb in November, he found 1,700
Indians, including 700 Comanches. His "first duty" was to provide a food
ration. Of primary importance were the coffee and sugar rations; "no attempt
at discontinuing them could be made without jeopardizing all that has been so
accomplished." Hazen also became involved in the politics of the ration
distribtion:

> There had been a custom, also, of giving equal numbers to each chief for
> his people without much regard to their numbers; also as issues had been
> made at long intervals, they had learned to expect quantities such that
> when a week's rations were given them based upon actual count, and a
> chief had forty followers, he was always disappointed, usually angry and
> always giving annoyance which had to be endured at the risk of revolt.
> [Hazen 1869]

But his immediate problem was to keep the Indians out of the way of the
impending Cheyenne campaign. That was not easy, as threats of large armies
had been made in the past but had come to naught. This time, however, the
threat was real. In December the largest American army ever sent against the
southern Plains peoples took to the field. Two battles were fought: one force
under Lt. Colonel George A. Custer attacked a Cheyenne camp on the
Washita River; nearby Comanches rallied to force back the attackers and to
surround and wipe out a small detachment (Attocknie 1965). Another force
operating out of Fort Bascom in New Mexico attacked a Comanche village at
Soldier Spring at the west end of the Wichita Mountains. Nye (1969:79) said
it was a Nokoni village, although the Nokoni chief, Terheryaquahip, was at
Fort Cobb.

Those battles were enough to effect the concentration of many, if not
most, Comanches and Kiowas, as well as some Cheyennes, at Fort Cobb. The
only ones who remained away were the "Staked Plains Indians"; they were
concentrated in a large intertribal village at the headwaters of the Pease River.
The village included Mowway's Kotsotekas and Paruacoom's Kwahadas; 140
lodges of Arapahos under Roman Nose, Big Mouth, and Bear Feather; 15
lodges of Cheyennes; Big Bow's Kiowas; and some Kiowa Apaches; in all
some 400 lodges and 1,000 warriors. In early 1869 they sent a delegation
consisting of Quahip, Tamar (possibly *taama* 'teeth'), and Quinanace (possibly *kwina nakl* 'eagle ears') to Fort Bascom with an offer to council with
General George W. Getty, commander of the Military Department of New
Mexico. They denied any connection with the recent Cheyenne hostilities;

rather they had "always restricted their incursions to middle Texas or thereabouts" (Getty 1869; Kobbe 1869).

Getty told them to go to Fort Cobb, as General Hazen "alone could receive them and assign them to a place of safety," but rather than going east, they went west, arriving in Santa Fe in early March. The delegation, now consisting of five Comanches, Quahip, Mowway, Buffalo Robe, Wild Horse —probably the man later known as Coby *kobe* 'mustang or wild horse'—and Ventura (the latter three Comanches were previously unmentioned), and two Kiowas, expressed a willingness to return to Fort Cobb, but during the night they slipped away. They were recaptured at Chaparito and, along with Paruacoom, were sent to Fort Union as prisoners of war (Getty 1869) and then on to Fort Leavenworth. How and where Paruacoom was taken prisoner was not recorded.

Another result of the 1868 campaign was the abandonment of Fort Cobb and the establishment of Fort Sill on Cache Creek, on a small plateau east of the Wichita Mountains. The area had been a Wichita village site and a Comanche camping area for the past century; there had been Comanche gatherings reported in the area since the 1780s, and nearby the dragoons had met the Tabequena's Comanches in 1834. Since the army had been given authority to disburse the Medicine Lodge moneys, the new post became the de facto agency.

In January 1869 the Penateka local bands of Tosawa, Esihabit, and several others, and the Yamparikas under Paruasemena and Puhiwitoya were present (Boone 1869). Present also were some of Terheryaquahip's Nokonis from the village at Soldier Spring. Sometime during the late winter or early spring, Quitsquip *(kutsƱkwepƱ* 'chewer'—sometimes called *parƱa kutsƱ-kwepƱ* 'chewing elk') arrived. He was later said to be the leader of the Detsakana local band, associated with the Yamparikas. In the summer the chiefs held at Fort Leavenworth were transferred to Fort Sill (Nye 1969:105).

Agent Boone resigned in the spring, exasperated at his lack of authority. In line with President Grant's Peace Policy—having religious denominations rather than the army provide the personnel for Indian agents—he was replaced by Lawrie Tatum, an Iowa Quaker with some interest in Indian affairs but apparently no direct experience (Hagen 1976:57). Meanwhile, Colonel Hazen's term as the army's agent expired. In his final report Hazen "regretted very much" that his circumstances required him to use his appropriation for food rather than for the other benefits of civilization as called for in the treaty: "With fifty thousand dollars I could have opened and fenced all the lands ever needed for the wants of the Indians, built good houses for all the chiefs and principal men, . . . done all that was essential for a permanent beginning on [the] reservation" (Hazen 1869).

Tatum arrived at Fort Sill in June; after a July meeting with Quitsquip, "who [was] spending his first summer on a reservation," Tatum noted that the Comanche "said he knows that the Indian road is bad but he knows of no other; after a while they will learn the white man's road but it will be by degrees" (Tatum 1869a). Later, in a perceptive comparison of Comanche and Anglo-American conditions, he noted, "I think every chief among the Indians here would like to control his young men, but they can no more do it than a magistrate can prevent white people from committing crimes" (Tatum 1870a).

The relations between Tatum and the army were cordial, although often strained. The army still acted as quartermaster, and Benjamin Grierson, commander at Fort Sill, had wanted to "issue [rations and annuities] in bulk to the agent and it was expected that the latter would attend to the immediate issue to the Indians. This however, he declined to do, stating that he had not sufficient assistance" (Grierson 1869). In August, post adjutant J. W. Walsh witnessed the ration distribution to the "Goa-ha-do-kuns, Coche-teghka, Quahada-tetchacoe, Tetchahkina, and Tamanarinds bands" (Walsh 1869). The first of those is an unknown ethnonym; the others are Kotsoteka, Quaharadachoko, Detsakana, and Tenewa.

Later that month a subcommittee of the recently appointed Board of Indian Commissioners—a "commission of citizens . . . to cooperate with the administrative departments in the management of Indian affairs" (Grant 1869) —arrived at Fort Sill. The subcommittee consisted of Felix Brunot of Pittsburg, and Nathan Bishop and W. E. Dodge of New York; none had any direct experience with Indians. In the evening of August 20 they met the assembled chiefs in council. The Comanches present included,

> of the Pe-na-teth-ca or Honey Eater band, Es-sa-hab-et (Milky Way) [Esihabit], Es-sa-too-yet or Grey Leggings [*esi toya* 'grey mountain'?]; Yam-hi-re-coe or Root digger band, Boo-e-wa-too-yah (Iron Mountain) [Puhiwitoya], Tip-pe-nah-bor (Painted Lips) [Tipenavon]; Ho-we-oh (Gap in the Woods) [Howea]; No-co-nie or Wanderer band, Ta-ha-yer-qua-hip (Horse Back) [Terheryahquahip]; Que-na-hea-vey (The Eagle) [Quenahewi]; Coo-cho-teth-ka or Buffalo eater band, Mow-wau (Shaking Hand) [Mowway], Pat-ro-o-kome (He Bear) [Paruacoom]; Titch-ah-ka-ne or Lewet [*sic*, Sewing People] band, Kutsquip (Chewer) [Quitsquip]. [Brunot, Bishop and Dodge 1869]

Although in other councils the Comanches had been told that the whites wanted to hear what they had to say, the meeting with the Board of Indian Commissioners was one of the few that actually recorded the Indians' remarks; the comments of the four Indian speakers—Esihabit, Satanta, the Waco chief Buffalo Good, and Mowway—probably reflect the spectrum of Indian opinion.

After a short prayer—apparently unique in negotiations with Comanches—Brunot began by saying that they had been sent by "the great father in Washington to inquire into the condition of things in the Indian country and to hear what the Indians had to say, and to report all they could learn to the Great Father in order that he might know what was best to be done for the benefit of both whites and Indians." But he also "urged strongly the necessity of their remaining at peace and submitting quietly to the authority of the United States Government"; they should "abandon their wandering and savage habits and learn to live like civilized people" (Brunot, Bishop, and Dodge 1869).

Esihabit was the first to reply. He said,

> I have been working with General Grierson and our agent trying to do good for my people. . . . But although I have been walking on this road some years, I have not seen a house on it yet, though we were promised that some should be built for us; we are trying to do what we were told to do, but the promises made to us have not been fulfilled. I think those who promise and do not fulfill their promises are not much captains.

Satanta then commented, probably with more than a hint of sarcasm,

> We have tried the white man's road and found it hard; we find nothing on it but a little corn, which hurts our teeth; no sugar; no coffee. But we want to walk in the white man's road. We want to have guns, breech loading carbines, ammunitions, and caps. These are part of the white man's road, and yet you want us to go back to making arrowheads, which are used only by bad foolish Indians, and have always been a mark of what was barbarous and evil. We want civilized weapons to hunt with. . . . All this country always belonged to us, all the way to the Arkansas, with all that is on it. But the white people have undertaken to divide it out to suit themselves. For some years . . . the great business of the whites has been to divide and apportion lands. . . . The commissioners who made the treaty at [Medicine Lodge] proved that they came from Washington and were chiefs by giving us presents. I hope you will give us the same evidence that you are chiefs.

In his turn Buffalo Good, the Waco chief, commented about the placement of Fort Sill on the site of an old Wichita village, "All the land around here belonged to us, our fathers lived and died here. Right where this house stands some of our chiefs are buried." He complained about the loss of their reservation in Texas, and the lack of rations at Fort Sill, "When we ask our agent for anything he says he has no money. We get nothing but promises . . . I had rather you had promised nothing than for you to promise and not perform." Finally Mowway, seemingly subdued after his imprisonment, said simply,

"My heart is like a woman's heart. I have little to say. My brother Esihabit has spoken for us. I hope the houses will be built for him and for us."

The four Indian speakers had touched on many matters, from specific complaints about rations to general complaints about the whites taking up all the land and about promises made but not kept. But the commissioners responded to only two points. The day after the council, Brunot wrote to Commissioner of Indian Affairs Ely S. Parker to

> urge . . . resuming the issue of coffee and sugar rations. . . . there is much reason to believe that the Kiowas and Comanches, in part, will again go to the plains if [the issue of coffee and sugar] is not adopted at an early day, and that the sugar and coffee will certainly hold them.

And in their final report, the commission noted, "It will be seen from the speeches that they are desirous to live in houses and have farms like white men" (Brunot, Bishop, and Dodge 1869). The larger issues were not addressed.

Within a week after the commission visited his agency, Tatum left for three months to purchase the steam sawmill and attachments specified in the Medicine Lodge Treaty, and to recruit employees. But, according to General Grierson, he left "no competant person in charge . . . Captain [N. D.] Badger has had to attend to the issues" (Grierson 1869).

In November Badger compiled the first accurate census of the Comanches (see table 7.12). In January 1870 the Comanches present at Fort Sill included Penatekas under Tosawa, Esihabit, Esitoya, and Ceachinika; Nokonis under Terheryahquahip; Tenewas under Quenahewi; and a "part of the Detsakana" under Quitsquip—who the others might have been is unknown (Walsh 1870). Late in the month Howea's and Hitetsi's Yamparika bands came in for rations (Grierson 1870a). In the spring, Mowway and Paruacoom were asked to persuade other Kwahadas to come in; and in April, they were reported to have "succeeded in getting a few more . . . to join them and I think they will be gradually induced to do so" (Grierson 1870b).

But by the summer, the fright of the previous year's winter campaign had worn off, and there were again raids and rumors of hostility. A major Indian council was held during the combined Comanche-Kiowa Sun Dance on the North Fork of the Red River (H. P. Jones 1870). Tabenanaka and Tokomi (*tuu kuhma* 'black male', Black Horse) declared for war, but Paruasemena, Terheryaquahip, Esihabit, and Tosawa were opposed. There was no consensus, and no chief had sufficient strength to impose a decision. In July Mowway and Paruacoom again went to the camps "with a view to induce them to cease hostilities" (Grierson 1870c). However, instead of persuading others to come in, they were apparently persuaded to stay out.

In September there were renewed Comanche raids into Texas and re-newed Anglo-American attempts to contact the Kwahadas. Howea, whose wife had been captured in Texas along with a number of his children—details of their capture are unknown—went in search of white captives among the Kwahadas to trade for the release of his relatives (Townsend 1870). In Octo-ber Pacer, the Kiowa Apache chief, went out, but he only went part way, and he reported that there were Mexicans in the Comanche camps encouraging them to steal cattle (Tatum 1870b).

In May 1871, when the Kiowa chiefs Satanta, Satank, and Big Tree were arrested for murders in Texas, a delegation of Comanches, including Paruase-mena, Tosawa, Puhiwitoya, Terheryaquahip, and A Man Not Living (pre-viously unmentioned), came in to ask if any of their people would be similar-ly arrested. They were told that since none of their people were directly in-volved, none would be so treated (Nye 1969:143). Later that month Mowway visited the agency for his annuities, but when he refused to relinquish a young captive, saying that his people had not stolen him, but merely bought the boy from New Mexican Apaches, the annuities were denied him and he left angry (Tatum 1871d). A week later Tatum reported a rumor that some Comanches had stolen a considerable number of horses from near one of the forts in Texas; he said, "I think [they] belonged to Tabenanaka's (He Bear's) [*sic*] band of Comanches, who has not been in for more than a year" (Tatum 1871e).

Tatum also attempted to recover several captives, including Rudolph Fisher, taken in 1860, and Temple Friend, taken in 1869, both said to be with Yamparikas (Tatum 1871c). In August he wrote to Colonels Grierson at Fort Sill and Ranald S. Mackenzie at Fort Richardson:

> Mowway's band of Comanches has a white captive child. He and his band have been here but once for more than a year and then gave me to understand that he should not deliver the captive to me. I wish to have the captive recovered if at all practicable and returned to its father who I suppose to be Henry M. Smith.[15]

He also noted

> Tabenanaka's and He Bear's bands have been away from here more than a year and are frequently raiding. . . . The [Kwahada] band of Comanche belong to this agency, but have never reported themselves here and are understood to be unfriendly to the whites, and much of the time engaged in raiding. . . . The last four named bands [Mowway's, Tabenanaka's, Paruacoom's, and the Kwahadas] are understood to be in the western part of Texas most of the time and are uncontrollable by me.

He concluded, "I wish you to take the stolen animals from them and bring the Indians to this agency and treat them as kindly as the circumstances will admit" (Tatum 1871g).

In the late summer and fall Colonel Mackenzie made several sorties onto the Staked Plains, but encountered Comanches only once. On October 9 his horses were stampeded, and his force was attacked by Kwahadas from Parua-coom's and Coby's villages. While the Kwahadas retreated through a blizzard to the Staked Plains, Mackenzie returned to Fort Richardson.

There was another movement of Comanches in 1871; some Penatekas moved from Fort Sill to the proposed Wichita reservation north of the Washita River. In February Tatum reported that "some of the Comanche Indians wish[ed] to have farms on the Washita River" (Tatum 1871a); it is not clear who those Comanches were, although in June Tosawa and Esihabit petitioned Jonathan Richards, newly appointed Wichita agent, for permission to transfer to his jurisdiction. Richards sent the request on to Commissioner Ely S. Parker, who voiced no objection (Parker 1871).

When informed of the request, Agent Tatum at Fort Sill was surprised, saying that was the first he had heard of it. Although he called Tosawa "faith-ful and reliable," he said:

> [There are] few chiefs if any among either of the tribes who are more expert at lieing and intransigence than [Esihabit], and I have taken more horses and mules away from his and Tosawa's people that they had re-cently stolen in Texas . . . than I have from any other Comanches in this agency. . . . I think the real motive of [Esihabit] wishing to leave here is to prevent having the stolen horses taken from him. . . . I write this mere-ly to let thee know the character of the Indians who are to be transferred. I hope they will do much better among the Wichitas. [Tatum 1871f]

Thus, in December 1871, Esihabit with 121 people and Tosawa with 75 moved north to the Wichita agency (Tatum 1871h). Other Penatekas, such as Esitoya, soon visited the Washita River, where Agent Richards gave them annuities and rations. Tatum was concerned that they were attempting to get double rations by collecting them at both the Fort Sill and Wichita agencies (Tatum 1872a). In response to a request for a policy decision, Superintendent Enoch Hoag noted that it was not so much a matter of at which agency they were registered, but of permanence of their settlement (Hoag 1872).

In February 1872, soon after his arrival on the Washita River, Tosawa persuaded Agent Richards that he was the "head and controlling chief" of the Penatekas, and that the other local bands under Esitoya, Ceachinika, and Ka-harawa,[16] still at Fort Sill should also be transferred to his jurisdiction. When Richards wrote to Tatum at Fort Sill with that request, Tatum responded that two of those bands did not want to go north—unfortunately he did not identify which ones. He observed, "That Tosawa is not a head and controlling chief is shown by his not taking the whole band" (Tatum 1872b). Moreover, he said, none of the "bands of Comanches have [a] head and controlling chief . . . [rather] each one acts independently . . . so far as it suits him" (Tatum 1872c). Later that month, when Esitoya returned to Fort Sill, ten lodges of Esihabit's people came with him (Tatum 1872d). Although several other Penatekas—including at least Kakarawa, although the details are unclear—did in fact move to the Washita, by 1874 he and several of his people "were dissatisfied with [Esihabit's] treatment and want[ed] to leave" (Haworth 1874b).

In March 1872 the army was given a first-hand account of how the Kwahada cattle trade worked. That month troops from Fort Concho captured a Comanchero named Polonio Ortiz. At first dissembling, under interrogation he admitted that in early February he and several others from the Pecos valley of New Mexico had left for the Indian country. With burros owned by the leader of the party and loaded with goods furnished by traders at Puerto de Luna and Cuesta, they traveled to Alamo Gordo Creek, where they were joined by others until the party numbered fifty or more. Crossing the Llano Estacado, they headed for Muchoque. There they found a village of Kwahada Comanches and Mescalero Apaches, numbering "100 lodges, perhaps 200" under "Pahween or Pachacunee." The former name is unknown, the latter is *paatsoko nehki* 'otter belt', usually spelled Patchokoni or Patchokoniki (plate 5); later Comanches suggested that his group was called *numukiowa* 'Comanche-Kiowa' (Gatschet 1893).

Whether they had no stock on hand or were simply waiting for an order is not known, but as soon as the traders arrived at Muchaque, the Indians sent out a party of 100 men to obtain cattle. The Mexicans, impatient at waiting for their return, went out on their own and were surprised and captured by the troops from Fort Concho. After telling his story, Ortiz guided troops back to Muchoque, only to discover that the village had left the day before (J. Hatch 1872a).

Mackenzie, ordered to suppress the raiding, established a base of operations near old Camp Cooper. With four companies of the Fourth Cavalry and one of the Twenty-fourth Infantry, he went on an extended expedition across the Staked Plains. A detachment scouted the Muchoque valley, "known to be a camping place of the Indians, and where large herds of cattle were collected and driven toward [New] Mexico," where they found "plenty of old 'signs' . . . but no Indians." On the Staked Plains itself,

Plate 5. Patchokoniki. Photograph by Willliam S. Soule, Fort Sill, Indian Territory. Ca. 1868-75. Courtesy National Anthropological Archives, Smithsonian Institution.

a plain travelled road was struck, with numerous cattle trails running parallel to it. This was followed some twelve days across the Staked Plains, when it was discovered that it led to the vicinity of a small town in New Mexico named Puerto del Luna, situated on the Rio Pecos, about thirty miles south of Las Vegas. . . . [B]ut one opinion was afterward expressed in the command, and that was the citizens of Puerto del Luna and its vicinity knew more about the broad cattle trail that the command followed than those who had so lately marched over it. [*Army and Navy Journal*, November 16, 1872]

They returned to Texas via Fort Bascom. Some distance east of that place they found another "plain trail made by cattle" leading to Quitaque. The correspondent to the *Army and Navy Journal* concluded that the roads were made by Indians and Mexicans "for no legitimate purpose."

In June, based on "information from a gentleman from [New Mexico]," Captain Hatch at Fort Bascom reported that "2000 head of cattle [were] at a lake on Staked Plains 40 miles northeast of Chisolm's ranch on Pecos." The "gentleman" got his information from "an officer at Stanton, who said these facts were known, but they were not authorized to interfere as the trade in Comanche cattle was a licensed one" (Hatch 1872c).

Because the army was "not authorized to interfere," that same summer Texas cattleman John Hittson decided to take matters into his own hands. With the full cooperation of the New Mexico military officials, Hittson and his cowboys spent three months in eastern New Mexico, bullying the population and restealing some six thousand head of cattle from the ranchers of the Pecos valley (Kenner 1962).

At about the same time it was decided to attempt another peaceful solution to the hostilities. In July Cyrus Beede, chief clerk of the Central Superintendency, met at Fort Cobb with Paruasemena, Tosawa, Terheryahquahip, Esihabit, and several Kiowa chiefs. Not much was accomplished at that meeting except that the Indian Office decided to hold another meeting and to bring another delegation to Washington. This time, two special commissioners were appointed, Edward Parrish, a Philadelphia Quaker, and Captain Henry Alvord, who had been associated with the Kiowas and Comanches since 1868 and had recently retired from the army. Although Parrish died before the meeting could get under way, Alvord continued the mission. Together with Terheryahquahip and the interpreter Horace P. Jones, he assembled a number of Comanche leaders for a conference. Besides those who spoke, noted below, the following individuals were present: Puhiwitoya, Hitetsi, Howea, Quitsquip, Terheryahquahip, and Tokomi (R. N. Richardson 1933:355).

On September 6 the meeting opened with Alvord berating the Indians for the recent raiding; he said that although the "good Indians" would be fed, the "bad Indians" would be punished. Esihabit led off the responses by pointing out the failure of Washington to keep its promises, and Pearekaeka (*pia tuhka eka* 'big red food', sometimes called simply Red Food) gave support to his comment. Tabenanaka told Alvord that although "you come here to do good, you say . . . yet the first thing you do is to pen us up in a narrow territory. I would rather stay out on the plains and eat dung than come in on such conditions" (R. N. Richardson 1933:356). Mowway noted, "When the Indians in here are better treated than we are outside, it will be time enough to come in." Finally Paruasemena suggested that since moving the Indians never seemed to work, perhaps they might try moving the Texans. The meeting adjourned without significant result.

Alvord did persuade forty Kiowas and Comanches to go to Washington. The Comanches included at least Paruasemana, his grandson Cheevers, with his wife and "mother"—but since Cheevers's mother had died in the 1849 cholera epidemic, the woman was probably another of Cheevers's wives— Quitsquip, Mowway, Esihabit and his wife, Esitoya, Timber Bluff (previously unmentioned, his Comanche name is unknown), Tosawa and his wife, Onaweah (*ona wia* 'salt gap' or 'worn spot') and his daughter, a young man named Jim (previously unmentioned, his Comanche name is unknown), and a boy called Buffalo Hump. There is no known relationship between the young Buffalo Hump and the Hois-Penateka chief Potsanaquahip of the 1830s through the 1850s. While in Washington, photographic portraits of them were made by Alexander Gardner (plate 6).

While in Washington they met President Grant and the cabinet and had a series of talks with the commissioner of Indian affairs, Francis J. Walker. After promising to release the Kiowa prisoners Satanta and Big Tree, still held in Texas, Walker told the Indians that by December they must establish residence within ten miles of Fort Sill or be considered hostile.

But when they returned to Indian Territory, they found that the army had again acted. On September 21 Mackenzie started from his supply camp on the Brazos, this time toward the headwaters of the Red River. On September 29, on the North Fork of the Red River near the mouth of McClellan Creek in the Texas panhandle, they found a trail leading to a village of 175 large lodges and a number of smaller lodges, 262 in all. Charging the village, the troops drove out the inhabitants, capturing "between 120 and 130 women and children." The horse herd was also captured, but it was later stampeded (Mackenzie 1872).[17] The prisoners were transported to Fort Concho, eight dying of wounds on the way, where they were held pending the good behavior of their relatives (Augur 1872).

Plate 6. Esihabit's wife. Photograph by Alexander Gardner, Washington, D.C. 1872. Courtesy National Anthropological Archives, Smithsonian Institution.

While there, Polonio Ortiz, the Comanchero, recognized many of the prisoners as being part of the band with whom he had traded at Muchoque the previous winter (Ortiz 1872); at that time he gave the leaders as "Pahween or Pachacunee." That identification was corroborated by Nye's informants of the 1930s, who said that the head chief of the McClellan Creek village was Kaiwotche (previously unmentioned), who was killed in the fight, and that he was seconded by Patchokoniki (1969:162).[18] The following April Lieutenant Matthew Leeper, Jr., son of the former agent at Fort Cobb, now an officer with the Fourth Cavalry, also recognized many of the women prisoners; he identified them as thirty-four Kotsotekas, thirty Kwahadas, eighteen Yamparikas, eleven Nokonis, and nine Penatekas (Leeper, Jr., 1873); unfortunately, Leeper did not name the individuals so identified. But the recognition was mutual: several of the Indians at McClellan Creek also recognized Leeper (Schofield 1872).

Mackenzie's attack in the heart of Comanchería sent many Indians searching for refuge. In early October Quahip—given as Cohepa—back out on the Staked Plains after his sojourn at Fort Leavenworth, sent word to Fort Bascom that he and his people, along with some Kiowas, would be willing to settle on a reservation in the upper Canadian or Pecos river valleys. The request was passed along to the Indian Bureau with the endorsement that he believed they were "acting in good faith" (Granger 1872). However, as in 1868, the policy was to concentrate the Comanches at Fort Sill.

Other Comanches did go to Fort Sill, where they endeavored to trade white captives for relatives held at Fort Concho.[19] By late October Paruacoom had moved his village to the banks of Cache Creek near Fort Sill; by early November Terheryahquahip had gathered a number of white captives to trade for some of his relatives at Fort Concho, including the mother of his present wife, a former wife, and her daughter (Tatum 1872i).[20]

In early December, Mowway, Paruacoom, and Tabenanaka, the "head chiefs of the roaming and heretofore uncontrollable Indians," came to visit Tatum (Tatum 1872j). In the "presence of several of the recent delegation to Washington," Tatum again told them that they must move onto the reservation or be considered hostile:

> After the Indians fully understood the interpreter, I separately asked Tabenanaka (head chief of the Quahada Indians), Mowway, and Paruacoom, and the other chiefs if they wished to comply . . . to which they all gave affirmative answers. [Tatum 1872j]

Later, some Kwahadas brought in twenty-five horses "in partial payment for the 53 stolen from the quartermaster," and Tatum issued them "their quota of annuity goods." Indeed, Tatum believed that "all the Indians of the agency are behaving better than ever before" (Tatum 1872k). Later that month, an order was received at Fort Concho authorizing the release of the first five on his list (Hatch 1872e), but one had died of pneumonia in November (Hatch 1872d).

There was one other major event of the winter of 1872. On his return from Washington, on December 21, Paruasemena became sick. He died two days later in a room in the agency office.

The Buffalo War, 1873–75

Many Comanches spent the winter of 1872–73 on the reservation. In January Tatum reported that because the grass had been burned from Cache and Chandler creeks the Indians were scattered. He attributed the burning to an intentional effort by the Indians to "make it impossible for them to camp on the streams near the agency" (Tatum 1872h), although it may simply have been to encourage the spring growth of the grass. The Penatekas Tosawa, Esihabit, Kakarawa, and Ceachinika, along with Mowway and Quitsquip, were on the south side of the Washita River about six miles below the Wichita agency. Paruacoom, "one of the most prominent of the Kwahada chiefs," with about five hundred followers, was camped in the Wichita Mountains, "within a reasonable distance of the agency." Terheryahquahip, "one of the most friendly of the chiefs," and several others were along the banks of Medicine Creek near Mount Scott (Tatum 1873b); that was the village photographed by William Soule (plate 8). Howea and Cheevers were north of Fort Sill near Chandler Creek (Nye 1969:164). Tabenanaka and his brother-in-law Esarosavit (*isa tosapitʉ* 'white wolf') were "camped off the reservation on the North side of the Washita varying from 4 to 10 miles from Wichita Agency," in the vicinity of old Fort Cobb (Tatum 1873b).

For the time being relative quiet held at the agency. In January 1873 Tomichicut (*tuu motso katʉ* 'he has a black beard') brought in three Mexican captives and asked for seven of his relatives among those at Fort Concho. Later that month Tabenanaka brought in two captives for four of his relatives.[21] Although there were occasional incidents—on March 15 scouts from Kicking Bird's Kiowa camp intercepted a Comanche party from Tabenanaka's and Esarosavit's village and threatened to shoot their horses if they continued (Nye 1969:165)—Tatum believed that the Indians "manifest a more docile and better disposition than they have ever done before, and give strong assurances of friendship." In March Cyrus Beede again visited Fort Sill and reported "an increased interest in farming . . . there are now nearly 50 small Indian houses" (Beede 1873a). After a council with Beede, about fifty Co-

Plate 7. Terheryaquahip's village on Medicine Creek, Indian Territory. Photograph by William S. Soule. Winter 1872–73. Courtesy Fort Sill Museum.

manche (table 7.5) and Kiowa chiefs and headmen signed a petition stating,

> You have taken . . . 100 women and children into captivity. Forgive us, allowing us to begin life anew and return to us our loved ones. If the Great Father will do this we will hereafter obey the wishes of the Great Father, we will go no more into Texas. [Esitoya, et al. 1873]

Meanwhile, Terheryahquahip continued to visit hostile camps to retrieve captives, and newly appointed agent James Haworth—another Quaker—wanted to reward Terheryahquahip with an army ambulance, saying that the chief was "faithful in working to carry out the will of the government and deserve[d] all encouragement" (Beede 1873a).

The Comanche women at Fort Concho were ordered released in April (Augur 1873), but there was a delay in obtaining transportation because of rain-swollen rivers (Haworth 1873k), and a detour around Jacksboro because of a rumored mob, so they did not reach Fort Sill until June (Haworth 1873c). In August Terheryaquahip, although suffering from hemorrhagic bleeding in the lungs, and Tomichicut recovered twelve more horses from the Kwahadas (Haworth 1873e). Other Comanches, including Quitsquip, Puhiwitoya, Tomichicut, Pearekaeka, Ohaumer (possibly *oha mʉa* 'yellow moon'), and Black Duck (the latter two previously unmentioned) brought in stolen horses (Haworth 1873f; Hoag 1873); even Paruacoom helped recover others (Haworth 1873g).

The Kiowa chiefs Satanta and Big Tree became the focus of another crisis. Since they were prisoners of the State of Texas, the state claimed authority in their case, but there was confusion and miscommuncation between Texas state officials and federal officials in Washington and at Fort Sill. At the core of the affair was the insistence by Texas officials of linking the Kiowas and Comanches together, each held accountable for the actions of the other; either the Texans took the Medicine Lodge Treaty's confederation of the Comanches and Kiowas literally, or they could not tell the difference between the two peoples. At the same time, there was the problem of the Kwahadas; they had not signed the Medicine Lodge Treaty, but at least some of them, represented by Paruacoom, Patchokoniki, and probably others, were nonetheless taking advantage of the opportunities provided by the reservation. In contrast to the Texans, federal authorities in Washington, St. Louis, and Fort Sill did not treat the Comanches and Kiowas as a single group, but dealt with each separately (Hagan 1976:94).

In early 1873, at the request of Secretary of the Interior Columbus Delano, Governor E. J. Davis of Texas agreed, pending compliance with conditions, to turn Satanta and Big Tree over to the army at Fort Sill. Those con-

Table 7.5

Comanche Signers of the March 1873 Petition Asking for the Release of the Comanche Women and Satanta and Big Tree

Esitoya	Terheryaquahip
Mowway	Paruacoom
Pearekaeka	Cheevers
Onaweah	Esasuat[a]
Little Captain [a]	Poyawatoya
Pyoh	Howea
Hitetitse	Wild Horse
Tosawa	Kahabewite
Blue Blanket [a]	Quitsquip
Bald Eagle [a]	White Eagle [a]
Esahabit	

[a] Previously unnamed.

SOURCE: Esotoya et al. 1873

ditions included the dismounting, disarming, and "close surveillance" of all Fort Sill Indians. When informed of the conditions, Terheryahquahip sullenly commented that they would be left "sitting like dogs on the prairie" (Beede 1873b). There was some confusion about the timing of the release, and the Modoc War intervened—it was not deemed politic to release hostiles in the midst of an Indian war, even if that war were as far away as Oregon. It was not until early October that Governor Davis arrived at Fort Sill with Satanta and Big Tree for a formal meeting.

After initial statements by Satanta and his father,[22] Davis gave a statement redolent with the Texan view of recent Indian affairs:

> For many years, Texas has been a part of the U.S. government and has been under the Government at Washington and a part of the Nation. Since when Lone Wolf was a little boy. The great Chief at Washington was bound to protect the lives and property of Texans as well as others of his children. But all these years the Kiowa and Comanche have been Killing and Capturing our women and children [and stealing] their horses. The Texans have not made captives of the women and children of the Kiowa, they have not stolen their horses. Nor gone to the country of the Kiowa to raid on them. The Texans have not made war on the Kiowa and Comanche, The Kiowa and Comanche have made war on the Texans. The Texans have remained at home to defend themselves and have not followed the Kiowa and Comanche to Capture and Kill them, but have staid home. They have not followed the Comanche and Kiowa

to capture them not because they are not powerful Enough to do so, for Satanta Can tell you that the Texans are as numerous as the leaves in the forest and a hundred times as many as the Kiowa and Comanche together. They have not followed because they are all children of the Great Father and they had made a treaty not to go to Texas. Some six years ago they the Kiowa and Comanche agreed in that treaty to remain on their reservation here and not go to Texas. They agreed in that treaty that they would not capture our women and children and not Scalp them or take the property of the white man. But they violate that treaty, they have been going to Texas all those years, taking their property and Killing their men. The Texans did not violate that treaty, they did not come to the reservation the Kiowa and Comanche alone went to Texas . . .

I am now going to tell you the terms I demand for Texas—Listen to them—The Kiowa and Comanche to go on that part of the reservation where they are permanently to remain on cultivatable land in the neighborhood of Fort Sill. Their location to be with a view of adopting the habits of the white man: cultivating the soil and raising cattle, and giving up the use of their horses and arms. This movement [is] to commence at once, and in the meantime, so as to prevent any misunderstanding of the conduct of the Indians on the part of the people of Texas or on the part of the United States Government and to prevent the possibility that the bad acts of other Indians be charged to them, they must have white men as agents remain with them constantly in their respective camps who can see all of them daily and see that none of them leave on raids. To make it impossible that they can go into Texas they are to draw their rations for not exceeding three days at a time each man personally present to answer his name and draw his rations.

Further, I demand that the Comanche who have recently been raiding into Texas be delivered up to the Texas authorities and to aid in effecting this those Comanche and Kiowa who have remained faithful shall put themselves under the direction of the United States troops to assist arresting those Comanches, so that they may be sent to the Texas authorities for trial and punishment. Horses that can be identified as having been stolen in Texas [are] to be delivered up to the Texas owner and also all captives that these Indians may have. [Winfrey and Day 1959-66, 4:352-53]

It was an amazing speech; indeed, Commissioner Edward P. Smith—or Agent Haworth (Nye 1968:170), the record is unclear—immediatedly disclaimed responsibility: "The Governor of Texas has given you these terms, not the Commisioner or Agents, who knew nothing about the Governor's terms until they heard them today" (Winfrey and Day 1959-66, 4:353). At the same time, Governor Davis's understanding of history is interesting, if only for its misrepresentations; his comment that "Texas has been a part of the U. S. . . . since when Lone Wolf was a little boy" greatly underestimated Lone Wolf's age: in 1873, Texas had been a state for only twenty–seven years, while Lone Wolf must have been at least forty years old at the time of the council. If this was indeed the case, then at his birth Texas was still Mexican, and the first Anglo-Americans had only just begun to arrive. Davis also conveniently ignored the recent unpleasantness between the Confederacy and the United States.

More significant were the differences between Davis's understanding of the Medicine Lodge Treaty as expressed in his speech and the document itself: specifically, except insofar as the signers said they would stay on the reservation, there was no stipulation that they "agreed . . . not go to Texas." Even more specifically, there was no treaty stipulation against capturing women and children, or taking property. That is, Davis was charging the Kiowas and Comanches with crimes against promises that did not exist.

Various Indians responded to Davis. Kicking Bird, the Kiowa, stated, "Turn over the chiefs [Satanta and Big Tree] and we will quit raiding in Texas." Terheryahquahip, Esitoya, and Quitsquip complained that the problem was as much Washington's as theirs; promises had been made but not kept. Quitsquip noted:

> You blame us for not getting on your road, but you have broken your promise to us about houses and farms, and you cannot blame us for breaking some of our promises. Why should I talk so much; I will try to get on the white man's road, but it cannot be done in a moment, we must have time. [Winfrey and Day 1959–66, 4:357]

Buffalo Good, the Waco, instigated the most discussion. In response to Davis's claim that "Texans did not come onto the reservations," he complained that Texans had indeed come to steal his horses; "we have been losing them all summer." Taken aback, Davis said, "if they will report the thing promply so that troops can pursue I will answer any requisition if they escape into Texas. As I do not wish to protect any bad Texans . . . they should be quick in reporting such stealing." This promise of assistance to Indians against Texans was off-the-cuff, but Davis quickly recovered, and returned to his theme: the "best way to compel Texans to behave themselves, as well as Indians, is to capture and punish them" (Winfrey and Day 1959–66, 4:358–59).

It is not clear what happened that night. According to Quaker schoolteacher Thomas Battey, Agent Haworth spent the evening pursuading Davis that his demands were unreasonable, and would lead to more trouble (Battey 1875:202–3). Meanwhile, the Indians, both Kiowas and Comanches, made plans for a sudden strike to free the prisoners (Battey 1875:202; Campbell

1926-28:637-38; Nye 1969:175).[23] The next morning, to everyone's surprise, Governor Davis released the prisoners on the guarantee of Commissioner Smith.

Following the meeting with Davis, Commissioner Smith demanded that five raiders be surrendered: if they were not, all rations would be stopped. It is not clear if Smith had five specific men in mind or simply the number.[24] In response to that surprise demand, Cheevers spoke:

> Tell that Washington Chief that I am a Comanche and that my people have been doing no wrong, and should not be asked to pay for any wrong done by the young men of other tribes. But I know that there are bad men among all people, among white men as well as Indians. Those among us who have persisted in bad actions, contrary to the wishes and orders of the chiefs, are renegades, and we have cast them out. They are the ones who are bringing all this trouble on the Indians. You will find them west of the Antelope Hills. [Campbell 1926-28:639; Nye 1969: 177]

Tokomi was more forward, "Tell that old man I am Black Horse, a soldier chief. He may take me if he can but he may have a little trouble doing it" (Campbell 1926-28:639; Nye 1869:177). Finally, a compromise was worked out: Cheevers would lead a party of Comanches and army troops in search of the raiders. They were given arms and uniforms and spent the month wandering around north Texas, but without success (Nye 1969:177-82).

On November 24, Commissioner Smith, back in Washington, finally lost patience. He instructed Haworth to halt immediately the distribution of rations, annuities, or ammunition—the office copy of the telegram told Haworth to "issue no *ammunition*" (E. P. Smith 1873a, my emphasis), but a synopsis of the telegram actually sent to Superintendent Hoag used the word *annuities* (E. P. Smith 1873b); the source of the confusion is unknown. The Comanches were given ten days to turn over the raiders, or else they would all be delivered over to the military. Receiving the telegram on November 30 (Haworth 1873h), the next day Haworth called in the chiefs and explained to them its contents; "most of them received it as a declaration of war and commenced at once to prepare for it" (Haworth 1873j). Nevertheless, on December 2 the order was rescinded (Clum 1873a) and Haworth was authorized to issue three-quarters rations pending the return of stolen property (Clum 1873b).

Haworth did not receive notice of the suspension until December 6, and by then some of the Comanche villages had already fled westward. Others stayed near the agency, meeting almost daily with Haworth. During the next two weeks, in letters to Superintendent Hoag and Secretary of the Interior

Delano, Haworth gave accounts of events, and although the accounts are slightly different, making an accurate reconstruction difficult, the statements provide a wide view of Comanche feelings.

Terheryaquahip told the agent he was too old and sick to run, and if Haworth would not issue rations to him, he must starve. But if he went with the others, he would be killed there, too. Thus, if he had to be killed, he would rather have a friend do it; he believed Haworth to be his friend so he would come in and take his chances near the agency (Haworth 1873j).[25]

Cheevers took a different approach. In a December 1 letter to Superintendent Hoag, Haworth quoted Cheevers—who himself quoted Commissioner Smith's telegram—as complaining that he was trying to get his people "to do right, but the white folks or Washington seemed determined to have war" (Haworth 1873h). A week later Haworth reported Cheevers's comments:

> I have tried very hard to do right. [I] have done everything I can to get my people to do as Washington asked us to. Only a few have done wrong. And they are now far out on the Plains and we can't catch them. Let us try as hard as we may. If the soldiers should kill them, we would not cry or care but Washington must be crazy to want to kill all the Comanches because a few have done wrong. I have done all I can. If Washington decides to make war I shall go with my people and fight until they kill me. [Haworth 1873j]

But it was the Penatekas who were most explicit about both their present circumstances and their own place in history. According to Haworth's letter of December 1, Esitoya said that his people

> had not done anything wrong and he could not see why they should be driven away or killed for what others have done. . . . the Penateka [have] kept separate from the wild Comanche, in fact they [have] never lived with them until after the white people had driven them from their homes on the Clear Fork of the Brazos in Texas. [Haworth 1873h]

That is, Esitoya made a clear political distinction between the Penatekas and the "wild" Comanches. It was the first step towards the story that culminated in Ceachinika's report of the Penatekas' "long separation" from other Comanches less than a decade later.

Esitoya also threatened to "take his people and go over to the Caddos"—that is, to the other Penatekas at the Wichita agency—until the trouble was over (Haworth 1873i). On December 8 Haworth gave Esitoya's statement:

> What [should] I do. I don't want to fight. [A] long time ago, [I] quit fighting. Now Washington says, "Asatoyet, you are an Indian, a Comanche, [and] because some of the mean young Comanches have done

wrong, we won't feed you or give you your annuities. You will have to go out on the Plains, and when the soldiers come [they will] make you fight." [I do not] want to fight. [I took the] white man's hand many years ago, and now [they have] let go [of] it and don't want it now. [Haworth 1873j]

Ultimately, on December 15, in a letter to Secretary of the Interior Delano, Haworth elaborated on Esitoya's reference to the Brazos reservation:

A part of them feel that they had rights in Texas from which they were forcibly driven. . . . They claim that when Samuel Houston was, as they regard it, the owner of Texas, he drew an imaginary line, the land on one side of which he gave to them to belong to them and their children for ever, [and] told them white men should never disturb them in their rights and that they must never cross over that line and disturb the people or their property. Subsequently, a certain district or reservation on the Clear Fork of the Brazos was set aside for them: for the Comanche, four square leagues of land, for the Caddos, eight square leagues. They lived peaceably upon these lands, had commenced to raise corn, their children were going to school around them. They had gathered cattle, hogs and chickens and as they express it, were getting far advanced in the white man's road when they were driven by a mob far from their homes, their hogs and cattle and many of their horses taken from them, property destroyed for which they have never been paid, though I am told the government did appropriate a certain sum for that purpose about the commencement of the war which however, I understand never reached in whole or in part the Indians for whom it was intended. [Haworth 1873k]

As he had done four years earlier, Esitoya recalled the losses sustained in the move from the Brazos reservation, recalling important elements in Penateka political history, Haworth had little knowledge of that history. Indeed, his own solution was to call for another council in which

all these matters might be satisfactorily adjusted and stipulations made in which it might be set forth that should thereafter any of their people go into Texas for unlawful purposes that they should assist in their arrest or themselves surrender them to their proper authorities which I believe could and would be done, at which time such other stipulations as might be thought important could be made and thereby a permanent peace be established on the border.

Haworth ended by noting that Indians were not the sole cause of violence among Texans, for whom "murders . . . are so common as yet not to attend much attention!" (Haworth 1873k).

The affair soon faded from immediate attention. There was still raiding into Texas, even a foray or two into Mexico, but most ended in disaster. In all, some thirty Kiowas and Comanches were killed that winter. In March, Hitetsi visited Agent Haworth; although he had not been explicitly named in the historical records since the Medicine Lodge council five years before, Haworth called him "a truthful Indian [who] has for several years stood well as a peaceable and friendly man," implying that he had been often present and visible at the agency, albeit not politically active.

Hitetsi told Haworth that

> 2 Kiowas [Lone Wolf's son, Tauankia, and nephew, Guitan] with three other Kiowas and some Comanches from 3 to 5 in number were in Mexico together. [They] were attacked. The 2 Kiowas were killed and one Mexican boy. . . . 2 of the Comanches after leaving the party met with another body of Comanches with whom, they were camped at some point near the Rio Grande when the soldiers surprised and killed a number of them, 9 men and 2 women. From the time he makes it, I suppose this is the fight of Lt. [Charles] Hudson. After which a portion of the same party had another fight in which about the same number were killed. I presume this to be the fight of Lt. Colonel [George] Buell near the Double Mountain. The Comanche do not claim the company of any Kiowas in either of the 2 fights in Texas. [Hitetitsi] seemed to be very certain that the 2 Kiowas were killed in Mexico. [Haworth 1874e]

The deaths of Tauankia and Guitan caused much mourning in the Kiowa camps, but it was the fights with Lieutenant Hudson on December 7 (to which Nye [1969:182] attributed the deaths of Tauankia and Guitan, although Hitetsi said there were no Kiowas present) and Colonel Buell on February 5 (in which four Kwahadas, four Kotsotekas, and three Yamparikas were killed [Haworth 1874m]) that had more lasting importance, for the reports received in the Comanche camps were that the soldiers were guided by Tonkawas.

There was much dissatisfaction in the Comanche villages that winter, and throughout the following spring Comanches were reported gathering all the weapons they could. The sale of arms and ammunition by the traders at Fort Sill had long since been banned, so many Comanches went to the traders at the Cheyenne Agency at Fort Supply. In the middle of March George Fox, a trader for J. S. Evans at Fort Sill, was in Kicking Bird's camp when Tabenanaka visited his trading tent, asking for arms and ammunition. When he was told there were none, "he coolly informed us that we could expect no trade from any of the Yamparika, stating that they could obtain all the arms and ammunition they wished at the Cheyenne or Wichita camps," and the chief flashed a new Colt revolver and a cartridge belt obtained from the Cheyenne traders. Patchokoniki received the same response from the Fort Sill traders;

several days later he returned from the Wichita camps with another pistol, fifty cartridges, and a mule load of ammunition (Fox 1874a).

In early May many Comanches stopped at Fort Sill to pick up their rations and then moved out to Elk Creek, also called Sweetwater Creek and Pecan Creek, near the North Fork of the Red River. The cause of the movement was not known until Terheryaquahip came in from the camp "very much excited":

> They have a medicine man who can accomplish wonders. [Terherya-quahip] says he can furnish an inexhaustible supply of cartridges suited for any gun from his stomach—certainly a very valuable man to have around in time of war—He can also raise the dead, having recently done so. He is himself, and can render all others bullet-proof. [Haworth 1874f]

Sometime the previous winter or late spring, a young Kwahada named Isatai *isatai* 'wolf's vulva'—he was also known as Quenatosavit *kwina tosapitʉ* 'white eagle', possibly the White Eagle who had signed the March petition, and whose uncle was reported killed in the Double Mountain fight (Nye 1969:182); the chronological order of those alternative names is unclear—announced plans for a ceremony to be held the next summer. He had, according to trader George Fox, ordered "all the Comanches . . . to join a grand Medicine Dance" (Fox 1874b)—Mooney later reported that Isatai "commanded the tribe to assemble in May" (1898:201); that was given by Nye as "all Comanches were invited—nay ordered—to attend" (1969:190)—but the nature of the command is unclear; clearly not all Comanches attended. Also present were some Cheyennes, a few Arapahos, Kiowas, and Apaches; Haworth felt the latter to be "still very strong in their professions and promises and unless something may happen to cause them to change I believe they will maintain this loyalty and do right" (Haworth 1874j). The Kiowas were also preparing for their own Sun Dance to be held later nearby (Mooney 1898:338). Several Comanches, notably Esasuat (*esa sootʉ* 'many wolves'), Onaweah, Quitsquip, and Mocksu (*makwɨsaʔ* 'sleeve'), did not attend, saying they did not want to "have any part of it lest it should involve them in trouble" (Haworth 1874h).

The only Comanche account of the 1874 ceremony has come from Joe Attocknie, whose grandmother, Querherbitty (*kwuhuru pitʉ* 'arrives to capture'), Cheevers's younger sister, was present. According to Attocknie, she described a

> gathering of mounted Comanches, both men and women, following the directions of [Isatai]. The Comanches were gathered around a tall pole set into the ground. The top of the pole was in the form of a cross. At his

signal, the mounted Comanches started singing and revolving around the cross. . . . The people nearest the center pole walked their horses slow. Those farther out from the center had to ride faster. A very dense dust cloud was raised as the riders at the very edge of the revolving mass had to whip and run their horses that much faster than those nearer the center of the singing revolving throng. [Attocknie 1965]

The gathering lasted for more than a month; several times Terheryaqua-hip, Onaweah, and Quitsquip came from the camp to report on its often confused progress (Haworth 1874g). The early reports emphasized a planned attack on the Tonkawas at Fort Griffen who had guided the soldiers against them during the winter (C. H. Carleton 1874); another report, based on information from Kicking Bird, said they had decided on a "war against whites in general and Texas and Texans in particular" (Fox 1874b). Quitsquip summarized the debate: "There are a great many hearts. They would make up their minds at night for one thing and get up in the morning entirely changed" (Haworth 1874i). A week later he reported that "with the exception of [the Kotsotekas] and Tabenanaka's people" the Comanches were opposed to making any trouble (Haworth 1874k).

On June 27 the "Kotsoteka and several other bands of Comanche [were] camped within a short distance of the agency—the main body of the Comanche were still on the Sweetwater" (Haworth 1874l). The identities of those Kotsotekas, either the ones acting with Tabenanaka or the ones camped near the agency, are not clear—by that time there were only two local bands consistently identified as Kotsotekas, Mowway's and Kawertzeme's, and both were apparently "hostile" during the events of 1875. Their apparently incon-sistent behavior probably reflects as much the fluid political identities of the time as it does the state of Haworth's knowledge of the Comanches. It was from those Comanches, however, that Haworth heard of the "great complaint . . . made by the Indians of the terrible destruction of the buffalo by hunting parties who were reported to be killing them by thousands taking the hides and leaving the bodies to rot on the Plains," and he asked, "Is there not some means by which it could be stopped" (Haworth 1874l).

That very day the associated Comanches and Cheyennes attacked a group of hide hunters operating out of the Bent's old adobe post on the Canadian River. Unfortunately, Isatai's *puha* 'power' did not work, and after a loss of six or seven Comanches and an equal number of Cheyennes, the attack was called off.

There are several uncertainties about those events that are important to their interpretation. Although it seems clear that there was much dissatis-faction in the Comanche villages, it is not clear whether the changes in the proposed targets—from anger at the Tonkawas, to anger at Texans, to a generalized anger at the whites, to a specific anger at the buffalo hunters, to a nationalistic revitalization movement—represented simply a reflection of the vagaries of reporting or corresponded to an evolution in political consciousness. Moreover, if the latter, the political dimensions of the emerging consciousness are uncertain; that is, it is not clear whether the nationalistic message was stated in divisional—Yamparika and Kwahada, but not Penateka—pan-Comanche, or even Pan-Indian terms—there were also Cheyennes present. The final selection of the buffalo hunters as a target points to political-economic considerations. But, since many Comanches did not concur in that movement—including the Nokoni leader Terheryaquahip, the Yamparika leader Cheevers, and most of the Penatekas (Haworth 1874m)—those political-economic goals did not correlate with a multi-divisional political identity. Rather, the selection of the buffalo hunters as a target probably reflected the immediate concerns of Tabenanaka and the Yamparikas: Tabenanaka was explicitly singled out as dissatisfied with the contemporary situation; indeed, his trade across the Arkansas River was put in immediate jeopardy by the hunters. Shrewdly, he was willing to let the Kwahadas take both the immediate leadership and the immediate risk while he could reap the benefits.

After a number of Comanche bands began to filter back into Fort Sill, General J. W. Davidson interviewed Esihabit and Esitoya asking "what did the Comanche have to complain of." They said they had

> nothing to complain of on the part of the Government, agent, troops, or whites, but that some 2 months ago a 'prophet' arose among them who told them that he had an interview with the Great Spirit who said that the Caddos, Wichita, and other Indians who were adapting the mode of life of the whites were going down hill fast, in mean [*sic*] and in population, and the Comanche would do the same if they followed the same road, and the way for them to be again a powerful nation they once were was to go to war and kill off all the white people they could. This, these two chiefs said, chimed in with the feeling and wishes of the evil disposed of the nation and the present war is the result. [Davidson 1874]

The Surrender

Taking authority over the Indians, the army ordered all "friendly" Indians to camp on the east side of Cache Creek, where they would be enrolled by name and subject to a daily roll call. Those who did not come in would be considered hostile. On July 23 Puhiwitoya, Howea, Cheevers, Paruacoom, and "10 other chiefs" sent a message that they were coming in (Haworth 1874n); the inclusion of Paruacoom in that list is puzzling, as he is usually said to have died during the move to the Adobe Walls (Nye 1969:190).

There was some resistance to enrollment by name—indeed, no individual name list has been found—but by August 11 Captain George Sanderson, detailed to complete the enrollment, and Agent Haworth described the situation:

> the following Indians [are defined] as hostile and those upon whom the troops will be justified in attacking:
> - The Kotsoteka Comanches.
> - The Quahada Comanches.
> - The Nokoni Comanches, except [Terheryaquahip][26] and 7 followers now enrolled unless others should hereafter be allowed to come in.
> - The Yamparika Comanche except Cheevers and 3 followers now enrolled . . .
> - [Puhiwitoya] and 6 followers . . .
> - [Ohaumer] and 9 followers . . .
> - Prairie Fire [previously unmentioned] and 3 followers . . .
> - Howea and 8 followers . . .
> - 4 Kotsotekas camped with the Yamparika . . .
> - unless [Hitetsi] and Esananaka and their followers should hereafter be allowed to come in on agreement.
> - The absent [Tenewas] including [Pearekaeka] and Black Duck . . .
> - Any absent [Detsakanas] including Tabenanaka and his followers.
> [Haworth 1874m]

Other Comanches were at Anadarko at the Wichita Agency, north of the Washita River. They included not only the Penatekas assigned there, but also other Penatekas not accounted for at Fort Sill; by mid-August a number of "hostile" Comanches and Kiowas, including, according to Nye (1969:205), Pearekaeka, Tabenanaka and his brother-in-law Esarosavit, Coby, Mowway, Hitetsi, Black Duck, and Isatai were camped near the Wichita agency.

On August 22, while the Indians assigned to the Wichita Agency were receiving rations, troops from Fort Sill arrived and demanded that Pearekaeka and the others surrender as prisoners of war. Initially agreeing, he bolted when the soldiers demanded all weapons, including bows and arrows. In the confusion that followed Pearekaeka escaped, but his village, with all its equipment, was burned.[27] However, the army soon found itself surrounded at the agency by Comanches, Kiowas, and assorted Caddos and Wichitas. For two days the Indians kept up a desultory siege, finally leaving upon hearing that troops were advancing from Fort Sill (Nye 1969:208).

The participants in the Anadarko affair fled west, having several skirmishes with soldiers from Fort Sill, Fort Richardson, and others. On September 27 Colonel Mackenzie's troops attacked a combined Kiowa, Comanche, and Cheyenne camp in the Palo Duro Canyon. Nye (1969:221) reported that the Comanches were under Ohamatai (possibly Ohaumer, it could also be based on *oha ma* 'yellow hand'); Utley (Pratt 1964:74 n74) reported the Comanches were with Mowway, Tabenanaka, and Coby, but the source of that attribution is unknown. Most of the Indians escaped, but Mackenzie captured the horse herd. Not willing to risk having the herd recaptured by the Indians as had happened after the McClellan Creek battle in 1872, he had the 1,400 horses shot.

The combined efforts of several army units forced most Comanches into the agency. By September about 480 Comanches and many Kiowas and Kiowa Apaches were at Fort Sill, with more coming in. Esananaka, with seventy-five followers, arrived at the end of the month. In October Tabenanaka, Esarosavit, Pearekaeka, and Hitetsi surrendered. By December Haworth reported that he had made a "complete census of the Indians to whom I am issuing rations"; of the Comanches, he listed 262 buffalo hide lodges and 41 cotton tents containing 162 men, 448 women, 144 boys, and 143 girls, a total of 897, and he estimated that there were about 135 warriors still out (Haworth 1874n).

The new arrivals were first divested of all military property, then held in Fort Sill's unfinished icehouse until a disposition was made. The most "incorrigible," such as Tabenanaka, Pearekaeka, Esarosavit, and Hitetsi, were held in irons. Others, against whom no accusation had been made, were released into the custody of the "friendly" Comanche chiefs Cheevers and Terheryahquahip and the Kiowa chief Kicking Bird (Davidson 1875a). By January most of the chiefs in irons had been released (Haworth 1875a); based on interviews with the "heads of tribes," Lieutenant Richard H. Pratt forwarded a list of "chiefs and the total number of men still out"; of Comanches chiefs, he included Blue Blanket, Coby, Tokomi, Kawertzeme, Esasoit, Soaring Eagle (previously unmentioned), Mowway, Tomichicut, and 177 followers (Pratt 1875). Hitetsi fled again in April, fearing reprisal for trying to hide some Kwahadas who had slipped into his camp (Haworth 1875g).[28]

At some point that winter Tabenanaka, Pearekaeka, and Cheevers visited Colonel John W. Davidson of the 10th Cavalry at Fort Sill. According to Davidson,

[they] represent to me that if a few of their men are permitted to go out to the Kwahadas to say to them that they may come in on the same terms

as [Pearekaeka], viz, unconditional surrender of their property, person and arms, that they may have reason to believe they will gladly come in. [Davidson 1875b]

Therefore, in the spring, Esarosavit went out; he returned in mid-April with Kawertzeme, Mowway, and Coby, with 36 men, 140 women and children, and 703 horses (Haworth 1875b).

Meanwhile, Ranald Mackenzie, who had taken command of Fort Sill, sent J. J. Sturm, now storekeeper at the Wichita agency, Coby, Habywake (*habi* 'lie down'), and Toveah (the latter two previously unmentioned) to contact the remaining Comanches (Sturm 1875). Traveling southwestward across the Red River and up the Pease River, they found Tomichicut's village of fifteen or twenty lodges on April 27. After dinner and a smoke, Sturm gave Mackenzie's message, "asking him to come and surrender himself and his people to the military authority of the United States." Sturm reported that Tomichicut "readily assented, saying that he was tired of war and anxious for peace." He would start for Fort Sill while Sturm went to on the main camp, "distant about two sleeps."

Following the trail of Mackenzie's wagons from the year before, they passed Muchoque. On May 1 they came in sight of the main camp, on the south side of the Staked Plains. Upon their arrival, their horses were turned over to the women, and they were escorted to a large tent where they distributed presents of tobacco, coffee, and sugar. Later, "after the usual preliminary of smoking," Sturm delivered Mackenzie's message; unfortunately, he did not name the individuals present. The Comanches declined to give an immediate answer, as they needed time to deliberate. That night Sturm was invited to Isatai's lodge for a "big talk." At that time Isatai, although a "very young man," was described as the "great medicine man . . . [with] a great deal of influence among his people." He said he would surrender as would his people. At the next day's council Quanah, a "young man of much influence with his people," made a speech in favor of surrender. Isatai then announced that they must all prepare to go in to Fort Sill, and "as his authority seems to be absolute they all agreed to start as soon as possible."

There were about thirty men out on a buffalo hunt, so Isatai left them a "letter" telling them where they had gone. Sturm reported that it showed

one white man and three Indians coming to the camp and the people running out to meet them. [Isatai] states that when the buffalo hunters see this letter they will know that messengers from Sill have visited their camp and brought "good words" and that they are all on their way to this place. The letter was written on a piece of buffalo skin and stuck on a pole.

The next day two of the hunters caught up with them. They had reached the old camp shortly after the others had left, and after reading the letter they threw away their packs of buffalo meat and hurried to join the village.

The movement was leisurely. There were pauses for buffalo hunting, chasing wild horses, and making an antelope surround—the only Comanche antelope surround mentioned in the literature. The women spent several days drying and packing meat, the men raced horses. The Comanches devoted May 4 to preparing for a celebration, the "last Medicine dance they ever expect to have." The women spent a day digging "a certain kind of vegetable of which they are very fond," while the men dug baking pits. Sturm said, "I am watching these proceedings and after the cooking is done shall eat my share of the mess and then be more able to judge the value of this food." Unfortunately, Sturm described neither the Medicine Dance nor the vegetable.

The young men found several two-horse wagons left by Mackenzie. To one they tied horses and, just at dark, came tearing into camp creating quite an excitement. Mules were hitched to the other and driven around with "half a score of Indians hanging to the wagon wherever they [could] get a hold."

One night there was "a pretty big row in camp": a horse had been in dispute for some time between a Mexican and a Comanche. Both parties had pistols. According to Sturm:

> The Comanche fired at the Mexican and the latter returned the fire and for a while they had a pretty lively skirmish. Shots and arrows flew pretty lively. The friends of each party rallied, some afoot some on horse back, and a general fight was in movement, but fortunately the old men and chiefs interfered and settled the dispute by bringing up the horse between the parties and killing him. It was a beautiful spotted horse. From what I can learn the Comanche was greatly at fault. As we were moving today the young Comanche came upon the Mexican and killed the horse he was riding, obliging the Mexican to walk to camp and carry his saddle. When he got to camp, his blood being hot from his tiresome walk he armed himself and went to kill a horse of the Comanche's to get even. The Comanche interfered and so the fight commenced. The Mexican got wounded by two arrows one in the arm and one in the breast both shot by a little boy, brother to the one he was fighting. He was the only one hurt but his wounds were not serious.

On May 20, they overtook Tomichicut.[29]

On hearing of their coming, the whole camp assembled and joined in a half circle and received them with drums, beating, singing and shouting and the messengers on reaching the circle rode inside then galloped out. This was done three or four times and then they rode to the middle of the circle and said they had brought good news, which was received with shouts. They then went to an arbor and after a general smoke told the news which was all well received with hah'as and approving grunts.

The next day Sturm sent Coby, Isatai, Esahabit, and Tahvemahnoe (given as Day Breaking, *tabe* 'sun' or 'day', previously unmentioned) to Mackenzie with the message that he hoped Isatai would be well received, because he "had been mainly instrumental in bringing his people in." The rest would stop at Signal Mountain west of the fort for further word. Thus, at about noon on June 2 108 men and 300 women and children (a total of 409), with 1,500 horses, were met by the army and quietly surrendered themselves and their arms (Haworth 1875e).[30] The surrendered horses and mules were sold at auction; one sale of 557 mules and 109 horses brought $5,000 (Haworth 1875c), another of 854 horses and 96 mules brought $15,339 (Haworth 1875f). With their surrender all of the Comanches were on the reservation, except for a few still out, including Hitetsi—who came in in November (Haworth 1875g, 1875h)—a few who joined the Mexican Kickapoos, and three or four families who had joined the Mescaleros.

In the meantime, a selection process had been underway at Fort Sill and elsewhere in Indian Territory:

> as fast as they were taken . . . the warriors [were] confined or paroled within close limits. All against whom good evidence of having committed crime could be found were taken out, and charges were alleged with a view to legal action. Another class, composed of those who were notoriously guilty of crime, but against whom no good evidence could be brought, and also of those who were notoriously insubordinate and stirrers up of bad feeling, was selected to be sent east for confinement at some fort. Not many of the first class could be found . . . When the time came to send them east, for some reason the first class accompanied the second, and all were sent [to Fort Marion, Florida] . . . they arrived on the 21st of May, 1875. [Pratt 1878:203]

That is, the Indian prisoners arrived at Fort Marion even before the main body of the Kwahadas had even approached Fort Sill. Furthermore, the prisoners were incarcerated as suspects, not as convicts; as Pratt noted, "the charges are only alleged and not proven" (Pratt 1878).

Sixty-four Cheynnes, Arapahos, Kiowas, Caddos, and Comanches were sent to Fort Marion, Florida. Although there were several prominent men among the Cheyennes and Kiowas, except for Tokomi—Black Horse—none of the eleven Comanches—nine men, and Tokomi's wife and daughter (plate 9)[31]—was particularly well known. Moreover, none of their crimes have been verified (table 7.6). At best, Tokomi was jailed for "talking defiantly" to Governor Davis of Texas. The rest of the charges against him were flimsy at best. For instance, inasmuch as there were apparently few Comanches near Fort Cobb in 1867, the charge that he had "killed a white man near Fort Cobb, Indian Territory, 1867" is difficult to substantiate. Further, the allegation that it was a contract killing at the behest of Agent Leavenworth—"Leavenworth and an inn-keeper named Lewis had engaged him to do the job on account of some trouble they had had with the man, who was a bad character"—is otherwise unsubstantiated. The references to Peehchip and his "fellows" shooting their father, being outlawed, and being sought by Captain Lee in 1873, are also apparently otherwise unnoted in the historical record.

It is sometimes said that when asked to point out the those who were guilty, Cheevers and other Comanche leaders sent only small-time raiders, while protecting the important men. However, as noted above, the selection was done before most of those important raiders had surrendered; it is not clear why a second deportation was not attempted. It is also sometimes said that some Comanches changed their names to avoid being identified; only one such case can be identified: before 1875, Black Horse was called Tokomi 'black male'. Afterward, however, he was called Tabeko (whose meaning is uncertain). But in his case the name change did not save him from the trip to Florida. Indeed, he was listed as *pukutue* 'little horse', a name by which he apparently was never known.

Comanche Resource Domains, 1860–75

During the fifteen years between 1861–75 Comanche political organization was reduced to two contrasting sets of resource domains: those based on political relations with the Anglo-American governments—ultimately with the federal government only—and all others. That historical trajectory resulted in the increasing encapsulation of Comanche political organizations within resource domains derived from and dominated by relations with the Anglo-American governments and the concomitant weakening of independent domains. Although some of that encapsulation was the result of individual decisions made by Comanche leaders hoping to establish domains based on political relations, most was the result of American military actions designed to close the independent trade and raiding domains.

Plate 8. Tokomi, Peahin, and Ahkes at Fort Marion. Ca. 1875–77. Photographer unknown. Courtesy National Anthropological Archives, Smithsonian Institution.

Table 7.6
Comanche Prisoners Sent to Fort Marion

Gno-yo-uh [Quoi-yo-uh]; given as Pile of Rocks; Warrior.
    Comment: Arrested at Fort Sill, Indian Territory, April 8, 1875. Bad man. Stealing horses. Stole thirty or more horses from the Chickasaws.

Pa-roo-rite [Pa-voor-ite]; given as Little Prairie Hill; Warrior.
    Comment: Mexican (Comanche Captive). Arrested at Wichita Agency, Indian Territory, December 25, 1874. Helped steal forty-six horses from near Fort Sill belonging to K[iowa] and C[omanche] Agency and John Madden, citizen, May 11, 1874. Threatened to kill Mr. Clark, Comanches inn-keeper, on the day of the Wichita disturbance, August 22, 1874. Drew pistol on Clark.

Eck-e-nah-ats [Eck-e-mah-ats]; given as Buck Antelope, possibly *eka* 'red', *wehkinitu* 'to look around for'; Warrior.
    Comment: Mexican (Comanche Captive). Arrested at Elk Creek, Indian Territory, October 26, 1874. Was in Texas with a party and stole horses about December, 1873.

Wy-a-ko [Wyako]; given as Dry Wood; Warrior.
    Comment: Mexican father, Comanche mother. Arrested at Elk Creek, Indian Territory, October 26, 1874. Has been in Texas stealing horses; was in Texas last in the winter of 1873-74.

Nad-a-with-t [Mad-a-with-t]; Warrior.
    Comment: Comanche. Arrested at Fort Sill, Indian Territory, March 7, 1875. Died July 1, 1877. A raider. A bad man. Always trying to persuade young men to go off into Texas, always going himself.

Po-ko-do-ah; given as Black Horse, it is *puku tue* 'little horse'; Chief.
    Comment: Comanche. Arrested at Fort Sill, Indian Territory, March 6, 1875. Talked defiantly in council with Governor Davis at Fort Sill, Indian Territory, 1873. Killed a white man near Fort Cobb, Indian Territory 1867. The man went in his company on a hunt, and it was thought at the time that Black Horse procured him to go for the purpose of killing him. That the Indian Agent Leavenworth and an inn-keeper named Lewis had engaged him to do the job on account of some trouble they had had with the man, who was a bad character.

Pe-e-chip [Peechip]; given as Tail Feather (possibly *pi* 'behind, tail', *sia* 'feather'); Warrior.
    Comment: Comanche. Arrested at Fort Sill, Indian Territory, April 18, 1875. He is one of the five fellows that shot their father and was outlawed; that Captain Lee (Tenth Cavalry) was sent down to Double Mountain after, in the fall of 1873. he has been on the war-path ever since.

Tischa-kah-da [Tischakahdah]; given as Always Sitting Down in a Bad Place (possibly *tuhtsu* 'bad' *karu* 'sit'); Warrior
    Comment: Comanche. Arrested at Fort Sill, Indian Territory, April 18, 1875. A bad man. Always trying to steal horses, or on the war-path, &c. He is one of the desperadoes Captain Lee (Tenth Cavalry) was sent down to Double Mountain after late in 1873.

Pe-ah-in; Mother.

Ah-kes; Small Child.

NOTE: This table follows the basic list in Pratt (1878). Spelling variations from Mooney (n.d.) are in brackets.

SOURCES: Pratt 1878; Mooney n.d.

The diversion of American attention during the Civil War, 1861-65, brought mixed blessings to the various Comanche groups. For the Penatekas, the Confederate agency at Fort Cobb held the promise of some respite from the general poverty of the Texas reservation. The 1861 Confederate treaties had promised quantities of goods, but the Confederacy was either unable or unwilling to supply the full amount of those goods, and extant accounts show only the distribution of subsistence goods, foodstuffs, soap, and tobacco; in the second quarter of 1861 Agent Matthew Leeper issued 550 pounds of coffee, 550 pounds of sugar, 650 pounds of soap, and 600 pounds of tobacco to the 380 Indians at Fort Cobb[32] (Abel 1915a:201). A year later, in February 1862, he issued 1,754 rations of beef, flour, coffee, sugar, soap, and salt for the "Indian soldiers" on his reservation (Abel 1915a:345). If those Indian soldiers were the scout company, the majority of whom were Comanches, their status clearly gave them access to goods above the other residents. The Comanches also had, according to Leeper, "a number of warm comfortable houses" (Abel 1915a:340). But after the attack of October 1862 and the Confederate abandonment of Fort Cobb, the Penatekas were apparently left on their own.

On the other end of Comanchería, the distribution of goods under the 1853 treaty of Fort Atkinson, supposed to last ten years, had long been ignored; there had been no distribution since 1858. Thus, those Yamparikas who attended the 1861 Confederate treaty council may have done so in hopes of the renewal of positive political relations with Anglo-Americans. Although it is not clear whether they understood the implications of the political separation of the Confederacy, it seems certain that they were genuinely surprised that when they tried to use the treaty as surety for goods at Fort Wise they found that they had been meeting with enemies of the United States. The 1863 reaffirmation of the Fort Atkinson and Fort Laramie treaties promised $25,000 in annuities, but there seems to be no evidence that such funds were requested let alone appropriated. In New Mexico, in contrast to earlier relations, Comanche visitors to the American posts received only "old clothing" amounting to no more than $206; when the Indian Bureau refused to pay the bill for Comanche subsistence, the army discontinued even that minimal support.

Some goods were given during the 1865 Little Arkansas Treaty council, and the treaty included the promise of continued annuities. But there are irregularities in the record of Comanche participation in that council that suggest political manipulation on both sides. Although the names of "representatives" of four divisions appear on the treaty, the record of negotiations focused mainly on the Nokonis Quenahewi and Terheryaquahip, with some later additions. It is possible that those chiefs were merely spokesmen—*tekwa-*

wapinᴴᴴ—for the other signatories, but that would have been extraordinary: Paruasemena and Tabenanaka seldom let anyone else do their talking for them; moreover, of those two prominent but silent Yamparikas, one "signed" as proxy for the other. Thus, it is possible that their silence in the record of negotiations is indicative of their absence from the meeting itself. That is, given the Yamparikas' apparently secure position in the Arkansas River buffalo hide trade, further discussion of political relations may have been of minimal importance. That is not to say that, given the opportunity, they would not take gifts if offered.

On the other hand, the Nokoni Comanches had had no political relations with Euroamericans for the previous five years; indeed, even their indirect relations through other Comanches and through other Indians of the Indian Territory had been severed during the war. Thus, like those Yamparikas who attended the Confederate council in 1861, the Nokoni participants on the Little Arkansas River may have been attempting to strengthen their own political positions through the reestablishment of political relations disrupted by the war. Similarly, Tosawa's involvement in the proceedings, albeit late, emphasized the precarious nature of his political position in the absence of Anglo-American political support.

The contrived 1866 Cheyenne war prevented the Little Arkansas Treaty from having its desired political results; moreover, there were white captives among the Kwahadas. Therefore, like the 1853 Fort Atkinson Treaty, for the Americans the 1867 Medicine Lodge Treaty was an attempt at an ultimate resolution of the entire political situation on the southern Plains (R. A. Smith 1971). And like the 1853 treaty, the Medicine Lodge Treaty was a Yamparika document: the only non-Yamparikas present were the Nokoni chief Terheryaquahip, and the Penatekas Tosawa and Ceachinika. Although the Yamparikas' participation reflects a change in attitude from 1865, whether it was political —realizing the benefits of association—or sentimental—setting aside any hard feeling from the Adobe Walls fight of the year before—is unknown; it did, however, result in an apparent protection of their principal resource, the buffalo, by allowing them to continue to hunt on the old Little Arkansas reservation and prohibiting Anglo-Americans from doing the same. Similarly, although the absence of the Kwahada was clearly due to circumstances in New Mexico rather than to an anti-American stance, whether the absence of the other groups was due to poor communication, as in Tosawa's case, or to a political decision to stay away, is unknown.

The Medicine Lodge Treaty involved the greatest one-time distribution of presents, approximately $120,000, to southern Plains Indians. They included

two thousand suits of uniform, two thousand blankets, fifty quarter boxes
tobacco, twenty bolts of Indian cloth, three bales domestics, one bale
linsey, twelve dozen squaw axes, one bale ticking, fifty revolvers (navy
size), besides an assortment of beads, butcher knives, thread and brass
bells, looking glasses, and sixteen silver medals worth $250. [Stanley
1967:288]

Navy revolvers were .36 caliber, smaller than the army models, which were
.44 caliber. They were the source of some concern on the part of the commission. Some commissioners suggested that they should not be issued at all,
as they could be used for offensive war. However, the army members of the
commission voiced no objection, and they were issued. A number of pistols,
made by the Union Arms Company, exploded on first firing. Those were
replaced by Colt revolvers from the 1865 annuity, which had been held up by
the commission. Fifty-four Henry repeating rifles had also been intended for
that earlier issue, but they were not distributed.

Although the treaty called for a thirty-year annual distribution of $25,000
in annuities, those efforts were defeated by several factors, not the least of
which was the continuing lack of funds. Although Congress appropriated
money for annuities, much of it was diverted to pay depredation claims; in
1869 those amounted to more than $150,000 in claims against the Comanches
and the Kiowas (Hagan 1976:68). What money was left was used to buy
rations, not specified by the treaty, but necessary for the support of the
Indians. In the beginning, the army's "Acting Commissary of Subsistence for
Indians" issued rations to the Agent, who issued to the Indians; after June
1870, the Agents had direct charge of the rations (Lee, Tatum, and Haworth
1869–77).

But the foodstuffs were often spoiled or short of weight, and the prescribed ration was small. After some experimentation, Colonel Hazen settled
on a ration rate of one hundred rations made up of "150 pounds of beef, 75
pounds of corn meal, 25 pounds of flour, 4 pounds of sugar, 2 pounds of
coffee, 1 pound of soap, 1 pound of salt." In winter the meat ration was
increased to 2 1/2 lbs per ration; according to Hazen, the ration gave "general
satisfaction" (Hazen 1869). But in July 1869 Quitsquip complained that
"seven days rations are gone in four" (Tatum 1869a). The new Quaker agent,
Lawrie Tatum, telegraphed the commissioner of Indian affairs that the Comanches "[could not] be kept upon their reservation without an increase in
rations" (Tatum 1869c), and in August Felix Brunot of the Board of Indian
Commissioners reported that "there is much reason to believe that the Kiowas
and Comanches, in part, will again go to the plains if [the issue of coffee and
sugar] is not adopted at an early day, and that the sugar and coffee will

certainly hold them" (Brunot, Bishop, Dodge 1869). Of other goods, Adjutant Walsh reported, "The Indians appeared well satisfied . . . but they desired to have blankets, cloth, turnips, brass kettles, camp kettles, knives, and axes in lieu of clothing which appears to be of a very inferior quality" (Walsh 1869); the inclusion of turnips in the list is unexplained. By the fall, the rations were increased, with the coffee and sugar restored. In March 1871 Agent Tatum complained, "The sugar is of very damp quality; if the barrels are not frequently rolled half way over, the molassas will run out of the sugar" (Tatum 1872e).

Table 7.7 consolidates the monthly ration returns for June 1870-June 1871.[33] By the end of that time Agent Tatum was anxiously awaiting the arrival of the wagon train of supplies, repeatedly bogged down by high water. Table 7.8 reproduces Haworth's June 1873 comparison of rations required with those on hand, showing significant shortfall in every category.

There were also structural conflicts in the alternative roles of the annuities and the buffalo as food and as elements of economic exchange. For example, sometimes beef was relatively abundant, as in early 1871. At that time, however, the cattle were superfluous as rations, since buffalo were still available. The Indians were allowed to sell the beef to the post traders in return for script, which could be used for luxury goods (Tatum 1871b). But by 1873 the beef supply was low, the Indians had been prohibited from hunting off the reservation, and the sale of surplus rations had been prohibited. That restricted not only the available food, but also the available luxury items. The problem was summarized by agent Haworth:

> They complain a great deal about the insufficiency of their rations. [They] say the requirements of the Government prevent them from leaving their reservation to hunt the buffalo or other game, and meat being their principal reliance, the beef falls short of satisfying their needs. [In addition], they claim that under a system practiced some time ago by my predecessor of buying back a portion of their rations by order on the traders they were enabled to buy many things for their families which now they cannot buy. As they have not the money, their hunting being cut off, they are without robes or furs to sell hence have to live entirely upon the rations issued by the government . . . without money to buy anything with it is hard to make them feel satisfied. [Haworth 1873a]

Of the other Comanches, as Haworth indicated, there were itinerent traders in their camps as well as traders at the Cheyenne and Wichita agencies who supplied "almost everything [they] need for subsistence, for which they can trade their furs and robes" (Haworth 1873l).

Table 7.7
Ration Accounts, Kiowa Agency, 1870–71

	BACON	BEEF	FLOUR	CORN	RICE	COFFEE	SUGAR	SOAP	SALT	TOBACCO
Rec'd 6/30/70	28,336	4,299	560,744	140,256	3,650	25,489	35,523	19,287	28,925	
Issued 7/70	6,333	254	318,030	22,260	400	3,321	8,830	725	1,773	
On hand	22,002	4,045	535,755	117,996	3,250	22,167	26,692	18,562	27,745	
Issued 8/70	8,220	386	59,552	36,329		3,250	4,028	10,229	651	1,642
On hand		13,782	3,659	456,452	53,395		18,139	16,462	17,911	26,103
Issued 9/70	4,755	340	43,118	33,334	-0-	3,623	8,702	476	1,333	
On hand	9,027	2,347[a]	413,339	10,341[b]	3,250	14,516	7,760	17,435	24,770	
Issued 10/15	3,026	152	22,500	587	100	2,447	4,846	230	611	
On hand	4,070	2,123	276,371	-0-	3,000	11,097	-0-	17,058	23,768	
Issued 10/31	1,474	107	47,553	-0-	2,241	212	560			
On hand	2,596	2,096	328,818	3,000	8,856	16,846	23,208			
Issued 11/15	2,181	105	84,580		800	2,490		560	622	
On hand		415	1,911	274,238		2,200	6,366	16,502	22,586	
Issued 11/30	415	39	57,485	800	1,806	87	452			
On hand	-0-	1,872	216,753		1,400	4,560	5,020[c]	16,425	22,133	
Issued 12/15		64	67,990			600	2,444	3,250	249	611
On hand			1,808	148,763		800	2,116	1,770	16,176	21,522

Table 7.7, *continued*

	BACON	BEEF	FLOUR	CORN	RICE	COFFEE	SUGAR	SOAP	SALT	TOBACCO
Issued 12/31			178	13,907		800	832	1,770	178	511
On Hand		1,630	134,856		-0-	1,284	-0-	15,998	21,011	
Issued 1/31	238	86,718	7,068	1,284	4,649	611	1,131			
On hand	1,392	48,137	1,200			-0-	9,146	15,387	19,880	
Issued 2/31		192	101,523	13,677		4,416	357	552		
On hand				171,614	26,199		1,500	6,581	14,937	18,862
Issued 3/31	8,723	342	117,116	9,765		1,500	6,581	1,678	2,258	400
On hand		1,276	858	94,498	16,434			-0-		-0-
		13,259	16,703	-0-						
Issued 4/31	3,319	787	111,126	7,650		6,044	18,999	927	1,519	600
On hand	-0-	71	97,172	8,784		196	1,504	12,332	15,184	-0-
Issued 5/31	4,615	130		89,513	6,975		969	2,504	720	863
On hand		1,184	568	35,159	1,809		-0-	-0-	11,612	14,321
Issued 6/31	8,686	173	15,875	7,020		2,660	5,320	506	540	270
On hand	71,127	395	413,438	33,181		18,625	54,151	11,106	17,140	3,214

a Loaned 972 lbs to Cheyenne Agent Darlington. c Borrowed from Cheyenne Agent Darlington.
b Some to herders. d Borrowed from Cheyenne Agent Darlington, plus received from Superintendent.

SOURCE: Kiowa Agency Records, 1869–77

Table 7.8

Estimates of Subsistence Needed for the Year Ending June 30, 1874

	BACON	BEEF	FLOUR	COFFEE	SUGAR	SOAP	SALT	TOBACCO	SODA
Required	72,000	4,000,000	700,000	57,600	115,200	14,400	14,400	7,200	3,500
On Hand 31 June 1873	10,000		30,000		20,000			3,000	500
To be Supplied	62,000	4,000,000	670,000	57,600	95,200	14,400	14,400	4,200	3,000

SOURCE: Haworth 1873d

In the relative absence of political support from the American governments, Union or Confederate, other resource domains took on relatively greater importance for Comanche political organizations. Along the Arkansas River the raiding of trains on the Santa Fe Trail offered the dual inducements of war honors as well as loot, but the dimensions of Comanche involvement in those raids remains unclear. It was the focus of debate between New Mexico agent Michael Steck and General James Carleton. Carleton argued that their involvement justified a military campaign against them while Agent Steck and Governor Connelly argued that there was no evidence of their involvement and that a campaign would needlessly "stir up this powerful tribe" (Connelly 1864). Carleton's position ultimately won out, resulting in the inconclusive first battle of Adobe Walls. However, there remains little documentary evidence for Comanche involvement in such raiding.

Of more importance for the Arkansas River tribes was the robe trade. Details of this domain, while it lasted, are scarce. There were licensed agency traders; at Fort Sill J. S. Evans was the post sutler and the licensed Indian trader. There were also itinerant traders, but details are unclear: by the 1870s the Comanche agents had prohibited such traders from visiting the Indians— although in March 1873 Tatum gave "J. S. Evans and William Mathiewson, the Indian traders here, permission to go to the Indian camps, believing that if they were there, the Mexicans would not be likely to go there to sell contraband goods" (Tatum 1873c)—the large wall tent visible in the lower left corner of plate 7 is probably Evans's "trading tents." However, by the time of Agent Haworth's tenure, later that year, Comanches specifically asked for a trader to come to their camps, ironically, "like the Cheyenne": almost seventy years earlier Cheyennes had visited Santa Fe asking for relations "as with the Comanches." Haworth clearly, but indirectly, justified the political nature of the request: with traders in their camps, "the necessity of visiting the agency for supplies is removed, which takes them from under the influence of the Agent" (Haworth 1873l).

As had been customary for the previous half-century, those traders included not only Anglo-Americans, but also Osages and other Indians. In 1873 Agent Haworth reported a rumor of a

> large train of goods being brought or taken from the Osage reservation by the traders following up the Osage Indians—a large part of whom are up on the Washita River among the Kiowas. Runners have been among the Kiowa and Comanche, and also the Apache offering them large inducements to bring their robes and trade. [Haworth 1873l]

The dimensions of that trade are also indistinct. William Mathiewson and Philip McCusker spent winter 1866-67 in the Indian camps, where they "acquired by trade about all the robes the Comanche had" (Hyde 1968: 268). In May 1867 a trader, C. W. Whittacker, arrived in Leavenworth, Kansas, with 1,600 robes and a "large amount of peltry" from Comanches (Leavenworth 1867b). In 1873 the Kiowas had over 1,000 hides (Haworth 1873j).

Only one account of the rate of exchange has been found. In 1869 it was reported that

> at Camp Supply the price paid for a buffalo robe is seven to ten cups of sugar, and two to five cups of coffee, according to quality. "Porcupine robes," which is the designation for robes finely ornamented with quills, sometimes command as high as fifteen cups of sugar. A cup of sugar contains three fourths of a pound. A cup of coffee, half a pound. [Brunot, Bishop and Dodge 1869]

It is clear that the robe trade constituted a political-economic domain with both political and domestic aspects, and which must be protected at all costs. The Yamparika participation in the Medicine Lodge council had the clear political goal of protecting that economy. When Paruasemena stated his preference for following the buffalo to life under civilization, he was making a statement both about the basis of his own political position and about the domestic economy. When he wrested the provision that the Comanches could continue hunting on the Little Arkansas reservation "so long as the buffalo may range thereon in such numbers as to justify the chase," together with the by then standard treaty clause prohibiting unauthorized trespass by whites, he had—hopefully—ensured the Yamparikas' political and domestic resource domain for years to come. Tabenanaka's insistence upon the protection of that domain led to the fight against the invading hide hunters at the Adobe Walls; the unfortunate outcome of that battle was the loss of the domain altogether as the army forced all the Comanches onto the reservation.

To the south, a raid-trade domain developed focusing on the horses and cattle of Confederate Texas traded to Federal New Mexico. The pragmatics of that trade, like those of the horse raid-trade domain of the late 1840s and of El Sordo before that—during a war and across an albeit disputed national boundary—resulted in the establishment of the powerful Kwahada organization, attracting members from many other divisions and tribes. Similarly, changes in those conditions effected changes in the viability of the domain.

Estimates of the size of that domain have varied greatly. In 1873 John Hittson said that in the previous twenty years 100,000 cattle were lost to the Indians (Kenner 1969:174). In 1875 William Steele, Texas adjutant general, reported "losses of about thirty millions [of dollars]" (Winfrey and Day 1959–66, 4:373). In 1886 the secretary of the interior reported to Congress that there were $1,706,244 in damage claims against the Comanches dating from as early as 1855 and ranging from Texas to Kansas and New Mexico; most of those claims were disallowed. The largest single claim was by L. A. Dickson, of Wise County, Texas, who claimed losses of $159,750 between 1868 and 1873.

The big cattlemen, such as Hittson and Charles Goodnight, reported whole herds lost during trail drives. Kenner (1969:167-9) listed nine such incidents, 1867-72, based on reports in the New Mexico newspapers (table 7.9). That accounts for 12,149 animals in five years. In 1873 Comanches admitted taking Adams's herd, and he was credited with $52,275 (Kenner 1969:168). Considering that figure, at $21.34 each, Dickson, mentioned above, must have lost 7,485 head of cattle.

In 1896 Charles Goodnight and John W. Sheek claimed that the Comanches had taken, between 1865 and 1868, some 5,000 horses and cattle worth over $66,000 (Goodnight and Sheek 1896) (table 7.10). Goodnight later presented Comanchero testimony that some 300,000 head of cattle and 100,000 horses had been stolen and transferred to New Mexico between 1860 and 1867 (Haley 1935:169). He also claimed that he "personally knew that Indians captured five herds . . . accounting for some five to ten thousand head" (McCarty 1946:12).

Many scholars have accepted those figures (e.g., Kenner 1969:174; Hagan 1976:24); Kenner himself noted, "the larger estimate [Goodnight's] is probably more accurate." Others are more critical; in comparing Goodnight's and Hittson's numbers, Roe (1955:7) noted that Goodnight postulated the loss of three times as many animals in one-fourth the time. Although evaluation of the figures has been hampered by the lack of data on losses, forcing a reliance on numbers such as Goodnight's, careful examination of depredation claims can provide a sense of scale to the raid-trade domain.

Relatively few reports of depredations in Texas seem to have survived from the pre-Civil War period. In the ten years between March 1847 and March 1857, citizens of Refugio County claimed losses of $18,107 (Winfrey and Day 1959-66, 3:264), an average of $1,810 per year; in the twelve years, 1849-1861, Nueces County residents claimed losses of 506 horses, worth $12,800, and 253 cattle, worth $1,265 (Winfrey and Day 1959-66, 4:64), an average of $1,172 per year; in the fifty months, April 1857-January 1861, residents of Montague County claimed losses of 135 horses worth $22,090 and 18 cattle worth $221.00 (Winfrey and Day 1959-66, 4:56), an average of $5,577 per year. The high average for Montague County is the result of the higher value they placed on their horses, $163 each, compared to the average of $20 for the Nueces County horses.

Table 7.9

Reported Comanche Cattle Thefts, New Mexico and Texas, 1867–71

New Mexico, 1867	
From A. M. Adams, three herds,	2,449
New Mexico, 1868:	
From John Chisum, lower Pecos trail	1,100
At Independence Spring 30 June	900
At Independence Spring 1 July	1,100
From "Another Party"	1,000
Texas, 1871	
12 Miles from Ft. Concho	800
Texas, 1872	
23 Miles above Horsehead Crossing	1,500
12 Miles west Fort Concho	2,600
Near Ballanger	700

SOURCE: Kenner 1969:168

Table 7.10

Charles Goodnight's Claim against the Comanches, 1867–72

September 1867		
300 steers, 4 years old and up	@ $25.00	$ 7,500.00
500 steers, 3 years old and up	@ $20.00	$10,000.00
1,200 stock cattle	@ 9.00	$10,800.00
1 mule		$15.00
15 horses	@ $75.00	$1,125.00
May 1867		
200 steers, 4 years old and up	@ $25.00	$5,000.00
400 steers, 3 years old and up	@ $20.00	$3,000.00
1,900 stock cattle	@ $9.00	$17,100.00
June 1867		
41 horses	@ $75.00	$3,075.00
June 1868		
47 horses	@ $75.00	$3,225.00

SOURCE: Goodnight and Sheek 1896

In the postwar period the Texas adjutant general's office made several surveys of county officials for details on the stock stolen, one in 1867, another in 1873, a third in 1875 (table 7.11). If there was no duplication in those figures, 14,535 horses and 45,443 head of cattle were lost by Texans to Indian raiders (Kavanagh 1986:354). But the Texas officials were also well aware of the discrepancies between those official numbers and the figures reported in the press, and they offered several explanations. In June 1870 W. Stuckler of Medina County noted that because "our settlers are too much scattered [and] time proves too short to make a complete report," the Medina County numbers were "at least one fourth behind real estimation" (Winfrey and Day 1959-66, 3:307). In 1875 the adjutant general argued, "The frontier people after a few reports which yielded to them no results, have discontinued reporting their losses. The newspapers teem with accounts of raids . . . of which my office has no official information" (Winfrey and Day 1959-66, 3: 391). Even if the reported totals were increased by Stuckler's twenty-five percent, they would still be well below both Goodnight's and Hittson's numbers. It should also be noted that many other groups were involved in the horse and cattle trade besides Comanches. Therefore, the judicious approach is to reject Goodnight's and Hittson's numbers as highly inflated, and while noting that the offically reported numbers are probably too low, they are likely closer to the mark than Goodnight or Hittson.

The other end of that economy was the trade into New Mexico, which, like the horse trade to the east during the earlier part of the century, was part of a larger commercial enterprise, including not only the general New Mexican population, but also suppliers of beef cattle to the forts along the Canadian River by such individuals as Mr. Goldbaum. It was also rumored in Texas that Kansas stock buyers, "no doubt to encourage them to depredate," kept the price low (Winfrey and Day 1959-66, 4:112).

Unfortunately, again there are few details of the operation at that end of the trade. The best data come from Polonio Ortiz, the Comanchero arrested in 1872, whose statement said:

[My name is] Polonio Ortiz, [my home is] in Chama, NM. A party of Fabriano Lucero, Juan María, Usebe Ortega, Marcial Gallegos, a peon named Esquipulo, and myself left Chama on February 10, 1872 for the Indian country on the eastern edge of the Staked Plains. Fabriano Lucero was the leader of the party, he furnished the animals and promised me two cows for my services. We took goods packed on burros. Passed through San Miguel and Vernal Springs to the Alamo Gordo (a point onthe Pecos 20 miles above Fort Sumner). We were joined by many other Mexicans. There were more than fifty of us and more following.

Table 7.11
Livestock Losses Reported in Texas, 1865–75

COUNTY	1865–67		BEFORE 1873[a]		1873–75	
	HORSES	CATTLE	HORSES	CATTLE	HORSES	CATTLE
Archer					7	
Bandera	135				62	
Bexar			25			
Blanco	185					
Bosque	94					
Brown					33	
Burnet	3		254			
Callahan					10	
Clay					137	250
Coleman			57	1,010	670	
Comal	16					
Comanche	75				24	
Concha	28					
Cooke	154	1,308				
Denton			1,195			
El Paso	110	238			10	
Erath	88				50	
Gillespie	40	1,000	1,177		66	
Hamilton	215	4	500			
Hood	46					
Jack	100	5,000	103		300	
Kendall	137		705	25		
Kenney					40	75
Kerr	70				182	710
Kimble				2,650	24	
Lampasas	409	400				
Live Oak			480			
Llano[b]	37	151				
Llano[b]	44				35	
Mason	38	500			10	
Maverick					4	
McCulloch[b]		4,000				
McCulloch[b]	44	827			4	
McMullen			474			
Medina	182					
Menard	57	2,720	562	5,000	271	
Montague[b]	191	1,100	32			
Montague[b]		11,625				
Palo Pinto	150		64		130	
Parker	454					
San Saba	75				476	125
Shackelford			37		25	

Table 7.11, *continued*

COUNTY	1865-67		BEFORE 1873		1873-75	
	HORSES	CATTLE	HORSES	CATTLE	HORSES	CATTLE
Stephens					98	
Tarrant	16					
Tom Green					445	
Uvalde	1,198	3,085			186	
Webb	88					
Wichita					12	
Wise			441		340	
Young			92		88	
Zavala					70	
Totals:	4,479[c]	31,958	6,198[d]	8,685	3,809	1,160

[a] It is unclear whether these were intended to be losses from 1867-73, or all losses prior to 1873.

[b] Duplicate entries for counties represent multiple reports.

[c] The official report (Winfrey and Day 1959-66, 4:236) gave the 1865-67 totals as 30,838 cattle and 3,781 horses

[d] The official report (Winfrey and Day 1959-66, 4:390) gave the 1866-73 totals as 11,365 cattle and 6,255 horses.

SOURCE: Kavanagh 1986:238, 354

Juan Gallegos of San Miguel and Gregorio Jaramillo of Puerto de Luna were among the principal men. We left the Pecos at Alamo Gordo and crossed the Staked Plains to a place called Mucho kwa [Muchoque]. There is plenty of water on the Staked Plains; it is permanent. The road is a good one. There is another road further north that leads to a place called Quitaque. Both are good roads with plenty of water. At Muchoque, the Comanche (Quahadies) and Mescalero Apache form a village of over 100 lodges, perhaps 200; they have many horses. The chief is called Pahween, or Pahchacunee. As soon as our people arrived at Muchaque the Indians started a party of 100 men to steal cattle. They left on the 19th of March, a few Mexicans with them. As soon as the cattle are brought in, the Mexicans bring them and return to New Mexico, but more will follow as it is a regular business. Two traders named Hughes and Church[34] living at Puerto de Luna furnished the goods and buy the cattle. The Mexicans take over to trade arms, ammunition, cloth, flour, bread, sugar, coffee, etc. [One] can ride a good horse from Alamo Gordo to Muchoque in five days; it would not be hard riding, about 200 miles. [J. Hatch 1872b]

In a later revision of his story, he called his supplier Adolph and noted that he had a store in La Cuesta that was a branch of a Santa Fe trading house (J. Hatch 1872c). The conclusion seems inescapable that, at least during the Civil War and for some period thereafter, Comanche cattle raids into Texas were inspired as much by the possibility of commercial transactions as by the desire to establish a war record.

Not all Comancheros were so connected; according to one of the few descriptions of late Comanchero trade goods, in August 1867 a party of Comancheros was arrested on the Canadian River by troops from Fort Bascom. Their packs were found to contain

> about 200 lbs. of corn meal, 500 of Mexican hard bread, 35 or 40 butcher knives, 9 files, vermillion, a lot of shirts, some red and white flannel, one vest, ticking, calico, some iron hoops, monte cards, shelled corn, tea, sugar, flour, letter paper, candy, one regalia [?], one box army [percussion] caps (100), about 400 percussion caps (small) [pistol caps], several pounds of lead, about 5 pounds of powder, 16 elongated balls cavalry cal. .58. [Letterman 1867a]

The small quantity of goods, consisting mostly in subsistence goods and hardware, suggests that the trade of that party was relatively low-level. The major army meat suppliers such as Goldbaum must have had larger stocks of merchandise, but their extent is unknown.

At the same time, however, the Comancheros were becoming the subject of political debate. In 1864, after the first Battle of Adobe Walls, Kit Carson reported:

> On the day of the fight I destroyed a large amount of powder, lead, caps, etc., and I have no doubt that this and the very balls with which my men were killed and wounded were sold by these Mexicans not ten days before. We saw the tracks of three wagons going down the river, and you may be sure they belonged to the traders. But I blame the Mexicans not half as much as I do Mr. Steck, superintendent of Indians affairs, who gave them the pass to go and trade, he knowing that the Mexicans would take what they could sell best, which was powder, lead, and caps, and Mr. Steck should have known better than to give passes to these men to trade when every one knows that ammunition is all the Indians want at this time. [Carson 1864]

Carson's evaluation is problematical. There is little evidence that anyone, let alone "every one," knew that "ammunition is all the Indians want at this time." Carson charged only "Mexicans" with trading ammunition to the Comanches, conveniently overlooking Mr. Goldbaum, who must also have been trading it to obtain the cattle that he sold to the army; since the military officers knew where he obtained his cattle, they must have known the full extent of his transactions. Moreover, if the packs confiscated by Captain Letterman in 1867 can be considered representative of Comanchero trade goods, ammunition was only a small component of the trade. Based on modern weights, the ammunition component of that 1867 load consisted of about 5 pounds of powder, one hundred musket caps (less than 4 ounces, including the can), four hundred pistol caps (about 2 ounces, including cans), several pounds of lead (presumably in bar form), and 16 "elongated balls cavalry cal .58" (about 18 ounces). That is, the entire load consisted of 700 pounds of foodstuffs; perhaps 100 pounds of miscellaneous clothing, iron, and playing cards; and only 10 pounds of "ammunition." That amount of ammunition is more consistent with what a subsistence hunter or trader might carry for his own use rather than as the stock in trade of an arms dealer.

Comanche Divisional Politics and Organization,

1860–75

The encapsulation of the Comanche within resource domains directly controlled by Anglo-Americans ultimately resulted in a reduction in the level of political organizations, forcing a concomitant reorganization of Comanche divisional politics. This trend can be demonstrated using the more detailed information available beginning around 1870.

Table 7.12 summarizes the divisional and band organizations and populations as reported 1869–74. Although there are a few names otherwise unknown, and some of the divisional attributions are based on assumptions and later attributions (Kavanagh 1989), the composition of the lists seems to be relatively accurate. At the same time, it is difficult to reconcile them with other data. For instance, Tatum's rations issue accounts include the December 31, 1870, issue:

> 842 Indians rationed to include December 1
> 3,117 Indians rationed to include January 4
> [total] 3,959 Indians to whom rations have been issued to date.
> [Tatum 1870c]

But Tatum's ration total is almost 1,000 less than the total reservation population—4,938—claimed on his "Nominal List containing the name of each head of Band in the Comanche and Kiowa Tribes of Indians" of the same date (Tatum 1870d)—the source for the data in table 7.12. That total also includes 1,896 Kiowas and 300 Apaches, but does not include the 1,000 "Quahada Co-

Table 7.12

Comanche Divisional and Local Band Populations, 1869–74

	NOVEMBER 1869	DECEMBER 1870	MARCH 1874
Yamparikas:			
Paruasemena	120	84	
Cheevers			186
Esananaka			100
Tabenanaka			100
Howeah	60	84	84
Puhiwitoya	180	102	120
Hitetsi		48	76
Tipenavon		66	
Tokomi	90	90	50
Moochi		60	37
Ohamer			90
Esarosavit			125
Onaweah			76
Detsakanas:			
Quitsquip	62	216	100
Tenewas:			
Puhiwiquasu	258[a]	102	
Pearekaekap	30[b]	186	50
Nokonis:			
Terheryaquahip	398	402	200
Pyoh	45	48	72
Quenahavy	108		
Kotsotekas:			
Mowway	300	300	100
Kawertzeme			60
Black Duck			50
Prairie Fire			100
Kwahadas:			
Paruakoom	300[a]	300	125
Jaw Breaker	21	24	
Tomichicut			100
Coby			100
Mocksu			37
Blue Blanket			72
Bald Eagle			67
Quenavike			61
Esasuat			87
Others, off res [est.]	1,960	1,000	

Table 7.12, *continued*

	NOVEMBER 1869	DECEMBER 1870	MARCH 1874
Penatekas:			
Asehabit	200	210	[at Wichita]
Tosaway	175	162	[at Wichita]
Kakarawa		60[c]	60[d]
Seichinicah	50	48	45
Asatoyet	90	150	150
Totals			
Comanches present	1,927[e]	2,742	2,643
Comanches absent	558		
Out	1,960	1,000	
Total Comanches	4,445	3,742	2,643
Kiowas and Apaches	2,120	2,196	

[a] Absent.
[b] Listed as Kwahada.
[c] Given as Kahabbywite.
[d] Given as Kahavawah.
[e] Badger's addition was off by 2.

SOURCES: Badger 1869; Tatum 1870d; Anonymous 1874

manches and Kiowas who have never reported"—listed on table 7.12 as "Others, off res."

Acceptance of both of Tatum's totals implies that either the number of Comanches off the reservation was closer to 2,000, that Tatum underestimated the number of Indians he was rationing, or that only 80 percent of those on the reservation were getting rations. It may also be noted that Tatum was relatively well stocked with supplies (table 7.7). The discrepancy cannot yet be satisfactorily explained. A similar, though more minor, discrepancy between ration and census lists involves the 1874 numbers. In January 1874 Agent Haworth reported he was issuing rations to 2,371 Comanches (Haworth 1874a). A month later he reported that he had sent "two young men out to take a census of the Comanche" (Haworth 1874c) and that he had confidence that their reported total of 2,643 was "not above their actual number" (Haworth 1874d).[35] However, the other records do not show that 72 people moved into the agency that month. But disregarding the estimated "never reported" figures, the three lists have remarkably similar totals for the Comanches: Badger (2,487), Tatum (2,742), and Haworth (2,643). Indeed, Tatum's total is only 99 more than Haworth's, while Badger's is 255 less than Tatum's; the difference between Badger's and Tatum's totals (354) is only 8 percent of Tatum's total.[36]

At the same time the differences in individual local band populations across the lists, while no doubt including some mistakes in attributions, represent in graphic form the sociopolitical and demographic reshuffling of personnel among bands and divisions. Certainly some of those shifts and reorganizations resulted from normal social processes, such as postmarital residence patterns, movement of individuals visiting relatives, movement based on political-economic motives, and the rarer case of new local band formation (ethnogenesis). Other shifts must have resulted from the stress of the continuing hostilities. All of those processes would result in local band populations composed of individuals whose origins often were in other local bands and divisions. That phenomenon is exemplified by the divisional distribution of the women captured at the McClellan Creek fight and held prisoner at Fort Concho: thirty-four Kotsotekas, thirty Kwahadas, eighteen Yamparikas, eleven Nokonis, and nine Penatekas.

The divisional political-economic processes are somewhat clearer. The principal chief of the Yamparikas at the 1853 treaty of Fort Atkinson, Shaved Head, died in 1858, and there was no clear holder of the status for several years. During that same period, there were no distributions of goods under the Fort Atkinson Treaty. None of the Yamparikas who participated in the 1861 Confederate treaty had been been mentioned before, and the only other mention of the "principal chief" of that treaty, Bistevana, was when he visited Agent Boone carrying the treaty. This suggests that their participation may not have been divisional policy, but rather an effort by local band leaders to establish or strengthen their own positions through domains based on political relations with Americans.

Although the connections are unknown, it was after the failure of the Confederate treaty that Paruasemena, a subordinate signer of the Fort Atkinson Treaty eight years earlier, emerged as the principal Yamparika chief. It was through him that several other truces, armistices, and treaties were successfully negotiated, resulting in the reestablishment of political relations with Anglo-Americans, albeit still with minimal direct support. Paruasemena died in 1872, and again there was no clear succession. Battey (1877:91) said that except for a son—unnamed—none of his people were present at his death, and he suggests that it was because he had been "thrown away." Nye (1969: 160) repeats the story with some elaboration. There is, however, no evidence that at his death Paruasemena had lost any prestige or power.

If Haworth's local band numbers are accepted, the Yamparikas were the largest Comanche division of the 1870s, with about 1,100 people. Following Paruasemena's death there was no Yamparika chief with sufficient stature to gather the support neccessary to gain recognition as principal chief, although several men apparently vied for the position. In 1868 Agent Leavenworth had suggested that Paruasemena's son Hitetsi was "aiming at the head of his father's band" (Leavenworth 1868a). Several of the Comanches interviewed by the 1933 Field Party emphasized the role of Esananaka, another son, suggesting that he had "called the first tribal council at time of the proposal of the Medicine Lodge Treaty" (Hoebel 1940:11). Although both Hitetsi and Esananaka lived into the early 1880s, after 1870 the historical record is relatively silent about their actions. Rather, it was one of Paruasemena's grandsons, Cheevers, and his distant relative Tabenanaka, who became the leading Yamparikas.[37] Although Cheevers sought political support from the agent and from the army, Tabenanaka remained the foremost proponent of the traditional life. It was the Yamparika factionalization—if that word can be used to refer to Cheevers's and Tabenanaka's rivalry—that often resulted in confusion about Tabenanaka's political identity: he was alternatively called "the head chief of the Quahada" (Tatum 1872i) or of the Detsakanas (Haworth 1874m; E. L. Clark 1881; W. P. Clark 1885).

While the Yamparikas successfully exploited the resources of the Anglo-Americans, the Penatekas experienced difficulty. Since 1855, when the Penatekas first tied themselves to an agency, they discovered the limits of its political potential, and the political-economic changes of 1860–75 brought about a splintering of that division. This can be seen in the varied history of the men recognized as its chiefs. At the time of the move to the reservation, Potsanaquahip—prominent in the events of the 1840s and 1850s—was reportedly staying with Kiowas, but after the Confederate treaty was signed the Kiowas drove him out of their camp (Davis 1861:23). He then stayed on or near the reservation, participating in some activities, but rarely visible. He was present at and signed the 1865 Little Arkansas Treaty, but again apparently played no prominent role. Ketumsee—principal chief on the Texas reservation—must have died soon after arriving at the new agency; indeed, he was not mentioned at all in connection with Confederate Fort Cobb. The Penateka treaty with the Confederacy was signed by Kakarawa as principal chief and Tosawa as second chief. However, within a few years the relative positions of the two men had reversed. Tosawa emerged as principal chief, but he had few political resources and placed much weight on the expectation that the government would fulfill its treaty obligations. In 1867, at the Medicine Lodge Treaty council, Tosawa was explicit in the assessment of his political situation: "My band is dwindling away fast. My young men are a scoff and a by-word" (Taylor et al. 1910:58). But even his frank admission of political embarrassment failed to bring support from the commissioners. In a final gamble in 1872 he attempted to change the political arena by moving the Penatekas from the agency at Fort Sill to the Wichita agency north of the Washita River, but that effort only further splintered the division.

The significance of Tatum's characterization of the Penatekas as lacking a "head and controlling chief" was not that he accurately described Penateka political organization as it existed in 1872. Rather, by denying the status of principal chief, a position that by Tosawa's time depended upon outside political support, Tatum ensured that it would not exist in the future.

Throughout the 1850s the Kotsotekas, once an important and powerful group, were virtually unmentioned. The ethnonym reemerges in the 1860s and 1870s with a greatly reduced population. Meanwhile, a new group, the Kwahadas, was gaining prominence in the same geographic area. That suggests that like the Eastern Kotsoteka-Hois-Penateka ethnogenesis sequence of the 1820s–1840s, in the 1860s and 1870s some Comanches—Kotsotekas, Yamparikas, and others—were transforming themselves into Kwahadas. But that ethnogenetic process makes it difficult to specify the number and leadership of either the Kotsoteka or Kwahada local bands. Mowway was the most prominent Kotsoteka mentioned in the documentary records—neither of the other two Kotsoteka signers of the Confederate treaty is known. Another Kotsoteka, Kawertzeme—Mowway's son-in-law, and probably Pike's Kewichhemah of 1861—headed a local band in the early reservation period and presumably before. Tatum called Paruacoom a Kotsoteka, and R. N. Richardson (1933:363, n.708) concured, although noting that "he spent so much time on the Plains with the wild Kwahadies that he is often referred to as a Kwahadi." Similarly, Joe Attocknie referred to Tokomi as a Yamparika, saying, "but he associated with the Quahada" (Attocknie 1965).

Conversely, according to New Mexican officials, there were at least four local bands who "made their home on the head of the Red River and its tributaries and on the eastern border of the Staked Plains," those of Puertas, Paruaquahip, Quajipe, and Maue. The latter is clearly Mowway, but whether the former three considered themselves Kwahadas or Kotsotekas is unclear. Similarly, Sheerkenakwaugh's political position is unclear. After the Battle of Adobe Walls he apparently acted as spokesman for the Yamparikas involved in that battle, but at the council with Colonel Bergmann at the Arroyo de Nuez, he was with Kwahadas. Paruaquahip died in the 1867 cholera epidemic, and Puertas was killed by Utes that same year; the fate of Quajipe and Sheerkenakwaugh is unknown. According to the Comanchero Polonio Ortiz, in early 1872 Patchokoniki was leader of a village of about 100 lodges engaged in the cattle raid and trade economy; later that year, in combination with another chief, Patchokoniki's village on McClellan Creek consisted of 262 lodges. But interestingly, he did not appear on Badger's, Tatum's, or Haworth's list of chiefs. The populations and single leaders for both the Kotsotekas and Kwahadas (Mowway and Paruacoom were listed as leaders of the two groups, respectively), reported on Tatum's 1870 list, probably represent the agent's limited knowledge of the internal composition of those groups, rather than an accurate account of their political organization.

The political economy of the Nokonis and Tenewas is unclear; as in the 1850s, they are conspicuous mostly for their absence from the documentary record. As before, they were often accused of raiding, but there is little direct evidence of involvement either in raiding or in a transshipment economy. The 1865 Little Arkansas Treaty was negotiated by the Nokonis Quenahewi and Terheryaquahip—the latter may have been one of signers of the 1861 Confederate treaty—and although not a major negotiator, Terheryaquahip signed the 1865 Medicine Lodge Treaty. In the years after that he maintained a policy of friendship and was the recipient of some support. Whatever the source of support, if Badger's and Tatum's numbers are correct, his policy was successful, allowing him to maintain a population equal to that of the identified Kotsotekas and Tenewas and only slightly less than that of the Kwahadas.

8

Political History of the

Comanche Tribes

Political organizations exist in multidimensional sociopolitical space. First, they are the on-the-ground manifestations of cultural structures by people in groups. Comanche political culture allowed for several structural poses— family groups, hunting parties, war parties, religious gatherings, small-scale medicine groups, large-scale military societies, diplomatic missions, and divisional political gatherings—on four levels of sociopolitical integration: the nuclear family, the extended family (*numunahkahni*), the residential local band, and the political division or tribe.

Second, political organizations are the on-the-ground manifestations of cultural structures by people in groups exploiting particular resources. Co-manche political organizations were based on four kinds of resources: (1) the exploitation of the buffalo by horse-mounted hunters, (2) warfare and raiding, (3) trade, and (4) political relations with others, including Euroamericans.

Conceptualized as axial coordinates—as in Villanueva's 1807 "Extract of the Quantity of Gifts for Each Class" (reproduced above as table 4.8)—those two dimensions, with their levels of organization and types of resources, present a paradigm of Comanche political organization. As a source of food, hunting supported nuclear families and *numunahkahni*, but it was usually not a direct element in the political economy of local bands or divisions. That is, although chiefs and military societies may have organized and controlled pre-hunt activities, they did not organize or control the distribution of the pro-ducts of the hunt. On the other hand, leaders of war expeditions controlled the distribution of war booty to members of the expedition, and successful warriors made further distributions of booty in such ceremonies as the Horse Dance. On the next higher level, local band chiefs controlled the transformation of buffalo products and war booty into trade items. Local band chiefs— and principal chiefs acting in their capacity as local band chiefs—controlled the distribution of subsistence gifts received during visits to Euroamerican towns, but prestige gifts of canes, flags, medals, and uniforms went exclusively to divisional principal chiefs.

Political organizations, as the on-the-ground manifestations of cultural structures by people in groups exploiting particular resources, are fluid and dynamic. They constantly form and dissolve in step with changes in their wider natural and social environments. That is, as the Comanches' resources varied, so did their political organizations. Some of that resource variation resulted from normal seasonal rounds, as populations organized and reorganized to exploit seasonally available resources; other variation resulted from longer-scaled fluctuations in the general climatic conditions. Still other variation was geographic, based on the localization of resources. Finally, some resource variation was political-economic, based on human political and economic decisions. Since different Comanches had differential contacts with Euroamericans—Spaniards, Frenchmen, Englishmen, Anglo-Americans, Yankees, and Confederates—there were corresponding variations in the political resources available to the various Comanche groups, with corresponding variations in their political histories.

The relation between political resource and resultant organization is not deterministic, leading unimpeded from resource variation to organization or disorganization. Rather, there are efforts, more or less successful, to manipulate and control that relation. For Comanches, those manipulations ranged from the Shakedown Dance—young women shaming their heros into redistributing the spoils of war—through the various magical efforts to draw the antelope and buffalo or to avoid arrows and bullets, to the pragmatic skills of the diplomatic negotiator trying to maintain a flow of political resources. The temporal expression of those processes is political history.

The Kotsotekas and Their Successors: Hois, Penatekas and Kwahadas

The earliest notices of the Comanches did not give specific ethnonyms, but since Shoshone political ethnonyms often labeled major food sources, the Kotsotekas—the Buffalo Eater Comanches—were probably among the first proto-Comanche Shoshones on the plains and were probably the first Comanches to have contacts with the Spaniards of New Mexico. By the 1740s two groups of Comanches were near New Mexico, and although details of their relationships with each other are unknown, it does seem clear that they followed radically different policies toward that province and toward other Euroamericans. One group, northeast of Taos, maintained trade with that pueblo and peacefully passed along French traders and travelers. The other group was east of Pecos and Galisteo and was particularly hostile toward those pueblos and toward any Europeans they met. Bernardo Miera y Pacheco's maps from the 1760s showed only a single group of Comanches in New Mexico proper; unfortunately, the maps did not extend far enough north or east to include other groups. By the next decade two concentrations of Kotsotekas were again recognized, one centered in northeastern New Mexico, the other near the Wichita groups on the Red River; the first of these was recognized on Miera's 1778 map as "Cuchan Marica." It is tempting to suggest that those latter localizations were continuations of the earlier groups, but there are no confirming details.

From 1786 through the 1820s the New Mexico Kotsoteka divisional organization was supported by the continuing lucrative trade with the Pueblos and the Spaniards, by the increasing Comanchero trade on the plains, and by the political gifts coming from Santa Fe. The strength of their organization is particularly evident in the apparent ease of succession of the several elected principal chiefs after Ecueracapa.

Soon after 1830 the Kotsoteka ethnonym virtually disappeared from the documentary records and did not reappear until the 1860s. Although there were several brief mentions of them in the intervening years, none was direct and none provided evidence of political organization. One possibility is that the entire group, or a major portion of it, decamped for Mexico—that is, that the otherwise unnamed, but apparently large, group of Comanches with Tabe Peté and Tabe Tuk were the Kotsotekas; one of their number was called Magüe, possibly the Kotsoteka man later called Mowway.[1] By the 1870s there were only four local bands that could be clearly identified as Kotsoteka.

Meanwhile, the political organization of the Kotsotekas in Spanish and Mexican Texas—those Comanches "near the Wichitas," sometimes called the Comanche Oriental—was supported by different resources than were their New Mexican cousins, and although some of their leaders approximated the stature of the New Mexican principal chiefs, they were often politically subordinate to the westerners. The uncertainty of their positions suggests an unstable or uncontrollable resource base; indeed, the Texas Spaniards themselves were chronically unable to receive a constant supply of goods, let alone ensure their consistent transmission to Comanches.

The few unsuccessful attempts—significantly, initiated by the Texas Kotsotekas themselves—to set up permanent and official traders with the

Texas Spaniards indicate the growing importance of trade in both the domestic and the political economies. For the Texas Kotsotekas the Anglo-American and contrabandista horse trade between Comanchería and Saint Louis, or between Comanchería and Louisiana by way of Natchitoches, was the eastern equivalent of the western Comanchero trade. That reliance on the horse trade forced the Texas Kotsotekas into a raiding economy focused on Mexico. Individuals such as El Sordo harassed the border settlements, transferring their booty to middlemen, such as Pisinampe, who transferred the horses on to traders—Anglo-Americans, contrabandistas, or Comancheros—in return for the European goods that were quickly becoming necessities in Comanche life. At the same time, however, the inability of the Texas Spaniards to deter those raids made the policy of political gifts appear to be giving in to extortion and further undermined their willingness to continue political gifts.

By the mid-1830s the political links between the Texas Kotsotekas and their New Mexico kinsmen had been broken. It seems that two groups of Texas Comanches emerged. In the east were the Comanches associated with Muguara, and later with Mopechucope and Potsanaquahip; initially they were known as Hois, but by 1846 they were being called Penatekas. The western group, unnamed in the records, was associated with Esananaka and Isawacony. For reasons yet unclear, after Muguara's assassination in 1840 the western group disappeared from the Texas annals.

Through its relations with the Republic of Texas , the eastern group was able to maintain a divisional organization, although the political relations between Mopechucope and Potsanaquahip are unclear. That organization was shattered by the 1849 smallpox and cholera epidemics and the ensuing contest for power among Potsanaquahip, Sanaco, and Ketumsee. The outcome was that Ketumsee, through his control of the rations distribution on the Texas reservation, maintained a modest organization of a few hundred people, while Potsanaquahip maintained another, apparently based on a raid-and-trade economy with the Indians and Anglo-Americans of Indian Territory. By the 1860s many of his people had been drawn off to other groups, particularly the newly forming Kwahadas. The Penateka organization was finally splintered in 1872 when Tosawa and Esihabit, successors to Ketumsee, moved to the Wichita reservation, while Ceachinika, Kakarawa (Kahabewite), and Esitoya remained at Fort Sill. It was at that time that agent Lawrie Tatum denied that there was any "head and controlling chief" of the Penatekas.

The Kwahadas were the last political organization to coalesce from the Kotsotekas, probably not coming into existence much before the 1860s. As is often noted, they had no official relations with any local, state, or federal government. That was probably not the result of an intentional policy on their part; rather, it was due to historical contingency and intentional policy on the part of the federal and state governments. While the Kwahadas certainly had relations with the federal army in New Mexico via Mr. Goldbaum and others like him, the government was not encouraging the establishment of formal and official relations. Moreover, after the Civil War, the absence of the Kwahadas from the Medicine Lodge Treaty council can be accounted for by disease, rather than by opposition to the treaty. But the result was the same: they had no access to political gifts. Their principal resource domain was the trade in stolen cattle. With the collapse of that market in 1872, their political fortunes collapsed. Isatai's 1874 ceremony may be seen as an attempt—ultimately unsuccessful—to create an ideological and charismatic resource, but by that time the Kwahadas lacked an economic base.

The Jupes, Yamparikas, and Tenewas

For most of the eighteenth century the Jupes and the Yamparikas were north of the Arkansas River, sometimes as far east as the Wichita villages below the Great Bend. The two groups were closely intertwined, but the specifics of the relationship are unclear. When they first appear in the Spanish records, their chiefs—especially those of the Jupes—wielded considerable power and authority. The two Cuerno Verdes of the 1760s-70s were both probably Jupes. Toro Blanco may have been Jupe, succeeding the second Cuerno Verde and continuing his predecessor's opposition to the Spaniards, ultimately leading to his assasination. His succesor was Paruanarimuco, the "lieutenant general" recognized by the Spaniards in 1786.

In the years before 1786, booty from raids on the New Mexico settlements was the Jupes' and Yamparikas' most visible political resource. There was some trade with the Wichitas, but it was often interrupted for long periods. In the years after 1786, Yamparikas and Jupes were familiar although infrequent visitors to Santa Fe, where they engaged in some trade and received some political gifts. More important was their position beyond the Arkansas River, which gave them control of the Spanish goods moving onto the Plains from the southwest. It is possible that the various "Snakes" reported exchanging Spanish horse equipment at the Upper Missouri trade fairs were not Shoshones per se, but were Yamparika and Jupe Comanches; similarly, it is likely that those whom the Cuampes envied in 1807—when they said they wanted trade "on the same terms as with the Comanche" (N. Salcedo 1807)—were Yamparikas or Jupes.

By 1820, the Jupe ethnonym had disappeared from direct reference, probably merging with Yamparika. By the end of that decade the Yamparikas had removed south of the Arkansas River, hastened by the advance of the Cheyennes and the Arapahos, who were themselves drawn south by inter-marriage and economic relations with the Bents' traders. The Yamparikas, supplied by Chouteau's traders in Indian Territory, resisted the advance, but after the death of Auguste Chouteau in 1839, that firm's western post at Camp Holmes was withdrawn. It was probably no coincidence that the next year, Yamparikas and Kiowas made peace with the Cheyennes and the Arap-ahos near Bent's Fort.

However, it is not clear how much the Yamparikas profited from that alliance. They were still infrequent visitors to the Bents' post on the Arkansas River. The Bents' "wood post" on the Canadian River was built in 1842, and the more famous adobe post was built in 1845, but the latter post was proba-bly manned for only two seasons. The next summer brought raids on the Santa Fe Trail, although it is not clear if they were related to the lack of trade. The year 1847 also brought the start of the major horse raids south of the Rio Grande, raids in which Yamparikas increasingly participated.

With the Fort Atkinson Treaty in 1853, American political gifts again became available to the northern Comanches; not since the collapse of Mex-ican New Mexico had they had direct access to such resources. Conversely, it is important to note that since those gifts were given on the Arkansas River, only the Yamparikas could benefit from them. By 1861, however, the distri-butions had not been made for several years, and the Yamparikas' participa-tion in the Confederate treaty of that year may be seen as an attempt to re-establish political relations with Euroamericans and renew access to a supply of resources. Although that effort failed, Paruasemena was able to accomplish the same goal on the Arkansas, remaining as political head of the Yamparikas for the next decade. Following his death in 1872, his grandson, Cheevers, solicited political support from the army, and Tabenanaka controlled the hide trade on the southern plains, but no single Yamparika was able to establish a secure position as a leading chief. Still, at the surrender in 1875, the Yampa-rikas were the most numerous Comanche division, with thirteen local bands.

About 1810 a splinter group of Yamparikas led by El Sordo, along with Taovayas, Wichitas, and others, established a new political organization on the middle Red River. To the Yamparikas upriver, they were the Tenewas, Downstream People. There has been some confusion between the ethnonyms Tenewa and Tanima, with some scholars (e.g., R. N. Richardson 1933:20) arguing that they referred to "distinct bands." But since the latter ethnonym occurs in only a few citations—five have been noted here (the 1826 Coman-che-New Mexico treaty, Ruíz's undated report of the 1830s, John Cameron's 1836 report, the 1865 Little Arkansas Treaty, and Butler, Sawyer, and Leyendecker's 1867 report), none of which co-occur with Tenewa, I believe that both ethnonyms referred to the same people, Tanima representing a typographical error or orthographic confusion.

There is significant evidence that the major political support for the Red River chiefs came from the horse trade. The earliest of those chiefs was El Sordo himself. Although David Burnet (1824) argued that the Tenewa trade was with New Mexico, most evidence points to an eastern trade with contrabandistas from Natchitoches, and particularly to the ex-revolutionaries from the failed 1810 Hidalgo uprisings. There is no record of any Tenewa visit to the major Euroamerican centers before 1820, nor is there evidence of Euroamerican political support for their chiefs. Thus, there is no evidence of support based on political gifts. However, after the 1821 Mexican Revolution, many of the exiled revolutionaries attained positions of power in Texas and through their previous connections with the Tenewas brought those Comanches with them. Thus, the Tenewa chief Paruakevitse became one of the principal Comanche chiefs in Texas. But the Mexicans had the same problems maintaining a supply of goods as had the Spaniards. Furthermore, the Tenewas maintained their connections with American horse traders, thereby ensuring the continuance of horse raids. After Paruakevitse's death in 1832, the Tenewas disappeared from the Texas Mexican records.

Early American contacts with the Tenewas came through the traders on the Red River, such as David Burnet. Later, official American contacts with the Tenewas were infrequent. The village visited by the dragoons in 1834 was probably Tenewa, under—or at least associated with—Tabequena. By the next year a power struggle between Tabequena and Isacony had emerged. The two cultivated divergent political strategies: Tabequena was particularly friendly toward the Anglo-Americans of eastern Indian Territory, whereas Isacony was notably unfriendly. Although the causes of the differences are unknown, with the disappearance of Isacony from the historical record about 1837, Tabequena became the principal Tenewa leader, favoring a policy of friendship, or at least communication, with the Americans. That policy was continued by Pahayuko. Although Pahayuko may have lived through the mid-1850s, there is little positive mention of the Tenewas during that decade; they were only mentioned by Agent Robert Neighbors in Texas in connection with raids.

This infrequent contact implies a minimal reliance upon Euroamerican political support and thus that the major source of Tenewa political capital came from the trade in horses, many of which were stolen from Mexico. The Comanches who frequented Chouteau's trading post at Camp Holmes were probably Tenewas, as were those who visited Edwards's trading settlement on Little River. Warren's post at the mouth of Cache Creek was in the heart of

Tenewa country. The height of the horse trade was in the late 1840s and early 1850s during the California Gold Rush. The subsequent decrease in the demand for horses coincided with the apparent decline in Tenewa fortunes.

The Nokonis

The origins of the Nokonis are unclear. The earliest appearance of the ethnonym is in Butler and Lewis's 1846 report; apparently the only mention in Spanish is in García-Rejón's 1865 vocabulary.

Based on Robert Neighbors's various reports from Texas, the Nokonis were apparently centered on the upper reaches of the Red River and the headwaters of the Pease River. They were closely associated with the Tenewas, but they had even fewer relations with the Americans than did the Tenewas. By the 1860s contacts increased, and in 1861 several Nokonis signed the Confederate treaty, but like the Yamparika signers, they probably did so in an effort to establish some political relations with Euroamericans and to gain access to goods. In 1864 Quinahewi received a peace medal from the United States and took part in the 1865 Little Arkansas Treaty proceedings. But as he was not able to control his young men, in 1866 his treaty goods were withheld "subject to his good behavior." After 1866 the most prominent Nokoni was Terheryaquahip, who continued the policy of peaceful but not submissive coexistence with Americans. The Nokonis were probably never very numerous and by the late 1870s there were only two local bands that could be identified as Nokoni.

Comanches and the Plains:
A Comparative Perspective

In this final section I want to draw out several more general implications of this examination of Comanche political-economic history. I have argued that the specific "problem" of the Comanches—the variation in ethnonyms through time—was the temporal reflection of their adaptations to changing conditions in the wider political-economic environments. Moreover, I have argued that the Problem of the Comanche is a special case of the Problem of Tribe, the tension resulting from the confusion of tribe as static widest-scaled cultural unit and tribe as dynamic and processual political organization.

The Comanches are not the only example of the Problem of Tribe on the Plains; indeed, the problem permeates the anthropology of the Plains. Many scholars follow Wissler's (1926) listing of eleven "true Plains" tribes: in

alphabetical order, the Arapahos, Assiniboines, Blackfeet, Cheyennes, Comanches, Crows, Gros Ventres, Kiowas, Kiowa Apaches, Sarsis, and Teton
Sioux. However, inasmuch as "tribe" referred to the widest-scaled cultural
unit, not to the operative political units, Wissler's list misrepresents the full
ethnographic record. For instance, neither the Blackfeet nor the Teton Sioux
were politically organized at the maximal level. Rather, like the mid-nineteenth century Comanche divisions—Yamparikas, Kotsotekas, Penatekas,
Kwahadas, Nokonis, and Tenewas—the political units of the Blackfeet were
the Piegans, Kainais, and Siksikas, while those of the Teton Sioux were the
Oglalas, Hunkpapas, Miniconjous, Brulés, Blackfoot, Sans Arcs, and Two
Kettles. Thus, in a political sense there were far more than eleven Plains
tribes.

Answering the question of how many tribes there were requires the
same preliminary response as the question of how many Comanche tribes
there were. It would be first necessary to specify a time period; a more detailed answer would require a processual approach, invoking such factors as
the parameters of resource availability, external political and economic relations, and the dynamics of group organization and reorganization. Ironically,
examples of those processual trajectories on the Plains have long been
known, but they are seldom considered as such in anthropological or historical discussions. Many Plains mythologies and oral histories, as well as ethno-
histories, describe fusions of varying strengths (several groups of western
Algonkians into the Arapahos, others into the Gros Ventres, others into the
Cheyennes, others into the Blackfeet; the Plains Apaches with the Cheyennes
and later with the Kiowas); and fissions (the Comanches separating from the
Shoshones, El Sordo from "his proper nation," two groups of Crows from the
Hidatsas, the Poncas from the Omahas, northern from southern Arapahos,
northern from southern Cheyennes, and Potsanaquahip and Sanaco from
Ketumsee and the main body of the Penatekas). There are groups of mixed
origins (the varied origins of El Sordo and his people, the so-called wandering nation, the Kwahadas), and otherwise unknown ethnonyms (Jumanos,
Aas, Orejones, Têtes Pelés), as well as disappearances of varying periodicity
(Cuampes, Jupes, Hois, Kotsotekas). There are major changes of political
relations: in the eighteenth century Comanches and Lipan Apaches were
mortal enemies, in the mid-nineteenth century Lipans and Kwahada Comanches raided together, and in the late nineteenth century two Lipans brought
what was to become the ritual of the Native American Church to the Comanches. Similar examples are the Comanche-Kiowa war and alliance and the
later Comanche-Kiowa—Cheyenne-Arapaho war and alliance. Finally, there
cases of battlefield annihilations of whole communities. Beyond the particularities of history, each of those examples reflects general processes of

sociopolitical organization and reorganization based on variations in the political and economic environments.

Moreover, the fact that a group is politically organized at a particular moment in time does not mean that it always has been, nor that it always will be; since contemporary political organizations result from contemporary political and economic forces, the mere existence of a political organization requires that its resource base(s) be examined. Such a view requires a radical shift in the way political organizations, including those of the Plains peoples, are conceptualized, and it requires that we be extremely careful of the words we use to describe them.

In attempting to specify the political processes and historical trajectories of the eighteenth- and nineteenth-century Plains leading to the historic Cheyenne "nation," John Moore (1988) identified five general political processes: fission, polarization, fusion, dispersion, and hybridization. More recently, Patricia Albers (1993) has suggested three general modes of intergroup political interaction: symbiosis, merger, and war. I find those suggestions provocative and useful, but I would also suggest that since the determination of which specific process, which mode of interaction, was operative at any specific historic moment is often difficult (cf. Albers 1993:117, 126), those processes and modes of interaction can be considered as specific aspects of the more general processes here called political organization and reorganization.

At the same time, I have serious reservations about aspects of Moore's presentation. For Moore, the major trajectory of recent Cheyenne political history has been *ethnogenesis*, the processual development of the Cheyenne "nation."[2] However, I find his discussion far too general to be useful for comparison, and unless one is careful, it can lead to a Problem of Nation as treacherous as the Problem of Tribe.

In Moore's analysis, ethnogenesis involves the processual development of four elements: citizenship (normative statements of membership, although the details may be subject to political debate); defended territory (although its boundaries may be variable and permeable); political unity (not only in major public policies, as in war making, but also in deciding more local matters); and a shared language (although which language is the national language may depend upon contemporary political conditions). To my mind, however, even though those elements certainly are involved in national development, they are also aspects of other kinds of political processes and their resulting organizations, and so they cannot serve to distinguish nations from those other kinds of organizations. Certainly, if an ad hoc group gathers for a purpose, some definition of the resources upon which that group is focused must develop. Moreover, if the group interacts for any length of time, some common language must develop, or else meaningful and productive group interaction cannot occur. Likewise, some mode for making political—group-wide —decisions must develop, some consensus on who "we"—the group making the group-wide decisions—are. But to call the resulting organization a nation based on those elements alone has the potential for seriously distorting ethnographic and ethnohistorical interpretation.

Moore emphasized one other aspect of national ethnogenesis: "nations begin by the conscious and explicit charter of their citizens" (1988:16). Scholars have chacterized that symbolic aspect of ethnogenesis in a number of ways; for example, although he called it "retribalization," Abner Cohen described the

> process by which a group . . . involved in a struggle for power and privilege with another [group] . . . manipulate[s] some customs, values, myths, symbols, and ceremonials from their cultural tradition in order to articulate a political organization, which is used as a weapon in that struggle. [1969:2]

Nancie Gonzalez paralleled Cohen: ethnogenesis was the "breaking down [of] old loyalties, and merging old symbols from diverse cultural patterns into a new and self-conscious ideological framework" (1975:120); Sturtevant (1971) called it the "establishment of [self-conscious] group distinctiveness." It is the use of invidious and chauvinistic Us-Them comparisons as political ammunition. In that form, like sodalities for tribes, chauvinistic nationalism is the threshold variable defining nations.

However, while it is clear that in the symbols of the Sacred Hat and Arrows the Cheyennes developed the kinds of national symbols intended by Cohen, Gonzalez, and Sturtevant, Moore also used the term *nation* in a much looser and more problematic way. For instance, he noted,

> I must continue to emphasize the importance of the Sun Dance as emblematic of national identity. Not only the Cheyennes, but all the tribal nations of the Plains symbolized the physical extent of their nations by assigning bands particular places in the tribal circle. [1988:318]

There are three problems with that assertion. In the first place, despite more than a century of such claims there is no clear evidence for the enduring organization of Plains camp circles reflective of larger tribal-national structures; as Moore himself noted, families and larger groups camped in different places in the circle at different times.

Second, despite the central role played by the Sun Dance in the traditional anthropological explanatory paradigm of the Plains, that role is more assumed and asserted than demonstrated. Like the emphasis given to the men's societies, I believe the emphasis on the Sun Dance is derived more from the *mass* of the American Museum's monumental comparative studies of those institutions (Wissler 1916; Spier 1921) than from the critical analysis of the *content* of those studies. In the case of the Sun Dance, beyond an inferred *communitas* created by shared participation in a ritual, there is no evidence for an explicitly political aspect—especially one expressing tribal nationalism —to the various nineteenth-century Sun Dances reported in the literature. Indeed, according to that literature, only two groups—the Cheyennes and the Kiowas—actually required attendance at an annual "tribal" ceremony; for others there could be several ceremonies in a season, and for still others several years could pass between ceremonies.

Finally, I believe Moore to be overly generous in granting nationhood to several of the Plains peoples. Although he never explicitly enumerated those groups he encompassed by the phrase "all the tribal nations," he periodically cited groups whose nationalism is at best questionable, if not negligible: for example, "[in comparison to the Cheyennes, there were other] nations that were more loosely organized, such as the Comanches and Shoshones" (1988: 222). I would argue that during the historic period the Comanche "nation" as a political organization was so loosely organized as to be nonexistent. There is little evidence of nationalism in Comanche political history, either on the level of the Comanches as a whole or on the divisional-tribal level. There were no symbols of national existence such as the Arapahos' and Gros Ventres' Flat Pipes, the Buffalo Calf Pipe held by the Miniconjou Lakotas, the Cheyennes' Sacred Hat and Arrows, or the Kiowas' *Taime*. Nor were there Comanche tribal-nationalistic ceremonies; at most, there is the possibility that Isatai's ceremony of May 1874 was part of a formative nationalistic movement that failed. To paraphrase the 1900 Supreme Court decision *Montoya vs. United States* (180 U.S. 266), "the word 'nation' as applied to the [Comanches] is so much of a misnomer as to be little more than a compliment." But if in those terms the Comanches were not a nation, they were not alone: neither were the Crows, the Lakotas, nor the Blackfeet—note the similarity with the question of "tribal" identity—although some of their component parts may have approached nationhood.

The immediate question is whether conceiving of all the Comanches as comprising a single nation without specifying the relevant time period helps in understanding their history (or histories). I think not; like the question of tribes, it confuses rather than clarifies the political question. Whether the late nineteenth- and twentieth-century Comanches developed into a nation is another matter.

The broader question is whether nationalism is an inevitable part of political evolution. Again I think not. Nation-forming ethnogenesis is logically a *secondary step* in a processual trajectory of political organization and reorganization. It occurs within groups that are already focused toward preexisting political-economic goals and whose achievement of those goals is perceived by them to be hindered by competitors. Certainly, although the primary political processes of organization and reorganization for resource exploitation may invoke a self-identification, it is at first as a subjective, collective, inclusive, and *communitas* identification, not the objective, chauvinistic, exclusive, and oppositional identification of nationalism.

Secondly, ethnogenetic chauvinistic nationalism is only one of several trajectories that might be followed by a group facing competition. When a group discovers a competitor for its resources, its options are to ignore the competition, to disperse (i.e., deciding that it was not worth the effort to maintain the organization in the face of competition), or to meet the challenge. Only if the group decides to meet the challenge are its options focused by the need to utilize existing social and cultural structures, or to develop new ones. Finally, of those latter choices, the focus on an explicitly nationalistic opposition is only one of several options.

If national ethnogenesis is only one of several possible trajectories, can the factors that impelled the Cheyennes in the direction of nationalism and the Comanches in another be clarified? One possibility is particularistic—the difference was that the Cheyennes received the prophet Sweet Medicine, who, as an individual, "created a multidimensional charter for the Cheyenne nation" (Moore 1988:318). Another possibility is cultural continuity. Of the clearly definable "tribal nations on the Plains"—Cheyennes, Arapahos, Gros Ventres, and Kiowas—three of the four are closely related groups of Algonkian speakers. That suggests the Galtonian situation of historical-cultural continuity masquerading as independent development and that at least some sources of Cheyenne nationalism might be sought in the Algonkians' pre-Plains culture history.

If I might borrow Oliver's terms—although rejecting his conclusions—it is true that both historical particularism and cultural continuity may be involved in Plains culture history, but I suggest a broader and more processual contemporary resolution: the eighteenth-century Comanches and Cheyennes faced different political problems and found different political solutions. Moore suggested that in the mid–eighteenth century the Cheyennes' problem was "lack of numbers, limited access to trade, and poverty in horses" (1988: 314). In contrast, at that time the Comanche divisional tribes did not face the first and third problems; the first because, if my analysis of the prehorse Plains is valid, the problem faced by Comanche chiefs in the early to middle eighteenth century was not how to organize a disparate population, but how to prevent the democratizing effects of the horse from dissolving preexisting organizations. The Comanche solution to the third Cheyenne problem was self-evident: they were generally horse-rich. The second Cheyenne problem

—limited trade—had its parallels, along with variations in the flow of political gifts, in the specific Comanche divisional histories. The Cheyennes' solution to all their problems was in ethnogenesis, tying the people together into a nation by means of ideology; in contrast, Comanches took the more pragmatic and political route of establishing and maintaining organizations through the creative cultivation of alternative political-economic resources. In evolutionary terms, the Cheyennes specialized in becoming a nation, the Comanches generalized in exploiting a variety of resources. In that context—and that context alone—Oliver's explanation that the Comanches were individualists, compared to others who were collectivists, makes some sense.

But in the final analysis, the historical Comanche and Cheyenne tribes, like all political organizations, resulted from the temporal intersections of historical, sociocultural, and environmental processes. Their political histories are the trajectories described by the exploitation of resources leading to the establishment, manipulation, competition, and potential but not inevitable collapse of organizations. Those processes continue today.

Notes

Chapter 1

1. The exceptions seem to be Jean Louis Berlandier's apparent references to Padilla's 1820 list and José Francisco Ruíz's 1828 list—see chapter 4—and Butler and Lewis's probable use of Robert S. Neighbors's information—see chapter 5.

2. There are scattered references to Comanches eating horses, mostly as a famine food, or as war party rations. In June, 1844, an English traveler through Texas, William Bollaert, noted in his journal, "The Comanches it is supposed have eaten 20,000 mustangs during the last five years. They *barbecue* mustangs sometimes whole by digging a large hole in the ground, putting stones in, making them hot, then in goes the mustang, other stones laid on, and then a big fire. Sometimes as a tid-bit, the head" (Bollaert 1956:361; emphasis in original). A number of scholars have used this comment as evidence for a widespread famine in Comanchería in the late 1840s and 1850s, causing the Comanches to eat their horses (e.g., Flores 1991:480). But Bollaert had no known contacts with Comanches, or with anyone knowledgeable about Comanches. Furthermore, there is no other evidence for serious famine between 1839 and 1844 in Texas—Bollaert's "past five years." Thus it is probable that the comment was more campfire speculation on what the Comanches did with all the horses they stole than it was the reporting of fact.

3. Anthropological interest in sociopolitical structure has its origins in the theories of Lewis Henry Morgan, and his follower John Wesley Powell, who argued that "primitive" society was structured through "clans" and "gentes," which were in turn structured through symbolic systems such as colors and natural directions (Kavanagh 1984). As director of the Smithsonian's Bureau of Ethnology, Powell encouraged researchers to identify tribal clans (matrilineal descent groups) and gentes (patrilineal descent groups); thus the early anthropological literature is full of lists of bands, gentes, and phratries. Unfortunately, research rarely passed beyond the game of "trace the band."

4. MacGowan is the earliest appearance of an element of a larger and more mythic story. In later years, the name "Pootnokoné" was usually given as Peta No-

492

kona, with the same or similar interpretation, e.g., 'lone camper'. But in either form the name seems to be composed of either *petu?* 'daughter', or *pitu?* 'to arrive' and *koni* 'to turn' or 'return', only vaguely translatable as either Solitary Roamer or as Lone Camper. The larger element is that in later years, the holder of that name was said to have been married to the captive Cynthia Ann Parker (DeShields 1886; Hacker 1990), father of Quanah Parker, principal Comanche chief in the later reservation period, and to have been killed either in 1858, 1860, or, following MacGowan, some time after the August 12, 1861 signing of the Confederate treaty with the Nokonis and other Comanches. The name Peta Nocona, or any variant, has not been found in any document earlier than MacGowan.

5. It seems odd that Coby offered this rather nonspecific example for the change from Awl People to Sewing People while making no mention of the specific incident which lead to his own people, the Movers (Returners) becoming the Poor Travelers.

6. Interestingly, when Hoffman reported the latter story in publication, it was with different ethnonyms. Now, instead of the "Pá'-ka-tsa—Headwater people"— hunting horses, it was the "Nau'niem":

> A new band was formed, after leaving the Rocky Mountain divide, which was composed of individuals from all [of the bands], and known as the Nau'niem— *Ridge People*—who remained behind to catch wild horses. When a sufficient number of animals had been captured they followed the tribe and the different individuals joined their respective bands. [Hoffman 1886:299–301]

7. Ceachinika's "well-authenticated tradition" of an early Penateka separation from the rest of the Comanches (E. P. Clark 1881; W.P. Clark 1885) is at variance with all other pre-1846 accounts of Comanche organization, either in the form of band lists or narratives; the name Penateka simply does not occur in the written record before 1846. Although that lack might be attributed to the vagaries of reporting, other Comanche ethnonyms occur with apparent regularity and meaningfulness from as early as the 1750s. Moreover, there is no other evidence of a "well-authenticated tradition"; it exists only in Ceachinika's statement. Therefore, it seems probable that the comments had less to do with an unbiased reporting of ancient tradition than they did with the contemporary politics of the late 1870s and early 1880s, when the Penatekas were trying to dissociate themselves from the other so-called wild Comanches.

8. The term is from science fiction, referring to a warp in space-time through which people can travel, emerging at a different space-time coordinate.

9. The word Yupe is meaningless in Comanche; in Spanish the ethnonym is Jupe *hupe* 'wood' [*hupenʉʉ* 'timber people']. The spelling with a 'Y' is an ortho-graphic error apparently originating in Pedro Garrido's transcription of Juan Bautista de Anza's reports of 1785–86, published by A. B. Thomas (1932). Although Thomas used the spelling Yupe in his text, in a note he gave the name as "Yupes or Jupes" (1932:105). From Garrido's error, and through a convoluted series of name equiva-

lences, Hyde (1959:60) correlated the mistaken term Yupe with Lewis and Clark's "Yep-ee," which was itself an untutored attempt at the Shoshone word *yapai* 'root'. As an ethnonym, *yapainʉʉ* 'root people' could refer to either Comanches or Shoshones. While that result was partially valid—the historical Comanche Jupes were closely associated with the Yamparikas, also called *yapainʉʉ*—Hyde's train of thought, and his conclusions, were hopelessly muddled.

10. Unfortunately, that dynamic aspect was not particularly evident in Service's major statement (1962) and only briefly in Sahlins (1968); rather it shows up in Sahlins's two articles peripheral to the evolutionary arguments (1961, 1963).

11. Fried's typology was explicitly concerned with the evolution of inequality, that is "political society." Sahlins's and Service's typology was inherently multidimensional. On a political-economic dimension, their tribes could range from social units linked by sodalities, but which might have no further political or economic functions, to what may be called tribal chiefdoms—residential units linked by sodalities—whose economies are dominated by redistribution. Some might also be tribal nations, tribes—residential units linked by sodalities—whose sociopolitical cultures included a sense of political chauvinism.

12. The major exceptions to that general rule are the ethnonyms. For those terms, except in quotations, I have conventionalized the spellings as Yamparika, Kotsoteka, Jupe, Tenewa, Nokoni, Hois, Penateka, and Kwahada. There will be a few other specific exceptions to the general rule noted in context.

Chapter 2

1. Honor is a particularly elusive concept among modern Comanches. While it is clear that honor is important in social interactions such as the powwow, where "honorings" and "specials" are a constant element (Kavanagh 1980:87), no specific Comanche term for honor, social standing, reputation, or "face" has been elicited from the Comanche speakers of the modern generation. Robinson and Armagost's dictionary (1990:201) includes the terms *mabitsiarʉ* 'honor' and *maritsiakutʉ* 'honored' ['possessor of honor'], but those terms were generally not recognized by contemporary speakers. One Comanche man offered the term *natsaawapI* as 'integrity', that one was urged to be *nʉmʉnʉʉ natsaawapI* 'the pride of the people', but that form has also not been confirmed.

At the same time, it is perhaps unnecessary to note that not all Comanches were absorbed with the politics of social standing; one woman at the turn of the twentieth century was notably disrespectful of many social conventions, but she is still remembered as an active participant in the community.

2. There are a few accounts of female Comanche warriors; none are as specific as the accounts of the "manly hearted women" on the northern Plains and thus which could allow an evaluation of the role of women in war.

3. References to notes from the 1933 Comanche Field Party are cited by consultant and date of interview.

4. The reference is possibly to a *tuepukunuu* 'little ponies/little horse' dance (see Comanche Field Party 1933: Post Oak Jim, July 11), although it may refer to a more generic celebration.

5. On their return to the Comanches, the brothers brought with them the ritual that was to become the foundation of the Native American Church.

6. I find Adams's term for the converse of skill authority—"power authority"— unwieldy as it conflates two separate concepts, but at this point I can offer no specific term for the kinds of indirect social authority exercised by Comanches.

7. Hoebel (1940:18–38) and Wallace and Hoebel (1952:210, 224) argued for a "constitutional" distinction between peace chiefs and war leaders. However, such a distinction is misleading, if not incorrect. At the most basic level of terminology, although Hoebel gave *paraibo* as 'peace chief', he gave no Comanche term for the gloss 'war chief', although he indirectly implied that *tekwuniwapI* 'brave man' or 'hero' was to be glossed as 'war leader'. However, no distinct and specific term for 'war chief' beyond *maimiana paraibo*, itself incorporating the term *paraibo*, has been uncovered. Further, although Anglo-Texans often labeled various men 'war chief', no version of the term (gefe de guerra, gefe militar, etc.) occurs in the Spanish documents, suggesting that the Anglo-Texan use resulted from the improper application of faulty knowledge of the eastern Indians to the Comanches.

The primary ethnographic source for the "constitutional" distinction of peace and war chiefs seems to have been comments by Howard White Wolf in 1933: "There were two *paraibo*, one for war, the other for civilian duties. The latter decided on moving camp, maintaining camp peace, etc. The former was in command when the tribe was at war. Tabenanaka and Esarosavit divided the duties of war and peace paraibo" (Comanche Field Party: August 1, 4). While those comments seem straightforward, evaluation of them is complicated by several factors. While Tabenanaka and Esarosavit were both Yamparikas—although Tabenanaka was sometimes called a Detsakana—and although they were sometimes reported as camping together) they were leaders of separate local residential kinship groups. Thus presumably their decisions about camp movements, etc., would have been made independently of one another. It is possible that Howard White Wolf may have been referring to differences in temperament and historical visibility: Tabenanaka was a signer of the 1865 Little Arkansas Treaty and played a major role in political events between 1865 and 1875 (a "war chief"), whereas Esarosavit is only rarely visible through the historical records (a "peace chief").

At the same time, there was a complex kinship dimension to Howard White Wolf's comments. Tabenanaka and Esarosavit were brothers-in-law: Esarosavit had married Tabenanaka's sister (Pohocsucut 1961). Then, after Esarosavit's brother, Howard White Wolf's father, was killed in 1875, Howard was raised by Esarosavit, taking his stepfather's name. That is, Howard White Wolf was not just speaking of generic peace and war chiefs, but of his *ahpu?* his father/father's brother and his *ara?*

his stepmother's brother. While it is unclear how much the Field Party knew of those genealogical relations, and although the concepts of British social anthropology had only just entered American anthropology—Ralph Linton, leader of the Field Party was a notable opponent of A. R. Radcliffe-Brown, the primary proponent of social anthropology—the immediate implications of those kinship relations were known to the Field Party. According to Nemaruibitsi,

> a father's brother was terminologically equated with father and often acted as disciplinarian . . . a man goes to his *ara?* if he gets in trouble. If the trouble is over a woman, all the *ara?*'s goods are at his disposal in settling the *nanuwokU*. He usually gets anything the *ara?* has even though the *ara?*'s wife objects. When the *ara?* becomes old and poor the nephew gives him horses. [Comanche Field Party, July 31]

Thus it is not clear whether White Wolf's comments were an unbiased presentation of historical and cultural generality, or whether they had they been influenced by the specifics of his own position in that cultural matrix.

A similar situation exists with Tahsuda's discussion of the two sons of Red Sleeve, Two Mountains and Cold. According to Hoebel (1940:20; the comments do not appear in the field notes),

> [Tahsuda] spoke with tender sentiment of Two Mountains, peace chief of the Water Horse band, "a fine gentle fellow never looking for trouble; whatever they did he was the leader of all." But it was of Two Mountain's brother, Cold, that [Tahsuda] waxed enthusiastic, for Cold was a famous war chief.

But according to the census lists, Tahsuda was speaking not just of a revered peace chief and his famous brother, but of his own father *wahatoya* 'two mountains' and therefore also of his father's brother *etseit* (*utsu?itU*) 'cold'.

Interestingly, in both cases it was the consultant's father who was the "peace chief," while the other was the "war hero."

8. There are multiple dimensions to the issue of Comanche political authority. Some of the cases in which observers noted that Comanche leaders had little authority involved a confusion of public and private matters. Thus Foster misplaced his criticism when he charged that I was "unable to demonstrate that the . . . leaders who were chosen as 'principal chiefs' by Euro-American authorities . . . had equal authority or power with respect to Comanche-Comanche relations" (Foster 1991:68): Comanche political (public) leaders would not normally be involved with domestic (private) Comanche-Comanche relations. Moreover, it should not have been surprising that certain individuals did not "obey the chief": those individuals may have been members of other groups.

9. -*wapI* is an agentive suffix with honorific overtones; -*katu* is a possessive suffix. Both *tekwawapI* and *tekwakutu* are from the same root as *tekwuniwapI* 'hero', and are often confused. It may be that *tekwawapI* and *tekwakutu* are literal descrip-

tions of the status of 'talker', while *tekwuniwapI* is a metaphorical extension of the 'talk' involved in 'counting coup'.

10. In 1984 Joe Attocknie gave me six names of Yamparika local bands of the mid-nineteenth century. His names and translations, along with other citations, are as follows:

Ketahtoh	Don't Wear Shoes (*ke* negative, *tahto* 'put on shoes', *tu* nominalizing suffix); García Rejón (1865) gave it as Ketatore; it is synonymous with Curtis's (1907–30, 19:187) *napwat* (*napu* 'shoe', *wah* 'without', *tu* nominalizing suffix) 'no shoes'.
Motsai	Joe Attocknie gave no translation; it is possibly related to *motso* 'beard'.
Pibianigwai	Loud Talkers; *pibia* 'large', *nigwai* 'to ask'. Once a deer wandered into the village, the people shouted so loud that the deer died of fright. Robinson and Armagost (1990:4) attribute the story with the *pihnanuu* 'honey people', a clear error.
Suhmuhtuhka	Eat Everything; *sumu* 'all, completely', *tuhka* 'eat'.
Wahkoh	Shell Ornament.
Wohoi	Joe Attocknie gave no translation, but he implied that that was the name Mooney (1896:1045) gave as 'Maggot' and that Hoebel (1940: 13) gave as *wo'ai* 'Lots of Maggots on the Penis' (*wo?a* 'worm'; *wua* 'penis').

It is not clear whether Joe Attocknie intended that list to represent all nineteenth-century Yamparika local bands, or just those group names he could remember.

11. My thanks to Jerrold Levy (personal communication, 1991) for that observation.

12. Hoebel (1940:40) called the smoke lodge the "old men's society," implying that smoke lodges formed a sodality. That was probably an over-formalization.

13. There is only one reference to succession in the 1933 notes—Wedel's notes of a conversation with Kwasia (July 5)—and although Hoebel and Carlson were present, the comment does not appear in their notes. The comment was "When the chief became old he retained the civil duties, his son took over the war tasks." The phrase clearly paralleled Josiah Gregg's comment, "When a chief becomes old and care-worn, he exercises but the 'civil authority' of his clan while his son, if deemed worthy . . . assumes, 'by common consent,' the functions of warchief" (J. Gregg 1844, 2:308). While it is possible that Kwasia had independently produced the sentence, it is also possible that Linton made the comment as a quote from Gregg.

There is another relevance to the Gregg quote to the analysis of Comanche politics. Hoebel (1940:20) called Gregg's comment "essentially correct"; he then noted, "Some tendency to hereditary succession is found. . . . Sons of Chiefs become chiefs with more than average frequency." But his source for that "tendency to hereditary succession" is uncited. Moreover, Hoebel attributed that tendency "not to any established rule . . . but by virtue of training and examples set by their fathers." Wallace and Hoebel (1952:211) attribute the "tendency for sons of chiefs to become chiefs" and the rationalization that sons were exposed to the "training and example set by their fathers" to "Gregg's penetrating perception." But it was Hoebel, not Gregg, who made the "training and example" link.

Wallace and Hoebel (1952:211) went on to note that the "chief was merged to some extent with his family, and people get used to looking to that family for leadership. The son, who is identified with the father, tends to become the focus of leadership expectancies." That appeal to psychological factors ignores the far simpler sociological fact that local bands were at base kinship networks in which there could be succession to status from within the network.

14. Mirsky's Comanche field notes have not been located, and so the context of the story of the Crow Tassel group cannot be further verified.

15. Lowie's consultant, Wakini, noted, "Offenders in bison hunt [were] never whipped, only reproved by whole party of hunters" (Lowie 1912).

16. There are minor variations, interesting but probably not significant, between the versions of the *tarja* described here (as recorded in the AGN) and that in the AGI; the AGI version was reproduced by Thomas (1929b, 1932:324). Both are copies of an as-yet-undiscovered original, and it is not clear which is the earlier copy.

17. Foster's terms "supraband" and "main band" (1991) are neologisms with little to recommend them.

18. It is perhaps from those per-lodge averages that the estimates of an aboriginal Comanche population in the several tens of thousands arises. There is, however, no good way to evaluate their accuracy; for lack of an alternative, I will simply report the estimates without further comment.

19. But it must be noted if the last *piakne nuhkana* was in 1878—the date fixed by reference to the total eclipse of the sun on July 29 of that year (Linton 1935: 420)—Post Oak Jim would have would been no more than nine years old. Moreover, it is almost certain that his account was colored by visits with his father to Kiowa and Cheyenne ceremonies. Thus, unfortunately, it is now impossible to disentangle the various threads of his accounts.

20. Interestingly, all of the recorded elections are of Kotsoteka (or its descendant division, Penateka) chiefs, suggesting a possible divisional difference in the process of selection.

21. See chapter 6.

22. That is not to argue that other species of fauna and flora were unimportant. For present purposes, I mean the phrase "the buffalo and the horse" to be inclusive of all aspects of the domestic household economy.

23. It would be surprising if an event with such major social and political consequences were not expressed in mythology. In 1933 several Comanches recounted versions of the story "The Owner of the Buffalo." In that story, when a man penned up all the buffalo, the people starved. The Hero, *kaawosA* 'fox', a changeling, turned himself into a puppy and tricked the man's daughter into letting him see the animals. He then jumped out of her arms and into the herd, stampeding it out of the pen. After that the people had plenty of meat.

That is a widespread Basin myth (Hultkrantz 1986:639), which is also reported from several other Plains groups—interestingly, most of whom Oliver characterizes as "Plains tribes of hunting and gathering background." The coordinate myth from the "Plains tribes of horticultural background" is the "Buffalo Wife and Corn Wife" (e.g., Dorsey 1890:147-62), which can be seen as legitimating the dual horticultural-hunting economies.

Chapter 3

1. A 1694 document gave Come Cibolo 'buffalo eater' as the name of an Indian group near the junction of the Rio Grande and Conchos Rivers (Hackett 1923-37, 2:395). Although *kutsuhtuhka* 'buffalo eater' was the name of a Comanche division, the location of a Comanche group in the far south at that early date is problematic; the name probably referred to the people also called Jumanos.

2. It is also interesting that Alvarez Barriero, engineer and cartographer on Rivera's expedition, made no mention of the Comanches or other "Yndios Barbaros" surrounding the province (Barnes, Naylor and Polzer 1988:215-18).

3. Twitchell (1914, 2:205) listed these documents under Torres's name. However, since the final page was signed by, and the sentencing was ordered by Governor Cruzat y Gongora, I have so referenced them.

4. The Aa Nation poses one of the more difficult problems in Plains ethnohistory.

5. Reported details of that fight are confused. Bishop Pedro Tamarón y Romeral, who had visited New Mexico only months later, reported that fifty-six women and children were taken captive, with a loss of forty-nine Comanches (E. Adams 1953:217). However, almost twenty years later, cartographer Bernardo de Miera y Pacheco, on his 1779 map of New Mexico, stated that "fourteen men with firearms . . . perished, and sixty-four persons, large and small of both sexes were carried off. Of the enemy, more than eighty died" (E. Adams and Chavez 1956:4).

6. The seat of government of Spanish and Mexican Texas was the presidio of San Antonio de Béxar, generally referred to by the Spaniards and Mexicans simply as Béxar. It was one of several governmental and ecclesiastical institutions within a small radius along the San Antonio River. San Antonio de Béxar should not to be confused with the modern city of San Antonio, which, after the Texas Revolution, developed from the nearby civil villa of San Fernando de Béxar. Also nearby was the mission of San Antonio de Valero, nicknamed the Alamo.

7. It was probably that battle that formed the core incident of the folk drama *Los Comanches*, allegedly composed by a participant in the battle (A. Espinosa 1907; G. Espinosa 1931; Campa 1942). Although the play gave the leadership of the Comanches to Cuerno Verde 'green horn'—and alluded to his death in the battle— there is no other evidence that the Spaniards knew their opponent's identity. Five

years later, Cuerno Verde, or another of the name, was killed by Governor Juan Bautista de Anza.

8. The river would later be called Napestle; the reason for the difference is unknown.

9. Most scholars seem to have translated this word as plural, 'rivers', to parallel 'lakes', but the words on the map are "el rio" not "los rios." The reference to a "wide river" is unknown.

10. Following current convention, I will spell it Kotsoteka.

11. In Spanish it reads "Causa por que se experimentan tantos daños, pues les falta su primer mantenimiento les obliga la necesidad a mantenerse con caballos y mulas." Herbert Bolton (1950:73) gave it as "In this way they have suffered so many losses that, lacking their chief means of support necessity compels them to maintain themselves by eating horses and mules," while Carl Wheat (1957–63:109) gave it as "since their primary lack of provisions is forcing them to subsist on horses and mules."

12. Robinson and Armagost (1990:58) have *naruʔuyapu* as 'mean, dangerous'.

13. The Spanish text reads: "que avian muerto, de las tres partes que eran, los dos."

14. Apparently a village of Arkansas Indians west of the Arkansas Post (Bolton 1915:394).

15. In the next few years, the name would be spelled several different ways, Camisa de Hierro, Camisa de Fierro, Camisa de Yierro, thus adding to the confusion.

16. The description possibly refers to having his hair shaved into a roach.

17. The chronology of events in New Mexico that follows is based on a summary "Account of Events" prepared by Pedro Garrido y Duran, secretary to the comandante general of the Provincias Internas in Chihuahua, which was in turn based on Anza's reports (Thomas 1932). Anza's original reports have not been found. Thus, it is not clear how much Garrido summarized the significant details.

18. The suffix *-tu* is both an aspect marker and a nominalizing suffix.

19. See chapter 2, note 16.

20. Thomas's translation (1932:315) of secretary Pedro Garrido's summary of that expedition designates Ohamaquea as Ecueracapa's "younger son," a clear error. Garrido's convoluted syntax may have confused both Thomas and John (1975:686).

21. John (1975:729 n. 55), citing Navarro García (1964:468), who in turn cited Ugarte's letter of January 4, 1787 to the viceroy (Ugarte's letter number 56; AGI 286), implied that the report of the battle came from the Comanche envoys in January 1787. However, other details of Navarro's narrative suggest that Ugarte was citing Menchaca's report. Unfortunately neither Ugarte's letter nor Menchaca's report are included in the extracts of the AGI available in North America, and therefore have not been directly examined.

22. John has argued that the two names referred to the same person, that "the [1785–86 Casa de Palo] council chose . . . Ecueracapa . . . long distinguished for exploits in war. . . . New Mexicans already knew him as Cota de Malla for the shirt of

armor that he wore in battle, and it was probably he whom Cabello's interpreter called Camisa de Fierro" (1975:668–69).

However, neither name, Ecueracapa nor Cota de Malla, occurs in the New Mexico records *before* the Casa de Palo council; therefore there is no evidence that the New Mexicans "already knew" him. While Pedro Garrido's summary of the events leading up to the 1786 Comanche-New Mexico peace included the phrase "he is the individual whom we know as Cota de Malla" (Thomas 1932:295), since there is no evidence that the New Mexicans "knew" him, the "we" can only have referred to Garrido and his superiors in Chihuahua. Moreover, that knowledge could only have been based on Domingo Cabello's reports from Texas, themselves derived from Pedro Vial's report. At the same time, while there is no prior New Mexican reference to Ecueracapa, let alone one describing him as wearing armor, Vial did refer to the Texan Camisa de Hierro so attired.

Much of John's case for the identity of Ecueracapa and Camisa de Hierro hinges on the conclusion that "certainly Vial and Chaves, who had known the Comanches in their home territory, believed Cota de Malla, Camisa de Fierro, and Ecueracapa to be one" (1975:716). But that appeal to the authority of Vial and Chavez founders on the uncertainty surrounding the actual extent to which they "knew the Comanches in their home territory." Vial himself admitted only to "passing through" their rancherías, and he conducted his negotiations with them in the Taovaya language, not in Comanche.

Finally it may be noted that of all of the documents about the singularity or multiplicity of Cota de Malla/Camisa de Hierro/etc., only Ugarte's January 1787 report of his interview with Ecueracapa's sons, the one in which the identity of Cota de Malla and Ecueracapa was denied—and despite John's indictment of the veracity of the interpreter (1975:715)—has the authority of being a firsthand report of a conversation with Comanches about the matter. All other reports of the identities of Cota de Malla, Camisa de Hierro, and Ecueracapa are at best only second-hand.

Chapter 4

1. In contrast to the numbered-paragraph report of his 1785 trip, Vial's report on his 1786-87 trip is more like a diary, with dated entries. It is not clear, however, whether Vial indeed kept a dated entry format on his journey or whether the diary was composed after his return. Loomis and Nasatir's version of the journey is based on a composite of three versions of Vial's diary (Loomis and Nasatir 1967:268). I have been able to examine only the version in AGN 43 (14). Any prior contacts Cristóbal de los Santos may have had with Comanches are unknown.

2. It may have been through Tanicón, Guaquangas's brother, that Vial learned of the identity of the Spanish commander who killed Camisa de Hierro.

3. There was also a Ute "general" named Ysampampi (Concha 1790).

4. That is, Pisimampat. The name was given this time as Tampisimanpe *ta* indefinite subject, *pisi* 'odor' *napɏ* 'shoe' which has the same meaning as Pisimampat *pisi* 'odor', *napʉ* 'shoe', *tʉ* suffix. From that time forward, the name was given simply as Pisinampe or a variant, i.e. Visinampa, Bixinampe, etc.

5. John (1985:387) explicitly equated El Ronco with Guik'ate, but was more cautious with her identification of the Comanche chief, merely noting that "current Kiowa memory of that Comanche chief's name agrees with Mooney's report" (1985: 396 n. 18). In part, that modern Kiowa agreement with Mooney is understandable by processes other than continuing oral history: Alice Marriott (1952:36) noted that in the 1930s, one of her Kiowa informants brought forth a copy of Mooney's *Calendar History of the Kiowa Indians* saying, "When we don't know for sure what happened we look him up in Mr. Mooney"; the same may be true sixty years later. While it is also clear that Joe Attocknie had read Mooney, the extent of his influence is uncertain.

6. Loomis and Nasatir's later suggestion that Ysambanbi "might mean Handsome Wolf" (1967:488 n 22a) is not warranted.

7. Carroll and Haggard (1942:128) title this section of their translation "Indian Problems." There is no such title in Pino's original. They also translate Naciones de Gentiles as "Wild Indian Tribes."

8. While most of the names remain nonspecific ethnonyms, some can be identified. Cahigua is clearly Kiowa; Panana is Pawnee or Wichita; Canseres, Kansa; and Guasachi, Osage. Of the Pananas, Pino reported, in what is probably a good example of how second-, third-, or fourth-hand information can get garbled and yet retain an element of truth, he said, "[they] live in underground caves and sometimes in huts covered with hay, weeds, or grass; they are very neat. These Indians are expert in the use of firearms; and have warehouses supplied with powder and ball, etc., furnished them by the United States. They raise corn, beans and certain fruits" (Carroll and Haggard 1942:128).

9. D. L. Flores (1985:23) reported that Sibley had licensed the party to trade not only with the Wichitas, but also with Comanches, and to invite both groups to come to Natchitoches for a conference. Unfortunately, Flores did not give a direct citation for either the licensing or the invitation.

10. In an earlier letter Sibley said Lewis had reported the Hietan camp as composed of "three thousand" souls (Garrett 1942–46, 45:381).

11. The points in English and American "point blankets," in this case 3-point, were a measure of quality. The points were marked in the blankets by lines woven into the fabric along the selvedge edge.

12. The *Houston Telegraph and Texas Register* (July 1, 1840) cited its source as "from the Texas Sentinel" indicating that the letters had been published at least one other time, but I have been unable to locate the exact date of publication in the *Sentinel*.

13. It was reprinted, under the heading "Indians on the Red River," in *Niles' Weekly Register* for October 28, 1820.

14. D. L. Flores commented (1985:23), but without direct citation, that Joseph Lucas, a Caddo-French métis, was "Nolan's sign language expert."

15. There are minor discrepancies in Diaz de Luna's arithmetic; in my dissertation I made other errors in transcribing the tables (Kavanagh 1986:261).

Chapter 5

1. The incident has been widely reported; in one version: "226 Comanche men, along with some women and children, . . . rode into San Antonio and stayed for six days, entering people's houses, insulting them, and carrying off what they fancied" (Weber 1982:89). While that account parallels the original report, it lacks the specificity of the original and is therefore open to over-estimating the resulting damage.

2. The term *genizaro* generally referred to Christianized Plains Indians living in New Mexico; it was used here as a personal name.

3. An article in *Niles' Weekly Register* for August 30, 1823, under the heading "Indian Hostilities," and reprinting an article from the *St. Louis Enquirer* earlier that month, stated:

> Mr. John McKnight, an old and respectable citizen of St. Louis, trading on one of the upper sources of the Arkansas, has been murdered by the Indians, and robbed of nearly all of his merchandise. He had fixed himself near the Spanish boundary, where he erected a fort, protected by a few men, with the intention of making an establishment in that quarter, and, opening a trade with the Indians. But in consequence of the unfortunate fate of Mr. McKnight, the post has been abandoned, and the party has returned to the settlements.

The implications of the differences between the two accounts, the locations of the fort: on the Canadian inside Mexico (James) or the upper Arkansas within the United States (Niles), and the fate of the post: kept up (James), abandoned (Niles), are uncertain. Both, however, agreed that the attackers were Comanches.

4. The identification of the ethnonym Towash is uncertain. On the one hand, it could be an untutored effort at Taovaya or one of its synonyms (Taguayaces, etc.). At the same time, *ta?wach* is 'man' in Ute (Jean O. Charney, personal communication). The former is more likely. In 1811 John Sibley reported that since visiting him, the "Tawaiche" chief had died, "since which a separation has taken place, a party of them have gone off and joined a Wandering Band of Ietans" (Garrett 1942–46, 49:403).

There are several other possible connections with incidents in Comanche history. It is possible that the "wandering band of Ietans" referred to El Sordo's mixed band of Comanches, Wichitas and others. Or, as *Niles' Weekly Register* extract from the *St. Louis Enquirer* (see previous note) continued:

> The Camanche are said to be under the direction of the celebrated Caddo chief, the same as was mentioned a short time since, that Iturbide wished to

form an alliance with for the purpose of getting his Camanches into the imperial service in return for which the Caddo was to have an 'empire' on his own footing.

The earlier mention of the "celebrated Caddo Chief" has not been located. Although James's "Alasarea the Towash" could be taken to be a Caddo, there is no direct linkage between him and Guonique, with whom Iturbide had negotiated the year before.

5. Benton left out the rest of the sentence from Storrs's report: "[the Camanche] Indians who lost one man in the battle. This robbery being committed in the Osage territory, was attributed to them, until the contrary was ascertained last summer" (Storrs 1825).

6. I have been unable to locate the exact data of publication in the *Intelligencer.*

7. Berlandier lived the rest of his life at Matamoros, drowning in the Rio Grande in 1850; thus, he could have made the collections during the interim.

8. Translation by Georgette M. Dorn, Library of Congress, for John C. Ewers, 1974. My thanks to Dr. Ewers for making it available to me.

9. The watercolors, now held by the Thomas Gilcrease Institute of American History and Art, were published in Berlandier (1969). José María died in 1834, Lino in 1838.

10. As noted earlier, Shoshones—Sonsoris—were reported on the Arkansas as late as 1831. Cameron wrote in 1836; eight years later, Josiah Gregg (1844, 2:251) noted that the "different bands of the Comanches and Shoshonies constitute [an] extensive [language] stock, speaking one language." Three years after that, in discussing the "two great roots from which have sprung all the different tongues spoken by the Indians," Thomas Fitzpatrick metaphorically "[crossed] the Rocky Mountains, by way of South Pass; and in going I shall like to take with me the Comanches and place them where they properly belong, among the Shoshone or Snake Indians, as I found their language exactly the same" (Abert 1846:48). Although only metaphorical, Fitzpatrick's was also the earliest explicit effort to lump the Comanches with the Basin peoples, "where they properly belong"—rather than on the Plains—a process some anthropologists have been attempting ever since. The otherwise earliest professional linguistic notice of the language similarity of Comanche and Shoshone was Robert Latham's 1862 *Elements of Comparative Philology*, as cited in Casagrande (1954–55:145).

11. Other observations by Cameron are noted in chapter 2.

12. McLean often treated names in Comanche as if they were Spanish rather than Comanche. Thus, he glossed the clearly identical Comanche name Mueracuita and Maraquita as two separate Spanish names, the first as "Death to Care," and the second as "Little Gourd Rattle."

13. The Béxar Archives at the University of Texas lists that document as 1835; it is probably from 1832.

14. According to George Bent's informant, Left Hand Bull, around 1825 or 1826 a group of Blackfeet and Gros Ventres had come south and stolen a Comanche horse

herd (Hyde 1968:32). The dates are so close that they might refer to the same incident.

15. In a much later context (1855) Houston referred to "Comanches of the
Woods" and "Comanches of the Prairies" (A. W. Williams and Barker 1938–43, 6:
125), but that usage was probably influenced by intervening events.

16. LeGrand's credentials for that delicate diplomacy are unclear. He was
captain of the 1824 Santa Fe caravan (*Franklin, Missouri Intelligencer*, April 3,
1824)—the June 5, 1824 *Intelligencer* gave the captain as "Augustus A. LeGrand,"
presumably a typographical error as Augustus Storrs was also on that trip. In the early
1830s, LeGrand was in and out of trouble with the local New Mexico officials (Sena
1832). He was later to claim that in the summer of 1833, while surveying a tract of
land in west Texas, he met a Comanche chief named Cordero (Kennedy 1841).
However, there are reasons to doubt his veracity in the matter: his published notes
state that he and a survey party had marked out the area from 32 degrees north, 102
degrees west (Midland, Texas)—which LeGrand said was thirty-nine miles south of
the "south fork of [the] Red River" of Texas, the Colorado—to the Arkansas River, a
distance of just under 600 miles, and westward to the mountains, in degree-by-degree
blocks in four months. If true, it was a monumental feat of civil engineering. As it is,
most of his reported topographic details do not match the area and thus cast doubt
upon both his survey and his claim of having met Comanches.

17. Wallace and Hoebel (1952:31) give his name as Bonville.

18. Mooney (1898:271–73) gave the 1838 fight as on Wolf Creek.

19. It is possible that distinction was the basis of Wallace and Hoebel's (1952:
210, 224) argument for a "constitutional" distinction not just between a chief's war
and peace duties, but between different individuals with different war and peace roles,
that is, "war chiefs" and "peace chiefs." See the comments in chapter 2 on Hoebel's
(1940) and Wallace and Hoebel's (1952) use of that quotation.

20. The wood post was about nine miles upstream from the later, better-known
adobe post.

21. Although the sixty-year gap between incident and inscription gives ample
reason to doubt the historical accuracy of Smithwick's memory, there are only a few
differences between Smithwick's account and the contemporary records.

22. While the second part of the name Potsanaquahip is clearly *kwahip∀* 'back',
the first part is problematic. Joe Attocknie (1965) gave the full name as 'Male
Buffalo's Back', implying that the first part, *potsana*, is 'male buffalo'; as such the
name and the traditional translation coincide. A possible alternative is *po?sana* 'crazy'
(Charney, personal communication), which, while closer to the phonetics, is farther
from the traditional gloss.

23. There is some question about the strength of Spain's, and later Mexico's,
acceptance of that doctrine, particularly in reference to the Comanches. Its historic
validity aside, the continuity of Spain's denial of aboriginal rights was a feature of
Texas land claims after the Revolution.

24. Kiowas called the winter of 1839–40 "Smallpox Winter" (Mooney 1898:274). According to Mooney, "it was brought by some visiting Osage, and spread at once through the Kiowa, Apache, and Comanche, killing a great number in each tribe."

25. One of the children had been named William Hockley by the Texans (Winfrey and Day 1959–66, 1:265); nothing more is known of his naming or his history.

26. The parallels between Eldredge's account of his meeting with Pahayuko and that of Vial's meeting about sixty years earlier in the same vicinity are striking. Both had been guided by Wichitas; both had been warned to stay in their tents during the preliminary debates, and both made their own speeches only after those initial discussions.

27. The latter article is one of the few articles in any treaty that gave the Comanches—or any Indians—authority to punish non-Indian offenders.

Chapter 6

1. The reference to mines may be evidence of the continued influence of the meteoritic "silver ore" found in Texas in 1808.

2. It is not clear who was actually present.

3. The account of the German-Comanche treaty given in Harston (1963: 145–50) is completely confused.

4. Following Montaignes's description they would have been somewhere northeast of modern Borger, Texas. According to Abert's astonomical observations of that date, they were at "latitude 35° 47′ 56″, longitude 101° 35′ 47″." The latter position is some ten miles away, north of the river.

5. Hatcher's contacts were clearly greater with the Kiowa than with the Comanches. Indeed, one woman in the Kiowa village "wept over him for joy when they met, and insisted on his receiving a bale of tongues and some pinole which she had manufactured from musquit. She always calls him son, having adopted him ever since his first trading with her nation" (Abert 1846:40). That would explain the several asides in both narratives:

> The Kioways are a people exceeding the Comanches in every respect and though far inferior to them in number, not counting more than 200 lodges in all, yet exercise almost absolute control over them. . . . The Kiowa sustain a character for bravery, energy, and honesty, while the Comanches are directly the opposite, being cowardly, indolent, and treacherous. [Abert 1846:39]

> The Camanches steal & their neighbors the Kioways . . . do not. I mention this on the authority of one who has had numerous opportunities of testing its truth and one who has for years been a trader among both nations. [Montaignes 1852–56:112]

6. Lecompte (1972:283) suggested that the adobe post was built by John Hatcher in the spring or summer of 1845. If so, it is strange that Hatcher and Abert's party stopped near the "former" wood post, which, if Montaignes was correct, was in a burned and ruined condition, rather than continuing on to the brand-new adobe post, a post Hatcher had just completed. It also seems strange that if the adobe post had just been completed, the ordinarily loquacious Hatcher was silent about his achievement.

On another point, Lecompte (1972:282) also noted that the adobe post was apparently never given a name by the Bents. Kit Carson (1964) would later called it Adobe Fort, as would George Bent. Lecompte suggested that the transposed name Fort Adobe apparently stems from Grinnell (1915).

7. There are at least two other contemporary reports that are not included in Barry's chronology. For both, the rumor factor is high: the July 3, 1847 *Niles National Register* copied from the *St. Louis Reveille* that on the evening of June[?] 21, a gentleman arrived at St. Louis from Westport, with the news that a Delaware Indian had just arrived, giving an account of the "wholesale murder of [38 or 40] teamsters, by a combined force of Arapahoes, Camanches, and Pawnees." That such a major incident is unattested elsewhere suggests it never actually happened, but it might have been included in Gilpin's count. In another incident, reported in *Niles' National Register* for July 31, 1847, and copied from the *St. Louis Courier and Enquirer*, on July 26 (only five days before the issue was published!) "Comanche Indians . . . and northern Mexicans" attacked an unidentified party on the banks of the Arkansas River, taking one hundred and thirty-five yoke of government oxen:

> it is evident that that their whole object is to cut off trains and destroy United States property. This is no doubt a part of guerrilla warfare. The amount of public property which we have heard of destroyed on this road, in the last eight days, will amount to very nearly $10,000.

Needless to say, unless that last statement includes the incidents listed in table 6.2, it is unattested elsewhere.

8. Grinnell (1923:54) gave the name of the attacker at Pawnee Fork as Red Arm, which would be *ekapuura*.

9. On the other hand, according to Tahsuda, one of the consultants for the 1933 Field Party (Hoebel 1940:20), his grandfather was named Red Sleeve, in which case the name may have been his own rather than an American nickname. A Plains Apache called Red Sleeve lived in the same vicinity in 1853 (Froebel 1859:259).

10. Fort Mann, or Mann's Fort, was built west of Dodge City by army wagonmaster Daniel P. Mann as a service depot for government trains.

11. It is possible that the group later called *numukiowa* 'Comanche-Kiowa' had formed at that early date, but there is no other evidence for it.

12. There is little mention of Comanches in the interim. In February 1851 Colonel Miles at Fort Washita reported:

> the Northern Comanches under the chieftainship of Pa-ya-ho-kee roam with his numerous bands through this district, like lords of the soil—all pay

> homage to him; all court his protection. Whatever he orders is obeyed, if even to cease war among the small bands and make peace. It is only late in the Fall and during the winter that the Comanches approach near here. The chief has been once to visit me [apparently the visit of August 1849] but brought no one with him but his servants. As he was encamped then not over 100 miles west of [the fort] with, as was estimated about 5,000 warriors, I considered his visit then as a reconnaissance and held myself in readiness to give him a proper reception should he come nearer. Since then no Comanche have visited the settlements. [Foreman 1934:128–29]

The sources for his generalizations on Pahayuko's political standing are unknown; they certainly could not be based on observation from a single visit some eighteen months before.

Rodney Glisan, a surgeon assigned to Fort Arbuckle for the period 1851–54, although noting periodic Comanche "scares," including practical jokes on newly arrived officers, reported only one actual Comanche visit—in September 1853—by a small ranchería suffering from dysentery (Glisan 1874:124).

13. There is no clear relation to the "Na-ó-ni-em or Ridge people" mentioned by Coby in 1880.

14. There is a degree of uncertainty with name Kakaraway. It is probably the same as Cariwah, the signer of the Rollins and Rogers Agreements, and is more grammatical (Cariwah drops the initial negative suffix). While the name Cariwah did not reappear after the Rogers Agreement, the name Kakaraway gradually underwent a spelling metamorphosis, through Kaharawa and Kahavwah to Kahabewite. Since none of those variations occur in the same context, the likelihood that they are the same name is increased. While Kekarawa (Carawa) is meaningful in Comanche, *kekaruwah* 'never sits', Kaharawa is not. But Kahabewite is *kehabewahtʉ* 'never lies down', a near synonym. In 1870 it was given as 'restless' (Tatum 1870d), and a later document gave "Kahabbywite" as 'won't stay with a woman' (Haworth 1878). It is not known if this progression was the result of an intentional name change, or of a series of gradual permutations, mispronounciations, and back-translations attempting to make sense out of the ever-compounding errors.

In 1870, Agent Lawrie Tatum reported that "Kahabbywite" was a Penateka local band chief with sixty members in his band (Tatum 1870d); four years later, "Kahavwah"—no translation was offered—was recorded as a Penateka local band chief also having sixty members in his band (Anonymous 1874). The similarites of names and sizes of populations suggest that they were the same. After about 1870, the name Kekarawa does not appear; the name Kahabbywite appears on the 1879 and 1881 censuses.

15. In another incident, in May, on hearing that Ketumsee was sick, Lee again visited the camps. But when he arrived,

> the medicine man rushed at me, made significant signs that I must disrobe before presenting myself before the august patient. I patiently sat on my

horse till I ascertained what garment they considered most inimical to the healing art, which I learned to be the cravat. Then alighting, unbuttoning my coat, and slipping off the noxious article, I displayed to their admiring eyes a blue check shirt, and was greeted by a general approving "humph." The charm was fully developed and I walked boldly in. [F. R. Adams 1955:123]

It seems likely that the cravat Lee was wearing was black, marking him as having medicine power. If that interpretation is correct, that is the earliest indication of "black handkerchief shamanism" among the Comanches (see Slotkin 1974).

16. That gloss is uncertain.

17. Although the Wichita Mountain area had been Comanche country for over a century, according to Anglo-American law, it had been assigned to the removed Choctaws and had to be leased from them for the Texan tribes, thus its name, the Leased District.

18. One of the variant pronounciations of *-tuhka* emphasizes the aspiration, resulting in the spelling "-tethka."

19. There is also the question of mutual influence. While George Bent did know James Mooney personally, it is not known if Joe Attocknie ever read any of the books resulting from the George Bent-George Hyde correspondence; he certainly knew the Kiowa calenders. But he also had independent information.

20. It is unclear why there should be such a radical difference in the claimed value of the horses between those two counties.

Chapter 7

1. The manuscript itself is unsigned. Pilling (1889:63) noted that it is "probably by General A. Pike," but the basis for that attribution is unknown, as is how it came to be at the National Anthropological Archives.

2. The story of the latter name is that an individual sat on top of the hill, watching for the traders, picking at his moustache with tweezers.

3. There are two photographs of Cynthia Ann Parker. One, with her daughter, was by A. C. Corning in 1861 soon after her recapture; the other, recently discovered, has no documentation, and although also said to date from 1861, shows a much plumper woman (Hacker 1990, cover and frontispiece). There are several other early photographs of Comanches in a number of collections, but the available document-ation on them is incomplete; several in the Smithsonian collections (originating in the Haverford College collections) were probably taken at the 1865 Fort Smith council with the former Confederate Indians.

4. For some reason the treaty was not submitted to the Senate for ratification until 1869, long after two other treaties had been submitted and ratified; therefore the Senate voted "not to advise and consent" to its ratification (Gorham 1869).

5. The parallel of Le-na-weets for Tenawa with the typographical error in Butler and Lewis's band list—Lenawoosh for Tenawoosh—is striking but unexplained.

6. Although Stanley had reported most other speeches exactly as given in the official transcript, suggesting he had access to the records, his report of this speech (H. M. Stanley 1967:285) and of subsequent incidents are but poor paraphrases of the official records suggesting that for some reason he was no longer a valued representative of the press.

7. From that point on the official transcript of the October 20 proceedings seems to be a paraphrase rather than a verbatim record; instead of the first person, "I am glad to be here," it is third person, "They were glad to hear the Indians." It is almost as if the stenographer was exhausted after recording Paruasemena's speech and could no longer take dictation. Stanley's reports, however, kept the first person; indeed, he claimed to have "copied it verbatim [sic]." There are other discrepancies. For instance, Stanley reported that after Paruasemena's long speech, Satanta, after a brief interlude trying to get Black Eagle, another Kiowa, to speak, went off sulking. Satanta returned in a short while and made another brief speech, demanding that two agents be assigned to the Kiowas—Leavenworth was adequate—but he wanted John Tappan, cousin to commission member S. F. Tappan, as agent for his band.

The official transcript, while recording Satanta's first brief speech and Black Eagle's reluctance to speak, did not record Satanta's sullen departure and return. It noted only that Satanta interrupted Henderson's speech to make his demand for a new agent. And instead of noting that John Tappan was a relative of a commission member, the official transcript specified that he was the sutler at Fort Larned (Taylor, et al, 1910:61). Then the transcipt noted that Paruasemena "lifted up his voice"—a reference to the "shrill" oratorical style noted by Stanley?—and said that Leavenworth was an old man, and that "while he lived he would like to have Leavenworth as his agent; when he was dead it mattered not" (Taylor, et al, 1910:61). Stanley made no mention of these words.

It is difficult to evaluate the discrepancies between the accounts. On the one hand Stanley's earlier exact quotation of the official record gave a degree of authenticity to his reports. But his poor paraphrase of Paruasemena's speech and the increasing discrepancies thereafter suggest that, at minimum, his access to the offical transcript had been restricted and that at times he may not even have been present at the events he reported. To be balanced, the opposite may have also been true, that he relied upon the offical transcript to cover those events when he was not present and that his later reports give a more valid account than did the official transcript. At this remove in time, the question must remain open.

8. Whereas the Little Arkansas reservation included what was to become the entire Texas panhandle, the Medicine Lodge reservation would be totally within the Indian Territory north and east of the Red River. Historian Ralph Smith (1972) has argued that those differences were not coincidental, but had wider political motivations. That is, in making the reservation described in the Little Arkansas treaty

encompass the Texas panhandle, the 1865 treaty commissioners "presumably . . . acted under the Conquered Province idea of the radical Republicans," i.e., that defeat in the Civil War made Texas conquered territory, thereby nullifying the 1845 Texas annexation treaty and its denial of aboriginal Indian land rights. In turn, that legitimated the giving away of "millions of acres of [Texan] public domain" to the Indians. By the time of the Medicine Lodge Treaty, however, the government had "probably" recognized the legal and political problems with the "Conquered Province" concept as applied to Texas and so modified the new reservation to remove it from Texas (R. A. Smith 1972). Although the new reservation was entirely outside of Texas, there is no evidence that the establishment of the Little Arkansas reservation within Texas, or the later modification of the boundaries of the Medicine Lodge Treaty reservation outside of Texas, were motivated by political considerations.

9. There is some confusion about his role in the proceedings. According to the official records he did not speak at the council, but at least one of the Comanches interviewed in 1933 believed that he was a most active chief. According to Kwasia (Comanche Field Party, July 5), "Esananaka called the first general meeting of all Comanche chiefs." Hoebel stated this as: "'Echo of the Wolf's Howl' convened the first tribal council at the time of the proposal of the Medicine Lodge Treaty in 1876 [sic, 1867]" (1940:11). Wallace and Hoebel modified those words to say: "The first assembly of chiefs representing all the bands, in the belief of Echo of the Wolf's Howl, was at the time of the proposal of the Medicine Lodge Treaty in 1867" (1952: 214). But inasmuch as there was no "tribal" council representing all the divisions at the Medicine Lodge (neither Kwahadas, Kotsotekas, nor Tenewas were apparently represented), both Hoebel and Wallace and Hobel are in error. Moreover, Wallace and Hoebel imply that they got their information from Esananaka, or from one who knew his beliefs, but that chief had died in the early 1880s. It may be that Kwasia was reporting a belief held by some of Esanaka's followers. That is, although Kwasia was born into Yuniwat's local band, ca. 1860, when he was a teenager and young adult, he was associated with people who had been members of Esananaka's local band in the 1860s and 1870s, and he may have picked up their version of the events.

10. The name on the treaty is Ah-te-es-ta, and was given as Little Horn. However, the similarity between the names *ahtutsi* 'little horn' and *hitutsi* 'little crow', and the absence of any other mention of a Comanche by the name of Little Horn suggests that rather than two men with similar names, the signer was Hitetsi, son of Paruasemena, and brother of Esananaka.

11. At this point in his narrative, Douglas C. Jones (1966:128) commented:

Any list of Indian names is interesting to speculate upon. Although little profanity was included in their language, the Plains Indians spoke obscenely by Europeans standards, and proper names were no exceptions. Some humor might have been added to an otherwise somber moment if the interpreters had translated Indian names literally.

While the first part of that comment may be correct, no such humor could have been derived from the Comanche or Kiowa signatories. None of the names is even remotely obscene or scatalogical.

12. Douglas C. Jones (1966:136) argued the gifts were given according to an agency roster prepared by Leavenworth, thus implying a list of names and numbers beyond Bogy and Irwin's very broad 1866 list. However, no such list has yet been found.

13. There is a degree of uncertainty around the name and person of Esitoya. As given, it seems clearly *esi toya* 'grey mountain'. According to Joe Attocknie, Esitoya was one of two Mexican brothers captured about 1850 by his grandfather, Attocknie. They were later offered their freedom but decided to remain with the Comanches. In later years Esitoya was a Penateka local band leader. A similar name, Esitoyate, sometimes occurs, usually glossed as 'grey leggings' or 'grey legging stripe', sometimes as 'striding through the dusk'; none of those glosses can be confirmed. If there were two individuals, Grey Leggings/Striding Through the Dusk did not survive to be named on a reservation census. For the present I must assume that only one individual was politically prominent.

14. In 1880, Coby told W. J. Hoffman of the Smithsonian Institution that "the former name of the Ku-a-ha-di was Na-ó-ni-em or Ridge people" (Hoffman 1880). But there is no clear relation between, on the one hand, the ethnonyms Kwahada and Na-ó-ni-em, and on the other the ethnonyms Nonaum (untranslated) reported by Neighbors, Noonah reported by Lewis as 'People of the Desert', or Nonah (untranslated) reported by Butler. None of those latter terms ever appeared in contemporary documents as direct references.

15. The captive was Clinton Smith, who with his brother Jefferson, later wrote a superficial captivity narrative (C. L. Smith and J. D. Smith 1927).

16. See chapter 6, note 14.

17. Mackenzie reported some three thousand animals taken, the correspondent for the *Army and Navy Journal* (Nov. 16, 1872) reported "from twelve to fifteen hundred horses and ponies."

18. Richardson (1933:362) cited several sources indicating that Mowway was the village chief and implying that it was a Kotsoteka village; Richardson also said, "It is spoken of as a Kwahadi village." Mowway, of course, was returning from Washington at the time of the attack. Nye's informants said, "Mowway not there, he with the Peace People" (1969:162).

19. Hagan, without citation, noted that some Comanches "vented their wrath by putting to the torch the houses of two chiefs on the Washington delegation, Tosawa and [Esihabit]. It must have been quite a disappointment to Tosawa to return from Washington and find in ashes the home for which he had pled for years" (1976:88). However, it is unclear whether those houses had yet even been built: in May 1872 Tatum had reported: "I have to my credit $750 for the purpose of building Tosawa a house. He did not wish to have a house while at this agency. He is now transferred to

the Wichita Agency. If it meets the approbation of the Department, please instruct me to transfer the said amount to Jonathan Richards" (Tatum 1872f).

20. According to Tatum (1872i), Terheryahquahip asked for the following individuals:

(1) Sekia, a Penateka, the mother of Horse Back's present wife;

(2) Worobeah, a former wife of Horse Back, and her daughter, the latter has but one eye;

(3) Edaika, a near relative of Horse Back, an old woman and her sister;

(4) Three nieces of Horse Back, one said to be wounded, the daughters of Chetoka, the mother not taken;

(5) Pahawits, an old woman whose nose has been cut off;

(6) Peebo, and child, daughter of No. 5;

(7) Saseka, daughter of No. 5, and child;

(8) Taquakema, a middle-aged woman;

(9) Taquiyou, sister of No. 8, and child;

(10) Yamahtakema, sister of No. 8 & 9;

(11) Peeya, a young woman;

(12) The mother of No. 11;

(13) The sister of No. 11;

(14) Voonet taka, a middle aged woman;

(15) Sister of Kotobe & child, Kotobe was not taken;

(16) Two wives and two children of Watsuah who is in Horseback's camp;

(17) Two young women both named Nimekiama;

(18) Tarena and her two children and her sister;

(19) Tarro and her two children and sister.

Unfortunately, none of those names can be identified on later census lists.

21. According to Tatum (1873a), Tomichicut asked for the following individuals:

(1) Chop-pay, Black Beard's mother;

(2) Toponypeah, Black Beard's wife;

(3) Sawwithtakqua, a boy about 8, Black Horse's son.

(4) Waschicksa, Esihabit's mother;

(5) Waaughpi, Mother of No. 3;

(6) Tay, sister of No. 4;

(7) Navonywoopatsa and her 2 children.

According to Tatum (1873c), Tabenanaka asked for the following individuals:

(1) Tassiapeah and child

(2) Quassuaere, a girl almost grown

(3) Kiamockka, a boy

(4) Woomockqua, a girl.

Unfortunately, as with Terheryaquahip's list, none of the names on these lists can be identified on later census lists.

The ransomed captives included three Anglo-Texan boys, Clinton Smith, Adolph Kohn, and Temple Friend; and five Mexican-Texans, four boys, Presleano

Gonzalez, Seferino Trevino, Juan and José María Benavides, and a girl who Tatum named Martha Day. Tatum (1899:138-54) has a highly romanticized account of the release of those captives. There were several other captives who stayed with the Comanches, including Rudolph Fisher. Corwin (1959) contains several accounts of them.

22. There are minor differences of wording between the reports of the council as printed in Winfrey and Day (1959-66:350-61) and that reported in Nye (1969: 168-75). The differences are probably due to different stenographic versions.

23. Nye's account (1969:175-76) closely parallels Campbell's account (1926-28:638-39), but it is not clear if there was another source both were following.

24. Nye (1969:167) reported that some young men from Esihabit's band had gone to San Antonio to steal horses, and other Comanches had killed a surveyor near the Red River. It is not known if they were part of Smith's demand.

25. Nye (1969:179) suggested that the chief had been "thrown away" by his people, but he gave no evidence for the claim; indeed, the chief lived for another five years with apparently great influence both with his people and with the Americans.

26. The names were given in their English translations.

27. Mooney (1898:205) and the Kiowa calendars (1898:339) imply that Pearekaeka was killed in the fight, but he died the following December (Haworth 1875a).

28. Pratt (1964:84-89) has an account of his attempt to arrest Hitetsi, but it has some peculiar details. Pratt said that together with some of his Wichita, Kiowa, Comanche and Apache scouts (unfortunately no listing of those scouts has been found), he went out to where the Indians were being taught how to plow a field. Upon being informed that he was wanted by the post commander, Hitetsi threw off his banket to reveal a gun belt and pistol, ran out into the plowed field, and facing the sun, shouted that he would not surrender. At that he "bounded off like a deer" with Pratt, his scouts, and an army detachment in pursuit. Behind them came Esananaka, Hitetsi's brother, with a strung bow.

Then, according to Pratt, "it so happened that one of my scouts was a younger brother to Little Crow. He told [Horace P. Jones, interpreter] to ask me to let him lariat his brother . . . It was a ruse to let him get away" (Pratt 1964:87). Upon reaching his camp, Hitetsi retrieved a rifle, as did Esananaka, and together they confronted Pratt and the soldiers. Then Cheevers showed up, and a lengthy argument ensued with Cheevers trying to pursuade Hitetsi to go with Pratt. Pratt finally told Jones to "tell Cheevers and Esananaka that I was not sent after them, but as Cheevers is the principal chief, and Esananaka is Little Crow's brother, I think they had better go with us to the commanding officer and talk it over with him." Apparently leaving Hitetsi in camp with no guard, Cheevers, Esananaka, and their wives, and Pratt's whole entourage went back to Fort Sill. Cheevers and Esananaka and their wives were placed in the guardhouse as hostages for Hitetsi, but he had already fled. Pratt said he went to the Kwahadas, but by late summer, Haworth (1975g) said he was with the Esikwita (Mescalero) Apaches.

The peculiar details are, first, by this time, April 1875, Hitetsi must have been at least middle-aged; it is difficult to imagine such a man "bounding off like a deer." Then, while Hitetsi and Esananaka were indeed brothers, there was no other "younger brother," and since no list of the scouts has surfaced, his actual identity is uncertain. Moreover, those two brothers were Cheevers's uncles, his mother's brothers. Finally, there seems to be no other evidence that Cheevers was placed in the guardhouse.

29. There is some confusion here, for Haworth had reported that "on [May] 15th, [Tomichicut] . . . and three others came in with one of the messengers who had been sent to the Quahada camp. They report all the Quahada and a few of the Esa-quita [Mescalero Apaches] are coming in" (Haworth 1875d).

30. Sturm's account is in marked contrast to the impression given by Wallace and Hoebel: "On a sultry summer day in June, 1875, a small band of starving Comanche Indians straggled in to Fort Sill" (1952:3). The number that surrendered that day, 400 people, was neither small (but cf. Wallace and Hoebel 1952:327, where they characterize it as a "large band") nor starving. Further, Wallace and Hoebel (1952:327) imply that the group that surrendered was under Quanah; Sturm was clear that Isatai was the leader.

31. It is not known why Peahin and Ahkes accompanied Black Horse.

32. Leeper made no census of the population present; the number is based on the number of Comanches brought from the Brazos reservation by Neighbors.

33. The complete returns for November 1869 through June 1877 are in Lee, Tatum, and Haworth (1869-77).

34. Otherwise unidentified.

35. It is thus obvious that the otherwise anonymous 1874 list in table 7.12 is Haworth's band census.

36. It is beyond the scope of this study to comment more fully on the significance of those population totals. At a minimum, they are less than one-eighth the population size estimated for the Comanches less than a century before. Indeed, the number would go lower: the 1879 census counted only some 1,400 individuals. The effective causes of the decline are unclear.

37. In 1933 Howard White Wolf had emphasized the role of his stepfather/father's brother, saying that Esarosavit and Tabenanaka divided the duties of peace and war chiefs between them. Although both men were prominent among the Yamparikas who were still out, both leading large local bands, the unequivocal attribution of those titles is misleading.

Chapter 8

1. For another possible identification of Tabe Peté's group, see the discussion of the Tenewas below.

2. The earliest use of the term ethnogenesis I have found is as the title of a poem by Henry Timrod (1861), celebrating the establishment of the Southern Confederacy.

There is an extensive literature on ethnogenesis by Soviet ethnographers, for whom the question of nations was of basic theoretical importance. Unfortunately, relatively few of the Russian materials have been translated into English (Bromley 1983, 1984, 1987), and those that have are more concerned with typology and with inter-ethnos processes than with the origins of ethnoses and nations; indeed, the Soviets explicitly asserted that the primordial human condition was "tribal," an assertion leading directly into the classic Problem of Tribe.

References

Abbreviations

AGI   Archivo General de Indias (Seville, Spain; microfilm copies, H. H. Bancroft Library, University of California, Berkeley, and Western History Collection, University of Oklahoma, Norman.)

AGN   Archivo General de la Nación (Mexico City; photographic copies, University of New Mexico [see NMA]; the AGN has been subsequently reorganized [see Civiera Taboada and Bribiesca Sumano 1977].)

AGN-PI   Archivo General de la Nación, Provincias Internas (See AGN.)

ARCIA   Annual Report of the Commissioner of Indian Affairs (Published separately by the Office of Indian Affairs and in the U. S. Congressional serial set; pagination varies [see Jones 1955].)

BA   Béxar Archives of Spanish and Mexican Texas (University of Texas, Austin; microfilm edition.)

MANM   Mexican Archives of New Mexico (New Mexico State Records Center, Santa Fe; microfilm edition [1969]. Wherever possible, cross-references to the NMA are provided.)

NAA   National Anthropological Archives (Smithsonian Institution, Washington, D.C.)

NARS   National Archives and Record Service (Washington, D. C.)

NMA   New Mexico Archives (Photographic reproductions of documents relating to Spanish, Mexican, and Territorial New Mexico, Zimmerman Library, University of New Mexico, Albuquerque. Documents from the AGN in the NMA are cited under their original numbering system [but see AGN note]. Wherever possible, cross-references to the MANM are provided.)

OHS-KA   Oklahoma Historical Society, Kiowa Agency Records (Oklahoma City.)

SANM   Spanish Archives of New Mexico (New Mexico State Records Center, Santa Fe; microfilm edition [1967]. Citations are given first to the Bandelier document number [e.g., T-1925; see Twitchell 1914], then to the microfilm edition.)

517

Abel, Annie H.
1915a   The American Indian as Slaveholder and Secessionist. Cleveland: Arthur H. Clark.
1915b   The Official Correspondence of James C. Calhoun. Washington, D.C.: Government Printing Office.
1916   The Journal of John Greiner. Old Santa Fe, 1916:189-243.
1939   Tabeau's Narrative of Loisel's Expedition to the Upper Missouri. Norman: University of Oklahoma Press.

Abert, James W.
1846   Journal of Lieutenant J. W. Abert, from Bent's Fort to St. Louis, in 1845. 29th Cong., 1st sess., Sen. Exec. Doc. 438. Reprinted as *Through the Country of the Comanche Indians in the Fall of the Year 1845.* Edited by John Galvin. San Francisco: John Howell, 1970. (Page citations are to the reprint edition.)

Abreú, Santiago
1834   [Letter to Ministerio de Guerra y Marina, Mar. 14, 1834.] (MANM 14: 690.)

Adams, Eleanor
1953   Bishop Tamarón's Visitation of New Mexico, 1760. New Mexico Historical Review 28:193-221.

Adams, Eleanor, and Fray Angelico Chavez
1956   The Missions of New Mexico, 1776: A Description by Fray Francisco Atanasio Dominguez with Other Contemporary Documents. Albuquerque: University of New Mexico Press.

Adams, Francis Raymond, Jr.
1955   An Annotated Edition of the Personal Letters of Robert E. Lee, April, 1855-April, 1861. Ph.D. Diss., University of Maryland.

Adams, Richard N.
1966   Power and Power Domains. America Latina 9:3-21.

Ahumada, Mateo
1825a   [Letter to Juan José Llanos, Aug. 8, 1825.] (BA 83:150.)
1825b   [Letter to Antonio Elozúa, Aug. 21, 1825.] (BA 83:599.)

Alamán, Lucas
1824a   [Letter to José María Zambrano, June 1, 1824.] (BA 77:196.)
1824b   [Letter to José Antonío Saucedo, Sept. 3, 1824.] (BA 77:745.)
1942   Historía de Mejico. Mexico, D.F.: Editorial Jus.

Alencaster, Joaquin del Real
1805   [Letter to Nemesio Salcedo, Nov. 20, 1805 (#30).] (SANM T-1925, 15: 993.)
1806   [Letter to Nemesio Salcedo, Jan. 4, 1806.] (SANM T-1942, 16:2.)

Allen, Henry Easton
1939   The Parrilla Expedition to the Red River in 1759. Southwestern Historical Quarterly 43:53-71.

Allen, Joel Asaph
    1877   History of the American Bison. Annual Report for the Year 1875, U.S. Geological Survey. Washington, D.C.

Andrade, Cayetano
    1825   [Letter to Antonio Elozúa, Nov. 20, 1825.] (BA 86:100.)

Anonymous
    1803   [Indian Expenses, Oct. 31, 1802.] (SANM T-1632, 14:1029.)
    1827   [Instructions for Juan Cristóbal Tenorío, Apr. 18, 1827.] (NMA 1827-359.)
    1830   [Accounts of the Indian Fund, Dec. 31, 1830.] (MANM 12:388; also NMA 1830-1212.)
    1844   [List of Indians Who Arrived in This Capital of Santa Fe, July 31, 1844.] (MANM 37:651.)
    1874   [Names of Chiefs and Headmen and Numbers in Bands; Delawares, Comanches, Apaches, Kiowas, 1874] (OHS-KA 1A:25.)

Anza, Juan Bautista de
    1786   [Letter to Jacobo Ugarte y Loyola, Nov. 18, 1786.] (AGN-PI, tomo 65, exp. 2.)

Aranda, Pedro
    1811   [Letter to José Menchaca, Feb. 26, 1811.] (BA 48:131.)

Arce, José Antonio
    1826   [Message to Chihuahua State Legislature, July 1, 1826.] (MANM 5:451.)

Archuleta, Juan Andres
    1840   [Letter to Guadalupe Miranda, May 3, 1840.] (MANM 27:1031.)

Armagost, James L.
    1989   An Interpretation of Comanche Names in an Eighteenth-Century Document. Tlalocan 11:367-73.

Armijo, Isidro, ed.
    1929   Information Communicated by Juan Candalaria, Resident of This Villa de San Francisco de Alburquerque, Born 1692, Age 82. New Mexico Historical Review 4:274-97.

Armijo, Manuel
    1839   [Letter to Juan Andres Archuleta, July 31, 1839.] (MANM 26:485.)
    1840   [Letter to Ministerio de Guerra y Marina, Sept. 7, 1840.] (MANM 27:1091.)
    1843a   [Letter to Ministerio de Guerra y Marina, Mar. 22, 1843.] (MANM 28:1522.)
    1843b   [Letter to Mariano Martínez, Oct. 22, 1843.] (MANM 33:543.)

Armiñan, Benito de
    1814   [Letter to Joaquin de Arredondo, Aug. 15, 1814.] (BA 54:122.)

Armstrong, Francis W.
    1835   [Letter to Elbert Herring, Mar. 6, 1835.] (Letters Received from the Western Superintendency. NARS microfilm pub. M234, 921:905.)

Armstrong, William

1839 [Letter to Crawford, June 8, 1839.] (Letters Received from the Western Superintendency. NARS microfilm pub. M234, 922:597.)

1845 [Annual report, Acting Supterintendent, Western Territory.] (ARCIA, 1845, doc. 15.)

Arocha, Juan José

1827a [List of the Effects Bought to Regale the Friendly Nations, June 11, 1827.] (MANM 7:554.)

1827b [Letter to Manuel Armijo, Oct. 1, 1827.] (MANM 6:1402.)

1828a [Letter to Alcalde, San Miguel del Bado, May 21, 1828.] (NMA 1828-495.)

1828b [Letter to Gefe Politico, Aug. 8, 1828.] (MANM 8:151; also NMA 1828-883.)

1829 [Diary of Expedition, Aug. 1, 1829.] (NMA 1829-460.)

Arocha, Juan José, José Francisco Ruíz, and José Cavallero

1828 [Ratification of 1826 Treaty, Aug. 28, 1828.] (MANM 7:1155; also NMA 1828-943.)

Arrambide, Juan Ignacio de

1810 [Letter to Bernardo Bonavia, Oct. 19, 1810.] (BA 46:953.)

1812 [Interrogation of Comanches, Aug. 2, 1812.] (BA 46:248.)

Arredondo, Joaquin de

1814 [Letter to Benito de Arminan, Jan. 31, 1814.] (BA 53:508.)

1821 [Letter to Juan Cortés, Mar. 16, 1821.] (BA 67:362.)

Arthur, George W.

1975 An Introduction to the Ecology of Early Historic Communal Bison Hunting among the Northern Plains Indians. Archaeological Survey of Canada 37. Ottawa: National Museums of Canada.

Attocknie, Francis Joseph

1965 [Life Sketch of Ten Bears.] Manuscript in Kavanagh's possession.

1969 [Interview T-508, June 9, 1969.] Doris Duke Oral History Project. Western History Collection, University of Oklahoma, Norman.

Auerbach, Herbert S.

1943 Father Escalante's Journal With Related Documents and Maps. Utah Historical Quarterly 11.

Augur, Christopher C.

1872 [Letter to Lawrie Tatum, Nov. 22, 1872.] (OHS-KA 42:99.)

1873 [Letter to John W. Davidson, Apr. 14, 1873.] (OHS-KA 42:130.)

Babb, Theodore Adolphus

1912 In the Bosom of the Comanches. Dallas: John F. Worley Press.

Baca, Bartolomé

1824a [Letter to Benjamin O'Fallon, Feb 24, 1824.] (Letters Received from the St. Louis Superintendency. NARS microfilm pub. M234, 747.)

1824b [Letter to Gaspar de Ochoa, Aug. 15, 1824.] (MANM 3:926.)

1825a [Letter to Gaspar de Ochoa, Mar. 5, 1825.] (MANM 3:955.)

1825b [Letter to Comandante General, 18 May 1825.] (MANM 3:963.)

1844 [Letter to Comandante General, July 31, 1844.] (MANM 35:650.)

Baca, Manuel

    1813 [Letter to José Manrrique, June 1, 1813.] (SANM T-2492, 17:731.)

Baca, Manuel Antonío

    1830a [Letter to José Antonío Chavéz, Jan. 30, 1830.] (NMA 1830-85.)

    1830b [Letter to José Antonío Chavéz, Aug. 27, 1830.] (NMA 1830-636.)

Backus, William H.

    1862 [Report, Dec. 1, 1862.] Official Records of the War of the Rebellion, ser. 1, vol. 15, 153.

Badger, N. D.

    1869 [List of Indians at Fort Sill, I.T., Nov. 30, 1869.] (OHS-KA 1a:857.)

Baker, T. Linsay, and Billy R. Harrison

    1986 Adobe Walls: The History and Archaeology of the 1874 Trading Post. College Station: Texas A & M University Press.

Bamforth, Douglas

    1988 Ecology and Human Organization on the Great Plains. New York: Plenum Press.

Bancroft, Hubert Howe

    1889a History of Arizona and New Mexico, 1530-1888. Reprint, Albuquerque: Horn and Wallace, 1962. (Page citations are to the reprint edition.)

    1889b History of the Life of William Gilpin. San Francisco: History Co.

Barker, Eugene C.

    1926 Life of Stephen F. Austin. Nashville and Dallas: Cokesbury Press.

Barnes, Thomas C., Thomas H. Naylor, and Charles W. Polzer

    1981 Northern New Spain: A Research Guide. Tucson: University of Arizona Press.

Barragán, Manuel Rudencindo

    1832a [Letter to Antonio Elozúa, Apr. 28, 1832.] (BA 149:642.)

    1832b [Letter to Antonio Elozúa, May 6, 1832.] (BA 149:822.)

    1833 [Letter to Antonio Elozúa, Feb. 22, 1833.] (BA 155:252.)

Barrera, Manuel

    1821 [Letter to José Angel Navarro, Dec. 3, 1821.] (BA 69:284.)

Bastrop, Felipe Enrique Neri, Barón de

    1823 [Letter to García, Aug. 15, 1823.] (BA 75:431.)

Battey, Thomas C.

    1877 The Life and Adventures of a Quaker among the Indians. Reprint, Norman: University of Oklahoma Press, 1968. (Page citations are to the reprint edition.)

Baugh, Timothy G.

    1991 Ecology and Exchange: The Dynamics of Plains-Pueblo Interaction. In Farmers, Hunters, and Colonists: The Interaction between the Southwest and the Southern Plains, edited by Katherine A. Speilman, 107-27. Tucson: University of Arizona Press.

Baylor, John R.
    1856   [Annual report, Special Agent, Texas Indians.] (ARCIA 1856, doc. 69.)

Beckwith, E. G.
    1855   Report of Exploration of a Route for the Pacific Rail Road near the 38th and 39th Parallels of Latitude from North of Kansas to the Sevier River in the Great Basin. Report of the Secretary of War Communicating the Several Railroad Expeditions. 33rd Cong., 1st sess., House Exec. Doc. 129.

Beede, Cyrus
    1873a   [Letter to E. P. Smith, July 1, 1873.] (Letters Received from the Kiowa Agency. NARS microfilm pub. M234, 378:344.)
    1873b   [Letter to E. P. Smith, July 31, 1873.] (Letters Received from the Kiowa Agency. NARS microfilm pub. M234, 378:385.)

Benavides, Adan
    1989   The Bexar Archives (1717-1836): A Name Guide. Austin: University of Texas Press.

Benavides, Placido
    1834   [Letter to Juan Nepomuceno Seguin, Aug. 22, 1834.] (BA 162:932.)

Bent, George
    1905   [Letter to George E. Hyde, Mar. 6, 1905.] (George Bent Papers. Western Americana Collection. Beinecke Rare Book and Manuscript Library, Yale University.)

Bent, William
    1859   [Annual report, Agent, Upper Arkansas Agency]. (ARCIA 1859, doc. 35.)

Benton, Thomas Hart
    1825   [Speeches on the Inland Trade between Missouri and Mexico, Jan. 3-25, 1825.] Register of Debates in Congress, 1825-37. 14 vols. Washington: Gales and Seaton.

Bergmann, Edward H.
    1865   [Letter to Assistant Adjutant General, Department of New Mexico, Jan. 21, 1865.] Official Records of the War of the Rebellion, ser. 1, vol. 48, pt. 1, 611-12.
    1866   [Letter to Cyrus H. DeForrest, Aug. 11, 1866.] (Letters Received, Military Department of New Mexico. NARS microfilm pub. M1088, 2:670; also Letters Sent, July 24, 1865-June 12, 1869, Military Department of New Mexico, no. 1866-98 . NARS Record Group 393, pt. 4, entry 93.)

Berkhofer, Robert F.
    1971   The Political Context of a New Indian History. Pacific Historical Review. 40:367-82.

Berlandier, Jean Louis
    1844   Caza del Oso y Cibalo en el Nor-oeste de Tejas. El Museu Mexicano. Tomo III:177-87.

1969   The Indians of Texas in 1830. Edited by John C. Ewers. Washington, D.C.: Smithsonian Institution Press.

1980   Journey to Mexico During the Years 1826 to 1834. Translated and edited by S. M. Ohlendorf, J. M. Bigelow, and M. M. Standifer. Austin: Texas State Historical Association.

Bieber, Ralph

1937   The Southern Trails to California in 1849. Glendale, Cal.: Arthur H. Clark.

Biesele, Rutolph L.

1930   The History of the German Settlements in Texas, 1831–1861. Austin: Van Boeckmann-Jones.

Bigelow, John

1856   Memoir of the Life and Public Service of John Charles Frémont. New York: Derby and Jackson.

Blair, W. Frank

1950   The Biotic Provinces of Texas. Texas Journal of Science 2:93–117.

Blake, George A.

1855   [Letter to W. T. Magruder, July 20, 1855.] (Letters Received, Military Department of New Mexico. NARS microfilm pub. M1120, 4:592.)

Bogy, Charles, and W. R. Irwin

1866a   [Letter to Lewis Bogy, Nov. 26, 1866.] (Letters Received from the Kiowa Agency. NARS microfilm pub. M234, 375:55.)

1866b   [Letter to Lewis Bogy, Dec. 8, 1866.] (Documents concerning Negotiation of Indian Treaties. NARS microfilm pub. T494, 7:699.)

Bollaert, William

1956   William Bollaert's Texas. Edited by W. E. Hollon and R. L. Butler. Norman: University of Oklahoma Press.

Bolton, Herbert Eugene

1913   Guide to Materials for the History of the United States in the Principal Archives of Mexico. Washington, D.C.: Carnegie Institute.

1914   Athanase de Mézières and the Louisiana-Texas Frontier. 2 vols. Cleveland: Arthur H. Clark.

1915a   French Intrusions into New Mexico, 1749–52. In The Pacific Ocean in History, edited by H. Morse Stephens and H. E. Bolton, 389–407. New York: The MacMillan Co.

1915b   Texas in the Middle Eighteenth Century: Studies in Spanish Colonial History and Administration. Berkeley: University of California Press.

1950   Pageant in the Wilderness: The Story of the Escalante Expedition to the Interior Basin, 1776. Utah Historical Quarterly 18.

Bonavia, Bernardo

1810a   [Letter to Nemesio Salcedo, Aug. 8, 1810.] (BA 46:312.)

1810b   [Letter to Manuel de Salcedo, Oct. 17, 1810.] (BA 46:936.)

1816   [Letter to Pedro Maria de Allande, 12 August 1816.] (SANM T-2667; 18:682.)

Bonnell, George W.

1838   Annual Report, November 3, 1838. (Reprinted in 30th Cong., 1st sess., Sen. Committee Report 171, 38–50.)

1840   Topographical Description of Texas. Reprint, Waco: Texian Press, 1964. (Page citations are to the reprint edition.)

Boone, Albert G.

1861a   [Truce between A. G. Boone, Tapowinewah and Cochaqua, Sept. 6, 1861. Enclosure in Boone to W. P. Dole, Sept. 7, 1861.] (Letters Received from the Upper Arkansas Agency. NARS microfilm pub. M234, 878:517.)

1861b   [Letter to A. M. Robinson, Mar. 14, 1861. Enclosure in letter from A. M. Robinson to W. P. Dole, Mar. 28, 1861.] (Letters Received from the Upper Arkansas Agency. NARS microfilm pub. M234, 878:587.)

1861c   [Annual report, Agent, Upper Arkansas Agency]. (ARCIA 1861, doc. 39.)

1862   [Letter to W. P. Dole, Feb. 2, 1862.] (Letters Received from the Upper Arkansas Agency. NARS microfilm pub. M234, 878:doc. B1086.)

1869   [Letter to N. G. Taylor, Jan. 6, 1869.] (Letters Received from the Kiowa Agency. NARS microfilm pub. M234, 376:58.)

Bradford, William

1819   [Letter to John C. Calhoun, Mar. 28, 1819.] (Letters Received by the Secretary of War Related to Indian Affairs. NARS microfilm pub. M221, 80:doc. B287.)

Bromley, Yulian V.

1983   Ethnic Processes. Moscow: Social Sciences Today Editorial Board, USSR Academy of Sciences.

1984   Theoretical Ethnography. Moscow: General Editorial Board for Foreign Publications.

1987–88 Ethnic Processes in the USSR. [Original Russian text, 1983.] Soviet Anthropology and Archeology, Winter.

Brown, Jacob

1827   [Relative to the Establishment of a Miltary Post for the Protection of the Trade to Santa Fé, in New Mexico.] American State Papers, Military Affairs, vol. 3, 615.

Brown, John Henry

1899   Indian Wars and Pioneers of Texas. Austin: L. E. Daniell.

Brown, William R., Jr.

1986   Comancheria Demography. Panhandle Plains Historical Review 59:1–17.

Browning, O. H.

1867a   [Letter to N. G. Taylor, Apr. 17, 1867.] (Records of the New Mexico Superintendency. NARS microfilm pub. T–21, 7.)

1867b   [Letter to N. G. Taylor, Dec. 19, 1867.] (NARS microfilm pub. M234, 375:475.)

Brunot, Felix, Nathan Bishop, and W. E. Dodge
1869   [Report of Board of Indian Commissioners, Nov. 23, 1869.] (ARCIA 1869, doc. C.)
Buchanan, James
1845   Message from Secretary of State James Buchanan to Chargé d'Affaires Donelson. 29th Cong., 1st sess., Sen. Exec. Doc. 1.
Buckner, Simon B.
1851   [Letter to I. McDowell, Nov. 26, 1851.] (Letters Sent, no. 1851-20, Post Records, Fort Atkinson. NARS Record Group 393, pt. 4.)
1852a   [Letter to I. McDowell, Feb. 8, 1852.] (Letters Sent, no. 1852-54, Post Records, Fort Atkinson. NARS Record Group 393, pt. 4.)
1852b   [Letter to I. McDowell, Mar. 10, 1852.] (Letters Sent, no. 1852-62, Post Records, Fort Atkinson. NARS Record Group 393, pt. 4.)
1852c   [Letter to D. D. Mitchell, Mar. 10, 1852.] (Letters Received from the Central Superintendency. NARS microfilm pub. M234, 55:157; also Letters Sent, no. 1852-68, Post Records, Fort Atkinson; NARS Record Group 393, pt. 4.)
1852d   [Letter to I. McDowell, Mar. 30, 1852.] (Letters Sent, no. 1852-70, Post Records, Fort Atkinson; NARS Record Group 393, pt. 4.)
1852e   [Letter to D. D. Mitchell, May 9, 1852.] (Letters Sent, no. 1852-85, Post Records, Fort Atkinson; NARS Record Group 393, pt. 4.)
1852f   [Letter to I. McDowell, May 10, 1852.] (Letters Sent, no. 1851-87, Post Records, Fort Atkinson; NARS Record Group 393, pt. 4.)
1852g   [Letter to I. McDowell, May 19, 1852.] (Letters Sent, no. 1852-95, Post Records, Fort Atkinson; NARS Record Group 393, pt. 4.)
1852h   [Letter to I. McDowell, May 30, 1852.] (Letters Sent, no. 1852-102, Post Records, Fort Atkinson; NARS Record Group 393, pt. 4.)
1852i   [Letter to I. McDowell, June 1, 1852.] (Letters Sent, no. 1852-105, Post Records, Fort Atkinson; NARS Record Group 393, pt. 4.)
1852j   [Letter to I. McDowell, June 9, 1852.] (Letters Sent, no. 1852-111, Post Records, Fort Atkinson; NARS Record Group 393, pt. 4.)
1852k   [Letter to I. McDowell, June 10, 1852.] (Letters Sent, no. 1852-112, Post Records, Fort Atkinson; NARS Record Group 393, pt. 4.)
1852l   [Letter to I. McDowell, July 11, 1852.] (Letters Sent, no. 1852-120, Post Records, Fort Atkinson; NARS Record Group 393, pt. 4.)
Burnet, David G.
1824   Indians of Texas. *Cincinnati Literary Gazette,* May 8.
1840   Indians of Texas, A Series of Letters Originally Addressed to Col. John Jamison, Deceased, Late Indian Agent at Nacogdoches. *Telegraph and Texas Register*, July 1.
1847   [Letter to R. S. Neighbors, Aug. 20, 1847.] (30th Cong., 1st sess., Sen. Committee Report, 7-8.)
1851   The Comanches and other Tribes of Texas. *In* Historical and Statistical Information Respecting the History Conditions and Prospects of the

Indians Tribes of the United States, edited by Henry R. Schoolcraft. Vol. 1, 229–41. Philadelphia: Lippincott, Grambo.

Bustamente, Anastacio, José Antonio Saucedo, Mateo Ahumada, Ramon Muzquiz, José Francisco Ruíz, José Mariano Guerra, Quellune, Yncoroy, and Quellucare

 1827 [Cease-Fire Agreement, July 28, 1827.] (BA 105:800.)

Bustamente, Juan Domingo

 1724 [Proceedings of Council of War, Jan. 24–Feb. 11, 1724.] (SANM T-324, 6:104.)

 1725 [*Bando* on Indian Trade, Sept. 17, 1725.] (SANM T-340, 7:357.)

Butler, H. B., A. A. Singer, and J. Z. Leyendecker

 1867 [Comanche Vocabulary, collected in Laredo, Texas.] (NAA ms. 767.)

Butler, Pierce M.

 1846 [Letter to W. Medill, Mar. 4, 1846.] (Misc. Letters Received by the Office of Indian Affairs. NARS microfilm pub. M234, 444:44.)

Butler, Pierce M., and M. G. Lewis

 1846 [Letter to W. Medill, Aug. 8, 1846.] (Documents concerning the Negotiation of Indian Treaties. NARS microfilm pub. T494, 4:259. 29th Cong., 2d Sess., House Doc. 76. Also 30th Cong., 1st sess., Sen. Committee Report 171, 29–37.) (Page citations are to House Doc. 76.)

Cabello y Robles, Domingo

 1780a [Letter to Teodoro de Croix, Feb. 12, 1780.] (BA 13:911.)

 1780b [Letter to Teodoro de Croix, July 10, 1780.] (BA 14:294.)

 1780c [Letter to Teodoro de Croix, Aug. 17, 1780.] (BA 14:370.)

 1781 [Monthly Report, Dec. 31, 1781.] (BA 14:888.)

 1783 [Monthly Cavalry Report, June 30, 1783.] (BA 15:512.)

 1784a [Letter to Felipe de Neve, July 20, 1784.] (BA 16:134.)

 1784b [Letter to Felipe de Neve, Aug. 19, 1784.] (BA 16:261.)

 1784c [Letter to Felipe de Neve, Sept. 20, 1784.] (BA 16:287.)

 1784d [*Ynforme* of the Governor of Texas Don Domingo Cabello on the Peace with the Lipan Apaches in the Colony of Nuevo Santander, Sept. 30, 1784.] (AGN-PI, tomo 64, exp. 1.)

 1785a [Letter to Joseph Antonio Rengel, Feb. 18, 1785.] (BA 16:447.)

 1785b [Inventory of Goods given by Pedro Vial to Comanche Chiefs, June 17, 1785.] (BA 16:744.)

 1785c [Letter to Joseph Antonio Rengel, Nov. 25, 1785.] (BA 17:68.)

 1785d [Letter to Joseph Antonio Rengel, Dec. 9, 1785.] (BA 17:88.)

 1785e [Letter to Joseph Antonio Rengel, Dec. 10, 1785.] (BA 17:97.)

 1786a [Letter to Joseph Antonio Rengel, Jan. 10, 1786.] (BA 17:181.)

 1786b [Letter to Joseph Antonio Rengel, Mar. 14, 1786.] (BA 17:324.)

 1786c [Responses of the Governor of Texas to the Questions which the Comandante General of the Provincias Internas Made in his Official Letter of January 27, 1786, Covering Various Circumstances of the Eastern Comanche Indians, Apr. 30, 1786.] (BA 17:417.)

 1786d [Letter to Jacobo Ugarte y Loyola, July 30, 1786.] (BA 17:607.)

 1786e [Letter to Jacobo Ugarte y Loyola, Sept. 24, 1786.] (BA 17:833.)

Calhoun, John C.
    1820a   [Circular Letter to Agents, Feb. 19, 1820.] (Letters Received by the Secretary of War Related to Indian Affairs; NARS microfilm pub. M15, 4.)
    1820b   [Letter to George Gray, May 16, 1820.] (Letters Received by the Secretary of War Related to Indian Affairs. NARS microfilm pub. M6, 11.)

Calvo, José
    1831   [General Order, Oct. 16, 1831.] (MANM, 13:483.)

Campa, Arthur L.
    1942   Los Comanches, A New Mexico Folk Drama. The University of New Mexico Bulletin. Language Series, vol. 7, no. 1.

Campbell, Charles E.
    1926-28 Down Among the Red Men. Collections of the Kansas State Historical Society, vol. 17, 623-91.

Capron, Horace
    1852   [Letter to George T. Howard, Sept. 30, 1852] (Letters Received from the Texas Agency. NARS microfilm pub. M234, 858:1069.)

Carleton, C. H.
    1874   [Letter to Commanding Officer, Fort Griffen, Tex., May 2, 1874.] (Letters Received from the Military Department of Texas, no. 1771 DT 74. NARS Record Group 393, pt. 1, entry 4875.)

Carleton, James H.
    1864a   [Letter to Michael Steck, Santa Fe, Oct. 29, 1864.] Official Records of the War of the Rebellion, ser. 1, vol. 41, pt. 4, 319-23.
    1864b   [Letter to Michael Steck, 1864.] Official Records of the War of the Rebellion, ser. 1, vol. 41, pt. 4, 497.
    1867   [Letter to W. S. Hancock, Jan. 23, 1867.] (Letters Sent, Military Department of New Mexico. NARS microfilm pub. M1072, 4:55.)

Carroll, H. Bailey, and C. V. Haggard
    1942   Three New Mexico Chronicles. Albuquerque: Quivira Society.

Carson, Christopher
    1864   [Reports on Engagement with Indians at Adobe Fort, on the Canadian River, N. Mex., Dec. 6, 1864, Dec. 16, 1864.] Official Records of the War of the Rebellion, ser. 1, vol. 41, pt. 1, 939-44.

Carter, Clarence Edwin
    1934-75 The Territorial Papers of the United States. 28 vols. Washington, D.C.: Government Printing Office.

Carter, John L.
    1966   John Hatcher. In The Mountain Men and the Fur Trade. Edited by Leroy R. Hafen. Vol. 4, 125-36. Glendale, Cal.: Arthur H. Clark.

Casagrande, Joseph B.
    1954-55 Comanche Linguistic Acculturation. International Journal of American Linguistics 20:140-51, 217-37, 21:8-25.

Cash, Joseph H., and G. W. Wolff
  1974   The Comanche People. Phoenix: Indian Tribal Series.
Cass, Lewis
  1834   Message of the Secretary of War. American State Papers, Military
            Affairs, vol. 5, 358–61.
  1835   [Letter to M. Stokes, M. Arbuckle, and F. W. Armstrong, Mar. 26,
            1835.] (Letters Received from the Western Superintendency. NARS
            microfilm pub. M640, 1:314.)
Castañeda, Carlos E.
  1936   Our Catholic Heritage in Texas, 1519–1936. 6 vols. Austin, Tex.: Van
            Boeckmann-Jones.
Catlin, George
  1841   Letters and Notes on the Manners, Customs, and Conditions of the
            North American Indians. 2 vols. Reprint, Minneapolis: Ross and
            Haines, 1965. (Page citations are to the reprint edition.)
Cavallero, José
  1823   [Adjustment and List of the Accounts of Gifts Given in Regaling the
            Gentile Indian Nations in Peace from 1 November 1822, until 31 Octo-
            ber 1823, Oct. 31, 1823.] (MANM, 3:114; also NMA 1823-151.)
Chacón, Fernando
  1797a   [Report on the Election of a Comanche General, Nov. 18, 1797.]
            (SANM T-1404, 13:467.)
  1797b   [Letter to Pedro de Nava, Nov. 19, 1797.] (SANM T-1405, 14:234.)
  1801   [Summary of Events, Aug. 6–31, 1801.] (SANM T-1565, 14:822.)
  1803   [Summary of Events, June 29, 1803.] (SANM T-1673, 15:71.)
  1804   [Letter to Nemesio Salcedo, May 16, 1804 (#6).] (SANM T-1724, 15:
            266.)
Chavez, Angelico
  1976   The Domínguez-Escalante Journal. Their Expedition through
            Colorado, Utah, Arizona, and New Mexico. Provo: Brigham Young
            University Press.
Chávez, José Antonio
  1829a   [Letter to Jefe Politico, July 14, 1829.] (MANM, 9:696; also NMA
            1829–378.)
  1829b   [Diary of Expedition, Aug. 2, 1829.] (NMA 1829-463.)
  1830a   [Letter to José Antonio Vizcarra, Jan. 15, 1830.] (NMA 1830-99.)
  1830b   [Letter to Lucas Alamán, Aug. 26, 1830. (#79).] (NMA 1830-632.)
  1831   [Letter to José Antonio Vizcarra, Oct. 23, 1831.] (MANM, 13:488;
            also NMA 1831-695.)
Chávez, José Antonío, Juan José Arocha, and José Francisco Ruíz
  1829   [Treaty with the Comanches, July 26, 1829.] (NMA 1829-443.)
Chilton, R. W.
  1852a   [Letter to D. D. Mitchell, Aug. 10, 1852.] (Letters Sent, no. 1852-130,
            Post Records, Fort Atkinson; NARS Record Group 393, pt. 4.)

1852b [Letter to A. N. Lea, Aug. 23, 1852.] (Letters Sent, no. 1852-134, Post Records, Fort Atkinson. NARS microfilm pub. M234, 55:67; also NARS Record Group 393, pt. 4.)

1853 [Letter to S. Cooper, July 27, 1853.] (Letters Sent, no. 1853-193, Post Records, Fort Atkinson; NARS Record Group 393, pt. 4.)

Chouteau, Auguste P.
1837 [Letter to C. A. Harris, Nov. 25, 1837.] (Letters Received from the Western Superintendency. NARS microfilm pub. M234, 922:159.)

1838 [Letter to C. A. Harris, June 28, 1838.] (Letters Received from the Western Superintendency. NARS microfilm pub. M234, 922:353.)

Chouteau, Paul Legeste
1837 [Letter to William Armstrong, Feb. 1, 1837; enclosure in W. Armstrong to C. A. Harris, Feb. 13, 1837] (Letters Received from the Western Superintendency. NARS microfilm pub. M234, 922:28.)

Civiera Taboada, Miguel, and María Elana Bribiesca Sumano
1977 Guia descriptiva de los ramos que constituyen el Archivo General de la Nación. Mexico, D. F.: Archivo General de la Nación.

Clark, Edward L.
1881 [Report to William P. Clark, May 18, 1881.] (OHS-KA 11:513; also 47:7.)

Clark, Wahnee C.
1988 The Grand Celebration: An Indian Delegation to Washington. Chronicles of Oklahoma 66:192–205.

Clark, William
1824 [Letter to Secretary of War, Feb 11, 1824.] (NARS microfilm pub. M234, 747.)

Clark, William P.
1885 The Indian Sign Language. Philadelphia: L. R. Hamersly.

Clarke, Mary W.
1969 David G. Burnet. Austin: Pemberton Press.

Clelland, R. W.
1853 [Letter to G. Manypenny, May 6, 1853.] (Letters Received from the Central Superintendency. NARS microfilm pub. M234, 55:292.)

Clifford, James
1988 The Predicament of Culture. Cambridge: Harvard University Press.

Clift, W. H.
1924 Warren's Trading Post. Chronicles of Oklahoma 2:129–40.

Clum, Henry R.
1873a [Telegram to J. M. Haworth, Dec. 2, 1873.] (Letters Sent by the Office of Indian Affairs. NARS microfilm pub. M21, 144.)

1873b [Telegram to J. M. Haworth, Dec. 2, 1873.] (Letters Sent by the Office of Indian Affairs. NARS microfilm pub. M21, 144.)

Codallos y Rabál, Joachín
1746 [Bando on Indian Trade, July 20, 1746.] (SANM T-495, 8:200–32.)

Cohen, Abner K.

1969   Political Anthropology: The Analysis of the Symbolism of Power Relations. Man, n.s., 4:215-35.

Colley, S. G.

1862   [Letter to William Dole, Aug. 11, 1862.] (Letters Received from the
Upper Arkansas Agency. NARS microfilm pub. M234, 878:668.)

1864   [Annual report, Agent, Upper Arkansas Agency.] (ARCIA 1864, doc.
94 1/2.)

Colson, Elizabeth

1954   Review of The Comanches: Lords of the South Plains, by Ernest Wallace and E. Adamson Hoebel. Man 8:13-14.

Comanche Field Party

1933   Field Notes of Gustav C. Carlson, E. Adamson Hoebel, and Waldo
Wedel, June 30-Aug. 16, 1933. (Carlson's and Wedel's notes are in
the National Anthropological Archives, Smithsonian Institution;
Hoebel's notes are in the American Philosophical Society Library,
Philadelphia.)

Concha, Fernando de la

1787   [Letter to Jacobo Ugarte y Loyola, Nov. 10, 1787.] (AGN-PI, tomo 65,
exp. 1.)

1788   [Ynforme to Jacobo Ugarte y Loyola, June 26, 1788.] (AGN-PI, tomo
65, exp. 5.)

1790   [Letter to Jacobo Ugarte y Loyola, Sept. 7, 1790.] (SANM T-1090, 12:
297.)

1791   [Ynforme Apr. 20, 1791.] (AGN-PI, tomo 65, no. 219.)

1792   [Letter to Viceroy Cónde Revilla Gigedo, July 20, 1792.] (SANM T-
1200, 13:111.)

1794   Advice on Governing New Mexico, 1794. Translated and edited by
Donald Worchester. New Mexico Historical Review 24:236-54.

Cónde, Alejo Garcia

1818   [Letter to Facundo Melgares, Nov. 9, 1818.] (SANM T-2771, 19:438.)

1819   [Letter to Facundo Melgares, May 11, 1819.] (SANM T-2819,
19:711.)

Connelly, Henry

1864   [Letter to Michael Steck, Nov. 16, 1864.] (Steck Papers, New Mexico
State Archives and Records Center microfilm pub..)

Cooley, Dennis N.

1865   [Official Report of the Proceedings of the Council with the Indians of
the West and Southwest, held at Fort Smith, Arkansas, in September,
1865.] (ARCIA 1865, doc. 106.)

1866   [Report of the Commissioner of Indian Affairs.] (ARCIA 1866.)

Cordero

1810   [Testimony of Chief Cordero, Oct. 25, 1810.] (BA 47:6.)

Cordero, Manuel Antonio

1806   [Letter to Nemesio Salcedo, June 20, 1806.] (BA 34:799.)

Cortés, Juan
    1821a   [Letter to Antonio Martínez, Oct. 16, 1821.] (BA 68:591.)
    1821b   [Letter to Antonio Martínez, Oct. 23, 1821.] (BA 68:664.)
Corwin, Hugh D.
    1959   Comanche and Kiowa Captives in Oklahoma and Texas. Guthrie, Okla.: Cooperative Publishing Co.
Cos, Martín Prefecto de
    1832   [Report on the examination of a battlefield, Feb. 11, 1832.] (BA 148:23.)
    1835   [Letter to Domingo de Ugartechea, May 8, 1835.] (BA 165:38.)
Cosio, Mariano
    1831   [Letter to Antonio Elozúa, Aug. 16, 1831.] (BA 143:781.)
Coues, Elliot
    1895   The Expeditions of Zebulon Montgomery Pike. New York: Francis P. Harper.
Creel, E. C.
    1928   El estado de Chihuahua: Su historia, geografia, y riquezas naturales. Mexico, D.F.: Tip. El Progresso-Nesones.
Croix, Teodoro de
    1783   [Letter to Governor of New Mexico, Mar. 8, 1783.] (SANM T-858, 11:567.)
Cruttenden, Joel
    1845   [Annual report.] (ARCIA 1845, doc. 24.)
Cruzat y Gongora, Gervasio
    1735   [Proceedings against Diego de Torres.] (SANM T-402, 7:364.)
Curbelo, Juan José
    1800a   [Gifts given to Captain Soxas and the two other Captains, Mar. 12, 1800.] (BA 29:403.)
    1800b   [Notice of Gifts given to Captains Soquina and Soxas, May 1, 1800.] (BA 29:481.)
Curtis, Edward S.
    1907-30   The North American Indian. Being a Series of Volumes Picturing and Describing the Indians of the United States and Alaska. Edited by Frederick W. Hodge. 20 vols. Norwood, Mass.: Plympton Press.
Dary, David
    1979   True Tales of Old Kansas. Lawrence: University of Kansas Press.
Davidson, J. W.
    1874   [Letter to Assistant Adjutant General, July 20, 1874.] (Letters Received from the Military Department of Texas, no. 2922 DT 74. NARS Record Group 393, pt. 1, entry 4875.)
    1875   [Letter to J. M. Haworth, Jan. 9, 1875.] (OHS-KA 7:344.)
Davis, Jefferson
    1861   Message of the President, and Report of Albert Pike Commissioner of the Confederate States to the Indian Nations west of Arkansas, of the Result of his mission. Richmond, Va.: Enquirer Book and Job Press.

Reprint, Washington, D.C.: 33°, Ancient and Accepted Scottish Rite, 1968. (Page citations are to the reprint edition.)

Dearborn, Henry

1804   [Letter to John Sibley, Dec. 13, 1804.] (Letters Sent by the Secretary of War. NARS microfilm pub. M15, 2.)

1805   [Letter to John Sibley, May 25, 1805.] (Letters Sent by the Secretary of War. NARS microfilm pub. M15, 2.)

DeConde, Alexander

1976   This Affair of Louisiana. New York: Scribner's Sons.

DeForrest, Cyrus H.

1864   [Letter to Commanding Officer, Fort Bascom, Sept. 27, 1864.] Official Records of the War of the Rebellion, ser. 1, vol. 41, pt. 3, 429-30.

1867   [Statement Showing the Indians within the Military Department of New Mexico. Enclosure in Carleton to Hancock, Jan. 23, 1867.] (Letters Sent, Military Department of New Mexico. NARS microfilm pub. M1072, 4:57.)

Deloria, Vine, Jr.

1970   We Talk, You Listen: New Tribes, New Turf. New York: Macmillan.

De Mun, Julius

1817   [Letter to William Clark, Nov. 25, 1817. Enclosure in James Monroe to the House of Representatives, Apr. 15, 1818.] (American State Papers, Foreign Relations, vol. 4, 207-13.)

De Shields, James T.

1886   Cynthia Ann Parker: The Story of Her Capture. St. Louis: private.

1912   Border Wars of Texas. Tioga, Tex.: Herald.

Detrich, William

1894   [Comanche vocabulary.] (NAA ms. 788.)

Dillehay, Tom D.

1974   Late Quaternary Bison Population Changes on the Southern Plains. Plains Anthropologist 19:180-96.

Dodge, Richard H.

1883   Our Wild Indians. Hartford, Conn.: A. D. Worthington.

Domínguez, Cristóbal

1812   [Letter to Manuel de Salcedo, Apr. 29, 1812.] (BA 51:128.)

Dorsey, James Owen

1890   The Ḉegiha Language. Contributions to North American Ethnology, no. 5. Washington, D.C.

Driver, Harold

1969   Indians of North America. Chicago: University of Chicago Press.

DuBois, John

1867a   [Letter to Assistant Adjutant General, May 10, 1867.] (Letters Sent, no. 1867-B168, Fort Bascom, New Mexico. NARS Record Group 393, pt. 4, entry 93.)

1867b   [Letter to C. H. DeForrest, July 12, 1867.] (Letters Received, Military Department of New Mexico. NARS microfilm pub. M1088, 5:470; also Letters Sent, July 24, 1865–June 12, 1869, no. 1867-187. Fort Bascom, New Mexico, Military Department of New Mexico. NARS Record Group 393, pt. 4, entry 93.)

1867c   [Letter to C. H. DeForrest, Aug. 31, 1867.] (Letters Sent, July 24, 1865–June 12, 1869, no. 1867-B128. Fort Bascom, New Mexico. Military Department of New Mexico. NARS Record Group 393, pt. 4, entry 93.

Duke, Philip, and Michael C. Wilson

1995   Beyond Subsistence: Plains Archaeology and the Postprocessual Critique. Tuscaloosa: University of Alabama Press.

Duran, Manuel

1821   [Letter to Facundo Melgares, Aug. 22, 1821.] (SANM T-3008, 20: 735.)

Duval, Marcellus

1849   [Letter to W. Medill, Mar. 25, 1849.] (Letters Received from the Texas Agency. NARS microfilm pub. M234, 858:334.)

Eggan, Fred

1937   Social Anthropology of North American Tribes. Chicago: University of Chicago Press.

1980   Shoshone Kinship Structures and Their Significance for Anthropological Theory. Journal of the Steward Anthropological Society 11:165–93.

Elguézabal, Juan Bautista de

1802a   [Letter to Pedro de Nava, Jan. 20, 1802. (#306)] (BA 30:484.)

1802b   [Letter to Pedro de Nava, Mar. 17, 1802. (#320)] (BA 30:491.)

1802c   [Letter to Pedro de Nava, Apr. 28, 1802.] (BA 30:498.)

1802d   [Letter to Pedro de Nava, July 20, 1802. (#367)] (BA 30:510.)

1802e   [Letter to Pedro de Nava, Nov. 24, 1802. (#397)] (BA 30:519.)

1803   [Letter to Nemesio Salcedo, Aug. 3, 1803.] (BA 31:470.)

Elguézabal, Juan José de

1831   [Letter to Antonio Elozúa, Aug. 9, 1831.] (BA 144:312.)

1833   [Letter to Antono Elozúa, Apr. 4, 1833.] (BA 155:952.)

Elias, Simon, Pedro María de Allande, Manuel José de Zuloaga, Luis Antonio Alfaro, José María de Valois

1826   [Treaty with the Comanches, Oct. 8, 1826.] (MANM, 5:425.)

Elozúa, Antonio

1825   [Letter to Monclova Paymaster, Apr. 10, 1825.] (BA 80:493.)

1828   [Letter to José Ventura Rámon, Oct. 8, 1828.] (BA 117:124.)

1829a   [Letter to Anastacio Bustamente, Mar. 2, 1829.] (BA 120:451.)

1829b   [Affidavit, Mar. 3, 1829.] (BA 120:513.)

1831a   [Letter to Commandants, Aug. 17, 1831.] (BA 143:824).

1831b   [Letter to Manuel Mier y Terán, Aug. 18, 1831.] (BA 143:857.)

1831c   [Letter to José Francisco Ruíz, Sept. 1, 1831.] (BA 143:529.)

1831d   [Letter to the Military Commander of Goliad, Oct. 12, 1831.] (BA 145: 309.)

1831e   [Letter to Manuel Mier y Terán, Oct. 14, 1831.] (BA 145:337.)

1832a   [Letter to Manuel Mier y Téran, Apr. 12, 1832.] (BA 149:375.)

1832b   [Letter to Juan José de Elguézabal, July 19, 1832.] (BA 151:731.)

1832c   [Letter to Comandante of Matamoros, Oct. 9, 1832.] (BA 153:62.)

1832d   [Monthly Report, 15 November 1832] (BA 153:965.)

Emory, William H.

1857   Report on the United States and Mexico Boundary Survey under the Direction of the Secretary of the Interior. 34th Cong., 1st sess., House Exec. Doc. 135.

Engels, Frederick

1884   The Origin of the Family, Private Property, and the State, in Light of the Researches of Lewis Henry Morgan. Reprint, New York: International Publishers, 1972. (Page citations are to the reprint edition.)

Esitoya, et al.

1873   [Petition, Mar. 28, 1873. Enclosure in E. Hoag to J. Clum, Apr. 7, 1873.] (Letters Received from the Kiowa Agency. NARS microfilm pub. M234, 378:219.)

Espinosa, Aurelio Macedonio

1907   Los Comanches: A Spanish Heroic Play of the Year Seventeen Hundred and Eighty. Critical Edition. University of New Mexico Bulletin, Language Series, vol. 1, 1.

Espinosa, Gilberto

1931   Los Comanches. New Mexico Quarterly (May):132–46.

Estep, Raymond

1950   The Military and Diplomatic Services of Alexander LeGrand for the Republic of Texas, 1836-1837. Southwestern Historical Quarterly 54: 169–89.

Evans, John

1864   [Annual report, Superintendent, Colorado Superintendency.] (ARCIA 1864, doc. 91.)

Ewers, John C.

1955   The Horse in Blackfoot Indian Culture. Smithsonian Institution, Bureau of American Ethnology Bulletin 159. Washington, D.C.

1965   Hair Pipes in Plains Indian Adornment: A Study in Indian and White Ingenuity. Smithsonian Institution, Bureau of American Ethnology Bulletin 164, Anthropological Papers 50. Washington, D.C.

Faulk, Odie B.

1964   The Last Years of Spanish Texas, 1778-1821. The Hague: Mouton.

1969   The Comanche Invasion of Texas, 1743-1836. Great Plains Journal 9: 10-50.

Fauntleroy, T. J.

1855   [Letter to M. Nichols, Sept. 20, 1855.] (Letters Received, Military Department of New Mexico. NARS microfilm pub. M1120, 4:605.)

Fehrenbach, T. R.
1974   Comanches: The Destruction of a People. New York: Alfred A. Knopf.
Fenton, William
1957   American Indian and White Relations to 1830. Chapel Hill: University of North Carolina Press.
Fernández, Carlos
1750   [Investigation of Comanche Depredations, Dec. 31, 1749–Jan. 7, 1750.] (SANM T-509, 8:947.)
Firth, Raymond
1954   Social Organization and Social Change. Journal of the Royal Anthropological Institute 84:1–20.
Fisher, M. C.
1869   On the Arapaho, Kiowa, and Comanche. Journal of the Ethnological Society of London, n.s., vol. 1, 274–87.
Fitzpatrick, Thomas
1847a   Annual Report. [Letter to T. H. Harvey, Oct. 19, 1847.] (Letters Received from the Upper Platte Agency, filed with letter H517-1848. NARS microfilm pub. M234, 889.) [Excerpted in Historical and Statistical Information respecting the History, Condition and Prospects of the Indian Tribes of the United States, edited by Henry R. Schoolcraft. Vol. 1, 260-64. Philadelphia: Lippincott, Grambo. Reprinted as "A Report from the First Indian Agent of the Upper Platte and Arkansas." Edited by Leroy R. Hafen. In New Spain and the Anglo-American West: Historical Contributions presented to Herbert Eugene Bolton. 2 vols. Edited by Charles W. Hackett, George P. Hammond, J. Lloyd Mecham, W. C. Binkley, Cardinal Goodwin, and J. Fred Rippy, 2, 121-37. Los Angeles: Privately printed, 1932]
1847b   [Letter to T. H. Harvey, Dec. 18, 1847.] (Letters Received from the Upper Platte Agency, filed with letter H517-1848. NARS microfilm pub. M234, 889.) [Excerpted in Historical and Statistical Information respecting the History, Condition and Prospects of the Indian Tribes of the United States, edited by Henry R. Schoolcraft. Vol. 1, 260. Philadelphia: Lippincott, Grambo.]
1848a   [Letter to W. Gilpin, Feb. 10, 1848; enclosure in Fitzpatrick to T. A. Harvey, Feb. 3, 1848.] (Letters Received from the Upper Platte Agency. NARS microfilm pub. M234, 889.)
1848b   [Letter to T. H. Harvey, Feb. 13, 1848.] (Letters Received from the Upper Platte Agency. NARS microfilm pub. M234, 889.)
1848c   [Letter to W. Medill, Aug. 11, 1848.] (Letters Received from the Upper Platte Agency, F86-1848. NARS microfilm pub. M234, 889.)
1853   [Annual report, Agent, Upper Platte and Arkansas Agency.] (ARCIA 1853, doc. 44.)
Flores, Dan L.
1985   Journal of an Indian Trader: Anthony Glass and the Texas Trading Frontier, 1790-1810. College Station: Texas A & M University Press.

1991   Bison Ecology and Bison Diplomacy: The Southern Plains from 1800
            to 1850. The Journal of American History (September):465–85.
Flores, Gaspar
1824   [Letter to Juan de Castañeda, Oct. 14, 1824.] (BA 78:108.)
Flores, José María
1835   [Letter to Angel Navarro, June 2, 1835.] (BA 165:451.)
Folmer, Henri
1942   Etienne Veniard de Bourgmond in the Missouri Country. Missouri
            Historical Review 36:279–98.
Ford, John S.
1963   Rip Ford's Texas. Edited by Stephen B. Oates. Austin: University of
            Texas Press.
Foreman, Grant
1926   Pioneer Days in Early Southwest. Cleveland: Arthur H. Clark.
1933   Advancing the Frontier. Norman: University of Oklahoma Press.
1934   The Five Civilized Tribes. Norman: University of Oklahoma Press.
1935   The Journal of Elijah Hicks. Chronicles of Oklahoma 13:68–99.
1936   Journal of the Proceedings at Our First Treaty with the Wild Indians.
            Chronicles of Oklahoma 14:393–418.
1937   Adventure on Red River. Norman: University of Oklahoma Press.
1939   Marcy and the Gold Seekers. Norman: University of Oklahoma Press.
1941   A Pathfinder in the Southwest. The Itinerary of Lieutenant A. W.
            Whipple During his Exploring Expedition for a Railway Route from
            Fort Smith to Los Angeles in the Years 1853–54. Norman: University
            of Oklahoma Press.
1948   The Texas Comanche Treaty of 1848. Southwestern Historical Quar-
            terly 51:313–32.
Foster, Morris
1991   Being Comanche. Tucson: University of Arizona Press.
Foster-Harris, William
1955   The Look of the Old West. New York: Viking Press.
Fowler, Jacob
1898   The Journal of Jacob Fowler. Edited by E. Coues. New York: Francis
            Harper.
Fowler, Loretta
1982   Arapaho Politics. Lincoln: University of Nebraska Press.
Fox, George W.
1874a   [Letter to J. W. Davidson, Apr. 3, 1874.] (Letters Received from the
            Military Department of Texas, no. 1433 DT 74. NARS Record Group
            393, pt. 1, entry 4875.)
1874b   [Letter to J. W. Davidson, May 20, 1874.] (Letters Received from the
            Military Department of Texas, no. 2034 DT 74. NARS Record Group
            393, pt. 1, entry 4875.)

Fried, Morton H.
1966 On the Concepts of Tribe and Tribal Society. Transactions of the New York Academy of Science 28:527-40.
1967 The Evolution of Political Society. New York: Random House.
1968 On the Concepts of Tribe and Tribal Society. *In* Essays in the Problem of Tribe, edited by June Helm, 3-20. Seattle: University of Washington Press.
1975a The Notion of Tribe. Menlo Park: Cummings Publishing Co.
1975b The Myth of Tribe. Natural History 84(4):12-21.
1983 Tribe to State or State to Tribe in Ancient China? *In* The Origins of Chinese Civilization, edited by David Keightley. Berkeley: University of California Press.

Frison, George C.
1971 The Bison Pound in Northwest Plains Prehistory. American Antiquity 36:77-91.

Froebel, Julius
1859 Seven Years Travel in Central America, Northern Mexico, and the Far West of the United States. London: R. Bentley.

Gaines, W. Craig
1989 The Confederate Cherokees. Baton Rouge: Louisiana State University Press.

Gálvez, Bernardo de
1951 Instructions for Governing the Interior Provinces of New Spain, 1786. Translated by D. Worchester. Albuquerque: University Press.

García, Francisco
1829 [Letter to Juan José Arocha, July 3, 1829.] (MANM 10:305.)

García, José María
1831 [Letter to Antonio Elozúa, Oct. 29, 1831.] (BA 145:494.)
1832a [Letter to Antono Elozúa, Apr. 21, 1832.] (BA 149:536.)
1832b [Letter to Antono Elozúa, May 5, 1832.] (BA 149:789.)

García, José Pascual
1822 [Letter to Comandante General, Provincias Internas, May 23, 1822.] (BA 71:687.)

García Rejon, Manuel
1865 Vocabulario del idioma comanche. Mexico, D.F.: Ignacio Cumplido.

Garrard, Lewis
1955 Wah-to-yah and the Taos Trail; or Prairie Travel and Scalp Dances. Norman: University of Oklahoma Press.

Garrett, Julia K.
1942-46 Dr. John Sibley and the Louisiana-Texas Frontier, 1803-1814. Southwestern Historical Quarterly 45:286-301, 378-82; 46:83-84, 272-75; 47:48, 160-61, 319-24, 388-91; 48:67-71, 275, 547-49; 49:116-19, 290-92, 399-430, 599-614.

Gatschet, Albert

1884   [Shoshonean Linguistic Family-Comanche Language. Comanche Vocabulary, collected on Kiowa Comanche Apache Reservation, Indian Territory, October, November, December 1884.] (NAA ms 748.)

1893   [Comanche Vocabulary; information from Philip Bloch, Indian scout.] (NAA ms. 751.)

Gearing, Frederick O.

1958   Structural Poses of an Eighteenth Century Cherokee Village. American Anthropologist 60:1148-57.

1962   Priests and Warriors: Social Structures for Cherokee Politics in the 18th Century. Memoirs of the American Anthropological Association 93. Menasha, Wisc.

Getty, George

1869   [Letter to C. McKeever, Mar. 13, 1869.] (Letters Sent, Military Department of New Mexico. NARS microfilm pub. M1072, 4:455.)

Gilpin, William

1848   [Report to General R. Jones, Aug. 1, 1848.] Annual Report of the Secretary of War. 30th Cong., 2d sess., House Exec. Doc. 1, 136-40.

Gladwin, Thomas

1948   Comanche Kin Behavior. American Anthropologist 50:73-94.

Glisan, Rodney

1874   Journal of Army Life. San Francisco: A. L. Bancroft.

Goetzmann, William H.

1966   Exploration and Empire. New York: Alfred A. Knopf.

Goldbaum, M.

1866a   [Letter to J. H. Carleton, June 7, 1866. Military Department of New Mexico] (Letters Received from the Kiowa Agency. NARS microfilm pub. M234, 375:63.)

1866b   [Letter to Assistant Adjutant General, June 22, 1866.] (Register of Letters Received, no. 1866-G19. Military Department of New Mexico. NARS microfilm pub. M1097, 1.)

González, Josef Manuel, and Juan Domingo Cordero

1814   [Proceedings against Josef Manuel González and Juan Domingo Cordero, June 8-Aug. 10, 1814.] (SANM T-2542, 17:992.)

Gonzalez, Nancie

1975   Patterns of Dominican Ethnicity. In The New Ethnicity, edited by John W. Bennet, 110-26. St. Paul: West.

González, José Rafael

1824   [Letter to Juan de Castañeda, Mar. 3, 1824.] (BA 76:939.)

1825   [Letter to Juan de Castañeda, Mar. 1, 1825.] (BA 79:663.)

Goodnight, Charles, and John W. Sheek

1896   Indian Depredation Claim 9133. Charles Goodnight and John W. Sheek vs. Comanche Tribe of Indians. Records of the Supreme Court. NARS Record Group 267. Washington, D.C.

Gorham, George
  1869   [Documents relating to the negotiation of the unratified treaty of April
          6, 1863, with the Kiowa, Comanche, and Apache Indians.] (NARS
          microfilm pub. T494, 8:930–38.)
Granger, G.
  1872   [Letter to Assistant Adjutant General, Military Department of the Mis-
          souri, Dec. 18, 1872.] (Letters Sent, Military Department of New Mex-
          ico. NARS microfilm pub. M234, 377.)
Grant, Ulysses S.
  1869   [Appointment of the Board of Indian Commissioners, June 3, 1869.]
          (ARCIA 1869, doc. B.).
Green, Mary Rowena Maverick
  1952   Samuel Maverick, Texan. San Antonio: Published by the author.
Greenwood, A. B.
  1859   [Letter to J. Thompson, Dec. 30, 1859. Enclosure in James Carleton to
          Michael Steck, Oct. 29, 1864.] Official Records of the War of the Re-
          bellion, ser. 1, vol. 41, pt. 4, 319–22.
Gregg, Josiah
  1844   Commerce of the Prairies. 2 vols. New York: H. G. Langley.
Gregg, Kate L.
  1952   The Road to Santa Fe: The Journal and Diaries of George Champlin
          Sibley, 1825–27. Albuquerque: University of New Mexico Press.
Greiner, John
  1852a   [Letter to Luke Lea, Apr. 30, 1852.] (Letters Received from the New
          Mexico Superintendency, no. 1852-G11. NARS microfilm pub. M234,
          546.)
  1852b   [Letter to Luke Lea, July 31, 1852.] (Letters Received from the New
          Mexico Superintendency, no. 1852-G41. NARS microfilm pub. M234,
          546.)
Griego, Felipe
  1822   [Nota de la existencia sin cargo costeados por la Hacienda Naciónal
          quartenecientas, Oct. 31, 1822.] (NMA 1822-551.)
Grierson, Benjamin
  1869a   [Letter to Assistant Adjutant General, Military Department of the Miss-
          ouri, Aug. 25, 1869.] (Letters Received from the Kiowa Agency.
          NARS microfilm pub. M234, 376:16.)
  1869b   [Letter to Assistant Adjutant General, Military Department of the Mis-
          souri, Sept. 25, 1869] (Letters Received from the Kiowa Agency.
          NARS microfilm pub. M234, 376:19.)
  1870a   [Letter to W. G. Mitchell, Jan. 28, 1870.] (Letters Received from the
          Kiowa Agency. NARS microfilm pub. M234, 376:558.)
  1870b   [Letter to W. G. Mitchell, Apr. 12, 1870.] (Letters Received from the
          Kiowa Agency. NARS microfilm pub. M234, 376:572.)
  1870c   [Letter to W. G. Mitchell, July 10, 1870.] (Letters Received from the
          Kiowa Agency. NARS microfilm pub. M234, 376:611.)

Grinnell, George B.
    1915   The Fighting Cheyennes. New York: Charles Scribner's Sons.
    1923   Bent's Old Fort and Its Builders. Collections of the Kansas State His-
            torical Society, vol. 15, 28–91.
Guerra, José Mariano
    1832   [Letter to Antonio Elozúa, May 10, 1832.] (BA 150:33.)
Gutierrez, Gabriel
    1799   [General Statement of Gifts Given to the Nations of the North and the
            Comanches, Jan. 1, 1794–July 27, 1799.] (BA 29:482.)
    1800   [Relación which Shows the Gifts Supplied by the Fondo de Mesteñas,
            Jan. 1, 1794–July 27, 1799, May 1, 1800.] (BA 29:485.)
Hacker, Margaret Schmidt
    1990   Cynthia Ann Parker: The Life and The Legend. El Paso: Texas West-
            ern Press, University of Texas-El Paso.
Hackett, Charles Wilson
    1923-37 Historical Documents Relating to New Mexico, Nueva Vizcaya and
            Approaches Thereto, to 1773, collected by Adolph F. A. Bandelier and
            Fanny R. Bandelier. 3 vols. Carnegie Institution of Washington, Publi-
            cation 300. Washington, D.C.
    1931-46 Pichardo's Treatise on the Limits of Texas and Louisiana. 3 vols.
            Austin: University of Texas Press.
Hafen, LeRoy R.
    1931   Broken Hand: The Life of Thomas Fitzpatrick. Denver: Old West Pub-
            lishing.
Hafen, LeRoy, and Ann W. Hafen
    1959   Relations with the Indians of the Plains, 1857–1861. In The Far West
            and the Rockies Historical Series. Vol 9. Glendale, Cal.: Arthur H.
            Clark.
Hagan, William T.
    1976   United States-Comanche Relations: The Reservation Years. New
            Haven: Yale University Press.
Haley, J. Evertts
    1935   The Comanchero Trade. Southwestern Historical Quarterly 38:157–76.
Hardee, William J.
    1851   [Letter to George Deal, Aug. 29, 1851.] (Letters Received from the
            Texas Agency. NARS microfilm pub. M234, 858:889.)
Harris, Carey A.
    1837   Report of the Commissioner of Indian Affairs. House Executive Doc.
            3, 25th Cong., 2nd sess.
Harston, J. Emmor
    1963   Comanche Land. San Antonio: The Naylor Co.
Hatch, Alexander
    1856   [Letter to Garland, Sept. 24, 1856.] (Letters Received, Military
            Department of New Mexico. NARS microfilm pub. M1120, 5:765.)

Hatch, John
  1872a   [Letter to Commanding Officer, Military Department of New Mexico, Mar. 31, 1872.] (Letters Sent, Fort Concho, Tex.; Post Records. NARS Record Group 393.)
  1872b   [Letter to Assistant Adjutant General, Apr. 15, 1872.] (Letters Sent, Fort Concho, Tex.; Post Records. NARS Record Group 393.)
  1872c   [Letter to Assistant Adjutant General, June 16, 1872.] (Letters Sent, Fort Concho, Tex.; Post Records. NARS Record Group 393.)
  1872d   [Letter to Assistant Adjutant General, Dec. 12, 1872.] (Letters Sent, Fort Concho, Tex.; Post Records. NARS Record Group 393.)
  1872e   [Letter to Lawrie Tatum, Dec. 12, 1872.] (Letters Sent, Fort Concho, Tex.; Post Records. NARS Record Group 393.)
Hatcher, Mattie Austin
  1919   Texas in 1820. Southwestern History Quarterly 23:46-68.
Haworth, James M.
  1873a   [Letter to Enoch Hoag, Apr. 7, 1873.] (Letters Received from the Kiowa Agency. NARS microfilm pub. M856, 47:658.)
  1873b   [Letter to Enoch Hoag, May 5, 1873.] (Letters Received, Central Superintendency. NARS microfilm pub. M856, 47:759.)
  1873c   [Letter to Enoch Hoag, June 12, 1873.] (Letters Received, Central Superintendency. NARS microfilm pub. M856, 47:832.)
  1873d   [Letter to Enoch Hoag, June 30, 1873.] (Letters Received from the Kiowa Agency. NARS microfilm pub. M856, 47:578.)
  1873e   [Letter to Enoch Hoag, Aug. 8, 1873.] (Letters Received from the Kiowa Agency. NARS microfilm pub. M856, 47:944.)
  1873f   [Letter to Enoch Hoag, Aug. 21, 1873.] (Letters Received from the Kiowa Agency. NARS microfilm pub. M856, 47:955.)
  1873g   [Letter to E. P. Smith, Nov. 14, 1873. Enclosure in Cyrus Beede to E. P. Smith Nov. 22, 1873.] (Letters Received from the Kiowa Agency. NARS microfilm pub. M234, 378:498.)
  1873h   [Letter to Enoch Hoag, Dec. 1, 1873. Enclosure in E. Hoag to E. P. Smith, Dec. 9, 1873.] (Letters Received from the Kiowa Agency. NARS microfilm pub. M234, 378:522; also Letters Received by the Central Superintendency, M846, 47:1044).
  1873i   [Letter to E. P. Smith, Dec. 1, 1873.] (Letters received from the Kiowa Agency. NARS microfilm pub. M234, 378:530.)
  1873j   [Letter to Cyrus Beede, Dec. 8, 1873.] (NARS microfilm pub. M856, 47:1062.)
  1873k   [Letter to C. Delano, Dec. 15, 1873.] (NARS microfilm pub. M856, 47:1079.)
  1873l   [Letter to Enoch Hoag, Dec. 27, 1873.] (NARS microfilm pub. M856, 47:1107.)
  1874a   [Letter to Enoch Hoag, Jan. 19, 1874.] (NARS microfilm pub. M856, 55.)
  1874b   [Letter to Jonathan Richards, Jan. 30, 1874.] (OHS-KA 47:85.)

542

REFERENCES

1874c [Letter to Enoch Hoag, Feb. 16, 1874.] (NARS microfilm pub. M856, 55.)

1874d [Letter to Enoch Hoag, Feb. 25, 1874.] (NARS microfilm pub. M856, 55.)

1874e [Letter to Enoch Hoag, Mar. 28, 1874.] (NARS microfilm pub. M856, 55.)

1874f [Letter to Enoch Hoag, May 6, 1874. Enclosure in Hoag to E. P. Smith, May 12, 1874.] (Letters Received from the Kiowa Agency. NARS microfilm pub. M234, 379:218.)

1874g [Letter to Enoch Hoag, May 9, 1874.] (NARS microfilm pub. M856, 55.)

1874h [Letter to E. P. Smith, June 1, 1874.] (NARS microfilm pub. M856, 55.)

1874i [Letter to Enoch Hoag, June 8, 1874.] (NARS microfilm pub. M856, 55.)

1874j [Letter to Enoch Hoag, June 11, 1874.] (NARS microfilm pub. M856, 55.)

1874k [Letter to Cyrus Beede, June 13, 1874.] (NARS microfilm pub. M856, 55.)

1874l [Letter to Enoch Hoag, June 27, 1874.] (NARS microfilm pub. M856, 55.)

1874m [Letter to E. P. Smith, July 2, 1874.] (NARS microfilm pub. M856, 55.)

1874n [Letter to E. P. Smith, Dec. 23, 1874.] (NARS microfilm pub. M234, 379:60.)

1874o [Annual report, Agent, Kiowa and Comanche.] (ARCIA 1874.)

1875a [Letter to Enoch Hoag, Jan. 1, 1875.] (NARS microfilm pub. M856, 62:276.)

1875b [Letter to Enoch Hoag, Apr. 19, 1875.] (NARS microfilm pub. M856, 62:413.)

1875c [Letter to Enoch Hoag, May 3, 1875.] (NARS microfilm pub. M856, 62:427.)

1875d [Letter to Enoch Hoag, May 17, 1875.] (NARS microfilm pub. M856, 62:474.)

1875e [Letter to Enoch Hoag, June 2, 1875.] (NARS microfilm pub. M856, 62:525.)

1875f [Letter to Enoch Hoag, Aug. 2, 1875.] (NARS microfilm pub. M856, 62:621.)

1875g [Letter to Enoch Hoag, Sept. 3, 1875.] (NARS microfilm pub. M856, 62:672.)

1875h [Letter to Enoch Hoag, Nov. 3, 1875.] (NARS microfilm pub. M856, 62:749.)

1879 [Comanche Census.] (OHS-KA 1A:86–113.)

Hayt, Edward A.

1878 [Letter to James M. Haworth, Mar. 1878.] (OHS-KA 1.)

Hazen, William B.
   1869   [Report, Headquarters, Southern Indian District.] (ARCIA 1869, doc.
             123.)
Hedgcoxe, H. O.
   1848   [Letter to Robert S. Neighbors, Feb. 18, 1848.] (30th Cong., 1st sess.,
             Sen. Committee Report 171, 14-15. Also ARCIA 1848, doc. 22-B.)
Henderson, J. Pinckney
   1847   [Letter to Robert S. Neighbors, Dec. 10, 1847.] (30th Cong., 1st sess.,
             Sen. Committee Report 171, 11-12.)
Herrera, Símon de
   1811a   [Letter to Nemesio Salcedo, Aug. 7, 1811.] (BA 49:126.)
   1811b   [Letter to Nemesio Salcedo, Aug. 21, 1811.] (BA 49:64.)
Heth, Henry
   1852   [Letter to Irwin McDowell, Nov. 4, 1852.] (Letters Sent, Post Records,
             Fort Atkinson, no. 1852-145. NARS Record Group 393, pt. 4.)
   1853   [Letter to Irwin McDowell, Apr. 10, 1853.] (Letters Sent, Post Re-
             cords, Fort Atkinson, no. 1853-164. NARS Record Group 393, pt. 4.)
Hildreth, James
   1836   Dragoon Expedition to the Rocky Mountains. Reprint, New York:
             Arno Press, 1973. (Page citations are to the reprint edition.)
Hinojas, Blas de
   1826a   [Indian Gifts, Dec. 31, 1826.] (MANM 15:637)
   1826b   [Indian Gifts, Dec. 31, 1826.] (MANM 15:715.)
Hoag, Enoch
   1872   [Letter to Lawrie Tatum, Feb. 15, 1872.] (OHS-KA 47:79.)
   1873   [Letter to E. P. Smith, Aug. 27, 1873.] (Letters Received from the
             Kiowa Agency. NARS microfilm pub. M234, 378:430.)
Hodge, Frederick W., ed.
   1907-10 Handbook of American Indians North of Mexico. Smithsonian Institu-
             tion, Bureau of American Ethnology Bulletin 30. 2 vols. Washington,
             D.C.
Hoebel, E. Adamson
   1936   Associations and the State on the Plains. American Anthropologist 38:
             433-38.
   1940   Political Organization and Law-Ways of the Comanche Indians. Mem-
             oirs of the American Anthropological Association 54. Menasha, Wisc.
   1941   The Comanche Sun Dance and Outbreak of 1873. American Anthro-
             pologist 43:301-3.
   1954   The Law of Primitive Man. Cambridge: Harvard University Press.
Hoffman, Walter J.
   1880   [Comanche Indians, June 28, 1880.] (NAA ms. 1214a.)
   1886   Remarks on Indian Tribes. Proceedings of the American Philosophical
             Society, vol. 23, 299-301.

Huebner, Jeffrey A.
    1991   Late Prehistoric Bison Populations in Central and Southern Texas. Plains Anthropologist 36 :343–58.

Hultkrantz, Åke
    1968   Shoshoni Indians on the Plains: An Appraisal of the Documentary Evidence. Zeitschrift fur Ethnologie 93:49–72.
    1986   Mythology and Religious Concepts. *In* Handbook of North American Indians, edited by William C. Sturtevant. Vol. 11, Great Basin, edited by Warren L. D'Azevedo, 630–40. Washington, D.C.: Government Printing Office.

Hyde, George E.
    1959   Indians of the High Plains. Norman: University of Oklahoma Press.
    1968   The Life of George Bent. Norman: University of Oklahoma Press.

Inman, Henry
    1897   The Old Santa Fe Trail. New York: Macmillan.

Irving, Washington
    1851   Adventures of Captain Bonneville, U.S.A., in the Rocky Mountains and the Far West. New York: G. Putnam.

Jackson, Andrew
    1831   Message of the President, In Compliance with a Resolution of the Senate concerning the Fur Trade and the Overland Trade with Mexico. Senate Executive Doc. 90, 22nd Cong., 1st sess.

Jackson, David
    1966   The Journals of Zebulon Montgomery Pike. 2 vols. Norman: University of Oklahoma Press.

Jackson, Jack
    1971   Comanche Moon. San Francisco: Ripoff Press.

James, Thomas
    1846   Three Years among the Indians and Mexicans. Reprint, Lincoln: University of Nebraska Press, 1984. (Page citations are to the reprint edition.)

Jamison, John
    1817a   [Letter to the Secretary of War, June 10, 1817.] (Letters Received by the Secretary of War Relating to Indian Affairs, no. 1817-J129[10]. NARS microfilm pub. M221, 74.)
    1817b   [Letter to the Secretary of War, Aug. 19, 1817.] (Letters Received by the Secretary of War Relating to Indian Affairs, no. 1817-J186[10]. NARS microfilm pub. M221, 74.)

Jenkins, John Holland
    1958   Recollections of Early Texas. Edited by John Holmes Jenkins, III. Austin: University of Texas Press.

Jenkins, John Holmes, III
    1973   The Papers of the Texas Revolution, 1835–1836. 10 vols. Austin, Tex.: Presidial Press.

John, Elizabeth A. H.

1975   Storms Brewed in Other Men's Worlds. College Station: Texas A & M University Press.

1982   Portrait of a Wichita Village, 1808. Chronicles of Oklahoma 60:412–37.

1984   Nurturing the Peace: Spanish and Comanche Cooperation in the Early Nineteenth Century. New Mexico Historical Review 59:345–69.

1985   An Earlier Chapter in Kiowa History. New Mexico Historical Review 60:379–414.

Johnson, Edward

1853   [Letter to Mr. Page, Sept. 10, 1853.] (Letters Received from the Upper Platte Agency. NARS microfilm pub. M234, 889.)

Johnson, R.

1855   [Letter to Robert Williams, Sept. 26, 1855. F55.] (Letters Received, Military Department of New Mexico. NARS microfilm pub. M1120, 4:613.)

Johnston, William Preston

1878   The Life of Albert Sidney Johnston, Embracing His Services in the Armies of the United States, the Republic of Texas, and the Confederate States. New York: D. Appleton.

Jones, David C.

1966   The Treaty of Medicine Lodge. Norman: University of Oklahoma Press.

Jones, David E.

1968   Sanapia: Comanche Medicine Woman. Master's thesis, University of Oklahoma.

1972   Sanapia: Comanche Medicine Woman. New York: Holt, Rinehart, and Winston.

Jones, Horace P.

1870   [Letter to Lawrie Tatum, May 20, 1870.] (Letters Received from the Kiowa Agency. NARS microfilm pub. M234, 377:179.)

Jones, J. A.

1955   Key to the Annual Reports of the United States Commissioners of Indian Affairs. Ethnohistory 2:58–64.

Kappler, Charles J.

1903   Indian Laws and Treaties. Reprint, New York: Interland Publishing Co., 1979. (Page citations are to the reprint edition.)

Kavanagh, Thomas W.

1980   Recent Socio-cultural Evolution of the Comanche Indians. Master's thesis, George Washington University.

1984   Problems with the Powell Paradigm: Anthropology at the BAE 1879–1902. Haliksa'i: Journal of the University of New Mexico Anthropology Society 3:22–35.

1985   The Comanche: Paradigmatic Anomaly or Ethnographic Fiction. Haliksa'i: Journal of the University of New Mexico Anthropology Society 4: 109-28.

1986   Political Power and Political Organization. Ph.D. diss., University of New Mexico.

1989   Comanche Population Organization and Reorganization, 1869-1901: A Test of the Continuity Hypothesis. Plains Anthropologist 34 (2):99-111.

1991   Whose Village? Photographs by William S. Soule, Winter 1872-73. Visual Anthropology 4:1-24.

Kendall, George W.

1844   Narrative of the Texan Santa Fé Expedition, Comprising a Description of a Tour through Texas, and Across the Great Southwestern Prairies, the Camanche and Caygua Hunting Grounds, with an Account of the Suffering from Want of Food, Losses from Hostile Indians and Final Capture of the Texans, and Their March, as Prisoners, to the City of Mexico. 2 vols. New York: Harper Brothers.

Kennedy, William

1841   Texas: The Rise, Progress, and Prospects of the Republic of Texas. London: R. Hastings.

Kenner, Charles L.

1962   The Great New Mexico Cattle Raid—1872. New Mexico Historical Review 37:243-59.

1969   A History of New Mexico-Plains Indian Relations. Norman: University of Oklahoma Press.

Kessell, John

1979   Kiva, Cross, and Crown: The Pecos Indians and New Mexico, 1540-1840. Washington, D.C.: National Park Service.

Kimball, Harry

1872   [Report on the Indians on the Kiowa, Comanche, and Apache Reservation.] (NAA ms. 1911.)

King, Irene. M.

1967   John O. Meusebach: German Colonizer in Texas. Austin: University of Texas Press.

Kobbe, William A.

1869   [Letter to A. W. Evans, Jan. 10, 1869.] (Letters Sent, Military Department of New Mexico. NARS microfilm pub. M1072, 4:424.)

Labadi, Lorenzo

1862   [Annual report, Agent, New Mexico Superintendency.] (ARCIA 1862, doc. 53.)

1867a   [Letter to A. B. Norton, Aug. 28, 1867.] (Letters Received from the New Mexico Superintendency, no. 1867-N141. NARS microfilm pub. M234, 554; also Records of the New Mexico Superintendency. NARS microfilm pub. T-21, 7; also ARCIA 1867, doc. 57.)

1867b   [Letter to A. B. Norton, Sept. 9, 1867.] (Records of the New Mexico Superintendency. NARS microfilm pub. T-21, 7.)

1867c   [Letter to A. B. Norton, Oct. 10, 1867.] (Records of the New Mexico Superintendency. NARS microfilm pub. T21, 7.)

Lafuente, Manuel

1831   [Diary, Nov. 30, 1831.] (BA 146:228.)

1832   [Letter to Antonio Elozúa, Feb. 9, 1832.] (BA 147:936.)

Lamar, Mirabeau Buonaparte

1921   The Papers of Mirabeau Buonaparte Lamar. Edited by C. A. Gulick, Katherine Elliott, Winnie Allen, and Harriet Smither. 6 vols. Austin: Van Boeckmann Jones.

Lane, William Carr

1853   [Letter to Commissioner of Indian Affairs, Feb. 24, 1853.] (Letters Received from the New Mexico Superintendency, no. 1853-N107. NARS microfilm pub. M234, 546.)

Lange, Charles H., and Carroll L. Riley, eds.

1966   The Southwestern Journals of Adolph F. Bandelier, 1880-1882. Albuquerque: University of New Mexico Press.

Lavender, David

1954   Bent's Fort. Garden City: Doubleday.

Leavenworth, Jesse

1865a   [Truce Agreement, Aug. 1865. Enclosure in Leavenworth to D. N. Cooley, Feb. 7, 1866.] (Letters Received from the Kioa Agency. NARS microfilm pub. M234, 375:165.)

1865b   [Letter to D. N. Cooley, Nov. 9, 1865.] (Letters Received from the Kiowa Agency. NARS microfilm pub. M234, 375:33.)

1866a   [Letter to D. N. Cooley, June 5, 1866.]. (Letters Received from the Kiowa Agency. NARS microfilm pub. M234, 375:249.)

1866b   [Letter to D. N. Cooley, Aug. 23, 1866.] (Letters Received from the Kiowa Agency. NARS microfilm pub. M234, 375:262.)

1866c   [Letter to T. Murphy; enclosure in Murphy to D. N. Cooley, Dec. 19, 1866.] (Letters Received from the Kiowa Agency. NARS microfilm pub. M234, 375:398.)

1867a   [Letter to N. G. Taylor, Mar. 6, 1867.] (Letters Received from the Kiowa Agency. NARS microfilm pub. M234, 375:491.)

1867b   [Extract from Leavenworth (Kans.) Conservative, May 13, 1867; Enclosure in J. Leavenworth to Mix, Dec. 6, 1867.] (Letters Received from the Kiowa Agency. NARS microfilm pub. M234, 375:657.)

1867c   [Letter to N. G. Taylor, July 1867.] (Letters Received from the Kiowa Agency. NARS microfilm pub. M234, 375:485.)

1868a   [Letter to N. G. Taylor, May 21, 1868.] (Letters Received from the Kiowa Agency. NARS microfilm pub. M234, 375:858.)

1868b   [Letter to N. G. Taylor, July 30, 1868.] (Letters Received from the Kiowa Agency. NARS microfilm pub. M234, 375:892.)

Lecompte, Janet
    1969   Julius and Isabelle De Mun. Bulletin of the Missouri Historical Society 26:24–31.
    1972   Bent, St. Vrain and Company among the Comanche and Kiowa. The Colorado Magazine 49:273–93.

Lee, S.P., Lawrie Tatum, James M. Haworth
    1869–77 [Monthly Returns of Provisions Received, Issued, and Remaining on Hand at Fort Sill, I.T.] (OHS-KA 6:12–144.)

Leeper, Matthew, Jr.
    1873   [Letter to Post Adjutant, Fort Concho, Tex., Apr. 3, 1873. Enclosure in C. Delano to E. P. Smith, May 1, 1873.] (Letters Received from the Kiowa Agency. NARS microfilm pub. M234, 378:592.)

Leeper, Matthew, Sr.
    1857   [Letter to R. S. Neighbors, Dec. 6, 1857.] (Letters Received from the Texas Agency. NARS microfilm pub. M234, 861:118.)
    1858a   [Letter to R. S. Neighbors, Jan. 28, 1858. Enclosure in Neighbors to C. E. Mix, Feb. 16, 1858.] (Letters Received from the Texas Agency. NARS microfilm pub. M234, 861:295.)
    1858b   [Letter to R. S. Neighbors, Feb. 12, 1858. Enclosure in Neighbors to C. E. Mix, Feb. 27, 1858.] (Letters Received from the Texas Agency. NARS microfilm pub. M234, 861:302.)
    1858c   [Letter to R. S. Neighbors, Apr. 9, 1858. Enclosure in Neighbors to C. E. Mix, Apr. 22, 1858.] (Letters Received from the Texas Agency. NARS microfilm pub. M234, 861:437.)
    1858d   [Letter to R. S. Neighbors, Apr. 16, 1858. Enclosure in Neighbors to C. E. Mix, May 14, 1858.] (Letters Received from the Texas Agency. NARS microfilm pub. M234, 861:450.)
    1858e   [Letter to R. S. Neighbors, June 11, 1858. Enclosure in Neighbors to C. E. Mix, July 29, 1858.] (Letters Received from the Texas Agency. NARS microfilm pub. M234, 861:484.)
    1858f   [Report, Special Agent, Comanche Agency.] (ARCIA 1858, no. 67.)
    1858g   [Letter to R. S. Neighbors, Aug. 31, 1858.] (Letters Received from the Texas Agency. NARS microfilm pub. M234, 861:864.)
    1858h   [Letter to Maj. G. H. Thomas, Nov. 15, 1858. Enclosure in Neighbors to J. W. Denver, Nov. 30, 1858.] (Letters Received from the Texas Agency. NARS microfilm pub. M234, 861:820.)
    1858i   [Letter to R. S. Neighbors, Nov. 23, 1858. Enclosure in Neighbors to J. W. Denver, Dec. 9, 1858. N565.] (Letters Received from the Texas Agency. NARS microfilm pub. M234, 861:837.)

Letterman, George W.
    1867a   [Letter to C. H. DeForrest, Aug. 31, 1867.] (Letters Received, Military Department of New Mexico. NARS microfilm pub. M1088, 5:471.)
    1867b   [Letter to E. Hunter, Oct. 5, 1867. B152.] (Letters Sent, July 24, 1865–June 12, 1869, Fort Bascom, no. 1867-31. NARS Record Group 393,

pt. 4, entry 93; also Letters Received, Military Department of New Mexico. NARS microfilm pub. M1088, 5:584.)

Levine, Francis, and Martha D. Freeman
1982   A Study of Documentary and Archeological Evidence for Comanchero Activity in the Texas Pan-Handle. Austin: Texas Historical Commission.

Levy, Jerrold E.
1959   After Custer: Kiowa Political and Social Organization from the Reservation to the Present. Ph.D. diss., University of Chicago.

Lewellen, Ted C.
1983   Political Anthropology. New York: Bergin and Garvey.

Lewis, M. G.
1846a   [Letter to W. Medill, July 13, 1846.] (Documents Covering the Negotiation of Indian Treaties. NARS microfilm pub. T494, 4:254.)
1846b   [Letter to W. Medill, July 16, 1846.] (Letters Received, Office of Indian Affairs. NARS microfilm pub. M234, 444:366.)

Lewis, M. G., and Pierce M. Butler
1846   [Letter to W. Medill, Apr. 1, 1846.] (Letters Received, Office of Indian Affairs. NARS microfilm pub. M234, 444:60.)

Linton, Ralph
1933   [Letter to Jesse Nusbaum, August 3, 1933.] (File 89SF3.013.1, Archives of the Laboratory of Anthropology. Museum of New Mexico. Santa Fe.)
1935   The Comanche Sun Dance. American Anthropologist 37:420–28.

Loomis, Noel H., and Abram P. Nasatir
1967   Pedro Vial and the Roads to Santa Fe. Norman: University of Oklahoma Press.

Lopez, Gaspar
1822a   [Letter to Béxar Ayuntamiento, Mar. 11, 1822.] (BA 71:8.)
1822b   [Letter to Antonio Martínez, Mar. 27, 1822.] (BA 71:204.)
1822c   [Letter to Béxar Ayuntamiento, Mar. 27, 1822.] (BA 71:213.)
1822d   [Letter to Antonio Martínez, Aug. 11, 1822.] (BA 72:165.)

Lowie, Robert H.
1909   The Assiniboine. New York: Anthropological Papers of the American Museum of Natural History, vol. 5, no. 4.
1912   [Comanche Field Notes.] Department of Anthropology Archives. American Museum of Natural History. New York.
1915   Comanche Dances. In Dances and Societies of the Plains Shoshone. Anthropological Papers of the American Museum of Natural History, vol. 11, no. 7.
1927   The Origin of the State. New York: Harcourt, Brace, and World.
1952   Indians of the Plains. Reprint, Lincoln: University of Nebraska Press, 1982. (Page citations are to the reprint edition.)

Lummis, Charles Fletcher
   1898   Some Unpublished History: A New Mexico Episode in 1748. Land of
             Sunshine 8 (Jan.):75–78, 8 (Feb.):126–30.
Luna, Miguel Diaz de
   1810   [Indian Gifts, Dec. 1, 1810.] (BA 47:420.)
MacGowan, D. J.
   1865   [Notes of a Brief Stay among the Comanches, Caddos and Wichitas.
             Fort Smith, Ark., Sept. 1865.] (Copy by George Gibbs. NAA ms.
             1814).
MacKenzie, Ranald
   1872   [Letter to Assistant Adjutant General, Oct. 12, 1872.] (Letters Receiv-
             ed Relating to Difficulties with Indians. NARS Record Group 393, pt.
             1, entry 4875.)
MacLeod, William C.
   1928   The American Indian Frontier. New York: Alfred A. Knopf.
Maese, Juan de Dios
   1828   [Letter to Juan José Arocha, June 28, 1828.] (MANM 8:68; also NMA
             1828–629.)
Magnaghi, Russell M.
   1970   The Indian Slave Trade in the Southwest. The Comanche: A Test Case.
             Ph.D. diss., University of Nebraska.
Manrrique, Josef
   1809   [Letter to Nemesio Salcedo, Aug. 31, 1809.] (SANM T-2249, 16:938.)
   1810a   [Letter to Nemesio Salcedo, Mar. 27, 1810.] (SANM T-2308, 17:61.)
   1810b   [Letter to Nemesio Salcedo, Mar.29, 1810.] (SANM T-2310, 17:66.)
   1810c   [Letter to Nemesio Salcedo, Mar. 31, 1810.] (SANM T-2313, 17:86.)
   1810d   [Letter to Nemesio Salcedo, June 30, 1810.] (SANM T-2331, 17:126.)
Manypenny, George W.
   1856   [Report of the Commissioner of Indian Affairs.] (ARCIA 1856.)
Marcy, Randolph B.
   1849   Report of Capt. R. B. Marcy's Route from Fort Smith to Santa Fe. 31st
             Cong., 1st sess., Sen. Exec. Doc. 64, 169–227.
   1856   Report of Captain Marcy to Major Porter. 35th Cong., 2d sess., Sen.
             Exec. Doc. 1.
   1859   The Prairie Traveler: A Handbook for Overland Expeditions. New
             York: Harpers. Reprint, New York: Time-Life Books, 1981. (Page cit-
             ations are to the reprint edition.)
   1866   Thirty Years of Army Life on the Border. New York: Harper Brothers.
Margry, Pierre, ed.
   1886   Découvertes et établissments des français dans l'ouest et dans le sud de
             l'Amérique septentrionale (1614–1754). Vol. 6. Paris: Imprimierie de
             D. Jouaust.

Marín del Valle, Francisco
  1758   [Description of the Province of New Mexico, with a map which shows
          its situation and towns, made under Governor Don Francisco Marín
          del Valle.] (AGN, Californias, tomo 39, exp. 1.)
Marriott, Alice
  1962   Greener Fields. Garden City, New York: Dolphin Books.
Marshall, Doyle
  1985   Red Haired 'Indian' Raiders on the Texas Frontier. West Texas His-
          torical Association Year Book, vol. 61, 88-105. Abilene.
Marshall, Thomas Maitland
  1928   The Journals of Julius De Mun (Part II). Missouri Historical Society
          Collections, vol. 5, 311-26
Martin, Mabelle Eppard
  1925-26 From Texas to California in 1849: Diary of C. C. Cox. Southwestern
          Historical Quarterly 29:36-51, 128-47, 201-23.
Martín, Mariano
  1827   [Letter to Manuel Armijo, Sept. 23, 1827.] (MANM 6:956; also NMA
          1827-1175.)
Martínez, Felix
  1716   [Council of War, Oct. 14-Dec. 10, 1716.] (SANM T-259, 5:625.)
Martínez, Juan de Dios
  1803   [Invoice of Gifts, July 20, 1803.] (BA 31:423.)
Martínez, Manuel
  1827   [Letter to Simon Elias, Sept. 20, 1827.] (NMA 1827-1161.)
Martínez, Mariano
  1845a   [Letter to Juez de Paz, San Miguel, June 8, 1845.] (MANM 38:932.)
  1845b   [Letter to Departmental Assembly, June 27, 1845.] (MANM 38:740.)
Martínez Pacheco, Rafael
  1788   [Letter to Jacobo Ugarte y Loyola, Jan. 21, 1788.] (BA 18:800.)
  1789   [Letter to Juan de Ugalde, May 25, 1789.] (BA 19:827.)
Maynez, Alberto
  1815   [Journal of Events, Apr. 1-Dec. 1, 1815.] (SANM T-2585, 18:29-32.)
McCarty, John Lawton
  1946   Maverick Town: The Story of Old Tascosa. Norman: University of
          Oklahoma Press.
McCusker, Philip
  1866   [Letter to Thomas Murphy, Sept. 7, 1866; enclosure in letter from
          Murphy to D. N. Cooley, Sept. 17, 1866.] (Letters Received from the
          Kiowa Agency. NARS microfilm pub. M234, 375:390.)
  1867   [Letter to J. H. Leavenworth, May 19, 1867.] (Letters received from
          the Kiowa Agency. NARS microfilm pub. M234, 375:929.)
  1868a   [Letter to J. H. Leavenworth, Apr. 6, 1868; enclosure in Leavenworth
          to Taylor, May 21,1868.] (Letters Received from the Kiowa Agency.
          NARS microfilm pub. M234, 375:862.)

1868b   [Letter to J. H. Leavenworth, Apr. 10, 1868; enclosure in Leavenworth to Taylor, May 21, 1868.] (Letters Received from the Kiowa Agency. NARS microfilm pub. M234, 375:866.)

1868c   [Letter to N. G. Taylor, June 5, 1868.] (Letters Received from the Kiowa Agency; NARS microfilm pub. M234, 375:868.)

McElhannon, Joseph C.

1949   Imperial Mexico and Texas, 1821-1823. Southwestern Historical Quarterly 53:117-50.

McKisick, A. H.

1857   [Annual report, Agent, Wichita Agency.] (ARCIA 1857, no. 111.)

McLaws, Lafayette

1850a   [Letter to John Buford, June 7, 1850.] (Letters Sent, 9th Military District. NARS microfilm pub. M1072, 1:119.)

1850b   [Letter to John Buford, June 23, 1850.] (Letters Sent, 9th Military District. NARS microfilm pub. M1072, 1:130.)

McLean, Malcolm

1974-93 Papers concerning Robertson's Colony. 18 vols. Austin: University of Texas Press.

McLeod, Hugh

1840   Richmond, Texas, *Telescope and Register*, April 4.

Medill, W.

1847a   [Letter to R. S. Neighbors, Mar. 20, 1847.] (30th Cong., 1st sess., Sen. Committee Report 171, 1-4.)

1847b   [Letter to R. S. Neighbors, Aug. 20, 1847.] (30th Cong., 1st sess., Sen. Committee Report 171, 5-7)

Melgares, Facundo

1821   [Letter to Manuel Duran, Aug. 22, 1821.] (SANM T-3010, 20:740.)

Mendoza, Gaspar Domingo

1742   [Order to Alcaldes, Feb. 20, 1742.] (SANM T-443, 8:107.)

Meriweather, David

1855a   [Letter to George W. Manypenny, May 28, 1855.] (Letters Received from the New Mexico Superintendency, no. 1855-N439. NARS microfilm pub. M234, 547.)

1855b   [Letter to George W. Manypenny, May 28, 1855.] (Letters Received from the New Mexico Superintendency, no. 1855-N440. NARS microfilm pub. M234, 547.)

Messervy, William S.

1853   [Affidavit of Goods Bought and Delivered to the Comanche and Apache Indians, April 1851.] (Records of the New Mexico Superintendency. NARS microfilm pub. T21, 1.)

Mexico, Republic of

1878   Tratados y convenciones concluidos y ratificados por la republica mexicana. Mexico, D.F.: Gonzalo A. Estura.

Middlebrooks, Audy J., and Glenna Middlebrooks
    1965   Holland Coffee of Red River. Southwestern Historical Quarterly 69: 145–62.

Miller, Robert C.
    1856   [Letter to A. J. Cummings, Nov. 29, 1856.] (Records of the Central Superintendency. NARS microfilm pub. M856, 3:467.)
    1857a   [Letter to William Bent, July 20, 1857.] (Records of the Central Superintendency. NARS microfilm pub. M856, 3:571.)
    1857b   [Letter to Lavertz, Oct. 1, 1857.] (Records of the Central Superintendency. NARS microfilm pub. M856, 3:593.)
    1857c   [Annual report, Agent, Upper Arkansas Agency.] (ARCIA 1857, doc. 60.)
    1858a   [Invoices of Goods Received for the Use of the Comanche, Kiowa, and Apache Indians of the Arkansas River for the Year 1858, May 12, 1858] (Records of the Central Superintendency. NARS microfilm pub. M856, 5:198.)
    1858b   [Annual report, Agent, Upper Arkansas Agency.] (ARCIA 1858, doc. 27.)

Mitchell, D. D.
    1852a   [Telegram to Luke Lea, Aug. 3, 1852.] (Letters Received from the Central Superintendency. NARS microfilm pub. M234, 55:178.)
    1852b   [Letter to Luke Lea, Aug. 3. 1852.] (Letters Received from the Central Superintendency. NARS microfilm pub. M234, 55:181.)

Mix, Charles E.
    1867   [Letter to A. G. Norton, Sept. 17, 1867.] (Records of the New Mexico Superintendency. NARS microfilm pub. T21, 7.)

Montaignes, François des
    1852–56 The Plains. Reprint, edited by Nancy A. Mower and Don Russell. Norman: University of Oklahoma Press, 1972. (Page citations are to the reprint edition.)

Mooney, James
    [n.d.]   [Report of Indian Prisoners Confined at Fort Marion, St. Augustine, Fla., during the Month of May, 1875.] (NAA ms. 1916.)
    1896   The Ghost-Dance Religion and the Sioux Outbreak of 1890. Fourteenth Annual Report of the Bureau of American Ethnology for the Years 1892–93, pt. 2. Washington, D.C.
    1898   Calendar History of the Kiowa Indians. Seventeenth Annual Report of the Bureau of American Ethnology for the Years 1895–96, pt. 1. Washington, D.C.
    1910   Tenawa. In Handbook of American Indians North of Mexico, edited by Frederick W. Hodge. Vol. 2, 728. Smithsonian Institution, Bureau of American Ethnology Bulletin 30. Washington, D.C.

Moore, John H.
    1980   Aboriginal Indian Residence Patterns Preserved in Censuses and Allotments. Science 207:201–2.

1988   The Cheyenne Nation. Lincoln: University of Nebraska Press.
Moorhead, Max
1968   Apache Frontier. Norman: University of Oklahoma Press.
Moreno, José Maria
1831   [Letter to Antonio Elozúa, July 27, 1831.] (BA 143:163.)
Morfi, Fray Juan Agustín
1935   History of Texas, 1673-1779. Translated by Carlos E. Castañeda. 2
            vols. Albuquerque: Quivira Society.
Morse, Jedidiah
1822   Report to the Secretary of War of the United States on Indian Affairs,
            Comprising a narrative of a Tour performed in the summer of 1820,
            Under a Commission of the President of the United States, for the Pur-
            pose of Ascertaining, for the Use of the Government, the Actual State
            of the Indian Tribes in Our Country. New Haven, Conn.: S. Converse.
Morton, Ohland
1948   Terán and Texas: A Chapter in Texas-Mexican Relations. Austin: Tex-
            as Historical Association.
Muñoz, Manuel
1791   [Letter to Juan Cortés, Sept. 9, 1791.] (BA 21:702.)
1792a   [Promissory note for tobacco, Mar. 1, 1792.] (BA 22:153.)
1792b   [Order for supplies, Mar. 3, 1792.] (BA 22:159.)
1792c   [Letter to Francisco Amangual, Mar. 27, 1792.] (BA 22:263.)
1795   [List of presents, Jan. 16, 1795.] (BA 25:261.)
Murphy, Thomas
1865   [Goods Distributed at Treaty Grounds, October 26, 1865; enclosure in
            letter to D. N. Cooley, Feb. 22, 1866.] (Letters Received from the
            Kiowa Agency. NARS microfilm pub. M234, 375:322.)
Múzquiz, Manuel
1801   [Letter to Juan Bautista de Elguézabal, July 29, 1801.] (BA 30:219.)
Músquiz, Ramón
1834   [Letter to Béxar Ayuntamiento, May 1834.] (BA 161:779.)
Narbona, Antonio
1825   [Letter to Tomas Sena, Sept. 21, 1825.] (MANM 4:827; also NMA
            1825-475.)
1826a   [Letter to Agustín Duran, July 6, 1826.] (NMA 1826-654.)
1826b   [Letter to Agustín Duran, Aug. 19, 1826.] (MANM 6:156; also NMA
            1826-720.)
1827   [Audit of the Indian Fund, July 1, 1827.] (MANM 7:548.)
Nava, Pedro de
1791   [Letter to Domingo Diaz, Jan. 11, 1791.] (SANM T-1112a, 12:505.)
1793a   [Letter to Fernando de la Concha, Aug. 8, 1793.] (SANM T-1247, 13:
            335.)
1793b   [Letter to Fernando de la Concha, Dec. 31, 1793.] (SANM T-1272, 13:
            467.)
1794   [Letter to Governor of Texas, Feb. 26, 1794.] (BA 24:523.)

1795   [Letter to Governor of Texas, June 4, 1795.] (BA 25:541.)
1797   [Letter to Fernando Chacón, Oct. 19, 1797.] (SANM T-1399, 14:202.)
1798   [Letter to Governor of Texas, Dec. 25, 1798.] (BA 28:601.)
1802   [Letter to Governor of Texas, Jan. 19, 1802.] (BA 30:536.)

Navarro, Angel
1835   [Letter to Béxar Ayuntamiento, Aug. 27, 1835.] (BA 166:470.)

Navarro García, Luis
1964   Don José de Galvez y la comadancia general de las provincias internas
          del norte de Nueva España. Seville: Consejo Superior de Investi-
          gaciones Científicas.

Neighbors, Robert S.
1847a   [Letter to W. Medill, Apr. 24, 1847.] (Letters Received from the Texas
          Agency. NARS microfilm pub. M234, 858:16.)
1847b   [Letter to W. Medill, June 22, 1847.] (ARCIA 1847, doc. 22.)
1847c   [Letter to W. Medill, Aug. 5, 1847.] (Letters Received from the Texas
          Agency. NARS microfilm pub. M234, 858:40; also ARCIA 1847, doc.
          23.)
1847d   [Letter to W. Medill, Sept. 14, 1847.] (ARCIA 1847, doc. 24.)
1847e   [Letter to W. Medill, Oct. 12, 1847.] (ARCIA 1847, doc. 25.)
1847f   [Letter to W. Medill, Nov. 18, 1847.] (Letters Received from the Texas
          Agency. NARS microfilm pub. M234, 858:110. Also 30th Cong., 1st
          sess., Sen. Committee Report 171, 9-10.)
1847g   [Letter to J. Pinckney Henderson, Dec. 10, 1847. Enclosure in Neigh-
          bors to W. Medill, Dec. 13, 1847.] (Letters received from the Texas
          Agency. NARS microfilm pub. M234, 858:121. Also 30th Cong., 1st
          sess., Sen. Committee Report 171, 10-11.)
1848a   [Letter to W. Medill, Jan. 20, 1848.] (Letters Received from the Texas
          Agency. NARS microfilm pub. M234, 858:133. Also ARCIA 1848,
          doc. 22-A.).
1848b   [Letter to W. Medill, Mar. 2, 1848.] (Letters Received from the Texas
          Agency. NARS microfilm pub. M234, 858:153. Also 30th Cong., 1st
          sess., Sen. Committee Report 171, 16-25. Also ARCIA 1848, doc. 22-
          C.).
1848c   [Letter to H. O. Hedgcoxe, no date.] (30th Cong., 1st sess., Sen. Com-
          mittee Report 171, 15-16).
1848d   [Letter to W. Medill, June 15, 1848.] (ARCIA 1848, doc. 22-E.)
1848e   [Letter to W. Medill, Oct. 23, 1848.] (Letters Received from the Texas
          Agency. NARS microfilm pub. M234, 858:212. Also ARCIA 1848,
          doc. 22-K.)
1849a   [Letter to W. Medill, Feb. 15, 1849.] (Letters Received from the Texas
          Agency. NARS microfilm pub. M234, 858:381.)
1849b   [Letter to W. Medill, June 18, 1849.] (Letters Received from the Texas
          Agency. NARS microfilm pub. M234, 858:391.)

1849c   [Letter to W. J. Worth, Aug. 9, 1849. Enclosure in Neighbors to O. Brown, Aug. 9, 1849.] (Letters Received from the Texas Agency. NARS microfilm pub. M234, 858:402.)

1852   The Naüni, or Comanches of Texas. *In* Historical and Statistical Information respecting the History, Condition and Prospects of the Indian Tribes of the United States, edited by Henry R. Schoolcraft. Vol. 2, 125- 34. Philadelphia: Lippincott, Grambo.

1853   [Letter to W. Medill, Nov. 21, 1853.] (Letters Received from the Texas Agency. NARS microfilm pub. M234, 859:306.)

1856   [Report, Supervising Agent, Texas Indians.] (ARCIA 1856, doc. 68.)

1857   [Quarterly Return of Property, Dec. 1857. Enclosure in Neighbors to Mix, Jan. 1858.] (Letters Received from the Texas Agency. NARS microfilm pub. M234, 861:167.)

1858a   [Letter to C. E. Mix, Jan. 17, 1858.] (Letters Received from the Texas Agency. NARS microfilm pub. M234, 861:131.)

1858b   [Letter to J. W. Denver, Dec. 9, 1858.] (Letters Received from the Texas Agency; NARS microfilm pub. M234, 861:839.)

Neighbours, Kenneth F.

1954   The Expedition of Major Robert S. Neighbors to El Paso in 1849. Southwestern Historical Quarterly 58:36-59.

1965   The Battle of Walker's Creek. West Texas Historical Association Year Book, vol. 41, 121-30. Abilene.

1975   Robert S. Neighbors and the Texas Frontier 1836-1859. Waco, Tex.: Texian Press.

Norton, A. B.

1866   [Annual report, Superintendent, New Mexico Superintendency.] (ARCIA 1866, doc. 47.)

1867   [Letter to N. G. Taylor, Nov. 26, 1867.] (Records of the New Mexico Superintendency. NARS microfilm pub. T21, 7.)

Nye, Wilbur S.

1968   Plains Indian Raiders. Norman: University of Oklahoma Press.

1969   Carbine and Lance. Norman: University of Oklahoma Press.

Ocaranza, Fernando

1934   Estableimientos franciscanos en el misterioso reino de Nuevo Mexico. Mexico, D.F.

Ochoa, Gaspar de

1825a   [Letter to Comandante Principal, Jan. 25, 1825.] (MANM 4:658; also NMA 1825-142.)

1825b   [Letter to Comandante Principal, Mar. 8, 1825.] (MANM 4:665; also NMA 1825-199.)

O'Fallon, Benjamin

1823   [Letter to Governor of New Mexico, Aug. 1, 1823.] (Letters Received from the St. Louis Superintendency. NARS microfilm pub. M234, 747.)

1824   [Letter to Governor of New Mexico, Dec. 13, 1824.] (Records of the
        Central Superintendency. NARS microfilm pub. M856, 2:46.)

Ohlendorf, S. M., J. M. Bigalow, and M. M. Stadifer
1980   Berlandier's Journey to Mexico during the Years 1826 to 1834. Austin:
        Texas State Historical Association.

Olavide y Micheleña, Henrique de
1737   [*Bando* on Indian Trade, Jan. 7, 1737.] (SANM T-414, 7:552.)

Oliver, Symmes C.
1962   Ecology and Cultural Continuity as Contributing Factors in the Social
        Organization of the Plains Indians. University of California Publica-
        tions in American Archeology and Ethnology, vol. 48, no. 1. Berkeley.

Opler, Morris
1983   The Apachean Culture Pattern and its Origins. *In* Handbook of North
        American Indians, edited by William C. Sturtevant. Vol. 10, South-
        west, edited by Alfonso Ortiz, 368-92. Washington, D.C.: Government
        Printing Office.

Orandain, Francisco
1796   [Report of Gunsmith, Mar. 30, 1796.] (BA 26:557.)

Ortiz, Polonio
1872   [Copy of Statement. Enclosure in Crosby to Secretary of the Interior,
        Nov. 23, 1872.] (NARS microfilm pub. M234, 375:108.)

Ortiz, Fernando, Santiago Ulibari, Rafael García
1835   [Report on Commission, Mar. 24, 1835] (MANM 19:527.)

Parker, Ely S.
1871   [Letter to Enoch Hoag, June 29, 1871.] (OHS-KA 47:72.)

Parker, William B.
1856   Notes Taken during the Expedition Commanded by Capt. R. B. Marcy.
        Philadelphia.

Pedraga, Gómez
1825   [Letter to Antonio Elozúa, Feb. 2, 1825.] (BA 79:299.)

Peña, Juan de Dios
1790   [Diary and Itinerary of a Campaign in Aid of the Comanches against
        the Pananas, June 12-Aug. 8, 1790.] (SANM T-1089, 12:262.)
1805   [Record of Military Campaigns, Aug. 14, 1805.] (SANM T-1874, 15:
        773.)

Pérez, Ignacio
1818a   [Letter to Antonio Martínez, Mar. 16, 1818.] (BA 60:685.)
1818b   [Letter to Antonio Martínez, May 31, 1818.] (BA 61:125.)

Perrine, Fred S.
1927   Military Escorts on the Santa Fe Trail. New Mexico Historical Review
        2:175-93, 269-304.
1928   Military Escorts on the Santa Fe Trail. New Mexico Historical Review
        3:265-300.

Perrine, Fred S., and Grant Foreman
1925   The Journal of Hugh Evans. Chronicles of Oklahoma 3:194-214.

Pettis, G. H.
  1908   Kit Carson's Fight with the Comanche and Kiowa Indians. New Mex-
            ico Historical Society Publications, no. 12. Santa Fe.

Piedras, José de las
  1832   [Letter to Antonio Elozúa, May 21, 1832.] (BA 150:180.)

Pike, Albert
  1833   [Letter to John Cass (sic), Mar. 16, 1833.] (Letters Received from the
            Western Superintendency. NARS microfilm pub. M234, 921:166.)

  1843   Prose Sketches and Poems. Reprint, Albuquerque: C. Horn, 1967.
            (Page citations are to the reprint edition.)

  1861a   Articles of a Convention . . . between the Confederate States of Amer-
            ica . . . and the Peneteghca band of the Neum. Official Records of the
            War of the Rebellion, ser. 4, vol. 1, 542–48.

  1861b   Articles of a Convention . . . between the Confederate States of
            America . . . and the No-co-ni, Ta-ni-ewah, Co-cho-tih-ca, and Ya-pa-
            ri-cah bands of the Neum. Official Records of the War of the
            Rebellion, ser. 4, vol. 1, 548–55.

  1862   Report, May 4, 1862. Official Records of the War of the Rebellion,
            ser. 1, vol. 13, 819–23.

  1866   [Comanche Gentes.] (NAA ms. 593a.)

  1886   [Autobiography of General Albert Pike.] (Manuscript. Library of the
            Supreme Council, 33°, Ancient and Accepted Scottish Rite, Washing-
            ton, D.C.)

Pilling, James C.
  1889   Bibliography of the Muskhogean Languages. Smithsonian Institution.
            Bureau of Ethnology Bulletin 9. Washington, D.C.

Pohocsucut, Sarah
  1961   Comanches. [Unpublished notes taken by Gillett Griswold. Fort Sill
            Museum, Fort Sill, Okla.]

Polk, James K.
  1910   The Diaries of James K. Polk during His Presidency, 1845 to 1849.
            Edited by Milo Milton Quaife. 4 vols. Chicago: Chicago Historical
            Society.

Pratt, R. H.
  1875   [Letter to J. W. Davidson, Jan. 11, 1875.] (Letters Received from the
            Military Department of Texas, no. 302 DT 75. NARS Record Group
            393, pt. 1, entry 4875.)

  1878   [Letter to Spencer F. Baird, Feb. 9, 1878; List of Indians; Notes on the
            Preceding List.] In Spencer F. Baird, Catalogue of Casts taken by
            Clark Mills, Esq., of the Heads of Sixty-Four Indian Prisoners of
            Various Western Tribes, and Held at Fort Marion, Saint Augustine,
            Fla., in Charge of Capt. R. H. Pratt, U.S.A. Proceedings of the United
            States National Museum, vol. 1, 201–13.

  1905   Some Indian Experiences. Journal of the United States Cavalry Asso-
            ciation 17:200-217.

1964   Battlefield and Classroom: Four Decades with the American Indian, 1867-1904. Edited by Robert M. Utley. New Haven: Yale University Press.

Ramirez, Alexander
1826   [Letter to Comandante Principal, Oct. 6, 1826.] (MANM 6:553; also NMA 1826-1002.)

Reher, Charles A.
1977   Adaptive Process on the Shortgrass Plains. *In* For Theory Building in Archaeology, edited by Lewis R. Binford, 13-40. New York: Academic Press.

Rengel, Joseph Antonio
1785   [Letter to José de Gálvez, Dec. 31, 1785. 116] (AGI, Guadalajara, Legajo 286.)
1786   [Letter to Domingo Cabello, Jan. 27, 1786.] (BA 17:222; also AGI, Guadalajara, Legajo 286.)

Rey, Ysidro
1810-11   [Accounts of the Santa Fe Company.] (SANM T-2372, 17:209.)
1814   [Letter to Bernardo Bonavia, Dec. 5, 1814.] (BA 54:498.)

Richardson, J. M.
1847   [Letter to W. Medill, Mar. 31, 1847.] (Letters Received from the Texas Agency. NARS microfilm pub. M234, 858:248.)

Richardson, Rupert N.
1929   The Comanche Reservation in Texas. West Texas Historical Association Year Book, vol. 5, 43-65. Abilene.
1933   The Comanche Barrier to South Plains Settlement. Glendale, Cal.: Arthur H. Clark.

Rister, Carl Coke
1955   Comanche Bondage: Beale's Settlement and Sarah Ann Horn's Narrative. Reprint, Lincoln: University of Nebraska Press, 1989. (Page citations are to the reprint edition.)

Rivera, Pedro de
1946   Diario y derrotero de lo camionado, visto y observado en la visita que lo hizo a los presidios de la Nuevo España septentrional. Edited by Vito Allesio Robles. Secretaria de la Defensa Nacional, Mexico, D.F.

Robinson, A. M.
1859   [Letter to A. B. Greenwood, Aug. 6, 1859.] (Letters Received from the Central Superintendency. NARS microfilm pub. M234, 56:999.)

Robinson, Lila Wistrand, and James Armagost
1990   Comanche Dictionary and Grammar. Arlington, Texas: Summer Institute of Linguistics and the University of Texas at Arlington.

[Rodriguez, Guadalupe]
1833-39   [Military Records of Guadalupe Rodriguez, 1833-39.] (NMA 1833-124.)

Roe, Frank Gilbert
1955   The Indian and the Horse. Norman: University of Oklahoma Press.

Roemer, Ferdinand
1935   Texas. San Antonio: Standard Printing Co.
Rogers, John
1839   [Letter to Matthew Arbuckle, May 3, 1839.] (Letters Received from
the Western Superintendency. NARS microfilm pub. M234, 922:593.)
Rollins, John H.
1850a   [Letter to Orlando Brown, May 8, 1850.] (Letters Received from the
Texas Agency. NARS microfilm pub. M234, 858:513.)
1850b   [Letter to Orlando Brown, May 30, 1850.] (Letters Received from the
Texas Agency. NARS microfilm pub. M234, 858:525. Also extracted
in ARCIA 1850, doc. 34.]
Ronquillo, José María
1832   [Letter to Ayudante Inspector, Oct. 31, 1832 (#386).] (MANM 14:914;
also NMA 1832-88.)
1833   [Letter to Ayudante Inspector, June 28, 1833 (#419).] (MANM 14:930;
also NMA 1832-117.)
Ronquillo, José María, and Donaciano Vigil
1831   [Report on Depredations near Tierra Blanca, Sept. 17, 1831]. (MANM
13:559.)
Ross, Sullivan P.
1858a   [Letter to R. S. Neighbors, Feb. 17, 1858. Enclosure in Neighbors to C.
E. Mix, Apr. 2, 1858.] (Letters Received from the Texas Agency;
NARS microfilm pub. M234, 861:311.)
1858b   [Letter to R. S. Neighbors, June 30, 1858. Enclosure in Neighbors to
C. E. Mix, July 28, 1858.] (Letters Received from the Texas Agency.
NARS microfilm pub. M234, 861:526.)
Rubio, Josef
1778   [Report on Military Operations, Jan. 8, 1778.] (SANM T-716, 10:965.)
Ruíz, José Francisco
1821   [Letter to Antonio Martínez, Oct. 15, 1821.] (BA 68:587.)
1822   [Letter to Béxar Ayuntamiento, Apr. 2, 1822.] (BA 71:283.)
1823   [Letter to Luciano García, Oct. 8, 1823.] (BA 75:411.)
1824   [Letter to Gaspar Flores, Oct. 18, 1824.] (BA 78:131.)
1828   Report on the Indian Tribes of Texas in 1828. Edited by John C.
Ewers. New Haven: Yale University Library, 1972.
Ruíz, [José Francisco]
1921   [Comanches; Customs and Characteristics.] In The Papers of Mirabeau
Buonaparte Lamar, edited by C. A. Gulick, Katherine Elliott, Winnie
Allen, and Harriet Smither. Vol. 4, 221-23. Austin, Tex.: Van Boeckmann Jones.
Sahlins, Marshall
1961   Segementary Lineage: An Organization of Predatory Expansion. American Anthropologist 63:322-45.
1963   Poor Man, Richman, Bigman, Chief: Political Types in Polynesia and
Melanesia. Comparative Studies in Society and History 5:285-303.

1968   Tribesmen. Englewood Cliffs, N.J.: Prentice Hall.

Salazar, Donacio

1841   [Letter to Manuel Armijo, Jan. 10, 1841.] (MANM 28:1195.)

Salcedo, Manuel de

1810   [Interrogation of Comanches, 1810.] (BA 47:701.)

1812   [Proceedings concerning Oso Ballo's conspiracy, Mar. 6, 1812.] (BA 50:627.)

Salcedo, Manuel de, Bernardo Bonavia, and Símon de Herrera

1810   [Council of War, October 1810.] (BA 47:123.)

Salcedo, Nemesio

1803a   [Letter to Fernando Chacón, May 14, 1803.] (SANM T-1656a, 15:40.)

1803b   [Letter to Fernando Chacón, Sept. 16, 1803.] (SANM T-1677, 15:102.)

1803c   [Letter to Juan Bautista de Elguézabal, Sept. 26, 1803.] (BA 31:642.)

1803d   [Letter to Juan Bautista de Elguézabal, Oct. 11, 1803.] (BA 31:712.)

1804   [Letter to Fernando Chacón, Jan. 16, 1804.] (SANM T-1703, 15:176.)

1805   [Letter to Governor of Texas, Aug. 3, 1805.] (BA 33:529.)

1806a   [Letter to Manuel Antonio Cordero, May 19, 1806.] (BA 34:665.)

1806b   [Letter to Manuel Antonio Cordero, June 3, 1806.] (BA 34:722.)

1807   [Letter to Joaquín del Real Alencaster, Sept. 17, 1807.] (SANM T-2076, 16:388.)

1811   [Letter to Símon de Herrera, Dec. 18, 1811.] (BA 49:756.)

1812a   [Letter to Manuel de Salcedo, Apr. 27, 1812.] (BA 51:84.)

1812b   [Letter to Manuel de Salcedo, June 8, 1812.] (BA 51:468.)

Sanborn, John B., William S. Harney, J. Steele, Thomas Murphy, and Jesse Leavenworth

1865   [Report of Treaty Commission, October 16-24, 1865.] (ARCIA 1865, Appendix 14A.).

Sánchez y Tapia, José María

1926   A Trip to Mexico in 1828. Translated by Carlos E. Casteñeda. Southwestern Historical Quarterly 29:249-88.

1939   Viage á Texas en 1828-29. Mexico, D.F.

Sarracino, Francisco

1833   [Letter to Secretarío de Estado, Nov. 30, 1833.] (MANM 16:381.)

Sarracino, José Rafael

1795   [Indian Expenses, Apr. 30, 1795.] (SANM T-1320, 13:677.)

Schlesier, Karl H.

1972   Rethinking the Dismal River Aspect and the Plains Athabaskans, A.D. 1692-1768. Plains Anthropologist 17:101-33.

Schofield, George W.

1872   [Copy of letter to Assistant Adjutant General, Dept of Texas, Oct. 10, 1872; enclosure in H. F. Crosby to Secretary of the Interior, Nov. 23, 1872.] (Letters Received from the Kiowa Agency. NARS microfilm pub. M234, 375:108].

Schoolcraft, Henry R.
    1851-57 Historical and Statistical Information Respecting the History, Condi-
            tion, and Prospect of the Indian Tribes of the United States. 6 vols.
            Philadelphia: Lippincott, Grambo.
Schroeder, Alfred
    1974   Apache Indians. New York: Garland.
Scott, Hugh L.
    1898   [Comanche notes.] (NAA ms. 2932.)
Secoy, Frank R.
    1951   The Identity of the Paduca: An Ethnohistorical Analysis. American
            Anthropologist 53:525-42.
    1953   Changing Military Patterns on the Plains. Monographs of the American
            Ethnological Society 21. Locust Valley, N.Y.: J. J. Augustin.
Seguín, Juan Nepomuceno
    1834   [Letter to Ramón Musquiz, Apr. 6, 1834.] (BA 161:13.)
Sena, Antonío
    1840   [Fondo de Aliadas, Aug. 19, 1840.] (NMA 1840-35.)
Sena, Miguel
    1832   [Letter, Feb. 13, 1832.] (NMA 1832-260.)
Sena, Tomas
    1825a   [Letter to Antonio Narbona, Sept. 8, 1825.] (MANM 4:730; also NMA
            1825-452.)
    1825b   [Letter to Antonio Narbona, Sept. 17, 1825.] (MANM 4:734; also
            NMA 1825-461.)
    1825c   [Letter to Antonio Narbona, Dec. 30, 1825.] (MANM 4:771; also
            NMA 1825-704.)
Service, Elman
    1962   Primitive Social Organization. New York: Random House.
Sherman, William T.
    1867   [Endorsement, June 25, 1867, on letter of May 14, 1867, from Mark
            Walker to C. McKeever] (Letters Received from the Kiowa Agency.
            NARS microfilm pub. M234, 375:714. Also Winfrey and Day
            1959-66, 4:209-10)
Shimkin, Demitri B.
    1940   Shoshone-Comanche Origins and Migrations. Proceedings of the Sixth
            Pacific Science Congress, vol. 5, 17-25.
    1941   Uto-Aztecan Kinship Terms. American Anthropologist 43:223-45.
    1947   Wind River Shoshone Ethnogeography. Anthropological Records, Uni-
            versity of California, vol. 5, no. 4. Berkeley.
    1980   Comanche Shoshone Words of Acculturation. Journal of the Steward
            Anthropological Society 11:195-248.
Sibley, John
    1805   [Letter to the Secretary of War, Apr. 5, 1805.] (Letters Received by the
            Secretary of War Related to Indian Affairs. NARS microfilm pub.

M271, 1:302. Also American State Papers, Indian Affairs, vol. 1, 721–25.)

1807a   [Letter to the Secretary of War, Sept. 7, 1807.] (Letters Received by the Secretary of War Related to Indian Affairs. NARS microfilm pub. M271, 1:417).

1807b   A Report from Natchitoches in 1807. Edited by A. H. Abel. Indian Notes and Monographs. New York: Museum of the American Indian. (Typescript in Letters Received by the Secretary of War Related to Indian Affairs. NARS microfilm pub. M271, 1:398.)

Siegel, Bernard J., and Alan Beals

1960   Pervasive Factionalism. American Anthropologist 62:394–417.

Simmons, Marc

1967   Border Comanches. Santa Fe, N.M.: Stagecoach Press.

1968   Spanish Government in New Mexico. Albuquerque: University of New Mexico Press.

1979   History of Pueblo–Spanish Relations to 1821. In Handbook of North American Indians, edited by William C. Sturtevant. Vol. 9, The Southwest, edited by Alfonso Ortiz, 178–93. Washington, D.C.: Smithsonian Institution.

Simpson, James

1849   [Report of Lt. James Simpson, Topographical Engineers.] (31st Cong., 1st sess., House Exec. Doc. 45.)

Slotkin, James S.

1974   The Peyote Religion: A Study in Indian–White Relations. New York: Octagon Books.

Smith, Clinton L., and Jefferson D. Smith

1927   The Boy Captives. Edited by J. M. Hunter. Bandera, Tex.: Frontier Times.

Smith, E. L.

1867   [Letter to O. D. Green, Feb. 16, 1867.] (Letters Received from the Kiowa Agency. NARS microfilm pub. M234, 375:516.)

Smith, E. P.

1873a   [Telegram to James M. Haworth, Nov. 24, 1873. Letter 167/493; page 474.] (Letters Sent by the Office of Indian Affairs. NARS microfilm pub. M21, 114.)

1873b   [Telegram to Enoch Hoag, Nov. 24, 1873. Letter 467/477; page 471.] (Letters Sent by the Office of Indian Affairs. NARS microfilm pub. M21, 114.)

Smith, Ralph A.

1959   The Comanche Invasion of Mexico in the Fall of 1845. West Texas Historical Association Year Book, vol. 35, 3–28. Abilene.

1960   Mexican and Anglo-Saxon Traffic in Scalps, Slaves and Livestock, 1835–1841. West Texas Historical Association Year Book, vol. 36, 98–115. Abilene.

1970   The Comanche Sun over Mexico. West Texas Historical Association Year Book, vol. 46, 25–62. Abilene.

1971   Many Mini Treaties. West Texas Historical Association Year Book, vol. 47, 62–77. Abilene.

1972   The Fantasy of A Treaty to End Treaties. Great Plains Journal 12:26–51.

Smithwick, Noah

1899   The Evolution of a State, or Recollections of Old Texas Days. Reprint, Austin: University of Texas Press, 1983. (Page citations are to the reprint edition.)

Sonnichsen, C. L.

1968   Pass of the North. El Paso: Texas Western Press.

Spier, Leslie

1921   The Sun Dance of the Plains Indians: Its Development and Diffusion. Anthropological Papers of the American Museum of Natural History, vol. 16, no. 7.

Stanley, F.

1953   Fort Union. St. Louis: Published by the author.

Stanley, Henry M.

1967   A British Journalist Reports the Medicine Lodge Councils of 1867. Kansas Historical Quarterly 33:249–320.

Stanley, John Mix

1852   Portraits of North American Indians, with Sketches of Scenery, etc., painted by J. M. Stanley. Deposited with the Smithsonian Institution. Washington, D.C.

Stearn, Ester A., and Allen E. Stearn

1945   The Effect of Smallpox on the Destiny of the Amerindian. Boston: Bruce Humphries

Steele, William

1849   [Letter to G. Deas, Sept. 23, 1849. Copy, enclosure in G. W. Bamford to Thomas Ewing, Oct. 20, 1849.] (Letters Received from the Texas Agency. NARS microfilm pub. M234, 858:440.)

Stephens, F.F.

1916   Missouri and the Santa Fe Trade. Missouri Historical Review 10:233–62.

Stem, Jesse

1851   Indian Population of Texas in 1851. In Historical and Statistical Information Respecting the History, Conditions, and Prospects of the Indian Tribes of the United States, edited by Henry R. Schoolcraft. Vol. 3, 635. Philadelphia: Lippincott, Grambo.

Steward, Julian H.

1955   Theory of Culture Change. Urbana: University of Illinois Press.

Stewart, John

1835   [Letter to W. Seawell, Mar. 28, 1835.] (Letters Received from the Western Superintendency. NARS microfilm pub. M234, 921:872.)

Stokes, Montford, and F. W. Armstrong
 1835 [Letter to Lewis Cass, Dec. 29, 1835.] (Letters Received from the Western Superintendency. NARS microfilm pub. M234, 921:1069.)

Storrs, Augustus
 1825 Answers of Augustus Storrs, of Missouri, to Certain Questions upon the Origin, Present State, and Future Prospects of Trade and Intercourse Between Missouri and the Internal Provinces of Mexico, Propounded by the Hon. Mr. Benton, Jan. 5, 1825. 18th Cong., 2d sess., Sen. Doc. 7.

Streeter, Thomas W.
 1983 Bibliography of Texas. Edited by A. Hanna. Woodbridge, Conn.: Research Publishing Co.

Sturm, Jacob J.
 1875 [Notes of Travel in Search of the Quah-di-ru Band of Comanches.] (Military Department of the Missouri, Letters Received, 1875-S248/2. NARS Record Group 98.)

Sturtevant, William C.
 1971 Creek into Seminole. In North American Indians in Historical Perspective, edited by Eleanor Leacock and Nancy Lurie, 92-128. New York: Random House.
 1983 Tribe and State in the Sixteenth and Twentieth Centuries. In The Development of Political Organization in Native North America, edited by Elizabeth Tooker, 3-16. 1979 Proceedings of the American Ethnological Society. Washington, D.C.

Sutton, Mark Q.
 1986 Warfare and Expansion: An Ethnohistorical Perspective on the Numic Spread. Journal of California and Great Basin Anthropology 8:65-82.

Straus, Anne S.
 1994 Northern Cheyenne Kinship Reconsidered. In North American Indian Anthropology, edited by Raymond J. DeMallie and Alfonso Ortiz, 147-71. Norman: University of Oklahoma Press.

Swagerty, William
 1988 Indian Trade in the Trans-Mississippi West to 1870. In Handbook of North American Indians, edited by William C. Sturtevant. Vol. 4, History of Indian-White Relations, edited by Wilcomb Washburn, 351-74. Washington, D.C.: Smithsonian Institution.

Swartz, Mark, Victor Turner, and Arthur Tuden, eds.
 1966 Political Anthropology. Chicago: Aldine.

Tatum, Lawrie
 1869a [Letter to E. S. Parker, July 24, 1869.] (Letters Received from the Kiowa Agency. NARS microfilm pub. M234, 376:290.)
 1869b [Telegram to E. S. Parker, Aug. 10, 1869.] (Letters Received from the Kiowa Agency. NARS microfilm pub. M234, 376:288.)
 1870a [Letter to E. S. Parker, May 7, 1870.] (Letters Received from the Kiowa Agency. NARS microfilm pub. M234, 376:892.)

1870b   [Letter to Enoch Hoag, Oct. 27, 1870.] (Letters Received from the Kiowa Agency. NARS microfilm pub. M234, 376:1042.)

1870c   [Letter to Enoch Hoag, Dec. 31, 1870.] (Letters Received, Central Superintendency. NARS microfilm pub. M856, 29.)

1870d   [Nominal List Containing the Name of Each Head of Band in the Comanche and Kiowa Tribes of Indians, December 30, 1870.] (OHS-KA 1A:865.)

1871a   [Letter to Enoch Hoag, Feb. 10, 1871.] (Letters Received, Central Superintendency. NARS microfilm pub. M856, 34:338.)

1871b   [Letter to Enoch Hoag, Feb. 10, 1871.] (Letters Received, Central Superintendency. NARS microfilm pub. M856, 34.)

1871c   [Letter to Enoch Hoag, May 12, 1871.] (Letters Received, Central Superintendency. NARS microfilm pub. M856, 34.)

1871d   [Letter to Enoch Hoag, May 13, 1871.] (Letters Received, Central Superintendency. NARS microfilm pub. M856, 34.)

1871e   [Letter to Enoch Hoag, May 20, 1871.] (Letters Received, Central Superintendency. NARS microfilm pub. M856, 34.)

1871f   [Letter to Enoch Hoag, July 13, 1871.] (Letters Received, Central Superintendency. NARS microfilm pub. M856, 34.)

1871g   [Letter to Colonels Benjamin Grierson and Ranald MacKenzie, Aug. 4, 1871.] (Letters Received, Central Superintendency. NARS microfilm pub. M856, 34.)

1871h   [Letter to Jonathan Richards, Dec. 12, 1871.] (OHS-KA 6:177.)

1872a   [Letter to Jonathan Richards, Jan. 20, 1872.] (OHS-KA 6:211.)

1872b   [Letter to Jonathan Richards, Feb. 1, 1872.] (OHS-KA 6:231.)

1872c   [Letter to Enoch Hoag, Feb. 3, 1872.] (OHS-KA 47:322; also OHS-KA 6:112; also Letters Received, Central Superintendency. NARS microfilm pub. M856, 41:494.)

1872d   [Letter to Jonathan Richards, Mar. 1, 1872.] (OHS-KA 6:260.)

1872e   [Letter to Enoch Hoag, Mar. 30, 1872.] (Letters Received, Central Superintendency. NARS microfilm pub. M856, 34; also OHS-KA 5:292.)

1872f   [Letter to Enoch Hoag, May 21, 1872.] (Letters Received, Central Superintendency. NARS microfilm pub. M856, 41.)

1872g   [Letter to Enoch Hoag, May 22, 1872.] (Letters Received, Central Superintendency. NARS microfilm pub. M856, 41.)

1872h   [Letter to Enoch Hoag, Oct. 10, 1872.] (Letters Received, Central Superintendency. NARS microfilm pub. M856, 41.)

1872i   [Letter to Enoch Hoag, Dec. 9, 1872.] (Letters Received, Central Superintendency. NARS microfilm pub. M856, 41.)

1873a   [Letter to C. C. Augur, Jan. 4, 1873.] (Letters Received, Military Department of Texas, no. 271 DT 73; NARS Record Group 393 Pt.1 Entry 4875.)

1873b   [Letter to Enoch Hoag, Jan. 11, 1873. Enclosure in Hoag to F. A. Walker, Jan. 18, 1873.] (Letters Received from the Kiowa Agency. NARS microfilm pub. M234, 378:129.)

1873c   [Letter to C.C. Augur, Jan. 16, 1873.] (Letters Received from the Military Department of Texas, no. 408 DT 73. NARS Record Group 393, part 1, entry 4875.)

1873d   [Letter to Enoch Hoag, Mar. 3, 1873.] (Letters Received, Central Superintendency. NARS microfilm pub. M856, 47.)

1899   Our Red Brothers and the Peace Policy of President Ulysses S. Grant. Philadelphia: J. C. Winston.

Taylor, Nathaniel G.

1868   [Letter to O. H. Browning, July 1, 1868.] (Letters Received from the Kiowa Agency. NARS microfilm pub. M234, 375:872.)

Taylor, Nathaniel G., John B. Henderson, Samuel F. Tappan, John B. Sanborn, William S. Harney, Alfred H. Terry, William T. Sherman, Christopher C. Augur

1910   Papers Relating to Talks and Councils Held with the Indians in Dakota and Montana in the years 1866-1869. Washington: Government Printing Office. (Original in NARS, Records of the Indian Division, Office of the Secretary of the Interior, Record Group 48.)

Tefft, Stanton K.

1960   Sociopolitical Change in Two Migrant Tribes. Proceedings of the Minnesota Academy of Sciences, vol. 28, 103-11.

1965   From Band to Tribe on the Plains. Plains Anthropologist 10:166-70.

ten Kate, H. F. C.

1885a   Notes ethnographiques sur les Comanches. Revue d'Ethnographie 4: 120-36.

1885b   Reizen en Onderzoekingen in Noord-Amerika. Leiden: E. J. Brill.

Thomas, Alfred B.

1929a   Documents Bearing on the Northern Frontier of New Mexico. New Mexico Historical Review 4:146-64.

1929b   An Eighteenth Century Comanche Document. American Anthropologist 31:289-98.

1929c   San Carlos: A Comanche Pueblo on the Arkansas River, 1787. Colorado Magazine 6:79-91.

1932   Forgotten Frontiers. Norman: University of Oklahoma Press.

1935   After Coronado. Norman: University of Oklahoma Press.

1940   The Plains Indians and New Mexico. Albuquerque: University of New Mexico Press.

1941   Teodoro de Croix and the Northern Frontier of New Spain, 1776-1783. Norman: University of Oklahoma Press.

Thompson, David

1916   David Thompson's Narrative 1784-1812. Edited by J. B. Tyrrell. Toronto: Champlain Society.

Thompson, Gerald
  1983   Edward F. Beale and the American West. Albuquerque: University of
            New Mexico Press.
Thurman, Melburn D.
  1980   Comanche. *In* Encyclopedia of Indians of the Americas, edited by
            Keith Irvine, vol. 4, 4-13. St. Clair Shores: Scholarly Press.
  1982   Nelson Lee and the Green Corn Dance: Data Selection Problems with
            Wallace and Hoebel's Study of the Comanches. Plains Anthropologist
            27:239-43.
  1987   Reply to Gelo. Current Anthropology 28:552-55.
Thwaites, Reuben Gold, ed.
  1904-7   Early Western Travels, 1748-1846: A Series of Annotated Reprints of
            Some of the Best and Rarest Volumes of Travel, Description of the
            Aborigines and Social and Economic Conditions in the Middle and Far
            West, during the Period of Early American Settlement. 38 vols. Cleve-
            land: Arthur H. Clark.
  1908   The French Regime in Wisconsin. Wisconsin Historical Collections 18.
            Madison.
Tiling, Moritz
  1913   History of the German Elements in Texas from 1820 to 1850. Houston:
            Moritz Tiling.
Timrod, Henry
  1861   Ethnogenesis. Charleston (S.C.) *Courier,* Feb. 4, 1861. Reprinted *in*
            Songs and Ballads of the Southern People, 1861-65, collected and
            edited by Frank Moore, 9-14. New York: D. Appelton, 1886.
Torrey, David K.
  1847   [Letter to A. Talcott, Sept. 6, 1847. Enclosure in W. S. Marcy to W.
            Medill, Sept. 10, 1847.] (Letters Received from the Texas Agency.
            NARS microfilm pub. M234, 858:78.)
Tosawa
  1868   [Statement of Toshona (*sic*) to W. B. Hazen, Mar. 6, 1868.] (Letters re-
            ceived from the Kiowa Agency. NARS microfilm pub. M234, 375:
            1012.)
Tosawa, et al.
  1868   [Petition to N. G. Taylor, Sept. 2, 1868.] (Letters Received from the
            Kiowa Agency. NARS microfilm pub. M234, 375:994.)
Townsend, E. D.
  1870   [Letter to Commanding Officer, Military Department of Texas, Sept.
            28, 1870.] (Letters received from the Kiowa Agency. NARS microfilm
            pub. M234, 376:658.)
Trespalacios, José Felix
  1822   [Letter to Gaspar Lopez, Nov. 8, 1822.] (BA 73:431.)
Tunnel, Curtis D., and W. W. Newcomb
  1969   A Lipan Apache Mission: San Lorenzo de la Santa Cruz: 1762-1771.
            Austin: Texas Memorial Museum.

Turner, Victor
    1957   Schism and Continuity on an African Society. Manchester: Manchester
            University Press.
Turpin, Solveig
    1987   Ethnohistoric Observations of Bison in the Lower Pecos River Region:
            Implications for Environmental Change. Plains Anthropologist 32:424–
            29.
    1988   More or Less Bison: Reply to Bamforth. Plains Anthropologist 33:
            408–9.
Twitchell, Ralph E.
    1914   Spanish Archives of New Mexico. 2 vols. Cedar Rapids: Torch Press.
Ugarte y Loyola, Jacobo
    1786a   [Letter to Domingo Cabello, Aug. 17, 1786.] (BA 17:706.)
    1786b   [Letter to Juan Bautista de Anza, Oct. 6, 1786.] (SANM T–943, 11:
            1058.)
    1787a   [Letter to the Marques de Sonora, Jan. 4, 1787.] (AGN-PI, tomo 65,
            exp 2.)
    1787b   [Letter to Juan Bautista de Anza, Feb. 8, 1787.] (AGN-PI, tomo 65,
            exp 2.)
Ugartechea, Domingo de
    1835a   [Letter to José González, Feb. 8, 1835.] (BA 164:60.)
    1835b   [Letter to Martín Prefecto de Cos, Feb. 9, 1835.] (BA 164:86.)
Valverde y Cosio, Antonio
    1719   [Proceedings of a Council of War, Aug. 11, 1719.] (SANM T–301, 5:
            922.)
Van Camp, Cornelius
    1858   [Letter to J. F. Minter, Sept. 2, 1858. Enclosure in Neighbors to
            Thomas J. Hawkins, Nov. 26, 1858.] (Letters Received from the Texas
            Agency. NARS microfilm pub. M234, 861:977.)
Veatch, James C.
    1865   [Compact Made and Entered into Between the Confederate Indian
            Tribes and the Prairie Tribes of Indians, made at Camp Napoleon, on
            the Washita River, May 26, 1865. Enclosure in Letter to J. Schuyler
            Crosby, July 20, 1865.] Official Records of the War of the Rebellion,
            ser. 1, vol. 48, pt. 2, 1102–3.
Vial, Pedro
    1787   [Diary which I, Pedro Vial, Start to Write From this Presidio of San
            Antonio to the Capital of the Villa of Santa Fe, July 5, 1787.] (AGN,
            Historia, tomo 43, exp. 14.)
Vial, Pedro, and Francisco Xavier de Chavez
    1785   [Diary of Trip from San Antonio to the Comanche Villages to Treat
            For Peace, Nov. 15, 1785.] (AGI, Guadalajara, Legajo 286.)
Viesca, José María
    1831   [Letter to Ramón Músquiz, Feb. 5, 1831.] (BA 138:557.)

Vigil, Juan Bautista
    1825   [Cuenta de los efectos comprados para el regalo de los Indios Aliadas
              de Paz, Aug. 1, 1825.] (NMA 1825-388.)
Villanueva, Vicente
    1807   [Indian Expenses, Oct. 31, 1807.] (SANM T-2084, 16:427.)
Vincent, Joan
    1990   Anthropology and Politics: Visions, Traditions, and Trends. Tucson:
              University of Arizona Press.
Viola, Herman J.
    1981   Diplomats in Buckskin: A History of Indian Delegations in Washing-
              ton City. Washington, D.C.: Smithsonian Institution Press.
Vivero, José Antonio
    1821   [Letter to Antonio Martínez, 1 August 1821.] (BA 68:1.)
Vizcarra, José Antonio
    1831   [Letter to Comandante General, Oct. 30, 1831 (#277).] (MANM 13:
              520; also NMA 1831-73.)
Vizcaya-Canales, I.
    1968   La invasion de los indios bárbaros al norte de Mexico en los años de
              1840 y 1841. Materiales para la ethnohistoria de noreste de Mexico,
              Monterrey: Publicaciones del Instituto Technologico y de Estudios
              Superiores de Monterrey.
Walker, Mark
    1867   [Letter to C. McKeever, May 14, 1867.] (Letters Received from the
              Kiowa Agency. NARS microfilm pub. M234, 375:714. Also Winfrey
              and Day 1959-66, 4:209-10)
Walkley, L. S.
    1868   [Letter to W. B. Hazen, Dec. 28, 1868.] (Letters Received from the
              Kiowa Agency. NARS microfilm pub. M234, 376:525.)
Wallace, Ernest
    1954   David G. Burnet's Letters Describing the Comanche Indians. West
              Texas Historical Association Year Book, vol. 30, 115-40. Abilene..
Wallace, Ernest, and E. Adamson Hoebel
    1952   The Comanches: Lords of the South Plains. Norman: University of
              Oklahoma Press.
Walsh, J. W.
    1869   [Letter to B. L. Woodward, Aug. 7, 1869.] (Letters Received from the
              Kiowa Agency. NARS microfilm pub. M234, 376:26.)
    1870   [Letter to J. L. Woodman, Jan. 5, 1870.] (Letters received from the
              Kiowa Agency. NARS microfilm pub. M234, 376:544.)
Weatherhead, L. R.
    1980   What is an "Indian Tribe": The Question of Tribal Existence. Ameri-
              can Indian Law Review 8(1):1-48.
Weaver, B. D.
    1980   Relations between the Comanche Indians and the Republic of Texas.
              Panhandle Plains Historical Review 53:17-33.

Weber, David J.
    1982   The Mexican Frontier, 1821–1846: The American Southwest under Mexico. Albuquerque: University of New Mexico Press.

Wedel, Mildred, and Raymond J. DeMallie
    1980   The Ethnohistorical Approach in Plains Area Studies. *In* Anthropology of the Great Plains. Editied by W. Raymond Wood and Margot Liberty, 110–28. Lincoln: University of Nebraska Press.

Weems, John E.
    1969   Men without Countries. Boston: Houghton Mifflin.

Wheat, Carl I.
    1957–61 Mapping the Transmississippi West. 5 vols. San Francisco: Institute of Historical Cartography.

Wheat, Joe Ben
    1972   The Olsen-Chubbock Site: A Paleo-Indian Bison Kill. Memoirs of the Society for American Archaeology, no. 26. Washington, D.C.

Wheelock, T. B.
    1835   Journal of Col. Dodge's Expedition from Fort Gibson to the Pawnee Pict Village. 3rd Cong., 2d sess., House Doc. 2.

Whitfield, John W.
    1854   [Annual report, Agent, Upper Platte Agency.] (ARCIA 1854, doc. 29.)
    1856   [Letter to C. E. Mix, Jan. 5, 1856.] (Upper Arkansas Agency. NARS microfilm pub. M234, 878:102.)

Wilbarger, J. W.
    1889   Indian Depredations in Texas. Reprint, Austin: Steck Co., 1935. (Page citations are to the reprint edition.)

Wilkinson, James
    1805   [Letter to Thomas Jefferson, Dec. 23, 1805.] (Thomas Jefferson Papers, folio 27050. Library of Congress.)

Willey, Gordon R., and Philip Phillips
    1958   Method and Theory on American Archaeology. Chicago: University of Chicago Press.

Williams, Amelia W., and Eugene C. Barker
    1938–43 The Writings of Sam Houston. 8 vols. Austin: University of Texas Press.

Williams, L. H.
    1849   [Letter to R. S. Neighbors, Oct. 9, 1849. Enclosure in Neighbors to O. Brown, Oct. 18, 1849.] (Letters Received from the Texas Agency. NARS microfilm pub. M234, 858:412.)

Winfrey, Dorman H., and James M. Day, eds.
    1959–66 The Indian Papers of Texas and the Southwest. 5 vols. Austin: Pemberton Press.

Wisehart, Marion K.
    1962   Sam Houston: American Giant. New York: Van Rees Press.

Wissler, Clark
    1911   Social Life of the Blackfeet. New York: Anthropological Papers of the
            American Museum of Natural History 7, pt. 1.
    1914   The Influence of the Horse on the Development of Plains Culture.
            American Anthropologist 16:1-25.
    1926   The Relation of Nature to Man in Aboriginal America. New York: Ox-
            ford University Press.
Wolf, Eric R.
    1982   Europe and the People Without History. Berkeley: University of Cali-
            fornia Press.
Wright, Gary A.
    1977   The Shoshonean Migration Problem. Plains Anthropologist 23:113-
            37.
Wright, Muriel H.
    1951   A Guide to the Indian Tribes of Oklahoma. Norman: University of
            Oklahoma Press.
Yoakum, Henderson K.
    1855   History of Texas from Its First Settlement to Its Annexation to the
            United States in 1846. 2 vols. Reprint, Austin: Steck Co., 1961. (Page
            citations are to the reprint edition.)
Young, Otis E.
    1952   The First Military Escort on the Santa Fe Trail, 1829. Glendale, Cal.:
            Arthur H. Clark.

Addenda

Barry, Louise
    1972   The Beginning of the West. Topeka: Kansas State Historical Society.
Becknell, William
    1823   Diary of William Becknell. *Missouri Intelligencer and Boon's Lick
            Advertiser.* Reprint, 1910, "The Journals of Captain Thomas [sic]
            Becknell from Boon's Lick to Santa Fe, and from Santa Cruz to Green
            River." Missouri Historical Review 4(2): 65-84.

Index

In *Studies in the Anthropology of North American Indians*